AMSCO® ADVANCED PLACEMENT

EUROPEAN
HISTORY

Contributors

Senior Reviewers

Lou Gallo
AP® European History Consultant
West High School
Knoxville, Tennessee

Robert Wade
AP® European History Consultant
John Paul II High School
Plano, Texas

Writers and Reviewers

Don Baeszler
AP® European History Consultant
Riverview High School
Sarasota, Florida

Alaina Brown
AP® European History Consultant
Novi High School
Novi, Michigan

Catherine Holden Desmond
AP® European History Consultant
Baltimore County Public Schools
Baltimore, Maryland

Sue Chaney Gilmore
College Board Consultant
Martin Luther King Academic Magnet High
School
Nashville, Tennessee

Alice Grant
AP® European History Consultant (retired)
Pelham Memorial High School
Pelham, New York

Bryan Henry
AP® European History Teacher
Kingwood High School
Kingwood, Texas

Gerald Hurd
AP® European History Exam Selector
Olympic High School
Silverdale, Washington

Jody Janis
AP® European History Teacher
J. Frank Dobie High School
Houston, Texas

Mark Klopfenstein
AP® European History Teacher
Palmer Ridge High School
Monument, Colorado

Ken LeSage
AP® European History Exam Table Leader
Lewis-Palmer High School
Monument, Colorado

Jamie Oleson
AP® World History Teacher
Rogers High School
Spokane, Washington

Lenore Schneider
AP® National Leader
New Canaan High School
New Canaan, Connecticut

Clara Webb
AP® European History Exam Table Leader
Boston Latin School
Boston, Massachusetts

Pam Wolfe
AP® European History Consultant
Yeshiva of Greater Washington
Silver Spring, MD

AMSCO® ADVANCED PLACEMENT®

EUROPEAN
HISTORY

AMSCO® SCHOOL PUBLICATIONS, INC. ,

a division of Perfection Learning®

AMSCO® Advanced Placement® European History is one of a series of
Advanced Placement® social studies texts first launched with the book now titled
AMSCO® Advanced Placement® United States History.

*Advanced Placement® and AP® are trademarks registered and/or owned by the College
Board, which was not involved in the production of, and does not endorse, this product.*

© **2019 Perfection Learning®**

Please visit our website at:
www.perfectionlearning.com

When ordering this book, please specify:
Softcover: ISBN 978-1-5311-1362-9 or **1340201**
Hardcover: ISBN 978-1-5311-3028-2 or **1340206**
eBook: ISBN 978-1-5311-1363-6 or **13402D**

2 3 4 5 6 7 PA 24 23 22 21 20 19

Printed in the United States of America

Contents

PERIOD 1: c. 1450 to c. 1648

PERIOD 2: c. 1648 to c. 1815

PERIOD 3: c. 1815 to c. 1914

PERIOD 4: c. 1914 to the Present

Preface

AMSCO Advanced Placement® European History provides a concise narrative, skills instruction and practice, multiple-choice questions, short-answer questions, long essay questions, and document-based questions designed to help students understand the significant content and develop the vital skills needed to master the subject. It can be used in classes as either the core textbook or along with other resources.

For teachers, an Answer Key is available from the publisher. It also includes correlations to standards identified by the College Board.

As of its publication, *AMSCO Advanced Placement® European History* was up to date with all standards and guidelines published by the College Board. For the latest information on Advanced Placement® European History courses and the exam, check the European history section of apcentral.collegeboard.com and advancesinap.collegeboard.org.

EUROPE TODAY

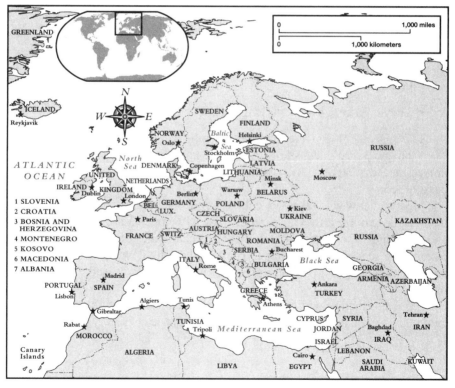

Introduction

Studying Advanced Placement®
European History

Enrollment in AP® courses such as this one has grown over the years. Students cite many reasons they want to take courses such as AP® European History:

- They provide evidence that the student has the ability to succeed as an undergraduate.

- They increase eligibility for scholarships.

- They help strengthen a student's college applications.

- They help reduce college expenses by earning college credit.

- They allow students to test out of introductory college courses.

- They reflect the fact that AP® students have better college graduation rates.

- They help enrich students' high school experience.

The placement and credits offered will vary from college to college. The College Board's website provides a comprehensive list of colleges and universities that accept AP® examinations and the credits they award for passing scores.

Most students who take AP® courses report that they are more challenging than regular courses; they also report that AP® courses are more interesting and gratifying. The rewards of taking on the challenges of an AP® program go beyond the scores and placement. They include the development of lifelong reading, reasoning, and writing skills, as well as an increased enjoyment of history.

This introduction will provide you with background information that will help you understand the structure of the AP® European History exam.

Overview of the AP® European History Exam

This textbook was created to prepare you for the current AP® European History exam. The exam emphasizes the history practices and reasoning skills used by historians, with a strong focus on themes and related concepts to help deepen your understanding of European history. It includes readings, images, and other data sources and requires 3 hours and 15 minutes to complete. The AP® European History exam will include the components shown in the table below.

Section	Question Type	Number of Questions	Timing	Percentage of Total Exam Score
I	Part A: Multiple-choice questions	55 questions	55 minutes	40%
	Part B: Short-answer questions	3 questions • Required Question 1: 1600–2001 • Required Question 2: 1600–2001 • Choose between Question 3 periods 1–2 OR Question 4 periods 3–4	40 minutes	20%
II	Part A: Document-based question	1 question: topics from 1600–2001	60 minutes (includes a 15-minute reading period)	25%
	Part B: Long essay question	1 question, chosen from three options on the same theme: • period 1 • periods 2–3 • periods 3–4	40 minutes	15%

Source: *AP® European History Course and Exam Description.*

Each of these exam components will be explained in this introduction, along with a guide to sequential skill development. AP® examinations, including the European History exam, score student performance on a five-point scale:

- 5: Extremely well qualified

- 4: Well-qualified performance

- 3: Qualified

- 2: Possibly qualified

- 1: No recommendation

An AP® score of 3 or higher is usually considered evidence of mastery of course content similar to that demonstrated in a college-level introductory course in the same subject area. However, the requirements of introductory courses may vary from college to college. Many schools require a 4 or a 5.

The AP® exams are built differently than typical classroom tests. For example, the developers of the AP® exams want to generate a wider distribution of scores. They also want higher reliability, which means a higher likelihood that test takers repeating the same exam will receive the same scores.

In addition, AP® exams are scored differently. The cutoff for a "qualified," or level 3, score varies from year to year depending on how well a group of college students who take the test do on it.

The writers of the AP® exam also design it to be more difficult. If you take a practice exam before you have fully prepared for the test, don't be surprised if you have difficulty with many of the questions. More importantly, don't be discouraged. AP® European History is challenging. But like many challenges, people can master it by breaking it down into manageable steps.

How This Book Can Help

The goal of this textbook is to provide you with the essential content and instructional materials needed to develop the knowledge and the historical reasoning and writing skills needed for success on the AP® European History exam. You can find these in the following parts of the book:

- *Introduction.* This section introduces the practices and historical reasoning skills, five course themes, and six chronological periods of the history program. A step-by-step skill development guide provides instruction for answering (1) the multiple-choice questions; (2) the short-answer questions; (3) the document-based essay question; and (4) the long essay question.

- *Concise History.* The 24 chapters of essential historical content and accessible explanation of events are the heart of the book. Summaries and key AP® concepts introduce each of the four periods.

- *Maps and Graphics.* Maps, charts, graphs, cartoons, photographs, and other visual materials also are integrated into the text to help students practice analytical skills.

- *Historical Perspectives.* Each chapter includes a section that introduces significant historical issues and conflicting interpretations.

- *Key Terms by Themes.* To assist reviewing, each chapter ends with a list of key terms organized by theme.

- *Multiple-Choice Questions.* Each chapter contains 8 multiple-choice questions to assess your historical knowledge and skills using a variety of sources.

- *Short-Answer Questions.* Each chapter contains two short-answer questions to provide practice writing succinct responses.

- *Document-Based Questions.* Each period includes two DBQs for practice.

- *Long Essay Questions.* Each period contains several long essay questions.

- *Practice Examination.* Following the final chapter, the book includes a complete practice examination.

- *Index.* The index is included to help locate key terms for review.

A separate Answer Key is available for teachers and other authorized users of the book and can be accessed through the publisher's website.

The Study of AP® European History

Historians attempt to give meaning to the past by collecting historical evidence and then explaining how this information is connected. They interpret and organize a wide variety of evidence from primary sources and secondary texts to understand the past. AP® European History should develop a student's ability to think like a historian: to analyze and use evidence, and to deal with probing questions about past events. Often there is no one "answer" for such questions any more than one historical source can provide a complete answer for a question. AP® teachers and readers are looking for the student's ability to think about history and to support ideas with evidence.

AP® candidates should appreciate how both participants in history and historians differ among themselves in their interpretations of critical questions in European history. Each chapter of this book includes a Historical Perspectives feature to introduce some of the issues raised and debated by historians. The AP® European History exam does not require an advanced knowledge of historiography—the study of ways historians have constructed their accounts of the past. Some people refer to historiography as "the history of history." Nevertheless, prior knowledge of the richness of historical thought can add depth to your analysis of historical questions.

Students planning to take the AP® European History exam also need to become familiar with and then practice the development of (1) history disciplinary practices and reasoning skills, (2) thematic analysis, and (3) the concepts and understandings of the four periods that provide the organization of the content. These three components of the course are explained below for orientation and future reference.

Don't become overwhelmed with this introduction or try to comprehend all the finer points of taking the AP® exam in the first few days or weeks of studying. Mastery of these skills and understandings takes time and is an ongoing part of the study of AP® history. This introduction will become more helpful as a reference after you have studied some historical content and have begun to tackle actual assignments.

The Practices and Skills of History

Advanced Placement® history courses encourage students to become "apprentice historians." The College Board, which creates the AP® exams, has identified two practices and four types of historical reasoning skills for AP® European History. Every question on the exam will require you to apply one or more of these practices or skills. Questions and features at the end of each chapter and period provide frequent opportunities to use them.

History Disciplinary Practices

There are two main history disciplinary practices taught in AP® European History and tested on the exam. They address the core of what historians do—use evidence to make an argument.

1. **Analyzing Historical Evidence** Historians explain and evaluate diverse historical sources, including written works, art, images, and artifacts from the period under study. They make judgments about each source's relevance, usefulness, and limitations. Students should be able to explain (1) the historical setting of the source, (2) its intended audience, (3) its purpose, and (4) the point of view of the original writer or creator. For example, an AP® exam question might ask, "Which of the following best reflects the point of view expressed by the author?" Another possible question is, "Briefly explain ONE characteristic of the intended audience for this image."

   Historians also learn from secondary sources. Analyzing secondary sources involves the ability to describe, analyze, and evaluate the diverse work of other historians. Students should be able to identify the author's argument and the evidence used to support it. This skill also involves understanding how particular circumstances might influence a work.

2. **Argument Development** The second practice is developing an argument. A strong argument is built on the ability to make a historically defensible claim or thesis that addresses the question and all of its parts. This claim or thesis then needs to be supported with specific and relevant historical evidence, and the writer needs to explain the relationship of the evidence to the thesis.

On the AP® exam, students might be asked to demonstrate their ability to recognize historical arguments through questions such as "Which of the following would best support the argument of historian A?" or "Briefly explain ONE major difference between the arguments of historian A and historian B."

In both long essay questions and document-based essay questions, the answer should recognize and address alternative arguments and conflicting evidence. For example, a French peasant in 1789 might view the French Revolution with hope that it will make life better. A French aristocrat of the same period might feel threatened. A well-written essay should recognize the differences between them.

Part of the study of history is to recognize the diverse arguments historians have made about the past. Views of the past continue to change as three factors influence historians:

- Their personal perspective or society's perspective changes. All historians are influenced by their personal experience in the world they live in. However, good historians are aware of these influences, and they attempt to account for them, so they can still present the past accurately.

- They discover new sources and information. Because uncovering a long-hidden diary or developing an innovative technique for determining the wealth of a community in the past can reshape how people see the past, all interpretations about history are tentative.

- They ask new questions. Questions reflect what historians want to know. Historians who ask questions about the causes of World War I will write very different works than historians who ask questions about the life of a typical soldier.

One common reason historians disagree is that not all evidence has equal value. Some observers and some data are more reliable than others. In writing an essay on an AP® exam, students should recognize that some evidence is more useful than other evidence in supporting an argument. Students should not focus on recalling a mass of facts. Rather, they should demonstrate a conceptual understanding of the evidence and an ability to link that understanding to the argument. For example, to support an argument comparing the economies in Great Britain and Russia, it is not enough to describe each one individually. In addition, a writer should make the comparison explicit.

History Reasoning Skills

There are four history reasoning skills taught in AP® European History and tested on the exam. These are the basic skills that historians use to understand the past.

1. **Contextualization** This skill is the ability to see how a specific event, policy, or source connects to larger historical developments. Often these developments are at a global level. For example, during the 19th century in Great Britain, working-class families organized to demand better social and economic conditions. Their efforts occurred in the context of intellectual changes in the 18th and 19th centuries known as the Enlightenment and the Romantic movements, which shaped how people felt about equality.

   The ability to use the skill of contextualization could be evaluated through an exam question such as, "The conditions shown in the photograph depict which of the following trends in the early 20th century?" Both the document-based questions and the long essay questions explicitly require contextualization. Strong answers to the short-answer questions will also incorporate contextualization, though it is not a required feature of the response.

2. **Comparison** This skill is the ability to describe, compare, contrast, and evaluate two or more historical events or developments in the same or different eras or periods or in the same or different locations. It requires an ability to identify, compare, contrast, and evaluate a given historical event or development from multiple perspectives.

   The ability to use the skill of comparison could be evaluated through an exam question such as "Which statement expresses a difference between communism and fascism in Europe in the 20th century?"

3. **Causation** This skill is the ability to identify, analyze, and evaluate the relationships among many historical events and developments as both causes and effects. Not all causes and effects are equally important. A key task of a historian is to determine which causes and effects are primary, and which are secondary. Showing persuasive evidence of causation is difficult. Many events are simply correlated, which means they occur at the same time or one occurs right after the other, but there is no persuasive evidence that one caused the other.

4. **Continuity and Change over Time** This skill is the ability to recognize, analyze, and evaluate the dynamics of history over periods of time of varying lengths, often investigating important patterns that emerge. The study of themes in history (explained later in this introduction) is often the tool of choice to understand continuity and change over time.

Britain's industrialization shows *continuities and changes over time* in class structure. Britain began the period as a highly stratified society with the monarch at the top; powerful nobles next on the social pyramid; a small middle class of bankers, merchants, and lawyers next; and small landowners and craftsworkers at the bottom. Through the upheavals of industrialization, stratification remained a *continuity*, but *change* did occur as new groups and classes arose. At the bottom now were factory workers and coal miners—the *working class*. Industrialization also expanded a new *middle class* of managers, office workers, small business owners, and professionals. Toward the top of the hierarchy (but still below the monarchy) were wealthy industrialists, who eclipsed the landed aristocracy in power.

On the AP® exam, a question about continuity and change over time might ask, "How was the development of new classes in the Industrial Revolution important to political movements of the late 19th and early 20th?"

Course Themes

Each AP® European History exam question also is related to one or more of six course themes. These six themes will help you think about the main ideas in European history. The themes include the study of interactions with the natural environment, the development and interaction of cultures, the building and expansion of states as well as the resulting conflict, the dynamics of economic systems, and the development and change of social structures and gender roles.

Each theme covers cross-period and cross-cultural investigations. They help identify trends and processes that have developed throughout centuries in different parts of Europe and the world.

Each chapter in this book includes a review list of important names, places, events, and concepts used in that chapter: Key Terms Organized by Theme. To help you recognize thematic connections in the chapter, the entries in the lists are grouped under subheads for each theme, with a code identifying the theme.

Theme 1: Interaction of Europe and the World (INT)

This theme focuses on Europe's growing interaction with the broader world after 1450. It focuses on the motivations that led to these interactions as well as the consequences for both non-European and European societies. The possible motivations were many, including the desire for economic gain, the broadening of each European nation's power, and the spread of Christianity. The consequences were even more numerous and wide ranging, and often devastating.

In the Americas, Europeans established colonies that would fundamentally and permanently alter both continents' people and societies. Civilizations were toppled, land was expropriated, and populations were decimated. Africa was profoundly affected by the European takeover of the Americas, as millions of Africans were captured and sold into bondage, working on colonial plantations. Europeans, too, were affected by the interaction of peoples, cultures, and environments. Many left to live abroad, never to return. The exchange of foods and goods between the new and old worlds changed how Europeans lived irrevocably.

European colonialism and imperialism developed and spread throughout Asia and Africa in the 19th and 20th centuries, fueling resistance by subject peoples and competition among the European colonial powers.

Theme 2: Poverty and Prosperity (PP)

This theme explores the ways in which the new global commercial network, developed and dominated by Europeans, eventually led to profound impacts on the continent's social and political systems. The commercial wealth that resulted from colonization fueled a further economic revolution in the 17th and 18th centuries. The growth of large-scale agriculture during this era also led to significant change, including a rise in European populations and a gradual shift in populations from rural to urban.

Over time, these changes resulted in rising levels of material prosperity for some Europeans, particularly in the era of technological advances after 1850. But this prosperity was distributed unequally, with often-stagnant working-class wages and the exploitation of workers and resources from the less-developed world. These inequalities gave rise to ideologies such as socialism that sought greater equality through the reform, or even replacement, of the capitalist system.

Theme 3: Objective Knowledge and Subjective Visions (OS)

This theme explores the ways in which knowledge has been created and transmitted throughout European history. Beginning in the 15th century, thinkers in multiple fields of inquiry tentatively began to question traditional sources of authority and knowledge, substituting a belief in direct inquiry and subjective truths.

With the advent of the Enlightenment in Europe, however, growing numbers of Europeans adopted a view of the world based on natural laws and objective scientific truths, in place of traditional and religious beliefs. This led eventually to a blossoming of scientific and mathematical knowledge and the application of scientific methods to social and political issues and systems. The 20th century saw another shift, from a belief in objective knowledge and truths to the exploration of subjective paradigms and nonrational forces (especially in psychology).

Theme 4: States and Other Institutions of Power (SP)

This theme focuses on the cultural, economic, and social impact of changes within European government and social institutions over time. The rise of sovereign states and the success of the Protestant Reformation signaled a shift away from traditional church power and toward secular and state control of many societal and governmental institutions.

Intellectual, political, and social aspects born of the Enlightenment fueled movements away from monarchies and aristocracies and toward the rule of law and representative governments. The participation of everyday people in governance, chiefly through broadening suffrage, increased over time. However, mass politics and the political and economic crises of the early 20th century combined to fuel the rise of totalitarian regimes and the expense of parliamentary governments. The latter half of the century saw the rise of international (the UN and other NGOs) and European (EU, NATO) organizations designed to promote worldwide and regional stability.

Theme 5: Individual and Society (IS)

Theme 5 focuses on changes to family and societal classes and groups across Europe. Movements such as the Protestant Reformation and the Industrial Revolution had massive consequences for European society. How and when people got married and started families changed, as did how those families functioned. Women's roles evolved markedly, with women seeking greater economic and legal rights by the 19th century. The development of middle and working classes fundamentally changed how people related to one another at home and otherwise.

World War I brought an end to the remnants of the old order, as empires were disbanded and democracy expanded. After World War II, welfare states developed in Western Europe, providing increased family support, reproductive choices, and universal health care. The end of the Cold War brought about the EU, which, while highlighting the shared values of European society, has experienced difficulty particularly over the question of immigration.

Theme 6: National and European Identity

This theme examines how Europeans' ideas of cultural, national, and regional identity have evolved over time. Early modern European identity was based on cultural elements such as shared language, history, and location, and it could be manifested in anything from a city-state to a small principality to an emerging nation-state.

While great 17th- and 18th-century monarchs built powerful nations around cultural and linguistic ties in places like France and Russia, England's continued growth was accompanied by the rise of an increasingly powerful Parliament. The ideas of the Enlightenment and the French Revolution gave rise to a European sense of shared values, based around citizenship, reason, and equality.

The growing sense of nationalism in the 19th century brought together new nations (Italy, Germany, and the Netherlands) but also served as a divisive force in multiethnic states, such as the Habsburg Empire. This nationalism carried through the 20th century, leading to the century's great conflicts and the eventual rise of independent nations and greater political fragmentation. This process was reversed, in a way, by the rise of the EU. But recent struggles within the EU show that European identity is ever changing.

Historical Periods

AP® European History also is based on a framework of four historical periods. According to the College Board, the instructional importance and assessment weighting for each period is equal. These periods are briefly described below, and each description includes the chapters of the book that address each period's content.

Period 1: c. 1450 to c. 1648 (Chapters 1–6) The period from the Renaissance to the Peace of Westphalia deals with the growth of science, mathematics, art, and philosophy in Europe. It also examines changes and conflicts brought about by major events and trends such as the Protestant Reformation, the Catholic Counter-Reformation, the overseas expansion of European power, and the Columbian Exchange. During this period, power in Europe was increasingly centralized and secular, and power also was increasingly open to men of talent and wealth, not just those who belonged to the hereditary nobility.

Period 2: c. 1648 to c. 1815 (Chapters 7–12) The period from the Peace of Westphalia to the Congress of Vienna deals with growth in Europe in a number of different avenues. In politics, a balance of power system between European states emerged, and was generally challenged only when one or another state sought to upset the balance. (Revolutionary and Napoleonic France represent major upsets of the system.)

Overall economic strength and individual standards of living grew as well, particularly in Atlantic countries. Further, the Scientific Revolution and the Enlightenment altered Europeans' ways of thinking, as reason increasingly challenged religion and literacy grew.

Period 3: c. 1815 to c. 1914 (Chapters 13–18) The period from the Congress of Vienna to the beginning of World War I saw industrialization grow and spread throughout Europe. This led to the growth of specific social classes, particularly the proletariat (working class) and the bourgeoisie (middle class). Rapid population growth and urbanization also followed, bringing their own challenges. During this period, responses to socioeconomic change led to the revolutions of 1848, which authorities eventually quelled.

Rising nationalism helped promote and consolidate state power, and led to the unification of both Germany and Italy. This nationalism spurred further imperial actions, and as a result, Africa was partitioned and came under the domination of various European powers. At the same time, European emigrants sought better lives, chiefly in the Americas, and brought their cultures with them.

Period 4: c. 1914 to Present (Chapters 19–24) The period from the beginning of World War I to the present was dominated by conflict, namely the two world wars and the Cold War. Great areas of Europe were devastated by war and tens of millions of people, mostly civilians, perished. Nazi Germany's genocidal Holocaust alone marks the 20th century as a grim period in European history. The problematic resolution of World War I led to resentment in Germany and elsewhere, where fascist dictatorships arose. The Great Depression of the early 1930s also helped fuel dissatisfaction and anger.

Out of World War II emerged a more unified Europe, which culminated in the European Union. The union grew after the end of the Cold War, as some former Soviet satellite countries joined. In general, the nations of Europe became more secular and their governments became increasingly involved in citizens' economic lives. New Europeans—migrants from former colonies and world conflict zones—added diversity to the continent's culture and bolstered populations in a period of low birth rates. However, these immigrants often found inhabitants unwilling to accept them, and questions of social justice and identity remain.

Answering the AP® Exam Questions

History, like any field of study, is a combination of subject matter and methodology. The history practices, reasoning skills, and themes are methods or tools to explore the subject matter of history. One cannot practice these skills without knowledge of the historical content and understanding of specific historical evidence. The following section provides suggestions for development of another set of skills useful for answering the questions on the AP® exam. Again, the "mastery" of these skills, particularly writing answers to AP® questions, takes practice. This section will suggest how to develop the skills related to each different kind of question on the exam:

- multiple-choice questions

- short-answer questions

- document-based questions

- long essay questions

1. Answering the Multiple-Choice Questions

The College Board asks 55 multiple-choice questions (MCQs) on the AP® European History exam, and students have 55 minutes to complete this section. The value of the MCQs will be 40 percent of the student's score; and each MCQ will assess a historical reasoning skill and also will require historical knowledge from the Concept Outline of AP® European History. Questions will be related to the analysis of a stimulus—a primary or secondary source, such as a passage, image, map, or table.

Each question will have one best answer and three distracters. The questions will emphasize the ability to analyze the source and use the historical reasoning skill the question requires.

This textbook provides preparation for the multiple-choice questions section of the exam through items at the end of each chapter and on the Practice Exam at the end of the book. The MCQs in this book are similar in form and purpose to those appearing on the AP® exam but also are designed to review the content and understanding of the chapter.

Analyzing the Stimulus On the AP® exam, multiple-choice questions will be introduced with a stimulus. When analyzing a stimulus, ask yourself basic questions to spark your thinking: Who? What? When? Where? and Why? Beyond these questions, one of the most important questions to ask is, "What is the point of view of the author, artist, or speaker?" Consider the following excerpt from the Nuremberg Charter, which defined war crimes and laid the foundation for trials following World War II:

> The following acts . . . are crimes coming within the jurisdiction of the Tribunal for which there shall be individual responsibility:
> . . . Crimes against humanity: namely, murder, extermination, enslavement, deportation, and other inhumane acts committed against any civilian population, before or during the war, or persecutions on political, racial or religious grounds in execution of or in connection with any crime within the jurisdiction of the Tribunal, whether or not in violation of the domestic law of the country where perpetrated.

The multiple-choice questions about this excerpt will test your understanding of it. (Answering this question will be easier after you have studied the World War II era.) In addition, the questions will focus on one or more historical reasoning skills. The following are topics of multiple-choice questions that could be asked about this excerpt:

- *Contextualization:* Why do you think this definition of "crimes against humanity" was created at this point in history?

- *Causation:* Why does the definition of "crimes against humanity" include the phrase "whether or not in violation of the domestic law of the country where perpetrated"?

- *Continuity or change over time:* Is the establishment of a postwar court to try officials of defeated nations an example of continuity or change?

Making a Choice You need to read the stem (the question or statement before the choices of possible answers) of any MCQ and all four choices carefully before you choose your answer. More than one choice may appear to be correct at first, but you must select the best answer. If you are not immediately confident which answer is best, start by eliminating answers you recognize as incorrect. Choices that include words that reflect absolute positions, such as *always*, *never*, or *exclusively*, are seldom correct, since historical evidence can rarely offer such absolute certainty. Keep in mind the need to make judgments about the significance of a variety of causes and effects.

Should you guess on the AP® exam? Yes: The exam format does not penalize for guessing, and points are not deducted for incorrect answers. So you should answer every question. Obviously, though, the process of first eliminating a wrong answer or two before guessing increases your chances of choosing the correct answer.

Budgeting Your Time The AP® European History exam allows 55 minutes to answer the 55 questions. Fifty-five minutes does not allow enough time to spend 2 or 3 minutes on difficult questions. For questions involving a passage, chart, or picture, read the question first. If you find a question is hard, make a guess and then come back to it later if you have time.

Recommended Activities Practicing sample multiple-choice questions is important before the exam, if for no reason other than to reduce the number of surprises about the format of the questions. However, for many students, the review of content through multiple-choice questions is not the most productive way to prepare for the exam. The purpose of the chapter content in this text is to provide a useful and meaningful review of the essential concepts and evidence needed for the exam. By reviewing the essential facts in the historical content, you will better recall and understand connections between events, which is extremely important for applying the historical reasoning skills.

2. Answering the Short-Answer Questions

The AP® European History exam will include four SAQs. You will have 40 minutes to answer three of them.

Short-Answer Question	Required	Primary Practice or Skill Assessed	Stimulus	Time Period
1	Yes	Analyzing secondary sources	Secondary source	1600–2001
2	Yes	Causation or continuity and change over time	Primary source text or visual source	1600–2001
3	Either 3 or 4	The practice or skill not assessed in question 2	No stimulus	Periods 1–2
4	Either 3 or 4	The practice or skill not assessed in question 2	No stimulus	Periods 3–4

Source: *AP® European History Course and Exam Description*

Each question consists of three parts (labeled a, b, and c). A single part might ask for either ONE or TWO examples. No thesis is required. The following is a sample stimulus and question:

"In capitalist society we have a democracy that is curtailed, wretched, false, a democracy only for the rich, for the minority. The dictatorship of the proletariat, the period of transition to communism, will for the first time create democracy for the people, for the majority, along with the necessary suppression of the exploiters, of the minority."

from The State and Revolution, Vladimir Lenin, 1917

3. a) Identify one <u>similarity</u> between the ideas of Vladimir Lenin and those of the French Revolution.

   b) Identify one <u>difference</u> between the ideas of Vladimir Lenin and those of the French Revolution.

   c) Explain a <u>difference</u> between the long-term effects of the French Revolution and the Bolshevik revolution in Russia.

3. Answering the Document-Based Question (DBQ)

The AP® European History exam consists of one document-based question (DBQ) that includes seven documents. It will focus on a topic from between 1600 and 2001 and target one historical reasoning skill, such as causation or continuity and change over time. The skill will vary from year to year. You will be given 60 minutes to answer the question, which includes 15 minutes for reading the documents.

For details on how responses are scored, see the *Course and Exam Description*. In short, you should state a clear thesis and provide support for it from the documents. To receive a top score, you will need to refer to at least six of the documents in your analysis. To strengthen the probability of earning the maximum point value for this question, however, use all seven documents. In addition, you should analyze one or more of these elements of three documents:

- the creator's point of view

- the creator's purpose

- the historical situation when the document was produced

- the intended audience for the document

Some teachers refer to this analysis of the elements as "sourcing" the document. Earning credit for sourcing a document requires more than a simple statement such as "The intended audience is the elite class." You also will need to state the significance of this analysis. In other words, give a reason or further explanation of the significance for the point of view, purpose, historical situation, or intended audience. To determine significance, ask yourself, "What is the creator's point of view?" "Why did the creator produce the document?" "In what historical situation was the document created?" "What audience was the creator addressing?" The answers to these questions often are overlapping.

Besides using evidence stated in the documents, you should include outside knowledge in your response. This consists of additional examples, details, and analysis that provide context or clarify what is in the documents or that provide new information that supports your thesis.

Answering a DBQ builds on the skills for writing responses to the essay questions. (These are discussed in more detail in the following section on the long essay question.) The same skills apply here:

- Write a thesis statement that addresses all parts of the question.

- Provide historical context for your argument.

- Build argumentation supported by relevant specific evidence.

- Use the historical reasoning skill targeted in the question.

- Use evidence in a compelling way.

The most important difference between a DBQ response and a long essay is that your DBQ response should refer to specific sources to support arguments. This sample DBQ prompt illustrates how important it is to identify and address all parts of the prompt. Read it closely.

To what extent did World War I affect the role of women in Europe?

An effective answer will address the targeted skill and period: causation in Europe during and after World War I.

A common mistake writers make in answering a DBQ is to write little more than a descriptive list of the documents. The order of the documents in the DBQ should not control the organization of the essay. Rather, group the documents based upon how they support your thesis. Analyze the documents for evidence they provide, and integrate them into an organized and persuasive essay.

In a strong essay, a writer groups pieces of evidence from the documents that relate to each other. However, grouping requires more than simply placing related evidence within the same paragraph. It also requires seeing commonalities and contradictions in the evidence, and explaining how they both fit your argument.

- Words and phrases such as *similarly*, *in addition*, and *as well as* alert the reader that you see a common element among the documents.

- Phrases such as *in contrast to* or *this is different from* alert the reader that you see contradictory evidence in the documents.

As you use this textbook, you will find two DBQs in the review section at the end of each of the four periods and another one in the Practice Exam at the end of the book. Use these practice DBQs to develop your historical reasoning skills as well as the writing skills needed for answering the DBQ on the exam.

Here are some tips for writing an effective DBQ:

1. Use the 15-minute reading period to make marginal notes on the documents. Underline key parts of the prompt to help keep you on track. Before writing, formulate a thesis that addresses all parts of the question. The key historical reasoning skills to be developed for the successful writing of a DBQ answer are contextualization, comparison, causation, and continuity and change over time.

2. Keep references to the documents brief. Because the exam readers know the content of the documents, you do not need to quote them. A reference to the document's author or title is enough. Many writers simply cite the document number in parentheses, such as (Doc. 1). Readers like this system as well because it is simple and clear.

3. Use all of the documents. (The scoring guidelines call for students to use all or all but one of the documents.) However, recognize that each document represents a point of view, and some might contain information that is not accurate.

4. Address contradictory evidence. Your thesis should be complex enough to account for evidence that does not support your argument, and you should demonstrate that you understand other points of view and the context in which documents were created. Demonstrate your judgment about the sources based on your knowledge of the historical period.

Recommended Activities As a prewriting activity for the DBQs, work with a small group of classmates to read and discuss a contemporary primary source document and two historical ones. For each, discuss the author's point of view, intended audience, purpose, and historical context.

Following is a practice scoring guide for DBQs based on the College Board's grading rubric. (Check apcentral.collegeboard.com for the full rubric and any updates.) Use this guide to evaluate your work and to internalize the criteria for writing a strong DBQ essay.

A. Thesis: 0–1 Point

- 1 point for a historically defensible thesis/claim that establishes a line of reasoning to address the question, and does not merely restate it. The thesis must be at least one sentence and located in one place, either in the introduction or in the conclusion.

B. Contextualization: 0–1 Point

- 1 point to describe the broader historical context of the question, such as developments either before, during, or after its time frame. Describing the context requires more than a mere phrase or reference.

C. Evidence: 0–3 Points

Evidence from the Documents: 0–2 Points

- 1 point for accurately describing the content of **three documents** that address the question.

OR (Either the 1 point above or the 2 points below, but not both)

- 2 points for accurately describing the content of **six documents** and using them to **support the arguments** used in response to the question. Using the documents requires more than simply quoting them.

Evidence Beyond the Documents: 0–1 Point

- 1 point for using at least one additional piece of specific historical evidence **beyond** those found in the documents that is relevant to the arguments for the question. The evidence must be different from evidence used for the contextualization point and more than a mere phrase.

D. Analysis and Reasoning: 0–2 Points (Unlike the LEQ scoring, both points can be gained)

- 1 point for using at least **three documents** to explain **how or why** the document's point of view, purpose, historical situation, and/or audience is relevant to an argument used to address the question.

- 1 point for demonstrating a **complex understanding** of the historical developments by analyzing the multiple variables in the evidence. This can include analyzing more than one cause, both similarities and differences, both continuity and change, and/or the diversity of evidence that corroborates, qualifies, or modifies an argument used to address the question.

4. Answering the Long Essay Question (LEQ)

Test takers will answer one of three questions with a long essay in 40 minutes. All three options will focus on the same theme and reasoning skill, but they will focus on different periods. The first will focus on Period 1, the second on Periods 2 and 3, and the third on Periods 3 and 4. Before you begin to write, take 5 to 10 minutes to identify key points and plan the structure of your essay. Your essay responses will be evaluated on the argument you present: provide a clear evaluative thesis and support it with evidence.

Development of Essay Writing Skills Begin developing your writing skills as soon as the course starts. Rather than simply writing and rewriting complete essays, break down the skills needed to write an effective AP® history essay into sequential steps and work on one of them at a time. Following are basic steps in writing an essay:

1. Analyze the question.

2. Organize the evidence.

3. Take a position and express it in a thesis and introductory paragraph.

4. Write the supporting paragraphs and conclusion.

5. Evaluate the essay.

Analyze the Question Some students rush to start writing and fail to grasp the question fully. Before writing, ask yourself two questions:

- What is the topic?
- What is the historical reasoning skill?

Read over the question or prompt two or more times. What are the key words or phrases in the question? Underline them. They could be verbs such as *evaluate, analyze*, *explain*, *support*, or *refute*. All questions have one thing in common: They demand the use of historical reasoning skills and analysis of the evidence. An essay answer will not receive full credit by simply reporting information: You need to demonstrate that you can use the targeted historical reasoning skill. For example, consider this sample long essay question:

Evaluate the reasons why Great Britain began industrializing in the mid-18th century, before any other country.

Note all of the parts of the prompt. What is the topic? Industrialization in Great Britain. What is the historical reasoning skill? Causation. What does the prompt ask you to do? Evaluate reasons. What type of evidence do you need to provide? It must be significant and it must include an evaluation of the causes.

An essay that fails to deal with all parts of the question will receive a lower score than one that addresses the entire question. The few seconds you take to identify the topic and key reasoning skills will help you avoid the mistake of writing a clear, information-rich essay that receives little or no credit because you answered a question that was not asked.

Recommended Activity As an initial skill-building activity, analyze the essay questions at the end of Period 1. Underline the key words that indicate what the writer should do, and circle the words that indicate the specific parts or aspects of the content that need to be addressed.

Organize the Evidence Directions for the AP® European History exam advise students to spend some time planning before starting to answer the essay question. This advice emphasizes how critical it is to first identify what you know about the question and then organize your information. A recommended practice is to spend five minutes to create a brief outline, table, or other graphic organizer summarizing what you know about the question. The following table shows one way to organize the information that could become the essay to answer the question about the Industrial Revolution in Great Britain.

Why did Great Britain lead the Industrial Revolution?	
Geographic Factors	**Nongeographic Factors**
Massive coal deposits, coal used to • power steam engines • boost iron/steel production Coal industry itself became huge	Investment capital accumulated during trans-Atlantic slave trade
An island nation, Britain's strong maritime tradition bolstered • importation of raw materials • export of finished goods	Well-established British legal system protected investors and private property
Enclosure movement eliminated most common farmlands • forced farmers off land and into cities • created low-cost industrial workforce	Agricultural Revolution improved diets, reducing infant mortality and prolonging lives • workers were healthier and could work more efficiently • population (number of industrial workers) grew
Network of rivers and streams for powering mills and transporting goods	Technological improvements • spinning jenny and water frame • gave rise to the factory system

Recommended Activity Practice identifying the type of evidence you will need to answer questions by creating an outline, table, Venn diagram, or other graphic organizer for each of the questions in Chapter 1.

Take a Position and Express It in the Thesis and Introductory Paragraph After you see the evidence that you know, you can write a thesis statement that you can support. A strong thesis, or argument, is an essential part of every AP® European History long essay answer. Writers usually state the thesis in the first paragraph (sometimes the second), and they often restate it in the final paragraph or final two paragraphs. A thesis must be more than a restatement of the question.

A thesis requires taking a position on the question. In other words, it must be evaluative. Many students have difficulty taking a position necessary to build a strong argument. Some are afraid of making a mistake. But think about the nature of history. History does not offer the certitude of mathematics or the physical sciences. Disagreement over the interpretation of historical evidence develops because of the limitations of the evidence available and the differing perspectives of both participants and historians. AP® readers are looking not for the "right answer" but for a writer's ability to interpret the evidence and use historical support for that interpretation. Consider this important advice for any AP® essay question: If you think that you can write an essay without making some judgment that results in a thesis statement, you have not understood the question.

Below is one example of a thesis statement based on the information in the table on the previous page.

Between 1750 and the early 19th century, Britain became the first European state to industrialize because it had a unique combination of geographic and political advantages, including access to coal, capital, workers, technology, shipping, and a supportive government.

This statement takes a position—Britain had unique characteristics—and it identifies causation for the events raised in the question. This interpretation will provide the organizing argument that guides the development of the essay.

Recommended Activity Work with one or two partners. Each of you should write a prompt that might appear on a test based on a current event in the news. Exchange prompts. Then write a thesis statement in response to your partner's prompt. Compare and discuss your thesis statements using these guide questions:

- Does the thesis take a position?

- Does the thesis offer an interpretation of the question?

- Does the thesis help organize ideas for an essay?

The main point of the first paragraph is to clearly state a thesis that addresses the question. Readers will look for a clear thesis that sets the organization for the rest of the essay. An effective introductory paragraph also may provide the context of the question and a preview of the main arguments that will be developed in the subsequent paragraphs. However, this additional information should not distract from the thesis statement.

You may have learned to write an argumentative five-paragraph essay: a one-paragraph introduction, three paragraphs of support, and a one-paragraph conclusion that ties back to the introduction. This model shows the importance of the introductory paragraph in shaping the full essay, including the arguments to be developed. However, the total number of paragraphs in your AP® essay is for you to determine. You are likely to need more than three paragraphs of support.

Recommended Activity Practice writing introductory paragraphs for the essay questions at the end of each period. Next, follow up the introductory paragraph with an outline of the supporting paragraphs. For each paragraph, list historical evidence that you will link to the thesis. The exercise of writing an introductory paragraph and an outline of your supporting paragraphs helps in two ways. First, it reinforces the connection of the main points in the introduction to the supporting paragraphs. Second, it requires you to think in terms of historical evidence before you start writing a complete essay.

Write the Supporting Paragraphs and Conclusion The number and lengths of the paragraphs forming the body of the essay will vary depending on the thesis, the main points of your argument, and the amount of historical evidence you present. To receive the highest score, you also must explain how specific historical evidence is linked to the thesis. Each essay also will have a targeted historical reasoning skill that you should use to analyze the historical development or process you identified in your thesis. The chart that follows shows the main focus of an essay based on key words in the prompt.

Key Words in the Question	What an Essay Should Do
Cause, causation	Describe, analyze, and evaluate reasons why something happened, using specific examples.
Compare, comparison	Describe, analyze, and evaluate specific examples that show similarities and differences.
Continuity and change over time	Describe, analyze, and evaluate similarities (representing continuity) and differences (representing change across time) with specific examples.
Describe, identify	Describe or identify a significant, specific example of the essay topic.
Explain, analyze, evaluate	Identify and comment on the nature and relationship of the parts of a topic in order to explain why things happened.
Contextualization	Describe, analyze, and evaluate the extent to which other specific, relevant events influenced historical developments or process.

Besides your ability to address the targeted reasoning skill, your essay will be assessed on how well you develop your argument. Readers will consider how well you use specific historical evidence, recognize the historical context, and include evidence from outside the theme and time period of the question prompt. For example, in the sample question, the context of the Age of Discovery and the colonial markets it created is essential to understanding the industrialization of Britain.

Your goal is not to fill a specific number of pages but to write an insightful, persuasive, and well-supported answer. Many students fail to achieve the full potential of their essay because they simply list a few generalities or a "laundry list" of facts, and they do not answer the full question. Keep in mind that the readers of your essay are not looking for a retelling of history, or "stories." They will be grading you on your ability to craft an analytical essay that supports an argument with specific evidence. A short yet concise essay in which every word has a purpose is better than an essay bloated with fillers, flowery language, and interesting stories.

Your conclusion should restate the thesis. In addition, it should answer the larger question of "So what?" That is, the conclusion should provide the context and explain why the question is relevant in a broader understanding of history.

General Writing Advice Here are some tips to keep in mind as you start practicing the writing of history essays for the AP® exam.

- *Write in the third person.* Avoid using first-person pronouns (*I, we*). Write your essay in the third person (*it, they, she*, etc.).

- *Write in the past tense.* Use past tense verbs, except when referring to sources that currently exist (e.g., *the document implies*).

- *Use the active voice.* Readers prefer the active voice over the passive voice because it is more effective in explaining cause and effect. For example, "Factories were built in Britain" is in the passive voice. It is weak because it fails to say who built the factories. "Wealthy investors built factories in Britain" is in the active voice. It is stronger because it states who was taking action.

- *Use precise words.* Use words that clearly identify persons, factors, and judgments. Avoid vague verbs such as *felt*. Use stronger verbs instead such as *insisted*, *demanded*, or *supported*. Also, avoid vague references, such as *they* and *others,* unless you are clearly referring to people already identified. Use specifics, such as *Louis XVI of France.* Use verbs that communicate judgment and analysis, such as *reveal, exemplify, demonstrate, imply*, and *symbolize*.

- *Explain key terms.* The majority of questions will deal with specific terms (such as *Agricultural Revolution* or *mercantilism*), and an essential part of your analysis should be an explanation of these terms.

- *Anticipate counterarguments.* Consider arguments against your thesis to show that you are aware of opposing views. The strongest essays confront conflicting evidence by explaining why it does not undercut the thesis. The statement of counterarguments is known as the concession or the conciliatory paragraph. Writers often present it directly following the introduction.

- *Remain objective.* Avoid opinionated rhetoric. The AP® test is not the place to argue that one group was the "good guys," while another was the "bad guys." And do not use slang terms such as "bad guys"!

- *Communicate your organization.* Each paragraph in your essay should develop a main point that is clearly stated in the topic sentence. It is also good practice to provide a few words or a phrase of transition to connect one paragraph to another. Each paragraph also should include a sentence that links the ideas in the paragraph to the thesis statement.

- *Return to the thesis.* Writers often restate their thesis in the final paragraph in a fresh and interesting manner or explain its significance. The conclusion should not try to summarize all the data or introduce new evidence. If you are running out of time but have written a well-organized essay with a clear thesis that is supported with evidence, your conclusion can be very short. As noted earlier, including your thesis in the first and the last paragraph helps you make sure you have stated it clearly.

Recommended Activity Your first effort to write an AP® European History essay will be a more positive experience if it is an untimed assignment. After gaining confidence in writing the essay, you should try your hand at a timed test similar to that of the AP® exam (40 minutes for the essay). The purpose of such practice is to become familiar with the time constraints of the exam and to learn ways of (1) improving the clarity as well as the efficiency of your writing and (2) gaining insight into the type of information needed. The feedback from these practice tests—whether from teachers, peers, or self-evaluation—is essential for making progress.

Evaluate Your Essay More essay writing does not necessarily produce better essays. Breaking down the process into manageable steps is one key for improvement. Peer evaluation as well as self-evaluation also can help you internalize the elements of an effective essay and learn ways to improve. The activity on the next page provides a set of questions about how effectively an essay achieves the elements that the AP® readers look for in their grading. The use of the essay-evaluation techniques can help AP® candidates better understand the characteristics of an excellent essay.

Activity: Evaluation of the Essay

1. **Introductory Paragraph** Underline the thesis and circle the structural elements identified in the introduction. How effectively does the introductory paragraph prepare the reader for the rest of the essay? How might you improve the introductory paragraph?

2. **Thesis** Is the thesis clear? Does it take a position and address all parts of the question?

3. **Analysis** Does the body of the essay provide analysis of the question? Does the body reflect the argument and controlling ideas stated in the introductory paragraph? Does the body acknowledge opposing points of view? How could the analysis be improved?

4. **Evidence** Is the thesis supported clearly with substantial, relevant information? Is the evidence clearly connected to the stated thesis through strong paragraph topic sentences? What significant additional information or evidence could have been used for support?

5. **Errors** What minor or major errors in fact or analysis does the essay display?

6. **Presentation** How well organized and persuasive is the essay? Do the supporting paragraphs and their topic sentences address all parts of the essay prompt and stated thesis? Does paragraph composition, sentence structure, word choice, or spelling add to or detract from the essay? Identify areas that need improvement.

Recommended Activity Evaluation by a teacher and self-evaluation of essay work is initially less threatening than peer evaluation, but once a level of confidence is established, peer evaluation can help you become a better writer and is often the most useful form of feedback.

This scoring guide for the long essay question is based on the College Board's grading rubric. (Check apcentral.collegeboard.com for the full rubric and any updates.) Use the guide to evaluate your work and internalize the characteristics of a strong long essay.

PRACTICE SCORING GUIDE FOR LONG ESSAY QUESTIONS

A. Thesis: 0–1 Point

- 1 point for a historically defensible thesis/claim that establishes a line of reasoning to address the question, and not merely restate it. The thesis must be at least one sentence and located in one place, either in the introduction or in the conclusion.

B. Contextualization: 0–1 Point

- 1 point to describe the broader historical context of the question, such as developments either before, during, or after its time frame. Describing the context requires more than a mere phrase or reference.

C. Evidence: 0–2 Points

- 1 point for identifying specific historical examples of evidence relevant to the question.

OR (Either the 1 point above or the 2 points below, but not both)

- 2 points for using specific and relevant historical examples of evidence that support the arguments used to address the question.

D. Analysis and Reasoning: 0–2 Points

- 1 point for using historical reasoning to frame or structure the arguments that address the question, such as causation, comparison, or continuity and change over time. Reasoning may be uneven or not as complex as needed to gain two points.

OR (Either the 1 point above or the 2 points below, but not both)

- 2 points for using historical reasoning and demonstrating a complex understanding of the historical developments by analyzing the multiple variables in the evidence. This can include analyzing more than one cause, both similarities and differences, both continuity and change, and/ or the diversity of evidence that corroborates, qualifies, or modifies an argument used to address the question.

Review Schedule

Plan how you will prepare to take the AP® European History exam. Set a schedule for your review of each period of history. You might spread your review over a long or a short amount of time. Many AP® candidates find that study groups are helpful. The following is a sample of a review schedule using this text. It assumes the review will take place over six weeks:

Week 1: Review writing skills

Week 2: Period 1, (Chapter 1–6)

Week 3: Period 2, (Chapters 7–12)

Week 4: Period 3, (Chapters 13–18)

Week 5: Period 4, (Chapters 19–24)

Week 6: Complete and review the Practice Exam

Staying with a schedule requires discipline. A study group that chooses a specific time and place to meet and sets specific objectives for each meeting can reinforce the discipline of all its members. Some individuals may find it more productive to create a review schedule for themselves. If this review text has been used in conjunction with a history course, your familiarity with the essential content and skills developed in this book should make it an even more convenient and efficient review tool.

PERIOD 1: c. 1450 to c. 1648

Period Overview

Between 1450 and 1648, Europeans began to change how they thought about the world. They were moving away from the beliefs of the Middle Ages about how to think and to organize society and creating the foundation for attitudes that people commonly share today.

Science, Religion, and Exploration This period saw the beginning of modern science. Instead of relying on long-held ideas about the natural world, people began to rely more on close observation and precise recording of information. The result was revolutionary. To start with, Europeans realized that the earth was not the center of the universe.

These years also witnessed the collapse of the one force that united Europeans: the leadership of the Roman Catholic Church. Reformers challenged Catholic teachings and power. One result was a century of religious warfare that cost millions of people their lives.

The mid-1400s were also the beginning of two centuries of European exploration outside the continent. Driven by dreams of wealth, desire to spread Christianity, and curiosity about the world, Europeans connected Europe, Africa, and Asia with North and South America for the first time. In doing so, they established colonies and trade relations that united the world as never before.

Society and Politics These changes laid the foundation for profound changes in society. In 1450, almost all Europeans lived in rural communities and survived on what they grew or made themselves. They accepted inequality as natural and were loyal to their king, regardless of whether he shared their culture. By 1648, the world of today, with large cities, equality, democracy, and strong government, was beginning to emerge.

Key Concepts

1.1 The rediscovery of works from ancient Greece and Rome and observation of the natural world changed many Europeans' view of their world.

I. A revival of classical texts led to new methods of scholarship and new values in both society and religion.

II. The invention of printing promoted the dissemination of new ideas.

III. The visual arts incorporated the new ideas of the Renaissance and were used to promote personal, political, and religious goals.

IV. New ideas in science based on observation, experimentation, and mathematics challenged classical views of the cosmos, nature, and the human body, although existing traditions of knowledge and the universe continued.

1.2 Religious pluralism challenged the concept of a unified Europe.

I. The Protestant and Catholic reformations fundamentally changed theology, religious institutions, culture, and attitudes toward wealth and prosperity.

II. Religious reform both increased state control of religious institutions and provided justifications for challenging state authority.

III. Conflicts among religious groups overlapped with political and economic competition within and among states.

1.3 Europeans explored and settled overseas territories, encountering and interacting with indigenous populations.

I. European nations were driven by commercial and religious motives to explore overseas territories and establish colonies.

II. Advances in navigation, cartography, and military technology enabled Europeans to establish overseas colonies and empires.

III. Europeans established overseas empires and trade networks through coercion and negotiation.

IV. Europe's colonial expansion led to a global exchange of goods, flora, fauna, cultural practices, and diseases, resulting in the destruction of some indigenous civilizations, a shift toward European dominance, and the expansion of the slave trade.

1.4 European society and the experiences of everyday life were increasingly shaped by commercial and agricultural capitalism, notwithstanding the continued existence of medieval social and economic structures.

I. Economic change produced new social patterns, while traditions of hierarchy and status continued.

II. Most Europeans derived their livelihood from agriculture and oriented their lives around the seasons, the village, or the manor, although economic changes began to alter rural production and power.

III. Population shifts and growing commerce caused the expansion of cities, which often placed stress on their traditional political and social structures.

IV. The family remained the primary social and economic institution of early modern Europe and took several forms, including the nuclear family.

V. Popular culture, leisure activities, and rituals reflecting the continued popularity of folk ideas reinforced and sometimes challenged communal ties and norms.

1.5 The struggle for sovereignty within and among states resulted in varying degrees of political centralization.

I. The new concept of the sovereign state and secular systems of law played a central role in the creation of new political institutions.

II. The competitive state system led to new patterns of diplomacy and new forms of warfare.

III. The competition for power between monarchs and corporate and minority language groups produced different distributions of governmental authority in European states.

Source: *AP® European History Course and Exam Description*

Polish astronomer Nicolaus Copernicus ignited a revolution in European thought in the 16th century with his arguments that the sun, not the earth, was the center of the known universe. This statue of him stands in Warsaw, Poland.
Credit: Getty Images

The Renaissance and the Scientific Revolution

We have made you neither of heaven nor of Earth, neither mortal nor immortal, so that with freedom of choice and with honor, as though the maker and molder of yourself, you may fashion yourself in whatever shape you shall prefer.

—Pico della Mirandola, from *On the Dignity of Man*

Essential Question: How did the worldview of European intellectuals shift in the 15th century?

Beginning in the mid-1300s, Europe entered a period of transition between the Middle Ages and the modern world. Since the 19th century, historians have called this period the **Renaissance**, from a French word meaning "rebirth." During the Renaissance, many intellectuals showed a renewed interest in the civilizations of Greece and Rome during the **classical** era, roughly 800 B.C.E, to 500 C.E. Scholars of the 15th century first used the term **Middle Ages** to designate the period between the end of the classical era and their own time.

The Renaissance began in northern Italy and spread throughout Europe. It was a time when scholars broke free of the religion-based thinking of medieval times toward a belief in the dignity and limitless potential of human beings.

The **Roman Catholic Church** and the **Holy Roman Empire** had been the dominant institutions of the Middle Ages. Throughout that period, members of the clergy and issues of **theology**, the study of ideas about God, dominated intellectual life. The Catholic Church was closely involved in all aspects of political and social life. The Holy Roman Empire sought to establish unified political control over Christian Europe. Over time, scandals and abuses weakened the power of the papacy and the Catholic Church. The Holy Roman Emperors based in Germany found it increasingly difficult to maintain control over the distant Italian peninsula. These conditions, freeing scholars from the religious and political controls of the Middle Ages, set the stage for a period of intellectual exploration that had lasting effects throughout Europe on education, the arts, politics, religion, and science.

Revived Interest in the Classical World

Throughout the Middle Ages, monks had preserved and studied many classical texts in monasteries throughout Europe. Yet during the Renaissance, the revived interest in classical texts took a new form. One major change was that many Renaissance scholars were not members of the clergy. In addition, they approached the texts in new ways.

Italian Renaissance Humanists

Renaissance intellectuals who studied classical civilization and its texts were later called **humanists** because they focused on human beings and their inherent dignity. Humanists began to break free of the medieval philosophy known as **scholasticism**, which was limited by the beliefs of Roman Catholicism and focused on religious inquiries, such as proving the existence of God.

A Shift in Ideas about Religion Although humanists remained Christians, humanists tended to emphasize different values than did medieval scholars. The content of classical texts was **secular**, or worldly, rather than religious. Humanists emphasized living a good Earthly life rather than a life of penance aimed toward an afterlife. In addition, there was growth of **individualism** or a focus on personal rather than institutional interests.

Petrarch One of the earliest humanists, sometimes called the Father of Humanism, was an Italian poet and scholar named **Petrarch** (1304–1374). He saw the Middle Ages as a period of darkness when knowledge of classical civilization was in decline. (Later historians would refer to this period as the Dark Ages.) A lover of language, he criticized medieval scholars for their inelegant use of the Latin language and he searched for forgotten Latin manuscripts in libraries throughout Europe. One key discovery was *Letters to Atticus* by the Roman statesman and orator **Cicero** (106–43 B.C.E.), which gave insights into political life in classical Rome. Petrarch, followed by many later humanists, adopted Cicero as a model for writing in Latin. Though he appreciated Latin, he was among the first scholars of his era to write in the language of his region, Italian.

Stemming from his work with ancient manuscripts, Petrarch developed new **philological** approaches, scholarly methods of analyzing texts with a focus on the history of language. One famous use of philology occurred in 1440 when Lorenzo Valla demonstrated that an important Roman Catholic document, the *Donation of Constantine*, supposedly written by the Emperor Constantine in the 4th century, was a forgery, because its language was not the 4th-century Latin the emperor would have used.

Petrarch also admired Cicero's life as an engaged citizen. As a humanist, Petrarch focused on how people behaved. He criticized medieval thinkers who had focused more on scholarly issues of logic than on everyday concern of ethics.

Challenges to Institutional Power

Many classical Greek texts in philosophy and science had nearly disappeared in Europe during the Middle Ages. However, Arabic-speaking Islamic scholars in the Middle East, North Africa, and Spain preserved these works. These scholars had translated the works into Arabic, and from Arabic into Latin. As Europeans came into increased contact with the Islamic world during the Crusades of the 12th century, the texts again became available in Europe. However, since books were still copied by hand at that time, access to them was limited.

Some Renaissance humanists began to study Greek so they could read classical texts in their original language. In addition, after the invention of the printing press around 1450, many more copies of books were available. With the spread of books and literacy, the influence of universities and the Catholic Church over intellectual life declined. Classical texts and new methods of scientific inquiry, rather than theological writings, became the focus of education.

Changes in Education Scholars in the 15th century expanded the revival of interest in Greek and Roman texts to include literature, drama, and history. These works had been unavailable or of little interest to medieval scholars who were primarily concerned with theological questions. During the 15th century, the **liberal arts** (areas of study required for general knowledge rather than for specific professional skills, such as becoming a lawyer or church official) of the Middle Ages began to be called the **humanities**, and humanists were known as teachers of the humanities. The chart shows that in spite of some similarity in medieval and Renaissance higher education, there was a different emphasis.

Liberal Arts Curriculum at European Universities	
Medieval Universities, c. 13th century	Renaissance Universities, c. 15th century
• Grammar • Rhetoric • Logic • Arithmetic • Geometry • Astronomy • Music	• History • Moral philosophy • Eloquence • Letters (grammar and logic) • Poetry • Mathematics • Astronomy • Music
Instructors read aloud from Latin texts because few books were available.	Students were required to know Classical Latin and Greek to read those works directly.

Humanists believed that education could help people achieve their full human potential and would prepare them to be active, productive citizens. Therefore, they created secondary schools to teach the humanities to students at younger ages. In addition, while universities continued to focus on their traditional fields of study, they also began to include the humanities. The ultimate goal for humanists was not the preparation of scholars in theology, law, or medicine, but the development of a **Renaissance man**, an individual who excelled in many areas. *The Book of the Courtier*

Challenges to the Catholic Church As popes became more concerned with their political and financial power and with secular Renaissance culture, they lost some of the spiritual authority they once held. This shift happened at the same time many Christian humanists, especially in northern Europe, began to focus on texts of the early Catholic Church. These humanists advocated a return to a simpler and more humane form of Christianity. They criticized religious practices that they believed were not based on Scripture. (See Chapter 2 for more information on humanism and the Catholic Church.)

Revival of Civic Humanist Culture

In the 15th century, a single, unified country did not control the Italian peninsula. Instead, it was a collection of small regional kingdoms and self-governing communities called **city-states**. Large city-states, such as the northern Italian cities of **Florence, Venice, and Milan** also controlled the surrounding regions. Some of the city-states were ruled by local dukes and others by powerful families. Invasions by French, Spanish, and German forces only added to the political instability and rivalry among city-states.

Greek and Roman Political Institutions As humanists studied classical texts, they developed renewed admiration for Greek and Roman political institutions. For example, the city-state itself was the common form of government in classical Greece with Athens and Sparta as the two largest examples. Athens had been the site of the birth of **democracy**, government in which the people hold power either directly or by electing representatives. The **Roman Republic** was an early example of **representative government,** government elected by, and thus representative of, the people.

Politicians such as Cicero became secular models of active, engaged citizenship and eloquent leadership. Humanists saw in the classical examples a **civic humanist culture** that they sought to promote in their own place and time.

Baldassare Castiglione One secular model for individual behavior by the aristocratic class came from a writer in Milan. **Baldassare Castiglione** (1478–1529) wrote *The Book of the Courtier,* which outlined how to act as a proper gentleman or lady. It remained influential among the nobility for centuries. According to Castiglione, the ideal courtier, or person in frequent attendance at the court of a ruler, was similar to a medieval knight but was also classically educated, skilled in the arts, and engaged in civic life by serving that ruler.

Niccolò Machiavelli In 1498, **Niccolò Machiavelli** (1469–1527) began serving as a diplomat for the republic of Florence, thus also becoming familiar with French and German politics. While earlier generations of diplomats had represented the Christian empire, Machiavelli observed that Renaissance diplomats worked on behalf of their own state.

The early 16th century was a time of violence and instability in Florence. In 1512, a shift in political power caused the exile of Machiavelli and others who supported a republic. Hoping to demonstrate his insight and persuade another leader to hire him, Machiavelli turned to political writing.

Machiavelli's most famous work, *The Prince* (1513), provided advice for rulers. Unlike medieval political teachings that focused on morality, *The Prince* separated politics from morality. Perhaps written as a satire on contemporary Italiain politics, *The Prince* stressed the need for an absolute ruler to use any means to achieve political unity and independence from foreign control. Machiavelli presented a cynical view of human nature that required the prince to be feared rather than loved. He emphasized the importance of maintaining the power of the state to provide citizens with peace and safety. To maintain stability, leaders often had to commit acts such as lying and bribery, Machiavelli explained, but should appear virtuous. A leader unwilling to act in such ways would fail to serve the community and would soon lose power.

In a later work, *The Discourses*, Machiavelli pointed to the Roman Republic as a model of a government under law, rather than under an authoritarian prince. Yet, whether Machiavelli himself favored republicanism or **despotism**, the exercise of oppressive and absolute power, his ideas were influential. The principles for achieving and maintaining power in *The Prince* became a guide for later authoritarian regimes. *The Prince* has become identified with the belief that "the end justify the means," or that any methods, however evil or dishonest, may be used to achieve positive results.

The Printing Press Revolution

One key feature of the Renaissance was access to written works. During the Middle Ages, books had been copied by hand. Printing from carved wooden blocks began in Europe toward the end of the 14th century. Such blocks were first used to print religious pictures and then small amounts of text. Renaissance scholars needed new technologies to make their ideas available beyond Italy.

Invention of the Printing Press A revolutionary printing technology— **movable type** made of metal—was developed by printers over the first half of the 15th century in Europe. With this new development, printers could compose whole pages of text by creating lines of type from individual letters. Once a page was printed, the printer could take the type apart and reuse it. **Johannes Gutenberg**, a German printer, devised a usable form of the new process between 1445 and 1450. In addition, Gutenberg developed a **printing press** that differed from earlier technology. The hand-operated wooden press was the beginning of a process of mechanizing printing and producing large quantities of books. The **Gutenberg Bible**, completed in 1456, is the first known example of a book produced from movable type.

Printing then spread rapidly throughout Europe, and within a few years there were printers throughout the Germanic states of the Holy Roman Empire.

By the 1470s, printing had spread throughout Europe. By 1500, Europe had more than 1,000 printers, and Venice alone had nearly 100. Most earlier printed works had been religious or classical and were often in Latin. However, the printing press made **vernacular literature**, written in the native language of a region, increasingly available. The availability of books in the language that ordinary people used increased the number of lay readers. Over the following centuries, reading caused people to identify more and more with their own national cultures. rates of literacy ↑

The Printing Press and Religious Reform Renaissance humanism spread to northern Europe in the late 15th century, and northern humanists focused more on religious concerns than did their Italian counterparts. By 1500, about half of the 40,000 titles that had been published were Bibles or other religious works. Humanists especially desired to reform the Catholic Church; but such calls had spread slowly at first, because they were written in Latin and had to be copied by hand.

However, by 1517, printing had become well established and would have explosive impact on Europe. That year, German monk **Martin Luther** (1483–1546) called for religious reform. Luther emphasized the Bible as the main source of religious truth and believed that people should be able to read and interpret the Bible themselves without the aid of priests. Luther's ideas were quickly translated into German, printed into pamphlets, and distributed throughout German-speaking lands. A local protest by one unknown scholar ignited a raging controversy.

95 Theses

Soon, additional reformers added to the debate sparked by Luther. The printing press allowed them to spread their ideas faster and more widely than ideas had ever spread before.

Within a decade, a revolutionary shift in European Christianity and politics, known as the Protestant Reformation, had begun. (See Chapter 2 for more information on the Protestant Reformation.) Scripture readings became an important part of the Protestant services that were replacing the Catholic mass. Since most people did not read Latin, if they were going to read the Bible, they needed one in their vernacular, or local language. With the spread of printing, affordable Bibles appeared in many vernaculars for the first time.

Renaissance Ideas in the Visual Arts

The revived interest in classical civilizations affected the visual arts just as it had other aspects of Renaissance culture. Artists of the Middle Ages had emphasized religious messages rather than portraying their subjects realistically. Paintings looked flat and were decorative. Renaissance artists, however, studied examples of classical art, and along with the influence of humanist ideas, brought a fresh emphasis and style to the visual arts. Renaissance artists began to promote not only religion, but also personal, political, and religious goals of the artists and their patrons.

Italian Art and Architecture

In addition to using classical themes and styles and focusing on human beings, Renaissance painters and sculptors incorporated new techniques and trends in their work. In contrast to the heavy use of symbolism in medieval painting, Renaissance artists tried to be more realistic in two ways:

- As artists observed the natural world more closely, they began to aim for **naturalism** in their works. Artists wanted to imitate nature.

- Artists mastered the technique of **geometric perspective**, which used mathematics to help them create the appearance of space and distance in two-dimensional paintings.

The Medici Family and Florence Italian Renaissance patrons of the arts were rulers and popes who commissioned works of art mainly to increase their own prestige. Among the most prominent of these patrons were leaders of the Medici family, which controlled Florence for decades. Their commissions of paintings, sculptures, and architecture made Florence the early center of much of the greatest Renaissance art.

The Church of San Lorenzo For example, **Cosimo de' Medici** commissioned **Filippo Brunelleschi** (1377–1446) as architect for the rebuilding of the Church of San Lorenzo in Florence (shown on the next page). The Church reflects the influence of Roman achitechture with its use of classical columns and rounded arches. Further, it is built to a more human scale than medieval Gothic cathedrals. Brunelleschi also incorporated into the church the largest dome built since classical Rome.

The cathedral in Cologne shows the impressive scale and complexity of Gothic churches.
Credit: Getty Images

Church of San Lorenzo reflected the human-scale church architecture during the Renaissance.
Credit: Getty Images

Botticelli The grandson of Cosimo de' Medici, known as **Lorenzo the Magnificent** (ruled 1469–1492), kept a large group of artists at his court, including **Sandro Botticelli** (1445–1520). Botticelli's famous painting, *Primavera (Spring)*, displays the artist's interest in classical mythology, featuring the figures of Venus, Cupid, Flora, and Mercury.

The High Renaissance The period 1480–1520, when Renaissance art reached its peak, is called the **High Renaissance**. During this period, the city of Rome became prominent as an artistic center. Three artists dominated this period, creative geniuses who advanced far beyond their art.

The first of these dominant artists was **Leonardo da Vinci** (1452–1519). Leonardo is often referred to as the model of the Renaissance man because of the range of his talents. He studied nature and conducted experiments, dissected human bodies to learn more about their structure, and drew designs for machines that were far ahead of his time. Leonardo urged artists to move beyond the earlier emphasis on realism to a portrayal of human beings that reflected their idealized or divine qualities. Two of his most famous paintings are the portrait *Mona Lisa* and *The Last Supper*, a **fresco**, or wall painting using watercolor on wet plaster. *The Last Supper* demonstrates Leonardo's mastery of perspective as well as his skill at depicting idealized human figures with psychological insight.

Michelangelo (1475–1564) was the second leading artist of the High Renaissance. Another Renaissance man, **Michelangelo** was a sculptor, painter, architect, and poet. In 1501, the government of Florence commissioned him to create the monumental marble sculpture *David*, in which he portrays the biblical figure of David to reveal the splendor of the human form. Michelangelo is probably best known for his commission from the pope to paint the ceiling of the **Sistine Chapel** in the Vatican. In the paintings, Michelangelo focused on scenes from the biblical book of Genesis, showing humans as reflections of the divine. In this commission and others, including plans to rebuild **St. Peter's Basilica** in Rome, the pope sought to revitalize the prestige of the papacy and the Papal States, the lands in central Italy that the pope ruled from 756 to 1870.

Raphael (1483–1520) was another dominant Renaissance artist who flourished under papal patronage. His many paintings of the Virgin Mary idealized her beauty. The pope commissioned Raphael to paint a series of frescoes in the Vatican Palace. Perhaps the most famous is *School of Athens*, (painted c. 1510–1511).. In this work, Raphael portrayed a gathering of classical scholars, including **Aristotle** and **Plato**, using perspective and other Renaissance techniques to demonstrate harmony, balance, and order—all principles central to both classical and Renaissance art.

Medieval paintings, such as this one of Mary holding Jesus, often appear flat and somewhat out of proportion

Credit: Getty Images.

This Renaissance painting of Mary, the mother of Jesus, shows the depth and complexity of art from that period.

Credit: Getty Images

The Northern Renaissance

Renaissance humanism and art spread to the regions north of the Alps later in the 15th century in a movement known as the **Northern Renaissance**. Northern humanists retained a more religious focus, which influenced artists of the region as well. The naturalism of their art was more human-centered and artists considered individuals and everyday life appropriate objects for their work. Artists in the north were less focused on the beauty of the human form and realistic settings and more on rendering exquisite details in smaller works such as illuminated manuscripts and altarpieces painted on wooden boards.

Flanders, a region in what is now part of France and Belgium, became the leading center of art in the north in the 15th century. The focus on individuals and everyday life as objects in art can be seen in the work of **Jan Van Eyck** (c. 1390–1441) and other northern artists who observed nature closely in order to depict details accurately, but did not display the skill of Italian artists in the use of perspective and proportion. However, after the spread of Protestantism in northern Europe, the number of religious works of art declined as they became associated with idolatry, or the worship of physical objects as divine.

Mannerist and Baroque Artists

In the 16th century, monarchies, city-states, and the Catholic Church commissioned works of art to promote their own stature and power. Artists continued to follow the High Renaissance principles by expressing themselves in new ways.

Mannerism The term "**Mannerism**" started as a criticism. It came from 16th-century critics who thought contemporary artists were painting in the "manner" of Michelangelo and Raphael but lacked the same substance. However, Mannerist artists did want to break away from some High Renaissance traditions. In particular, they wanted to replace the principles of balance and harmony with more distortion and illusion to add drama to their works.

Like the Renaissance, Mannerism spread from Italy to other parts of Europe. Mannerism also reflected the spiritual and political turmoil following the Protestant Reformation in the 1520s and 1530s. Perhaps the highest example of Mannerism was the work of **El Greco** (1541–1614). He was originally from Crete, studied in Italy, and later settled in Spain where he became a church painter. His elongated figures and dark, eerie colors created feelings of intense emotion.

Baroque Around 1570, Mannerism gave way to **Baroque**, also beginning in Italy. Baroque art and architecture brought together Renaissance classical traditions and the strong religious feelings stirred up by the Reformation. It departed from the realism and naturalism of Renaissance works, however, in its dramatically complex appeal to the senses.

Baroque architecture and sculpture became important to Catholic rulers and clergy in central and northern Europe, who resisted the Reformation and commissioned dramatic Baroque architecture and sculpture to stimulate religious devotion in their followers. The courts of Madrid, Vienna, Prague, and Brussels were patrons of Baroque artists. The grand scale and splendor of their palaces, including elaborate decorations, were intended to reflect their power and evoke awe. In the same way, the Catholic Church wanted to reflect the power of the faith in its new churches.

Baroque art spread beyond central and southern Europe and included painting, sculpture, and architecture:

- **Peter Paul Rubens** (1577–1640) became the most prominent Baroque painter from northern Europe. His paintings, which exemplified Baroque style, were dramatic in their use of light and color and dynamic movement and were known for richly sensual nude forms.

- **Gian Lorenzo Bernini** (1598–1680) was a famous Italian Baroque architect and sculptor. He completed the work on St. Peter's Basilica, begun during the High Renaissance.

Observation-Based Science

Renaissance humanism and art laid the groundwork for new ideas in science to emerge in the 16th and 17th centuries. Humanists' emphasis on learning Greek led later scholars to read a broader range of classical texts, providing a source of ideas that challenged the existing worldview. In addition, artists' close observations of the natural world and use of mathematics to develop techniques, such as perspective, established a new way to learn about the world. Later thinkers expanded the use of experimentation that Leonardo da Vinci and others developed in the late 15th century. These new methods for studying the natural world were the core of the **Scientific Revolution**, which developed slowly between the mid-16th and late-18th centuries.

New Ideas in Astronomy

Since ancient times, scholars have tried to understand their world and the cosmos. The word **astronomy** comes from the ancient Greek word meaning "arrangement of the stars." It is a general term for the study of the universe beyond the earth. **Cosmology** is the branch of astronomy concerned with the origins and structure of the universe.

Medieval Worldview The classical cosmology of the Greek philosopher Aristotle and astronomer **Ptolemy** (2nd century C.E.) went unchallenged for more than 1,400 years, forming the basis of the worldview of medieval scholastic philosophers. Aristotle and Ptolemy portrayed a **geocentric** universe—one with the earth at the center of a system of concentric spheres, including the sun, circling around it. According to this worldview, the planets were bodies of light. Medieval scholastic philosophers accepted this view and, in line with their Christian beliefs, taught that God and the souls of those who had been saved existed beyond the outermost sphere of the system.

Copernicus's New System Among the first Europeans to challenge the classical view was **Nicolaus Copernicus** (1473–1543), a Polish mathematician and **natural philosopher**, a scholar who studied the physical world. In classical writings, Copernicus found references to ancient Greeks who questioned the geocentric views of Aristotle and Ptolemy and believed instead in a **heliocentric**, or sun-centered, universe. ⟶ What we know today

Copernicus then applied advanced mathematics to earlier astronomical observations to confirm the idea that the planets, including the earth, revolved around the sun. He proved that the perceived motion of the sun came from the earth's spinning on its axis and its annual orbit around the sun. Although he still accepted many of Aristotle's ideas, Copernicus feared that other astronomers would criticize his heliocentric system. Therefore, he only published his work, *On the Revolution of the Heavenly Spheres*, shortly before his death.

Building on Copernicus Later natural philosophers built on Copernicus's work, including German astronomer, **Johannes Kepler** (1571–1630). By analyzing precise measurements of planetary orbits, Kepler found them to be elliptical rather than circular. By demonstrating these elliptical orbits, Kepler further supported Copernicus's still-controversial heliocentric model and disputed the religious belief (which even he had originally held) that the circle was the "perfect shape" and reflected the Divine order.

Kepler shared his published work with the Italian mathematician **Galileo Galilei** (1564–1642) in 1597. Galileo then extended Kepler's ideas through use of a new method to observe the planets. He became the first European to build and use a **telescope** for this purpose and thus discovered details that had never been known, such as the moons that circled Jupiter as well as the craters on Earth's moon. With these observations, Galileo showed that the planets were not ethereal bodies but were similar to Earth in their composition. Galileo's book *The Starry Messenger*, published in 1610, reaffirmed the heliocentric system and brought wide attention to these new ideas.

The Catholic Church rejected Galileo's work and found him guilty of heresy. They placed him under house arrest until his death. Although Galileo retracted his ideas publicly, his works continued to circulate. Later, Galileo's work on bodies in motion further challenged Aristotle's views of the universe.

A New Worldview The Catholic Church's condemnation of Galileo diminished the growth of science in Italy. The scientist who later brought together the ideas of Copernicus, Kepler, and Galileo was the English mathematician, **Isaac Newton** (1642–1727). Among Newton's many accomplishments was the discovery of the **universal law of gravitation**. Newton published his proofs for this law in *Principia* (1687), demonstrating that gravity applied to objects on Earth and in space and was the force that held the planets in orbit around the sun.

Newton saw the universe as a giant machine with God as the prime mover who set the planets in motion. While Newton's ideas were accepted rather quickly in England, it took almost a century after *Principia* before they were generally accepted on the continent of Europe.

Over a period of approximately 200 years, astronomers had developed a radical new cosmology, challenging the ideas of Aristotle and Ptolemy that were so widely held for about 1,400 years. Such rapid change in such fundamental beliefs shook the foundations of knowledge, but it was just an early step in replacing trust in tradition with reliance on observations and data.

Anatomical and Medical Discoveries

Much like medieval astronomy, medicine of medieval times was dominated by ideas from ancient Greece and was transformed in the 16th and 17th centuries. The work of the Greek physician **Galen** (2nd century C.E.) dominated the fields of anatomy and physiology. **Anatomy** refers to the structure of the bodies of humans, animals, and plants. **Physiology** refers to how those systems function.

Traditional Theory of Medicine Because Galen dissected animals rather than humans, his ideas of human anatomy were often incorrect. He thought there were two different systems of blood flowing through the arteries and veins that controlled different systems of the body. Galen also put forth the **humoral theory** of the body and disease. According to this theory, the body was composed of four humors, namely blood, yellow bile, phlegm, and black bile. Each humor had different combinations of the qualities of warm, cold, wet, and dry. According to Galen's theory, disease was caused by an imbalance of the humors.

Challenges to Galen's Ideas Three physicians were most notable in challenging Galen's theories:

- **Paracelsus** (1493–1531) used observation and experiments to develop a theory of disease based on chemical imbalances in specific organs that could be treated with chemical remedies in careful dosages.

- **Andreas Vesalius** (1514–1564) emphasized anatomical research, including dissection of the human body.

- **William Harvey** (1578–1657) corrected Galen's ideas on the **circulatory system**, describing the body instead as an integrated system. Harvey's experiments demonstrated that the heart was the starting point for the circulation of a single system of blood that makes a complete circuit through the body's arteries and veins. Modern physiology is based on Harvey's ideas.

The Scientific Method

As part of the Scientific Revolution, some thinkers promoted a more systematic approach to acquiring knowledge about the natural world. They laid the foundations for the **scientific method**, an approach based on observation, experimentation, and reasoning. It combines two different but complementary types of reasoning.

Two Types of Reasoning An English lawyer named **Francis Bacon** (1561–1626) encouraged scientists of his time to build their knowledge on the foundation of **inductive reasoning**, which moves from the specific to the general. For example, a scientist might observe many individual flowers and then come up with a general conclusion about flowers based on those observations. Bacon believed that scholars should combine careful observation and systematic experimentation to collect small bits of information. Then they could use the information to support valid general conclusions. Bacon encouraged the growth of an international community of natural philosophers who would share the information from their research. The area of work of these scholars came to be called **natural science**.

use evidence to hypothesize

In contrast, **deductive reasoning** moves from the general to the specific. A leading advocate of this approach was the French philosopher **René Descartes** (1596–1650). He wanted scientists to think like students of geometry. They should start with general principles, similar to geometric axioms, and then apply them using strict logic to understand particular cases.

Isaac Newton brought these two complementary forms of reasoning together into the scientific method. A scientist might begin by conducting experiments that involved observation and data collection. Over time, general conclusions could be drawn from this data. Then these general conclusions might be extended by deductions that led to new hypotheses that could be tested through further experimentation. The goal of this new scientific endeavor was the formulation of general principles about the way the world worked, called **natural laws**, often based on mathematical proofs or expressed as mathematical formulas. Newton's universal law of gravitation provides one example of a natural law.

LEADERS IN THE SCIENTIFIC REVOLUTION

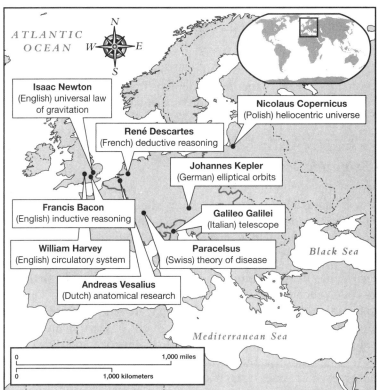

Exploration and Science When laying out his method of inductive reasoning, Francis Bacon clearly stated that his goal was for humans to gain practical benefits from scientific knowledge and "conquer nature in action." An example of this scientific approach can be seen in Europeans' encounters with the Western Hemisphere that began in the late 15th century (see Chapter 3).

These encounters provided new impetus to formulating natural laws based on a wealth of data gained through direct observation, including new information about geography, types of plants and animals, and different races and cultures. Gathering such data through direct observation supported the new endeavor of expanding scientific knowledge in general.

Science Before and After the Renaissance		
Area	**Medieval Science**	**Post-Renaissance Science**
Goal	To demonstrate the truth of traditional Christian beliefs	To understand the natural world
Background of Natural Philosophers	Most were clergy members	Most were secular
Classical Sources	Relied on Aristotle, Ptolemy, and Galen	Drew on a broad range of classical sources
Methods	Relied primarily on logical analysis	Combined observation and experiments with logic and mathematical calculations
Relationship with Religious Authorities	The Catholic Church judged the validity of scientific ideas	Science and religion were separate paths of inquiry

Persistence of Traditional Views

The acquisition of knowledge through inductive and deductive reasoning makes up an inquiry-based **epistemology**, or philosophy of knowledge—a way of understanding what we know and how we know it. While this new method dominated the thinking of natural philosophers during the 16th and 17th centuries, it did not generally clash with more traditional ideas about how people learned. Europeans continued to believe that spiritual forces governed the cosmos. Most scientists of the time believed in God and accepted a role for religion. Only later, in the 19th century, did people disagree over the boundary between science and religion.

Scientists of the 16th and 17th centuries also continued to accept two other traditional explanations about the world: alchemy and astrology.

- **Alchemy** was a medieval and Renaissance approach to chemistry primarily focused on discovering a method to turn common metals into gold. In a broader sense, alchemy was concerned with transformation and saw the world as filled with divinity.

- **Astrology** was originally synonymous with astronomy, but during the Renaissance it came to mean the study of the heavenly bodies as they influenced human activity.

These traditional ideas continued to appeal to elites and to some natural philosophers. For example, Kepler studied astrology and was interested in the idea of a sacred geometry in the universe. Newton wrote extensively about his experiments in alchemy. Paracelsus's view that a human being was a small reflection of the larger universe was similar to the basis of astrology. These traditional views persisted partly because, like the new science, they supported the idea that humans could understand the universe and make predictions about it.

HISTORICAL PERSPECTIVES: WHAT MADE PEOPLE CIVIL?

Since at least the days of the classical Greeks and Romans, writers in what is today Europe have been commenting on what social behavior is proper. However, not only have ideas of civility changed, but also people have changed their ideas about the roles of men and women in setting the standards.

Defining Civility Baldassare Castiglione's *The Book of the Courtier* (1528) was one of the most influential books in 16th-century Europe. Castiglione told an engaging story about an after-dinner conversation among gentlemen in the court of the duke who ruled Urbino, a 16th-century Italian city. The men discussed the qualities of the perfect courtier and how one achieves civility. *The Book of the Courtier* provided guidance for men throughout Europe who aspired to serve and influence powerful princes and kings. Castiglione focused on the causes and results of individual behavior.

In contrast to Castiglione, 20th-century German sociologist Norbert Elias, in *The Civilizing Process* (1939), focused on the social context of civility. He explored how development of manners and individual personality was part of the formation and centralization of power within modern states. Civility was part of the taming of individual passions in order to create a stable government.

The Influence of Women On the surface, women did not seem to play a major role in Castiglione's *The Book of the Courtier*—the discussion was among men. However, under the influence of feminism in the late 20th century, scholars took a closer look at gender roles in the book. They pointed out that women, though not key participants in the discussion, were important. They were not only present, but they determined the guest list, set the rules of the "game," and influenced the men to behave with civility.

Some historians argued that women of the Renaissance represented a higher standard of civility than men. As mothers, wives, and teachers, women worked behind the scenes to provide men with models of behavior to use when trying to work with and impress a ruler. If women failed to provide such models, the men would not become good courtiers. Then a ruler would lack the skilled advisors necessary to lead the state. Whether women became more or less influential than men during the Renaissance depends, in part, on the point of view of the historian about what determines influence.

KEY TERMS BY THEME

Knowledge

Aristotle
Plato
Ptolemy
Nicolaus Copernicus
Johannes Kepler
Galileo Galilei
Isaac Newton
Galen
Paracelsus
Andreas Vesalius
William Harvey
Francis Bacon
René Descartes
Scientific Revolution
astronomy
cosmology
geocentric
natural philosopher
heliocentric
telescope
universal law of
    gravitation
anatomy
physiology
humoral theory
circulatory system
scientific method
inductive reasoning
natural science
deductive reasoning
natural law

epistemology
alchemy
astrology

States

Holy Roman Empire
city-state
Florence
Venice
Milan
democracy
Roman Republic
representative
    government
Niccolò Machiavelli

Society: Individuals

Petrarch
Cicero
Baldassare Castiglione
Johannes Gutenberg
Martin Luther
Cosimo de' Medici
Sandro Botticelli
Leonardo da Vinci
Michelangelo
Raphael
Jan Van Eyck
El Greco
Peter Paul Rubens
Lorenzo Bernini
Filippo Brunelleschi
Lorenzo the Magnificent

Society

Renaissance
classical
Middle Ages
Roman Catholic Church
theology
humanists
scholasticism
secular
individualism
philological
liberal arts
humanities
Renaissance man
civic humanist culture
despotism
movable type
printing press
Gutenberg Bible
vernacular literature
Protestant Reformation
naturalism
geometric perspective
High Renaissance
fresco
Sistine Chapel
St. Peter's Basilica
Northern Renaissance
Mannerism
Baroque

Questions 1–3 refer to the passage below.

"The foundations of all true learning must be laid in the sound and thorough knowledge of Latin: which implies study marked by a broad spirit, accurate scholarship, and careful attention to details . . . Without it the great monuments of literature are unintelligible, and the art of composition impossible. . . .

But we must not forget that true distinction is to be gained by a wide and varied range of such studies as conduce to the profitable enjoyment of life . . .

First amongst such studies I place History: a subject which must not on any account be neglected by one who aspires to true cultivation . . . For the careful study of the past enlarges our foresight in contemporary affairs and affords to citizens and to monarchs lessons of incitement or warning in the ordering of public policy. . . .

The great Orators of antiquity must by all means be included. Nowhere do we find the virtues more warmly extolled, the vices so fiercely decried. . . .

I come now to Poetry and the Poets. . . . For we cannot point to any great mind of the past for whom the Poets had not a powerful attraction."

Leonardo Bruni, *On Learning and Literature*, c. 1405

1. The passage most clearly shows the influence of which development?
   a) The use of the scientific method to critique traditional knowledge
   b) The development of mandatory systems of public education
   c) A renewed interest in classical Greek and Roman texts among humanist thinkers
   d) The increase of publications questioning Papal authority

2. The methods of learning described in this passage contributed most directly to which change in thinking?
   a) Political revolutions based on the idea of natural rights
   b) The discovery of gravity and the laws of motion
   c) New ideas about government and individual behavior
   d) The rediscovery of secular ideas from ancient Greece and Rome

3. Compared to Bruni's view of education in the 15th century, intellectuals in the 18th century tended to:
   a) emphasize intuition and emotion more than formal education.
   b) be less reliant on classical sources of knowledge.
   c) reject education as a means of social progress.
   d) place more faith in religious authorities.

Questions 4–5 refer to the excerpt below.

"I think that in discussions of physical problems we ought to begin not from the authority of scriptural passages but from sense experiences and necessary demonstrations; for the holy Bible and the phenomena of nature proceed alike from the divine Word the former as the dictate of the Holy Ghost and the latter as the observant executrix [a female who carries out orders of another] of God's commands. . . .

From this I do not mean to infer that we need not have an extraordinary esteem for the passages of holy Scripture. On the contrary, having arrived at any certainties in physics, we ought to utilize these as the most appropriate aids in the true exposition of the Bible and in the investigation of those meanings which are necessarily contained therein, for these must be concordant [in agreement] with demonstrated truths. I should judge that the authority of the Bible was designed to persuade men of those articles and propositions which, surpassing all human reasoning could not be made credible by science, or by any other means than through the very mouth of the Holy Spirit . . .

But I do not feel obliged to believe that the same God who has endowed us with senses, reason and intellect has intended us to forego their use and by some other means to give us knowledge which we can attain by them. He would not require us to deny sense and reason in physical matters which are set before our eyes and minds by direct experience or necessary demonstrations."

Galileo Galilei, "Letter to Madame Christina de Lorraine,
Grand Duchess of Tuscany," 1615

4. This passage most clearly demonstrates the influence of which of the following developments?

    a) Christian humanist interest in original translations of the Bible
    b) The Scientific Revolution's promotion of reasoning and experimentation
    c) Renaissance thinkers' reliance on classical Greek and Roman sources
    d) The Protestant Reformation's emphasis on the authority of scripture

5. This passage best demonstrates which of the following about scientific thinkers in the 17th century?

    a) They continued to hold religious worldviews as they pursued scientific inquiry.
    b) They received substantial support from political authorities.
    c) They developed mathematical models to prove scientific ideas.
    d) They rejected the role of divine forces in the universe.

Questions 6–8 refer to the image below.

In this 1435 painting, Dutch artist Jan Van Eyck shows Nicolas Rolin, a wealthy contributor to the Catholic Church, seated with the Virgin Mary, who is holding Jesus.

Credit: *http://www.lou-vre.fr/en/oeuvre-notices/virgin-chancellor-rolin*

6. This painting reflects which of the following developments in the Northern Renaissance?

    a) The portrayal of individuals interacting with nature

    b) The portrayal of the everyday life of common people

    c) The portrayal of subjects from classical mythology

    d) The portrayal of religious content as the subject matter

7. Based upon the image and its intended audience, the inclusion of Rolin in the painting was most likely a reflection of

    a) the artist's belief in the divine right of kings.

    b) the desire of secular rulers to control Church institutions.

    c) the effort of elites to enhance their prestige by supporting the arts.

    d) the use of art to promote civic virtue.

8. The emergence of Baroque and Mannerist artistic styles were different than the style that influenced the above painting in which of the following ways?

a) The depiction of landscapes rather than people as the focal point

b) The inclusion of more dramatic and exaggerated human forms

c) The rejection of religious subjects and symbols

d) The use of abstract shapes and colors to convey the artist's vision

SHORT-ANSWER QUESTIONS

1. Use the passage below to answer all parts of the question that follows.

"The dissemination of new humanist learning during the Renaissance typically included five methods: tutoring and self-directed study in families, education in schools, humanist lecturing, conversations in small private groups and larger coteries, and correspondence. . . . In the fifteenth century and early sixteenth century many Italian women displayed the highest technical competence in the study, interpretation, and exposition of the revived humanist learning. Some [of] them . . . could hold their own in matters of scholarship with the best of their male contemporaries and . . . were accepted and even acclaimed elsewhere."

Mary R. Beard, *Women as a Force in History,* 1946

a) Explain how ONE piece of evidence supports Beard's argument regarding the effects of the Renaissance on women in Europe.

b) Explain how ONE piece of evidence undermines Beard's argument regarding the effects of the Renaissance on women in Europe.

c) Explain how ONE feature of 20th-century life life might have influenced Beard's interpretation of the Renaissance.

2. Answer all parts of the question that follows.

a) Identify ONE way in which classicism influenced the development of the Renaissance in Europe from 1450 to 1550.

b) Explain ONE difference between the Italian Renaissance and the Northern Renaissance in the period from 1450 to 1550.

c) Explain ONE similarity between the Italian Renaissance and the Northern Renaissance in the period from 1450 to 1550.

LONG ESSAY QUESTIONS

1. Evaluate to what extent changes in technology influenced European life in the 14th to 16th centuries.

2. Evaluate to what extent changes in how people viewed history influenced European life in the 14th to 16th centuries.

REFLECT ON THE CHAPTER ESSENTIAL QUESTION

1. In one to three paragraphs, explain how the worldview of European intellectuals shifted in the 15th century.

WRITE AS A HISTORIAN: UNDERSTANDING THE PROMPT

When answering an essay question, try to think as a historian does by understanding complex relationships and analyzing information to support a position. Read the prompt slowly. Circle direction words, such as *analyze, evaluate, validate or refute, or compare or contrast.* Each of these words has its own meaning:

- *Evaluate* means to identify positive and negative aspects or determine something's significance.
- *Analyze* means to examine causes and effects, to explain why something happened; more broadly, in means to examine the structure of something in order to explain or interpret it.
- *Validate* means to show support for an idea. *Refute* means to argue against it.
- *Compare* means to explore similarities and differences between ideas or things. *Contrast* means to explore differences. Some questions ask for compare and contrast.
- *Examine continuity and change over time* means to understand how and why some things have changed in a given period of time while other things have remained the same.

Identify the reasoning skill that each statement requires.

1. Explain the social and economic changes in Europe that resulted from the increase in wealth produced by overseas trade.

2. Compare and contrast Catholicism and Protestantism in terms of doctrine and practice.

3. What effects did the values of individualism, subjectivity, and emotion have on changing traditional political ideologies' artistic forms?

Writing notes in the margins is one way to plan your response to a question. If you use accurate historical evidence and clearly organize your thoughts, writing will be easier, and your argument will be easier for readers to identify.

For each of the following prompts, which statement below it would be most useful in the argument answering it?

4. Analyze the ways in which the revival of classical texts influenced Italian society during the Renaissance.

   a. Classical Greek and Roman texts were written by people such as the playwright Euripides, the epic poet Homer, and the satirist Horace.

   b. The intellectuals of the Renaissance, later known as humanists, used their knowledge of Greek and Latin to revive classical ideas that put humans at the center of all things.

5. Compare and contrast the styles of the visual arts in Italy and in the Northern Renaissance.

   a. Although both Italian and Northern Renaissance artists depicted religious subjects, Northern Renaissance artists focused more on everyday life and human-centered themes.

   b. The Italian Renaissance produced some of the most famous artists in history, including Michelangelo, Donatello, and Raphael.

6. Analyze the ways in which the invention of the printing press affected European society during the Renaissance.

   a. The printing press spread Renaissance ideas beyond Italy and created more vernacular literature, which led to a rise in national cultures and a lasting challenge to the power of the Catholic Church.

   b. Europe was affected by a movement called the Protestant Reformation, started by Martin Luther in Germany in 1517.

2

Conflicts over
Religious Pluralism

It is certainly the pope's sentiment that if indulgences, which are a very insignificant thing, are celebrated with one bell, one procession, and one ceremony, then the gospel, which is the very greatest thing, should be preached with a hundred bells, a hundred processions, a hundred ceremonies.

—Martin Luther, *95 Theses*, 1517

Essential Question: How did religious pluralism challenge the concept of a unified Europe?

One early reason for **Martin Luther**'s demands for religious reform stemmed from concerns over the Catholic Church's policy of selling **indulgences**, a practice that had come to mean the buying of forgiveness for sin. However, over time, many reformers called into question other Catholic practices and doctrines, such as papal infallibility—the belief that the word of the pope is supreme on matters of faith. Such concerns fractured the unity of Christianity in Central and Western Europe, bringing the emergence of differing and often competing sects of Christianity in the 16th century, a religious revolution known as the **Reformation.**

Reforms in the Christian Church

The growing Renaissance interest in **secular**, or nonreligious, matters strongly affected the Roman Catholic Church in Europe. The desire for fine art and material wealth caused the Church to be a patron for painters such as Michelangelo and to build grand cathedrals. Thus, in the view of the reformers, many Church officials, especially the high clergy, had turned away from their true religious responsibilities. In response to this and other practices, **Christian Humanists** called for religious reform.

Christian Humanists Seek Religious Reform

While influenced by the Italian Renaissance, Christian Humanists in Northern Europe wanted to use their intellectual achievements and love of the classics to inspire the Christian beliefs. Christian Humanists were critical of the growing secular spirit of the Church and wanted to restore what they considered a purer Christian dogma. Embracing the motto "*Ad fontes* (back to the source)," Christian Humanists began reading the Bible in Greek and Hebrew as well as studying writings of early Christian leaders.

Erasmus Pleads for Reform One of the best representatives of Christian Humanism was the Dutch scholar **Desiderius Erasmus.** He acquired a traditional scholastic education as well as a new liberal arts education at the University of Paris. Erasmus called for the reading of the New Testament in Greek, Latin, and Hebrew in order to understand its original meaning. With a deep understanding of Roman Catholic teachings, Erasmus began writing extensively about the need for reform. Particularly important was his book *In Praise of Folly* (1509), in which he addressed Church abuses such as the lack of knowledge among much of the clergy and the focus of the papacy on material rather than spiritual concerns.

While Erasmus called for reform, he feared splintering the Roman Catholic Church. Although Erasmus agreed with concerns raised by Martin Luther, he felt Luther's manner was too harsh and his action too defiant.

Thomas More Calls for a Utopia An English Christian Humanist and close friend of Erasmus's, **Thomas More** had studied at the University of Oxford. This helped him gain government positions such as a member of Parliament and adviser to **Henry VIII**, king of England. In 1516, More wrote the book *Utopia* about an imaginary land that possessed a perfect, orderly society. Calling for the creation of a more just society, More argued in favor of education for women and abolition of private property.

Martin Luther Establishes New Doctrine

As Christian Humanists called for Church reform, one of them, **Martin Luther**, demanded change so strongly he threatened Christian unity. Growing up, Luther had attended a school run by the Brethren of the Common Life, a group that taught Christian Humanism. He later attended the University of Erfurt, receiving a strong liberal arts education and embracing the religious slogan "Back to the source." Studying the book of Romans in the Bible, Luther was struck by the emphasis on God's grace—an emphasis he believed the Catholic Church had lost. After earning a master's degree, Luther entered an Augustinian monastery, where he continued his studies and arrived at his belief in *sola fide*, that people gained eternal salvation "by faith alone."

Salvation, Luther believed, came from God's grace rather than from actions people performed. Luther agreed that attending church and helping the poor were good works but believed that they did not in themselves bring salvation. To Luther, faith alone brought salvation. Good works were the result of faith, not steps on a path to eternal life.

Luther Presents Religious Grievances Luther argued that any religious practices encouraging the belief that good works led to salvation were misleading. For example, he strongly disagreed with the practice of seeking salvation through the buying and selling of indulgences. Luther presented his document known as the **95 Theses** after Pope Leo X proclaimed a Jubilee Indulgence to raise money for the restoration of St. Peter's Basilica. The most famous indulgence preacher was Johann Tetzel. He was hired to sell indulgences in the German states of the Holy Roman Empire. According to legend, Tetzel said, "As soon as the gold in the casket rings, the rescued soul to heaven springs."

In response, according to legend, an angry Luther nailed his theses to the door of the Wittenberg church, denouncing indulgences and other Church practices. More likely, according to the custom of the time, Luther simply wanted to prompt his archbishop and other scholars to discuss possible reforms within the Catholic Church. But as a result of the printing press, within months his document was circulating throughout Europe. Luther, an unknown monk, quickly became the key figure of a rapidly growing protest movement. In addition to indulgences, Luther and other reformers objected to

- *simony*: the buying and selling of Church appointments and offices
- *pluralism*: the holding of multiple Church positions at the same time
- *nepotism*: the appointment of family and friends to Church positions
- *immorality*: the decline in moral standards of clergy and monks

The Catholic Church Responds Catholic officials responded forcefully, accusing Luther of heresy. In 1518, after being allowed to defend his position in a debate in the imperial city of Augsburg, the Church ordered Luther to recant his protests. (An imperial city was one that was subject only to the authority of the emperor.) Luther refused and returned to Wittenberg.

The pope issued a decree demanding that Luther recant or be excommunicated—exiled from the Catholic Church. In April 1521, Luther appeared before a diet, or assembly of leaders, that convened in the city of Worms with the choice to either recant or affirm his beliefs. Luther's case was so important that presiding over the **Diet of Worms** was the newly chosen emperor of the Holy Roman Empire, **Charles V.** According to legend, when confronted with his writings, Luther refused to back down, declaring, "Here I stand. I can do no other." His actual words were less dramatic, but the message was the same: He refused to recant. The Catholic Church excommunicated Luther, and Charles V declared him an "outlaw of the empire."

Protestant Doctrines and Practices In an age when religious dissent could mean death, Luther's strong stand took courage. However, he was supported by many German rulers. Some cared little about theology, but hoped the religious controversy would help them reduce Rome's political power. Luther's prince, Frederick III of Saxony, protected him in the prince's castle known as the Wartburg. There, Luther began to work out his ideas more fully. For example, he believed that the Bible was the sole authority for Christians. To make the New Testament easier for people to read, Luther translated it into common German.

While many of Luther's religious ideas were radical for his time, his ideas on politics and economics were not. He called for harsh treatment of people who wanted to reform society, and he expressed strongly anti-Semitic views.

Luther Versus the Catholic Church		
Issue	Luther's Beliefs	Catholic Teachings
How God Judges People for Salvation	Faith alone, although faith leads to good works	Faith and good works
Source of Religious Authority	The Bible alone	The Bible, the pope, and centuries of religious interpretation
Organization of the Clergy	Pastors are independent	Strict hierarchy
Role of Mary, Mother of Jesus	Honored, but not considered holy	Revered
Church Art and Architecture	Simplicity, so people will focus on God	Beauty, to glorify God

Zwingli and Calvin Bring New Interpretations

Even before Luther challenged the Catholic Church, the group of states known as the Swiss Confederation sought independence from the leaders of the Catholic Church and the Holy Roman Empire. In 1499, the Swiss Confederation won enough autonomy to allow Swiss merchants and crafts workers to flourish economically and politically.

In 1519, Huldrych Zwingli, a pastor of the People's Church in Zurich, Switzerland, began criticizing the Catholic Church and its abuse of power after reading Erasmus's texts. Following in Luther's footsteps, Zwingli criticized the papal authority and clerical celibacy, or abstaining from marriage and sexual relations. In addition, Zwingli demanded a simplified service based on the principle of "faith alone."

Zwingli Challenges Luther and the Catholic Church Zwingli challenged both Luther and the Catholic Church on the necessity of the sacraments (rites such as communion, believed to be a way to attain divine grace). For example, both Luther and traditional Catholics believed in the presence of Christ in the communion. Luther believed that the communion's bread and wine were both bread and wine *and* the body and blood of Christ (consubstantiation). In the traditional Catholic belief, the bread and wine of communion actually *became* the body and blood of Christ (transubstantiation). Zwingli rejected both beliefs, insisting that the ritual of communion was symbolic.

The Protestant leader Philip of Hesse, in hope of uniting Protestants, invited Luther and Zwingli to meet to discuss their disputes. In what became known as the Marburg Colloquy, the two vehemently disagreed, permanently dividing Protestants. Zwingli rejected Luther's reforms and insisted on abolishing the spiritual necessity of ritual sacraments, such as baptism, confirmation, and penance. Luther and Zwingli had never merged their movements by the time of Zwingli's death in 1531.

Calvinism Takes Root in Switzerland In 1536, French-born theologian **John Calvin** published his book *Institutes of the Christian Religion*, calling for religious and political reform. Calvin had studied the ideas of Luther and other dissidents, and he agreed with many of their criticisms of the Catholic Church. However, Calvin developed two unique ideas: **predestination** and his concept of **the elect**. In predestination, Calvin believed that an omnipotent (all-knowing) God already knew who would be saved and that, even at birth, a person's eternal fate was set. From this belief, Calvin later developed his concept of the elect—those chosen by God to be saved—in order to ensure people would live according to God's law. Their pious behavior would be an outward sign that such people were part of the elect, and their accumulation of wealth would be another sign of God's favor.

The year Calvin published *Institutes of the Christian Religion*, the leaders in the Swiss city of **Geneva** invited him there to live and preach. In Geneva, Calvin's doctrines transformed not only the practice of Christianity but also the role of the government. The Bible served as the highest law in Geneva, and sinning was a civil offense. The city required residents to denounce the Catholic faith and to attend church services five times a week. People could be punished for missing church, playing cards, or dancing. People who failed to follow the religious laws could be forced to leave the city. While laws enforced religious practices, they also required churches to provide social services for the city's poor and sick.

Anabaptists Reject the Secular World In 1525, another strand of Protestantism emerged in Zurich. Unlike Catholics, Lutherans, and Calvinists, **Anabaptists** rejected baptism of infants. They stressed that only adults could make the decision to believe, and they thus required all adults to be rebaptized. Anabaptists also excluded themselves from society because they believed that sin existed everywhere. This seclusion placed them in direct conflict with many governments because Anabaptists refused to serve in the government or the military. Because of the Anabaptists' unique doctrine and solitary lifestyle, both Catholics and Protestants targeted them. When Anabaptists established an old-world theocracy (a government based on religious law) at Münster, an army of both Catholics and Protestants captured the city, torturing and killing the leaders.

Division Among European Christians

The Reformation caused the Catholic Church to reflect on its doctrines and policies. While the Church mostly reinforced its established belief system, it also made some changes. This period of change is known as the **Counter Reformation** or the Catholic Reformation.

The Counter Reformation Cements Division During the Middle Ages, the Catholic Church had established several institutions, known together as the Inquisition, to defend its official doctrines. The Inquisition searched for and punished heretics, Christians who denied important Church doctrines. In 1542, the pope introduced the **Roman Inquisition** to stop Catholics from converting to Protestantism.

Calvinist churches were often very plain so they would not distract people from worshipping God.

Credit: Getty Images

Roman Catholic churches were often very ornate so that the beauty would inspire people to worship God.

Credit: Getty Images

Seventeen years later, the pope took another step to stop the spread of Protestantism, establishing the *Index of Prohibited Books*, a list of books that Catholic printers were not to print and Catholics were not to read. Together, the Inquisition and the *Index* cemented the growing religious divide in Europe.

The Counter Reformation Revives the Church The Catholic response to the Reformation included establishment of new religious orders. Each order had its own focus. For example, in 1540, Ignatius Loyola established the **Jesuits**, an order that emphasized obedience to authority, prayer, and communal living. The Jesuits provided soldiers to fight Protestants and missionaries to spread Christianity in the Americas and East Asia. They became famous for their rigorous scholarship. Many of the most prestigious universities in Europe were founded by Jesuits. This commitment to research and learning would later bring them into conflict with Roman Catholics who disliked their willingness to question traditional teachings.

Another influential order, the Ursuline Sisters, was established in 1544. It focused on educating girls.

To promote the unity of the Catholic faith, Pope Paul III convened the **Council of Trent**. Meeting three times between 1543 and 1563, the council was responsible for reaffirming traditional Catholic doctrine while addressing issues such as clerical pluralism and simony. Church officials discussed the official beliefs of the Catholic Church and the criticisms of Protestant reformers. The Council of Trent mostly reaffirmed established Catholic doctrine by:

- emphasizing the need for the seven sacraments (baptism, confirmation, communion, penance, annointing the sick, matrimony, and holy orders)
- stressing the role of both faith and good works
- affirming Latin as the language of the Church
- continuing clerical celibacy
- maintaining the art in churches
- upholding the power of the papacy

The Council of Trent did make some minor reforms related to pluralism, celibacy, and education of the priesthood. The actions of the Catholic Reformation revived Catholicism, particularly in Southern and Central Europe, in what are today the countries of Spain, Italy, and Austria. Many regions that had been Protestant reverted back to Catholicism.

State Power and Religion

In some places, leaders and religious groups used the religious changes of the Reformation to promote political unity. In others, such changes led to partisan turmoil and challenges to a leader's authority.

Top Down Religious Reform in England

Unlike Central Europe, where religious reforms started with a variety of monks and preachers and spread to the upper reaches of society, in England, reform started at the top. The king of England changed the religious practice of his subjects by edicts and laws.

Henry VIII Defends Catholicism In 1509, Henry VIII assumed the throne of England. During his thirty-eight-year reign, he would become one of England's most influential monarchs. When Martin Luther began criticizing the Catholic Church, Henry VIII quickly came to the support of Pope Leo X. Henry VIII, with the help of his trusted advisor Thomas More, argued in favor of the supremacy of the pope and the importance of the sacraments. For this loyalty, the pope gave Henry VIII the title of "Defender of the Faith."

Henry VIII Breaks with the Pope However, Henry VIII soon had his own criticism of the papacy. In 1527, after more than twenty years of marriage, Henry VIII desired to end his marriage to Katherine of Aragon, the youngest daughter of Ferdinand and Isabella of Spain and the aunt of Holy Roman Emperor Charles V. During their marriage, Katherine gave birth to six children, but five died and the only one who survived to adulthood was female, Mary Tudor. Without a clear male heir, Henry VIII feared for the stability of the Tudor Dynasty after his death, especially since he was only the second Tudor king. He asked Pope Clement VII for an annulment, or cancellation, of his marriage on the grounds that it should never have been allowed. Katherine had been married to Henry's brother before he died, and Henry argued that his marriage to her was improper. The pope, pressured by Charles V and unwilling to offend Spain's Catholics, refused to grant the annulment.

Henry VIII of England was known for his strong will and self-confidence.

Credit: Getty Images

In 1533, Anne Boleyn, the mistress of Henry VIII, became pregnant. Henry VIII divorced Katherine—knowing the pope would object—so he could marry Anne Boleyn, who gave birth to Elizabeth, another female. Pope Clement VII declared Henry and Anne's marriage illegal. Henry VIII responded by denouncing the authority of the pope. In November 1534, the English Parliament passed the **Act of Supremacy**, making the king of England the head of the Church of England. England was no longer officially a Catholic country. Under Henry, Anne Boleyn was executed for adultery. He later married Jane Seymour, who finally presented Henry with a son, Edward. Seymour died shortly after giving birth, and Henry married three more times but had no more children.

While the Church of England was no longer officially part of the Roman Catholic Church, many people in England remained loyal Catholics. To enforce his power, Henry VIII enacted additional religious reforms. One of these was the Treason Act, which made refusing to recognize the Church of England as the state religion an act of treason. Violating this act was punishable by death.

While Henry broke away from the control of the pope, he continued to support most of the doctrine of the Roman Catholic Church. In 1539, the government reaffirmed core Catholic doctrines on the celibacy of clergy, importance of confession, and transubstantiation in communion—doctrines that divided Catholics and Protestants.

The Church of England became known as the Anglican Church. Anglicans did not all agree with how closely they should keep to Catholic traditions and doctrine. Those who wanted to remain close to the Catholics were known as "High Church," while those who were more influenced by Protestant doctrines and practices were known as "Low Church."

Two Brief Reigns Following Henry's death, his young son Edward became king. He reigned for only six years (1547–1553) before dying at 15. During these years, the government became more Low Church.

However, his successor, Mary Tudor (reigned 1553–1558), took the country in the oppposite direction. She tried to restore Catholicism to England. Those in England who had never supported the break with Rome supported her, as did her powerful husband, the Spanish king Philip II. Mary's persecution of some Anglican bishops earned her the nickname "Bloody Mary."

Elizabeth Takes Control After Mary Tudor's death, her half-sister, **Elizabeth I** (reigned 1558–1603), tried to find a middle ground, sometimes called the Elizabethan Settlement, that would end religious turmoil. She returned to Anglicanism, rejecting both Roman Catholicism and strong Calvinism. During her long reign, she avoided harsh persecution of people who practiced their own beliefs quietly.

Legal Support for the Church of England Under Elizabeth I		
Act	**Year**	**Provisions**
Act of Supremacy	1558	• Redeclared the King of England the head of the Church of England • Acknowledged Elizabeth as the head of the Church of England
Act of Uniformity	1559	• Reestablished the *Book of Common Prayer* • Noted the need for subjects to attend church services once a week
Thirty-Nine Articles	1571	• Reestablished English as the language of the Church of England

Elizabeth was determined to restore the Anglican Church in England and keep England from returning to Catholicism while at the same time she wanted to prevent more radical forms of Protestantism from growing. One such radical group, the **Puritans,** wanted to "purify" the Church of England, demanding the elimination of clerical dress and removal of Catholics from England. To accomplish many of her goals, Elizabeth employed diplomacy and often used marriage proposals to form alliances.

Other Monarchs Initiate Religious Reform and Control

While Henry VIII and Elizabeth I responded to the Reformation by establishing and strengthening a new state religion in England, other rulers made different choices. Some loosened restrictions to allow religious pluralism. Others, such as Philip II of Spain, became strong advocates for Catholicism.

France's Agreement with the Pope In France in 1516, King Francis I (reigned 1515–1547) signed the **Concordat of Bologna** with Pope Leo X in which the Catholic Church continued to collect income from French churches. In return, the king gained the power to tax the clergy and appoint Catholic bishops in France. Because the king created such a powerful relationship with the Catholic Church, the Reformation initially had a limited impact on France.

The Holy Roman Emperor Implements Peace By the reign of Holy Roman Emperor Charles V (reigned 1506–1556), the Habsburg Dynasty encompassed a large landmass throughout Europe and the Americas. His 1.5-million-square-mile empire included territory in Spain, Italy, the Netherlands, Austria, the Holy Roman Empire, and South America.

Charles had to spend much of his rule confronting the expansion of the Ottoman Empire. He also fought a series of wars with France, as French monarch Francis I threatened his power. These concerns prevented him from dealing more forcefully with Lutheranism, and by the time he tried to do so, it had become too entrenched. In 1555, Charles established the **Peace of Augsburg** in the German states, a legal agreement allowing each German ruler to determine whether residents of that state would be Catholic or Lutheran. The faith of the ruler would become the faith of all. This agreement did not acknowledge Calvinism or Anabaptism as options.

Religious Challenges to Monarchical Power

Martin Luther published the _95 Theses_ to prompt religious reform. He had little interest in politics. However, religion and politics were thoroughly intertwined in Europe during his lifetime. His challenges to religious authority created an environment that prompted others to challenge political authority. In the German Peasant Wars of 1525 and 1526, farmers rebelled against the feudal power of the nobles. The peasants were crushed, and around 200,000 were killed. Though they were unsuccessful, the rebellions demonstrated how the Reformation could lead to unrest.

Puritans Challenge the English Crown The same day that England's Queen Elizabeth died in 1603, James I took the throne. The son of Mary Tudor, James was part of the Stuart family and already king of Scotland. Since he had been raised as a Roman Catholic, Puritans feared he would reinvigorate Catholicism in England. As ruler, James was sympathetic to Catholics, but only those who publicly supported the Church of England.

James's successor, Charles I, also worried Puritans. He married a French Catholic, Henrietta Maria, and he did not aid the Protestants in their battle against Catholics known as the Thirty Years' War (see pages 41–42).

The struggle between the Puritans and the Stuart monarchy came to a head in the English Civil War (1642–1649) when the Puritans supported the Parliamentarians against the Royalists. In 1649, the Parliamentarians successfully overthrew the Stuart monarchy and executed Charles I.

Conflicts Among Religious Groups

The growing religious tension between Catholics, Lutherans, Calvinists, and Anabaptists throughout Europe, combined with political rivalries that often fell along religious lines, brought nearly a century of warfare. Between 1562 and 1648, millions would be slaughtered or would die from hunger and disease related to internal rebellion, civil war, and international conflicts.

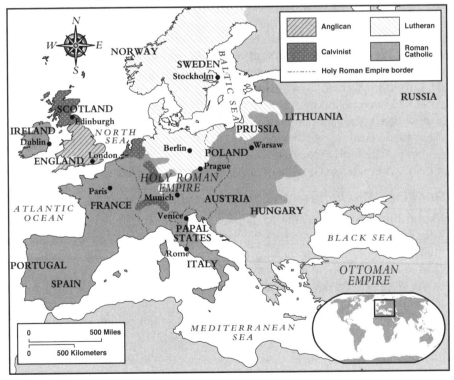

DOMINANT FAITHS IN WESTERN EUROPE, 1560

The French Wars of Religion

The Concordat of Bologna signed in 1516 worked for several decades, as long as nearly all French were Catholics. However, by 1562, French Calvinists, known as **Huguenots**, represented 10 percent of the country's population, or about 2 million people. More importantly, an estimated 40 percent of the French nobles identified as French Calvinists and sought to gain more political rights.

Origins of the Religious Conflict The French monarchy persecuted the Huguenots in order to diminish the power of the nobility and protect Catholicism. In 1559 and 1560, France suffered the death of two monarchs, which brought 11-year-old Charles IX to the throne. His mother, Catherine de' Medici, acted as regent and ruler. The ascension of Charles IX caused a power vacuum in which religious and political persecution flourished. With religious and political motivations, the French Wars of Religion continued to escalate leading to nine civil wars from 1562 to 1589.

Religious Violence In 1562, after a massacre of Huguenots at Vassy, French Calvinists took to the streets and looted Catholic Churches, destroying artwork and breaking stained-glass windows.

Tensions between Catholics and Huguenots reached a peak in 1572 at the marriage of Margaret of Valois, the sister of the king of France, to **Henry of Navarre**, a leading Calvinist. Henry Navarre invited many wealthy and influential Huguenots to the wedding in Paris. Catherine de' Medici, in collaboration with the reactionary Catholic Guise family, ordered the massacre of the Huguenots, which pleased the pope and other reactionary Catholics. Starting in Paris and spreading outward, an estimated 10,000 to 20,000 people were killed in an event known as the **St. Bartholomew's Day Massacre.** *— @ their wedding*

[handwritten in left margin: aka Henry the IV]

Political Rivalry As civil war persisted in France, three men, each named Henry, vied to be king.

- **Henry III** of Valois was a Catholic. He was the fourth son of King Henry II and supported by his mother, Queen Catherine de' Medici, who was Italian. Henry III became king of France in 1574 after the death of Charles IX. Catherine was influential throughout his reign.

- Henry of Navarre, the husband of Margaret of Valois, was a Huguenot with support from Elizabeth I of England. He was heir-presumptive to the throne after Henry III of Valois.

- Henry of Guise was a Catholic with support from Philip II of Spain. He established the Catholic League, which wanted to ensure that only Catholics ruled France.

The War of the Three Henrys was settled by assassinations. In 1588, the bodyguards of Henry III killed Henry of Guise. A year later, a Catholic monk, on the orders of Henry of Guise's brother Louis, assassinated Henry III, who left no direct male heir to the throne. The Huguenot Henry of Navarre ascended the French throne and took the name Henry IV.

Political Ending Henry IV took power in a French society torn by religious conflict. Raised as a Protestant but ruling a majority-Catholic country, he looked for a compromise that would end religious conflict. In 1593, he took a bold step by converting to Catholicism. This angered his Huguenot supporters, but reassured Catholics. His conversion demonstrated that he was a **Politique,** a French moderate who valued unity and peace more than any particular religious group.

Reacting against four decades of bloodshed over religion, Henry IV took a historic step in 1598 toward religious toleration with the **Edict of Nantes.** Under this policy, the government recognized Catholicism as France's official religion. However, the policy also allowed Huguenots to worship freely in certain provinces. This ended much of the religious violence in France.

However, many people rejected toleration of beliefs they found not just wrong but dangerous. In 1610, Henry IV, like Henry III and Henry of Guise before him, was assassinated. His killer was a Catholic extremist.

Decline of the Habsburgs

Like England and France, the Habsburg Empire faced deadly political and religious tensions in the 16th and 17th centuries. These tensions became worse after 1556, when the Holy Roman Emperor Charles V abdicated his throne.

Troubles in Eastern Europe Charles V's younger brother, Ferdinand, took control empire's eastern European lands, including Austria. Ferdinand ruled in the middle of a 230-year conflict between Austria and the **Ottoman Empire**. In 1453, Ottoman forces had captured Constantinople, completing their conquest of the Byzantine Empire. The Ottomans then attacked Habsburg lands in central and eastern Europe. In 1683, the Habsburgs successfully defended Vienna against an Ottoman siege, finally stopping the Ottoman's advance. The long conflict used up valuable resources of each empire, weakening both. As a result, Catholics lost some power in Eastern Europe.

Troubles in Western Europe Charles V's son, **Philip II** acquired his German lands and was elected the new emperor. Philip II was was fiercely anti-Protestant, and he devoted his rule to making all of Europe Catholic again.

Philip's first conflict over religion emerged in the Spanish Netherlands, Many members of the Dutch middle class there had converted to Calvinism. They embraced Calvin's emphasis on hard work. Under Philip's father, the Dutch had remained loyal. However, Philip ignored the local customs, demanded strict adherence to Catholicism, and raised taxes to fund exploration in the Americas and Asia.

Then, in 1566, Philip began to persecute Dutch Calvinists as heretics. In response, William of Orange took leadership of the Dutch resistance movement. In 1581, under his leadership, the seven northern provinces of the

Netherlands declared their independence and established a Dutch Republic that was Calvinist rather than Catholic.

England's Protestant queen, Elizabeth I, supported the Protestant rebellion in the Netherlands. Encouraged by the pope, Philip II responded by attacking England. He sent the Spanish Armada, a large fleet of ships, to invade England in 1588. Because of bad weather and the use of English fire ships (ships filled with explosives, set on fire, and floated toward enemy ships), the Armada was defeated. The English victory, like the Dutch rebellion, strengthened the Protestant government. Such victories enabled Protestant groups to gain both religious and political strength in Europe.

The Thirty Years' War

Religious conflicts continued in central Europe in the 17th century because of a weakness in the 1555 Peace of Augsburg. That agreement allowed the German princes the power to determine whether their state would be Catholic or Lutheran. However, it excluded other Protestants, particularly Calvinists, from the same power.

In 1618, a German Calvinist leader, Frederick I, refused to accept the Catholic absolutism of Holy Roman Emperor Ferdinand II. The conflict between Frederick I and Ferdinand II touched off the **Thirty Years' War**. The war had four phases:

- During the Bohemian Phase (1618–1625), armies of Holy Roman Emperor Ferdinand II defeated Frederick I at the Battle of White Mountain, allowing Ferdinand to reimpose Catholicism in many of the empire's German states and the province of Bohemia.

- During the Danish Phase (1625–1630), the Lutheran king of Denmark took up the Protestant cause, but overwhelming victories by the armies of Ferdinand II enabled him to issue the Edict of Restitution, which was designed to force Protestant princes to return to Catholicism or pay huge sums of money for taking control of Catholic lands.

- During the Swedish Phase (1630–1635), King Gustavus Adolphus of Sweden, a brilliant military leader, took control of Protestant forces, funded to a large degree by **Cardinal Richelieu** of France, who was the chief minister to King Louis XIII. Winning several important victories before being mortally wounded at the Battle of Lutzen, Gustavus Adolphus was able to reverse many of the gains made by the Catholic forces in the previous phases.

- During the French Phase (1635–1648) and with the death of Gustavus Adolphus, the French entered the war directly, on the side of the Protestants. The Spanish entered on the side of the Catholics, and this phase saw the French fighting the Spanish primarily in the northern German states, with the French ultimately gaining the upper hand.

The Thirty Years' War ended with the **Peace of Westphalia** in 1648. This was a set of treaties that included the following provisions:

- Officially recognized independence of the Netherlands and the Swiss Confederation

- Strengthened French, Swedish, and German rulers

- Took Italian regions from the Holy Roman Empire, which caused them to focus on their traditional holdings in Central and Eastern Europe

- Confirmed Peace of Augsburg

- Added Calvinism as an officially recognized religion

[handwritten margin note: princed could choose btwn: Calvinism, Catholicism, & Lutheranism]

Political Uses of Religion While the Thirty Years' War was a religious conflict between Protestants and Catholics, it was also a political and economic conflict. Rulers exploited the fight over beliefs in order to strengthen themselves. For example, France was led by a Catholic king, Louis XIII, and his chief minister was Cardinal Richelieu. However, they sided with the German Protestants against the Catholic Habsburgs of Austria. France was more concerned with weakening their political foes the Habsburgs than with rolling back Protestantism.

The Thirty Years' War, which cost between three and six million lives, was the last large religious war in Europe. The Peace of Westphalia was a turning point in European history. France had become the dominant continental power, and Calvinism had joined Catholicism and Lutheranism as a major force.

Carl Wahlbom, The Battle of Lutzen. 1632. National Museum of Sweden.
The turmoil portrayed in this painting captured the chaos of the Thirty Years' War.

Credit: Wikimedia Commons

Emergence of Religious Pluralism

With the 1648 Peace of Westphalia, the religious wars of Europe had come to end. Yet rivalries among different versions of Christianity continued, and many still faced discrimination and persecution for beliefs that dissented from the official religion of their state. However, the large-scale bloodshed had ended. European rulers had accepted that the continent would be home to various types of Christians. These rulers accepted religious pluralism—but not religious freedom.

Further, by 1648, the boundaries of political states and the boundaries of cultural areas were more aligned than before the Reformation had begun. Europe was moving toward becoming a land where most people who shared a culture lived under the same government, and most people who lived under a government shared a culture. The map of Europe was beginning to look like the map of today.

Christians, Jews, and Muslims

Besides conflicts among Christians, Europe also suffered from conflicts between Christians and other faiths. These began before the Reformation had divided Christianity. In Spain, Muslims had ruled since the 8th century. Christian armies had slowly pushed them out, with the last Muslims expelled in 1492. Over a period of 200 years, England, France, and Spain had expelled Jews. Most moved to Central or Eastern Europe or to the Middle East. Jews often faced discriminatory laws and sometimes violent persecution.

HISTORICAL PERSPECTIVES: HOW GERMAN WAS LUTHER?

Just over 500 years ago, Martin Luther posted his *95 Theses* at the University of Wittenberg, inviting his fellow scholars to a debate. Luther's relationship with German culture and politics has been controversial ever since.

Unintentionally Political Writing a few years after World War II, the British historian, G. R. Elton, portrayed Luther as strongly shaped by his cultural heritage as a German. In *The New Cambridge Modern History*, Vol. II, *The Reformation*, Elton argued that Luther saw a Roman-based church exploiting Germans and rebelled against it. Elton focused on political rather than cultural aspects, pointing out that the Reformation took root only where princes and lords supported it. To Elton, Luther was a benefactor of the German princes seeking to establish modern states independent of Rome's influence. Luther himself may not have been interested in politics, but his ideas provided support for those who were.

A Friend of Germans By the early 21st century, the focus on German pride shifted. Germany had evolved into a solid member of an internationalist, integrated Europe that downplayed particular national identities. In *Martin Luther: Renegade and Prophet* (2016), another British historian, Lyndal Roper, portrayed Luther as a man neither looking backward toward a German past nor as a tool of political leaders. Roper focused on the personal life of Luther as a man. She saw significance in Luther's friendship with those who were proud to be German. Protestant artist friends such as Albrecht Dürer, Hans Holbein, and Lucas Cranach surrounded him. Luther was part of an intellectual trend to see pride in their identity as Germans as the answer to their problems. In the words of one reviewer, "Luther's campaign to 'restore' Biblical Christianity to 16th-century Germany was a battle for land and national supremacy."

KEY TERMS BY THEME

States

Henry VIII

Act of Supremacy

Elizabeth I

Concordat of Bologna

Charles V

Peace of Augsburg

Edict of Nantes

Politique

Philip II

Ottoman Empire

Henry III

War of the Three Henrys

Thirty Years' War

Peace of Westphalia

Cardinal Richelieu

Society

indulgences

Reformation

secular

Christian Humanists

Desiderius Erasmus

Thomas More

Martin Luther

95 Theses

Diet of Worms

John Calvin

predestination

the elect

Geneva

Counter Reformation

Anabaptists

Roman Inquisition

Index of Prohibited Books

Jesuits

Council of Trent

Puritans

Huguenots

Henry of Navarre

St. Bartholomew's Day Massacre

Questions 1–3 refer to the passage below.

So it was determined to exterminate all the Protestants and the plan was approved by the queen. They discussed for some time whether they should make an exception of the king of Navarre and the prince of Condé. All agreed that the king of Navarre should be spared by reason of the royal dignity and the new alliance. The duke of Guise, who was put in full command of the enterprise, summoned by night several captains of the Catholic Swiss mercenaries from the five little cantons, and some commanders of French companies, and told them that it was the will of the king that, according to God's will, they should take vengeance on the band of rebels while they had the beasts in the toils. Victory was easy and the booty great and to be obtained without danger. The signal to commence the massacre should be given by the bell of the palace, and the marks by which they should recognize each other in the darkness were a bit of white linen tied around the left arm and a white cross on the hat.

> —Jacques de Thou (1553–1617), French historian describing
> the St. Bartholomew's Day Massacre, August 24, 1572

1. What was the "new alliance" made by the king of Navarre that is referred to in the passage?

   a) A marriage between the Protestant king and a Catholic princess

   b) A treaty between the French monarch and Swiss mercenaries

   c) A pledge by the royal family to grant more power to each region

   d) An agreement between the king and nobles to end religious toleration

2. Which statement best describes the context in the 16th and 17th centuries for the events described in the passage?

   a) Tension between France's central government and local governments

   b) An alliance between Roman Catholics in France and Ireland

   c) Emigration from Europe to North and South America

   d) Violent conflict between Roman Catholics and Protestants

3. What was the relationship between the events of 1572 described in the passage and the Edict of Nantes issued in 1598?

   a) Both were examples of deadly religious persecution.

   b) Both were examples of greater religious toleration.

   c) Reaction against the events of 1572 led to more persecution in 1598.

   d) Reaction against the events of 1572 led to more toleration in 1598.

Questions 4–6 refer to the passage below.

> The king's Majesty justly and rightfully is and ought to be the supreme head
> of the Church of England, and so is recognized by the clergy of this realm
> in their convocations… and to repress and extirpate [eliminate] all errors,
> heresies, and other enormities and abuses heretofore used in the same, be it
> enacted, by authority of this present Parliament, that the king, our sovereign
> lord, his heirs and successors, kings of this realm, shall be taken, accepted,
> and reputed the only supreme head in earth of the Church of England, called
> Anglicana *Ecclesia*; and shall have and enjoy, annexed and united to the
> imperial crown of this realm, as well the title and style thereof, as all honors,
> dignities, preeminences [signs of superiority], jurisdictions, privileges,
> authorities, immunities, profits, and commodities to the said dignity of the
> supreme head of the same Church belonging and appertaining; and that our
> said sovereign lord, his heirs and successors, kings of this realm, shall have
> full power and authority from time to time to visit, repress, redress, record,
> order, correct, restrain, and amend all such errors, heresies, abuses, offenses,
> contempts and enormities, whatsoever they be.
>
> —The Act of Supremacy, issued by the English Parliament, 1534

4. How do the ideas in this passage compare to those of Martin Luther?

   a) This passage focused on the power of a monarch over a church,
      while Luther focused on theology and doctrine.

   b) This passage wanted church leaders to eliminate errors in belief,
      while Luther did not think Christians should criticize each other.

   c) This passage thought profits and commodities of a church belonged
      to its leader, an idea that Luther agreed with.

   d) This passage described a national church for English Christians, and
      Luther rejected the idea of a single, universal form of Christianity.

5. Which best describes the context in which the passage was issued?

   a) Economic change threatened the power of English religious leaders.

   b) Several countries had already established a national church.

   c) Reformers on the continent were challenging the Catholic Church's
      power.

   d) Europeans were becoming more tolerant of religious diversity.

6. Which English monarch did some Protestants perceive as a threat to
   reverse the action taken in this document?

   a) Henry VIII (reigned 1509–1547)

   b) Edward VI (reigned 1547–1553)

   c) Mary I (reigned 1553–1558)

   d) Elizabeth I (reigned 1558–1603)

Questions 7–8 refer to the passage below.

Let no one think that this Commandment entirely forbids the arts of painting, engraving, or sculpture. The Scriptures inform us that God Himself commanded to be made images of Cherubim [a category of angel], and also the brazen serpent. The interpretation, therefore, at which we must arrive, is that images are prohibited only inasmuch as they are used as deities to receive adoration, and so to injure the true worship of God. . . .

He [the pastor] will also inform the unlettered . . . of the use of images, that they are intended to instruct in the history of the Old and New Testaments, and to revive from time to time their memory; that thus, moved by the contemplation of heavenly things, we may be the more ardently inflamed to adore and love God Himself. He should, also, point out that the images of the Saints are placed in churches, not only to be honored, but also that they may admonish us by their examples to imitate their lives and virtues.

—Council of Trent: Catechism for Parish Priests, 1566

7. Who would most strongly disagree with the passage?
   a) Charles V
   b) John Calvin
   c) The pope
   d) King Henry VIII

8. What was the context in which this passage was written?
   a) Roman Catholics were rejecting earlier positions and adopting the ideas proposed by Protestants.
   b) Roman Catholics were attempting to find compromises that would persuade Protestants to accept papal authority.
   c) Roman Catholics were trying to explain that they and Protestants actually agreed on most issues.
   d) Roman Catholics were defending their views against the challenges posed by Protestants on how to interpret the Bible.

SHORT-ANSWER QUESTIONS

1. Use the passage below to answer all parts of the question that follows.

> The repudiation of ordination as a sacrament demolished the caste system of clericalism and provided a sound basis for the priesthood of all believers since, according to Luther, ordination is simply a rite of the Church by which a minister is installed to discharge a particular office. He receives no indelible character, is not exempt from the jurisdiction of the civil courts, and is not empowered by ordination to perform the sacraments. At this point what the priest does any Christian may do, if commissioned by the congregation, because all Christians are priests.
>
> —Roland H. Bainton, *Here I Stand: A Life of Martin Luther*, 1950

   a) Describe ONE way Bainton thought that Luther's view on ordination challenged the structure of the Roman Catholic Church.

   b) Describe ONE specific piece of evidence that supports the view that Luther did not want to challenge the structure of the Roman Catholic Church.

   c) Explain ONE Roman Catholic response to Luther's teachings that challenged traditional doctrines.

2. Answer all parts of the question that follows.

   a) Describe ONE religious cause of the English Reformation.

   b) Describe ONE political cause of the English Reformation.

   c) Explain ONE significant outcome of the English Reformation.

LONG ESSAY QUESTIONS

1. Evaluate the extent to which nation-states or individual rulers differed in their attempts to resolve the conflicts between Protestants and Catholics during the 16th and 17th centuries.

2. Evaluate the extent to which reform movements transformed Christian beliefs or practices during the 16th and 17th centuries.

REFLECT ON THE CHAPTER ESSENTIAL QUESTION

1. In one to three paragraphs, explain how religious pluralism challenged the concept of a unified Europe.

Evidence is specific information based on facts or reasons, not a generalized or unsupported opinion. The most accurate evidence for an essay uses specific names of people, places, and events.

Which evidence below each question would be most useful in answering it? Explain your choice.

1. How did Protestant Reformation change Christian theology?

   a. Martin Luther and John Calvin criticized Catholic teachings, leading to new beliefs such as the priesthood of all believers, the primacy of scripture, predestination, and salvation by faith alone.

   b. Protestant leaders charged that the Catholic Church was corrupt and that its leaders used their positions to gain wealth and power.

2. How did religious reform result in increased state control of religious institutions in England?

   a. One Reformation idea was to implement a top-down approach to centralize power and bring about religious reform.

   b. The English monarchs initiated reform that gave them more control over religious life.

Evidence must be relevant. It should focus on the right culture, time period, and topic. For example, if a question asks about religious intolerance in France, facts about the persecution of the Huguenots would be more relevant than facts about the Versailles palace.

For each claim below, evaluate the relevance of the evidence.

3. Conflicts among religious groups overlapped with political and economic competition among states.

   a. The Thirty Years' War was Europe's most deadly religious war, but it became also a rivalry between France and the Habsburgs for political domination of the European continent.

   b. Members of the House of Habsburg ruled the Holy Roman Empire for three centuries. During this time, they fought off both foreign challengers and domestic opposition.

4. The principle of religious toleration emerged over time.

   a. The Peace of Augsburg (1555) allowed princes in the Holy Roman Empire to choose Catholicism or Lutheranism for their subjects, but not Calvinism or Anabaptism.

   b. Groups like the Huguenots, the Puritans, and the nobles of Poland all challenged the monarchs' control over religious institutions in the regions they lived in.

3

Exploration and Encounters Overseas

"I believe that . . . you will achieve the conversion of a great number of peoples to our holy faith, with the acquisition of great lordships and riches and all their inhabitants for Spain. For without a doubt there is a very great amount of gold in these lands."

—Christopher Columbus, Letter to King Ferdinand and Queen Isabella, **1493**

Essential Question: How did European's overseas explorations affect both them and indigenous populations?

During the Renaissance, Europeans became more interested in the world around them. Intellectuals of the time studied classical texts and observed the natural world in order to understand it better. By the late 15th century, educated Europeans knew that the earth was round. Yet they had little understanding of the size of their world, as few Europeans had traveled beyond their own region. This new era of exploration and expansion would have profound effects on Europe and the rest of the world. However, it was more than curiosity that sparked the era of exploration and colonization beginning in the 15th century and continuing well into the 19th century.

Motives for Exploration

In the 15th century, Europe was not a particularly wealthy or intellectually advanced region of the world. Two overarching reasons historians sometimes give to explain why European states took the lead in exploration were "God and gold." Yet behind these reasons also was the desire to gain power and glory for monarchs and emerging centralized states.

Christianity Stimulates Exploration

The desire of Europeans to spread and strengthen the Christian faith affected events both within and beyond the continent. Between the birth of Jesus and 1492, Christians had spread the faith throughout the Mediterranean world and into northern and eastern Europe. After Muslims won control of Spain in the 8th century, Spanish Christians spent the following seven centuries reconquering the region. After defeating the Muslims in 1492, the Spanish monarchs ordered that Jews either convert to Christianity or leave their kingdom.

Then, as Europeans began to explore the world, many wanted to spread Christianity. The split in Europe resulting from the Protestant Reformation increased the desire of some countries to spread their faith. Portugal, Spain, and France, which remained largely Catholic, were interested in both commerce and spreading their beliefs. For those countries, religion was a powerful factor in exploration and colonization. However, people from England and the Netherlands, mostly Protestant, focused more on commerce. In the 17th century, English groups sought refuge in North America from the Anglican Church: Puritans in Massachusetts, Catholics in Maryland, and Quakers in Pennsylvania. As Christians carried their faith throughout the world, some used it as justification for subjugating the indigenous people they encountered.

Commercial Motives for Exploration

Though Europeans were geographically confined during the Middle Ages, they were exposed to goods and ideas from Asia and Africa. For example, Venetian merchant **Marco Polo** published an account of his travels throughout Asia in the late 13th century, giving medieval Europeans their most detailed information about that region.

Search for New Routes to the East Europeans were aware of exotic products and luxury goods such as spices, silk, and jewels from Asia and Africa, and knowledge of these products increased as a result of the Crusades. Yet, European access to such products was limited. In the 14th century, the Muslim rulers of the **Ottoman Empire** gained control of trade routes connecting Asia to Europe both by land and by the Mediterranean Sea. Traders from Venice were the only Europeans who had direct access to the Muslim ports. Therefore, Europeans had to purchase spices, such as ginger and cinnamon and other foreign goods, from Muslim traders at very high prices. For example, in Spain, nutmeg was as expensive as gold.

Europeans hoped to discover an all-water route connecting Europe to Asia, which would not only bypass Ottoman-controlled lands, but also would be less expensive. Transporting heavy goods over water was much cheaper and easier than transporting them over land.

Europe's monarchs also hoped to find an all-water route to Asia in order to enhance the power of their states and increase their personal wealth. As explained later in this chapter, countries explored different paths to Asia:

- The Portuguese traveled south along the coast of Africa and then east across the Indian Ocean.

- The Spanish tried to reach Asia by sailing west across the Atlantic and Pacific Oceans.

- The French searched for an ice-free water route through the Arctic Ocean.

Mercantilism One important economic idea that motivated the search for a route to the East was **mercantilism**, which measured the wealth of a country by how much gold and silver it accumulated through trade. Mercantilism developed in 16th-century Europe, particularly England and France, and began to lose supporters in the 19th century. It includes these principles:

- The world's wealth is like a pie. It is a limited size, and the only way to get a larger share is for another state to get a smaller share. This belief reflected the world as it existed before the 19th century. Life changed very little from one generation to the next, and economic growth was normally slow. In contrast today, people assume that technological change will make the global economic pie larger and larger.

- A country grows wealthier if it has a **favorable balance of trade**, which means it **exports** (sells to other countries) more than it **imports** (buys from other countries). If it does, then it will receive more in payments of gold and silver than it pays out. Today, economists do not use the balance of trade to measure a country's wealth. A wealthy country might have an unfavorable balance of trade because it can afford to import many goods.

- A **colony**, or a separate land controlled by a **parent country**, can enrich the parent country by providing precious metals, crops, and other products. (See Chapter 9 for more information on mercantilism.)

Governments that followed mercantilist policies attempted to regulate trade to encourage exports, discourage imports, and justify seizing colonies. However, starting in the late 1700s, people began to believe that countries could prosper with fewer restrictions on trade. In particular, consumers benefited by the opportunity to buy less expensive products made in other countries. An ideology of free trade began to replace the belief in mercantilism.

Exploration and Advances in Knowledge

European interest in finding new trade routes and establishing overseas colonies converged with growth of knowledge about geography and **navigation**, the science of plotting the course of a ship. In the 13th and 14th centuries, European navigators had developed detailed charts (which were actually early maps) called *portolani* that gave sailors accurate information about the location and distances between European ports. These charts, however, were not sufficient for extended ocean voyages.

Advances in **cartography**, or the making and study of maps, grew in the 15th century, as early explorers created detailed maps based on their observations as they traveled farther and farther from their shores. The invention of printing in the mid-15th century made more copies of maps available to navigators in different countries.

To sail long distances in unknown waters, Europeans adopted Middle Eastern and Chinese navigational technology:

- Europeans developed a new type of ship, the caravel, that was larger than earlier ships. They also began replacing their traditional square sails with triangular-shaped lateen sails, developed by Arab sailors. Lateen sails allowed more flexibility for sailing regardless of wind direction.

- Europeans adopted the sternpost rudder from China. It was a steering device attached to the ship's main beam at the rear that made the ship more maneuverable.

- Europeans used navigational aids including the **compass**, which likely came from China in the 12th century, and the **astrolabe**, from Muslim navigators, to determine latitude more accurately.

Advances in military technology, such as gunpowder weapons and steel swords, also assisted Europeans in establishing overseas colonies and empires. Caravels were large enough to support mounted cannons and maneuverable enough to engage in naval warfare. Horses gave Europeans an advantage when colonizing the Americas, where there had been no horses before Europeans arrived in the 15th century.

Overseas European Empires

As Europeans established new trade networks, they sometimes negotiated agreements that benefited both themselves and local people in Africa, Asia, and the Americas. However, Europeans often used coercion to establish overseas empires by subduing native populations or enforcing trade monopolies.

Portuguese Trading Network

The Portuguese were the first to begin systematically exploring to increase overseas trade. Under the leadership of **Prince Henry the Navigator** (1394–1460), the Portuguese wanted to spread Christianity and to obtain direct access to gold, ivory, and slaves from sub-Saharan Africa. Henry was known as "the Navigator" for his support of sailing on the open seas. However, he never sailed beyond the sight of land. Henry established a school for navigators on the country's southwest coast in 1419. The work there formed the basis of Portuguese explorations of the 15th and 16th centuries.

Africa Beginning in the 1430s, Portuguese sailors explored the western coast of Africa looking for gold. The combination of winds and currents made traveling along this coast dangerous. In 1441, the Portuguese brought the first enslaved Africans to Europe from the Senegal River region. African leaders along the coast realized their kingdoms could benefit economically by selling captives, and sometimes their own people, as slaves to the Portuguese. Finally, in 1471, the Portuguese found a new source of gold in western Africa. Europeans later referred to the area as the **Gold Coast**. Trade in gold, ivory, and slaves continued to grow, and the Portuguese developed a trading network based in forts along the African coast. The Portuguese negotiated with local landowners to obtain land for their forts.

South Asia The Portuguese heard that there was a possible trade route to Asia around the southern tip of Africa, then called the Cape of Storms. In 1488, the explorer **Bartholomeu Dias** (c. 1450–1500) was the first European to sail around the Cape, but Dias turned back as his crew refused to go on against attacks from shore and powerful currents. Ten years later, **Vasco da Gama** (c. 1460–1524) rounded the Cape, which he renamed the **Cape of Good Hope**, and explored the coast of East Africa. Da Gama then sailed to the southeastern coast of India by crossing the **Indian Ocean**, then called the Arabian Sea. There, in the port of Calicut, he acquired a cargo of spices that would yield huge profits.

In later years, the Portuguese sought to dominate the spice trade and eliminate Muslim traders from the market. The country used its maritime strength to defeat its rivals and set up a port in Goa on the western coast of India, just north of Calicut.

Pressing Eastward After reaching South Asia, the Portuguese continued eastward. They started to travel more extensively throughout Asia seeking to expand their access to the spice trade. In 1511, they captured the city of Malacca on the Malay Peninsula from the Muslim inhabitants. They used that port as a base to extend their lucrative trading network to China and the **Spice Islands**, now called the Moluccas, and part of Indonesia. In the Spice Islands, the Portuguese negotiated a treaty that allowed them to export cloves to Europe. However, the Portuguese did not have the desire, population, or political power to establish colonies in Asia.

Dividing the World In the **Treaty of Tordesillas** (1494), Spain and Portugal agreed to establish separate spheres of colonial influence. They separated their interests along a line that divided the world through eastern South America. East of the treaty line, Portugal received control of trade routes around Africa's Cape of Good Hope and a portion of South America that became eastern **Brazil**. The explorer **Pedro Álvares Cabral** (1467/68–1520) claimed Brazil as a colony for Portugal in 1500. The Portuguese began to establish settlements there in the 1530s and eventually set up large sugar cane plantations. A **plantation** is a large farm that usually grows a single cash crop such as sugar, tobacco, or cotton.

Plantations need large workforces. At first, the colonists enslaved the native people and forced them to work on the plantations. Later, they imported enslaved people from Africa as well. The sugar that was exported from Brazil and sold in Europe created tremendous wealth for Portugal, which ran its colony in Brazil along mercantilist principles. Eventually, coffee also became a valuable export from Brazil.

Spanish Colonies

Spain was Portugal's more powerful neighbor on the Iberian Peninsula. Like Portugal, Spain also wanted direct access to the Asian spice trade. Spain had the wealth and resources not only to compete for trade but also to establish a vast empire of colonies. While this empire would generate great wealth for Spain, it would also spread Christianity, either by persuasion or force, throughout the Americas and parts of Asia.

Early Explorations Christopher Columbus (1451–1506) was a devout Christian and an experienced sea captain. From his study of the Bible and sea charts, he concluded that the earth was small enough that the shortest route to Asia from Europe was by sailing west across the Atlantic Ocean. He tried to persuade Portugal to support his plan, but the Portuguese realized that Columbus had miscalculated the size of the earth. They knew that sailing west was the long route to Asia.

Columbus then approached the Spanish monarchs, **King Ferdinand and Queen Isabella** of Spain (ruled 1469–1516), who were willing to take a risk on his plan. They backed his first expedition, and he set sail in August 1492. After a two-month voyage, he landed in the Bahamas and also explored parts of Cuba and Hispaniola (present-day Haiti and the Dominican Republic) in the **Caribbean Sea**. Columbus believed he had reached Asia and claimed the lands for Spain. Because he thought the lands he had reached were the Indies, he called the area the **West Indies** and referred to the people as **Indians**.

Columbus made three later voyages between 1493 and 1502 trying to find a way to reach the Asian mainland, but he was unsuccessful. He never acknowledged that he had found a landmass that was previously unknown to Europeans. Columbus did explore all the major islands of the Caribbean and what is now **Central America**. Spain gained control of all these lands that were west of the line established by the Treaty of Tordesillas.

The Italian explorer **Amerigo Vespucci**, who traveled along the eastern coast of South America between 1499 and 1504, was the first to refer to this area as the **New World**. A mapmaker used Vespucci's first name to refer to the lands he explored, and they have been called the Americas ever since.

Mexico In the early 16th century, Spanish **conquistadors**, or conquerors, began subduing the indigenous populations in the Americas. Conquistadors led military expeditions sponsored by the government but privately funded. Conquistador **Hernán Cortés** (1485–1547) first reached what is now Veracruz on the Gulf of Mexico in 1519, when the **Aztec Empire** ruled most of the region. The Aztecs had an advanced civilization, yet Cortés conquered them and destroyed their capital, **Tenochtitlán**, within two years. Though he had a small force of soldiers, Cortés had horses and guns. He also got help from native groups who were enemies of the Aztecs. Perhaps the most important factor helping Cortés was disease, which killed millions of native people. (See page 61 for more on the effects of disease on indigenous populations.)

By 1550, the Spanish controlled northern Mexico and part of Central America. They built **Mexico City** on the ruins of Tenochtitlán, and it became the capital of **New Spain**, which included Mexico, Central America, and the Caribbean. To ensure a labor supply, the Spanish under Queen Isabella had established a system called the *encomienda*. Large landowners, *encomienderos*, forced indigenous people to work on plantations for food and shelter. The Spanish also forced indigenous groups to send men for the dangerous work in gold and silver mines. With this supply of labor, tremendous wealth flowed to Spain. The imposition of Catholicism on the native population only served to strengthen the power of the Spanish over them.

Jesuit missionaries tried to save the indigenous people from some of the horrors of the conquistadors, while Spanish Dominican missionary **Bartolomé de las Casas** insisted that the encomienda system and forced labor were unjust. The arguments of las Casas persuaded Charles V to call the Council of Valladolid in Spain, where a group of Catholic Church leaders agreed that the Spanish policies were cruel and had to change. However, their decision brought no change to Spain's harsh policies in its American colonies.

South America Spanish explorer **Vasco Nuñez de Balboa** crossed the **Isthmus of Panama** in 1513. He and his expedition were the first Europeans to reach the eastern shore of the **Pacific Ocean**.

Our Lady of Guadalupe is a depiction of Mary, the mother of Jesus. To many people, she also represents aspects of indigenous faiths practiced in Mexico before the arrival of Christianity.

Credit: Getty Images

Spain then became interested in the western coast of South America. Conquistador **Francisco Pizarro** (c. 1475–1541) arrived in the region in 1530 and found the **Inca Empire** in the **Andes Mountains** of Peru in a weakened condition. European disease had already killed a large proportion of the population, including the emperor. The empire then became embroiled in civil war. Pizarro took advantage of the situation. With his force of fewer than 200 men and his superior weapons, he defeated the Inca and took control of their capital.

Within five years, Pizarro established a new Spanish capital in **Lima** that governed **Peru**, the part of the empire that covered much of western South America. The Spanish used a similar system to control the indigenous population and extract wealth as they had in New Spain.

The Pacific A Portuguese explorer sailing for the Spanish named **Ferdinand Magellan** (1480–1521) set out in 1519 to explore the eastern coast of South America and the Pacific Ocean. Magellan and his crew survived the storm-ravaged straits at the southern tip of South America and headed west. Because of the lack of wind to push them westward, they nearly starved to death on the voyage. But in 1521, they reached the islands later named the **Philippines** after the Spanish king. Magellan died in the islands, but one of his ships continued the voyage across the Indian Ocean and around Africa. It completed the first voyage around the world.

At first, the Spanish saw the Philippines primarily as a stop on the way to the Spice Islands. Not until 1565 did they establish a permanent settlement there, founding their capital of **Manila** in 1571. As in the Americas, Catholic missionaries set out to convert the native people, many of whom had embraced Islam shortly before the Spanish arrived. Manila became a center of commerce, as traders exchanged Chinese silk for Mexican silver. The trade drew Chinese merchants along with a growing number of Spanish settlers.

The Spanish in the Americas and the Pacific: 16th Century			
Territory	**Explorer**	**Economic Activities**	**Religious Issues**
Mexico	Hernán Cortés	Plantation agriculture; gold and silver mines	Imposition of Catholicism strengthened hold of Spanish over natives as cheap labor
Peru	Francisco Pizarro	Plantation agriculture; silver mines; trade for Inca gold products and fabrics	Imposition of Catholicism strengthened hold of Spanish over natives as cheap labor
Philippines	Ferdinand Magellan	Trade (Chinese silk for Mexican silver); other commercial activities	Conversion to Catholicism after many had previously adopted Islam

The breadth and wealth of the Spanish Empire made Spain a dominant power in Europe in the 16th century. Between 1492 and the mid-1500s, Spain established an empire that stretched from northern Mexico through much of South America and the Caribbean islands, and into the Philippines. By the 17th century, Europeans had begun to build a global trade network. Over time, they pushed out the Muslims and Chinese who had dominated trade in the Indian Ocean and the western Pacific.

Global Exchanges Reshape the World

Before the era of expansion, the Mediterranean Sea was the center of European maritime trade and naval power. States that bordered the Mediterranean, such as the Italian city-states, Spain, and France were the most powerful. Foreign trade around the Mediterranean focused on the region to the east controlled by the Ottoman Empire. For example, the Italian city-state of Venice had been especially powerful as the port where trade from Asia entered Europe.

Shifts in Economic Power

In the 16th century, Portugal challenged Venetian dominance in trade for most luxury goods from the East. In the 17th century, the Dutch wrested control of the spice trade away from Venice. The global exchange of goods thus shifted its center of economic power from the Mediterranean to the Atlantic states.

Shift to the Atlantic Prior to the discovery of new trade routes that originated on the Atlantic Ocean, Europeans thought there was little benefit to having ports on the Atlantic coast. They had believed that there was little of value that could come from the West. But Portuguese and Spanish explorations opened their eyes to a far different possibility. In the 17th century, the Dutch were the first to grasp this possibility and gain ascendancy in the new global trading network; yet by the early 18th century, the English surpassed the Dutch.

Leading Atlantic Ports The shifting of economic power to the northern Atlantic states can be seen in the shifting location of leading port cities. The Portuguese began their exploration and trade from the port city of **Lisbon** in the 15th century. It became clear in the early 16th century that Lisbon's distance from northern and central Europe made it less than ideal as a place from which to ship goods from Asia throughout the continent.

The Portuguese then set up a trading center in the city of **Antwerp** on a river near the North Sea in what is now northern Belgium. At that time, this region was part of the Netherlands, then under the control of Spain. Antwerp was the financial and commercial center of northern Europe. The city benefited from the emerging trade from Spanish and Portuguese overseas colonies. Portugal faced stiff competition in the city from other European traders.

By the early 17th century, the northern parts of the Netherlands had become independent of Spain. The Dutch port city of **Amsterdam** then surpassed Antwerp and became the major trading port in Europe. The Dutch had large fleets of ships that traded both regionally and internationally. Though the Atlantic states became part of an expanding world economy, trade within Europe still accounted for most of European trade volume even at the end of the 17th century. However, the goods that were traded from overseas, such as pepper, spices, sugar, tea, and coffee, tended to be more valuable.

Changing Role for China The development of European-based trading empires led to a decline in the relative power of China by the 19th century. For many centuries, China had been a center of innovation and prosperity. It had dominated trade and political events in eastern Asia. This changed as Europeans applied what they learned from people in other parts of the world and aggressively spread their influence.

The Columbian Exchange

The **Columbian Exchange** (so named because it began with the voyages of Columbus) refers to the exchange of plants, animals, and germs between the **Old World**—Europe, Africa, and Asia—and the New World. American historian **Alfred Crosby** first explained the concept in the 1970s. A vast ocean separated the Old World from the New World, so different plants, animals, and germs evolved in each region. The exchange thus had enormous consequences, both positive and negative.

As Europeans established colonies around the world, they began to trade goods between Europe, the Americas, Asia, and Africa. These goods included spices, luxury goods, precious metals, crops, and livestock. Tomatoes, potatoes, corn, and squash were introduced to Europe from the Americas, while Europeans brought cattle, horses, pigs, and sheep to the Americas and introduced the cultivation of wheat. The exchange of foods throughout the world led to better nutrition and increased population. Tea from Asia, coffee from Africa, and chocolate from Mexico, along with sugar and tobacco from the Americas changed European life.

Cultural practices were also exchanged. Spanish colonization in the Americas and the Philippines brought a new language and religion, including the institutions of the Catholic Church, along with its churches, schools, and hospitals.

Furthermore, the relative ease with which Europeans conquered indigenous populations reinforced the Europe-centered belief that they had a superior civilization. European expansion marked a shift toward European dominance beyond the continent.

Columbian Exchange				
Direction	Plants	Animals	Disease	Ideas and Technology
From Africa and Eurasia to the Americas	• Wheat • Sugar • Coffee • Oranges	• Horses • Pigs • Cows • Sheep	• Typhus • Influenza • Measles • Smallpox	• Alphabet • Gunpowder weapons
From the Americas to Africa and Eurasia	• Potatoes • Tomatoes • Chocolate • Corn • Tobacco	• Turkeys • Llamas • Alpacas • Guinea pigs	• Syphillis	• Rubber • Quinine

Economic Opportunities Europeans profited in many ways from the Columbian Exchange. For example, by establishing plantations to grow sugar cane, coffee, tobacco, and cotton in different parts of the Americas, Europeans cultivated lucrative cash crops that could be sold directly to a growing European market. Because the Europeans relied largely on forced labor of indigenous peoples and enslaved Africans, their costs to grow the crops were minimized. In addition, the slave trade itself was a source of profit.

Livestock, including cattle, sheep, pigs, and horses, provided another economic opportunity for Europeans. Settlers brought animals from the Old World to the New World, where they had ample space to graze and few natural predators. Herds were raised for their meat, hides, and wool, which could all be sold at a profit.

Ecological Disasters Old World plants, animals, and diseases came to the New World along with European settlers. The results were often devastating. Plants and animals in the New World were destroyed, as the introduction of Old World plants, including weeds, often edged out native species. Extensive grazing by European livestock eroded the soil in many areas and made it difficult for native species to grow. Some areas began to look like deserts as the soil eroded. Europeans also cleared forests, often by large-scale burning to create open land for settlements, grazing, and crops, further damaging the environment.

Diseases By far, the worst disaster was the introduction of European diseases, such as **smallpox** and **measles**. Peoples of the Americas had never been exposed to these diseases. As a result, their bodies had not built up **immunity,** or resistance, to them as Europeans had over several centuries. As soon as Europeans arrived, epidemics began devasting the native population. Historians estimate that because of epidemics caused by European diseases, the native population declined between 50 percent and 90 percent within a century of contact.

Death from disease was a major reason Europeans dominated Native Americans as quickly as they did. The deadly effect of European diseases occured first in the West Indies, where Columbus landed. It continue in Mexico and South America when Spanish conquistadors conquered the Aztecs and the Inca. By the time the English began colonizing North America in the 17th century, diseases had already spread to the region and killed many Native Americans.

African Slave Trade Expands

The growth of the African slave trade was another result of the expanding Atlantic trading system and the colonization of the Americas. When the Portuguese brought their first cargo of enslaved Africans to Europe in 1441, they sold the enslaved people within Europe. The slave trade grew gradually as the Portuguese continued to explore and trade along the west coast of Africa.

In the 16th and 17th centuries, as Europeans began establishing a plantation economy in the Americas, plantation owners first turned to indigenous peoples as slave laborers and forced them to work under cruel conditions. Deaths from European diseases and harsh treatment created a **demographic**, or population, catastrophe among indigenous peoples. Europeans thus sought another form of labor, turning to enslaved Africans and bringing a marked change to the Atlantic slave trade.

Europeans realized that supplying labor to plantations in South America and the West Indies and later in North America could be a lucrative venture. The Portuguese and the Spanish brought slaves to the Americas, especially to Brazil and the islands of the West Indies in the early 16th century. The first English slave-trading expedition of 1562 sold slaves to the Spanish West Indies. English slave-trading voyages increased after the establishment of the English colonies in North America. The first enslaved Africans were brought to Virginia in 1619. The slave trade continued to expand throughout the 17th and 18th centuries. (See Chapter 9 for more information on the transatlantic slave labor system from 1648 to 1815.)

Competition Among Atlantic States

Spain administered a vast empire in the Americas and explored parts of what later became the United States, including Florida and several southeastern and southwestern states. Though the Spanish wanted to claim all of North America for their empire, they were challenged in the early 17th century by the Atlantic states of France, England, and the Netherlands.

Shortly after the voyages by Columbus, explorers of other states doubted his conclusion that he had reached Asia. Because the sea routes to Asia controlled by the Portuguese and the Spanish were long and difficult, these explorers sought alternative routes, sailing north and then either west or east looking for a passage to Asia. In their explorations, they found and claimed other parts of the New World.

The Netherlands The Dutch became the leading maritime power around 1600 and dominated 17th-century European trade. They were the first to benefit from the weakening of Spain and Portugal and were later challenged by France and England. Like the Portuguese, the Dutch focus for expansion overseas was on developing a trade network rather than a colonial empire. They established two trading companies:

- The **Dutch East India Company**, founded in 1602, focused on Asian trade and established a strong presence in the Spice Islands.

- The **Dutch West India Company**, created in 1621, focused on the Americas and established the colony of **New Amsterdam** in 1624. The colony stretched from the mouth of the **Hudson River** north to present-day Albany, New York. The only Dutch North American colony, New Amsterdam, was taken over by the English in 1664 and became **New York**.

England One of the early explorers for England was the Venetian **John Cabot**. Sailing across the North Atlantic in 1497, Cabot reached the eastern coast of Canada. His explorations gave England a basis for claiming land in North America.

After Cabot's voyages, the English became consumed with domestic issues and colonizing Ireland. They did little exploring of the Americas for the next century. By the time they did, the French and the Spanish controlled the most profitable regions: the fur-bearing territories in the north and the sugar islands, gold mines, and silver mines in the south. Finally, in 1607, the English established their first permanent settlement in North America, **Jamestown**, Virginia. By 1670, England had established colonies in eastern Canada and several smaller islands in the West Indies, including Barbados and Bermuda. They had also founded eleven of the thirteen colonies along the Atlantic coast of North America that would later be part of the United States.

The English were also interested in expanding their trade to compete with the Portuguese and the Dutch in Asia, so they established the **British East India Company** in 1601.

France The French sent out early expeditions to explore the Americas looking for a passage to Asia:

- In 1524, the Italian navigator **Giovanni de Verrazano**, who sailed on behalf of France, explored the Atlantic coast from North Carolina to Newfoundland.

- From 1534 to 1536, **Jacques Cartier** became the first European to explore the **St. Lawrence River** in Canada.

Neither explorer found a passage to Asia, but Cartier's explorations established French claims to the territory.

It took decades before the French established a permanent North America settlement. In 1608, **Samuel de Champlain** founded **Quebec** as a prosperous fur-trading post in eastern Canada. He continued to explore the surrounding region and strengthened French claims to Canada, then called **New France**.

France also established colonies in the West Indies beginning in the 1620s. While the islands such as Martinique and Guadeloupe that the French colonized were small, the sugar these islands produced made them very valuable.

The Atlantic States in the Americas and Asia, 15th to 17th Centuries			
Atlantic Nation	Explorers	Lands Claimed	Economic Activities
England	John Cabot	Parts of Canada; Jamestown; smaller islands in West Indies (including Barbados and Bermuda); by 1670, 11 of the 13 colonies that would become the United States	British East India Company, established 1601; competed with Portuguese and Dutch for trade in Asia
France	Giovanni Verrazano, Jacques Cartier, Samuel de Champlain	Area of St. Lawrence River in Canada; established trading post at Quebec, 1608; established New France in Canada; colonies in West Indies, including Martinique and Guadeloupe	Fur trading in Quebec; sugar plantations in West Indies
The Netherlands	Willem Schouten (discovered route to Pacific around southern tip of South America, 1615–1616)	Established colony of New Amsterdam, which was taken over by England and renamed New York	Focused on developing trade network; established Dutch East India Company (1602) for Asian trade and Dutch West India Company (1621) for trade in the Americas

Rivalries among European Powers

As European states competed for trade around the world, rivalries and conflicts developed among them in the 17th and 18th centuries. Because countries adopted the mercantilist idea that the amount of worldwide wealth was limited, they believed that their wealth could only grow at the expense of their neighbors.

Growing Trade Rivalries For example, the Portuguese had first sought to dominate the trade in spices and silk from Asia in the early 16th century. When the Spanish colonized the Philippines after 1570, they began to compete with the Portuguese for this lucrative trade. At the beginning of the 17th century, the Dutch successfully challenged the Portuguese for dominance of the spice trade when they established a strong presence in the Spice Islands. While Portuguese military efforts had been successful against Muslim traders in the region, they were less successful against the Dutch. In addition, even though the British East India Company had been established before the Dutch came to the region, the Dutch were strong enough economically to force the British to cede the trade in the islands and to shift their focus to India, which was ruled by the Mughal Empire.

During the 18th century, Britain became the dominant European power in Asian trade. France also established trading companies in Asia in the 17th century, but it had little success with them.

Conflict over American Colonies Based on the Treaty of Tordesillas of 1494, Spain and Portugal attempted to avoid conflicts by dividing their colonizing efforts. Each wanted to monopolize trade and colonize based on explorations in their assigned regions. However, other European states such as England, France, and the Netherlands did not consider themselves bound by the treaty. They soon began their own explorations that led to the establishment of trading companies and colonies in the early 17th century.

Rivalries over land in the Americas led to conflicts later in the 17th and 18th centuries. Great Britain and France fought a series of wars in the 18th century that included battles over North American colonies. As a result of these wars, France lost control of most of its territories in Canada and the United States to the British. (See Chapter 7 for more information on military conflicts among European powers in the period 1648 to 1815; see Chapter 9 for more information on commercial rivalries in that same period.) In the 19th century, the legacy of these colonial conflicts continued, as the United States and Mexico fought over territory that ended up being the southwestern United States.

European exploration caused dramatic changes in the Americas and Africa. The native population of the Americas plummeted and millions of Africans were enslaved and forcibly relocated. These developments, as well as the increasing wealth and power of Europe, were captured by William Blake's 1796 illustration "Europe supported by Africa and America." Portrayed as women, Africa and America prop up a female Europe who quietly threatens them with a whip. Blake suggests that the suffering of Americans and Asians contributed to European prosperity.

Advantages for Western Europe To dispel the belief that western Europeans dominated the world due to their superior culture, Jared Diamond explained in his book *Guns, Germs, and Steel* (1997) that Europeans benefited from geography. They had better access to the animals, innovations, diseases, and ideas of the more advanced societies in eastern Asia. European access to horses and cows improved the efficiency with which they could use the land and travel and trade across it. Guns and steel in European hands became more advanced, and this combined with years of plague developed well-armed and resistant peoples ready to dominate a part of the world that lacked these advantages.

However, advantages alone were not enough to establish the reality reflected in Blake's illustration. Helen Nader, an expert in medieval history, argued in the article "The End of the Old World" (1992) that Europeans couldn't just impose their ideas on others. They had to adapt to the weather, people, and the environment. This meant developing new ways of trading. From the beginning, success and profit in the Americas was about innovation. For the Spanish monarchs Ferdinand and Isabella to profit from the Americas, they had to infuse it with a strong competitive spirit.

Early explorers obscured this goal by following tradition and maximizing their own wealth. But by 1504, the Spanish crown saw the need for high-volume trade, which required numerous investors, not that of single explorers. As a result, Spanish America was full of family farms, run by households with a degree of local control, and acceptance of free trade. This brought the Spanish their wealth, at least in the short term. Their acceptance of competition, trade, and sometimes self-rule would soon be seen as a characteristic of the modern world.

Impact on the World Andre Gunder Frank challenged explanations of history that he found too centered on Europe. In *ReOrient: Global Economy in the Asian Age* (1998) he argued that exploration changed the world because European capitalism provided the needed wealth for Europe to rise (in the form of crops, silver, and gold) simultaneous to the decline of the East. Ultimately, European exploration established a new world system that placed Europe at the center. This system became so ingrained in the western worldview that it has taken historians the past 60 years to break with the Eurocentric tradition and explain the realities and complexities of Europe's rise and the resulting impact.

KEY TERMS AND NAMES

Movement

Marco Polo

Prince Henry the Navigator

Bartholomeu Dias

Vasco da Gama

Pedro Álvares Cabral

Christopher Columbus

King Ferdinand and Queen Isabella

Amerigo Vespucci

New World

conquistadors

Hernán Cortés

Aztec Empire

Vasco Nuñez de Balboa

Francisco Pizarro

Ferdinand Magellan

John Cabot

Giovanni de Verrazano

Jacques Cartier

Samuel de Champlain

Geography

Ottoman Empire

Gold Coast

Cape of Good Hope

Indian Ocean

Spice Islands

Brazil

Caribbean Sea

West Indies

Indians

Central America

Tenochtitlán

Mexico City

New Spain

Isthmus of Panama

Pacific Ocean

Inca Empire

Andes Mountains

Lima

Peru

Philippines

Manila

Lisbon

Antwerp

Amsterdam

Jamestown

British East India Company

St. Lawrence River

Quebec

New France

Dutch East India Company

Dutch West India Company

New Amsterdam

Hudson River

New York

Economics

mercantilism

favorable balance of trade

exports

imports

colony

parent country

plantation

encomienda

Technology

navigation

cartography

compass

astrolabe

Governance

Treaty of Tordesillas

Global Exchange

Columbian Exchange

Old World

Alfred Crosby

smallpox

measles

immunity

demographic

Questions 1–3 refer to the following passage.

"Upon which assurance of your royal love I have given my general command to all the kingdoms and ports of my dominions to receive all the merchants of the English nation as the subjects of my friend; that in what place soever they choose to live, they may have free liberty without any restraint; and at what port soever they shall arrive, that neither Portugal nor any other shall dare to molest their quiet; and in what city soever they shall have residence, I have commanded all my governors and captains to give them freedom answerable to their own desires; to sell, buy, and to transport into their country at their pleasure.

For confirmation of our love and friendship, I desire your Majesty to command your merchants to bring in their ships of all sorts of rarities and rich goods fit for my palace; and that you be pleased to send me your royal letters by every opportunity, that I may rejoice in your health and prosperous affairs; that our friendship may be interchanged and eternal."

Jahangir, ruler of the Mughal Empire, letter to King James I of England, 1617

1. Which phrase best describes the form of British colonial activity that is referred to in the excerpt above?

   a) A case of a crown monopoly

   b) An example of missionary colonization

   c) An investment by a private stock company

   d) A case of government-approved privateering

2. Which country's colonial activities in East Asia most resembled the British practices described in the passage?

   a) Netherlands

   b) France

   c) Spain

   d) Portugal

3. The most significant reason among the following for the decline of Portuguese influence in India was

   a) French interest in expanding their trade in Asia

   b) the establishment of the British East India Company

   c) the location of a Portuguese trading center in Antwerp

   d) the inclusion of Bombay in the dowry of a Portugues princess to England's king

Questions 4 and 5 refer to the following passage.

"The common ways mainly employed by the Spaniards who call themselves Christian and who have gone there to extirpate [eliminate] those pitiful nations and wipe them off the earth is by unjustly waging cruel and bloody wars. . . . When they have slain all the native rulers and young men (since the Spaniards usually spare only the women and children, who are subjected to the hardest and bitterest servitude ever suffered by man or beast), they enslave any survivors. . . .

Their reason for killing and destroying such an infinite number of souls is that the Christians have an ultimate aim, which is to acquire gold, and to swell themselves with riches in a very brief time and thus rise to a high estate disproportionate to their merits. It should be kept in mind that their insatiable greed and ambition, the greatest ever seen in the world, is the cause of their villainies. And also, those lands are so rich and felicitous [suitable], the native peoples so meek and patient, so easy to subject, that our Spaniards have no more consideration for them than beasts. And I say this from my own knowledge of the acts I witnessed. But I should not say "than beasts" for, thanks be to God, they have treated beasts with some respect; I should say instead like excrement [waste matter] on the public squares. And thus they have deprived the Indians of their lives and souls, for the millions I mentioned have died without the Faith and without the benefit of the sacraments.

Bartolomé de Las Casas, the Spanish conquest of the native
peoples of the Americas, 1542

4. The excerpt best supports which conclusion about the Spanish conquest of the native peoples of the Americas?

    a) Nearly all leaders of the Catholic Church opposed the practices of the conquistadors.

    b) The conquistadors converted the native peoples through their practice of Christianity.

    c) Some Spaniards believed that the Spanish used barbaric practices to control the native populations.

    d) The Spanish faced great difficulty conquering the native peoples.

5. Which is the most important factor leading to the reduction of native populations that could be added to Las Casas' first-hand account?

    a) The conflicts among native populations over how to respond to the Spanish

    b) The introduction by the Spanish of nonnative diseases to the Americas

    c) The decision by native individuals to move to lands not controlled by the Spanish

    d) The employment by the Spanish of native peoples in wars against British colonists

Questions 6–8 refer to the following chart.

Imports of Enslaved Africans		
Colonial Region	**Modern Countries in this Region**	**Percentage of Total Imported Slaves**
Portuguese Colonies	Brazil	39%
British West Indian Colonies	Jamaica, Barbados	18%
Spanish Colonies	Dominican Republic	18%
French Colonies	Haiti	14%
British Mainland Colonies	United States	6%
Other	Surinam	5%

Source: Adapted from Stephen D. Behrendt, et al. *The Encyclopedia of the African and African American Experience*

6. Which is the most likely explanation for the high percentage of enslaved people brought into Brazil and the West Indies?

   a) Sugar plantations in those regions could profitably employ the greatest numbers of laborers.

   b) Brazil and the West Indies were the ports closest to Africa.

   c) People in other colonies were too poor to afford to purchase enslaved workers.

   d) All other colonies already had a large supply of of labor.

7. Which of the following best explains why the labor of enslaved Africans was established in the European colonies?

   a) Most Native Americans had succumbed to disease or overwork.

   b) Native Americans had rebelled and refused to perform labor without compensation.

   c) Europeans had found that the slave trade itself was a source of profit.

   d) Europeans gave Native Americans the choice of whether to work.

8. The importation of slaves into the New World was part of a process known as

   a) mercantilism

   b) the Treaty of Tordesillas

   c) triangular trade

   d) the Columbian Exchange

1. Use the passage below to answer all parts of the question that follow.

> Too often, we historians tend to tell our story with the knowledge of the end
> result to come… But it is strangely liberating to look at the old maps, and see
> the vast stretches not-yet-filled-in, and populated instead with mermaids and
> unicorns and other figments of Europe's overheated imagination. Champlain's
> earliest and supposedly scientific renderings of the new world include a
> large winged dragon, ready to take flight. Well into the 18th century, maps
> of the Atlantic continued to include completely fictitious islands that had
> been legends for centuries, but never existed—the Sunken Land of Buss, St.
> Brendan's Isle, Hy-Brazil, the Island of the Seven Cities, and a dozen others.
>
> Ted Widmer, *Navigating the Age of Exploration*, 2007

   a) Provide ONE piece of historical evidence (not specifically mentioned in the passage) that would *support* Widmer's interpretation about the Age of Exploration.

   b) Provide ONE piece of historical evidence that would *undermine* Widmer's interpretation about the Age of Exploration.

   c) Explain how the Age of Exploration reflected the changing ideas about individuals and society in 15th- and 16th-century Europe.

2. Answer all parts of the question that follows.

   a) Explain ONE economic development that shifted the exchange of goods from the Mediterranean Sea to the states on the Atlantic Ocean from 1450 to 1650.

   b) Explain ONE political development that shifted the exchange of goods from the Mediterranean Sea to the states on the Atlantic Ocean from 1450 to 1650.

   c) Explain ONE geographic reason that shifted the exchange of goods from the Mediterranean Sea to the states on the Atlantic Ocean from 1450 to 1650.

LONG ESSAY QUESTIONS

   1. Evaluate the extent to which competition between Spain and Portugal affected overseas exploration in the 15th and 16th centuries.

   2. Evaluate the extent to which the interactions with Europeans affected native peoples during the Age of Exploration.

1. In one to three paragraphs, explain how Europe's overseas explorations affected both Europeans and indigenous populations.

WRITE AS A HISTORIAN: DISTINGUISH TYPES OF SOURCES

Historians use many types of sources to help explain the past. They range from very personal diaries to works of later scholars analyzing events. One way to think about this range of sources is to distinguish between primary and secondary sources. These are described in the chart below.

Differences Between Primary and Secondary Sources		
Characteristic	**Primary Source**	**Secondary Source**
Description	A first-hand account of an event or of what a person thought	A later description of an event or of what a person thought
Examples	• A journal kept by a Spanish priest in Mexicot • A a speech by an Aztec leader • The legal charter of the British East India Company • The clothes, pottery, tools and other possessions owned by people living in the West Indies • The records of a bank in Amsterdam showing deposits and loans • Paintings showing European merchants	• A book written by a historian in the 20th century anaylzing mercantilism in the 17th century • A painting created in the 19th century showing the first meeting between Pizarro and an Incan • A table created in the 21st century summarizing the population decrease among indigenous people after their first contact with Europeans
Strengths	• They reflect how people perceived an event at the time it was happening • They provide details about how people acted	• They reflect how people view an event after they have seen some of its results •They provide context based on other events happending at the same time in other places
Weaknesses	• They reflect the point of view of the observer	• They reflect the point of view of the historian or other person who created the source

Identify each item as either a primary or a secondary source.

1. *The Economy of British America,* by historian Cathy D. Matson, which analyzes economic developments in the colonies belonging to Great Britain in the Americas

2. *Representations of Slavery,* by historian Douglas Hamilton, which analyzes how museums, movies, and websites have portrayed slavery as it developed in European colonies

3. *Columbus,* by historian Felipe Fernández-Armesto, a biography of Christopher Columbus published in 1991

4. The journal kept by Christopher Columbus of his voyages to the Americas

5. *De varietate fortunae,* an account of the voyages of Nicolò de Conti, who travelled in the Indian and Pacific Oceans in the 15th century

6. Drawings and other artwork in the *Sino-Spanish Codex,* created in 1590, showing people in Japan, China, and the Philippines as portrayed by Spanish explorers, missionaries, and traders

7. A chapter about the astrolabe in *Champlain: The Birth of French America,* by Raymonde Litalien and Denis Vangeois, published in 2004

8. The astrolabe shown below, which was made in Spain during the Middle Ages

4

Tradition and Capitalism in Economic Life

"London, the Metropolis of England, is perhaps a Head too big for the Body, and possibly too strong."

—John Graunt, "Natural and Political Observations" 1662

Essential Question: How did capitalism combine with earlier structures to shape economic life during the 16th and 17th centuries?

Modern Europe emerged in the period that began around 1500 with European expansion through trade and colonization. As European society became more closely connected to the wider world, many aspects of daily life were shaped more and more by commercial and agricultural capitalism. **Capital** is wealth in the form of money that can be invested to create more wealth. **Capitalism** is an economic system characterized by private ownership of the **means of production** such as tools, buildings, and machines. In economic terms, the **market** is where buyers and sellers freely exchange goods and services. In capitalism, the market, rather than the government, determines what to produce, how to produce it, and who produces it. Thus, capitalism is sometimes called a **market economy**.

Forms of capitalism emerged long before 1500. At that time, **entrepreneurs**, individuals who assumed the risk of a business venture, generally acquired capital for their ventures as merchants. For example, the European woolen industry emerged in the 13th and 14th centuries. Entrepreneurs purchased raw wool from numerous sources, hired home-based workers to process it, and sold the finished products throughout northern Europe. In the 16th century, this system of producing goods was spread over a wider area, especially in rural England and the western Holy Roman Empire. Indeed, the commercial capitalism, or capitalism used for large-scale trade or business, that emerged in the 16th and 17th centuries extended to more-distant international markets. At the same time, traditional economic and social structures remained important throughout Europe.

Economic and Social Patterns

Economic changes that came to Europe after 1500 had widespread consequences for the economy and society. New patterns emerged while traditional hierarchies and status relations continued to define the roles of individuals in many groups.

Changes in Banking and Finance

To handle the global trade market, banking and finance needed new tools. In the 15th and early-16th centuries, prominent families such as the **Medici** in Italy and the **Fuggers** in central Europe had largely run Europe's banking; but as ever-larger amounts of capital flowed into Europe in the form of trade profits and precious metals from the Americas, banks needed to meet the new requirements of commercial capital markets. Such changes helped grow the **money economy**, an economy based on cash for investment, for wages, and for buying and selling goods. The money economy replaced the earlier economy, in which people grew or made most of what they used.

Joint-stock Companies One important financial innovation of the late-16th and early-17th centuries was the **joint-stock company**, which raised large amounts of capital for international trade and colonization ventures. In these enterprises, numerous investors bought **stock**, or shares, in a company and received **dividends**, or payments, as a return on their investment based on the company's profits. Investors could receive high returns from such ventures. For example, the **Dutch East India Company** was a joint-stock company formed in 1602 to finance Dutch trade in Asia. During the first ten years of its operation, the company paid investors a return of about 30 percent.

Urban Financial Centers As banking and finance changed, new capital markets emerged based in several urban financial centers, such as **Genoa, Amsterdam**, and **London**. Bankers in these centers could tap into capital throughout Europe.

Urban Financial Centers in the 16th and 17th Centuries		
City	Location	Economic Importance
Genoa	On the Mediterranean Sea near the current border of Italy and France	Genoa gained new importance in the later 16th and 17th centuries as the center of capital for the Spanish empire. Through central trading fairs and letters of exchange (authorizations of payments), bankers helped money flow from Spain to Spanish soldiers in the Netherlands.
Amsterdam	On the North Sea along the Amstel River	In 1609, the Dutch formed the **Bank of Amsterdam**, owned by many investors. Individuals, companies, and governments could deposit money in the bank and transfer capital to one another. The Dutch also established the **Amsterdam Exchange** for stock trading, and it was the center of European business by the mid-17th century, as Amsterdam became Europe's financial capital.
London	In southeast England along the Thames River, inland from the English Channel	London became England's financial center as trade expanded with the establishment of joint-stock companies starting in the middle of the 16th century. As the Dutch weakened late in the 17th century, London's importance grew as a European financial center.

New Economic Elite

The growth of towns and **commerce**, or large-scale buying and selling, made merchants and bankers more powerful in some places than nobles who owned land. In some states, rulers granted titles of nobility to the most powerful merchants and bankers, such as the Fuggers in central Europe.

In 17th-century Amsterdam, wealthy merchants, manufacturers, and shipyard owners were at the top of the social scale. These elites controlled the city government and the nation's legislative body. Nobles who owned land were a step below the city's new economic elite, although there were intermarriages between these groups.

London was similar to Amsterdam in this period, as a small number of wealthy merchants controlled the city. Increase in wealth could improve a person's rank in society. In spite of London's growing importance in international trade, England remained about 80 percent rural by the early 17th century. The landed nobility still had the highest status in the English countryside. However, a growing number of **gentry**, wealthy landowners who did not have inherited titles, were gaining in influence.

Established Hierarchies

Even with the growth of new economic elites, people in 17th-century Europe understood their places in established hierarchies that had long been based on class, religion, and gender. These hierarchies determined the ways people viewed each other's status in urban and rural settings.

Class Traditionally class was determined by birth and wealth, which placed monarchs and the nobility with inherited titles at the top of the scale. However, the expanding commercial economy created opportunities for some **social mobility**, or movement among classes, as wealthy merchants, manufacturers, and bankers rose in class in some societies. In France, for example, some Nobles of the Robe, people holding administrative or judicial offices, were not landowners and could pay for their positions to become hereditary. Yet some privileges and perceptions remained attached to ownership of land, as the composition of Britain's Parliament of the time illustrates.

- Nobles served in the **House of Lords**, the upper house of Parliament, and were often close advisers to the king. They were also the leaders of the counties where their vast estates were located.

- The wealthy but untitled gentry made up about 5 percent of the rural population and could be chosen to serve in the **House of Commons**, the lower house of Parliament. They also served as local magistrates.

Religion In most places, Christians who dissented from a country's established church suffered discrimination. In addition, Jews were expelled from many countries or forced to practice their religion in secret. Amsterdam was an exception. The city had a diverse population, which encouraged religious toleration but also boosted trade and economic growth.

Gender European society remained generally **patriarchal**, as men controlled government and public life as well as private households, while women were under the authority of their fathers or husbands. Women had value as workers in home-based businesses, but their earnings belonged to the men in the family.

In limited instances women had some economic independence and status. For example, in Amsterdam, widows of **artisans**, or skilled craftsmen, could take their husband's place in a guild and engage in business. **Guilds** were organizations of artisans or merchants that originated in the Middle Ages and that controlled production and distribution of goods in Europe until the advent of commercial capitalism.

Subsistence Farming and Commercial Agriculture

In pre-industrial Europe, most people lived in rural communities and made their living from agriculture. For landowners and agricultural workers, social customs and class relations had remained largely the same since the Middle Ages. By the 1600s, however, the economic changes of commercial capitalism reached the countryside of Western Europe where they began to transform the traditional way of life.

Subsistence Agriculture

In the Middle Ages, the social **hierarchy**, or ranking, and economic patterns in Western Europe still revolved around the system of feudalism, in which a lord would grant land (a fief) to a vassal, a person who accepted the land in exchange for loyalty and military service. Life in the European countryside revolved around the **manor**, a large agricultural estate under the control of a noble, or lord. The term **landlord** originally meant the lord who owned and controlled a certain amount of land. Although the nobility made up a small minority of the population, they owned most of the land and maintained their power through a system in which land and titles were inherited from one generation to the next. **Peasants**, who made up the vast majority of the population, farmed the land and occupied the lowest rung of the social order.

Changing Status of Peasants During the early Middle Ages, the majority of European peasants labored under **serfdom**, in which they were legally bound to the land and subject to the authority of their landlord. Many peasants, or serfs, labored three days a week for the lord and paid rent for the land that they farmed, often in the form of a portion of crops they grew or products made from livestock grazed on the lord's land. Serfs did have traditional rights, unlike slaves who were considered property and had no rights.

A Subsistence Economy During the Middle Ages peasants typically lived in small village communities within or near the manor. Day-to-day life was oriented around the seasons and annual cycles of planting and harvest. Despite the relentless toil of peasants, scarcity of suitable land for farming and lack of scientific knowledge limited how much food they could produce.

From the Middle Ages through the 17th century, **subsistence agriculture**, or farming for survival, was the norm in most of Europe. Peasants worked hard just to grow enough food to feed themselves and their families. They had very little food in reserve. In this precarious existence, a bad harvest could lead to food shortages and, at worst, deadly famine.

For example, Europe as a whole began to experience changes in the weather in the early-14th century, a period sometimes called the **"Little Ice Age"** that lasted until about 1850. Cooler temperatures, frequent storms, and heavy rains led to shorter growing seasons. Harvests, which had never been large, dwindled. These conditions resulted in famines throughout northern Europe in the period from 1315 to 1317. Widespread hunger and malnutrition likely made the surviving population more susceptible to diseases such as the plague that arrived in 1347.

Devasating Disease During the late Middle Ages, the status of peasants did improve, though, particularly in Western Europe. A variety of economic and demographic factors disrupted the balance of power between peasants and lords and contributed to the decline of serfdom. One of the main demographic factors was the **Great Plague** or **Black Death**, an outbreak of bubonic plague that began in 1347 and reduced the population of Europe by as much as one-third, with around 25 million people dying of the disease. That plague basically

THE GREAT PLAGUE IN EUROPE, 1347–1351

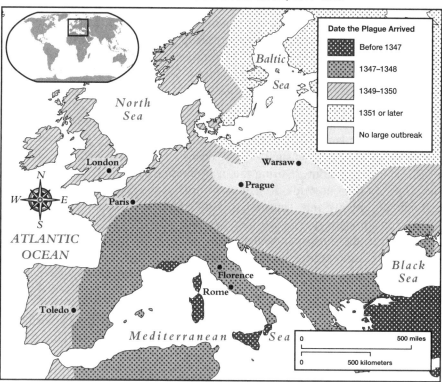

ended serfdom in Western Europe, bringing a severe labor shortage and thus freeing many peasants from serfdom. These free peasants could move, marry, and sell their land without their lord's permission. The decrease in the labor pool also allowed the remaining laborers to demand higher wages. Despite these new freedoms, social mobility was still limited, and much of the medieval social order persisted. Many peasants still paid rent or provided labor to their lord in exchange for the right to live and farm on his land.

The Open-Field System Farming methods that developed in the Middle Ages continued to organize rural food production well into the 1600s. Most villages adopted the **open-field system**, in which farmland was divided into two or three large fields. Within each field, land was further divided into narrow strips, and individual peasant families owned or rented several strips scattered in different places throughout the fields. The fields were "open" in the sense that there were no fences separating individual plots, and the scattering of plots ensured that areas of good and poor soil were evenly distributed. A portion of land was also set aside as common land, known as **the commons**, which could be used by all for livestock grazing. The open-field system contained elements of both private and communal land ownership. The arrangement required villagers to make collective decisions about what was to be grown and when. The survival of the village thus depended on community cooperation.

Crop Rotation A major obstacle to continuous farming was **soil exhaustion**—as multiple planting cycles of the same staple crop such as wheat depleted the soil of nutrients and resulted in successively smaller harvests. To confront this challenge, a system of **crop rotation**, or planting crops in different fields at different times, developed during the Middle Ages. In the traditional **two-field system**, half the land lay **fallow**, or empty and unused, in each growing season, so the soil could recover the nutrients depleted during the previous season.

In northern Europe, the **three-field system** became widespread. In the fall, the village planted grains such as wheat or barley in one field, and in the spring, they planted crops such as oats, beans, or peas in a second field. They left the third field fallow. During the next planting season, the village rotated the crops to different fields, so that two-thirds of the land was always in use, and one-third recovering. This system resulted in a significant advance in food production compared to the two-field system.

However, the three-field system was not practical in all parts of Europe. The Mediterranean region did not get enough spring and summer rainfall for a second spring planting, so the less productive two-field system continued there.

Commercialization of Agriculture

The growth of colonization and overseas trade in the 16th century contributed to the rise of commercial capitalism in Europe. Rather than deriving wealth from inherited land, merchants made their money from trade, the profits of private investment, and the selling of goods to a market of consumers.

The Price Revolution Beginning in the early 16th century, vast quantities of gold and silver entered Western Europe from the Spanish colonies in the Americas. That influx of precious metals and the resulting greater circulation of money, along with population growth, contributed to a period of rising prices of food and other basic necessities in Europe. The widespread rise in prices over an extended time period, known as **inflation**, also contributed to the growth of commerce in the 16th century. This inflationary period, the **price revolution,** lasted from the late 15th century to the mid-17th century and was pivotal in the commercialization of agriculture.

While rising prices made life difficult for ordinary people, merchants and bankers benefited tremendously from the higher returns on their investments and loans. As they accumulated more capital, they looked for new opportunities for investment and found them in the agricultural countryside.

As peasants migrated to towns, an increasing number of Europeans no longer grew their own food. They needed to buy it. Starting in the 1600s, middle-class investors and large landowners initiated a series of changes intended to shift the rural economy toward **commercial agriculture**, the production of food and livestock products, such as wool, for profit rather than subsistence. These changes had a profound impact on the peasant way of life.

The Enclosure Movement From the viewpoint of a large landowner or capitalist investor, the open-field system of peasant agriculture was inefficient and wasteful. Many scientists who applied their methods to agriculture agreed. With the availability of land limited, those involved in commercial agriculture needed to find other methods to increase crop yields. England passed legislation that allowed investors and commercial farmers to purchase land, including previously public land, the commons. **Enclosure** (also called inclosure) involved consolidating the various strips into larger fenced-in fields and establishing individual titles of ownership for each field. Most widespread in England, enclosures had started as early as the 12th century and had developed rapidly from the 15th to 18th centuries. The enclosure movement involved more than one thousand pieces of legislation in England alone.

Effects of Enclosure Over time, enclosure increased agricultural productivity and benefited the large landowners. The creation of privately owned, fenced-in fields made it easier for eager investors to buy more land and expand their holdings. In doing so, landowners could engage in large-scale production of crops and livestock, adopt new farming practices, and generate a surplus that could be sold in the market economy. However, the enclosure movement also profoundly disrupted traditional village life and created hardship for many peasants.

Enclosure increased rural poverty and contributed to a growing population of landless peasants. Some became laborers or tenant farmers on large estates owned by wealthy landowners. Others, hoping to find enough work to survive, migrated to towns and cities, leading to rapid urbanization. In some cases, peasants attempted to reassert their traditional rights by resisting enclosure, and farmer revolts swept England in the 1500s and 1600s.

Serfdom, Peasants, and Revolts

Although the growth of commercial agriculture often harmed Western Europe's peasants, most were no longer legally under the control of a landlord. They could make choices about how to adapt to the new economy. These choices included the freedom to move from one place to another and to change occupations.

Serfdom in Eastern Europe

As serfdom declined in Western Europe, an opposite trend occurred in Eastern Europe. By the early 16th century, the status of peasants in the east deteriorated, and serfdom became more entrenched. As centralized absolutist states eventually emerged in Austria, Prussia, and Russia during the 17th century, monarchs secured the cooperation of the aristocracy by incorporating them into the state bureaucracy or administrative structure. Landlords assumed bureaucratic positions as tax collectors, judges, and military officers; in turn, the state protected the serfdom from which the aristocracy benefited. In Russia, serfdom was codified into law in 1649.

Peasant Revolts

Peasants had long fought against attempts by landlords to become wealthier at the expense of peasants' rights. In the late Middle Ages, peasants revolted when landlords tried to re-impose conditions that existed before the Great Plague had devastated the population. In the revolt known as the **Jacquerie** in France in 1358 and the **English Peasants' Revolt** of 1381, peasants burned nobles' homes and murdered members of the upper classes. The landed nobility ultimately put down the revolts. In France, the forces of the nobility killed about 20,000 peasants. The failure of these revolts revealed the limit of what the peasants could achieve.

More than a century later, a much larger revolt occurred in the Holy Roman Empire. Serfs, influenced by the teachings of Martin Luther, revolted in an effort to gain greater economic and social freedom. Artisans and craftsmen joined the revolt. The forces of the nobility and Roman Catholic Church crushed the revolt, massacring thousands.

Commerce and the Growth of Cities

As commercial capitalism grew in the 16th and 17th centuries, population began to shift slowly from rural to urban areas. In 1500, less than 6 percent of the population lived in cities of 10,000 people or more. By 1650, more than 8 percent did. Some peasants took advantage of their increased mobility and moved to towns to find work. Artisans, merchants, and professionals had regularly been based in towns, and their numbers continued to grow. Wealthy nobles also began to establish homes in growing cities, especially the urban financial centers. Such changes placed stress on the traditional political and social structures of cities.

Population and Prices

In the mid-16th century, European population finally reached levels that had existed before the Great Plague that began in 1347. Population estimates increased from around 60 million people in 1500 to about 80 million in 1600. There was some leveling off in the early 17th century largely due to the Thirty Years' War. The Dutch, English, and French experienced the most growth. Much of the growth occurred in cities, which grew to unprecedented sizes for post-classical European cities. In 1500 only the largest cities in Europe, including Paris, Constantinople, and four Italian cities, had populations of more than 100,000 people. By 1600, Naples was up to 300,000, and more Italian cities, including Rome, had reached 100,000. Paris was the largest city with a population of 500,000.

As population grew, prices increased unevenly. Prices of **agricultural commodities** such as wheat rose more rapidly than workers' wages. Higher population meant a greater demand for food, which led to higher food prices. However, the greater number of workers meant competition for jobs, so wages stayed low. The resulting disparity between wages and the prices of food and other necessities reduced the standard of living for wage earners, including both agricultural laborers and urban salaried workers. In addition, the disparity grew worse as rulers increased taxes to build up their military forces.

Migrants and Cities

From the 12th to the 15th century, merchant and craft guilds had been the the economic and political leaders in European communities. While merchants were wealthier, craft workers were more numerous. The two groups competed for influence. However, with the growth of commercial capitalism, the power of guilds declined. Merchants became entrepreneurs, and guilds had a difficult time maintaining control of the production of goods as changes in manufacturing and trade occurred. Non-guild **migrants** in the cities challenged the merchant elites and the craft guilds for power. Merchants resented the influx of both the landed nobility and lower-wealth classes into the cities.

As more people migrated into cities, population density increased dramatically, which led to crowded and difficult living conditions for members of the lower classes. Cities generally lacked the resources to deal with this rapid growth and the problems that came with it, such as insufficient housing.

London In the early 17th century, city leaders in London tried to limit the city's population by outlawing the subdivision of older buildings into smaller and smaller dwellings. Their efforts were unsuccessful. Many people had to live in crowded and unsanitary conditions, which brought deadly diseases, such as outbreaks of plague and tuberculosis, as well as generally poor health. More than one-third of London's children died before the age of six. In 1666, the Great Fire of London burned for four days, ravaging much of the city because of the overcrowding and shoddy construction. In addition, the lack of clean water and food combined with high food prices and stagnant wages made it difficult for people to thrive in the city.

Many new businesses came into existence throughout this period. The businesses that caused the most pollution, such as slaughterhouses, were set up outside the city walls. When new shipping docks were built along the river, poorly built huts arose nearby to house workers.

London's population grew steadily. In 1600, it was 250,000. By 1815, it reached 1,500,000.

Amsterdam In Amsterdam, migrants doubled the population between 1570 and 1610, greatly contributing to the Dutch economy. Many came to escape religious persecution. Because Amsterdam was limited in area, the city developed a plan to more than triple the size of its territory in 1613. By 1660, the population had filled the new territory. Amsterdam was in its "Golden Age" and one of the wealthiest cities in Europe. 17th century

AMSTERDAM, 1635.

Ships crowding the harbor in Amsterdam in 1635 demonstrated the prosperity of the city.

Credit: *Getty Images*

Regulating Public Morals

During the Middle Ages, the Catholic Church set rules on **public morality**, or behavior that affected other people or society in general. During the Reformation, this role of the Church was diminished or destroyed completely in many Protestant countries. The rise of commercial capitalism and agriculture led to social dislocation, as people were either forced off their land or chose to move in search of economic opportunity. One issue of public morality thus became the treatment of beggars.

Some clergy and humanists of the 16th century blamed commercial capitalism, the market economy, and enclosures for destroying village life and increasing the number of beggars on the road and of poor people in towns. While the Roman Catholic Church, especially the monasteries, had cared for the poor in the Middle Ages, the increasing number of poor strained the traditional systems of charity and social control. The poor became the responsibility of city governments in the 16th century. For example, London began poor relief in 1547 after the decline of agencies previously run by the Catholic Church. Beggars were increasingly seen as threats to public order in the 16th century and were often forcibly removed from towns or even publicly whipped. People officially referred to as the "deserving poor," those seen as willing to work, were sent to public workhouses. As different institutions began to regulate public morals, many maintained a strong religious influence:

- New secular laws regulated private life.

- Stricter codes punished prostitution and begging.

- Regulations restricted or abolish celebrations.

In **Geneva**, Switzerland, there was no separation between the Protestant Church and the city when it came to regulating moral behavior. The city council adopted John Calvin's **Ecclesiastical Ordinances** in 1541. Under this church document, different groups of clergy and laymen were responsible for maintaining order and regulating public morals. Geneva's **Consistory**, or church council, served as a court that judged lapses in moral behavior and handed out punishments that included public whippings or banishment from the community. The Consistory might also refer some cases involving more serious offenses to the city council for justice. (See Chapter 2 to review the role of Calvinism in Geneva's city government.)

HISTORICAL PERSPECTIVES: WHY DID CAPITALISM EMERGE?

Max Weber (1864–1920) grew up under parents with very different approaches to understanding the world. His father was very intellectual and politically liberal. His mother followed strict Calvinist beliefs and more traditional German culture. Weber showed the influence of both parents in his explanation for why Protestantism and capitalism developed together. His book on this topic, *The Protestant Ethic and the Spirit of Capitalism* (1904–1905), was one of the most powerful writings of the time and remains widely read and debated today.

Liberal Government and Capitalism Like Weber, Robert L. Heilbroner (1919–1995) was a trained economist, interested in the institutions associated with economic activity, particularly with capitalism. However, he approached the development of the modern economic system from a different point of view from Weber's. As an American writing at the height of the Cold War, he focused more on economic and political institutions than on religion. In *The Making of Economic Society* (1962) he explained why England was first to industrialize. He suggested that England was the richest nation in the world, but that this wealth was not in the hands of the monarch or nobles. Rather, it was controlled by the rising middle class, which was supported by the English political structure. Heilbroner explained all the ways that the liberal English political environment supported the development of capitalism: from property laws that ended feudalism and allowed for enclosure, to the Royal Society encouraging innovation, to Parliament protecting innovation with patents.

Individualism and Capitalism As powerful as the political environment was, Heilbroner seemed to argue that it was an excited and motivated group of entrepreneurs born in this liberal political environment that led to the birth of capitalism. Christopher Castaneda, a modern historian, emphasized the central role of individualism to the development of capitalism. Castaneda, writing in *The History of World Trade* (2006, edited by John J. McCusker), cited the publication of the Declaration of Independence and Adam Smith's *Wealth of Nations,* both written in 1776 as evidence of the simultaneous rise of freedom and capitalism. During the Enlightenment, individualism became a secular, political value in Europe. The mercantilist governments of the time had inhibited individualism, but once liberalism took root, individualism gained political recognition, and capitalism thus thrived.

KEY TERMS BY THEME

Economics

capital

capitalism

means of production

market

market economy

entrepreneur

commercial capitalism

Medici

Fuggers

money economy

joint-stock company

stock

dividend

Dutch East India Company

Bank of Amsterdam

Amsterdam Exchange

commerce

subsistence agriculture

open-field system

the commons

soil exhaustion

crop rotation

two-field system

fallow

three-field system

inflation

price revolution

commercial agriculture

enclosure

agricultural commodities

Geography

Genoa

London

Amsterdam

Little Ice Age

Geneva

Social Structures

gentry

social mobility

patriarchal

artisan

hierarchy

guild

manor

landlord

peasant

serfdom

Great Plague

Black Death

migrants

merchant elites

public morality

Governance

House of Lords

House of Commons

Jacquerie

English Peasants' Revolt

Ecclesiastical Ordinances

Consistory

Questions 1–2 refer to the following passage.

"For in whatever parts of the land sheep yield the finest and thus the most expensive wool, there the nobility and gentry, yes, and even some abbots though otherwise holy men, are not content with the old rents that the land yielded to their predecessors. Living in idleness and luxury without doing society any good no longer satisfies them; they have to do positive evil.

For they leave no land free for the plough: they enclose every acre for pasture; they destroy houses and abolish towns, keeping only the churches–and those for sheep-barns…. Thus one greedy, insatiable glutton, a frightful plague to his native country, may enclose many thousands of acres within a single hedge. The tenants are dismissed and compelled, by trickery or brute force or constant harassment, to sell their belongings. One way or another, these wretched people–men, women, husbands, wives, orphans, widows, parents with little children and entire families … are forced to move out. They leave the only homes familiar to them, and can find no place to go. Since they must leave at once without waiting for a proper buyer, they sell for a pittance all their household goods …. When that little money is gone (and it's soon spent in wandering from place to place), what remains for them but to steal, and so be hanged–just, you'd say!–or to wander and beg?….

'To make this hideous poverty worse, it exists side by side with wanton luxury…. If you don't try to cure these evils, it is futile to boast of your severity in punishing theft. Your policy may look superficially like justice, but in reality it is neither just nor practical.'"

Thomas More, *Utopia,* 1516, George M. Logan and Robert
M. Adams, eds, (1989)

1. The passage describes developments resulting most directly from which trend in 15th-century Europe?
   a) The long tradition of subsistence agriculture
   b) The increase in peasant revolts in Western Europe
   c) The exploration of lands beyond Europe
   d) The beginnings of the commercialization of agriculture

2. Which of these individuals would most likely have agreed with More?
   a) An owner of a textile manufacturing company
   b) An entrepreneur in commercial agriculture
   c) A peasant who depended on subsistence agriculture
   d) A noble who gained control of more land because of an enclosure

Questions 3–5 refer to the following painting of the Great Fire of London in 1666 by an unknown artist and lyrics from a song called "The Londoner's Lamentation."

"Pitch, Tar, Oyle, Flax and ancient Wood/did make the raging fire so rant"
Source: *Wikipedia*

3. What is the context in which the event shown in the painting occurred?

   a) European cities were growing rapidly in population.

   b) The Little Ice Age was making the problem of fires worse.

   c) Uprisings such as the English Peasants' Revolt were common.

   d) The shift from monarchy to republicanism caused problems in providing public services.

4. Why was the event shown in the painting so destructive?

   a) Cramped housing conditions made fire spread rapidly.

   b) Damges to the Parliament building prevented the House of Commons from meeting.

   c) The destruction of warehouses led to an economic collapse.

   d) Fear of fires discouraged people from starting businesses.

5. To what extent was the event shown in the painting a problem in London in the 17th century?

   a) Fires were unusual because public services were strong.

   b) Fires were more of a concern in smaller communities than in cities.

   c) Fires were more common in other cities than in London.

   d) Fires were one of several problems faced by residents.

Questions 6–8 refer to the following passage.

"People went over and along the Thames on the ice, from London Bridge to Westminster. Some played at the football [soccer] as boldly there, as if it had been on dry land; . . . and the people, both men and women, went on the Thames in greater numbers than in any street in the City of London. On the third day of January, at night, it began to thaw, and on the fifth there was no ice to be seen between London Bridge and Lambeth, which sudden thaw caused great floods, and high waters, that bear down bridges and houses and drowned many people in England, especially in Yorkshire."

adapted from Raphael Holinshed, *Chronicles,* 1577, reporting on the unusual weather of 1564-1565

6. Which best identifies the trend in early modern Europe described in this passage?

   a) Discontinuation of the church enforcing communal norms

   b) Resistance by the urban poor against abolishing celebrations

   c) Influences of the Little Ice Age on Europe's climate

   d) Spread of pandemic illnesses such as the Great Plague

7. As a result of the changes described in the passage, which of the following effects had the greatest impact on the rural population of Europe?

   a) Good harvests amidst abundant rainfall helped increase family size.

   b) Subsistence farmers faced famine and malnutrition.

   c) Ties to the land strengthened because of the open-field system.

   d) Higher food production gave farmers independence from feudal ties.

8. Which was a long-term consequence in urban areas of the conditions reported by Holinshed?

   a) The formation of joint-stock companies

   b) The development of a more powerful gentry class

   c) The emergence of Genoa, London, and Amsterdam as financial centers

   d) The increase in wages for workers

SHORT-ANSWER QUESTIONS

1. Use the passage below to answer all parts of the question that follows.

"The orthodox [standard] view of the causes of the Price Revolution points to the large quantity of the precious metals, at first of gold, but later and principally of silver, shipped from Spanish possessions in the New World to Europe, and links this with the behaviour of prices in European countries."

> J. D. Gould, "The Price Revolution Reconsidered." *The Economic History Review.* NS, 17: 2 (1964).

a) Describe ONE specific piece of evidence that supports the orthodox view of the causes of the Price Revolution.

b) Describe ONE specific piece of evidence that provides an alternate explanation about the causes of the Price Revolution.

c) Explain ONE effect of the Price Revolution on the social or economic structure in Europe.

2. Answer all parts of the question that follows.

a) Describe ONE significant continuity from medieval European agricultural practices to European agricultural practices by the mid-17th century.

b) Describe ONE significant change from medieval European agricultural practices to European agricultural practices by the mid-17th century.

c) Explain ONE reason for change that took place from medieval European agricultural practices to more modern European agricultural practices by the mid-17th century.

LONG ESSAY QUESTIONS

1. Evaluate the extent to which commercial capitalism in the 16th century changed the European social hierarchy and standard of living.

2. Evaluate the relative importance of the different factors that produced a new urban commercial and banking elite in the 16th and 17th centuries.

REFLECT ON THE CHAPTER ESSENTIAL QUESTION

1. In one to three paragraphs, explain how capitalism and earlier structures shaped economic life during the 16th and 17th centuries.

Historians combine information from diaries, newspapers, census data, and other sources to answer questions. A credible source should be from a reliable observer or expert on the topic. While every source reflects a point of view, a credible source does not ignore clear facts or attempt to mislead others. Every source also has limitations. For example, no observer can see every action or know what every person is thinking. To decide how useful evidence is for advancing your arguments, ask: Is the source relevant to the topic? Will it tell readers something they need to know? Does it provide facts or informed opinions? Is it credible? What are its limitations?

For each topic below, which item is the least *useful bit of evidence?*

1. The growth of commerce produced a new economic elite in Europe.

   a. household bookkeeping records from a member of England's gentry

   b. a painting of a French noble that includes symbols of wealth

   c. a diary entry from a Spanish friar in Mexico about spreading Christianity

2. Commercialization of agriculture benefited landowners in Europe.

   a. legal records showing the number of commons converted during the enclosure movement

   b. a ledger entry detailing the transactions of a farming enterprise over the course of a year

   c. a series of maps depicting villages' features over time and their diminishing common space

   d. sketches of peasants working in the fields using farm tools of the period

For the statement, identify which response most strongly supports it and which most clearly refutes it.

3. A number of Renaissance and Reformation writers advocated against female education and an equal role for women.

   a. Juan Luis Vives's *Instruction of a Christian Woman* concluded that Catherine of Aragon's daughter, the future Mary I, should not be allowed to rule because women are inherently weak.

   b. Supporters of Elizabeth I published arguments that God had made her queen because she was unique. Elizabeth chose to remain unmarried so that she would never have a "master" in the eyes of society.

   c. John Knox, a Calvinist minister in Scotland, wrote *The First Blast of the Trumpet Against the Monstrous Regiment of Women* while women were on the thrones of France, Scotland, and England.

5

Tradition and Capitalism in Society

"A woman . . . is God's creature and her divine station is that she should bear and care for and rear children. So I am a man created for another office and work. But should I [think] . . . I am better in the sight of God?"

—Martin Luther, 1483–1546

Essential Question: How did capitalism and the persistence of earlier structures shape family life and traditional ideas during the 15th and 16th centuries?

The family was central to European society in the **early modern period**—roughly the early 15th century through the end of the 18th century. Many of its functions made the family central to the period. It was the main institution for reproduction and the raising of children, both essential elements of the economy of rural areas. Property also was primarily transferred through families, which passed on land and possessions through inheritance. Family units provided needed services, such as the care of land and resources, as well as tending to the sick, young, and aged. Every family member contributed labor and resources to the individual family economy. Important changes in the Church and European society would affect the family structure, as well as the economy and cultural traditions. As the quotation from Martin Luther showed, it was a time when people were rethinking the roles of men and women. New roles within the family and society took shape. As they did, the structure and purpose of the family itself changed.

Changes in the Family

Beginning in the mid-15th century, traditional culture in Europe changed significantly as a result of the social upheaval of the Protestant Reformation, natural disasters, and emerging capitalism. While family continued to be crucial to the preservation of the social order, the roles of men and women were changing within the **nuclear family,** the unit of a married couple and their children. The way the family itself fit into broader society also transformed during these years of change, as the family was becoming a new economic, social, and legal unit—but not without resistance based on age-old traditions.

Regulations on Families

Family laws and customs were at the center of religious, cultural, and legal issues of the early modern period. Though the structure and purpose of the family changed, it remained the primary social and economic institution in Europe. States and religious institutions were therefore nervous about any changes to the order and purpose of the family and made frequent attempts to regulate it.

Political and Religious Influences on Family Life		
Type of Regulation	Methods	Example
Direct	• Laws and traditions that determined the components of and legitimacy of a marriage • Laws that forbade people marrying someone of another class	In Venice, Italy, during financial difficulties, tradition required that only one son of a patrician family could marry. Other sons worked as family employees.
Indirect	• Government policies that offered fiscal incentives to encourage couples to have more children	In late-17th century France, Louis XIV tried to stimulate the birthrate by offering tax concessions to large families.
General	• Examples that showed images of family authority, such as portrayals of the king as a loving father	Churches, particularly in Roman Catholic countries, made obtaining a divorce very difficult.

Primogeniture States also regulated how family property could be divided, supporting the traditional model of a father passing land and other forms of wealth to his oldest son, a practice called **primogeniture**. This family structure caused younger sons to become members of the clergy or **artisans**—workers in a skilled trade. After the Reformation, fewer men sought lives within the church, leading to an increase in artisans that would eventually help fuel an emerging capitalistic structure.

Patriarchalism The political theory of **patriarchalism** from 17th century England defended the power of the absolute monarch by comparing him to a father. Those loyal to Kings James I and Charles I emphasized the paternal—or fatherly—power of the king over the state and his subjects. Patriarchs such as Sir Robert Filmer argued that the **conjugal family ideal**—the traditional family hierarchy that placed the father at the top of the family unit—was necessary for the monarch to maintain his own power and authority.

Gender and Class Roles

Family structure during the early modern period reflected the patriarchal structure of the larger social order. For example, in England, in wealthier families, the father had to ensure that the family's wealth remained intact, which meant his oldest male child inherited most of his estate through primogeniture. The only claim a daughter would have to her parental estate would come with her **dowry**, or the transfer of property or money that she would receive upon marriage. Wives could usually determine who should receive their dowry upon their death, and husbands typically could not claim ownership to more than one-third of the dowry during the marriage. Women even had the right to sue their husbands if they thought the dowry was being used improperly.

This gendered male-dominated structure existed most typically in the upper class. The merchants, business owners, and others who did nonphysical labor had more options in how to structure their lives than did poorer people. Husbands and wives in the class of people doing physical labor earned less. They needed to perform difficult, essential daily tasks just to survive. Families in rural areas—who were also largely proletarian—had even fewer choices. Poor rural households were run in a much more egalitarian fashion than households in urban centers, as men and women engaged in different but

The Merry Family by Jan Steen, a Dutch painting from the 17th century, portrays a lively scene in the home of a prosperous family.

Credit: Getty Images

complementary tasks. Regardless of the family's class, location, or need to work, families in the early modern period functioned as economic units, with husbands and wives contributing with tasks that, together, accomplished the needed work.

Women's Intellect and Education

Before the Reformation, Catholic convents were havens for unmarried women, offering them a chance to study, write, and exert leadership. However, unmarried women still had few other options. After the Reformation, women in Protestant countries lost many of the opportunities provided by convents. However, women had more freedom to explore other options. For example, many women used their homes to teach the gospel and feed the hungry. Some took to writing—from poems to theology to memoirs. Divorce become an option for married women in some places, though typically with many restrictions.

As women's roles started to change, the traditional family unit became even more important. The family—not a church or a monastery—was now the center of Christian life. Both men and women were thought to be able to communicate directly with God. No one needed a male priest or other intermediary to pray or confess sins. Women were encouraged to gain education, though typically mainly as a means of raising educated children who were good Christians and citizens. The question of how much education women should receive became an ongoing discussion, primarily in Italy and England in the mid-17th century.

The Woman Question An academic debate began in France in the 1530s over whether women were fit to attend university. It expanded into broader questions about gender relations, and became known as the **Querelle des Femmes**, or the Woman Question.

- One side argued that women were naturally inferior to men, and this was unchangeable. They cited three reasons: God created man first, men were physically stronger, and Eve—the woman created from Adam—deceived him and ultimately brought on humanity's downfall.

- The other side argued that men oppressed women to maintain their own social status and power. Eve was actually the one who was deceived. Women's inferior position was due to a lack of education, and was therefore changeable.

This became the fundamental question regarding the limits placed on women: Were the limits set by God or by humans? In limiting the opportunities for women, was the male-dominated society maintaining an unchangeable sanctified order, or was it oppressing women?

Limitation on Women Though this period provided more options for women than they were afforded previously, there were still many restrictions. Single women might have been able to choose to live outside a convent, but they were still not allowed to serve as preachers. They also were not allowed to hold positions of authority within the church. Instead, even single woman were expected to serve as models of obedience and Christian charity. Most importantly, they were expected to be quiet.

Anabaptists Compared to Catholic, Lutheran, and Calvinist churches, **Anabaptist** churches were less patriarchal. For example, women held some leadership positions. They were even preachers. They led worship services, taught the Scriptures, and were regarded as elders and prophets. Because of this stark contrast to the accepted practices of the time, many Anabaptist women were martyred for their behavior.

Marriage and Childbirth

The 14th century had been among the hardest on Europe's population. War, famine, and disease killed millions. In contrast, the 15th and 16th centuries were a period of growth. France's population doubled from 10 million to 20 million from 1450 to 1550. Europe still relied on human power to produce goods, so the increased population helped bring economic growth. Europe's population growth also meant farmers and artisans had greater incentive to bring more food and other essentials, as well as luxury items, to market.

Population growth affected marriage patterns also. Europeans in the early modern period typically did not marry out of love. Rather, they married for economic reasons, such as to have children and run a farm.

Strains on Resources

After catastrophic periods of famines or epidemics, when large numbers of people died from starvation and disease, marriage rates typically rose. During the **Black Death**—or plague—in the mid-14th century, more than 20 million people, or one-third of the population of Europe, died. Immediately afterward, Europe desperately needed to repopulate. The marriage rate rose and the age at marriage fell. During times of prosperity, however, couples typically waited for land and employment opportunities before marrying. As a result, the marriage rate fell and the age at marriage rose.

By the early modern period, Europe's population had rebounded from the Black Death so sufficiently that economic resources could no longer keep pace with demand for products. Couples married at an increasingly older age (between 26 and 27 for men and between 24 and 25 for women), as they waited to obtain land and opportunity. Acquiring a plot of land usually depended upon the death of the man's father, so some couples waited even longer.

Harsh Winters and Poor Harvests As part of the Little Ice Age, beginning around 1300 (see page 77), a series of unusually harsh winters led to poor harvests in the 1600s. Scarcity of food brought malnutrition and widespread disease. To cope with their poverty, members of the agricultural class started to have smaller families. They waited until they could become financially established before marrying, and thus married at a later age.

Decline of Multigenerational Households While it was once common to find several generations of one family living in the same household, this practice became increasingly less common in western Europe during the early modern period. In fact, a family would likely look very similar to today's nuclear family: two parents marrying in their late-twenties and raising a small number of children.

Influences on Family Size

A number of factors contributed to the low rate of live births and high infant mortality in the early modern period. These included cultural and economic factors, as well as scientific and medical knowledge of the time.

- When women married at a later age for economic reasons, they had fewer childbearing years.

- The number of miscarriages and stillbirths was high, reflecting both to lack of medical knowledge and extreme working conditions that strained a woman's body.

- Infant mortality was high. About one in four babies died in infancy, while another one in four died before puberty. A woman in the early modern period would see roughly two children survive to adulthood.

Birth Control and Family Planning Even after considering how delays in marriage reduced the number of childbearing years, European birthrates were below that of other world region of he time. Couples might have taken steps to avoid having children. For example, one form of natural birth control was that women are generally not as fertile as usual for six months after having a baby. People might also have used medications and other methods to reduce births. However, advising people on birth control could be risky. Some people opposed artificial methods of preventing pregnancy for religious reasons. Others considered birth control methods a form of witchcraft.

Persistence of Folk Ideas

Folk ideas and celebrations varied greatly throughout Europe, ranging from festivals marking rites of passage, such as births and marriages, to feasts at a specific time of year such as harvests, saints days, or religious holidays. When the Protestant Reformation brought religious upheaval, it also changed many traditions. Hoping to maintain their way of life, many held tightly to folk ideas and customs, especially in Germany, where the Reformation began and where its effects were felt most.

Carnival

The Christian period of Lent spans the six weeks before Easter, and **Carnival** is the three- to six-day period of celebration immediately before Lent. In the early modern period, Carnival's lavish feasting and celebrations served as a balance to Lent's fasting and purification. Carnival and Lent were polar opposites, but they were also meant to mutually support each other. The extreme feasting and celebrating during Carnival emphasized humans' multitude of sins from the previous year. It also was a way to release impulses by allowing people to live all those sins simultaneously. Carnival also helped reinforce the social order by temporarily allowing individuals to live outside that order: women posing as men, for example, peasants as aristocrats, and people as animals. Lent, in contrast, was a time of fasting and purification to serve **penance**—the voluntary self-punishment or confession for having done wrong.

After the Reformation, Protestant leaders rejected penance as a sacrament. Carnival, therefore, quickly became another target for anti-Catholic attacks. Even the Catholic Church came to reject Carnival when it did away with public confession.

Still, individuals fought to maintain the folk tradition of Carnival, especially in rural areas where the reach of the church and state was less strong. Carnival continues to exist today—most notably in the cities of Rio de Janeiro, Brazil, and New Orleans, Louisiana—but it has virtually no religious significance.

Blood Sports

Some popular entertainment in the early modern period were **blood sports,** also called "butcherly sports" because of their violent nature. These activities pitted humans against each other in jousting matches. Though not intended as deadly events, many participants did die in them. Other activities pitted animals against each other in dogfights or cockfights.

Saints' Day Festivities

All Saints' Day, also known as the Feast of All Saints, is celebrated every year on November 1 to commemorate all the saints. It is preceded by All Hallow's Eve, from which modern Halloween is descended. All Hallow's Eve was celebrated at the same time as the pagan holiday of Samhain, and like Samhain, it was a feast or vigil for the dead. Following All Saints' Day is All Souls' Day to honor faithful Christians who had died and whose souls were going to join the saints. Customs for these holidays included making "soul cakes" to give to beggars in exchange for their prayers for the dead and lighting candles to help sinners' souls escape from purgatory.

Challenges to Communal Norms

The success of the Reformation promoted the spread of humanism, with its increased emphasis on critical thinking rather than acceptance of traditional beliefs. While people adapted many folk ideas and maintained them beyond the early modern period, the Reformation and humanism challenged other practices that eventually became obsolete. However, certain forms of control and punishment survived from earlier times and were used by both local and church authorities.

Punishment and Control During the Early Modern Period	
Method	**Description**
Charivari	• **Charivari** was a loud, public mock parade, with clanging pots and pans to make **rough music**. It was a form of social intimidation or shaming, particularly in small communities in Western Europe. • As populations grew and capitalism began to replace subsistence agriculture, the social structure that supported charivari eventually disappeared with the rise of more official forms of social control, such as police and courts.
Stocks, Pillory and Pranger	• The **stocks** were a form of public punishment from medieval times. The offender sat on a bench with ankles closed into holes in boards for several hours. The wrists and neck might similarly be restrained. Townspeople might throw waste at the prisoner. • The **pillory**, also with medieval roots, entrapped the victim's head and wrists as he stood or walked around an upright wooden bar. Passersby often threw waste and otherwise tortured the prisoner, depending on the severity of the crime. • In a related device, the **pranger**, the victim's neck was chained to restraints around the ankles, placing the victim on in an uncomfortable half-kneeling position. In a less ominous form, the offender was chained to a column in the town center. • Public punishment with these devices remained common until at least 1748.
Flogging	• Flogging, or whipping, was often accompanied by punishment in the stocks, pillory or pranger. Like the blood sports and executions of the period, it drew many spectators.

Witchcraft

The many changes brought about by the religious and social upheaval of the Protestant Reformation contributed to increased accusations of witchcraft. Before Europeans used science to understand causes of illnesses, famines, and other misfortunes, they often attributed such events to witchcraft. Accusations of witchcraft peaked between 1580 and 1650, years of religious turmoil following the Reformation. As many as 100,000 people were accused and 40,000 executed on charges of practicing witchcraft. Exact numbers are not available, because detailed records were not kept. Most of the accused were women. As religious controversies became less deadly and knowledge of science spread, fear of witches declined.

Religious Upheaval The Reformation brought the church into people's homes, but it also brought thoughts of the devil and witchcraft. After the Reformation, Catholic rituals to defeat evil lost much of their perceived effectiveness. Many Protestants and Catholics were left feeling powerless against evil, so some invented ways to regain control. The medieval belief that the devil could assume a physical form was resurrected as individuals saw the devil in other people and accused them of witchcraft.

Social and Economic Upheaval Witchcraft accusations were also a result of social and economic upheaval. In the county of Essex in England, for example, most accusations were brought after a dispute regarding charity. The alleged witch, usually an older, poorer woman, would come to a wealthy home to ask for money, food, or work. The family might turn her away, with the woman muttering angry words as she left. If an unexplained illness or some other disaster later came upon the wealthy family, they would accuse the woman of witchcraft.

Accusations also came between members of poorer classes. In fact, the major peasant concern throughout Europe at this time was with **maleficium**, the harm supposedly brought on by witches. Accusations usually came after arguments over land use or resources. These disputes, many of which seemed petty, always had been a normal part of village life. They rose to a level of concern as Europe changed from an agriculture economy to a capitalistic one. Individuals did not have the same control over their land and resources as they once did. In this way, witchcraft accusations also highlighted the breakup of the traditional village community and economy.

Prominence of Women Roughly 80 percent of those killed for witchcraft were women, and many of them were elderly. Midwives were also accused of witchcraft as a means to provide blame when a couple lost a pregnancy or because they practiced a science that was unfamiliar at the time.

Women were not only more likely to be accused of witchcraft, but they were also more likely to be accusers. Some historians believe this happened because so many of the issues surrounding witchcraft related to women's concerns: child rearing, issues within the home, and the politics of reputation. Many accusations came after the death of a child, usually with the mother as accuser. Postmenopausal women, or those of an older age, often were the accused.

Regional Variation Witch hunts were not uniform throughout Europe. Witchcraft in French lands was less intense, but still provided some of the most dramatic trials of the era. In the countries of the British Isles, witch hunts occurred frequently in Scotland, seldom in England, and almost never in Ireland.

The death rates from witch hunts were the highest by far in the German-speaking states of the Holy Roman Empire and their immediate neighbors, especially Poland. About three-fourths of all executions for witchcraft occurred in the Holy Roman Empire. In some places, executions became widespread. For example, in the late 1670s, about 140 beggars and poor children were executed for witchcraft in the Austrian city of Salzburg alone. In other Germanic areas, entire towns were almost completely wiped out. The Reformation had started in Germany, and individuals in these areas felt its effects most intensely. Their way of life changed most quickly and most dramatically, so they had the strongest incentive to try to regain control over what was lost, lashing out at suspected witches.

Researching family history gives people a way to create and elaborate their own personal histories. Perhaps that is why searching for family history is the third most popular Internet activity, and why millions of Americans have sent their DNA for analysis. But the history of family history is much deeper than individuals' interests in who they are and how best to tell their personal stories.

Emergence of Family History Interest in these stories began in the 1960s as an outgrowth of sociological studies of kinship and legal units based on marriage and/or biology. Centered largely in France, sociologists collected and analyzed quantitative demographic data based on church registries. This data became particularly useful at a time when historians were looking for ways to explain the lives of common people who left behind little written record. Historians compared the statistics uncovered by these sociologists to the social, economic, and even cultural norms of the day. From these comparisons, historians were able to identify relative ages at marriage, pregnancy, and death (for both adults and children) and construct theories about general trends. By the 1970s, historians began comparing legal records (court documents and wills), as well as material evidence and architecture, to timelines of individuals and families across time to determine how social and economic changes impacted families. Toward the end of the century, family historians looked at the family as the intersection of the public and private spheres, examining how state and institutional expectations regulated behaviors within families.

But the emphasis in the 21st century seems to be on the stories shared by studying family history. Despite the popularity of genealogy searches, historian Joseph Amato argues that there is more to family history than DNA and statistics, because it is a "complex, constantly mutating, and ongoing historical creation."

Family History and Everyday Life Amato explained that until about one hundred years ago, the European family was merely an economic unit. People were bound by the responsibilities and lack of individual identity inherent in the "Great Chain of Being," a belief that the universe was made up of a series of connected forms (including humans) on a hierarchy from the lowest to the perfect being—or God. But as many stopped believing in the "chain," and circumstances, institutions, and understandings changed, so too did the family. People became responsible for making their own place in the world, and, through the analysis of genealogy, history, and the stories passed down through the generations, we can understand the attitudes, beliefs, situations and choices our family made. Amato suggests that these stories, with all the appropriate historical contextualization, can help us better understand history itself. In this sense, the history of common people gives the people themselves a voice as they try to live in a world defined (politically, economically, socially, and possibly culturally) by elites.

Continuity and Change conjugal family ideal

early modern period   Querelle des Femmes

Social Structure

nucelar family

artisans

primogeniture

dowry

patriarchalism

Identity

Anabaptists

humanism

Civic Ideals

Carnival

penance

charivari

rough music

stocks

pillory

pranger

flagellation

maleficium

MULTIPLE-CHOICE QUESTIONS

Questions 1–3 refer to the table below.

Average Age of First Marriage in England		
Period	**Men**	**Women**
1600–1649	28.1	25.6
1650–1699	28.1	26.2
1700–1749	27.2	25.4
1750–1799	25.7	24.0

Source: E. A. Wrigley and R. S. Schofield, *The Population History of England, 1541–1871* (Cambridge, England: Cambridge Unversity Press, 1989). Averages are the mean based on data from 13 communities.

1. What trend in marriage age from 1600 to 1700 does the table reflect?

   a) Marriage age for men increased.

   b) Marriage age for women changed less than marriage age for men.

   c) The age difference between men and women decreased.

   d) Marriage age for men and women declined.

2. Which is the most likely change to demographic patterns How did changes in the average age of first marriage affect demographic patterns in Western Europe before 1750?

   a) It caused a migration to towns and cities.

   b) It led to the continuation of serfdom.

   c) It tended to increase birth rates.

   d) It increased the occurrence of births to unmarried parents.

3. Which factor most influenced the context in which people made decisions about family life in the the years from 1600–1700?

a) Multigenerational households were more common than in earlier centuries.

b) Parents paid less attention to child-rearing practices than they did in earlier generations.

c) Religious leaders discouraged couples from having large families.

d) The Reformation caused the structure and purpose of the family to change

Detail from Pieter Bruegel the Elder, *The Fight Between Carnival and Lent.* The left shows Carnival, a period of drinking and carousing before the start of Christian season of Lent. The right shows Lent, a period of fasting and piety. Credit: Wikimedia Commons.

Questions 4–5 refer to the image and detail below.

4. A historian could best use this painting as evidence of which of the following features of 16th-century life?

a) The communal nature of leisure activities in preindustrial Europe

b) Growing tensions between religious and secular authorities

c) Efforts by religious reformers to challenge Catholic Church doctrine

d) The breakdown of the social and religious order

5. What important function of Carnival does the painting show most prominently?

a) Social and economic upheaval leading to accusations of witchcraft

b) Conflicts between communal norms and popular folk rituals

c) Enforcement of restrictions on celebrations by local authorities

d) Emphasis of the religious idea of humans' multitude of sins

Questions 6–8 refer to the passage below.

"Since the message of the Reformation, like that of the earlier religious movements, meant a loosening of hierarchies, it had a particular appeal to women. By stressing the individual's personal relationship with God and his or her own responsibility, it affirmed the ability of each to find truth by reading the original Scriptures. Thus, it offered a greater role for lay participation by women, as well as men, than was possible in Roman Catholicism . . . .

[Nevertheless], the Reformation did not markedly transform women's place in society, and the reformers had never intended to do so. To be sure, they called on men and women to read the Bible and participate in religious ceremonies together. But Bible-reading reinforced the Pauline [St. Paul's] view of woman as weak-minded and sinful. When such practice took a more radical turn in the direction of lay prophesy, as occurred in some Reform churches southwest of Paris, or in the coming together of women to discuss "unchristian pieces," as was recorded in Zwickau [a city in eastern Germany], reformers—Luther and Calvin alike—pulled back in horror."

Marilyn J. Boxer and Jean H. Quataert,
Connecting Spheres, 1987

6. The historians' statement most directly supports which interpretation?
   a) The most important causes of the Reformation were economic and political, rather than religious.
   b) The Reformation idea of spiritual equality failed to spark a profound social transformation.
   c) The Reformation primarily expanded the power of the existing elite and state authorities.
   d) The ideas of the Reformation were rooted in earlier efforts to reform the Catholic Church.

7. Which statement provides the strongest counterevidence to the authors' argument in the first paragraph?
   a) Women preaching in Protestant sects such as the Anabaptists
   b) Protestant women serving as assistants in religious schooling
   c) Luther's opposition to clerical celibacy
   d) The closing of convents in Protestant countries

8. Which statement about Protestants best supports the authors' argument in the second paragraph?
   a) Their emphasis on marriage and obedience by wives
   b) Their decision in many countries to legalize divorce
   c) Their support for primary education for both boys and girls
   d) Their rejection of Papal authority

SHORT-ANSWER QUESTIONS

1. Use the passage below to answer all parts of the question that follows.

> "Since the beginning of the early modern era, family formation processes in most western European societies . . . have been linked to the assumption of the headship of a household . . . newly marrying couples were not absorbed into pre-existing households, but instead set up their new residence apart from their [birth] families . . . .[F]or western Europeans, achieving independence entailed carrying all of the start-up costs associated with acquiring housing and equipping the household with the necessary material possessions. . . . [B]oth marriage and headship occurred relatively late in the life-cycle, when the couple had been able to accumulate capital through many years of living outside the parental homes and working as servants . . . .By contrast . . . in east-central and eastern Europe, new couples generally . . .[went] to live with the groom's [birth] family . . . . Here, the key feature was not only that marriage took place at a younger age, but that it hardly ever led to the establishment of a new independent householding unit, but rather resulted in the enlargement of the existing parental household."

> Mikolaj Szoltysek, *The Oxford Handbook of Early Modern European History, Vol. 1*, Hamish Scott, ed., 2015

a) Explain ONE difference between the family formation process in western Europe and that in east-central and eastern Europe.

b) Provide ONE piece of historical evidence that would support the explanation of the family formation process in western Europe.

c) Explain ONE piece of historical evidence that would show a difference in family patterns in western and eastern Europe in the early modern period.

2. Answer all parts of the question that follows.

a) Explain ONE economic cause of witchcraft accusations in the 1600s.

b) Explain ONE religious cause of the accusations of witchcraft.

c) Explain ONE possible reason the accusations of witchcraft were usually made against women.

LONG ESSAY QUESTIONS

1. Evaluate the extent to which family structure, social interaction, and community norms changed during the 15th and 16th centuries.

2. Evaluate the extent to which religion influenced gender roles and family demographics during the period from 1450 to the mid-1600s.

1. In one to three paragraphs, explain how capitalism and the persistence of earlier structures shaped family life and traditional ideas during the 15th and 16th centuries.

WRITE AS A HISTORIAN: ANALYZE AN ARGUMENT

One way to analyze an argument is to frame within one of the six thematic learning objectives for AP® European History:

- Interaction of Europe and the World (INT)
- Poverty and Prosperity (PP)
- Objective Knowledge and Subjective Visions (OS)
- States and Other Institutions of Power (SP)
- Individual and Society (IS)
- National and European Identity (NI)

For instance, if you are writing on the role that sovereign states and secular systems of law played in the creation of new political institutions, you could frame your essay in terms of the SP or NI themes.

Which theme(s) might provide the best framework for the following topics?

1. Describe how advances in military technology led to new forms of warfare, heavier taxation, and a larger bureaucracy.

2. Analyze how local and regional identities based on culture led to resistance against the dominant national group within states.

3. Explain how the English Civil War exemplified the competition for power between monarchs, Parliament, and the elite.

An essay is structured around a central argument called a thesis statement, which is usually presented in the introduction. Each paragraph then needs its own topic sentence related to the thesis, as well as supporting evidence.

Framing the topic sentences around a central theme can provide cohesion, or the feeling that all the paragraphs tie together.

For the prompt in question 4, which topic sentence best fits the SP theme?

4. How did the competitive state system change diplomacy and warfare?

   a. The Peace of Westphalia in 1648 ended the wars of religion by establishing a diplomatic congress and a system of sovereign states.

   b. Greater use of infantry, mobile cannons, and elaborate fortifications all were new forms of warfare during this time.

6

Struggles Over Sovereignty and Centralization

Since love and fear can hardly exist together, if we must choose between them, it is far safer to be feared than loved.

—Niccolò Machiavelli, *The Prince*, published in 1532

Essential Question: How did the struggle for sovereignty result in varying degrees of political centralization in early modern Europe?

Three major changes in the early modern period—approximately the 15th century through the 18th century—shaped its political development.

- the shift from **decentralized power** spread among many groups and individuals to **centralized power** in which a small group held control

- the shift in from the landed nobility who had inherited their position to people with education, skills, and wealth

- the shift from law and justice dictated by religion to rules of law dictated by a secular system

Sovereign States and Secular Laws

During the medieval period, monarchs gained and held power through the support of the landed nobility and clergy who were loyal to them. Further strengthening the power of these monarchs, the Holy Roman Empire dictated that they ruled with religious authority. But the Empire was unable to maintain such a model, which was especially challenged by two important developments:

- **political localism:** local control of governments, history, and culture

- **religious pluralism:** acceptance of diverse religions

In 1648, by the end of the **Thirty Years' War,** the deadliest religious conflict in European history (see Chapter 2), a new state system had emerged. Because of its widespread destruction, the Thirty Years' War had completely reshaped the religious and political map of central Europe.

This engraving was based on a 17th century painting by Dutch painter Philips Wouwerman. It captured the plight of homeless people displaced by the Thirty Years' War.

Credit: Getty Images

During the early modern period, professionals such as merchants and lawyers gained increased power in European states. This centralization of power ushered in a new form of diplomacy in which the sovereign state and secular systems of law played a central role in the creation of new political institutions.

The Emergence of New Monarchies

The states that emerged during the early modern period that featured greater royal control and centralization were known as **new monarchies**. They laid the groundwork for the centralized **modern state**. These monarchies established bureaucratic methods of tax collection, created strong military forces, implemented systems of justice, and even determined their subjects' religion. Especially in Spain, France, and England, monarchs controlled nearly every aspect of people's lives.

Spain During the first 75 years of the 15th century, the Spanish region of Aragon, home to King Ferdinand, was one of the most important areas of Europe. It was the main maritime power of the western Mediterranean, with an impressive fleet of ships. On the other hand, the Castile region of Spain, home to Queen Isabella, was in disorder. The marriage of Ferdinand and Isabella in 1469 began the process of the unification of Spain. This consolidation of power revitalized Spain.

Using national taxes such as the *alcabala* (a tax on the sale or exchange of property), Ferdinand and Isabella began to centralize power. To restore order in Castile they used *coreregidores* (magistrates who collected taxes and worked to strengthen royal authority) to carry out justice in the name of the monarch. The defeat of Muslim Granada in 1492 completed the *Reconquista,* or the driving of Muslims from Spain. Jews who had not converted to Christianity were expelled at the same time. With a uniformly Christian population, combined with the beginning of Spanish exploration of the New World by Christopher Columbus, Ferdinand and Isabella had begun transforming Spain into a unified and dominant world power.

France The Hundred Years' War had left France in a shambles, yet it had awakened a national feeling that kings could use their positions to centralize state power. Using the *taille* (a land tax organized under King Charles VII), French kings gathered royal income to establish an army, thus increasing royal power. To carry out the law, the king sent officials known as bailiffs out into the provinces. Later kings also brought the duchy of Burgundy as well as the provinces of Anjou, Provence, and Maine under royal control, adding valuable land and income to the crown. Ruling from 1461–1483, Louis XI, son of Charles VII, helped France recover from the damage of the Hundred Years' War and also weakened the power of the aristocracy, strengthening the power of the Crown.

The French Crown also was strengthened through an agreement between French King Francis I and Pope Leo X in 1516. The **Concordat of Bologna** permitted the pope to collect all the income that the Catholic Church made in France. However, it also gave King Francis I more direct control over French Catholic leaders by restricting their ability to communicate directly with Rome and by confirming the king's right to nominate church leaders, such as archbishops, bishops, abbots, and priors.

In 1598, King Henry IV of France promoted French unity by issuing the **Edict of Nantes**. This order granted the Calvinist Protestants of France, known as **Huguenots,** rights that had not been afforded to them previously. By no longer treating Huguenots as heretics, or individuals who reject the faith of the church, the edict helped unify France. It gave Huguenots civil rights, including the right to worship as they chose, work in any field, work for the state, and bring grievances directly to the king. It marked the end of the religious wars that had been fought in France throughout the second half of the 16th century.

England Combined with the Hundred Years' War, the Wars of the Roses had largely rid England of much of its feudal nobility. This period of civil warfare between the House of York and the House of Lancaster ended with the death of Richard III and the establishment of the Tudor monarchy. Henry VII, the first Tudor monarch, increased royal power in a number of ways. He used diplomacy to avoid expensive wars. He avoided overtaxing the landed gentry and middle class. He sent justices of the peace into the various counties to hear cases and "dispense justice in the name of the king." He also created the Royal Council made up primarily of the gentry to advise the king.

Henry also used the Court of the Star Chamber to control the actions of irresponsible nobility. Named for the pattern of stars on the ceiling of the room, the **Star Chamber** was an English law court that was created in the late 15th century. It was run by advisors to the monarch and judges. When created, its purpose was to hear cases aginst wealthy and powerful individuals that regular courts might have been unwilling to convict. It evolved into an appeals court, one that could overturn decisions of lower courts.

However, the Star Chamber became increasingly powerful and subject to political influence. It used its unchecked power to oppress social and political enemies without any real trial. Friends of the monarch were encouraged to bypass lower courts to receive a favorable judgment from the Star Chamber. The body was disbanded in the year after the British Parliament passed the Habeas Corpus Act in 1640. The term "Star Chamber" is still in use today. The term refers to secretive, upper-level government meetings that excerpt arbitrary power.

German Territories and the Peace of Augsburg Also called the Augsburg Settlement, the Peace of Augsburg was signed in the city of Augsburg, Germany, in 1555. It was a treaty between Holy Roman Emperor Charles V and the **Schmalkaldic League,** an alliance of Protestant territories within the Holy Roman Empire. The Schmalkaldic League formed to defend those German territories against the directives of the conference known as the **Diet of Augsburg** of 1531, which gave them a deadline to convert to Catholicism. The Peace of Augsburg officially ended this religious struggle, as it allowed individual rulers to choose whether their subjects would practice the Lutheran or the Roman Catholic form of Christianity.

Charles V signed the Augsburg agreement because he was worried that the Schmalkaldic League would align itself with France. Though France was primarily Roman Catholic, it feared the power Charles V was amassing more than it wanted to advance the spread of Catholicism.

Secular Laws

The **Peace of Westphalia** in 1648 involved a series of treaties among the Holy Roman Empire, France, Sweden, and other states that brought peace by ending the Thirty Years' War. The treaties that made up the Peace of Westphalia had important results, as they

- ended the major European religious wars.

- ended the medieval Christian ideal of a universal Christendom. Calvinism became officially recognized within the Holy Roman Empire. While Christianity was already divided, the treaties recognized that the unity of European Christians was shattered.

- recognized the decline of the Holy Roman Empire by granting individual leaders control over their states' religion. About 300 sovereign German states emerged, with Prussia and Austria dominating.

Gains in Power During the rule of the Holy Roman Empire, the Catholic Church was the primary influence on daily life, as it was a primary financier. For example, it had enough wealth to commission artwork, which is why so much of the art produced before the Renaissance was religious art. Innovations in banking and finance promoted the growth of urban financial centers and of a money economy. As a result, commercial and professional groups, such as merchants, lawyers, and other educated and talented individuals, acquired increasing power in the state, often in alliance with the monarchs.

In Northern Europe, the development of commerce and finance led to a golden age of art. For example, in the Netherlands, Dutch artists painted for private collectors rather than the Catholic Church. These private individuals supported a large number of painters and a wide range of styles. While many artists contined to use religious themes, they often showed the influence of Protestantism. Others portrayed wealthy individuals

Merchants and financiers also led developments in Renaissance Italy. One of the most prominent families based in what is today Italy were the Medici of Florence. Even before the Peace of Westphalia, no other family was so important in financing the Italian Renaissance. Medici were independent patrons of the arts, providing greater artistic freedom that was previously unknown. They also commissioned writing on political theories that directly influenced political leaders, of the Renaissance and for generations to come. The Medici family itself also produced three popes and two queens and founded the Medici Bank, one of the most prosperous institutions in Europe at that time.

Gentry Reform in England also saw noble titles moving toward a reward for personal or professional accomplishment. The gentry was the class of prosperous families who made their money through commercial ventures rather than inheritance, though they did sometimes include rural aristocrats, or landed gentry. The gentry in England often allied with the king to increase their political standing.

Secular Political Theories

The political fragmentation of the Holy Roman Empire allowed for new ideas on politics throughout Europe. Several writers developed theories to support the emerging secular state, or a government not primarily based on religion. In Renaissance Italy, Nicolò Machiavelli in *The Prince* provided for new concepts of the state. As power transferred away from traditional religious bodies and toward larger secular states, such political theories strengthened the state institutions.

These political theories focused on two types of relationships—those between individuals and those between individuals and the state. The theories also explored the responsibilities inherent in such relationships, especially the state's duty to take care of its people.

New Ideas about Politics		
Writer	**Theory**	**Significance**
Niccolò Machiavelli Florentine 1469–1527	**Machiavellianism:** Rulers should be willing to use cunning and deceit to keep themselves in power. Doing so will also help society by providing security and stable government. His most famous work, *The Prince,* was written as a handbook for rulers and aspiring political leaders.	• He is considered the father of modern-day political science. • He argued that ambition and therefore conflict are an inevitable part of human nature. • He advocated for republicanism—the belief in states ruled by the consent of citizens through elected leaders rather than monarchs.
Jean Bodin French 1530–1596	**Absolute Sovereignty:** Rulers of the **sovereign state**, operating by the doctirine of the divine right of kings, maintain peace by issuing laws and dictating religion, regardless of whether the people consent. His book *Colloquium of the Seven* is a conversation about truth among men from seven religious and intellectual traditions, including skepticism.	• He spread the idea of the modern state as different from the personal holdings of the monarch. • He viewed families (patriarchy) as the model for the state. • He was an early advocate for religious tolerance.
Hugo Grotius Dutch 1583–1645	**Natural Law:** Humans are born with certain innate rights. Leaders should govern by rational laws or ethical principles based in reason. His book *On the Law of War and Peace* outlined the rules of war. Grotius argued that there are three just causes of war: self-defense, reparation of injury, and punishment.	• He laid the foundation for international law and diplomacy, including freedom of the seas and humane treatment of civilians during war. • He defined the idea of one society of states, governed by laws and agreement, not by force and warfare. • His vision of an international society influenced the Peace of Westphalia.
Thomas Hobbes British 1588–1679	**Social Contract:** Power comes from an agreement among people rather than from divine right. A society needs a very powerful government to keep order. His book *Leviathan* was written during the English Civil War, a time of turmoil and violence.	• He promoted the idea of the rights of individuals. • He argued for the natural equality of all humans. • He believed that people had the right to do whatever the law does not forbid.

New Diplomacy and New Warfare

The **Peace of Westphalia** in 1648 brought the end of the Age of Religious Wars in Europe. With the end of those wars, a new concept, **balance of power,** became important, affecting how European states interacted and playing an important role in diplomatic and military objectives. A nation or group of nations maintains balance of power by assuring that its strength equals that of potential adversaries, such as through military might or alliances.

Advances in military technology and tactics also changed warfare. The development of artillery and mobile cannons was revolutionary. Knights with swords riding on horseback gave way to troops shooting rifles and marching in lines. Armed forces became professional organizations under control of a sovereign, not a noble aristocrat. Larger units fighting for a single state replaced small militias fighting for their local leader.These changes gave more power to the states and to state leaders willing to adopt those advancements.

This great military revolution favored the rulers who could manage the resources necessary to build increasingly complex fortifications, or defenses. Successful leaders were also skilled at managing increasingly complex groups of troops. Monarchs who were able to increase taxes enough to build a military outmaneuvered those who could not. This was especially true in Sweden, France, and Spain.

Sweden under Gustavus Adolphus

By the end of the 17th century, infantry units in Sweden resembled those that would persist well into the 20th century. Small militias faded away, replaced by standing armies—larger, more permanent military units. Military ranks, from private to general, also began to develop. One ruler, **King Gustavus Adolphus** of Sweden (1594–1632), was primarily responsible for most of these changes.

Gustavus Adolphus ran his military units like machines. A master of organization, he gave his infantry and cavalry the capacity for offense, providing increased firepower so they could strike first. He made his artillery mobile, and he organized linear formations of soldiers to be more flexible and responsible to commands.

France

The military revolution of this time reached its peak in France. After the Thirty Years' War, the French army became Europe's dominant land force. Up until this point, Spain had been the prevailing military power. The French army adopted the basic infantry formation from King Gustavus Adolphus's Swedes, but in much greater numbers.

Louis XIV helped make the French army superior to others of the time. He enacted reforms to bring individual field commanders under control, built 33 new fortresses, and remodeled 3,000 others. These fortresses were fully equipped. An army on the march could make camp at any of them and find everything they needed, including food and heavy artillery.

Spain under the Habsburgs

Even with France's great power, Spain under the Habsburgs dominated Europe politically and militarily for much of the 16th and 17th centuries. The Habsburg family created a dynasty, producing emperors and kings for the Holy Roman Empire and throughout Europe, including Phillip II of Spain (see page 40). Spain under the Habsburgs comprised several smaller kingdoms, including Aragon, Castile, León, Navarre and, beginning in 1580, Portugal.

The Habsburg influence also ushered in the "Siglo de Oro," Spanish for "Golden Century," a time of great art and culture in Spain. The Habsburgs were great patrons of the arts in both Austria and Spain, the primary areas of their control. Painting, sculpture, architecture, music, and literature all thrived in Spain under the Habsburgs. The works produced in Spain during the Siglo de Oro rivaled those of the great Italian masters of the Renaissance.

Challenges to Monarchs

Influential, successful monarchs such as those in England, France, and Spain were not universal, however. Throughout the rest of Europe, small factions of individuals challenged their monarchs and resisted political centralization, a form of government in which a single person or small group exercises control. In eastern and southern Europe especially, the traditional elites—the landed nobility—fought hard to maintain their positions. This struggle for power ultimately produced varied types of government systems across Europe.

Monarchies seeking enhanced power faced challenges from nobles who wished to retain traditional forms of shared governance and regional autonomy. Competition between monarchs and nobles was fierce and ongoing, especially in England, France, and Spain.

The English Civil War

The **English Civil War** erupted as a result of the Stuart monarchs' efforts to make England an absolute monarchy. Succeeding Elizabeth I, James VI of Scotland became King James I of England. His son **Charles I,** who succeeded him, constantly argued with Parliament over taxes and other issues; as a result, in 1642, civil war broke out between **Parliamentarians,** also called "Roundheads," who wanted change, and **Royalists,** also called "Cavaliers," who supported the monarchy. The Parliamentary army, under **Oliver Cromwell**, was victorious, and in 1649, Parliamentary forces executed Charles I. Cromwell established a Commonwealth but spent much of his energy putting down Royalist revolts. In 1653, he became Lord Protector and ruled until his death in 1658. After his son Richard ruled briefly as lord protector, England's Parliament restored the monarchy. Charles II became king in 1660.

Timeline of the English Civil War		
Date	**Event**	**Significance**
1603	James I succeeds Elizabeth I	• James I spent extravagantly with little oversight from Parliament.
1625	Charles I succeeds James I	• Charles I tried to fulfill his father's wish to unite England with Ireland, which made Parliament suspicious that such a move would strengthen royal power and weaken the power of Parliament. • James believed in the divine right of kings, which caused conflict with Parliament.
1642	Civil War begins	• Supporters of Charles I fought supporters of the so-called **Long Parliament** because it lasted from 1640 to 1660.
1649	Charles I executed	• Execution of a monarch was rare and shocking.
1649–1653	Parliament creates the Commonwealth of England	• Parliament and the Council of State replaced the monarchy.
1651	Civil War ends	• Supporters of Charles I fought supporters of the **Rump Parliament**, a broad term for any part of Parliament left over from a preceding Parliament. Fighting ended with the Parliamentarian victory at the Battle of Worcester on September 3, 1651.
1653–1658	Protectorate reigns	• England was ruled for a short time as a republic, not a monarchy. • Oliver Cromwell was named Lord Protector over the Commonwealth of England, Scotland, and Ireland. • When Oliver Cromwell died, his son, Richard, became Lord Protector. He was unable to carry on his father's policies, and the protectorate failed.
1660	Restoration begins	• Parliament's New Model Army removed Richard and reinstated the Rump Parliament and the monarchy. • English, Scottish, and Irish monarchies were restored under Charles II.

Contrast the appearance of King Charles I (left) and Oliver Cromwell (right). These differences reflected not just ideas about clothing and hairstyle but deep-seated religious views as well.

Credit: Getty Images

France under Louis XIII and Cardinal Richelieu

In France, a far different outcome emerged after a challenge to the monarch: absolutism, based on the political theory of Jean Bodin. During the reign of King Louis XIII, from 1610 to 1643, France was ruled as a Catholic country. As a result, the French monarch was able to cement an alliance with both the clergy and the middle class to build a powerful centralized government.

Cardinal Richelieu Louis XIII relied on his chief minister, Cardinal Richelieu, to oversee the consolidation of his power. As chief minister from 1624 to 1642, Richelieu used the royal army to disband the private armies of the great French aristocrats and to take away independence from the few remaining Protestant towns. More significantly, Richelieu stripped provincial aristocrats of their administrative powers by dividing France into about 30 districts. Each district was under the control of an "intendent," or royal administrator, and every intendent was under the control of Richelieu.

Richelieu died in 1642 and was succeeded by Cardinal Mazarin. When Louis XIII died in 1643, his successor, Louis XIV, was only five years old. Mazarin became young Louis's regent, or caretaker.

The Fronde Violent civil uprisings against the monarchy erupted between 1648 and 1653 to check the growing power of France's royal government. This series of uprisings was known as The Fronde (French for "slingshot" after the rocks protesters threw). The Fronde was not successful, but it ultimately scarred young Louis XIV so deeply that he intensified his absolutism for the rest of his reign. The failure of The Fronde did reveal the inability of the French nobility and Parliament to lead the nation effectively at that time.

The Catalan Revolt in Spain

In 1640, Spain faced increased military threat from its neighbor to the north, France. Spain's King Philip III therefore attempted to centralize his power and raise taxes to fund the ongoing wars. He also sent Count Olivares, one of his favored ministers, into the Spanish region of Catalonia with roughly 9,000 troops to gain access to the region's people and resources to fight the French. Instead, he was met with fierce Catalan backlash. The **Catalan Revolt** ultimately caused the downfall of Olivares.

Dutch Resistance in the Spanish Netherlands

The decline of Spain as an economic power partially resulted from growing competition from the Netherlands, a region under Spain's control. The **Dutch Revolt**, also known as the Dutch War for Independence, lasted 80 years, from 1568 to 1648, leading to Dutch independence being officially recognized by the Peace of Westphalia.

The Netherlands had already achieved a central role in inter-European trade as a result of its geographic position and large merchant marine fleet. For example, the Netherlands provided a connection between the Baltic region of north-central Europe and the rest of the continent. Increasingly, the Netherlands' capital of Amsterdam outstripped Spanish-controlled Antwerp as northern Europe's center of commerce.

Conflicts Among Identity-Based Minorities

While the English Civil War and the conflicts in France, Spain, and the Netherlands pitted nobles against monarchies, groups of citizens fought among themselves in conflicts in other areas of Europe. Minority groups with identities based on a unique language or culture resisted the dominant national group, often with far-reaching consequences, including inflaming conflicts that brought the Thirty Years' War.

Czech identity in the Holy Roman Empire In the 17th century, the Bohemian Estates—located in modern-day Czech Republic—was under control of the Habsburgs and represented the different regions and interests of the Czech people. Czech nobility also dominated the region. The Bohemian Estates tried to maintain its Czech identity and social status, despite the Habsburgs' attempts to mandate Catholicism and centralize their power. In 1618, the Bohemian Estates rose against the Habsburgs, signaling the start of hostilities of the Thirty Years' War, but were defeated in 1620 at the Battle of the White Mountain.

One of the primary influences in this movement was **Jan Hus**, though he had lived two centuries earlier. Hus was a voice for reforming the Catholic Church long before the Protestant Reformation led by Martin Luther and John Calvin. His teachings had a strong influence on the states of Western Europe, most immediately in the approval of the reformed Bohemian religious denomination. Hus was burned at the stake for heresy in 1415.

Celtic Regions of Scotland, Ireland, and France Clashes between traditional Celtic societies in modernizing European states began in the 17th century and stemmed from both religious and economic conflicts. Traditionally religious people, Celts were affected by various states' attempts to limit religious nonconformity. Celtic farmers were removed from their land as militaries expanded their infrastructure, such as the fortifications built by Louis XIV in France.

HISTORICAL PERSPECTIVES: WAS WESTPHALIA A TURNING POINT?

Friedrich von Schiller was a German literary icon in the 18th century, long before the modern German state existed. By the time he wrote his comprehensive *History of the Thirty Years' War* (1790), Europeans had more than one century to evaluate the war's significance.

Westphalia Changed Europe's Direction As a late 18th century writer, Schiller viewed history as the inevitable outcome of particular events and was especially interested in freedom. As such, he believed in the great significance of the Peace of Westphalia and suggested at the end of his work that "A mere abridgment of [the Peace of Westphalia] would reduce to a mere skeleton one of the most interesting and characteristic monuments of human policy and passions, and deprive it of every feature calculated to fix attention of the public, for which I write, and of which I now respectfully take my leave." Scholars have shared his view of the power of this document, but they are now questioning if the reality lives up to the legend.

In 1948, Leo Gross, an expert in international relations with experience in both the League of Nations and the United Nations, shared Schiller's view of the significance of the Peace of Westphalia. Nearly every article about the legacy of its treaties begins with the claim by Gross that the Peace of Westphalia was the basis for ideas of national sovereignty and balance of power. He viewed the document as the "starting point for the development of international law" at a time when the world was on the brink of Cold War divisions. Gross's argument fit so well into the stories historians and other scholars of international relations wanted to tell that few questioned it.

Even in the globalized world of today, Jason Farr, a modern scholar interested in global interactions, has emphasized the staying power of national identification and sovereignty rooted in the Westphalian system. Such was the obsession about the Peace of Westphalia, the recognition of sovereignty and the balance proposed between newly established sovereigns.

Not a Turning Point However, historian Andreas Osiander argued in 2001 that since "most of the states in question had been around for a long time, neither their survival nor even their independence [sovereignty] was at stake in this war." Osiander postulated that neither France, Sweden, nor any European state faced aggression by the Habsburgs, and yet the idea that the Habsburgs were abusing their power seemed widespread in all analyses of the Thirty Years'

War. In piecing together the sources, Osiander concluded that this view was largely shaped by French and Swedish propaganda. He placed partial blame on Swedish diplomat Johan Adler Salvius, who traveled and provided farfetched evidence of an aggressive Habsburg empire to the German principalities. To further challenge the Westphalian myth, Osiander turned to the actual terms of the Peace and noted that it made no mention of sovereignty, independence of European states, the power of the emperor or pope, or even establishing a balance of power. Osiander concluded that the current notions of nation-state sovereignty are so powerful that it has been difficult to understand a much more complicated relationship among the state actors of the 17th century. As a result, he concluded, international relations scholars have imposed false meaning and significance on the Peace of Westphalia to serve modern needs.

KEY TERMS BY THEME

Governance
English Civil War
Charles I
decentralized power
centralized power
political localism
religious pluralism
Thirty Years' War
New Monarchies
modern state
Star Chamber
Concordat of Bologna
Peace of Augsburg
Schmalkaldic League
Diet of Augsburg

Edict of Nantes
Huguenots
social contract
absolutism
Peace of Westphalia
gentry
secular state
Machiavellianism
sovereign state
natural law
absolute sovereignty
balance of power
King Gustavus Adolphus
political centralization
English Civil War

Charles II
Parliamentarians
Royalists
Oliver Cromwell
Long Parliament
Commonwealth of England
Rump Parliament
protectorate
The Fronde
Catalan Revolt
Dutch Revolt
Jan Hus

Questions 1–3 refer to the following passage.

"II. And forasmuch as all matters examinable . . . before the said judges, or in the court commonly called the star-chamber, may have their proper remedy and redress, and their due punishment and correction, by the common law of the land, and in the ordinary course of justice elsewhere;

(2) and forasmuch as the reasons and motives [for creating] that court do now cease:

(3) and the proceedings, censures and decrees of that court, have by experience been found to be . . . an arbitrary power and government. . . .

III. Be it ordained and enacted by the authority of this present parliament, That the said court commonly called the star-chamber . . . be . . .clearly and absolutely dissolved, taken away and determined."

adapted from Act by the English Parliament, July 5, 1641

1. The topic of the excerpt was a sign of which development?

   a) The creation of new monarchies in Europe

   b) The decline in power of Oliver Cromwell

   c) The increasing religious turmoil in Scotland

   d) The ongoing struggle for power between monarchs and other groups

2. Who would have most strongly supported this Act of Parliament?

   a) Critics of the monarch

   b) Roman Catholics

   c) People who owed taxes

   d) Members of the clergy of all denominations

3. Which contributed most to the change described in the excerpt?

   a) The court contributed to the start of the Anglican Church.

   b) The court contributed to the start of the French Wars of Religion.

   c) The court oppressed the monarch's enemies.

   d) The court oppressed the monarch's supporters.

Questions 4–6 refer to the following passage.

"The first attribute of the sovereign prince therefore is the power to make law binding on all his subjects in general and on each in particular. But to avoid any ambiguity one must add that he does so without the consent of any superior, equal, or inferior being necessary. If the prince can only make law with the consent of a superior he is a subject; if of an equal he shares his sovereignty; if of an inferior, whether it be a council of magnates or the people, it is not he who is sovereign…

But because *law* is an imprecise and general term, it is as well to specify the other attributes of sovereignty comprised in it, such as the making of war and peace. This is one of the most important rights of sovereignty, since it brings in its train either the ruin or the salvation of the state…

The third attribute of sovereignty is the power to institute the great officers of state…

The fourth attribute of sovereignty, and one which has always been among its principal rights, is that the prince should be the final resort of appeal from all other courts."

Jean Bodin, *Six Books of the Commonwealth*, 1576

4. Which of the following is the historical context in which the theory of sovereignty expressed in the passage emerged?

   a) The defeat of the Spanish Armada

   b) The Fronde uprisings in France

   c) The Peace of Westphalia

   d) The fragmentation of the the the Holy Roman Empire

5. Which group or individual would agree most strongly with the political theories about sovereignty expressed in the passage?

   a) Catholics

   b) Huguenots

   c) Hugo Grotius

   d) Machiavelli

6. Based on the writer's view of an absolute monarchy, which power of the ruler would the writer consider most important?

   a) To reflect the will of the people

   b) To issue laws

   c) To obey the Church

   d) To heed outside influences

Questions 7–8 refer to the map below.

RELIGIOUS DIVISIONS IN EUROPE, 1648

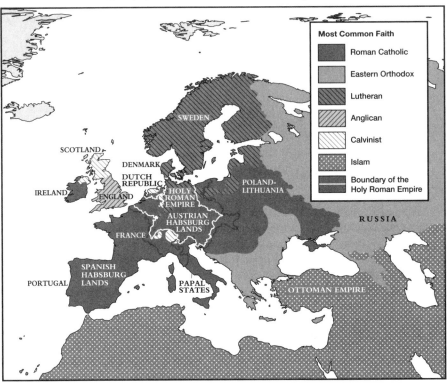

7. The map most directly shows the results of which agreement?

   a) The Peace of Augsburg

   b) The Concordat of Bologna

   c) The Edict of Nantes

   d) The Peace of Westphalia

8. What effect on the practice of religion did the settlement shown on the map have in Europe?

   a) The Habsburg rulers were successful in restoring Catholicism throughout Europe.

   b) Princes, bishops, and other local leaders within the Holy Roman Empire were granted control over religion.

   c) Religious tolerance was granted to Muslims in the Holy Roman Empire.

   d) Freedom of conscience was guaranteed in lands of Eastern Orthodox rulers.

1. Use the passage below to answer all parts of the question that follows.

> "The clear loser in 1648 was the Holy Roman emperor. The Peace of Westphalia, in reaffirming the terms of the Peace of Augsburg, effectively created about 1,800 sovereign states within the boundaries of the empire. The extent to which the Holy Roman Empire and its emperor were crippled over the remaining 150 years of its existence is a matter of some debate among historians. While some politically motivated historians have tried to claim that all of Germany's ills can be traced to the Thirty Years' War, it is indisputable that the war left the emperor with reduced power and a reduced role in administering his empire."
>
> "The Peace of Westphalia Ends the Thirty Years' War: 1648."

a) Describe ONE piece of evidence that supports the author's views on the effect of the Thirty Years' War on the Holy Roman Empire.

b) Describe ONE piece of evidence that suggests a different influence on weakening the Holy Roman Empire.

c) Describe one way that another European state gained influence at the expense of the Holy Roman Empire.

2. Answer all parts of the question that follows.

a) Describe ONE significant political cause of the English Civil War.

b) Describe ONE significant religious cause of the English Civil War.

c) Explain ONE significant result of the English Civil War.

LONG ESSAY QUESTIONS

1. Evaluate the extent to which the commercial revolution led to an increase in political centralization in the 16th and 17th centuries.

2. Evaluate the extent to which a New Monarch's policies changed the relationship between the monarch and the nobles in the 16th and 17th centuries.

REFLECT ON THE CHAPTER ESSENTIAL QUESTION

1. In one to three paragraphs, explain how the struggle for sovereignty resulted in varying degrees of political centralization during the early modern period.

In a historical essay, the writer lays out a clear and logical point of view and then defends it with supporting arguments and evidence. The sentence or sentences that state the argument for the essay is the thesis statement. It usually appears in the first paragraph.

A thesis statement should never simply rephrase the prompt. The prompt is usually a neutral statement, while a thesis statement states a position. A thesis statement should (1) respond directly to the prompt, (2) be specific and engaging, (3) take an evaluative position, (4) make a point that can be supported by several main subtopics, and (5) explain both how and why something happened.

All other paragraphs, except the conclusion, should provide information to support the thesis statement. The conclusion should summarize the support for the thesis and may restate the thesis in revised wording.

For each prompt, choose the more effective thesis statement.

1. Analyze how challenges to absolutism resulted in alternative political systems.

   a. Challenges to absolutism resulted in alternative political systems because people were tired of monarchs ruling all aspects of their lives.

   b. In events such as the English Civil War and the rise of the Dutch Republic, the gentry and the aristocracy forced a change from absolute monarchy to a constitutional type of government to protect their rights.

2. Explain how Louis XIV's policies provoked a coalition of European powers to oppose him.

   a. Louis XIV attempted to gain control over much of Europe by waging nearly continuous war. Because of this, the Dutch, the Holy Roman Empire, Austria, Spain, and England often combined forces to combat his influence.

   b. Louis XIV, also known as the Sun King, reigned for 72 years, which was longer than any other European monarch. He built the Palace of Versailles and initiated a golden age of arts and literature in France.

3. Evaluate the most significant effect of the Peace of Westphalia on the ideal of a unified Christian Europe.

   a. The Peace of Westphalia ended the Christian ideal of a universal Christendom, because it accepted Calvinism and allowed each ruler to determine their state's religions.

   b. The Peace of Westphalia ended the major European religious wars and established a balance of power among European nations.

PERIOD 1: Review

DOCUMENT-BASED QUESTION 1

Directions: Question 1 is based on the accompanying documents. The documents have been edited for the purpose of this exercise. You are advised to spend 15 minutes planning and 45 minutes writing your answer.

In your response you should do the following:

- **Thesis:** Make a defensible claim that establishes a line of reasoning and consists of one or more sentences found in one place.
- **Contextualization:** Relate the argument to a broader historical context.
- **Document Evidence:** Use content from at least six documents.
- **Outside Evidence:** Use one piece of evidence not in the documents.
- **Document Sourcing:** Explain how or why the point of view, purpose, situation, or intended audience is relevant for at least three documents.
- **Analysis:** Show the relationships among pieces of historical evidence and use them to support, qualify, or modify an argument.

1. Analyze the beliefs and attitudes that arose as a result of the Age of Discovery and the effects of those beliefs and attitudes on both Europe and the lands and people encountered.

Document 1

Source: Christopher Columbus, letter to the King and Queen of Spain, 1494.

[All gold shipped from the island to Spain] should be taken on board the ship, both that belonging to your Highnesses and the property of everyone else; . . . that there should come with the gold, for a testimony, a list of all that has been put into the said chest, properly marked, so that each owner may receive his own; and that, for the faithful performance of this duty, if any gold whatsoever is found outside of the said chest in any way, be it little or much, it shall be forfeited to your Highnesses.

That all the ships that come from the said island shall be obliged to make their proper discharge in the port of Cadiz, and that no person shall disembark or other person be permitted to go on board until the ship has been visited by the person or persons deputed for that purpose, in the said city, by your Highnesses, to whom the master shall show all that he carries, and exhibit the manifest of all the cargo, it may be seen and examined if the said ship brings anything hidden and not known at the time of lading [loading]. That the chest in which the said gold has been carried shall be opened in the presence of the magistrates of the said city of Cadiz, and of the person deputed for that purpose by your Highnesses, and his own property be given to each owner.

Document 2

Source: Amerigo Vespucci, letter to Lorenzo di Medici, 1503.

They have no cloth, either of wool, flax, or cotton, because they have no need of it; nor have they any private property, everything being in common. They live amongst themselves without a king or ruler, each man being his own master, and having as many wives as they please. The children cohabit with the mothers, the brothers with the sisters, the male cousins with the female, and each one with the first he meets. They have no temples and no laws, nor are they idolaters. What more can I say! They live according to nature, and are more inclined to be Epicurean than Stoic. This statement implies that the inhabitants pursue pleasure rather than consider philosophical matters. They have no commerce among each other, and they wage war without art or order. The old men make the youths do what they please, and incite them to fights, in which they mutually kill with great cruelty. They slaughter those who are captured, and the victors eat the vanquished; for human flesh is an ordinary article of food among them.

You may be the more certain of this, because I have seen a man eat his children and wife; and I knew a man who was popularly credited to have eaten 300 human bodies. . . . I say further that they were surprised that we did not eat our enemies, and use their flesh as food, for they say it is excellent. Their arms are bows and arrows, and when they go to war they cover no part of their bodies, being in this like beasts.

Document 3

Source: "The Lion of the Sea," the Algarve History Association.

The island of Goa is also fertile and could supply food to the Portuguese navy; it has a good harbour and was a centre for shipbuilding.   The timing was perfect since the new Khan was away on the mainland establishing his authority…
After an extraordinary piece of reconnaissance under fire by a junior officer, Albuquerque sailed into the harbour and the city quickly surrendered. But within weeks, the new Khan returned and, overwhelming the Portuguese defence, forced them back into their ships. The summer monsoon had arrived and Albuquerque found that his ships could not cross the harbour bar. From 1 June to 16 August, Albuquerque and his fleet were immobilised in the river and the Portuguese were subjected to surprise attacks, lack of food and water and the heat of an Indian summer. They finally managed to emerge from the river after 77 uncomfortable days and gathering his forces, a determined Albuquerque renewed his attack three months later. The new Khan was again away and Albuqerque's victory was swift and his reprisals terrible. His captains were told to 'reconnoitre the whole of the island and to put to the sword all Mohammedans, men, women and children'. Christians and Hindus joined the slaughter and for four days 'they poured out the blood of the Moors'. The Khan tried for three years to reoccupy his city but after a campaign of 33 months, the Muslims finally accepted the permanent loss of Goa.

Document 4

Source: Charles V, Emperor and King of Spain, Instructions for the Viceroy Mendoza, a Spanish colonial official, 1535.

Also, you should see if the towns are able to pay more gold, silver, and other things of value than they currently pay; [and if so], you should inform them that their assessment will be increased, payable in silver, gold, or its equivalent. Since I have been informed that the Indians of that country pay their tributes in blankets, corn, and other local goods that are difficult to turn into revenue, you should find a manner in which their tributes can be paid by converting all those things into a certain quantity of gold or silver yearly. This should be accomplished in such a manner that it increases Our revenue but not their labor, and since this is a very important matter, you should place great care in it, listing what they pay in tribute presently and what Our officials get for it when they sell it or use it in payment, and what its value would be if commuted to gold or silver; and you should send this list along with your report on the first ship to come...

Also, We are informed that in many places in the said province there are large and wealthy mines of gold, silver, and other metals, and that in addition to the fifths paid by private individuals who mine them with Our license and permission, We could increase Our revenues greatly if Our officials in the said mines purchased for Us a large number of slaves, either blacks or people purchased from the Indians who are held and reputed to be slaves. And because this is a matter of great importance and We could receive great benefit if it is correct.

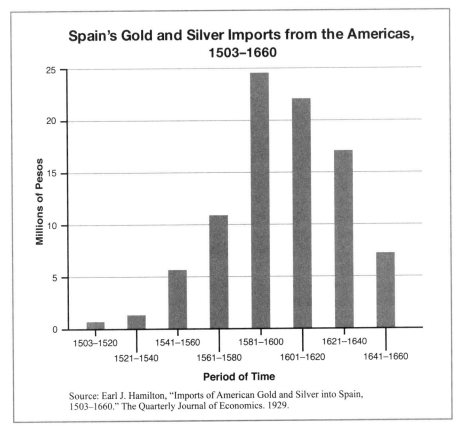

Spain's Gold and Silver Imports from the Americas, 1503–1660

Source: Earl J. Hamilton, "Imports of American Gold and Silver into Spain, 1503–1660." The Quarterly Journal of Economics. 1929.

Document 6

Source: Bartoleme de Las Casas, "The Devastation of the Indies," 1542.

They are very clean in their persons, with alert, intelligent minds, docile and open to doctrine, very apt to receive our holy Catholic faith, to be endowed with virtuous customs, and to behave in a godly fashion. Some of the secular Spaniards who have been here for many years say that the goodness of the Indians is undeniable and that if this gifted people could be brought to know the one true God they would be the most fortunate people in the world....Yet into this sheepfold, into this land of meek outcasts, there came some Spaniards who immediately behaved like ravening wild beasts, wolves, tigers, or lions that had been starved for many days. And Spaniards have behaved in no other way during the past forty years, down to the present time, for they are still acting like ravening beasts, killing, terrorizing, afflicting, torturing, and destroying the native peoples, doing all this with the strangest and most varied new methods of cruelty, never seen or heard of before, and to such a degree that this Island of Hispaniola once so populous (having a population that I estimated to be more than three million), has now a population of barely two hundred persons.

Document 7

Source: St. Francis Xavier, writing from Japan to the Society of Jesus in Europe, 1552.

[The Japanese said,] God therefore, if He were good, could never have done such a thing as create beings so evil (as Devils). To these arguments we replied that the devils were created good by God, but became evil by their own fault, and that in consequence they were subject to eternal punishment and torment.

Then they objected that God, who was so severe in punishing, was not at all merciful. Again, how could He, if He created the human race in the manner we taught, allow men sent into the world to worship Him to be tempted and persecuted by the devil? In like manner, if God were good, He ought not to have made man so weak and so prone to sin, but free from all evil. Again, it could not be a good God, they said, who had created that horrible prison of hell, and was to be forever without pity for those who suffer therein the most fearful torments from all eternity. Lastly, if He were good, He would not have imposed on men those difficult laws of the Ten Commandments. Their religious traditions, on the contrary, taught that all who should invoke the authors of their religion would be delivered even from the torments of hell.

They were quite unable to digest the idea that men could be cast into hell without any hope of deliverance.

DOCUMENT-BASED QUESTION 2

Directions: Question 2 is based on the accompanying documents. The documents have been edited for the purpose of this exercise. You are advised to spend 15 minutes planning and 45 minutes writing your answer.

In your response you should do the following:

- **Thesis:** Make a defensible claim that establishes a line of reasoning and consists of one or more sentences found in one place.
- **Contextualization:** Relate the argument to a broader historical context.
- **Document Evidence:** Use content from at least six documents.
- **Outside Evidence:** Use one piece of evidence not in the documents.
- **Document Sourcing:** Explain how or why the point of view, purpose, situation, or intended audience is relevant for at least three documents.
- **Analysis:** Show the relationships among pieces of historical evidence and use them to support, qualify, or modify an argument.

2. Analyze the continuity and change over time that occurred in the interpretation and practice of Christianity in 16th century Europe.

Document 1

Source: Desiderius Erasmus, *In Praise of Folly,* 1509.

Almost all Christians being wretchedly enslaved to blindness and ignorance, which the priests are so far from preventing or removing, that they blacken the darkness, and promote the delusion: wisely foreseeing that the people… would part with less if they knew more.

Document 2

Source: Huldrych Zwingli, Protestant reformer, on Communion, 1517.

Christ who gave himself once and for all upon the cross is a sacrifice and victim making satisfaction in eternity for the sins of all the faithful. Hence the Mass is not a sacrifice, but a commemoration of the sacrifice made once for all upon the cross and is, as it were, a sign of our redemption in Christ.

Document 3

Source: Martin Luther, Address to German nobles, 1520.

To his most Serene and Mighty Imperial Majesty and to the Christian Nobility of the German Nation.

It is not out of mere arrogance and perversity that I, an individual poor man, have taken upon me to address your lordships. The distress and misery that oppress all the Christian estates, more especially in Germany, have led not only myself, but everyone else, to cry aloud and to ask for help, and have now forced me too to cry out and to ask if God would give His Spirit to anyone to reach a hand to His wretched people. Councils have often put forward some remedy, but it has adroitly been frustrated, and the evils have become worse, through the cunning of certain men. Their malice and wickedness I will now, by the help of God, expose, so that, being known, they may henceforth cease to be so obstructive and injurious. God has given us a young and noble sovereign, and by this has roused great hopes in many hearts; now it is right that we too should do what we can, and make good use of time and grace.

Document 4

Source: John Calvin, *Institutes of the Christian Faith,* 1536.

Our prayer must not be self-centered. It must arise not only because we feel our own need as a burden we must lay upon God, but also because we are so bound up in love for our fellow men that we feel their need as acutely as our own. To make intercession for men is the most powerful and practical way in which we can express our love for them....God preordained, for his own glory and the display of His attributes of mercy and justice, a part of the human race, without any merit of their own, to eternal salvation, and another part, in just punishment of their sin, to eternal damnation.

Document 5

Source: Henry VIII, "An Act Abolishing Diversity in Opinions," 1539.

Where the King's most excellent Majesty is by God's Law Supreme Head immediately under him of this whole Church and Congregation of England, intending the conservation of the same Church and Congregation in a true, sincere, and uniform doctrine of Christ's Religion, calling also to his blessed and most gracious remembrance as well the great and quiet assurance, prosperous increase, and other innumerable commodities which have ever ensued, come, and followed of concord, agreement, and unity in opinions, as also the manifold perils, dangers, and inconveniences which have heretofore in many places and regions grown, sprung, and arisen of the diversities of minds and opinions, especially of matters of Christian Religion.

Document 6

Source: The Peace of Augsburg, 1555.

The Holy Empire's estates have remained continually in bitterness and distrust toward each other, from which much evil has arisen in the Holy Empire, and above all the administration of justice has produced many complaints and deficiencies. . . .

And in order that . . . peace is respected and maintained despite the religious chasm, as is necessary in the Holy Roman Empire of the German nation and between his Roman Imperial Majesty and Us, on the one hand, and the electors, princes, and estates of the Holy Empire of the German nation, on the other, therefore His Imperial Majesty, and We, and the electors, princes, and estates of the Holy Empire will not make war upon any estate of the empire on account of the Augsburg Confession and the doctrine, religion, and faith of the same, nor injure nor do violence to those estates that hold it, nor force them, against their conscience, knowledge, and will, to abandon the religion, faith, church usages, ordinances, and ceremonies of the Augsburg Confession, where these have been established, or may hereafter be established, in their principalities, lands, and dominions. Nor shall We, through mandate or in any other way, trouble or disparage them, but shall let them quietly and peacefully enjoy their religion, faith, church usages, ordinances, and ceremonies, as well as their possessions, real and personal property, lands, people, dominions, governments, honors, and rights.

Document 7

Source: Francois DuBois (1529–1584), Huguenot painter, "St. Bartholonew's Day Massacre."

PERIOD 2: c. 1648 to 1815

Period Overview

Between the Peace of Westphalia in 1648 and the Congress of Vienna in 1815, European monarchs continued to go to war to expand their territory. However, at the same time, governments began representing the will of the people.

Politics and Economics Europe's political structure began to shift away from governments based on absolute monarchs who felt they ruled by the will of God. People began to believe that governments should have limits and that they ruled by the will of the population. This shift became dramatically evident in 1789 with the outbreak of the French Revolution. It overthrew the French monarchy and led to the rise of Napoleon. He started as an advocate for popular government but evolved into the sole ruler of the country. Even though conservatives regained much of their power within 30 years, ideas about governance never fully returned to those from before the revolution.

In economics, Europe became more closely linked to overseas markets than it had been before. While these links increased prosperity in Europe, they also included the trans-Atlantic slave trade. Europeans transported millions of enslaved Africans out of their homeland. Most who survived the horrific voyage to the Americas were sold to owners of plantations that produced sugar, coffee, or other crops. Rivalries over trade and land led to war between Europeans, particularly between the English and the French, in India, Canada, and elsewhere.

Toleration, Reason, and Science By the mid-1600s, after more than a century of warfare based partly on conflicting views of Christianity, people began to tolerate religious diversity. A growing reliance on reason and evidence replaced trust in traditions and beliefs. This shift led to great advances in science. In reaction against the emphasis on reason, many writers, painters, and composers reasserted the importance of emotion.

Impact on Everyday Life These changes in politics, economics, and thought affected everyday life. For example, the rise of science resulted in more efficient machines and better techniques for planting and harvesting crops. The result was a revolution in agriculture. As farmers became more productive, fewer were needed. People saw greater opportunities in cities, and urban areas began to grow.

Key Concepts

2.1 Different models of political sovereignty affected the relationship among states and between states and individuals.

    I. In much of Europe, absolute monarchy was established over the course of the 17th and 18th centuries.

    II. Challenges to absolutism resulted in alternative political systems.

    III. After 1648, dynastic and state interests, along with Europe's expanding colonial empires, influenced the diplomacy of European states and frequently led to war.

    IV. The French Revolution posed a fundamental challenge to Europe's existing political and social order.

    V. Claiming to defend the ideals of the French Revolution, Napoleon Bonaparte imposed French control over much of the European continent, which eventually provoked a nationalistic reaction.

2.2 The expansion of European commerce accelerated the growth of a worldwide economic network.

    I. Early modern Europe developed a market economy that provided the foundation for its global role.

    II. The European-dominated worldwide economic network contributed to the agricultural, industrial, and consumer revolutions in Europe.

    III. Commercial rivalries influenced diplomacy and warfare among European states in the early modern era.

2.3 The spread of Scientific Revolution concepts and practices and the Enlightenment's application of these concepts and practices to political, social, and ethical issues led to an increased but not unchallenged emphasis on reason in European culture.

    I. Enlightenment thought, which focused on concepts such as empiricism, skepticism, human reason, rationalism, and classical sources of knowledge, challenged the prevailing patterns of thought with respect to social order, institutions of government, and the role of faith.

    II. New public venues and print media popularized Enlightenment ideas.

    III. New political and economic theories challenged absolutism and mercantilism.

    IV. During the Enlightenment, the rational analysis of religious practices led to natural religion and the demand for religious toleration.

    V. The arts moved from the celebration of religious themes and royal power to an emphasis on private life and the public good.

    VI. While Enlightenment values dominated the world of European ideas and culture, they were challenged by the revival of public expression of emotions and feeling.

2.4 The experiences of everyday life were shaped by demographic, environmental, medical, and technological changes.

   I. In the 17th century, small landholdings, low-productivity agricultural practices, poor transportation, and adverse weather limited and disrupted the food supply, causing periodic famines. By the 18th century, the balance between population and the food supply stabilized, resulting in steady population growth.

   II. The consumer revolution of the 18th century was shaped by a new concern for privacy, encouraged the purchase of new goods for homes, and created new venues for leisure activities.

   III. By the 18th century, family and private life reflected new demographic patterns and the effects of the commercial revolution.

   IV. Cities offered economic opportunities, which attracted increasing migration from rural areas, transforming urban life and creating challenges for the new urbanites and their families.

This engraving is based on a famous painting, *The Oath of the Horatii* (1784), by French artist Jacques-Louis David. It shows Roman soldiers preparing for war. The painting reflected the interest of many artists in the late 18th century in classical culture, and how they were portrayed in using clear figures and balanced composition.

Credit: Getty Images

7

Monarchies and Models of Sovereignty

"L'état, c'est moi." ("I am the state.") – Louis XIV, the Sun King

Essential Question: How did different models of political sovereignty affect relationships among states in early modern Euroupe?

By signing the Treaty of Westphalia in 1648, Europe's monarchs ended centuries of religious conflict that had taken a terrible toll on human life and financial resources. From 1648 to 1815, the principal form of political organization across Europe was in the process of becoming the nation-state. Catholic and Protestant political leaders alike agreed that the object of state-craft was a **balance of power** maintained through diplomacy—a system in which no one empire, kingdom, or country would dominate, either on the continent or in the New World.

In this period, monarchs advanced the needs of their sovereign states through the political system known as **absolutism**. Many though not all absolute monarchs believed that they ruled by **divine right**—that their power derived directly from God, as Jean Bodin had asserted. They amassed power by creating bureaucracies with enough resources to wage wars intended either to maintain the balance of power or to disrupt it. States that centralized control and expanded their borders generally fared better than those that did not. States that failed to centralize control tended to break down.

Though absolute monarchs believed they wielded unlimited power, in reality they did not. They needed ways to pay for their unending wars, and they were forced to subdue key elite groups within their regimes. The stronger the monarch was, the less powerful the elites—and vice versa. The monarch-elite relationship determined the nature of a monarch's reign.

These challenges facing absolute monarchies both on the European continent and in the Americas ultimately weakened absolutism. As a result, Britain was poised to dominate Europe and much of the rest of the world for 150 years. Britain's constitutional government, with its constrained monarchy, strong Parliament, religious and intellectual toleration, and healthy finances all made it strong. It had advantages that the absolute monarchies of France, Spain, and the Habsburg lands could not match.

Absolute Monarchies

Absolutism arose in Europe's new states as the old medieval order broke up. It began in 16th-century Western Europe with monarchs who wielded absolute power over both church and state. The system became widespread in the 17th and 18th centuries. Several factors contributed to a general acceptance of absolutism:

- A weakened Catholic Church provided no rival authority.

- The expansion of trade led to the rise of cities, whose merchant and middle classes hoped absolutism would bring stability and prosperity.

- Absolutist rulers favored the merchant class and middle class and weakened the nobility as a result.

- New weaponry, such as gunpowder, gave monarchs greater power to destroy nobles' lands and castles, keeping them in check and limiting opposition.

Because monarchs claimed a divine right to rule, no one was permitted to argue against their decisions, which were often tyrannical and threatened the financial stability of their nations.

Monarchs and the Aristocracy

Under absolutism, a state's power was directly connected to the strength of its ruler. Strong monarchs didn't accept restrictions on their authority—not by nobles, legislatures, churches, citizens, the courts, the military, or agencies, such as a finance ministry. Absolutism posed problems for several reasons:

- Inefficient leaders resulted in chaotic nations.

- Without checks on the ruler from other forces, royal decisions could be based on whims and favoritism rather than on the choices of an efficient government bureaucracy staffed by public servants.

- The nobility that surrounded the monarch did not represent the needs and viewpoints of the vast majority of citizens.

When France's Louis XIV said that he *was* the state (*"l'etat, c'est moi"*), he meant that he alone had the authority to rule the kingdom. In contrast, modern nations belong to "the people," with power divided in a system of checks and balances among a chief executive, a law-making body, and the courts—all of which are meant to serve the public good. Some examples of absolute monarchs who reigned with varying degrees of success were James I of England, Peter the Great of Russia, and Philip II of Spain.

James I of England

Unlike France or Spain, England during the Middle Ages developed a participatory system of government at both the local and parliamentary levels. England's Parliament had two chambers:

- the **House of Lords**: nobility selected by the monarch

- the **House of Commons**: those elected to represent the tax-paying subjects of counties and boroughs

Parliament had a monopoly on deciding how to spend taxes. **James I** (reigned 1603–1625) ran into problems because he overspent and wanted Parliament to cover his personal debts. The members of Parliament (MPs) disapproved and set a precedent by implementing stringent rules over the king's finances and establishing their own greater independence.

James I also needed tax money to pay for war against Spain. Because the MPs were anti-Catholic and anti-Spanish, they agreed to his request but drew up a petition that said James's son, Charles, would have to marry a Protestant. James felt Parliament had overstepped its bounds. In defiance of Parliament, he had Charles marry a Catholic, Henrietta-Maria, the sister of the French king. James's conflicts with Parliament laid the groundwork for a rebellion against his successor, **Charles I,** and for the English Civil War (see Chapter 6).

Peter the Great of Russia

Russia, which had broken free of Mongol control in the 1400s, was a multiethnic empire with its capital in Moscow. The empire grew as it conquered people of many nationalities and languages. Russian monarchs, called **tsars**, or czars, established control over all these varied people by granting the land back to local elites, or nobles, in exchange for their support. The tsars married their children into the families of these nobles, who were given positions of trust and power, in order to build loyalty and familial relationships. In turn, the nobles agreed to cede control to the central government.

Studying Western Europe Tsar **Peter the Great** (reigned 1682–1725) saw Russia as a medieval state that had not learned from technological advances made by the Western European powers. He believed that these differences threatened Russia's strength and independence. In 1697, Peter traveled to Europe with the **Grand Embassy**, a group of about 250 people, mainly to see firsthand how the more advanced Western European countries operated. In disguise as Sergeant Pyotr Mikhaylov, Peter visited shipyards, factories, arsenals, Parliamentary sessions, museums, and schools. He returned home convinced Russia had to modernize.

As one way to accomplish this modernization, he allied with Saxony and Denmark-Norway in the **Great Northern War** (1700–1721) against Sweden to gain access to the Baltic Sea and acquire a seaport access so that Russia could compete for trade and naval power. Peter's main prize from his victory in the war with Sweden became the seaport city of St. Petersburg, which he

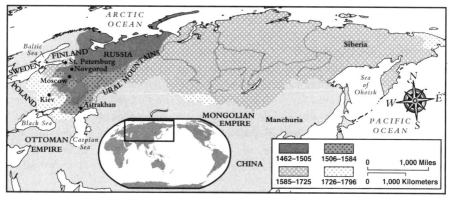

began planning and building as his "window on Europe." He brought architects and artisans from around the world to help build his magnificent new capital. He also rerouted trade through the new capital, and by 1726 the city hosted 90 percent of Russia's foreign trade.

In addition to building the new capital, Peter the Great instituted modern reforms in science, technology, industry, and education:

- promoting science and technology so that Russia's military, industry, transport, and trade could compete with those of western Europe

- founding the St. Petersburg Academy of Sciences (later the **Russian Academy of Sciences**)

- establishing guilds with special privileges to increase economic activity

- sponsoring secular education

- inviting foreign experts to teach at St. Petersburg Academy

Reorganizing Institutions In his quest to westernize and strengthen his empire, Peter the Great reorganized government, the Church, and the military under his absolute rule. To pay the great expenses for warfare and modernization, Peter tripled taxes. He conscripted peasants into lifetime service in the army and forced them to work in mines or manufacturing. The nobles had to serve for life in either the army or in government. To modernize the Russian bureaucracy, Peter created the "Table of Ranks" so that nobles could achieve status in either the military or government service. The ancient landed aristocracy, known as the **boyars**, and the clergy resisted Peter's changes, and both groups were severely punished. For example, Peter personally forced the boyars to cut their long beards and to stop wearing heavy skirtlike coats.

Peter also reorganized the Russian Orthodox Church. He abolished the Patriarch, the Orthodox Church's traditional leader, and established the **Holy Synod**, made up of officials and priests obedient to the tsar. Church lands were disposed of at the tsar's will, occasionally to placate the aristocracy.

Philip II of Spain

Under **Philip II's** reign from 1556 to 1598, Spain reached the height of its power, although a revolt by the Netherlands and the loss of the Spanish Armada in Spain's attempted invasion of England (1588) signaled its eventual decline. Philip II disliked travel, so he stayed in Spain and made all decisions based on reports from his ministers. Because he ruled on all matters both grand and trivial, the work of government slowed down, especially when he failed to make decisions. He was notoriously suspicious and condoned murder against his enemies, so his court was filled with factions and treachery. Philip wanted glory and power for both Spain and Catholicism, but he earned the enmity of most of the rest of Europe in the process. After the death of Philip II, Spain began a slow period of decline.

Louis XIV of France, the Sun King

No monarch embodied the concept of absolutism better than **Louis XIV** of France (reigned 1643–1715), known as the Sun King. Louis XIV inherited the throne when he was five years old and ruled for 72 years. Until he was crowned, his mother, Anne of Austria (1601–1666), and godfather, **Cardinal Jules Mazarin** (1585–1642), ruled a country that was fractured and unstable. To counter such problems, Louis XIV followed a system in which royal representatives called **intendants** went into the countryside to run the country on behalf of the king. Cardinal Richelieu, chief minister of the previous king (Louis XIII), had stripped provincial officials of their power when he divided the country into districts, each administered by an intendant (see Chapter 6). Because the king appointed the intendants, they displaced local authorities.

Eventually, the local authorities and the nobility fomented an unsuccessful uprising called **The Fronde** (1648–1653), but its lasting effect was to convince the young king that his power must be absolute.

French Society Louis XIV surrounded himself with **courtiers**—wealthy, powerful nobles who vied for his favor. In doing so, he eventually brought them under his control. Louis lived lavishly, building the **Palace of Versailles** outside of Paris, as well as several other expensive *chateaux*, or castles.

His military campaigns made France both powerful and multicultural. His army seized land in the north (Flanders), the east (Lorraine and Alsace), and the south (in the Pyrenees). By the end of his reign, many of his subjects spoke Spanish, Dutch, German, or a smaller, distinct regional language.

The French Economy To expand France's borders, Louis XIV needed a strong army, which meant he also needed a strong economy that generated tax revenues. Finance minister **Jean–Baptiste Colbert** (1619–1683) instituted mercantilist policies to decrease France's debt and revitalize its industries, working to expand France's colonies and create a favorable balance of trade. (For more about mercantilism, see Chapter 3 and Chapter 9.) However, most of Colbert's work was undone by Louis XIV's endless wars. Louis XIV also renewed France's war against its own Protestants, the Huguenots, revoking in

1685 the rights they had been granted in the Edict of Nantes. This loss of rights caused up to 800,000 Huguenots to flee the country. Their departure depleted the French middle class and further hurt the economy.

Absolutist rule in France was costly. By the time Louis XIV died in 1715, France supported a modern army of 350,000. Paying for this military resulted in crippling taxation for the poorer classes, who couldn't afford to buy food or basic necessities. In contrast, the nobility were only lightly taxed since they made the laws and wanted to keep their wealth. The country became impoverished and famine-ridden. The public turned against the Sun King and the royal family, setting the stage for later uprisings and the French Revolution.

Examples of Absolute Monarchs			
State	Leader	Reign	Accomplishments
England	James I	1603–1625	• Believed monarchs ruled by divine right • Dissolved Parliament • Married his son to a Catholic
Russia	Peter the Great	1682–1725	• Conscripted peasants into the military and supporting industries • Forced nobles to serve for life in the military or government • Westernized Russia • Built a new capital, St. Petersburg
Spain	Philip II	1556–1598	• Controlled Spanish Netherlands • Launched Spanish Armada • Worked tirelessly and conscientiously • Controlled political appointments
France	Louis XIV	1643–1715	• Used intendants to spread his control • Brutally suppressed rebellions • Increased the military • Expanded France's borders • Levied high taxes against the peasants

Enlightened Monarchs

During the 18th century, Enlightenment ideals spurred a number of rulers to engage in **enlightened absolutism**, also known as enlightened or benevolent despotism. Enlightened monarchs including Catherine the Great of Russia, Frederick II of Prussia, and Joseph II of Austria, maintained absolute power but often used it to promote industrial, educational, societal, and legal reforms.

Catherine the Great Catherine II, known as **Catherine the Great** (reigned 1762–1796), was the wife of Peter the Great's grandson. She took the throne by orchestrating a coup against her husband, Peter III—a cruel and ineffective ruler who often suffered bouts of insanity. To avoid being overthrown herself, she made amends with the Orthodox Church (by restoring its lands) and the military (by recalling troops from Denmark). She was an enlightened absolute monarch who promoted reforms to outlaw torture and the death sentence and initially tried to improve the conditions of Russia's serfs, which the Senate opposed. She formed a legislative commission to hear ideas about legal reform. She also reformed education and supported the arts.

In her later years, Catherine became more conservative. In response to a peasant uprising, Pugachev's Rebellion (1773–1775), and to the French Revolution, she gave the wealthy class permission to oppress their serfs. She also claimed the Russian Orthodox Church and all its holdings to be under the control of the state and therefore subject to taxes. In the end, she failed to improve conditions for the peasant class.

Catherine the Great was born in Germany and worked to win acceptance from the subjects she ruled as leader of the Russian Empire.

Credit: Getty Images

Frederick II of Prussia Also known as Frederick the Great, **Frederick II** (reigned 1740–1786) believed the king's duty was to protect and serve his people through efficient government and prosperity:

- He expanded Prussia's territories (especially into Silesia); this enabled the treasury to collect more taxes and thus pay for a strong army.

- He created new departments to manage mines, forests, and commerce.

- He reformed the judiciary and initiated competence exams for judges and other civil servants.

- He began the work that would become the Prussian Common Law.

However, despite being enlightened in the sense of instituting important reforms, Frederick II believed that only the nobility had a sense of honor, and during his reign the peasants continued to live in a state of serfdom.

Frederick II also believed that a good ruler must be personally involved and not simply rely on his ministers. His mistrust of allowing others to govern had its downside. Though people in his administration were honest and hardworking, they avoided taking initiative. Decisions and ideas came from the top and thus were limited.

Though remembered as a successful military leader, Frederick was more interested in the arts than in war. He was considered an excellent flute player and he composed sonatas and symphonies that are still played by orchestras today. Frederick was so impressed with French culture that when he built a new palace, he gave it a French name, Sanssouci, which means "without concerns." Among his friends were Voltaire, Rousseau, and other French thinkers.

Joseph II of Austria Another enlightened absolutist ruler, **Joseph II** (reigned 1765–1790) became Holy Roman Emperor upon the death of his father. His mother, **Maria Theresa** (1717–1780), was ruler of the Habsburg Empire, so Joseph II became her co-regent, though the two were often at odds. Joseph II believed in religious toleration, but his mother did not. After her death in 1780, Joseph II issued numerous royal decrees to speed reform. These reforms were his most important accomplishments:

- limiting the power of the Catholic Church

- providing more freedom for the press

- abolishing serfdom

- signing the **Edict of Toleration** (1782), which protected religious freedom for Jewish, Protestant, and Greek Orthodox citizens

Joseph II ran into opposition, though, because he did not seek the approval of the nobles or the clergy before making these rapid reforms. He alienated citizens in the Austrian Netherlands by trying to trade their land to regain control of Bavaria, a move that was stopped by Frederick II of Prussia (Maria Theresa's bitter enemy). He heavily taxed the peasants, who were more concerned about the high taxation than about gaining freedoms.

As domestic unrest mounted, Joseph II forged a military alliance with Catherine II of Russia to counter Prussia's growing strength. However, the alliance brought his empire into conflict with Turkey and the Ottomans, who wanted to control Hungary. With his resources stretched thin and his health failing, Joseph II abolished his own reforms in Hungary in order to regain more absolutist control.

Joseph II died alone, feeling his reign had been a failure. However, his actions paved the way for the abolition of feudalism in 1848. His views on religious toleration were progressive for his time. They were embraced by much of the rest of Europe after his death.

Partitions of Poland

While Prussia continued to rise as a great military power under Frederick II, Poland moved toward collapse. Poland was divided internally, as landed elites controlled the representative assemblies and key leadership positions in government. These elites defied the king, exempted themselves from taxation, and exploited the peasantry. Poland had neither a powerful monarchy (like France's) nor an effective government bureaucracy (like Britain's) to unite the country. People felt more connection to their region than to the abstract idea of a country called Poland.

Poland's neighbors took advantage of its weakness. During a period of 25 years, Poland was completely annexed by neighboring countries. Poland did not again appear as a nation on European maps until 1918.

The Three Polish Partitions, 1772–1797		
Causes	**Losses**	**Empires that Gained Land**
First Partition of Poland, 1772 • Russia approved partition of Habsburg lands because Austria opposed Russia's expansion into southeastern Europe. • Austria approved the partition, hoping to regain part of Silesia from Prussia.	About 80,000 square miles, which was one-third of the country and home to one-half of the population	• Prussia gained the territory of West Prussia through Frederick II negotiating with Russia and Austria. • Austria acquired part of "Little Poland," or Małopolska, western Podolia, and the area that became Galicia.
Second Partition of Poland, 1793 • In the 1790s, in response to Poland's new liberal constitution, a conservative Polish group asked Russia to intervene. • Russia accepted the invitation as Prussia invaded Poland, and the two powers created the Second Partition.	About 115,000 square miles	• Russia gained most of Lithuanian Belorussia and western Ukraine. Prussia gained several large cities and more territories.
Third Partition of Poland, 1797 • Russia and Prussia put down a 1794 uprising for Polish independence.	About 45,000 square miles, which was all the remaining land	• Russia and Prussia split the rest of Poland, except the remaining land of "Little Poland," which went to Austria.

Challenges to Absolutism

Absolutism worked in the short run to centralize control within Europe's new states, but it was a system fraught with problems. A more stable system evolved in Britain and the Dutch Republic. These nations flourished by supporting religious toleration, political liberty, representative government, and an efficient bureaucracy to manage such tasks as tax collection and budgeting.

England's Glorious Revolution

England was distinct from other European nations in that it had both a strong monarchy and a powerful Parliament. In governments on the European continent, different groups, or estates, shared influence, each corresponding to a special interest group, such as the clergy. England's two houses of Parliament more closely represented the country as a whole and served as a check on the monarch's power.

This English system was tested during the English Civil War (1642–1651), a series of bloody and expensive battles pitting royal forces against Parliament. (For a review of the conflict, see Chapter 6.)

Restoration and Abdication As a result of the Civil War, England was ruled for a short time as a republic, with Oliver Cromwell its Lord Protector. Two years after Cromwell's death in 1658, after his son Richard's inability to maintain the Protectorate, Parliament restored **Charles II** to the throne during the **Restoration** period. After Charles II's death, his brother James II, a Roman Catholic, became England's monarch.

When James II's wife gave birth to a son, anti-Catholic nobles rebelled. They called on James II's Dutch son-in-law **William of Orange,** a Protestant, to invade and depose the king. James II fled, abdicating the throne. William of Orange ruled as King **William III** with his wife, **Mary II.** The accession of William and Mary to the throne became known as the **Glorious Revolution**.

The English Bill of Rights When the new monarchs took power in 1689, Parliament required that they accept a **Bill of Rights.** This document, also known as the Declaration of Right, limited the monarchs's powers by protecting some of Parliament's: _no absolutism_

- Parliament had the power to meet frequently.

- Parliament needed to approve any change in the law.

- Parliament needed to approve taxes.

In addition, the Bill of Rights declared that some members of Parliament would be chosen through elections (by a small part of the population), that the monarch could not keep a standing army, and that government could not use excessive fines or cruel punishments. However, it did not grant equality for Catholics. By forcing the monarch to share power with Parliament, this document created a constitutional monarchy. It had a major impact on the writing of the United States Constitution and Bill of Rights.

The Dutch Republic

The Dutch Republic (1588–1795) was formed during the **Eighty Years' War** (1568–1648), when the Dutch battled for independence from Spain. Stemming from the military agreement known as the **Union of Utrecht** (1579), the Dutch Republic consisted of provinces that won independence from Spain between 1568 and 1609.

During the 16th century, the Dutch Republic was Europe's leading cargo shipper and engaged in an ongoing rivalry with Britain that sometimes led to maritime wars. The Dutch Republic also fought land wars, usually against the French. The republic generally fared well in these conflicts. It was a wealthy center of shipping and finance with a profitable trade empire in the Americas, Asia, and throughout the Indian Ocean (see Chapter 3).

The Dutch Republic was a world power during its Golden Age in the 17th century. Dutch artists such as Rembrandt (1609–1669), Frans Hals (1583–1666), and Johannes Vermeer (1632–1675) painted their masterpieces during this time.

Dutch Oligarchy The Dutch Republic did not have a monarch. Instead, estates representing the seven provinces each selected a provincial leader, or *stadholder*. The estates sent these delegates to meet in a legislative body called the Estates-General, which decided military and foreign policy issues. However, this was not truly a representative government but an **oligarchy** made up of urban gentry and rural landholders. An oligarchy is government by the few, usually to promote selfish causes. In this case, the ruling class wanted to protect the wealth they had gained through trade.

Dutch East India Company Merchants and financiers held most of the power in the Dutch Republic. To promote trade, these merchants and financiers formed the Dutch East India Company in 1602 as a private enterprise. Known by its Dutch initials, VOC, it was a **joint-stock company**, similar to a modern corporation, in which shareholders could buy stock. The company was professionally managed by a board of directors, enabling it to raise capital and spread risk across a wide pool of investors.

The profits of the VOC made Amsterdam one of the richest cities in the world. The influx of wealth helped keep the Dutch Republic peaceful and stable, in part because it offered upward mobility for workers and peasants. Even though the lower classes did not share in political power, their standard of living was higher than that in other European countries. However, when investors dumped their VOC shares in the 18th century due to worries about British competition, the company went into bankruptcy. As a result, the Dutch Republic declined in world influence and power.

European Wars and Diplomacy

Following the Peace of Westphalia in 1648, the Holy Roman Empire split into about three hundred sovereign princedoms, each with its own dynastic, political, and ethnic interests. Because of the competition for territory and resources both in Europe and in colonies worldwide, these states frequently found themselves at war. Attempts at diplomacy often failed, and alliances shifted as countries tried to keep a precarious balance of power. New nations arose while old empires, such as the Ottomans, saw their power decline in a changing political landscape.

Prussian and Habsburg Rulers

One nation to arise at this time was Prussia, made up of areas in eastern and central Europe. From 1701 the Hohenzollern dynasty ruled Prussia, after Frederick III of Brandenburg gained the title "king of Prussia" from the Holy Roman Emperor, and became Frederick I of Prussia (reigned 1701–1713).

Frederick William I The son of Frederick I, **Frederick William I** (reigned 1713–1740), expanded Prussia's territories by creating a large and powerful army financed by taxation. He persuaded the Prussian estates—legislative bodies composed of representatives from cities and towns—to allow him to impose taxes at will on the peasants. In exchange, he promised leaders of the estates that peasants would work the land for minimal pay. Peasants were also conscripted into the army. Prussia's army numbered 38,000 soldiers in 1713, but by 1740, it numbered 83,000. By the time of his death in 1740, Frederick William I had turned Prussia into a prosperous and efficient nation.

Frederick the Great The son of Frederick William I was Frederick II, known as **Frederick the Great**. He inherited his father's prosperous nation and turned it into Europe's leading military power.

When the Habsburg Holy Roman Emperor Charles VI died in 1740, he left as his heir a daughter, the Archduchess **Maria Theresa.** Frederick the Great sensed the empire's weaknesses: a disorganized army and poor finances. He thus decided to attack its territories. First, he invaded Silesia, an area in Central Europe to which his Hohenzollern dynasty had weak claims. Facing a hostile alliance, Maria was forced to give Lower Silesia to Prussia. Time after time, if Frederick II saw that Maria Theresa's armies were growing stronger or developing new alliances, he preemptively attacked Habsburg territories.

Frederick II's own alliances, especially with France, were based mostly on mutual hatred for the Habsburgs. When Britain and Russia agreed to protect the electorate of Hanover against a possible French or Prussian attack, it resulted in a new Franco-Austrian alliance. A worried Frederick II once again invaded preemptively, this time into Saxony and Bohemia in 1756. The attack began the **Seven Years' War** (1757–1764). Prussia found itself facing opposition from France, Russia, Sweden, and several small German states. Only two things saved it: subsidies from Britain and the death of Russian Empress Elizabeth, Frederick II's archenemy. Her successor, Peter III, admired the Prussians and signed a Russo-Prussian armistice, even as Berlin itself was besieged by the armies of France, Austria, and Russia.

The war cost Prussia 180,000 men and devastated its countryside. Prussia signed a peace agreement with Russia that lasted until 1780, but Prussia's conflicts with Austria continued.

The End of Ottoman Expansion in Europe

The Ottoman Empire spread quickly out of Asia Minor in its early centuries and engaged in wars with the Habsburg Empire for 300 years. The Ottomans first reached the outskirts of Vienna, capital of the Habsburg Empire, in 1529. They wanted the city in order to control trade routes along the Danube River to the Black Sea and overland to Germany. They already controlled much of Hungary and southeastern Europe.

In 1681–1682, border skirmishes escalated between the Ottomans and the Holy Roman Empire over control of Hungary. The Ottomans attacked Vienna in 1683, causing the Holy Roman Empire, the Habsburg monarchy, and the Polish-Lithuanian Commonwealth to unite against the invaders. The Ottomans lost the **Battle of Vienna** (1683), and over the next sixteen years they lost control of the rest of Hungary. The Battle of Vienna marked a turning point in history—the end of Ottoman expansion in the Christian world.

One of many legends about the origin of the shape of the curved rolls or pastries known as croissants is related to the Battle of Vienna. According to this story, bakers in Vienna celebrated the Hungarian victory over the Ottomans by making rolls in the shape of the crescent moon. The crescent moon is a symbol of Islam, and the Ottoman Empire was led by Muslims.

Credit: Getty Images

The Wars of Louis XIV

During Louis XIV's long reign, he kept France engaged in a series of wars. He challenged Britain, the Dutch Republic, Spain, the Habsburg rulers, and their allies in his quest to expand his power. The wars were expensive, and Louis left his successors large debts. These wars also created problems for the rest of Europe.

Wars Against the Dutch and Others France, aided by England, fought the **Dutch War** (1672–1678) to gain the Spanish Netherlands (now Belgium and a portion of northern France). The Dutch stopped French advances, though, and France eventually made peace. Still, Louis XIV remained the most powerful monarch in Europe. The **Nine Years' War** (1688–1697) pitted France against the Dutch Republic, Spain, England, Austria, the Holy Roman Empire, and Savoy (a region near the Alps). It was fought in multiple places including northern Europe, Ireland, and Scotland, as well as in colonial areas.

Unprepared for a protracted war on multiple continents, all parties signed a treaty in 1697. While this treaty stoppped the fighting, it did not solve the problem. It did not end the ambitions of Louis XIV and other monarchs to expand their territory.

War of the Spanish Succession One of Louis XIV's goals in fighting the Nine Years' War was to weaken and even conquer the Habsburgs. His other goal was to establish the right of his grandson **Philip**, **Duc D'Anjou** to rule Spain as **Philip V** (reigned 1701–1746; left throne briefly, January–August 1724) following the death of the childless Charles II. Emperor Leopold I of Austria had an equally strong claim to the Spanish throne by birth and marriage.

Alarmed by Louis XIV's plans, England and the Dutch Republic allied with Austria in the **War of the Spanish Succession** (1702–1713). Spain and France, both Catholic countries, were allies, along with Savoy and Portugal (both of which later changed sides). Throughout most of the war, the English and Dutch (both Protestant countries) prevailed over the French, on land and at sea.

All the parties concluded the war with the **Peace of Utrecht** (1713), a series of treaties that accomplished several goals:

- Britain won territories in Spain and the Americas, as well as the sole right to import enslaved Africans into America for thirty years.

- Other states recognized Philip V as the king of Spain.

- Spain obtained control of Milan, Naples, and parts of the Netherlands.

- France agreed to acknowledge Protestant succession in England.

These treaties assured a period of peace and balance of power between Britain and France in Europe. However, conflicts between the rivals continued in North America.

Colonial Rivalry between Britain and France

The Seven Years' War in Europe spilled over to North America, where it became known as the **French and Indian War** (1754–1763). Britain and its American colonists wanted to counter French expansion along the western frontier of the Ohio River Valley. In the war, both sides allied with different Indian tribes, each making promises to the Indians that would be broken. Britain won the war, and territorial changes resulted:

- Britain received all lands east of the Mississippi River plus Canada from France.

- Britain received Florida from Spain.

- Spain received Louisiana and France's lands west of the Mississippi.

- France kept its sugar-producing islands, including Haiti, in the Caribbean.

The war's end marked the beginning of Britain's world dominance and resulted in North America becoming a mainly English-speaking land.

However, the British-French rivalry in North America was not over. During the American Revolution (1775–1783), one important factor in the colonists' success was their alliance with France. The French took advantage of the rebellion to gain revenge for losses in the Seven Years' War. The American colonial government sent representative Benjamin Franklin to negotiate a treaty that kept Spain out of the war and prevented any European powers from entering into secret alliances with Britain. The French provided arms, ammunition, military training, and troops to the Americans. French naval support assured American victory at the Battle of Yorktown, where the British finally surrendered in 1781.

The period of rivalry from around 1689 to 1815 between France and Britain became known as the **Second Hundred Years' War**. However, on a larger scale, this period of warfare encompassed all of Europe, as states fought to keep each other in check—or to expand their dominance on the world stage. The era ended with Napoleon's defeat at Waterloo and the **Congress of Vienna** (1814–1815).

HISTORICAL PERSPECTIVES: WHY DID RUSSIA AND WESTERN EUROPE DIVERGE?

As the question in the title suggests, historians debate over whether Russia ever made a definitive break from the rest of Europe. Arguments often reflect whether a particular historian's perspective is based on beliefs tied to the Cold War, a broader world-history perspective, or the viewpoint of the post-Cold War period.

The Mongol Influence Historian Robert Strayer credited the Mongols with helping to establish modern Russia and the founding of Moscow. Strayer explained how Russians adopted Mongol weapons, diplomatic rituals, court practices, taxation, and the military draft.

Richard Pipes went further to suggest that Mongol influence in Russia was critical because it cut Russia off from Catholic Western Europe, the Byzantine Empire, and the Islamic Empire. This break established a patrimonial system in which nobles answered only to the tsar and lacked exposure to the cornerstones of Western political thought—Roman law, Catholic theology, feudalism, and commercial culture. This break was critical, Pipes believed, because it prevented the rise of an independent noble or middle class and respect for private property that would allow for the rise of the state as a public institution. To Pipes, this cemented a separate, conservative past and future for Russia.

Divergence or Similarity Angela Rustemeyer, a German historian writing during and after the Cold War, however, tried to find greater similarity between Russia and the West. In her article in the journal *Kritika* (2010), Rustemeyer traced recent historiographical shifts, highlighting four historians discussing closer Russian ties to Europe than previously understood.

As a result, Rustemeyer directly challenged the arguments popularized by Pipes. First, she demonstrated not the absence of feudalism, but the evolution of a system in which the Russian nobles, much like their Western European counterparts, owed loyalty to the tsar. And much like Western Europeans, the tsar increasingly had to respond to the nobles' demands—thus establishing a public sphere of interaction. Second, Rustemeyer compared the support of Russian abbots for economic expansion to that of the Calvinists, and Peter the Great's control of religion to that of Henry VIII.

Third, Rustemeyer cited the work of historian Donald Ostrowski as she noted a direct and intentional shift by Russia away from the Mongols toward Western Europe. Ostrowski had explained, for example, how the shift from useful bows and arrows to rudimentary and relatively ineffective guns represented a reorientation not only of Russian foreign policy, but also military practices and structure. Rustemeyer's conclusion was that Russia, prior to and accelerated by Peter the Great, was embarking on a path of modern state building much like that of the rest of Europe.

A Contextualization Challenge The historiography of Russia from the Western perspective always faces a challenge. Classifying a vast territory that covers one-sixth of the earth, spanning Europe and Asia, was never easy for historians. The challenge was complicated by Cold War tensions and uncertainty of the motivations of leaders such as Vladimir Putin. The result leaves historians trying to remain objective on a topic and goal that very much reflects crucial issues of their time. Historical viewpoints about Russia present an important lesson in contextualization, as the questions historians ask and the answers they develop are shaped by the times in which they write.

KEY TERMS BY THEME

Governance

balance of power

absolutism

divine right

House of Lords

House of Commons

James I

Charles I

tsar

Peter the Great

Grand Embassy

Great Northern War

Russian Academy of Sciences

boyars

Holy Synod

Philip II

Louis XIV

Cardinal Jules Mazarin

intendants

the Fronde

courtiers

Palace of Versailles

chateaux

Jean-Baptiste Colbert

enlightened absolutism

Catherine the Great

Frederick II

Joseph II

Maria Theresa

Edict of Toleration

First Partition of Poland

Second Partition of Poland

Third Partition of Poland

Restoration

William of Orange

Glorious Revolution

William III

Mary II

Declaration of Rights

English Bill of Rights

Eighty Years' War

Union of Utrecht

oligarchy

Frederick William I

Frederick the Great

Seven Years' War

Battle of Vienna

Dutch War

Nine Years' War

Philip, Duc D'Anjou

Philip V

War of the Spanish Succession

Peace of Utrecht

French and Indian War

Second Hundred Years' War

Congress of Vienna

Economics

joint-stock company

Questions 1–2 refer to the image below.

Grigory Musikiysky,
Portrait of Emperor Peter the Great,
Hermitage Museum, Russia, 1723

Credit: This image is in the public domain in the United States. https://en.wikipedia.org/wiki/Grigory_Musikiysky. Musikiysky, Grigory Semyonovich - http://www.hermitagemuseum.org/wps/portal/hermitage/digital-collection/02.+Dra wings/2645503/?lng=ru

Grigory Musikiysky's portrait of Peter the Great included several symbols of Peter's interests.

1. This image is best understood within the context of which of the following developments in Russia?

    a) Urbanization and rapid population growth in Eastern Europe

    b) Military reform and growth of mercantile trade

    c) Educational reform to revise Russian traditions

    d) The spread of Slavic independence movements

2. This image most clearly represents which of the following trends in Europe in the 17th and 18th centuries?

    a) The consolidation of royal power and state sovereignty

    b) The persistence of medieval military organization and technology

    c) The development of scientific knowledge and new technology in Eastern Europe

    d) The growth in commercial wealth fueled by the Atlantic slave trade

Questions 3–5 refer to the passage below.

"One must attempt, above all, to know the special genius of the people which one wants to govern in order to know if one must treat them leniently or severely, if they are inclined to revolt...

[The Prussian nobility] has sacrificed its life and goods for the service of the state; its loyalty and merit have earned it the protection of all its rulers... In such a state no factions or rebellions need be feared . . . it is one goal of the policy of this state to preserve the nobility.

A well-conducted government must have an underlying concept so well integrated that it could be likened to a system of philosophy. All actions taken must be well reasoned... However, such a system can flow but from a single brain, and this must be that of the sovereign.

Catholics, Lutherans, Reformed, Jews and other Christian sects live in this state, and live together in peace. If the sovereign, actuated by a mistaken zeal, declares himself for one religion or another, parties spring up, heated disputes ensue, little by little persecutions will commence and, in the end, the religion persecuted will leave the fatherland, and millions of subjects will enrich our neighbors by their skill and industry.

It is of no concern in politics whether the ruler has a religion or whether he has none. All religions, if one examines them, are founded on superstitious systems, more or less absurd."

Frederick the Great of Prussia, "Political Testament," 1752

3. The ideas expressed in this passage best illustrate which of following 18th century trends?

   a) The application of scientific and rational principles to government

   b) The establishment of representative government based upon a social contract

   c) The conservative reaction to the French Revolution

   d) The expansion of the commercial economy

4. The second paragraph of the excerpt best reflects which characteristic of the governing philosophy of Frederick the Great?

   a) The ultimate decision-making must come from the monarch.

   b) The ultimate decision-making must come from the honorable nobles.

   c) Representatives of the peasantry should be involved in all important decisions.

   d) All decisions should be arrived at democratically even if the monarch disagrees.

5. Which of the following would best explain Frederick the Great's attitude toward the nobility?

   a) He believed that the peasantry had a sense of honor as strong as the nobility's.

   b) He believed that the nobility had a sense of honor, but peasantry did not.

   c) He supported the spread of Enlightenment ideals that undermined nobles' privileges.

   d) He feared that oppressing the peasants would bring a revolution similar to France's.

Questions 6–8 are based on the following document.

- The pretended [assumed] power of suspending the laws or the execution of laws by regal authority without consent of Parliament is illegal…

- It is the right of the subjects to petition the king, and all commitments and prosecutions for such petitioning are illegal…

- The raising or keeping a standing army within the kingdom in time of peace, unless it be with consent of Parliament, is against law…

- The subjects which are Protestants may have arms for their defense suitable to their conditions and as allowed by law…

- Election of members of Parliament ought to be free…

- Freedom of speech and debates or proceedings in Parliament ought not to be impeached or questioned in any court or place out of Parliament…

- Excessive bail ought not to be required, nor excessive fines imposed, nor cruel and unusual punishments inflicted…

- Jurors ought to be duly impaneled and returned…

- And that for redress of all grievances, and for the amending, strengthening and preserving of the laws, Parliaments ought to be held frequently…

English Bill of Rights, 1689

6. The creation of this document resulted most directly from which of the following?

   a) Demands for Parliamentary representation by British American colonists

   b) The spread of Enlightenment ideas during the French Revolution

   c) The decline in power of the British aristocracy relative to the monarchy

   d) The overthrow of James II during the Glorious Revolution

7. What type of government does the excerpt reflect?

    a) Democratic republic

    b) Enlightened despotism

    c) Absolute monarchy

    d) Constitutional monarchy

8. Which individual would probably be most supportive of the provisions of the English Bill of Rights?

    a) James I of England

    b) Louis XIV of France

    c) Philip II of Spain

    d) Oliver Cromwell

SHORT-ANSWER QUESTIONS

1. Use the passage below to answer all parts of the question that follows.

"In the 17th century, European governments devoted more attention to the public image of the ruler than at any time since the later Roman Empire. Among these governments, it was the French who were the most concerned with the ways in which the king was represented. The most elaborate and self-conscious attempts at projecting a favorable image of the ruler were those made by a group of officials, artists and men of letters, during the reign of Louis XIV, especially in the period of his personal rule, which lasted for more than half a century (1643—1715). The term "propaganda" is all the more appropriate to describe these favorable images because the government was concerned not only to present the king in a heroic light but also to spread official interpretations of specific events of the reign.

                                  Peter Burke, *Fabrication of Louis XIV*, 1992

    a) Explain ONE piece of evidence that *supports* Burke's argument regarding the power of absolute monarchs in Europe.

    b) Explain ONE piece of evidence that *undermines* Burke's argument regarding the power of absolute monarchs in Europe.

    c) Explain ONE example of a new monarch in the 15th or 16th centuries that provoked a similar political system to those described by Burke.

2. Answer all parts of the question that follows.

    a) Describe ONE action or event in England from 1600 to 1700 that challenged absolutism by providing an alternative political system.

    b) Describe ONE action or event in Netherlands from 1600 to 1700 that challenged absolutism by providing an alternative political system.

    c) Explain ONE similarity in the actions or events discussed in parts a and b.

LONG ESSAY QUESTIONS

1. Evaluate the extent to which the governmental structure of France and England differed during the 17th century.

2. Evaluate the extent to which religious and economic reasons led to England's Glorious Revolution.

REFLECT ON THE CHAPTER ESSENTIAL QUESTION

1. In one to three paragraphs, explain how different models of political sovereignty affected relationships among states during the early modern period.

WRITE AS A HISTORIAN: USE CHRONOLOGICAL ORDER

Writing in chronological order means structuring an essay by presenting the supporting evidence in the order it occurred. (In Greek mythology, the god *Chronos* governed linear, orderly, predictable time.) Chronological organization helps the reader of a historical essay in several ways. First, it organizes the material sensibly. Second, it helps explain cause and effect, or how things built upon each other. Third, it can aid a smooth transition into the next main idea.

Which words in the sentences below cue the reader that the writer is using chronological order?

1. In the early 17th century, the English King James I believed in a divine right monarchy. His son and successor, Charles I, continued this absolutism by dissolving Parliament and attempting to rule without it for 11 years.

2. As a result of the Glorious Revolution in the late 17th century, English co-monarchs William of Orange and his wife, Mary, accepted a limited monarchy and Parliament's Bill of Rights.

3. In 1689, Russian monarch Peter the Great claimed power and began his program of Westernization.

4. After sending Russians to study in the West and bringing foreigners to Russia, he effected changes such as forcing men to shave, adopting Western court processes, and creating an Academy of Sciences.

5. In 1697, he traveled incognito to the West and learned about Western science and industry. He was credited with moving Russia from the medieval world into the modern world.

6. Peter was an absolutist who governed by subduing the nobles. Later, in the second half of the 18th century, Catherine the Great continued Peter's program of growth through conquest and diplomacy, but she gave increased freedom back to the nobles and was considered an enlightened despot.

Based on cue words and transitions, put the following ideas into chronological order.

7. During the 17th and 18th centuries, absolute monarchies were established throughout much of Europe, but they were not equally successful.

   a. Other examples of absolute monarchies were those of England's James I of England and Phillips II, III, and IV of Spain.

   b. Eventually, challenges to absolutism led to alternative political systems.

   c. However, not all monarchies were absolutist. Weak leadership and poor policies, like the *liberum veto*, plagued Poland. Poland also suffered uprisings that led to massacres of noblemen, Jews, and Catholic priests. A weak monarchy led to Poland's partition by Prussia, Russia, and Austria and its disappearance from the map of Europe for 123 years.

   d. Two results of these alternative systems were the English Bill of Rights, which gave Parliament sovereignty, and the Dutch Republic, established by a Protestant revolt of urban gentry and rural landholders to promote trade and protect traditional rights.

   e. Louis XIV epitomized the idea of absolute monarchy. Even though his finance minister, Jean-Baptiste Colbert, improved French manufacturing, Louis bankrupted France with his incessant wars.

8

The French Revolution and Napoleon

"Liberty, equality, fraternity, or death; – the last, much the easiest to bestow, O Guillotine!"

—Charles Dickens, *A Tale of Two Cities*

"Impossible is a word to be found only in the dictionary of fools."

—Napoleon Bonaparte

Essential Question: How did events in France challenge the existing political and social order and provoke nationalism?

The Revolution in France

The **French Revolution** (1789–1799) was a period of dramatic change that posed a fundamental challenge to Europe's political and social order. Before the Revolution, absolute monarchs ruled France as an extension of their own private property. They answered to no one, waged wars to increase their power and wealth, and heavily taxed the poorest people. The aristocracy and the Catholic Church had privileges and riches unknown to the common people, including exemption from taxation.

As Enlightenment ideals (see Chapter 10) took hold in France, support grew for individual rights and a republican form of government. A **republic** is a state in which the people create the government, give it authority, and elect representatives. The representatives as well as civil servants run the government for the public good—not simply to build another palace for a king or paint his walls with gold. France's revolutionaries found inspiration from the successes of the American Revolution and the United States Constitution.

The French Revolution began as a popular uprising against the king and the aristocracy, one that was supposed to bring an end to tyranny. Instead, violence and turmoil led to a period known as the **Reign of Terror**, when leaders of the revolt crushed resistance to it and executed as many as 40,000 people. During this period, revolutionaries suppressed by force the very rights many people desired—free speech, free thought, and freedom from excessive government power.

While the French Revolution had some success, it was not durable. During the next 100 years, France would be governed alternately as a republic, a dictatorship, a constitutional monarchy, two empires, and a monarchy. It would take more revolutions before modern France would emerge as a democratic nation. Despite these setbacks, during the first half of the 19th century, France's revolutionary ideals spread throughout Europe and into the Americas, challenging traditional politics and diplomacy.

Causes of The French Revolution

Many of the root causes of the French Revolution stemmed from economic crises. During the reign of Louis XIV, France fought many expensive wars. To finance these wars, the king had to raise money—either through taxation or borrowing. The nobility had exempted themselves from taxation, but they were willing to lend money to the crown at high interest rates. Up to 60 percent of all tax revenues—collected from commoners—went to repay these rich creditors. The remaining budget was still not nearly enough to govern a country of 25 million people and to fight its endless wars.

France had colonized many parts of the world, and while these colonies did generate wealth through trade, it was not enough to offset the costs of defending and managing them. During the Seven Years' War (1756–1763), the French crown lost vast territories in the Americas and India to Britain. Britain had now become the dominant trading power in Europe.

France's Involvement in the American Revolution France saw a chance for revenge when the American colonies declared their independence from Great Britain. With the American victory at Saratoga, the French provided money and weapons to the colonies. Their aid helped the American colonies win the war, but France ended up in a deepening financial crisis.

Problems with the Estates-General France was on the verge of collapse, in large part because it still operated in the same fashion as it had since the Middle Ages. This was referred to as the *ancien régime*, France's feudal social and political system from the 15th century until 1789. Under this system, the Church and nobility, who made up a small percentage of the population, controlled the economic, political, and social systems, including taxes and the courts, for their own benefit. Yet, like much of Europe, France had changed greatly during that time.

To deal with this financial crisis **Louis XVI** (1754–1793) was forced to call into action the **Estates-General**, which had been inactive for almost 200 years. The Estates-General was an assembly made up of three bodies:

- First Estate: the Catholic clergy—1 percent of the population owned 10 percent of land

- Second Estate: the nobility—2 percent of the population owned 30 percent of land

- Third Estate: the commoners—97 percent of the population owned 35 percent of land

As an unpopular ruler of a bankrupt state, Louis XVI felt he had to agree to revive the Estates-General. The people resented the wasteful extravagance of the Palace of Versailles, personified by the queen, **Marie Antoinette** (1755–1793), who spent lavishly on frivolous things when many of her subjects were starving. It became popular to blame Marie Antoinette, but in reality, France's problems began long before her arrival.

Though many in France hoped the Estates-General would resolve the country's problems, the governing body was ineffective for several reasons:

- Each of the three estates had one vote, even though the vast majority of French citizens were members of the Third Estate.

- The First Estate, the clergy, had already lost public confidence with the rise of secular and scientific beliefs during the Enlightenment.

- The Second Estate, the nobility, did not want to give up its privileges and power, which would involve taxing itself.

- The First and Second Estates always voted together since their interests were the same.

- Members of the Third Estate were forced to wear black robes and enter the meetings through a side door, reinforcing the perception that they were less important than the other two estates.

Eventually, the Third Estate realized that it could use its greater size to pressure the rest of the government to make significant changes.

Peasant and Bourgeoise Grievances The First and Second Estates feared mass rebellion by the peasants, who lived in poverty under feudal conditions. Peasants had already been rioting and looting. But the **bourgeoisie** of the Third Estate—the urban middle class who lacked noble titles and therefore weren't exempt from taxation—also spoke out against the excesses of the system. Many members of the bourgeoisie were wealthier than the nobility, but they lacked the same status. They wanted to dress and act like nobles, but the nobility wanted to preserve class distinctions. The aristocrats refused to share their titles or their tax exemptions.

Between March and April of 1789, each of the three Estates had compiled **cahiers**, or notebooks, declaring their grievances and their hopes for change. The French of the Third Estate asked for the following changes:

- a fairer taxation system

- a fairer voting system

- an end to the requirement that peasants provide unpaid labor to landowners

- the elimination of fees levied by nobles on peasant land holdings

- a halt to **tithes**, a 10-percent tax paid to the Church

After six weeks of negotiations that had started May 5, 1789, nothing was resolved. The Third Estate walked out and declared itself the official representative government, called the **National Assembly**, insisting that the French people deserved liberty, equality, and fraternity. As a start, the National Assembly granted themselves authority over taxation.

Reasons for the French Revolution		
Category	**Short-Term Causes**	**Long-Term Causes**
Economic	• In the French budget for 1789, 40 percent was for interest on loans and 30 percent was for the military. • The urban poor spent 80 percent of their income on bread. • Nobles and clergy were exempt from taxation, so the burden fell on farmers and workers.	• Taxes were not increased to repay debts and military expenditures. • Nobles and clergy exempt from taxation, were a burden on commoners • The wars of Louis XIV, Louis XV, and Louis XVI had drained the economy without material gains.
Social	• Bad harvests of 1787-1788 hurt the poor. • The divide between bourgeoisie and peasants was growing. • People disliked Queen Marie Antoinette.	• Land ownership was concentrated in the hands of the clergy and nobles. • Most people were peasants, but had little status.
Political	• Few reforms helped the growing number of poor. • King Louis XVI was not a strong leader. • The bourgeoisie demanded reforms to help them. • Each estate, regardless of size, had one vote in the Estates-General.	• Provincial Parliaments wanted more power after the death of Louis XIV. • Kings refused to address basic problems of inequality. • The ideas of the philosophes and criticism of privileges and institutions grew during the Enlightenment.

The Tennis Court Oath In June 1789, the National Assembly met at an indoor tennis court after being locked out of its traditional meeting hall, and the members swore an oath not to disperse before achieving a new constitution. Some members of the clergy and liberal nobles joined the cause. Louis XVI grudgingly accepted this new government, but secretly, the army was mobilizing around Paris and Versailles to disband it. To some historians, the **Tennis Court Oath** marked the beginning of the French Revolution— though most people at the time did not realize it.

Bread Shortages All of this political maneuvering took place during France's worst economic conditions in decades. People were starving and unable to find one of the staples of their diet: bread. Bread shortages began as a result of a drought in 1788. Louis XVI decided to remove price controls on grain, thinking that if farmers could get higher prices, they would choose to grow more wheat, thus increasing the supply and keeping prices stable.

However, France's antiquated farming system didn't have the technology and efficiency to produce any additional food. As a result, prices skyrocketed. In addition, the king also allowed more grain to be exported. The exports, along with several years of bad weather, further reduced the grain supply and created a starvation crisis.

Pamphleteers distributed written articles denouncing the king and queen. Some claimed that Marie Antoinette's response to learning of the peasants' bread crisis was unsympathetic. She reportedly said, "Let them eat cake." She probably did not make that statement. However, people believed the propaganda and anger at the gap between the hardships of the poor and the luxury of the wealthy widened.

The Liberal Phase of the Revolution

The first phase of the French Revolution (1789–1791) produced liberal reforms. The National Assembly abolished hereditary privileges for the aristocracy, increased popular participation in voting, nationalized the Catholic Church, and established a constitutional monarchy. However, as the people continued to express their rage, the Revolution became increasingly violent and intolerant of moderate opinions.

Declaration of the Rights of Man and Citizen On July 14, 1789, only a few weeks after the Tennis Court Oath, a group of rebels redirected the course of events. They were known as *sans-culottes* (French for "without knee-breeches") because they could not afford to buy the style of pants worn by more prosperous men. Hearing that the king was going to forcibly disband the National Assembly, the rioters stormed the Bastille, a prison in Paris. While the prison held only seven inmates (five forgers and two criminally insane), it symbolized the repression exercised by the French government. July 14, known as **Bastille Day**, has become France's equivalent of the Fourth of July in the United States. It is widely celebrated as the start of the Revolution.

Throughout the summer of 1789, peasants rose up, destroying the manorial records, looting and burning the homes of tax collectors and elites. Nobles fled the country during what became known as **The Great Fear**. These actions were, however, mostly crimes against property, not people.

On the night of August 4, the National Assembly officially abolished feudalism by voting to end seigniorial rights and fiscal privileges of the nobility, clergy, and towns. Interestingly enough, this marked the end of the Revolution for the vast majority of French peasants, who only wanted freedom from traditional ties to the outdated manorial system.

On August 26, the National Assembly took matters a step further by issuing the **Declaration of the Rights of Man and Citizen**. Much like the English and American Bills of Rights, it affirmed the "natural rights of man," so important to John Locke and Thomas Jefferson. It called for equality, free speech, representative government, and popular sovereignty. The day was a turning point in history. In just a few years, these ideals would spread throughout the rest of Europe.

The Bastille was often used to house political prisoners, although it was nearly empty when it was seized by revolutionaries on July 14, 1789.

Credit: Getty Images

Women's March on Versailles In October 1789, nearly 7,000 women marched 14 miles from Paris to Versailles in the pouring rain. Carrying pitchforks, pikes, and other weapons, they chanted "Bread! Bread!" Upon arrival, they got past a royal guard force of 20,000 men and broke into the palace searching for Marie Antoinette. Eventually, Marie Antoinette—using her children as a human shield—stood on a balcony before the rabble and allowed them to scream their frustrations at her.

The women didn't kill the queen, though they had beheaded two of her guards and stuck their heads on pikes. Instead, they demanded that the king agree to the following terms:

- distribute all the bread the palace had hoarded

- accept the Declaration of the Rights of Man and Citizen

- accompany the women back to Paris to see how real citizens lived

The king was forced to agree. The October march by the women of Paris ended the days of the king's reign from the lavish Palace of Versailles. From that point until their executions, Louis XVI and Marie Antoinette lived as virtual prisoners of the Revolution.

Civil Constitution of the Clergy One issue facing the new government was the role of the Church. Already, the National Assembly had abolished all monastic orders and confiscated the Catholic Church's lands within France. The **Civil Constitution of the Clergy** (1790) expanded the law in the following ways:

- placed the Catholic Church completely under the authority of the state

- eliminated the 10-percent tithe (tax) paid by the peasants

- demanded that the clergy owe allegiance to France (not to outside interests such as the Pope)

- regulated dioceses to align them with new administrative districts

- stated that bishops and priests would be elected by the people

The new government sold Church property to raise money for the government. France was largely a Catholic nation, so all these acts restricting the Church angered the Church's strongest supporters, and many turned against the French Revolution.

Abolition of Provinces and Division of France into Departments In 1790, the National Assembly abolished the provinces of the *ancien régime* to achieve greater national unity. After 1792, the country was divided into *départements,* or **departments**, based on geographical features more than on historical territories that had their own loyalties. The departments established in 1792 continue to exist today.

Constitution of 1791 France's first constitution established a constitutional monarchy that placed lawmaking power in the hands of the new legislative assembly. It also gave the king a limited veto and allowed him to appoint his own ministers. However, many French citizens did not trust that their monarch would abide by the terms of the constitution.

The War of 1792 Louis XVI and his family became captives in their palace. One night in June 1791, they disguised themselves and attempted to flee the country. After they were caught and forced to return to Paris, their captors discovered that the king had written a letter denouncing the Revolution. In addition, a group of émigrés, people who had left the country, and much of the French army loyal to the king, had urged Prussia and Austria to invade France to restore the monarchy to its previous power. Despite its internal struggles, the new French government declared war on those nations in 1792.

The Revolution's leaders convinced the French people that defending the country and supporting the Revolution were tied together. Working-class Parisians stormed the Tuileries Palace where the king's family lived in constant terror. The rioters killed 600 members of the king's guard and threatened the legislative assembly.

The Radical Revolution

By 1790, political parties had begun to spring up, organized as clubs. Foremost among these were the **Jacobins**. The Jacobins included members of the National Assembly and radical leaders such as **Maximilien de Robespierre** (1758–1794).

Following the summer violence of 1792, the National Assembly dissolved itself, calling for elections to form a new parliament called the **National Convention**. All adult men—but no women—would be permitted to vote. However, rumors had spread that prisoners planned to join up with the approaching Prussian army. Radical *sans-culottes* such as **Jean-Paul Marat** (1743–1793) whipped the people into a frenzy of violence known as the September Massacres, in which crowds attacked the prisons and slaughtered more than 1,000 inmates.

The Jacobins seized control of the National Convention from the more moderate **Girondins** and implemented the following changes in 1793:

- They abolished the monarchy and declared France a republic.

- They adopted a new calendar.

- They officially eradicated Christianity in France.

- They publically beheaded Louis XVI and Marie Antoinette by guillotine.

The other nations of Europe, horrified by the killing of the monarchs, allied against France. France stood alone, divided against itself. The Jacobins and Girondins couldn't compromise to rule the country and quell the violence. Fearful that the Revolution was in danger, the Jacobins began the **Reign of Terror**, a 10-month attempt to quash or kill the opponents of the Revolution, during which they guillotined 16,000 in Paris alone. The total in all of France reached 50,000.

The Committee of Public Safety When the Reign of Terror began, the **Committee of Public Safety** was created. It suspended the new constitution and controlled the National Convention. Robespierre and **Georges Danton** (1759–1794) headed the Committee. Its job was to defend against foreign attacks and domestic rebellions. Because of the threats to France from across Europe and from within its own borders, the Committee assumed great powers.

As Robespierre's vendettas against the counter-revolutionaries grew more extreme, people began to denounce the Committee for acting like a dictatorship. Those critics were arrested and executed. Danton, who strongly disapproved of the suppression of dissent, retreated from public life. However, soon Danton was drawn back into politics as a leader of the moderate opposition. For example, he argued against the complete elimination of Christianity. Robespierre had Danton arrested on charges of corruption and executed. At the guillotine, Danton said, "Show my head to the people. It is worth the trouble."

The Execution of Robespierre Eventually, Robespierre himself was challenged by opponents on the Committee of Public Safety. Some thought he was too radical while others considered him too moderate. He was sent to the guillotine in 1794. After the execution of Robespierre, the Reign of Terror subsided.

Revolutionary Armies and Mass Conscription

The Jacobins were an unstable force, but they did change French society. They promoted a strong sense of patriotism and created an enormous army. All able-bodied, unmarried men aged 18 to 25 were conscripted to serve, in a draft called the *levée en masse*. Despite some draft evasions and desertions, the army grew to more than 1,000,000 men by 1794—the largest Europe had seen.

Previous wars had been fought by professional soldiers of governments or dynasties. But this French force was an army created by a people's government, and the entire nation was involved in the war. Civilians were killed on a larger scale than ever before, and the door was opened to the total war of the modern world.

The French army was responsible for not only preserving the Revolution in France, but also for spreading its ideals through Europe. With fair pay and benefits, soldiers and their families were committed to the Revolutionary movement to spread wealth more equally and to abolish poverty. Families of soldiers received stipends. Men injured in battle were given generous veterans benefits. France's goal became not only to reinvent itself but also to spread its beliefs throughout Europe using its army of believers.

Women in the French Revolution

The Declaration of the Rights of Man and Citizen was aptly named since the French Revolution did not extend equal rights to women. Women couldn't vote, own property, make a will, file a lawsuit, or serve on a jury. However, in the early stages of the Revolution, women were hopeful about gaining rights. They participated by forming clubs and debating politics.

Olympe de Gouges Writer and reformer **Olympe de Gouges** (1748–1793) fought for the rights of women and minorities during the Revolution. Her most famous work was the **Declaration of the Rights of Woman and of the Female Citizen** (1791)—a response to the failure of Revolutionary ideals to extend to women. She once said, "Women have the right to mount the scaffold; they should likewise have the right to mount the rostrum [a podium for political speeches]." She herself often made speeches advocating divorce rights for women and the right of children whose parents were not married (as hers were not) to inherit parental property.

Though de Gouges was initially enthusiastic about the Revolution, its excesses dismayed her. As with many famous figures during this time, her death date gives a clue to her fate. She was beheaded by guillotine during the Reign of Terror for aligning herself with the moderate Girondists.

Credit: Alexander Kucharsky, portrait of Olympe de Gouges, c. 1790

Society of Republican Revolutionary Women The group known as the **Society of Republican Revolutionary Women** lasted only five months, but it raised issues important to women of the time. Founded in 1793, it consisted largely of working-class women who vowed to "rush to the defense of the Fatherland" and "to live for the Republic or to die for it." Women of the group wore decorated red bonnets to signal their membership, which often provoked violence against them. In 1793 during the Reign of Terror, when the Jacobins turned against one of the women's leaders, the society dissolved itself.

The De-Christianization of France

The National Assembly pursued a policy of de-Christianization as part of its attempt to establish a new order based on Enlightenment reason rather than faith. *Saint* was removed from all street names, the cathedral of Notre Dame was renamed the Temple of Reason, and a new republican calendar was adopted with year one beginning on September 22, 1792, the day on which the National Convention had proclaimed France a republic. Each year would have 12 months of three 10-day weeks. The remaining days were designated as festival days. The calendar also had the added benefit of reducing the number of nonworking days from 56 to 35. The new calendar faced much opposition from the beginning and eventually it was abandoned.

The Directory The Reign of Terror came to an end in 1794 with the arrest and execution of Robespierre. The moderate Girondins who had survived returned to power and wrote a new constitution that did the following:

- established France's first bicameral (two house) legislature

- gave executive power to a five–member committee called the **Directory** (or *Directoire*)

- allowed Parliament to appoint the members of the Directory

The Directory was yet another unsuccessful attempt at government. It lasted only four years and was riddled with corruption. It came to rely on the French army to enforce its authority. When radical factions such as the Jacobins protested, they were shut down by the army, now led by a young general named **Napoleon Bonaparte** (1769–1821). Napoleon and other generals wielded much of the national power as the French army pacified the country and also defeated the Prussians, Austrians, Spanish, and Dutch.

The Consulate In 1799, Napoleon staged a **coup d'état**, a sudden overthrow of the government. He abolished the Directory. He replaced it with a governing system called the **Consulate** in which three consuls, or chief magistrates, would lead the French government. Napoleon appointed himself one of the consuls. The system lasted just five years, from 1799 to1804.

The Revolution Outside of France

Napoleon's coup ended the era of the French Revolution and ushered in the Napoleonic era. Under Napoleon's military leadership, France dominated the European continent and spread its revolutionary ideals across the world. This sometimes resulted in France's own colonies fighting for independence against their colonial rulers.

The Haitian Independence Movement

As Napoleon was rising through the military ranks, the French Revolution inspired rebellions in other regions of the world. Partly, people felt inspired by the power of the Revolution's egalitarian ideals. In addition, while France was embroiled in domestic strife, its colonies were vulnerable to unrest. One major uprising began as a slave revolt in the French colony that would become the nation of Haiti.

Toussaint L'Ouverture (c.1743–1803) was a black man born a slave on Saint-Domingue, the western half of the Caribbean island of Hispaniola. Today the island is composed of Haiti and the Dominican Republic. L'Ouverture's master taught him to read and later freed him in the mid-1770s. L'Ouverture possessed several traits that made him a great leader. He was intelligent and literate and could speak several languages. Further, he was a skilled military commander and a shrewd diplomat. Like Napoleon, L'Ouverture was influenced by the Enlightenment and ascended to power during a revolution.

Toussaint L'Ouverture, the leader of the Haitian Revolution, used guerrilla tactics effectively against the French colonial rulers.

Credit: Getty Images

Slave Revolt Saint-Domingue was perhaps the world's most lucrative colony. The sugar it grew and exported made plantation owners very wealthy. However, 89 percent of its inhabitants were enslaved Africans who led horrible lives, as owners worked slaves to death and often used torture to punish them. One owner said it was more profitable to work a slave to death and buy another one than to treat a slave humanely.

In 1791, a slave rebellion spread through the colony. Though L'Ouverture was already free, he shared the slaves' rage and took command of the revolt. First, he shipped his wife, sons, and former master off the island and to safety. Then, he trained his troops in **guerrilla warfare** tactics. Guerrilla warfare involves quick, small military actions against larger regular army or police units.

While France fought its own Revolution, Spain and Britain invaded and tried to seize Saint-Domingue. Initially, the black rebel commanders joined with the Spaniards from the eastern side of Hispaniola, while the British occupied the island's coasts. France's hold on its most profitable colony was in danger. However, in 1794, the French National Convention did what neither Spain nor England would: they declared the slaves free. L'Ouverture returned to the French side.

Haiti After the Revolt The French governor of Saint-Domingue appointed L'Ouverture lieutenant governor. The British began losing ground, and the Spaniards were expelled from Saint-Domingue. L'Ouverture became a popular figure who advocated for reconciliation between the races. Though L'Ouverture forced people to work, the laborers were free and shared in plantation profits. The European plantation owners were permitted to return and run their businesses.

L'Ouverture pushed his rivals aside and appointed himself military governor over the newly renamed nation of Haiti. First, he signed trade treaties with Britain, much to the displeasure of France. Then, his forces invaded the Spanish portion of the island and freed all the slaves there. Napoleon distrusted L'Ouverture and began plotting against him. A French army arrived on the island, and L'Ouverture was tricked and arrested. He died in a French prison in 1803. However, his trusted followers feared France would reestablish slavery. They fought the French army and won, leading to Haiti's independence in 1804.

British Opponents of the French Revolution

Because France's Enlightenment impulses didn't match the violent reality of its actions, some condemned the French Revolution. One of the most influential writers of the time was the Englishman **Edmund Burke** (1729–1797). Burke wrote *Reflections on the Revolution in France.* In it, he cautioned Britain against engaging in the types of excesses occurring in France. Burke began writing his book in 1789 before the Reign of Terror; however, his warnings of anarchy came to pass. Britain managed to subdue its own radical reformers who demanded greater freedoms both at home and for British subjects in India. Britain's stable representative government and healthy economy allowed it to remain peaceful.

First Consul and Emperor

Born on the Italian island of Corsica, Napoleon Bonaparte came from humble circumstances. He went to French schools and the military academy. During the Revolution, he rose quickly as an officer, achieving the rank of brigadier general in 1794 at age 25. After saving the National Convention from the Parisian mobs, he defeated the Austrians in Italy. Returning to France as a hero, Napoleon was given command of an army to invade Egypt. Suffering defeats to the British on both land and sea, Napoleon returned to France, leading the coup to overthrow the Directory. He then became first consul of the three-member Consulate, the new governing body. In 1800, he led his army against Austrian forces in Italy and won. This victory cemented his power. He signed a peace treaty with Britain. By 1802, he had the government name him first consul for life, but that title was not enough to feed his hunger for power. In 1804, he crowned himself Napoleon I, emperor of France.

Domestic Reforms under Napoleon

Napoleon wanted to stabilize France after the violent excesses of the Revolution. One important step he took was to create the **Napoleonic Code**, a body of law governing people, property, and civil procedures. Prior to the Code's completion in 1801, France had a confusing, disorganized set of regional regulations based on feudal traditions. The Napoleonic Code reinforced revolutionary principles by recognizing the equality of all citizens under the law, guaranteeing religious toleration, and protecting property rights.

Centralized Government and the Merit System Napoleon also created a centralized national government, in which merit, rather than ancestry or social position, determined advancement. The French bureaucracy grew more efficient. For the first time it applied a tax system fair to all. When Napoleon became first consul, the government had a debt of 474 million francs and it had only 167,000 francs in the treasury. Napoleon hired professional tax collectors who maintained accurate records and didn't skim from the money they collected. Gradually, indirect taxes increased on various items. Reducing expenses and increasing revenues helped stabilized the government's budget.

Educational System Under Napoleon, France opened schools called *lycées* for boys ages 10 to 16. The middle class now had more educational opportunities, with the idea that these young men would then move into the military and the government. Scholarships were also given to those who could not afford to attend. The *lycées'* primary purpose was to indoctrinate an entire generation into the Napoleonic way of thinking.

Religious Reform The **Concordat of 1801**, an agreement between Napoleon and representatives of the Catholic Church in Paris and Rome, reconciled some of the animosity caused by the earlier eradication of Christianity and confiscation of Church lands:

- The Church was reestablished in France, but it gave up claims on its former land holdings (which had already been sold by auction).

- Napoleon would nominate bishops, who would appoint priests, but the government would pay both Catholic and Protestant clergy.

- Napoleon recognized that Catholicism was the religion of the majority of French citizens, without making it the official state religion.

Economic Reforms Napoleon's goals to promote economic health were straightforward: increase foreign trade and strive for full employment. Agriculture was a key to achieving both ends. Before the Revolution, France's agricultural system was so antiquated that the country imported staples such as butter and cheese. By 1812, France had become an exporter of these goods. Textile exports boomed as well. Napoleon discouraged unions and closely regulated the trade guilds, thinking that unhappy workers in unions could plant the seeds of rebellion. Instead, he focused on improving worker conditions to preempt any desire to unionize.

Curtailment of Rights under Napoleon

Napoleon succeeded in creating national laws, reforming the economy, and affirming the redistribution of land once held by the Catholic Church. However, he was no longer a proponent of liberty, equality, and fraternity. To maintain power and build his empire, he used secret police, censored free speech, and limited individual rights. Abroad, he reinstituted slavery on the French islands of Martinique and Guadalupe in the Caribbean. In name, France was a republic that became an empire. In reality, it was a dictatorship.

Secret Police During Napoleon's reign, royalist and radical plotters threatened the government and its leaders. The man responsible for uncovering these plots was Minister of Police **Joseph Fouché** (1759–1820), who acted as chief of espionage. Fouché ran a vast network of spies and was adept at gathering and using information. He even kept a dossier on Napoleon.

Fouché, a former priest, hated the Catholic Church and refused to support the Concordat of 1801. His strong views cost him his job at one point, but his skill in discovering dissenters made him valuable to Napoleon. Fouché assured Napoleon that all possible threats to the emperor were eliminated— either publically or privately. Some innocent people were assassinated simply to send a message to potential plotters. Napoleon didn't worry about these deaths. He believed that the ends of maintaining order justified such means.

Censorship and Restrictions Press censorship became more and more important to Napoleon as he came under increased public criticism. Paris had four major newspapers, each of which was required to maintain an on-staff censor to suppress the expression of opposition to Napoleon's politics or to his military expansions across Europe.

Limitation of Women's Rights Under Napoleon's reign, women did not have the same rights as men. For example, husbands had the legal power to:

- control their wives' wages

- control the property their wives brought into marriage

- divorce wives for adultery (even have them imprisoned)

- control all jointly held property

- control their wives' ability to file suits in civil court, take loans, or sell property

Further, while men could obtain a divorce easily, women could do so only with difficulty. All these rules were part of the Napoleonic Code.

Spread of Revolutionary Ideals across Europe

Between 1799 and 1815, Napoleon fought a shifting alliance of European countries during the period of the **Napoleonic Wars**. Using his large army of patriotic citizens, Napoleon won nearly all his early battles against Austria, Prussia, and Russia. By 1806, much of central and southern Europe was under French control.

As Napoleon's armies traveled across Europe, they spread ideals of the Revolution. They proved that ordinary citizens could overthrow a monarchy and strip the aristocracy of their traditional privileges. Peasants now owned lands formerly controlled by the Church, signaling the end of serfdom in France. When Haitian slaves rebelled, France had abolished slavery there. When the Haitians learned that the French had reintroduced slavery on the nearby island of Guadeloupe they revolted against French rule, and in 1804 won their independence. Despite setbacks and missteps, the trajectory was clear: The old order was ending and the time of the common people had arrived. This notion changed European politics and societies forever.

Nationalistic Responses

The period from 1804, when Napoleon crowned himself emperor, until 1814, when he abdicated for the first time (but soon returned to power), became known as the First Empire. Napoleon abolished the Holy Roman Empire and redrew the map of Europe. The armies of Napoleon spread the ideas of the French Revolution, abolishing feudalism as they conquered territory. He heavily taxed conquered peoples to spare the French while he continued his wars. Unable to defeat Britain militarily, Napoleon created the **Continental System**, a blockade of British goods being shipped to European ports.

Napoleon's actions awakened a new identity in the people he conquered. People began to feel a stronger sense of **nationalism,** a pride in one's cultural heritage that later led to a desire to have a single political state for that culture. Before the spread of nationalism, people identified more with their city or region than with all people who shared their culture. Their political loyalty was more to an individual ruler, such as a king, than to the state in general. People commonly were loyal to a ruler who did not even speak their language.

Guerrilla War in Spain Napoleon invaded Spain in 1808, forcing King Charles IV to abdicate. Unwilling to bend to French rule, the Spanish were joined by British troops to fight the French. The British effectively used small bands of Spanish fighters to harass the French army. These small groups used guerrilla tactics to harass the French army of 200,000 men. By 1814, Napoleon had lost what was called the Peninsular War.

Nationalism in German States Nationalism also arose in German states, especially Prussia, where intellectuals called for cultural nationalism based on the unity of the German people. Prussia, which had been crushed by the army of Napoleon, undertook a series of political and military reforms. These included the abolition of serfdom and the creation of a larger standing army.

Russian Scorched Earth Policy Napoleon, declaring he wanted to free Poland from Russian power and hoping to end Russian support for Great Britain, invaded Russia in June 1812 with an army of about 600,000. Russia had an army of about equal size, but had the advantage of knowing the land and how to survive the harsh Russian winters.

As French forces moved deeper into Russia, the Russian army made the strategic choice to retreat, never allowing the French to defeat them decisively. Further, the Russians burned everything behind them. This was called a **scorched earth policy** and prevented the French army from living off the land. Napoleon managed to reach Moscow, but the city had been evacuated and was ablaze. Lacking food and supplies, Napoleon began to retreat in October. However, his decision to retreat came too late. As the Russian winter set in,

French troops and their horses began dying from cold and starvation. Fewer than 40,000 French soldiers returned home. French **hegemony**, or authority over others, had ended.

End of the Napoleonic Era

As his army retreated during the Russian winter, Napoleon learned of an attempted coup back in France. He was also defeated by a revived opposing coalition led by Prussia and Austria. Napoleon was forced to abdicate in 1814 and sent to the Mediterranean island of Elba. He returned to France in 1815. He raised yet another army, only to be defeated at the Battle of Waterloo in present-day Belgium. He abdicated a second time and this time was exiled to St. Helena, a remote island in the South Atlantic Ocean, where he remained until his death. Approximately 750,000 French soldiers and citizens died from warfare during the time Napoleon had pursued his dreams of domination.

From 1814 to 1815, the Congress of Vienna met, guided by two principles: legitimacy and balance of power. The leaders of Austria, Great Britain, Prussia, and Russia met under the leadership of Prince Klemens von Metternich of Austria. Their goals were simple. First, redraw Europe's borders to where they were prior to 1792. Second, restore legitimate monarchs to the thrones of Europe. Guided by the ideology of conservatism, their efforts, both internationally and domestically, brought an era of stability to Europe.

MONUMENT TO NAPOLEON!

Napoleon was portrayed by artists in contrasting ways—as a noble Roman emperor, a tyrannical murderer, or an inspiring general—depending on which aspect of his life they wanted to emphasize.

Credit: Getty Images

Napoleon's historical importance is undeniable. But different historians depict him as various combinations of hero, tyrant, military genius, and heir to the French Revolution.

An Opportunist Conservative British historian and journalist Paul Johnson argued in a 2002 biography that Napoleon was merely an opportunist. Though Johnson gave him credit for his early military successes, he ascribes Napoleon's ultimate political and diplomatic failures to continued military campaigns.

A Machiavellian French historian and journalist Laurent Joffrin concluded in a 2004 article that "Despite the blood and death, despite the wars and repression, his taste for rule and his mania for state building have meant that the despot [Napoleon] is seen as the favorite dictator of the French republic," meaning they like him better than Robespierre, best remembered for subjecting the French to the Reign of Terror. Joffrin explained that Napoleon accomplished more in three years than any of his predecessors. However, the beneficial results resulted from Napoleon's anger "more suited to the boxing ring" than an administrative office. He once threatened an opponent with a whip. Joffrin also noted Napoleon's use of repression to reestablish rule of law. In conquered territories, this meant executions without trials, burning villages, and imprisoning opponents. In France, repression included setting up spy networks in order to manipulate opinion and keep Napoleon informed.

Despite Napoleon's flaws, Joffrin saw some positive accomplishments. He explained that the Civil Code was Napoleon's proudest achievement and that "if he made war, it was only in order to govern better." But in the end, according to Joffrin, Napoleon's rationalism broke down and personal glory took root.

A Complex Hero By 2004, with the publication of Napoleon's complete correspondences, an even more complex picture of the French leader emerged. Oxford historian Michael Broers attempted to revisit the story of Napoleon, after having already written *Europe Under Napoleon* (1996) and analyzing Napoleon's elite paramilitary force—the *Gendarmerie*—in 1999, with the publication of the article "The Napoleonic Police and Their Legacy." In these earlier works, Broers described a Europe that only knew the horrors of war. French soldiers were hated, because they were seen as not fighting for universal revolutionary ideals, but for the nation of France, a France that had an ugly history of war with its neighbors. But as Napoleon took charge, the battle lines moved, and the "inner empire" (France) was free from war, and from 1801–1812, it remained stable and secure, leaving Napoleon free to establish stable civilian administration, expand his prefect system, implement the Napoleonic Code, end guilds, and protect freedoms.

However, the "outer empire"—Spain in particular—resisted stability despite the efforts of the *Gendarmerie*, and remained unstable even after the defeat of Napoleon, whereas the inner empire quickly recovered and continued pursuing the ideas of the Napoleonic Code. Life in the inner empire was regulated by a clear, rational, and usually fair legal code. All these characteristics of the Napoleonic Empire are still at work in Europe because they remain effective. Broers even suggested that Napoleon ingrained these ideals and values so successfully that they remain central to the values of the European Union today.

Already noted for fair treatment of Napoleon, with new sources at his disposal, Broers described the political philosophy of Napoleon as based on the goal of persuading reactionaries to support the new regime *(ralliament)* and joining it *(amalgame)*. While Joffrin did credit Napoleon for listening to his advisers early, he stressed Napoleon's desire to be the one to always make decisions and increasingly did so with little advice; whereas Broers used the letters to document Napoleon's consistent effort to seek the counsel of his advisers, govern by committee, and promote based on talent. Much like Johnson, Broers concluded that Napoleon's success was military, but not because of the land conquered, instead, because of his successful political policies of *ralliament* and *amalgame*.

KEY TERMS BY THEME

Governance

French Revolution

republic

Reign of Terror

ancien régime

Louis XVI

Estates-General

Marie Antoinette

tithes

National Assembly

Tennis Court Oath

pamphleteers

Bastille Day

The Great Fear

Declaration of the Rights of Man and Citizen

Civil Constitution of the Clergy

departments

Jacobins

Maximilien de Robespierre

National Convention

Jean-Paul Marat

Girondins

Reign of Terror

Committee of Public Safety

Georges Danton

levée en masse

Olympe de Gouges

Declaration of the Rights of Woman and of the Female Citizen

Society of Republican Revolutionary Women

Directory

Napoleon Bonaparte

coup d'état

consulate

Toussaint L'Ouverture

guerrilla warfare

Edmund Burke

Napoleonic Code

lycées

Concordat of 1801

Joseph Fouché

Napoleonic Wars

Continental System

nationalism

scorched earth policy

Social Structure

bourgeoisie

cahiers

sans-culottes

hegemony

Questions 1–3 refer to the following passage.

"The representatives of the French people, organized as a National Assembly, believing that the ignorance, neglect, or contempt of the rights of man are the sole cause of public calamities and of the corruption of governments, have determined to set forth in a solemn declaration the natural, unalienable, and sacred rights of man, in order that this declaration, being constantly before all the members of the Social body, shall remind them continually of their rights and duties; in order that the acts of the legislative power, as well as those of the executive power, may be compared at any moment with the objects and purposes of all political institutions and may thus be more respected, and, lastly, in order that the grievances of the citizens, based hereafter upon simple and incontestable principles, shall tend to the maintenance of the constitution and redound to the happiness of all. Therefore, the National Assembly recognizes and proclaims, in the presence and under the auspices of the Supreme Being, the following rights of man and of the citizen:

1. Men are born and remain free and equal in rights. Social distinctions may be founded only upon the general good.

2. The aim of all political association is the preservation of the natural and imprescriptible rights of man. These rights are liberty, property, security, and resistance to oppression.

3. The principle of all sovereignty resides essentially in the nation. No body nor individual may exercise any authority which does not proceed directly from the nation."

Declaration of the Rights of Man and Citizen, the National
Assembly of France, August 26, 1789

1. The governing body that approved this declaration represented which sector of French society?

   a) First Estate

   b) Second Estate

   c) Third Estate

   d) Estates-General

2. With which statement would the writers of this declaration most agree?

   a) No king or legislative body can truly recognize the rights of man.

   b) Christians will respect religious leaders who address the rights of man.

   c) Kings and legislatures must respect the rights of men and women equally.

   d) Citizens will respect a government that recognizes the rights of man.

3. This declaration is most similar in meaning and intent to which of the following?

   a) The English Bill of Rights

   b) Machiavelli's *The Prince*

   c) The American Declaration of Independence

   d) Burke's *Reflections on the Revolution in France*

Questions 4–5 refer to the political cartoon below.

In English, the caption means "Good-bye Bastille." This art was created in 1789.

Credit: Library of Congress

4. What is the context in which this cartoon was drawn?

   a) The Bastille symbolized the members of the Third Estate.

   b) An attack on the Bastille marked the start of the French Revolution.

   a) The king had moved into the Bastille for safety.

   b) The Bastille was where the Reign of Terror was carried out.

5. What do the the two figures on the right who appear to be fighting probably symbolize?

   a) The king and the common people

   b) France and the Holy Roman Empire

   c) Protestants and Catholics

   d) The nobles and the clergy

Questions 6–8 refer to the following passage.

"Chapter VI: Of the Respective Rights and Duties of Married Persons

214. The wife is obliged to live with her husband, and to follow him to every place where he may judge it convenient to reside: the husband is obliged to receive her, and to furnish her with every necessity for the wants of life, according to his means and station…

217. A wife, although …separate in property, cannot give, pledge, or acquire by free or chargeable title, without the concurrence of her husband in the act, or his consent in writing…

267. The provisional management of the children shall rest with the husband, petitioner, or defendant, in the suit for divorce, unless it be otherwise ordered for the greater advantage of the children, on petition of either the mother, or the family, or the government commissioner…

1421. The husband alone administers the property of the community. He may sell it, alienate and pledge it without the concurrence of his wife…

1427. The wife cannot bind herself nor engage the property of the community, even to free her husband from prison, or for the establishment of their children in case of her husband's absence, until she shall have been thereto authorized by the law…

1549. The husband alone has the management of the property in dowry… He has alone the right …to enjoy the fruits and interest thereof, and to receive reimbursements of capital. Nevertheless, it may be agreed, by the marriage contract, that the wife shall receive annually… a part of her revenues for her maintenance and personal wants."

Code Napoleon, 1804

6. Which best describes the historical context for understanding the creation of this document?

   a) Napoleon thought women should have the same property rights as men, but not the same political rights.

   b) Napoleon hoped to overturn advances in women's rights made during the Revolution.

   c) Napoleon believed that granting rights to women would undercut positive changes made in the Revolution.

   d) Napoleon planned to push for rapid progress in gaining rights for French women.

7. Which best describes France's system of laws just before the implementation of the Napoleonic Code?

    a) A disorganized set of laws and regulations based on feudal traditions

    b) A compromise set of laws and regulations that maintained special rights and privileges for the monarch

    c) An organized system of laws and regulations based on Revolutionary principles

    d) A system of laws and regulations that recognized the complete equality of men and women in France

8. The passage represents the continuation of which view of women that was commonly held prior to the French Revolution?

    a) The wife can take over the family business if the husband dies.

    b) The wife is economically dependent on the husband.

    c) The wife is at the level of a slave in the family.

    d) The wife is an equal economic partner in marriage.

SHORT-ANSWER QUESTIONS

1. Use the passage below to answer all parts of the question that follows.

"The evil which besets us," declared Jeanbon Saint-André on 1 August, "is that we have no government." As a member of the Committee of Public Safety, he ought to have known. But when Danton proposed, in the same session, that the Committee be recognized formally as France's provisional government, the Convention would not agree . . . It never did become the government, or enjoy undisputed executive authority. But in the course of the next twelve months it was to give the country the leadership to mobilize its resources with unprecedented assurance, and put the crisis of 1793 behind it.

William Doyle, *Oxford History of the French Revolution* 1989

    a) Describe ONE specific argument used by people who thought Jacobin policies expressed the ideals of the French Revolution.

    b) Describe ONE specific argument used by people who thought Jacobin policies undermined the ideals of the French Revolution.

    c) Explain how Doyle views the Committee of Public Safety.

2. Use the image below to answer all parts of the question that follows.

J. B. Belley was a leader in the Hatitian Revolution who also served in the French government. In this portrait, he is standing in front of a bust of Guillame-Thomas Raynal, a writer who supported the French Revolution.

Credit: Anne-Louis Girodet de Roucy-Trioson. Wikimedia Commons

a) Describe ONE way that the above image shows the influence of the French Revolution on the Haitian Revolution.

b) Describe ONE way that conditions in Haiti were a cause of one of the events Belley was involved in.

c) Explain ONE effect of the Haitian Revolution on Europe's existing political order.

LONG ESSAY QUESTIONS

1. Evaluate how new Enlightenment ideas were used during the French Revolution to challenge existing hierarchies in France.

2. Evaluate the extent to which the French Revolution and reign of Napoleon altered existing hierarchies in Europe.

REFLECT ON THE CHAPTER ESSENTIAL QUESTION

1. In one to three paragraphs, explain how events in France challenged the existing political and social order and provoked nationalism.

Napoleon is commonly portrayed as short. Was he? The answer depends on the context. Compared to average men in France today, he was short. However, compared to average men in France in the 1790s, he was not. When you write as a historian, placing events in context is very important. To contextualize means to look at an idea, event, person, or situation together with everything that relates to it. Only when events are shown in context can you show historical themes and patterns accurately.

Contextualization is the skill of presenting historical facts and processes in relationship to other historical facts and processes. These other facts and processes provide the background to help historians recognize themes and patterns as well as to recognize what is significant.

For each prompt below, select the two *statements that best state the context for understanding it.*

1. Analyze the impact of the French Revolution on European politics up to the 1848 Revolutions.

   a. The French Revolution changed French society dramatically, and it had a great impact on colonial revolutions in the Americas.

   b. The French Revolution was part of a larger movement toward self-government that included the replacement of monarchies with republican governments and the decline of feudalism.

   c. The French Revolution was inspired by Enlightenment ideals and in turn inspired later revolutions in other European countries, particularly Italy, Belgium, Netherlands, and Austria.

2. Evaluate Napoleon Bonaparte's abilities as a military and political leader.

   a. Napoleon desired a stable and dominant French empire, so he exploited military power, information, diplomacy, and economic might to vanquish all opponents of France.

   b. When Napoleon returned to power in 1815, the United Kingdom, Austria, Russia, and Prussia joined forces to form the Seventh Coalition—the combined armies that defeated Napoleon at the Battle of Waterloo.

   c. Napoleon rose as a military leader during the French Revolution when he became associated with the Jacobins, a pro-democracy political group that influenced his later vision for a just and equitable French society.

Another application of context involves sources. When examining a source, think about the setting under which it was written.

- Consider the author: Who created this source and what was the person's point of view?
- Consider the place and time: When and where was the evidence produced? How does this affect the meaning?

For the following question, identify the three documents that best provide context for the prompt.

3. Why was the French Revolution significant?

   a. letters written by Napoleon explaining why he decided to crown himself emperor

   b. the Civil Constitution of the Clergy

   c. a map of the Louisiana territory sold to the United States to finance French wars

   d. an audio recording and printed lyrics for the French national anthem, "The Marseillaise"

   e. the Declaration of the Rights of Man and Citizen approved by the National Assembly of France in 1789

The Arc de Triomphe in Paris includes this dramatic frieze, which was created in 1832 by François Rude. It shows Lady Liberty calling on volunteers to defend the French Revolution in a time of crisis, 1792.

Credit: Getty Images

9

Commerce in a Worldwide Network

"It is not by augmenting the capital of the country, but by rendering a greater part of that capital active and productive than would otherwise be so, that the most judicious operations of banking can increase the industry of the country."

— Adam Smith, *The Wealth of Nations*

Essential Question: How did the expansion of European commerce accelerate the growth of a worldwide economic network in early modern Europe?

The Emergence of a Market Economy

Modern Europe began to emerge around 1500 with the expansion of trade and colonization. During the 17th and 18th centuries, life for ordinary Europeans changed even more dramatically because of the **Commercial Revolution**, a period of unprecedented expansion of commerce and trade. The seeds for this were originally sown by a desire for silks and spices from Asia, which drove advances in shipping and exploration during the 15th and 16th centuries. Countries bordering the Atlantic Ocean took advantage of their port cities to conduct trade that sent them around the southern tip of Africa to Asia and across the Atlantic to the Americas. The nations that prospered most during this period were those that established colonies in these far-flung regions.

Greater Prosperity

Colonies provided new opportunities for trade. They were a source of precious metals, raw materials, and agricultural products. They also provided markets for Europe's finished goods. This new system of commerce allowed businesses to thrive in the 17th and 18th centuries. Institutions such as charter companies, insurance companies, and national banks evolved to provide investment capital and spread the risks inherent in overseas trade. Governments passed laws to regulate trade, protect property rights, and manage taxation.

Over a remarkably short time, economies shifted from a feudal model of traditional farming to a system driven by wages and consumer demand. The more demand for products grew, the more quickly technology advanced to supply that demand. This, in turn, fed further consumption as goods became cheaper, more plentiful, and more easily transported.

The physical and material well-being of Europeans rose to a level never before seen, but these changes came at a price. As European nations competed to conquer and colonize, they came into conflict with native populations and with one another. The transatlantic slave trade resulted in the deaths and dislocation of millions of Africans. Europe became more sharply divided between the wealthier Atlantic nations engaged in overseas trade and the more traditional central and eastern European nations that had less economic growth. Despite these challenges, the European Commercial Revolution laid the groundwork for the Industrial Revolution and modern society.

Mercantilism and Colonies

Europe dominated the worldwide economic network, beginning with its voyages of discovery in the 16th century and continuing on through the 19th century. Two major factors enabled it to do so: mercantilism and colonization.

Mercantilism From the 15th through the 18th centuries, European nations believed that their economic growth and well-being were best served by following a policy of **mercantilism**, which limited imports by using tariffs and taxes on foreign products and maximized exports by forcing its colonies to trade only with the ruling nation. (For more about mercantilism, see Chapter 3 and Chapter 7.) Such policies brought a positive balance of trade and thus boosted monetary reserves, the accumulation of gold and silver in the treasury. The increase in reserves enabled a country to pay for a strong military. The goal was to exploit the cheap labor and raw materials from colonies in order to secure advantages over rival nations.

more export than import

Colonization Mercantilism drove European nations to colonize large swaths of the globe. **Colonization** permitted nations to increase their power by inhabiting new territories—or by gaining political or economic control—usually through force. In general, colonial empires were established through settlements in the New World and through trading empires in Asia and Africa. England, Spain, and France had both settlements and trading empires. Five colonial powers (identified below by their present names) divided the world:

- Portugal claimed Brazil.

- Spain claimed Latin America (other than Brazil) and the Philippines.

- Netherlands claimed parts of Indonesia.

- France claimed parts of Canada and the central part of what is today the U.S.

- England claimed parts of eastern North America, eastern Australia, and New Zealand.

- All five claimed islands in the Caribbean.

- Russia did not colonize, but it did expand its borders significantly from Eastern Europe across to the Pacific Ocean.

Colonies in Latin America were mined for vast amounts of silver and gold. *caused inflation*
Those in Canada and what is now the northern United States were a source of timber, fish, and furs. Colonies in the Caribbean and what is now the southern United States provided plantation crops such as sugar, rice, and cotton. Those in Asia and Africa supplied silks, teas, spices, and minerals. Everywhere, native people were used for cheap labor and used as a market where colonizing powers could sell finished goods.

The Transatlantic Slave-Labor System

As a result of their geographic isolation, native peoples in the Americas had not engaged in the types of exchanges that had been taking place for centuries among Europe, Africa, and Asia. One extremely deadly exchange between Europe and the Americas, however, involved disease and antibodies. Anywhere the first European explorers landed, native populations without immunities died off from smallpox, measles, typhus, and other common pathogens. Those who survived were enslaved but were not well suited to the hot, exhausting labor of plantation farming or mining.

As the deaths of Native Americans increased, Europeans looked for a new source of labor. They turned to Africa.

From the 15th to the 19th centuries, an estimated 12 million to 15 million Africans were forcibly transported to the Western Hemisphere. Millions more Africans died during raids, wars, and the overseas passage. Approximately 5 million Africans were taken to Brazil; another 5 million went to the sugar plantations of the Caribbean. About 10 percent were transported to North America. Britain engaged in more slave trade than the other major European colonial powers, transporting 2 million to 3 million enslaved people in the 18th century alone. However, influenced by the ideals of the Enlightenment, in 1807 Britain became one of the first European states to ban slave trading.

The Middle Passage The **Middle Passage** was the name given to the transatlantic slave-trade journey from West Africa to the West Indies. Raiding parties led by Europeans and Africans captured free people and forced them into captivity. The slaves were held in dungeons along the Guinea Coast, sometimes for up to a year, until a ship could carry them to the New World. While awaiting their fate, the captives were subject to epidemics, physical and sexual abuse, pirate raids, storms, and raids by hostile tribes.

Once aboard ships, the slaves were packed in rows below decks. Chained to platforms stacked in tiers, each person had a space about the size of a coffin: 6 feet long, 16 inches wide, 3 feet high. It was impossible for them to stand up or turn over in these bunks where they stayed nearly 24 hours a day. Many grew sick from dysentery and other diseases due to bad sanitation and hideous fumes from a lack of ventilation in the hold. Others mutinied or tried to commit suicide by jumping overboard or by refusing to eat. If the ship's progress stalled due to bad weather or a lack of wind, water and food rations were cut so much that many slaves starved. In one case, when water ran low, the British captain of the slave ship *Zong* threw 133 slaves overboard to save

The murder of slaves on the *Zong* was among the most infamous events of the transatlantic slave trade.

Credit: Shutterstock

the remainder and then filed an insurance claim on his "cargo." So many bodies were tossed into the ocean during these journeys that sharks learned to follow the slave ships.

Triangle Trade The trade linking Europe, Africa, and America is known as the **triangle trade** because the three parts of the route—from Europe to Africa, from Africa to the Americas, and from the Americas back to Europe—traced a triangular shape. From the 16th through the early 19th centuries, the name became synonymous with a form of colonial commerce that managed imports and exports to enrich European slave-trading nations.

Trade winds caused European ships to need to sail south before trying to cross the Atlantic Ocean. This became the first leg of history's most famous triangular trade route, as traders picked up captives in Africa. On the second leg of the journey, the ships transported the slaves from Africa to the New World, where they were sold or traded for the products that other slaves had produced: sugar, molasses, cotton, rice, indigo, tobacco, hemp, and rum. These items were then shipped from the Americas back to Europe on the final leg of the journey. The raw materials and crops were sold and the profits used to purchase finished goods—such as cloth, knives, guns, tools, copper, and brass items—which were sold back to the colonies or traded in Africa for additional enslaved people.

Plantation Economies in the Americas Many European families practiced primogeniture—the system in which the oldest son inherited everything. One result was that ambitious younger sons left home to become prosperous. Many emigrated to the Americas and established **plantations**, or agricultural estates that used mostly slave labor to produce cash crops. In the Caribbean, this meant sugar production. Because the production of sugar was so labor intensive, operating expenses were high. Many plantation owners believed that working slaves to death was more profitable than providing humane living conditions. During the 18th century, one-third of newly imported slaves died within three years of their arrival.

Plantations helped build family fortunes and dictated social and economic roles on the islands. Plantation owners controlled the legislature and militia and even the public calendar, all of which revolved around sugar production. By the 1830s, Britain acquired additional plantation territories following the Napoleonic Wars. The increased supply sent sugar prices down. That, along with reduced demand and increased anti-slavery sentiment, eventually weakened the Caribbean plantation economies.

Impact on European Consumers and Markets

The effect of a steady flow of raw materials from trade with the Americas, India, and Asia changed life for European consumers. Slave labor kept costs low. Improved technologies converted these raw materials into plentiful finished goods. Affordability and abundance led people to desire improved social status—which they could display by having beautiful furnishings and clothes and all the latest available conveniences. The trade products that most expanded purchasing opportunities for European consumers were sugar, silks and other fabrics, tobacco, rum, tea, and coffee.

Sugar Sugar, more than any other product, drove transatlantic trade, colonialism, and slavery. It was a rare commodity for Europeans before 1492. But as Britain established Caribbean plantations, it became easily available. People started to consider it as a necessity. Plantation owners bought provisions from British manufacturers, so factory owners benefited as well.

Britain protected its sugar growers with mercantilist policies. For example, the 17th century **Navigation Acts** protected the monopoly to sell British goods in the empire. Sugar tariffs helped enrich the British government but were a source of controversy as they raised consumer prices. The Navigation Acts and the tariffs were not repealed until the mid-1800s.

Fabrics Britain specialized in cotton and wool production for the masses, spurring the Industrial Revolution. France had its own textile industry, geared toward the wealthy. France became Europe's leading silk producer. Silk had long been a closely guarded treasure in China until the Silk Road linked China to the Roman Empire in the 2nd century B.C.E. But it was not until the Industrial Revolution that weaving silk became more feasible for the French. In 1801, **Joseph-Marie Jacquard** (1752–1834) invented a machine to create patterned silk textiles for luxury clothing and furnishings.

Because working conditions on sugar plantations were so harsh, the life expectancy for slaves there was about 10 years shorter than for slaves working on tobacco plantations.

Credit: Getty Images

Tobacco Tobacco was originally introduced to Europe by the Spanish, who learned to smoke it from Native Americans. By the end of the 16th century, tobacco use had spread across Europe. The Spanish and the British originally grew tobacco in the Caribbean, where it became a key item in the triangle trade. Later, Spain and Portugal expanded operations into Cuba and Brazil. In the early 17th century, **John Rolfe** (1585–1622) planted tobacco in Virginia, where it became an economic force for colonial development. In 1624, the Jamestown colony sold 200,000 pounds of tobacco to England. By 1680, the yearly total was more than 100 times that. European governments levied taxes on tobacco and attempted to maintain trading monopolies through tariffs.

Rum Britain and France first made rum—a profitable use for sugar by-products— in the 17th century on their sugar islands, and European colonists quickly started drinking it. By the 18th century, British rum makers sold their product throughout Europe and North America. However, three developments made Britain's rum trade less profitable:

- the American Revolution

- competition from Europe and the United States

- the growing tide of anti-slavery sentiment

At the same time, rising demand in France's cities helped Martinique become a major rum producer.

Rum production led to a second trade triangle: New England merchants bought molasses from the Caribbean and distilled it into rum. They shipped the rum to Africa in exchange for slaves, and then they traded the slaves in the Caribbean for more molasses.

Tea Tea was first imported as a rarity from China in the early 1600s. However, the use of tea in Britain increased two hundredfold by 1750. The British government levied a tax on tea that accounted for about 10 percent of the nation's annual revenues. British mercantilist policies prevented competition from the Dutch and the Russians but also brought protests. In the American colonies and elsewhere, tea smuggling became widespread to avoid taxes. In 1773, Britain tried to help the struggling British East India Company by passing the Tea Act, which allowed the company to sell directly to North America rather than warehousing its tea in England. Colonists, however, were still required to pay a tax on the tea. Their famous tax protest—the Boston Tea Party—helped spark the American Revolution.

Coffee Coffee was unknown in Europe before the 16th century, until an Arab pilgrim introduced it to traders. The Dutch were the first Europeans to enter the coffee business, with plantations in Sri Lanka, Ceylon, and Java. The French grew coffee in the Caribbean, and the Spanish and Portuguese grew it in Central and South America. Following the protests against Britain's tea monopolies, coffee became America's hot beverage of choice.

Agricultural Exchanges and European Nutrition

A host of new foods from the New World became part of Europeans' diets. While Europeans once had only wheat as a major source of carbohydrates, after the late 15th century, they had corn, potatoes, and cassava. An acre of any one of these New World crops yielded twice as many calories as wheat. Other new foods included avocados, beans, cacao, chilies, papayas, peanuts, pineapples, pumpkins, squashes, sweet potatoes, tomatoes, and turkeys. This exchange of crops across the Atlantic and around the world enriched both Europe and its colonies and provided the following benefits:

- Starvation, which had previously limited Europe's population growth, largely disappeared. The productive and plentiful potato crop helped alleviate the famines that had plagued Europe for centuries. A half-acre planted with potatoes could feed a family for a year.

- People's tastes and dietetic diversity expanded, contributing to better health and longevity.

- Europe's soaring population resulted in greater immigration to the New World and more agricultural trade.

- Old World crops thrived in the Americas, giving the colonists even better food choices than their counterparts in Europe.

Opportunities from Foreign Trade

Colonial expansion and trade fueled economic and social growth in Europe from the 16th through the 19th centuries. On the import side, European factories and industries benefited from the influx of raw materials, and people's health improved with new food crops. Cheap labor—whether from slaves or from indentured servants—helped generate massive fortunes and huge amounts of taxable wealth. On the export side, mercantilist monopolies and tariffs secured ready markets for European finished goods. Europe was growing into an economic powerhouse.

Worldwide Commercial Rivalries

With European nations engaged in ongoing wars for land and power on the continent, it was no wonder that these struggles spilled over in a quest to control the rest of the world. A combination of military and economic factors influenced commercial rivalries in the 18th century:

- the worldwide growth of trade and mercantilism

- the dominance of Europe's growing industrial power

- a rising need to find markets for machine-made goods

- a reliance on the use of Africans to ensure European wealth and industrialization

- the build-up of the British and French navies to control the seas, resulting in an increase in naval wars

- the declining naval dominance of Spain, Portugal, and the Netherlands

European Sea Powers

Increasingly, European powers jockeyed for power over trade between Africa and the Americas. Whether ships carried human cargo, raw materials, or finished goods, they were targets for piracy. This included attacks by **privateers**, armed ships licensed to attack other nations' vessels.

From 1701 to 1763, the greatest of these naval rivalries was between Britain and France. By establishing colonial settlements and trade outposts, they vied for control—either directly or by controlling trade—in North America and the Caribbean, as well as in Africa, India, and Asia.

Rivalries in the East Indies

With the land routes connecting Europe with India and East Asia long controlled by the Ottomans, European powers turned to the sea. During the 15th and 16th centuries, Spain and Portugal were rivals in colonizing and exploiting the resources around the world. The Spanish ruled Mexico, most of South America, parts of Africa, and the Philippines. The Portuguese ruled Brazil, parts of Africa, and key ports in India and China.

The Dutch In the 17th century, the Dutch Republic rose to power with a strong fleet of ships and the creation of the **Dutch East India Company**, known by its Dutch initials as the VOC. The VOC sold shares to stockholders and was considered the first transnational corporation. Through a series of confrontations with the Portuguese, the VOC established a principle of freedom of the seas for trade. They instituted a trading monopoly in the Indonesian archipelago as well as in hundreds of other places. However, by 1799, the VOC had collapsed, in part because of competition from a strong British fleet.

The British During the 18th century, the British established their own **East India Company** to trade with India, which at that time was the world's leading producer of textiles and spices. A combination of taxation, control of the local textile and shipbuilding industries, and trade restrictions helped Britain support its own industrial and economic growth, but the British presence in India devastated that country's economy and autonomy.

The Costs of Wealth

Throughout this period of history, Europe's commercial dominance grew because of **human capital** and rapid advances in technology. Human capital refers to the skills and resources of people and groups in a society. Europe's commercial success accelerated the growth of a worldwide economic network. However, growth came at a steep human cost for native peoples.

Dutch-made coins used in the East Indies included Arabic writing because of the strong influence of Islam in the region.

Credit: Getty Images

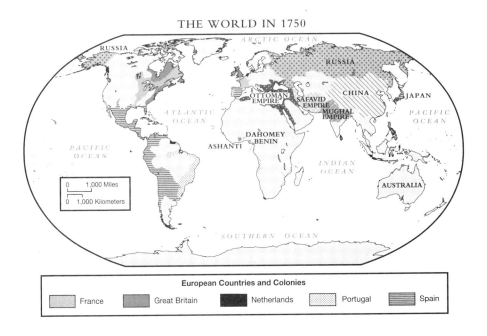

THE WORLD IN 1750

European Countries and Colonies

France | Great Britain | Netherlands | Portugal | Spain

Labor and Trade Freed from Traditional Restrictions

Nowhere did commercial changes occur as dramatically as in Britain. What enabled Britain to develop a market economy and a high level of prosperity? Britain enjoyed a combination of factors that created **self-sustaining growth** for the first time in history. Self-sustaining growth is an economic cycle in which a nation produces products that then drive more economic activity. One example involves Britain's woolens market.

Textiles Britain's wool was by far the finest in Europe. The high quality of the wool was thanks to excellent grazing lands that resulted in long, healthy fleeces on the sheep. British wool was so superior that most of its competitors on the continent dropped out of business. The more that Europeans desired British wool, the more wool the country produced.

People moved capital to where they could make a profit. Farmers specialized in raising sheep or producing wool. Merchants bought the wool, and spinners wove it into thread. Weavers used looms to join the threads into bolts of fabric. Dyers added color and patterns to the fabric. Seamstresses turned the bolts of woolen cloth into garments. Warehouse workers stored clothes and fabrics warehouses. Clerks and agents provided insurance for all the good and buildings.

At every stage of the textile industry, these newly created jobs paid relatively high wages, leading to a money-based economy. This step toward prosperity was all based on well-fed sheep.

Market-Driven Wages and Prices During medieval times and through the mid-16th century, most people lived and worked on farms. Their output sustained only their families and local communities. Cities remained small, and money was a rare commodity for three reasons:

- limited availability of gold and silver for coinage

- limited economic growth because countries were fighting costly wars

- limited productivity because everything was made by hand

Workers' Wages Workers were forced to join **guilds**, or associations of craftsmen that controlled certain industries. The guilds kept production low so prices would remain high. High prices did not translate into high wages, however. The guild system benefited wealthy merchants but did not generate a good standard of living for ordinary laborers.

Britain's woolens industry changed this model by paying wages directly to workers. Being paid wages by the pieces produced gave workers an incentive to increase productivity. The more pieces they produced, often in their homes in cottage industries, the more money they made. No longer working as subsistence farmers, people used their wages to purchase food and household goods. These changes created more new, specialized jobs—often in fast-growing cities—where urban laborers also earned and spent wages. London's population grew from 50,000 in 1500 to 1 million in 1800. Workers in London earned three times as much as workers in Vienna or Florence, cities that had not experienced a switch to wage-based jobs.

Le Chapelier Law During the period when Britain's industrial economy was booming, places such as France and the German states remained relatively agrarian as a result of their unstable governments. Consequently, industry and workers in those countries did not benefit to the extent that those in Britain did. At the start of the French Revolution, the National Assembly passed the **Le Chapelier Law** (1791), banning guilds or any similar gathering of citizens in the same trade (such as unions) and declaring free enterprise as the new norm in France. It also banned the right to strike on the belief that workers should not demand wage increases during a time of national crisis. The law was overturned in 1864, and the rights to strike and associate were restored.

The Agricultural Revolution

In Britain, fewer and fewer people worked on farms because they were migrating to cities. Yet, farm output nearly tripled between 1500 and 1700. In 1500, one farmer could feed approximately 1.4 people. By 1700, one farmer could feed 3.0 people. Other countries in Europe needed twice as many farmers to feed a comparable population. One reason for Britain's success was the climate. Atmospheric patterns change in the-17th century, so the weather became drier and warmer.

But Britain also utilized science and technology—the cornerstones of Enlightenment thinking. For example, scientific breeding of livestock improved agricultural production, as British farmers practiced the selective breeding of beef cattle and sheep.

Mixed Farming The British began using a **mixed farming** system. Most crops pull nutrients out of the soil, so fields were traditionally allowed to recover by lying fallow—or unused. Scientists discovered that crops such as turnips, alfalfa, or clover would restore depleted nitrogen to the soil. These crops also made excellent grazing for Britain's famous sheep. As the animals grazed, they deposited manure, which further enhanced the soil. When the manure and cover crops were tilled under, fields that used to have to rest became more productive than ever.

The Dishley breed of ship was one of the breeds developed using the techniques of scientific breeding.

Credit: Getty Images

The Dutch originally discovered this mixed farming method. The British, out of necessity, utilized it most extensively. With so many people leaving the countryside to take urban jobs, the remaining farmers had to use all the tools at their disposal to create enough food to feed a growing population.

Enclosure Movement Another change to farming was the **enclosure movement**—a series of laws allowing for the sale of public lands, including the public lands known as the commons, which were often purchased by large landowners. Small fields were consolidated into larger landholdings surrounded by hedges or fences (see Chapter 4). The enclosure movement contributed to a growing population of landless peasants. Some worked on the new larger farms, while many others migrated to towns and cities in search of work. Whether by choice or by force, more and more small farmers sold out to prosperous independent **yeoman farmers**, who had sufficient resources to put into food production. This led to more efficient and profitable farms with professional managers to keep up with the latest developments.

Advances in Farm Machinery Until the early 18th century, all farm tasks—from tilling the soil to sowing seeds to harvesting crops—were done by hand using people and animals. That began to change as British farmers met the challenges of providing food for domestic consumption and for exports to other nations. The Age of Enlightenment once again inspired technological solutions:

- In 1701, **Jethro Tull** invented a **seed drill** and **mechanical hoe.** The seed drill metered out the seeds in straight lines and then covered them with dirt. The mechanical horse-drawn hoe removed weeds from between the seed rows.

- In 1730, **Joseph Foljambe** created a cast iron plow based on earlier Chinese and Dutch designs. Soon Foljambe's plows were being fashioned by blacksmiths throughout Europe and North America. The smiths used interchangeable parts and standard patterns.

- In 1784, Andrew Meikle invented the **thresher**—a machine that separated grains from plants.

National Markets Because farmers no longer supplied only their families and immediate communities, agricultural products needed to be transported to and sold in cities, spurring an entirely new realm of economic activity involving merchants, middlemen, transporters, lines of credit, insurance, and banks. New legislation addressed weights and measures and ways to prevent price fixing.

Britain also eliminated **internal tariffs, customs barriers,** and **feudal tolls**, which gave it Europe's largest and best-organized market system.

- Internal tariffs were taxes on items or properties sold within the country. These hurt the average person by raising the price of essential goods. Eliminating internal taxes lowered prices and gave people more money to spend. In France, finance minister Jean-Baptiste Colbert (1619–1683) reduced internal tariffs as part of his mercantilist policies to decrease France's debt and revitalize its industries (see Chapter 7).

- Customs barriers were measures designed to protect British trade. One example was the **external tariff** on French wines. This tariff made importing wine very expensive, which is one reason the British became beer brewers and whisky distillers.

- Feudal tolls were fees imposed by medieval robber barons. These tolls were collected much as tolls are today—at stations where merchants or other people needed to use a road, bridge, or river. Once cities demanded more agricultural products, the government eliminated these feudal tolls. Instead, governments began their own transportation projects.

Transportation and Land Conversions To provide better infrastructure for commerce, the British borrowed several kinds of technology from the Dutch, who had developed these technologies after working with flooded lowlands for centuries. The following ideas improved British transportation and land usage:

- Between 1500 and 1700, the British expanded inland waterways through a canal system and tripled the number of usable roadways, helping move products to market more efficiently.

- Britain drained and reclaimed lands to make them arable for farming, adding from 10 to 30 percent additional farmland.

- They created **water meadows**, or fields of grass near rivers. Using planned irrigation, they could periodically flood the meadows. The river nutrients improved the grasses. This allowed farmers to move animals onto these pastures earlier in the spring. As a result, the animals produced more meat, milk, and hides. The manure from the pastured animals then improved the summer grasses, which were cut to make hay for winter feeding.

The Cottage Industry System

Before the widespread growth of factories during the Industrial Revolution, the main production system in the 17th and first half of the 18th centuries in Western Europe was called the **cottage industry system**. Merchants employed people such as spinners and weavers to work from home making finished products, and the workers were paid on a piece basis. Historians call this time period **proto-industrialization**. The prefix *proto* means "first" or "original." The system was the earliest example of industrialization in Europe.

The advantages for the workers were that they could remain in their rural villages while bringing in wages. They needed no investment other than their own time and labor. For the first time, women and children earned money on a widespread basis, and rural economies prospered.

The advantages for the merchants were lower wage costs and greater efficiencies because workers specialized in the tasks they did best. Merchants could now sell finished goods at higher prices than they had been able to charge for raw wool.

New Financial Practices and Institutions

In 1700, industry was a rarity. However, growing demand drove innovation. New technologies allowed investors to move production out of cottages and into mills and factories.

In particular, the burgeoning cotton textile industry grew rapidly, making use of several new inventions. During the mid-18th century, entrepreneurs thus began processing textiles in factories, which were first run by water-powered machines.

New Technologies in the Textile Industry, 18th Century		
New Technology	**Main Inventor**	**Significance**
Spinning jenny 1765	James Hargreaves	Spun multiple spools of thread simultaneously
Water frame 1769	Richard Arkwright	Used water power to drive spinning wheels
Spinning mule, 1779	Samuel Crompton	Multiple-spindle spinning machine; enabled a single worker to operate more than 1,000 spindles at the same time
Cotton gin 1793	Eli Whitney	Separated cotton fibers from seeds

Other industries spurred even more inventions. **Steam engines** powered machinery for extracting coal from the mines and crushing iron ore. Across England, industrial centers sprang up, specializing in textiles, mining, knives and tools, toys and nails, hats, stockings, and shipbuilding. All these goods had to be transported and marketed. As more opportunities emerged, the need arose for financial supports, such as business legislation, insurance, and banks.

Property Rights and Protections During the Glorious Revolution of 1688, the government committed to protecting and preserving private property. With this assurance, the elites felt confident that they could own land, add to it, or make improvements on it without risking having it confiscated. This meant that they had an incentive to find new ways to profit from that land, which was another factor driving economic growth.

With a representative Parliament, Britain's wealthy class shared power with the monarch. The Glorious Revolution had created an economic aristocracy made up of both landed nobles and the commercial class. Unlike the French aristocracy, these British aristocrats invested in commercial and industrial ventures. They were thus willing to tax themselves and fund public works if those choices meant they could somehow profit. Profiting would thus result from cheaper transportation costs due to better roads or a stronger navy that protected shipping lanes during the import and export of their wares.

Britain's financial and political stability stood in direct contrast to France's. France had no viable national parliament, and taxes often went to subsidize the luxurious lifestyle of the king. Stability was an important factor that gave Britain economic advantages and a head start during the Commercial and Industrial Revolutions.

Insurance Property insurance—especially fire insurance in an era of wooden buildings—was integral to economic success. Insurance offered security to entrepreneurs and encouraged them to accumulate wealth in the form of factories and inventories. In an era of extensive maritime trade, insurance also offered security to merchants engaged in commercial shipping. Joint-stock companies issued insurance in case of damage to shipments.

However, the insurance industry itself also provided investment opportunities. Private investors insured other people's businesses in exchange for premium payments. As long as the premiums were larger than the payouts, the insurers made money. This required them to develop special skills to assess risks and price their products. One of the earliest insurers was Lloyd's of London, founded in 1688. It remains still one of the world's largest and most respected insurance companies.

Turning Private Savings into Venture Capital Prior to the start of the Industrial Revolution, most major business transactions were conducted in gold or silver. Copper was used for smaller daily commerce. When people needed a business loan, they turned to merchants or family members, because a more organized system for investment capital had not yet been required. Before 1750, banking in Britain was limited to three tiers of institutions:

- The Bank of England: founded in 1694 by King William III to fund war costs, based on the Dutch model in Amsterdam, the banking capital of the 17th century

- Approximately 30 private banks: mainly used by merchants and industrialists

- Approximately 12 county banks: served local areas

However, as commerce boomed, entrepreneurs needed loans to build mills and factories and also to meet short-term operating expenses, such as payroll. Private industrialists and the British government needed loans to expand the infrastructure of roads, railways, and canals. Merchants needed a place to deposit their profits. Specialty banks arose to serve various industries. These banks made money by keeping cash reserves on hand from the deposits and then lending the money out at a certain rate of interest. This ready availability of capital fueled expansion because now there was money to get businesses up and running.

Bank of England The **Bank of England** became the model for modern banking. From 1688 to 1946, it was privately owned by stockholders. Its original mission was to gather enough subscriptions from wealthy investors that the cash-poor government could borrow £1.2 million at 8 percent interest, with a service charge of £4000 per year. Half of this loan went to rebuild the British navy following a major defeat by France at the Battle of Beachy Head in 1690.

Because the British developed this financial resource, the nation experienced several advantages:

- The navy quadrupled in size and positioned Great Britain to become a world power and empire during the 18th and 19th centuries.

- The resulting industries—ironworks and agriculture to feed the sailors—drove increased economic expansion.

- The bank became a **limited-liability corporation** that had the sole right to issue government notes, which were used as readily available paper money secured by either government bonds or gold deposits. *Limited-liability* refers to the principle that an investor was not responsible for a corporation's debts or other liabilities beyond the amount of the original investment, thus making investment safer.

The bank was such a profitable venture that George Washington remained a stockholder even during the Revolutionary War. However, the fact that banknotes were tied to gold reserves meant that growth was limited to the amount of gold in the vaults. For this reason, most banks went off the gold standard in the 1930s.

Europe's Commercial Revolution of the 17th and 18th Centuries	
Diet	Europeans experienced better nutrition thanks to food products imported from the Americas, Asia, and Africa beginning in the 15th and 16th centuries.
Weather	By the early 17th century, the weather became warmer and drier, and this, along with new crops, led to improved health and a population recovery.
Demography	Although Europe in 1700 was still largely rural and somewhat depopulated from waves of plague, Britain (and, to a lesser extent, the Dutch Republic) used trade within Europe and overseas to begin a Commercial Revolution.
Education	The growing population became more literate and was inspired by Enlightenment ideals to manipulate their world through scientific discoveries and technological innovation.
Machinery	After a brief period of proto-industrialization, factories and mines powered by machines and engines spread rapidly throughout Britain, generating jobs in urban centers. This Industrial Revolution started around 1750.
Agriculture	Urbanization meant that the remaining farmers had to become even more efficient, leading to the Agricultural Revolution, which accompanied urbanization and other important changes.
Money	A money-based economy emerged, and the standard of living—in Britain especially—improved so that for the first time, people used wages to purchase food and factory-made consumer goods.
Trade	Increasing trade among European nations and with overseas colonies led to increased wealth due to mercantilist policies. The growing merchant middle class wanted to share power with the elites and the monarchy.
Colonies	Britain's successes in the colonial phases of the wars of the 18th century expanded its profitable colonial empire and made Britain the foremost world power.

Some of the earliest human writings mention slavery, so historians assume slavery has long been a part of human society. But the notion of "modern" slavery begins with the transatlantic slave trade that became central to the rise of Europe on the back of African slavery.

How did modern slavery emerge? Prior to the 15th century, those enslaved were prisoners of war; and among Muslims, this often meant Christians. As a result, Christians came to believe they should not enslave each other. However, when the Portuguese began setting up trading posts along the African coasts, where the captives were not Christian, their ruler, Prince Henry, saw an opportunity to weaken the Muslim hold on the slave trade, increase profits for Portugal, and convert non-Christian Africans to Christianity. Both Africans and Muslims were already participating in the practice of the slave trade, and the European presence just increased the competition and scale.

How did Europeans come to dominate the slave trade? By the 19th century, Europeans used various metrics to prove their superiority to the rest of the world. In the field of history, G. W. F. Hegel provided a view that became so powerful, even historians aware of its limitations still fell into a Hegelian trap. Hegel used European history to demonstrate the phases of historic advancement of societies. In doing so, Hegel made the European path to modernity the only path, and those that were not already on that path, like Africa, were in "the land of childhood" according to an 1837 lecture. This view allowed "superior" Europeans to see slavery as Prince Henry did, as a chance to Christianize and modernize "inferior" Africans. It is this view that dominated the pro-slavery opposition to the growing abolitionist efforts throughout the century. Such racially biased viewpoints were continued in the 19th-century ideas of Social Darwinism and the "white man's burden," which held that the powerful nations and cultures were "superior" to those they dominated and should help "improve" those "inferior" nations and cultures.

Unequal Development At the height of decolonization in the 1960s and 1970s, historian Walter Rodney tried to avoid the Hegelian trap of European superiority by focusing on the economic argument. However, his explanation of the unique development of commercial capitalism in Europe, as compared to the subsistence economy of Africa, again showed a modernizing Europe dominating an underdeveloped Africa.

Market Power By the late 20th century, John Thornton represented the growing voice of historians interested in the history of the developing world. They tried to look at it outside the framework of an evil or benevolent Europe. Thornton refuted Rodney's portrayal of Africans as victims of European power. Instead, Thornton emphasized the self-sufficiency of Africa prior to and during initial trade with Europeans, the long history of African slave trade of prisoners of war, and the African choice in escalating both of those already established trading networks. Thornton showed that African leaders were not tricked into trading their own people. Rather, they responded to market demands.

Importance of Identity Heather Andrea Williams, a leading scholar in African studies, added one more point to explan how Africans could participate in the slave trade as much as they did. She argued that "these rulers did not think of themselves as Africans or as black people; their identities instead derived from being members of a specific village or an ethnic group. Therefore, they did not sustain a sense of unity with, or loyalty to, captives from other people." They were motivated by profit and access to new weapons, which increased tension in Africa and allowed for the capture of more prisoners who were then sold into slavery. It was this that ultimately weakened Africa and allowed later imperialists to dominate the continent so easily. European domination was not inevitable.

KEY TERMS BY THEME

Economics		Technology
Commercial Revolution	guilds	Jethro Tull
mercantilism	Le Chapelier Law	seed drill
colonization	mixed farming	mechanical hoe
Middle Passage	enclosure movement	Joseph Foljambe
triangle trade	yeoman farmers	thresher
plantations	internal tariffs	spinning jenny
Navigation Acts	customs barriers	James Hargreaves
Joseph-Marie Jacquard	feudal tolls	water frame
John Rolfe	external tariff	Richard Arkwright
privateers	water meadows	spinning mule
Dutch East India Company	cottage industry system	Samuel Crompton
East India Company	proto-industrialization	cotton gin
human capital	Bank of England	Eli Whitney
self-sustaining growth	limited-liability corporation	steam engines

Questions 1–3 refer to the passage below.

"[T]he Manufacturer sends the poor Woman combed Wool, or carded Wool every Week to spin, and she gets eight Pence or nine Pence a day at home; the Weaver sends for her two little Children, and they work by the Loom, winding, filling quills . . . and the two bigger Girls spin at home with their Mother, and these earn three Pence or four Pence a Day each: So that put it together, the Family at Home gets as much as the Father gets Abroad, and generally more . . . [T]he Family feels it, they all feel better, are cloth'd warmer, and do not so easily nor so often fall into Misery and Distress;... and as they grow, they do not run away to be Footmen and Soldiers, Thieves and Beggars . . . but have a Trade at their Hands, and every one can get their Bread."

Daniel Defoe, "A Plan of the English Commerce," 1728

1. Defoe's plan is best understood as a response to which developments?

   a) The cottage industry system that developed in Western Europe

   b) The expansion of the market economy in rural areas

   c) The Enlightenment debate over women's rights and education

   d) The implementation of new technology in textile factories

2. The author's point of view is most similar to

   a) a mercantilist's critique of capitalism

   b) John Locke's theory of natural rights

   c) Adam Smith's support for free trade

   d) Mary Wollstonecraft's criticism of traditional gender roles

3. A historian could best use this source as evidence of which of the following features of the early 18th century?

   a) The emergence of new class divisions between capital and labor

   b) The increase in tariffs passed by Parliament

   c) The improved standard of living brought about by new technology

   d) The development of new upper-class attitudes toward the poor

Questions 4–6 refer to the passage below.

"I was not long suffered to indulge my grief; I was soon put down under the decks, and there I received such a salutation in my nostrils as I had never experienced in my life; so that with the loathsomeness of the stench, and crying together, I became so sick and low that I was not able to eat, nor had I the least desire to taste any thing. I now wished for the last friend, Death, to relieve me; but soon, to my grief, two of the white men offered me eatables; and, on my refusing to eat, one of them held me fast by the hands, and laid me across, I think, the windlass, and tied my feet, while the other flogged me severely. . . . In a little time after, amongst the poor chained men, I found some of my own nation, which in a small degree gave ease to my mind. I inquired of them what was to be done with us? They gave me to understand we were to be carried to these white people's country to work for them."

Olaudah Equiano, describing conditions on a slave ship, *The Interesting Narrative of the Life of Olaudah Equiano; or, Gustavus Vassa, the African, Written by Himself* (1789)

4. The conditions on the slave ship described by Equiano were most directly a result of which of the following developments?

   a) The economic and geographic isolation of the African continent

   b) The ideas of the Enlightenment and the ban on the slave trade

   c) African demand for New World products such as tobacco and sugar

   d) European conquest and colonization of Africa and the Americas

5. The context in which this passage was written was most influenced by

   a) Enlightenment ideas about natural rights

   b) interest in African culture and history

   c) socialist critiques of capitalism

   d) liberal critiques of mercantilism

6. Which of the following contributed to reduced support for the practices described in the excerpt?

   a) Recognition by the British government of the principle of self-determination

   b) New theories in biology that challenged racial inequality

   c) An increase in the migration of Europeans to the Caribbean

   d) A decline in the profitability of the sugar industry

Questions 7–8 refer to the painting below.

In this etching based on a 1746 painting by Francois Boucher, a French fashion merchant shows articles of clothing to her client.

Credit: Metropolitan Museum of Art, Harris Brisbane Dick Fund, 1953

7. The economic activity reflected in this painting was largely a result of which of the following?

    a) Enlightenment debates over women's role in society

    b) The exclusion of women workers from urban guilds

    c) The passage of the Le Chapelier Law in France

    d) The increased availability of products from overseas trade and colonies

8. The painting best illustrates which of the following developments in the 18th century?

    a) Growing demand for consumer goods and services

    b) The employment of women as domestic servants

    c) The marketing of fashion to lower-class women

    d) The emergence of cottage industry in rural areas

SHORT-ANSWER QUESTIONS

1. Use the passage below to answer all parts of the question that follows.

> For many years the agricultural revolution in England was thought to have occurred . . . due to a group of heroic individuals. . . ." These men are seen as having triumphed over a conservative mass of country bumpkins. They are thought to have single-handedly, in a few years, transformed English agriculture from a peasant subsistence economy to a thriving capitalist agricultural system. . . . There is general agreement that the role of the "Great Men" as pioneers and innovators has been exaggerated.
>
> Mark Overton, *Agricultural Revolution in England*,
> published in 1996

a) Explain ONE piece of evidence that supports Overton's argument regarding the Agricultural Revolution.

b) Explain ONE piece of evidence that undermines Overton's argument regarding the Agricultural Revolution.

c) Explain ONE way in which the Agricultural Revolution affected the English economy.

2. Answer all parts of the question that follows.

a) Describe ONE significant *continuity* in commercial rivalries among European states in Early Modern Europe (1648–1815).

b) Describe ONE significant *change* in commercial rivalries among European states in Early Modern Europe (1648–1815).

c) Explain ONE significant effect of change in commercial rivalries among European states in Early Modern Europe (1648–1815).

LONG ESSAY QUESTIONS

1. Evaluate the success of two European countries in establishing a mercantilist empire.

2. Evaluate the extent to which slavery in the Americas influenced the economies of Europe.

REFLECT ON THE CHAPTER ESSENTIAL QUESTION

1. In one to three paragraphs, explain how the expansion of European commerce accelerated the growth of a worldwide economic network in Early Modern Europe.

Most essays written for AP® exams follow the same basic structure:

- The first paragraph sets the context and ends with the thesis statement.

- Each body paragraph starts with a topic sentence that introduces the main idea of the paragraph and includes evidence to support the thesis.

- The last paragraph recaps the evidence and restates the thesis.

For each thesis statement, choose the best topic sentence that supports it.

1. In its early stages, modern Europe developed a market economy that provided the foundation for its global role.

   a. Trade was freed from traditional restrictions, and wages and prices became more market-driven.

   b. Because workers had more geographic mobility, they were not as tied to traditional family and community traditions.

2. European domination of the worldwide economic network had several negative social consequences.

   a. Products such as sugar, tea, tobacco, and rum were widely enjoyed by Europeans.

   b. Triangle trade among Europe, Africa, and the Americas caused the slave trade to increase.

For each of the topic sentences below, choose the best supporting evidence.

3. The importation and transplantation of agricultural products from the Americas contributed to increases in food supply and trade.

   a. France's growing climate was hospitable to crops from the Americas such as beans, peppers, corn, squash, tomatoes, and potatoes.

   b. England's plantations produced crops such as rice, tobacco, and sugar that enriched a growing merchant class.

4. England's mercantilist policies provoked rebellion in its American colonies.

   a. The majority of profits from plantations flowed back across the sea to absentee owners in England.

   b. The colonists, in many ways, enjoyed a higher standard of living as a result of their greater economic opportunities.

10

The Age of Reason
Enlightenment

"Judge a man by his questions rather than by his answers"

—Voltaire

Essential Question: How did spreading the principles of the Scientific Revolution lead to an emphasis on reason?

The scientific advances that began with Copernicus's theory of a sun-centered solar system continued through Isaac Newton's discovery of the laws of gravity. These laid the groundwork for a dramatic shift in thinking about the universe and humanity's place in it. Before Copernicus, the accepted view of the universe was a religious one. People accepted the seemingly obvious geocentric (earth-centered) view that the church had promulgated for centuries. When Newton demonstrated that the laws of nature controlled how apples fell and how planets orbited the sun, the universe suddenly seemed both knowable and predictable.

The **Scientific Revolution** was thus more than a revolution in science. It was also a revelation about the nature of knowledge itself and about ways of thinking. During the 17th and 18th centuries, European thinkers applied reason and the scientific method to all aspects of life, producing an across-the-board **paradigm shift**—a radical and important change in the established conceptual framework.

The **Enlightenment**, or **the Age of Reason**, was the period of intellectual history set in motion by the work of these thinkers in such diverse fields as economics, politics, religion, education, and culture. The application of the scientific method to political, social, economic, and religious institutions transformed European society. Although the Enlightenment took different forms in various nations, two unifying themes emerged:

- a rational questioning of prevailing institutions and patterns of thought

- a general belief that human progress was possible

Old ideas were open to question. The French thinker Voltaire summed up the new skepticism with the quotation that opens this chapter. However, developments of the Enlightenment did not go unchallenged; feudal, despotic, and religious restrictions continued to exist, and clerics in particular remained bulwarks of the old ways of thought.

Rational and Empirical Thought

Beyond the field of science itself, the Scientific Revolution had its greatest impact in the area of philosophy, where it led to two schools of thought, **Rationalism** and **Empiricism**. The two schools differed in their understanding of how people know what they know.

- Rationalism focused on innate reason, the concept that people know independently of what they observe. It emphasized that humans have the ability to recognize and understand the world through reason. Rationalism was very strong in France, led by philosopher **Rene Descartes** and his use of **deductive reasoning**, or drawing conclusions from general principles.

- Empiricism was based on the idea that all human knowledge comes through what the senses can experience. Empiricism became prominent in England by **Sir Francis Bacon** with the use of **inductive reasoning**, or drawing conclusions from specific observations.

Examples of Inductive and Deductive Reasoning		
Starting Point	**Conclusion**	**Type of Reasoning**
Greek, Roman, and Italian republics all failed.	Therefore, republican governments do not work.	Inductive
The paths of Mercury, Venus, Mars, and Earth through space do not form perfect circles.	Therefore, the orbits of the planets are not circles.	Inductive
All humans are rational. Descartes is a human.	Therefore Descartes is rational.	Deductive
Humans are born with natural rights.	Therefore, England should pass laws that respect the rights of individuals.	Deductive

Both Rationalism and Empiricism argued that what people *knew* was more important than what they *believed,* and that investigation and reflection were more important than faith. In their emphasis on rational thought, both groups of thinkers were influenced by the classical Greek thinkers such as Socrates and Aristotle.

While this belief in the use of logic and reason undermined superstition and prejudice, it also set up a conflict with religious authorities. Revolutionary advances in physics and mechanics brought about a new conception of God, as the creator of a universe that operated deterministically, like a machine. **Deism** is the belief in the existence of a supreme being, specifically a creator who does not intervene in the universe.

The workings of natural law could be investigated by anyone, while religious teachings relied on improvable hypotheses. Obedience, fear, and dependence on ritual gave way to open-mindedness and autonomy. Enlightenment thinkers questioned religious institutions, arguing that human reason, not faith, was the key to improving society. The goal of many Enlightenment thinkers was to reduce the power of the church in society.

The emphasis on human reason led to a high value on human dignity. Intellectuals denounced slavery. Some argued for an end to the use of torture of criminals and for reserving capital punishment to the most abhorrent crimes, as well as making prisons more humane.

Philosophers theorized that people lived together through a **social contract**, an agreement to submit to a government for their mutual protection. Unlike earlier thinkers, who believed that the authority to rule came from God, social contract thinkers, such as **John Locke** (1632–1704), argued that such authority came from the people of a country, who retained natural rights that no government could take away.

The British Empiricists

Political philosophers tried to use the methods of the Scientific Revolution to analyze society's problems. Like mathematicians, they established basic facts as a starting point and systematically built upon them. People such as **Thomas Hobbes** (1588–1679) and John Locke believed that just as the natural world followed **natural laws**—laws that applied to everyone and which humans could discover and understand through observation and reason—so did human society. Both were empiricists who emphasized the importance of knowledge gained through experience, but because of when they lived they reached radically different conclusions about how governments should operate.

Hobbes's *Leviathan* Like many philosophers, Hobbes wrote in reaction to events he witnessed. He lived during the violent upheaval of the English Civil War and was appalled by the execution of King Charles I in 1649. In his book *Leviathan* (1651), Hobbes wanted to create a government that could guarantee peace and security for citizens. He argued that in a state of nature—in a society without government—humans would pursue their own survival and self-interest with no respect for the needs or rights of others. Each individual's life would be "solitary, poor, nasty, brutish, and short." In order to form "society", individuals would give up some of their rights to a sovereign authority. This authority must be very powerful—similar to a great sea monster from the Bible called a *leviathan*. Hobbes espoused that once this new government was created then the people must live under the rules of that government. He favored an **absolute monarchy**, although not one based on "divine right." He feared that a government with limits on its power could not command the respect and fear necessary to tame and control humans' naturally violent, self-seeking nature.

John Locke In contrast to Hobbes, John Locke argued that people are not naturally dangerous to each other. In his *Essay Concerning Human Understanding* (1690), Locke insisted that a person's mind at birth is a blank slate, often refered to by its Latin name, **tabula rasa**. According to Locke, people are neither bad nor good; they derive all knowledge from what they experience with their senses, and they are thus capable of learning and improving themselves. Therefore, Locke emphasized the importance of education in creating a stable society.

Locke believed that since humans are governed by natural law endowed by a creator, they possess **natural rights** that come from the creator as well. These rights are independent of any particular society or government. Many of his beliefs were shaped by his Puritan upbringing. Unlike Hobbes who saw the horrors of the English Civil War, Locke lived through the peaceful transformation of power brought about by the Glorious Revolution in which absolute monarchy gave way with minimal bloodshed to Parliamentary sovereignty. Locke thus presented a more positive view of human nature than Hobbes.

In his most important work, *Two Treatises of Government*, Locke argued that people are born with basic and inalienable rights, including life, liberty, health, and property. Like Hobbes, Locke argued that people willingly came together to form governments, forming a social contract. Unlike Hobbes, however, Locke believed that the purpose of such government was to protect people's natural rights. Should the government fail in this regard, the people could replace it with a new government. In fact, government only exists because of the tacit consent of the governed, and it is answerable to the people. Civil and political rights reside with the people and are not bestowed upon them by God or king. Locke's ideas about natural rights and limited government were influential with the American founders who wrote the *Declaration of Independence* and the Constitution.

The French Philosophes

The 18th-century intellectuals who popularized this new scientific attitude toward reason were known as the **philosophes** (French for "philosophers"). In the spirit of the Enlightenment, they criticized France's **ancien régime**— its feudal social and political system under which the monarch, church, and nobility controlled society for their own benefit. (See Chapter 8 for more on French society.) The philosophes sought social reform of the systems, believing that natural laws governed social institutions similarly to those laws that governed the physical universe. Their task was to discern these natural laws and use them as the basis for reform. With their faith in reason and belief in fundamental natural laws, philosophes for the most part embraced progress, earthly happiness, and liberty as innate rights.

Voltaire The most influential philosophe was François-Marie Arouet (1694–1778), known by his pen name **Voltaire**. He was a brilliant writer, an accomplished historian, and an aggressive and vocal deist. Voltaire fiercely advocated tolerance and freedom of religious belief and was known for his witty satirical critiques of the French clergy and aristocracy, which he deemed ignorant and corrupt. Voltaire coined the slogan *"écrasez l'infâme,"* meaning "crush the loathsome thing," a reference to the Roman Catholic Church. In his

Treatise on Toleration, Voltaire criticized religious fanaticism and superstition.

Voltaire was exiled from Paris for a time and was twice imprisoned in Paris's most famous prison, the Bastille. Upon his release, he moved to England, where he received a warm welcome from the leading literary figures of the day. He was fascinated with English society, with its greater tolerance of freedom of thought, and he learned English in order to read the works of John Locke. Voltaire was so impressed by English society that during his exile he wrote *"Letters on the English,"* a bitter satire that extolled the virtues of the English while demeaning French society.

Eventually Voltaire returned to France, where he published his masterwork, the short novel *Candide*. It was his bitter commentary on the hope for progress. The new scientific discoveries had led to widespread optimism that social progress was inevitable. Many Enlightenment intellectuals argued that if God was not controlling human society, then humans could shape their future. Through reason, they could improve it. However, given the evidence of widespread human suffering, Voltaire rejected this optimism as unrealistic and unwarranted.

Denis Diderot Another French philosophe, **Denis Diderot** (1713–1784) was fascinated by the idea that everything in the natural world could be catalogued and described. He spent 26 years gathering contributions from more than 150 writers on science, technology, politics, religion, art, and virtually every other human endeavor. The result was a 28-volume work, the ***Encyclopédie***—literally, "the circle of teachings." Diderot's *Encyclopédie* was controversial by its very premise, because it placed human reason as the foundation of all knowledge. All other forms of knowledge, including theological, were mere branches. Despite attempts at censorship, the *Encyclopédie* was widely disseminated across Europe and the Americas.

Montesquieu The Baron de Montesquieu, better known as simply **Montesquieu** (1689–1799), was a French lawyer and writer. As an aristocrat, Montesquieu was critical of the monarchs' usurpation of the traditional prerogatives of the aristocracy. Unlike other philosophes, he espoused a more favorable view of the Middle Ages, a time when the king's powers were balanced by nobility and clergy.

Inspired by the achievements of scientists in explaining the natural world, Montesquieu attempted to apply scientific principles to political institutions and theory. In particular, he focused on the law. Montesquieu, who wrote *On the Spirit of Laws,* argued that the best system of government featured a **separation of powers**, a division of governmental authority into separate branches, such as the legislative, executive, and judicial. To Montesquieu, the British Constitutional Monarchy was a prime example of this; having a king, parliament, and judiciary. Each branch was granted specific powers, creating a system of **checks and balances**, the ability of each branch to limit the power of the other branches. This concept influenced the American founders, especially James Madison, the father of the Constitution.

Montesquieu explored such ideas in his *The Spirit of the Laws*, a groundbreaking study of comparative law and political theory. He made the case for greater civil liberties, abolition of slavery, the elimination of religious persecution, and limits on the arbitrary application of state power. Montesquieu's work inspired modern political science and sociology.

Cesare Beccaria One of the most influential Enlightenment thinkers from southern Europe was an Italian jurist and philosopher, **Cesare Beccaria** (1738–1794). Beccaria sparked a criminal justice reform movement when he brought scientific reasoning to bear in the field of criminal justice in his influential treatise *On Crimes and Punishments*, inspired by Montesquieu and published with a detailed introduction by Voltaire. In this essay, Beccaria called for an end to the use of torture, a common tactic of the time applied to suspects to obtain confessions. He argued that torture was irrational because it might lead an innocent person to confess. He also denounced capital punishment as not only unnecessary but also a violation of basic rights, as the state does not have the right to take lives. His **deterrence theory** was based on Enlightenment views of man: as men are rational beings, punishment should be just severe enough to outweigh the possible rewards derived from committing the crime. Beccaria is considered the father of modern criminal law and the father of criminal justice.

Jean-Jacques Rousseau One of the most unusual French philosophes was the Geneva-born thinker **Jean-Jacques Rousseau** (1712–1778). Rousseau is famous for his treatise *The Social Contract*, with its striking assertion that "man is born free, but everywhere he is in chains." Although the words seem like a call to revolution, Rousseau's next sentence went on to say he would now "show how they [the chains] are legitimate."

In contrast to those philosophers who saw education as a key to happiness, Rousseau viewed people in their natural state as free and happy. He argued that humanity enters into civil society to secure this freedom and happiness. His concept of the social contract was of an agreement among free individuals that creates and gives government its legitimacy. The state exists to promote the liberty and equality of its citizens, and its laws should be respected only when they are supported by the **general will** of the people. Rousseau strongly opposed the idea of a republican form of government. Instead, he insisted that citizens should make laws directly, and the ideal state would be small enough that an assembly of all citizens would be possible.

Some politicians and historians have interpreted Rousseau's beliefs as upholding the principle that all citizens are bound by the general will with no possibility of dissent; in other words, they are "forced to be free." This interpretation could lead to a tyranny of the majority, and his ideas were later used to justify France's Reign of Terror.

Rousseau's views on education were distinctive for his time. While other thinkers saw education as training, he did not. In his book titled *Emile, or On Education,* he defined the proper role of education as fostering the innate curiosity of each child, who should not be regarded simply as a small adult.

Children should learn by following their own interests and reaching their own conclusions. Society's institutions corrupted humans and the aim of education should be to preserve the original, perfect natural state of the child.

Unlike many of his contemporaries, however, Rousseau maintained an ambivalent attitude toward reason and emphasized human emotion and sentiment–ideas that would connect him to the origins of Romanticism. (See Chapter 11.)

Women During the Englightenment

Before the Enlightenment, Europeans generally did not believe that men and women were naturally equal intellectually or morally. A few Enlightenment thinkers argued that women were equal to men, but the majority believed that women were still inferior in many ways.

Marquis and Madame de Condorcet One thinker who made progressive arguments on behalf of equal rights for women as well as for people of all races was **Marquis de Condorcet**. In his essay "On the Admission of Women to the Rights of Citizenship," he reasoned that if the natural rights are based on the innate capacity to reason, it is logical that women possess the same natural rights. There was, therefore, no excuse for excluding women from the public sphere, including education and the right to vote. His wife, Sophie de Condorcet, also an Enlightenment thinker, held similar views and translated works of Adam Smith and Thomas Paine into French.

However, most other philosophes disagreed with the Condorcets. Rousseau had argued that nature itself gave men power over women, justifying women's unequal treatment in society and exclusion from the sphere of politics. Their proper sphere, he argued, was as helpers to men. However, the language of natural rights used by the philosophes naturally aroused visions of equality.

Mary Wollstonecraft English writer **Mary Wollstonecraft** vehemently challenged Rousseau's position on women. Born into poverty and struggling later to raise a daughter born secretly out of wedlock, Wollstonecraft needed to earn a living and was frustrated by the limited options available for women. She became a governess and then a writer, supplementing her income by translating French and German texts. A fervent supporter of the French Revolution, Wollstonecraft used the language of equality espoused by the philosophes to affirm that women were human beings, and as such they were endowed with the same natural rights as men. If they appeared inferior, that was because of the systematic denial of educational opportunities to women, not an innate characteristic.

In her most famous work, *Vindication of the Rights of Woman* (1792), Wollstonecraft, a self-taught woman who had received little formal schooling herself, made a powerful argument for better education for women so they could, like men, cultivate their natural capacity to reason. Her reliance on the primacy of reason placed Wollstonecraft firmly in the Enlightenment tradition, but she extended its sphere by advocating for women's rights, becoming one of the founding feminist philosophers.

Comparing and Contrasting Major Enlightenment Thinkers		
Individual	**Key Idea**	**Major Writings and Legacy**
Hobbes	• People give up individual freedoms for security • Government must be powerful to keep peace	*Leviathan* • Established the concept of the social contract
Locke	• Government must protect citizens' natural rights to life, liberty, and property • People have a right to revolt if government abuses its power	*Second Treatise on Civil Government* • Influenced Thomas Jefferson and the Declaration of Independence
Voltaire	• Freedom of religion • Freedom of speech • Defense of enlightened despotism	*Letters Concerning the English Nation* • Supported the separation of church and state • Advocated for individual freedoms
Montesquieu	• Three branches of government • The separation of powers to check absolutism	*On the Spirit of Laws* • Influenced the U.S. Constitution
Rousseau	• The social contract • The concept of general will (but intolerant of dissent from the general will, an attitude later used to justify tyranny)	*The Social Contract* • Influenced the French Revolution and the doctrine of socialism
Diderot	• Tried to articulate the essential principles of every art and science	*The Encyclopédie* • Changed the way society views, organizes, and accesses knowledge • Spread Enlightenment thinking across Europe
Beccaria	• Criminal justice, abolition of torture • Punishment consistent with crime committed, regardless of class	*On Crimes and Punishments* • Led to criminal law reform and limits on the use of torture in parts of Europe
Wollstonecraft	• Women's equality	*A Vindication of the Rights of Woman* • Led to formation of women's rights groups
De Gouges	• Women's equality	*Declaration of the Rights of Woman* • Emphasized the rights of women, as the French Revolution did not include women's rights

Spread of Enlightenment Ideas

Spurred by the Enlightenment's intellectual community that crossed beyond national boundaries, the period saw the creation and growth of new civic institutions outside of government and the traditional university setting for the purpose of spreading and debating new social and political concepts.

The Growth of Civil Society

Coffeehouses and **salons** were popular and important new institutions that spread Enlightenment ideas. For a penny, coffeehouse customers could buy coffee, read newspapers, and discuss news and ideas. Political groups and societies often formed and met in coffeehouses. For the most part, coffeehouses were a male sphere. On the other hand, French discussion groups known as **salons**, were often mixed gatherings, frequently hosted by an influential woman in her own home. Female *salonnieres* often provided crucial financial support and protection to intellectuals promoting reform. One famous *salonniere* was Madame Sophie de Condorcet.

Other new civic institutions appeared during the Enlightenment. **Academies** were specialized groups, sometimes funded or protected by wealthy individuals or royalty, to investigate and promote knowledge, often in the areas of science, technology, and the arts. In addition, the first modern **lending libraries** emerged across Europe and the Americas, with the goals of collecting information and educating the citizenry, a condition seen as crucial to democracy. As the power of the church diminished, secret organizations such as the fraternal brotherhood of Freemasonry became popular; members met in chapters known as **masonic lodges**. The movement spread from Europe to the United States, where at least nine signers of the Declaration of Independence were Freemasons.

The Spread of the Printed Word

What made the spread of ideas possible during this time was not only new urban institutions where people could meet and discuss ideas, but a revolution in **print culture** brought about by technology and supported by improved transportation. As the literacy rate rose significantly during the Enlightenment, there was widespread demand for newspapers, periodicals, scholarly books and engravings, novels, pamphlets, and, of course, Diderot's *Encyclopédie*, which was a bestseller in its time.

Not surprisingly, the new freedom of expression often met with censorship. Conservative religious and political institutions sought to prevent the spread of ideas they considered radical and dangerous. Voltaire's printer was arrested, while Diderot desperately edited page proofs of the *Encyclopédie* on his own in an attempt to avoid censorship.

Salons reflected both the intellectual passions driving French culture and the expanding opportunities for women during the Enlightenment.

Credit: Getty Images

Often, authorities tried to be discreet in their efforts to censor, as bans were both difficult to enforce and likely to stir up public opposition. However, the **Republic of Letters**—the network of letters, journals, and other publications exchanged among Enlightenment thinkers--transcended national boundaries, and thus disrupted censorship. Books banned in one country were printed in another and smuggled in. French authorities were unable to destroy the print plates of the *Encyclopédie* as they were housed in Switzerland.

Challenges of New Cultures

During the Scientific Revolution, as European natural scientists and explorers traveled across the globe, their discoveries sparked new ways of thinking about humanity, religion, and nature, and led to the establishment of new fields such as physical anthropology. Yet there was disagreement about the nature of the societies these scientists and explorers were encountering. Rousseau proposed the idea of the "**noble savage**," who lived in a joyful state of nature that was as yet unspoiled by civilizing forces, while others, such as the French naturalist Georges-Louis Leclerc De Buffon, depicted the "ignoble savage," living in a backward condition, intellectually and morally inferior to more advanced European society.

Challenges to Absolutism and Mercantilism

New political and economic theories based on the Enlightenment ideals challenged existing systems of absolutism and mercantilism.

Absolutism

As philosophers reevaluated the political realm in light of the new ideas of the Scientific Revolution, movements in favor of limits on government power swept across Europe and the Americas. However, **absolutism** still dominated European nations in the 1600s and 1700s. Under this system, monarchs held total, or absolute, power, which many claimed as a divine right granted to them by God. Therefore, they saw themselves as answerable only to God, and not to the people they ruled.

The Challenge of the New Theories

Some philosophes themselves, including Hobbes, believed that a strong monarchy was a good form of government. However, they rejected the idea that the monarch had a divine right to power. Instead, even the more conservative Enlightenment thinkers tended to agree that monarchs were entrusted with power by means of the social contract and that the state originated from the consent of the governed.

Such thinkers believed that as long as both the ruler and the ruled followed the social contract, the government was right. But what was the recourse if the monarch did not act for the good of the people? Civil and political rights are lodged in the people, the philosophes believed. Once formed, government's role was to secure its citizens' liberty and happiness, rights derived from natural law before the formation of government. Humans had an inalienable right to pursue their own happiness. These beliefs about human nature, in particular John Locke's ideas of the social contract, and the political ideologies derived from those beliefs were used to justify many revolutions, beginning with the Glorious Revolution of 1688 in England. Thomas Jefferson, in the *Declaration of Independence,* set them forth as the rights of "Life, Liberty, and the pursuit of Happiness."

Enlightened Absolutism

While the ideals of the Enlightenment found voice in political revolution, most philosophes advocated not revolution, but political reform—and unsurprisingly, considering their education, and sophistication, they tended to look for this reform from above, not below. Many European rulers, looked to the philosophes for fresh ideas about how to strengthen state control and streamline bureaucracy, reform and modernize social institutions, better manage resources, and increase national prosperity. These rulers comprised the **enlightened absolutists**, or **enlightened despots**, of the 18th century. (To review enlightened rulers, see Chapter 7.) Such rulers embraced Enlightenment ideals to the extent that they could further these goals, while the rulers rejected concepts that expressly limited their own political power. The philosophes were not hostile to enlightened absolutism, since most did not oppose monarchy unless the monarch violated the social contract.

Enlightened Rulers The attitudes of rulers toward Enlightenment thinkers varied considerably from country to country. Ironically, the monarchies of Britain and France, nations with the most visible and influential public intellectuals, regarded the movement with indifference (as in Britain) or hostility (as in France, in many cases censoring or exiling movement leaders). In contrast, **Catherine the Great** of Russia, **Frederick the Great** of Prussia, and Holy Roman Emperor **Joseph II** welcomed Enlightenment philosophes to their courts, providing financial support and embracing such reforms as religious toleration and an end to capital punishment.

Important Reforms While each enlightened monarch focused on concerns specific to his or her nation and interests, common threads link their achievements. In general, the enlightened despots were drawn to reforms that weakened the Church and the aristocracy, whose power they recognized as a potential threat to their own. To this end, they limited the ability of the nobles to punish the peasants, abolished certain tax exemptions for the clergy and nobility, established a measure of legal protection for religious toleration, worked to codify laws, and supported internal improvements. For example, King Frederick of Prussia ordered the cultivation of potatoes to help the soldiers' diet and also to respond to rising bread costs. Frederick reportedly described his reforms by saying "I am the first servant of the state." When contrasted with Louis XIV's declaration a century earlier that "I am the state," Frederick's words neatly summarize the shift in attitude during the Age of Reason.

Mercantilism

From the 16th to the 18th centuries, **mercantilism**—the economic policy based on amassing wealth through trade—was bound to the belief that power equals wealth. A key goal of mercantile policy was the accumulation of monetary reserves, particularly gold and silver. Without a reserve of such wealth, a nation would be unable to maintain an army or navy, weakening its influence. To prevent wealth from flowing out of the country, protectionist policies were put into place imposing high tariffs on imports, unless they were raw materials to be transformed into finished goods for export. The goal was to produce a favorable balance of trade. Production was regulated and monopolies enforced.

Mercantilism encouraged the establishment of colonies, which could be a source of precious metals and raw materials, as well as a captive market for manufactured goods from the home country.

The Challenge of New Economic Theories

Like absolutism in the political sphere, mercantilism required strong state power to regulate economic activity so a nation could compete against other nations for the earth's fixed supply of gold and silver. And like absolutism, mercantilism considered the interests of subjects as subservient to the interests of the monarchy, an attitude that would be called into question by the Enlightenment concepts of natural rights and the social contract.

Physiocrats Challenges to the importance of the monarch also came from French thinkers who focused on the economy. **Physiocrats** argued that land and labor were sources of wealth. Like Locke, they saw government's function as the protection of life, liberty, and property.

- **Anne Robert Jacques Turgot** (1727–1781) was an advisor to King Louis XV of France. He advocated for **laissez-faire**, a phrase that means "leave alone." He thought government should not interfere in the economic sector by imposing regulations, particularly on trade. Turgot thought the economy would work best when all individuals were free to determine what goods they wanted and what work they would contribute. He rejected the mercantilist theory about the importance of building up gold reserves in the treasury.

- **François Quesnay** (1694–1774) was a doctor and economic theorist. He believed that a state's economic strength derived not from gold and silver but from agriculture. Industry and manufacturing, he felt, were "sterile" activities that ultimately did not produce wealth. While this idea would prove misguided, Quesnay demonstrated how to apply scientific reasoning to studying the economy. Quesnay called for reduced taxes, elimination of tolls, and an end to government restrictions on trade.

Adam Smith The most influential economic reformer was Scottish philosopher, **Adam Smith** (1723–1790). Paralleling the scientists of his day who searched for natural laws governing the physical world, Smith searched for natural laws governing economic behavior. One of these laws, Smith believed, was that people were naturally social. For example, they cared if others suffered and they were inclined to gather with each other and to trade goods.

Based on these beliefs, Smith laid out a series of principles of economic behavior that together formed a single, complete system. His book, *An Inquiry into the Nature and Causes of the Wealth of Nations* (1776), marked the start of modern economic thought. Smith tried to answer basic economic questions, such as why some countries were wealthier than others. Like the physiocrats, Smith attacked mercantilism for over-regulating trade in an attempt to accumulate gold. Smith argued that the wealth of a nation came not from gold, but from the productivity of its workers. He believed that Great Britain and other countries would be wealthier if they had fewer restrictions on trade. Unlike the physiocrats, who thought agriculture was the primary source of wealth, Smith thought all forms of labor were valuable.

Another question Smith tried to answer was how an economy worked at all. Without any central authority allocating resources, raising or lowering prices, or setting wages, economies somehow adjusted to changing desires of people. It was as if an **invisible hand**, a force that no one could see, guided all economic decisions. Individuals made choices such as to buy or sell goods or to take or leave jobs based primarily on their own self-interests. When everyone did so, the competing self-interests balanced each other.

Smith recognized an important role for government in protecting property rights, preventing powerful businesses from misusing their influence, taking care of the disadvantaged, and promoting trade. But he is best remembered for his attacks on the excesses of government regulation under mercantilism.

HISTORICAL PERSPECTIVES: HOW RADICAL WAS THE SCIENTIFIC REVOLUTION?

Historians often portray the Scientific Revolution as a radical break with the classical and religious beliefs of the past, with Copernicus, Galileo, Descartes, Newton, and others as the leaders of this break. In the early 19th century, French scholar Auguste Comte argued that to be modern meant one rejected a view of the world rooted in religion and adopted one based on science. The revolution was less in what people believed and more in how they determined what was true. Rather than trust the works of Greeks, Romans, and early Christians, they relied on their own observations, reason, new formulations of physics, and the creation of calculus to understand the natural world. Scientific methodology was a revolutionary way of knowing.

Galileo's trial provided an example of a conflict between faith and science. His scientific ideas changed long-held religious views, and one side would win and one would lose. Historians thought science was both revolutionary and destined to win.

Science as Not Revolutionary However, in recent years, historians have argued that modern science was not so revolutionary, and its victory was never inevitable. Historian Robert Strayer noted that most of the scientists remained Christian. Further, they believed they were developing a greater understanding of the perfect universe that God created. Strayer quoted Newton, "This most beautiful system of the sun, planets, and comets could only proceed from the counsel and dominion of an intelligent Being."

Historian and philosopher Maurice A. Finocchiaro also argued that Christians were not anti-science. In *Defending Copernicus and Galileo: Critical Reasoning in the Two Affairs* (2010), Finocchiaro points out that the objections to Galileo were not only based on theology, but also on the inability to reconcile his ideas with those of the trusted Aristotelian physics. In addition, as scientific theories described the world more accurately, the Catholic Church gradually accepted them. The Jesuits taught many of these ideas.

The Strength of Religion Further, the victory of science began to appear less inevitable as the world became more globally connected. Historians began seeing the past in the global context as part of an ever-changing story with no determined end, unlike the scholars of the nineteenth century. While religion did decline in Europe in the 19th and 20th centuries, it remains a powerful force in the United States and most of the world. Historian Peter Harrison concluded that science would not destroy religion, but that both will have a place in today's world.

KEY TERMS BY THEME

Identity
Scientific Revolution
Enlightenment
Age of Reason
rationalism
empiricism
Rene Descartes
deductive reasoning
Sir Francis Bacon
inductive reasoning
deism
coffeehouse
salon
academy
lending library
masonic lodge
print culture

Continuity and Change
paradigm shift

Civic Ideals
social contract
John Locke
Thomas Hobbes
natural law
tabula rasa
natural rights
philosophe
ancien régime
Voltaire
Denis Diderot
Encyclopédie
Montesquieu
separation of powers
checks and balances
Cesare Beccaria
deterrence theory
Jean-Jacques Rousseau
general will
Marquis de Condorcet

Mary Wollstonecraft
Republic of Letters
noble savage
absolutism
enlightened absolutist
enlightened despot
Catherine the Great
Joseph II
King Frederick of Prussia

Economics
mercantilism
physiocrat
Anne Robert Jacques Turgot
laissez-faire
François Quesnay
Adam Smith
invisible hand

Questions 1 and 2 refer to the following passage.

Average Tariffs on Imports in Great Britain and France		
Year	Great Britain	France
1820	50%	20%
1830	45%	22%
1840	32%	19%
1850	30%	21%
1860	16%	14%
1870	10%	5%
1880	6%	6%

Source: Adapted from A. Imlah, *Economic Elements of the Pax Britannica* (1958), and M. Levy-Leboyer and F. Bourguignon, *L'Economie Francaise au XIXe siecle* (1985).

1. The change in tariff rates supports the argument that between 1820 and 1880 the British moved toward a policy advocated by

   a) physiocrats

   b) mercantilists

   c) supporters of free trade

   d) supporters of socialism

2. Comparing tariffs in Great Britain and France supports the argument that between 1820 and 1840

   a) Great Britain relied more on imports than France did.

   b) Great Britain protected its industries less than France did.

   c) Great Britain was more concerned about providing low-cost food for consumers than was France.

   d) Great Britains tariff policies help explain why it industrialized faster than France did.

Questions 3–5 refer to the following passages.

"Her circle met daily from five o'clock until nine in the evening. There we were sure to find choice men of all orders in the State, the Church, the Court—military men, foreigners, and the most distinguished men of letters. . . . Politics, religion, philosophy, anecdotes, news, nothing was excluded from the conversation, and, thanks to her care, the most trivial little narrative gained, as naturally as possible, the place and notice it deserved. News of all kinds was gathered there in its first freshness."

Baron de Grimm, *Historical and Literary Memoirs and Anecdotes, 1815*

"[W]hither shall a person, wearied with hard study, or the laborious turmoils of a tedious day, repair to refresh himself? Or where can young gentlemen, or shop-keepers, more innocently and advantageously spend an hour or two in the evening, than at a coffee-house? Where they shall be sure to meet company, and, by the custom of the house, not such as at other places, stingy and reserved to themselves, but free and communicative; where every man may . . . begin his story, and propose to, or answer another, as he thinks fit."

"In Praise of Coffee-houses," 1675

3. Which best describes the context in which these passages were written?

   a) Political debate took place in civic institutions and commercial sites.

   b) The Catholic-Protestant conflict was growing more violent.

   c) Governmental power was becoming more decentralized.

   d) People were moving out of cities and into rural areas.

4. What characteristic do coffeehouses and salons have in common?

   a) They were intended only for entertainment.

   b) They were designed for all people to attend.

   c) They were important aspects of the Enlightenment.

   d) They were focused only on political discussions.

5. What was the common attitude towards female participation in political discussions in England and France during the 17th and 18th centuries?

   a) Men in both countries often discouraged women from taking part in political discussions.

   b) English women wanted to participate in public debates, while French women preferred expressing their opinion in writings.

   c) French women were discouraged from taking part in political discussions, while English women were encouraged to do so.

   d) Both English and French women hoped that organizing political events would lead to serving in public office.

Questions 6–8 refer to the following passage.

"Throwing aside, therefore, all those scientific books, which teach us only to see men such as they have made themselves, and contemplating the first and most simple operations of the human soul, I think I can perceive in it two principles prior to reason, one of them deeply interesting us in our own welfare and preservation, and the other exciting a natural repugnance at seeing any other sensible being . . . suffer pain or death. It is from the agreement and combination which the understanding is in a position to establish between these two principles, without its being necessary to introduce that of sociability, that all the rules of natural right appear to me to be derived — rules which our reason is afterwards obliged to establish on other foundations, when by its successive developments it has been led to suppress nature itself. In proceeding thus. . . . Whatever moralists may hold, the human understanding is greatly indebted to the passions."

Jean Jacques Rousseau, The Origin of Inequality, 1751

6. Unlike many Enlightenment thinkers, Rousseau believed strongly in
    a) logic and reason
    b) absolutism and divine right
    c) the scientific method
    d) feeling and sentiment

7. Which statement would Rousseau most strongly support?
    a) Improvement of the self would lead to a better society.
    b) Improvement of education would make government better.
    c) Improvement of child-rearing would result in greater economic stability.
    d) Improvement of women's rights would strengthen marriage.

8. As described in the above passage, what other author developed a new political model based on "rules of natural right"?
    a) Thomas Hobbes
    b) Voltaire
    c) John Locke
    d) Denis Diderot

1. Use the passage below to answer all parts of the question that follows.

"It is helpful to . . . think about the Enlightenment as a series of interlocking, and sometimes warring problems and debates. These were problems and debates which affected how the Enlightenment worked not only in Europe, but also in the rest of the world. . .This presentation of the Enlightenment sees this movement as a group of capsules or flashpoints where intellectual projects changed society and government on a world-wide basis.

However, this is a new interpretation. Until quite recently, it was normal to understand the Enlightenment as ultimately a unitary phenomenon, as if there was an entity called the Enlightenment. This version of Enlightenment saw it as a desire for human affairs to be guided by rationality, rather than faith, superstition or revelation, a world view based on science, and not tradition."

Dorinda Outram, *The Enlightenment,* 2013

a) Describe ONE example that supports the author's interpretation that the Enlightenment was "guided by rationality."

b) Describe ANOTHER example that supports the author's intepretation that the Enlightenment was "guided by rationality."

c) Explain ONE way that events of the 18th century contradicted the view that the Enlightenment was "guided by rationality."

2. Answer all parts of the question that follows.

a) Describe ONE significant change in economic theory during the 17th and 18th centuries.

b) Describe ONE significant continuity in economic theory during the 17th and 18th centuries.

c) Explain how new economic theory during the 17th and 18th centuries changed European economic development.

LONG ESSAY QUESTIONS

1. Evaluate the extent to which the medieval worldview differed from the modern worldview of the Scientific Revolution and Enlightenment.

2. Evaluate the extent to which the Scientific Revolution and Enlightenment altered how people perceived education and the discovery of knowledge.

1. In one to three paragraphs, explain how spreading the principles of the Scientific Revolution led to an emphasis on reason.

WRITE AS A HISTORIAN: CONCLUDE THE ESSAY

A strong conclusion should summarize how the evidence supports the thesis and demonstrate a complex understanding of the topic. A writer has some options in how to accomplish these goals in an effective conclusion.

- Restate the thesis in a broader chronological context. That is, remind the reader how the point made in the essay was connected to, or distinctive from, what came before or what would come later in history. For example an essay on the French philosophes might compare them to Montaigne (1533–1592) or John-Paul Sartre (1905–1980).
- Restate the thesis in a broader geographical context. That is, remind the reader how the point made in the essay was similar to or unlike events elsewhere in the world. For example, the French philosophes were less focused on empirical data than were thinkers in Great Britain.

Another way to strengthen the conclusion is to expand on the thesis without taking the essay in a new direction. For example, if your thesis is that Enlightenment beliefs brought new optimism to European thought, you could conclude, "The Enlightenment philosophes' belief that science would result in progress brought renewed optimism to Europe after two centuries of religious conflicts."

Another method is to lay the groundwork for what came next as a result of the topic you've written about. This is called causation. For instance, "Ultimately, Enlightenment thinking laid the groundwork for the French Revolution."

It's also possible to end your essay by putting your argument into the framework of continuity and change over time. How is it part of a larger historical theme? An example of this is, "If history is a pendulum swinging back and forth between emotion and reason, the Enlightenment fully embodied the latter."

A fourth way to end an essay is with a quotation (or a paraphrase of one) that summarizes your thesis statement. In this case, a direct quote by Voltaire easily ties back to the thesis: "Voltaire captured the Enlightenment spirit when he urged people to judge men by their questions rather than their answers."

Choose the three sentences that best conclude an essay on the topic of "The Philosophes' Impact During the Enlightenment," and then identify which concluding method these sentences use.

1. Although the Enlightenment initially reached only the intellectual elite, it eventually spread to change European society at all levels.

2. Philosophers, such as Voltaire, Smith, Kant, and Hume, had major impacts on Europe during the Enlightenment.

3. The philosophes might not have brought about a paradise of reason and toleration, but they successfully challenged powerful institutions.

4. Hume questioned whether a tree falling in a forest made a sound if no one was there to hear it; the world continues to hear the philosophes.

Salons reflected both the intellectual passions driving French culture and the expanding opportunities for women during the Enlightenment.

Credit: Getty Images

11

Religion, Art, and Sentiment

"Know then thyself, presume not God to scan.
The proper study of mankind is Man."

—Alexander Pope, *Essay on Man, 1734*

Essential Question: How did the Scientific Revolution encourage religious toleration and cause a new emphasis on sentiment?

During the 17th and 18th centuries, the rationalism of the Scientific Revolution penetrated all aspects of European society. Whereas the previous age had exalted church and monarchy, Enlightenment intellectuals now questioned religious and royal authority. Their confidence in humanity led to an increase in toleration, after centuries of crushing religious warfare. The new emphasis on reason also transformed culture, as artists and writers turned away from narrow religious focus to rediscover the ideals embodied in classical civilization.

Enlightenment rationalism thus produced a host of new ideas, including deism, skepticism, and neoclassicism. Inevitably, a backlash followed, in the form of a series of religious revivals and a growing turn to feeling and emotion in art and literature. By the start of the 19th century, this movement, known as **Romanticism,** had displaced the "cold" rationality of the Enlightenment.

Religion and Toleration

As the Scientific Revolution progressed, a **secular**, or nonreligious, culture began to expand across Europe. The Enlightenment can be characterized, in fact, by its strong aversion to the institutions of the church. This is not to say, however, that Enlightenment thinkers opposed religion entirely, even if they opposed its trappings.

Natural Religion and New Ideas

Whereas traditional Christianity saw God as beyond human comprehension, most philosophes believed that human reason provided a path to understanding God. This **natural religion** argued that God exists in nature, not separate from it. His laws are natural laws that can be discovered through scientific study. Natural religion represented a challenge to the revealed religion of the church, in which God could be known only through revelation, faith, and miracles.

French philosopher Pierre Bayle (1647–1706), exiled to Holland due to religious persecution, espoused natural religion in his massive *Historical and Critical Dictionary*. Bayle's dictionary, which used scientific analysis to highlight irrationality and contradictions in Christian doctrines, was extremely influential among Enlightenment intellectuals, including Voltaire and Diderot.

Deism The French philosophe **Voltaire** (see Chapter 10) is well-known for using satire and wit in fighting religious hypocrisy. In *Candide*, he attacked superstition and made fun of clerics; his *Treatise on Toleration* advocated religious toleration; and in *Letters on the English*, he praised England's limited religious tolerance (although ignoring its intolerance of Roman Catholics), contrasting it to the stranglehold of the Catholic Church in France.

However, Voltaire argued (at least for a time) that there must be a God. He espoused **deism**—the belief that God had created the world and set it in motion—as a watchmaker may make a watch and start it up—and then left it to run on its own according to natural law. While deists accepted God, they rejected organized religion and its insistence that those who disobeyed its strictures would face eternal damnation. Deism became widely accepted by the educated elite during the Enlightenment, and for a short time during the Terror of the French Revolutionary period, it became the national religion of France. Among European nations, France was especially drawn to deism after centuries of religious wars and domination by the Catholic Church.

Atheism Voltaire's writings were highly influential on the evolving religious attitudes of Enlightenment intellectuals, among them **Denis Diderot** (see Chapter 10). Diderot, who was inspired by Bayle's dictionary to produce the *Encyclopédie*, had received a Jesuit education but turned to deism, following Voltaire's example, and then to **atheism**, the complete rejection of God and religion.

One of the first and most outspoken atheists of the Enlightenment was **Baron d'Holbach** (1723–1789), a French philosopher and contributor of science articles to the *Encyclopédie*. In his 1770 book, *The System of Nature*, d'Holbach proposed a materialistic godless universe in which everything could be understood through scientific reasoning, particularly physics. God, he thought, was an invention created by human ignorance and fear.

Skepticism The brilliant Scottish philosopher **David Hume** (1711–1776) went further by advocating **skepticism**, which asserted that all knowledge and beliefs should be approached with doubt. In *Inquiry into Human Nature* (1748), Hume undermined the religious texts by using logic to argue against miracles. In *Dialogue Concerning Natural Religion*, he argued that human reason was not sufficient to prove the existence of God. He also disputed the idea of an afterlife and made a strong case that religion corrupts rather than contributes to morality. His critiques provided a devastating systematic argument against religious authority.

Hume's skepticism was more radical than deism or even atheism. In fact, it threatened not only religious authority but also the prevailing principles of the

Enlightenment. To Hume, the fact that human senses were fallible called all experiences into question. Therefore, it was by no means certain that human reason could reveal universal truths, or that any universal truths even existed.

Emerging Belief Systems of the 17th and 18th Centuries		
Idea	Main Proponents and Influential Works	Beliefs
Deism	Voltaire *Candide* (1759) *Dictionnaire Philosophique* (1764)	• Believed that God had created the world, set it in motion, and then left it to run on its own according to natural law • Rejected organized religion
Atheism	Baron d'Holbach *Christianity Unveiled* (1761) *The System of Nature* (1770)	• Completely rejected God and religion • Proposed a materialistic godless universe in which everything could be understood through scientific reasoning
Skepticism	David Hume *An Enquiry Concerning Human Understanding* (rev. 1758)	• Argued that all knowledge and beliefs should be approached with doubt • Argued that human reason was not sufficient to prove the existence of God • Argued against religious authority • Threatened both religious authority and Enlightenment principles

An Emphasis on Private Revelation

As deism, atheism, and skepticism were taking firm root in 18th-century Europe, new faith movements developed in reaction. Under the influence of Enlightenment thought, religion—formerly a matter of public allegiance to the established church—was held to be a matter of individual conscience. The new religious movements embraced this distinction, as it meant every conversion was proof of "true" belief.

Methodism Among those troubled by the new nonreligious *-isms* was the British Anglican priest **John Wesley** (1703–1791). Wesley experienced an intense personal revelation that led him to form the **Methodist** movement, which spread across England and beyond. Methodism is a Protestant Christian theology that focuses on a personal experience with God, through which any individual can earn salvation. This concept had great appeal to the working classes, as did Methodism's stress on the importance of charitable works. Wesley preached in the open air, in fields and public spaces where all could hear his message.

Pietism Around the same time, another Christian religious movement, also responding to the desire for a personal relationship with God, sprang up in Germany and spread across Northern Europe. **Pietism**, which began among German Lutherans, emphasized mystical personal experience and the primacy of the Bible. This emphasis on personal piety predated and paved the way for the acceptance of Lutheranism in Northern Germany. However, in keeping with the Enlightenment view of humans as creatures of reason, Pietism also regarded individual moral behavior as the key to salvation and considered all believers as lay priests of the church. Pietism was known for its enthusiastic and emotional religious services that welcomed members of every social class. The pietist movement promoted many educational reforms in 18th-century German-speaking Europe. Its members were encouraged to undertake evangelizing missions. John Wesley was influenced by the pietist movement when he encountered it in the American colonies, where he spent two years as a missionary.

Faith Movements of the 18th Century		
Faith Movement	**Main Proponents**	**Beliefs**
Methodism	John Wesley (British Anglican priest)	• Considered religion a matter of individual conscience • Focused on personal experience of God and salvation • Stressed charitable works
Pietism	Began among German Lutherans	• Sought personal relationship to God • Emphasized mystical personal experience and primacy of the Bible • Regarded individual moral behavior as the key to salvation and considered all believers as lay priests of the church • Promoted educational reforms • Encouraged members to undertake evangelizing missions

A New Toleration

The Enlightenment influence could be seen in a new **religious tolerance.** The influential **John Locke** (see Chapter 10) argued the concept of fundamental natural rights, which were seen by many to include freedom of religion. As well, Locke's advocacy of separation between church and state naturally promoted tolerance, as the state was no longer tethered to a single religion. The growing sentiment that religion was a matter of individual private conscience rather than public concern was only one of many factors that led to greater religious tolerance in the Enlightenment era.

A related Enlightenment influence was the growth of nationalism, the belief that an individual's primary loyalty should be to the nation. Nationalism thus deemphasized religious differences, as devotion to the church declined and devotion to the state increased. In addition, a general sense of fatigue had set in after centuries of religious warfare. Lastly, a shift in the relationship between state and church authority took place under both democratic governments and enlightened despots.

Many governments implemented policies of religious toleration:

- England passed a Toleration Act in 1689. It included most Protestants but excluded Roman Catholics and Unitarians.

- France issued the Edict of Tolerance, signed by Louis XVI, in 1787. It gave Protestants freedom of worship and other legal protections. During the French Revolution, the *Declaration of the Rights of Man and Citizen* (1789) proclaimed complete freedom of religion across France. In 1791, the French National Assembly offered full civil equality to Jews, setting a model for the rest of Europe.

- Prussia, during the reign of Frederick the Great of Prussia (1740–1786), accepted exiled religious groups from elsewhere in Europe, including French Huguenots and Polish Jews.

- Austria, under Joseph II, enacted religious toleration for Christians of any denomination. The following year, he issued an edict extending this tolerance to Jews.

- Russia's Tsar Catherine the Great recognized Jews as Russian subjects and granted them many civil liberties, but restricted them to living in the Pale of Settlement, a region in the western part of the empire.

By 1815, most European nations had enacted legal protections for religious toleration for Christian minorities, and some had included Jews as well. Despite this, the progress toward full religious freedom and civil equality

JEWS IN EUROPE, c. 1800

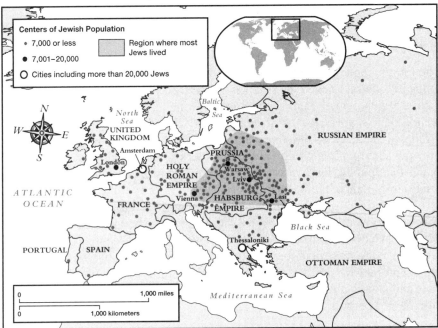

Source: Information adapted from map created for the International Institute for Jewish Genealogy by Sandra Crystall based on the research of Laurence Leitenberg, iijg.org.

for Jews was gradual and uneven. They were still prohibited from entering some occupations and living in some areas. It was not until the 20th century that Jews were extended full citizenship everywhere in Europe.

The Private Life and the Public Good in Art

During the 17th and 18th centuries, a new artistic movement spread. In painting, architecture, and music, the focus became grandeur, ostentation, and unimaginable opulence.

The Baroque Movement

In the 17th and early-18th century, the **Baroque movement** which had been inspired by the religous fervor of the Protestant Reformation dominated European art. Royal courts and religious leaders, hoping to awe viewers and listeners with the power of art, provided patronage to support painters, architects, and musicians, Some states established official "academies" to exhibit the works of artists judged suitable.

Baroque Art and Architecture Baroque architects constructed royal palaces, such as the Palace of Versailles in France, with its impressive entrance halls, magnificent staircases, lavish reception rooms, and extravagant decorative gilding. In painting, Baroque artists concentrated on religious themes and portraits of royalty. King Philip IV appointed the great Spanish artist **Diego Velásquez** (1599–1660) as the official painter of the Spanish court. Velásquez's work includes numerous portraits of members of the royal family, including his masterpiece, *Las Meninas*. Italian sculptor and architect

This sculpture by Bernini of an angel holding a cross is one of a series of 10 he planned for a bridge in Rome. Like other Baroque sculptors, he tried to portray energy and movement in his works.

Credit: Getty Images

Gian Lorenzo Bernini (1598–1680) was commissioned by the pope to renovate Saint Peter's Basilica and create several ornate chapels and piazzas near the Vatican. His designs included monumental open spaces flanked by sculptures in marble and bronze.

Baroque Music Baroque composers also depended on the patronage of royalty and aristocrats, and they wrote many compositions to be performed either as part of church services or at the royal court. **Johann Sebastian Bach** (1685–1750) wrote numerous *cantatas,* vocal pieces featuring instrumental accompaniment, for the Leipzig church that supported him. He received a commission from a Brandenburg nobleman to compose his famous *Brandenburg Concertos.*

Along with the cantata, the Baroque period saw the development of other musical forms, particularly opera and oratorio, large-scale dramatic concert pieces based on religious subject matter. The prolific composer **George Frideric Handel** (1685–1759) wrote nearly 50 operas and 30 oratorios. He composed *Water Music* at the behest of King George I of England, who desired a concert on the Thames River. Handel's masterpiece, *Messiah* (1741), is renowned for its dramatic and stirring "Hallelujah Chorus."

The Evolution Away from Baroque Style

As the authority of the church and monarchy continued to wane in Europe, by the 18th century art and literature increasingly reflected the values of the growing middle class. As it did, Baroque move in new directions.

Dutch "Golden Age" While appearing during the Baroque period, the art from the "Golden Age" of Dutch painting highlighted the increasing emphasis on private life and the growing importance of the middle class.

- **Frans Hals** (1582–1666) created realist paintings of a wide swath of humanity. He portrayed wealthy and influential aristocrats, clerks and members of guilds, colorful entertainers, and typical working-class men and women.

- The prolific Dutch painter and printmaker **Rembrandt van Rijn** (1606–1669) painted mainly portraits and biblical scenes, including such figures as Jesus and David, early in his career, but many of his most respected works focus on common people in everyday domestic settings or in nature. His paintings reveal a deep sense of humanity, regardless of the subject's station in life.

- **Johannes Vermeer** (1632–1675) painted mostly domestic interiors, often, as in *The Kitchen Maid*, showing women engaged in simple chores. *Girl with the Pearl Earring* is another of his famous paintings.

None of these artists received royal patronage, as perhaps is indicated by their broad choice of subject matter. Regarded today as among the finest artists in history, all three men had difficulty earning a living and died in poverty.

Rococo By the mid-18th century, the Baroque style had begun to evolve, and a looser, more graceful art form known as **Late Baroque** or Rococo spread across Europe. In contrast to Baroque glorification of churches and castles, Rococo art was secular, exuberant, and hedonistic. It reflected a general shift in emphasis from the public to the private sphere. This made it well-suited to the private interiors of upper-class homes and salons. It featured fluid lines; light, airy colors with gilt touches; painted ceilings; decorative mirrors; small sculptures; and a fascination with Chinese figurines and screens. Representative artists working in this style included the French artists Jean-Antoine Watteau (1684–1721) and Jean-Honoré Fragonard (1732–1806).

Neoclassicism

The Rococo period was short-lived. Near the end of the 18th century, as the Enlightenment focus on the individual continued to grow, the Rococo movement gave way to **Neoclassicism**. In contrast to Baroque glorification of church and court, Neoclassicists honored the secular values of reason and order and upheld the classical ideals of simplicity and symmetry. Neoclassicism was inspired by the cultural values of ancient Greece.

Neoclassicism in Art and Architecture Neoclassic artists and architects avoided ornamentation, preferring simple harmonious forms that revealed an underlying proportion and harmony. The French artist **Jacques-Louis David** (1748–1825), whose works inspired many during the French Revolution, produced perhaps the quintessential expression of Neoclassical ideals in *Oath of the Horatii*, painted in Rome and based on an ancient Roman legend. The painting, which depicts three brothers saluting their father as he hands them their swords before a deadly battle, forcefully evokes stoic self-sacrifice, calm inner strength, and devotion to duty.

The Neoclassic influence in architecture can be seen in the **Pantheon** in Paris, which is modeled on the ancient Pantheon in Rome. Originally intended as a Jesuit church, it was given new secular purpose during the French Revolution as a mausoleum for great French citizens, among them Voltaire and Rousseau.

Neoclassicism in Music In the 18th century, music also went through a profound stylistic transition. Composers such as **Wolfgang Amadeus Mozart** (1756–1791) reflected the ideas of the Enlightenment. His music often focused on secular rather than religious themes, and it emphasized order and balance rather than drama and emotion.

Neoclassicism in Literature England produced the most influential writers of this period, also known as the Augustan Age for its imitation of the classical Roman writers Horace and Virgil. It also saw the development of a number of literary forms, including political satire, melodrama, and the modern novel (including many new subgenres).

Neoclassical Authors	
Author	**Selected Works and Style**
Daniel Defoe (1660–1731)	• Written as a series of letters, the story *Robinson Crusoe* describes adventures of a shipwrecked man on a deserted island who learns to survive and finds redemption—in nature, without guidance from the church • The novel explores economic issues of that time
Alexander Pope (1688–1744)	• *The Dunciad* and *The Rape of the Lock* • "Mock-epic" narrative poems in the style of antiquity but promoting a modern sensibility
Samuel Richardson (1689–1761)	• *Pamela* and *Clarissa* feature women who defend their chastity • Originated the *epistolary novel,* a fictional work written in the form of letters
Henry Fielding (1707–1754)	• Novelist and dramatist famous for humorous novel *Tom Jones,* in which the protagonist faces a colorful cross-section of social classes • Major theme is the struggle to maintain virtue confronted with rogues, hypocrites, and villains
Johann Wolfgang von Goethe (1749–1832)	• Portrayed idyllic pastoral life and emphasized emotions over reason • *Faust,* about a man who sells his soul to the devil for knowledge and wealth, also treats man's search for meaning
Jane Austen (1775–1817)	• Novels included *Sense and Sensibility, Pride and Prejudice,* and *Emma* • Focused on the morals and social behavior of the English middle and upper class at the turn of the 19th century

The Revival of Public Emotion

Until the late 18th century, Enlightenment ideals of reason and science were the central theme of European culture. But rationalism was falling out of favor, as society experienced the seductive appeal of passion, danger, intensity, drama, feeling, and the lure of the sublime. The Age of Reason was giving way to Romanticism.

Historians debate the sources of this transformative shift. Some suggest that the cataclysm of the French Revolution led to a loss of faith in man's ability to solve problems by reason alone. Others argue that industrialization and agrarian reform had created a new social class untethered by convention or traditional historic roles. Some argue that Romanticism was less a reaction against the Enlightenment than a natural outgrowth of the Enlightenment's emphasis on the individual.

Rousseau and the Challenge to Reason

Like other Enlightenment philosophes, **Jean-Jacques Rousseau** (see Chapter 10) criticized the existing social order and argued vehemently for individual freedom. Unlike them, however, Rousseau did not put all his faith in reason. Instead, he managed to alienate deists, atheists, skeptics, and Catholics leaders alike by rejecting both natural religion's concept of an impassive "clockmaker" God and the church's emphasis on dogma and obedience. Instead, Rousseau envisioned God as a benevolent force that one could experience subjectively through personal experience and inner feelings.

An eclectic figure, Rousseau was involved with the *Encyclopédie* but also composed music and wrote novels and poetry. His writings celebrate nature, spontaneity, individualism, and passion. This, along with his emphasis on the subjective, has led many historians to describe him as the "Father of the Romantic movement."

The Romantic Movement

The **Romantic movement** spanned roughly the last decade of the 18th century through the first half of the 19th. Romantics departed in key ways from the orderly, rational science-based thinking of the Enlightenment. They did not entirely reject reason but considered it inadequate. Humans, they insisted, not only thought rationally, but also felt with emotion. Thus, sentiment and imagination were vital for a truer understanding of the world.

This explains to some degree why this period is famous for an outpouring of genius in the fine arts. Beyond mere sensual pleasure, fine arts represented the expression of personal truth and spiritual experience. Artists and writers were no longer content to catalog the world, as in the *Encyclopédie*; their aim was to mine the depths of imagination and personal experience to produce a new vision. The Romantics were particularly preoccupied with the beauty of nature and the sense of wonder and awe it produced. Their art favored wild landscapes, exotic peoples, fantastic and spiritual experiences, and heart-stirring deeds of heroism and romance, often set in the Middle Ages.

Romantic Literature The Scottish author **Sir Walter Scott** (1771–1832) is known for colorful folk poems set in rural Scotland, and narrative poems, including "The Lady of the Lake," that describes deeds of chivalry and the culture of the Highlands region. However, Scott is most famous for his novel *Ivanhoe*. Set in 12th-century England and based on the legend of Robin Hood, *Ivanhoe* contains many of the themes that were hallmarks of Romantic art:

- fascination with the medieval period, and chivalric values, such as honor and valor
- free-spirited heroes
- religious feeling and imagery
- romantic love, passion, and emotion
- nationalism, a strong feeling of pride in a culture

Ivanhoe was very popular and influential. One distinctive feature of it for its time was that Scott depicted Jewish characters as brave and intelligent. In this, he reflected the growing religious tolerance of the era.

The poet and artist **William Blake** (1757–1850) was notable because he scorned organized religion as a perversion of true spirituality. Yet, he insisted his art was divinely inspired. His poems and etchings were emotional, deeply subjective, and rich in symbolism and prophetic visions. They were so unusual that some people considered him mentally ill.

William Wordsworth (1770–1850) was a dominant figure in Romantic literature. Wordsworth argued for "common speech" in poetry and decried the old emphasis on epic poetry, preferring an emphasis on emotion and the imagination. Published anonymously in 1789, *Lyrical Ballads* was a joint collection of poetry that is recognized as Wordsworth's masterpeice. Poet and friend **Samuel Coleridge** contributed four poems to *Lyrical Ballads*, including his most famous work *The Rime of the Ancient Mariner.*

One writer recognized by Wordsworth for her contributions to the Romantic movement was **Charlotte Smith** (1749–1806). As a woman, she defied social expectations by becoming a poet and novelist. Smith responded to the French Revolution by challenging social injustice and advocating for class equality. Her works revived interest in a form of poety with 14 lines called an English sonnet. For example, Smith composed a collection titled *Elegiac Sonnets* while in prison with her husband and twelve children for his debts.

William Blake's painting from 1800 shows a story from the Hebrew tradition in which the ghost of a prophet named Samuel appeared to a king, Saul. Like other Romantic artists, Blake often portrayed mystical scenes. Credit: *The Ghost of Samuel Appearing to Saul,* c. 1800 by William Blake, Rosenwald Collection, National Gallery of Art

Among the many writers influenced by Wordsworth and Coleridge was a friend of Coleridge's, **Mary Robinson** (1757–1800). She responded to *Lyrical Ballads* by titling one of her own works *Lyrical Tales*. In her writing, Robinson often explored themes of people pushed to the margins of society or who suffered abuse.

Percy Bysshe Shelley (1792–1822) was a social reformer and pamphleteer before turning more to poetry. His lyrical drama *Prometheus Unbound* and the poems "Ode to the West Wind" and "To a Sky-Lark" expressed several Romantic themes: the quest for love and beauty, social justice and political rights, and hope arising from natural beauty. **John Keats** (1795–1821) often expressed his emotional response to nature in his poems. However, his most famous work, "Ode to a Grecian Urn," reflected his interest in classical culture.

Also in the tradition of Romanticism were the German writers, brothers **Jacob** (1785–1863) and **Wilhelm Grimm** (1786–1859). The Brothers Grimm were folklorists and linguists who collected tales from various cultures, particularly German, and brought them together in *Grimm's Fairy Tales* (1812–1822). Influenced by the social and political turmoil of their time, the brothers looked to the past to understand contemporary social institutions—yet without advocating a return to that past. Instead, they hoped to convey the richness, imagination, and beauty of those traditional cultures.

Romantic Music Music, particularly emotional symphonic and piano music, flourished during the Romantic era. German **Ludwig van Beethoven** (1770–1827) is among the most influential of all composers. While his early works sound like those of Mozart, his later works changed the direction of European music. Beethoven was prolific, writing nine symphonies, more than 30 **sonatas** (short compositions written for solo piano), numerous concertos, masses, and an opera. His Sixth Symphony, known as the Pastoral, expressed his love of nature. His Ninth Symphony incorporates the words of the German Romantic poet Friedrich von Schiller's "Ode to Joy." Beethoven's intense personality, wild dark hair, and tragic hearing loss made him the symbolic embodiment of Romanticism.

Frédéric Chopin (1810–1849) was a Polish composer and skilled virtuoso on the piano. He wrote numerous concertos, mazurkas (Polish folk dances), ballades (piano compositions), and nocturnes (pieces that evoke the spirit of the night), and three sonatas that are still among the most popular classical works. Often turbulent and passionate, Chopin's music stands out for its intimacy and expressiveness.

Romantic Art Like poets and novelists, Romantic artists were also striving to give form to an intense emotional reaction to the beauty of the natural world. The German artist **Caspar David Friedrich** (1774–1840) painted atmospheric natural landscapes, sometimes featuring allegorical or symbolic elements, such as ruins or leafless trees. Human figures do not face forward but rather out into the distance, inviting the viewer to join them in contemplating the scene. One

John Constable's painting of Salisbury Cathedral (1820) demonstrates the interest of Romantic painters in elements of nature, including trees, clouds, and shadows. **Credit:** "Salisbury Cathedral from Lower Marsh Close," 1820 by John Constable, Andrew W. Mellon Collection, National Gallery of Art

of his best paintings shows a solitary traveler standing on mountain summit, staring into a vast mysterious landscape of rugged mist-covered peaks.

John Constable (1776–1837) and **J.M.W. Turner** (1775–1851) were important English landscape artists. Constable's favorite subject was the local countryside, with its ancient castles, working farms, waterways, and agricultural laborers. He used a broader color palette than was typical at that time, trying to represent the *chiaroscuro*—the contrast between *chiaro* (bright) and *scuro* (dark) that he saw as a principle feature in nature. Likewise, Turner favored a radical color palette and innovative techniques, some of which laid the groundwork for modern abstraction. Turner is known for his expressive depictions of turbulent, storm-swept seas and luminous skies.

A New Religious Revival

The Romantic era's emphasis on feeling and intuition fed into a widespread **religious revival**. The very magnificence of the natural world, many felt, was proof enough of the existence of God. Generally, these revival movements shared a belief in the truth of personal spiritual experience, mysticism as a gateway to ultimate truth, and an emotional yearning for connection with God. At the same time, the Enlightenment ideal of religious tolerance and the view that religion was a matter of private conscience had taken root and now became part of the fabric of the new movements.

Evangelical Movements As the locus of faith moved from the state church to voluntary associations of believers, evangelical movements began to spring up across Europe, especially England, Germany, and France. Members actively shared their religious message in an effort to persuade outsiders to voluntarily and sincerely commit to Christianity. Methodism had become a mass movement, sometimes drawing crowds of 25,000. Its fervent adherents were sometimes regarded as extremists. However, they were also leading the charge in many social causes, including the abolition of slavery, prison reform, relief for the poor, improvements in education, and the creation of libraries. Poverty and disease were widespread in England, and the charitable work of the Methodists earned them respect.

A similar situation existed in Germany, where the rationalism of the Enlightenment era was surpassed by a new personal religiosity that emphasized emotion, feeling, and the mysteries of the spirit. Pietist revivals competed with a neo-Lutheran movement focused on liturgy (prescribed religious service) and confession.

France In France, religious fervor was tempered by political events. One of the primary goals of the French Revolution was ending the corruption and greed of the Catholic Church. As the Revolution progressed, policies were put in place to achieve these goals, ranging from confiscation of Church wealth to the nationalization of Church-owned property to fully outlawing the Church and deporting or murdering many of its priests and clerics. However, as a reaction to the anti-clericalism of the Enlightenment and the religious persecution during the Revolution, France experienced a Catholic revival in the early 19th century, as reflected in the writing of François-Auguste-René, vicomte de Chateaubriand.

Nationalism and Mass Uprisings

Modern nationalism emerged during the late 18th century, inspired by Enlightenment ideals. It was ushered in by the ideals of the French Revolution:

- individual liberty rather than subordination to government

- equality among all citizens rather than special privileges for aristocrats

- fraternity among all people of a state rather than loyalty to a small local region

As Napoleon's army spread through Europe after the French Revolution, it undermined the old feudal structure. In some areas, Napoleon essentially liberated people from the control of nobles. In others, particularly in German-speaking areas where people were divided into hundreds of separate states, people united around a national identity to resist Napoleonic domination.

Mass uprisings were another distinguishing feature of the late 18th century. They were the driving force propelling the French Revolution forward, beginning with the march on Versailles and on through the storming of the Bastille, the peasant revolts of the Great Fear of 1789, and the massive national mobilization for the war effort. For the first time in history, a mass movement of the people had formed to overthrow an authoritarian regime and replace it with a representative government.

Both of these emerging forces were fueled by the emotions and sentiment the Romantic movement held in high value. These forces would become increasingly powerful in Europe in the decades to come.

HISTORICAL PERSPECTIVES: WHAT LED TO RELIGIOUS TOLERATION?

During the long wars over religion in Europe, to say someone tolerated religious diversity was a criticism. It meant they tolerated untruthful and dangerous ideas. The attitude toward toleration began to change with Voltaire and other Enlightenment thinkers. In the 19th century, British historians began to see the rise of religious toleration throughout Europe not only as positive but also as inevitable. It was part of a general march toward human improvement that had reached its peak in the present. In other words, the historians were viewing history through the lens of their own beliefs, not on its own terms.

Challenging the March of Progress That optimistic view of the past in general and toleration in particular changed in the 20th century. The horrific destruction in World War I caused many intellectuals to rethink the belief that history was a march of progress. In 1931, a young British historian at Cambridge University, Herbert Butterfield, published *The Whig Interpretation,* a direct challenge to the rosy view of earlier historians, whom he identified as Whigs. For example, they had praised the development of religious toleration that grew out of the Reformation—because it was a value the historians held—and ignored the painful realities of the post-Reformation world.

One cost of this Whiggish view, according to Butterfield, was that historians judged people by the values of the historians' time rather than of the historical period. For example, historians condemned rulers such as the 16th-century Queen Mary for trying to uphold the long tradition of religious unity as a way to keep the state together and at peace.

Political Necessity By 2000, Butterfield's ideas were widely accepted. Historians tried to understand the past on its own terms, without making it a story of progress that led to the present. Cary J. Nederman, a professor of political science at the University of Arizona, pointed out that the Protestant Reformation and the resulting fragmentation of Christian Europe did not provide a direct line toward greater toleration. Luther and Calvin, the most influential leaders of the Reformation, did not advocate for religious toleration. For Nederman, early steps toward toleration such as the Peace of Augsburg (1555) and Edict of Nantes (1598) were the result of political necessity. During the 17th century, writings by Thomas Hobbes and

John Locke that supported religious toleration were ratifying a belief that it was a sensible policy. There was nothing inevitable about it.

Centralized Government More recently, economist Mark Koyama focused on how political conditions after the Reformation led to religious toleration. Once a monarch no longer needed the pope's blessing, persecuting heretics became politically irrelevant and economically unwise. They could allow religion to become a private matter. They did not need to expend money and lives trying to enforce religious unity. In addition, as the state became centralized and standardized, rulers found it more efficient and economically advantageous to treat everyone the same regardless of their faith. Centralization and standardization drove equality and toleration slowly but steadily. Religious toleration was not part of the story of a steady progress in human history nor part of an improvement in human morality. Rather, it was just a practical response to changes in political structures.

KEY TERMS BY THEME

Identity

Romanticism

secular

natural religion

Voltaire

deism

Denis Diderot

atheism

Baron d'Holbach

David Hume

skepticism

John Wesley

Methodist

Pietism

religious tolerance

John Locke

nationalism

Baroque movement

Diego Velásquez

Gian Lorenzo Bernini

Johann Sebastian Bach

George Frideric Handel

Frans Hals

Rembrandt van Rijn

Johannes Vermeer

Late Baroque

Neoclassicism

Jacques-Louis David

Pantheon

Wolfgang Amadeus Mozart

Alexander Pope

Samuel Richardson

Henry Fielding

Johann Wolfgang von Goethe

Daniel Defoe

Jane Austen

Jean-Jacques Rousseau

Romantic movement

Sir Walter Scott

William Blake

William Wordsworth

Lake Poets

Samuel Coleridge

Charlotte Smith

Mary Robinson

Percy Bysshe Shelley

John Keats

Jacob and Wilhelm Grimm

Ludwig van Beethoven

sonatas

Frédéric Chopin

Caspar David Friedrich

John Constable

J.M.W. Turner

religious revival

Civic Ideals

mass uprisings

MULTIPLE-CHOICE QUESTIONS

Questions 1–3 refer to the following passage.

"A miracle is a violation of the laws of nature; and as a firm and unalterable experience has established these laws, the proof against a miracle, from the very nature of the fact, is as entire as any argument from experience can possibly be imagined. Why is it more than probable, that all men must die... that fire consumes wood, and is extinguished by water; unless it be, that these events are found agreeable to the laws of nature, and there is required a violation of these laws, or in other words, a miracle to prevent them? Nothing is esteemed a miracle, if it ever happens in the common course of nature. It is no miracle that a man, seemingly in good health, should die on a sudden: because such a kind of death, though more unusual than any other, has yet been frequently observed to happen. But it is a miracle that a dead man should come to life; because that has never been observed in any age or country. There must, therefore, be a uniform experience against every miraculous event; otherwise the event would not merit that appellation."

David Hume, *An Enquiry Concerning Human Understanding,* 1748

1. On what basis did David Hume reject the existence of miracles?

   a) Miracles are too unusual to be true.

   b) The permanent laws of nature contradict miracles.

   c) Miracles are a product of an attempt to deceive people.

   d) Miracles are based on religion, not science.

2. The philosophical theory that is the underlying basis of this passage is known as

   a) absolutism

   b) mercantilism

   c) skepticism

   d) humanism

3. Which viewpoint about the role of God and religion developed as a result of Enlightenment rationalism?

   a) Agnosticism

   b) Romanticism

   c) Deism

   d) Skepticism

Credit: *The Syndics of the Amsterdam Drapers' Guild,* by Rembrandt von Rijn,1662, Rijksmuseum, Gallery of Honous

4. This painting represents a shift from paintings of earlier eras because its subject matter

   a) emphasized religious themes more

   b) focused more on everyday life

   c) reflected a more idealized view of the world

   d) portrayed things and people more realistically

5. What shift in society and economics enabled art such as this to appear at this time?

   a) The patronage of commercial elites

   b) The patronage of monarchs and nobles

   c) The influx of gold and silver into Poland and Eastern Europe

   d) The ability of the Catholic Church to withstand Protestant encroachment

Questions 6–8 refer to the passage below from "The Tables Turned," by William Wordsworth. It was first published in 1798.

"Up! up! my Friend, and quit your books;

Or surely you'll grow double:

Up! up! my Friend, and clear your looks;

Why all this toil and trouble?

The sun, above the mountain's head,

A freshening lustre mellow

Through all the long green fields has spread,

His first sweet evening yellow.

Books! 'tis a dull and endless strife:

Come, hear the woodland linnet [a type of bird],

How sweet his music! on my life,

There's more of wisdom in it.

And hark! how blithe the throstle [a type of bird] sings!

He, too, is no mean preacher:

Come forth into the light of things,

Let Nature be your Teacher."

6. The poem best exemplifies which intellectual trend of the 18th century?
   a) The spread of deism and atheism among elites
   b) The belief in the outdoors as a source of truth about the world
   c) The use of satire to criticize political authorities
   d) The emphasis on individual emotion as a challenge to rationality

7. The poem's themes are a response to which development?
   a) Peasant movements to revive communal agriculture
   b) The growth of industrialization and urbanization
   c) Demands for suffrage and Parliamentary reform
   d) Rising literacy rates among the working class

8. The inspiration for this poem is most similar to the inspiration for some of the music by which composer?
   a) Bach
   b) Mozart
   c) Beethoven
   d) Chopin

1. Use the passage below to answer all parts of the question that follows.

> Baroque art (derived from the Portuguese word "Barrocca," meaning rough or imperfect pearl) originated in Italy and a few other countries as an imperceptible passage from the late Renaissance, which ended about 1600. It was occasionally seen as a variation and brutalization of the Renaissance style and sometimes conversely as a higher form of its development, and it remained dominant until approximately the middle of the 18th century. Conventionally, Baroque style is not emphasized in the global history of art because the time period when it flourished—between 1550 and 1750—is correctly viewed as an enclosed time period in which various directions were expressed.
>
> Klaus Carl and Victoria Charles, *Baroque Art*, 2009

a) Explain how ONE piece of evidence supports the argument by Carl and Charles regarding the *change* in art in the Baroque period.

b) Explain how ONE piece of evidence supports the argument by Carl and Charles regarding the *continuity* in art in the Baroque period.

c) Explain how Neoclassicism marked either a continuity OR a change from Baroque artistic style.

2. Answer all parts of the question that follows.

a) Explain ONE way the Enlightenment influenced the development of religious tolerance.

b) Describe ONE way political institutions expanded religious tolerance in Europe in the 1700s.

c) Describe ONE way religious tolerance marked a change from policies held by absolute monarchs of the 1600s.

LONG ESSAY QUESTIONS

1. Evaluate the most significant change in the interaction between religion and science in Europe in the three centuries following the Reformation.

2. Evaluate the most significant impact the Scientific Revolution had on religious tolerance.

1. In one to three paragraphs, explain how the Scientific Revolution encouraged religious toleration and a new emphasis on sentiment.

WRITE AS A HISTORIAN: COMPARISON AND CONTRAST

The skill of comparison includes evaluating both similarities and differences in events in the past. Suppose a prompt asks you to compare Baroque and Neoclassical art. One way to organize such an essay would be by broad topic:

- describe Baroque art
- describe Neoclassical art
- identify the similarities and differences between the types

A second way to organize the essay would be by relationship:

- describe similarities
- describe differences

A third way, the most commonly used in essays on exams, would be by issue:

- the time period in which each style was dominant
- the geographic regions where each style was popular
- the subject matter commonly portrayed in each style
- the political significance of works created in each style

As in other essays, the thesis should present an argument. A statement such as "Baroque and Neoclassical art are two very different styles that both emerged during the Enlightenment period" is a weak thesis. It simply restates the prompt. Instead, try to find a deeper historical idea: "Until about 1750, monarchs used Baroque art to promote religious sentiment and the power of the state. That changed as Enlightenment philosophies gave rise to the more linear and rational Neoclassical style that emphasized private life and the public good over traditional institutions."

Organize information as directed for the following topics.

1. Contrast Baroque vs. Neoclassical art: Create two categories—one for subject matter and one for style characteristics.

2. Compare the impact of Enlightenment thinking on the lives of people belonging to various religious groups: Create two categories—one for religious reforms and one for political changes.

12

Revolutions in Everyday Life

"We are born weak, we need strength; helpless, we need aid; foolish, we need reason. All that we lack at birth, all that we need when we come to man's estate, is the gift of education.

Jean-Jacques Rousseau, *Emile, or on Education,* 1762

Essential Question: What factors shaped the experiences of everyday life in the 18th century?

The economy of preindustrial Europe had been based on cottage industry, merchant guilds, and subsistence agriculture produced on small landholdings and dependent on peasant labor. Most people lived in villages rather than cities. The population, slowly increasing for centuries, had been held in check by periods of famine, epidemic, disease, and war. Agricultural productivity had seen little improvement for hundreds of years. Europe was still in the clutches of the **Little Ice Age**, generally cold weather that extended from the 16th to the mid-19th century, causing extensive crop, livestock, and human death.

Then suddenly—just as the economy began to transition in the early stages of industrialization—the population of Europe began to increase rapidly. This burgeoning populace would experience life much differently from previous generations. Overall, levels of prosperity and material well-being rose, reflected in changing social and cultural behavior. At the same time, there was a vast increase in the numbers of poor, as displaced agricultural workers migrated to cities for work, cutting them off from traditional extended-family networks.

Population Growth

One revolution in modern history was the shift in **demographic patterns,** the trends in birth and death rates and population size, that emerged during the 18th and 19th centuries. One was a dramatic increase in population. In preindustrial Europe, the growth rate averaged less than 1 percent per decade, more or less. In the 1800s, that rate jumped to nearly 10 percent per decade.

In 1700, roughly 110 million people lived on the European continent. By 1800, the figure was about 190 million; in 1900, it was 423 million. Demographers measure population growth by comparing birth rates to death rates (mortality). In 1700, birth rates were slightly higher than death rates. However, by 1750, while birth rates remained stable, death rates began to plummet. Infant mortality decreased and life expectancy became significantly higher. By 1820, the birth rate was substantially greater than the death rate, creating a population explosion.

The new demographic pattern alarmed political economist Thomas Malthus (1766–1834). Like other Enlightenment thinkers, Malthus tried to apply scientific tools to what he observed around him. In 1798, he published *An Essay on the Principle of Population*, in which he demonstrated that while populations grew *geometrically* (by a constant multiple), the food supply could only increase *arithmetically* (by a constant amount). The population would inevitably run out of food, Malthus argued, unless severe limits could be placed on population growth.

Examples of European Population Growth				
Country	Population in 1700	Population in 1900	Percentage of World Population in 1700	Percentage of World Population in 1900
Great Britain/UK	8 million	40 million	1.2%	2.3%
British Empire	9 million	436 million	1.3%	26.0%
France	21 million	39 million	3.1%	2.3%
French Empire	21 million	79 million	3.1%	4.6%

Source: Data summarized from multiple sources

The Agricultural Revolution

For centuries, most Europeans had experienced chronic undernourishment, living on a **subsistence diet**—just enough food to sustain life. This was a major cause of the high mortality rate. During the Enlightenment, thinkers used science to approach the problem of food shortages and famine. As a result, the late-17th and the 18th centuries saw a second revolutionary transformation in Europe, the **Agricultural Revolution**, a series of breakthroughs that increased agricultural production.

Changes in Farming

The Agricultural Revolution changed how people farmed. It greatly increased food production, reducing the number and frequency of food-related crises.

Land Use Additional land became available for agricultural use through land reclamation, particularly in England and the Netherlands, where reclamation often required building dykes, or walls to prevent flooding from the sea. The engineering of dykes in the Netherlands was so successful that England hired Dutch engineer Cornelius Vermuyden (1595–1677) to drain the marshy fens in East Anglia. The resulting farmland was some of the most productive in the country. Other European states followed the same methods to clear and plant their woodlands and forests and drain their wetlands.

The Dutch led the way in **crop rotation,** the practice of growing different crops in a specific area so that the land could remain in continuous use without depleting the soil. This contrasted with traditional farming techniques in use since the Middle Ages, when land was left fallow, or uncultivated, for a period to restore nutrients. First, farmers in Flanders (a Dutch-speaking area in what is today Belgium) discovered that a four-year, four-crop rotation of wheat, barley, turnips, and clover would result in dramatically higher crop yields. Turnips and clover were rich in nitrogen, which replenished the soil. Turnips were especially important because they could remain in the ground in winter and their tops provided fodder for grazing livestock.

The idea of crop of rotation then spread thoroughout Europe. For example, the British aristocrat Charles Townshend (1674–1738) observed crop rotation when he served as ambassador to the Netherlands. He established the process in Britain, starting on his own estates.

Advances in Technology and Science Several advances in farming combined to create the Agricultural Revolution (See Chapter 9 for more about this development):

- British agriculturist Jethro Tull (1674–1741) developed a horse-drawn mechanical seed drill that planted seeds in rows.

- Tull also created a horse-drawn steel hoe that could till weeds between the rows and overturn the soil for planting.

- Scottish engineer Andrew Meikle (1719–1811) invented the threshing machine in 1786, which removed the outer husks from grains of wheat, greatly reducing the number of workers required for the harvest.

- British engineer Robert Bakewell (1725–1795) and reformer Thomas Coke (1754–1842) pioneered selective breeding of livestock for desirable characteristics, such as size and health.

New Crops The effects of **Columbian Exchange**—the interchange of plants, animals, diseases, and culture between the Americas and Europe—had been reflected in European diets since the 16th century. The exchange brought important new crops, including tomatoes, corn, and perhaps most importantly potatoes, which became a staple in Ireland by the 1750s. The potato had a shorter growing season than most grains, grew well in poor soil and cold climates, and was highly nutritious. (See Chapter 3 for more information about the Columbian Exchange.)

Enclosures The **enclosure movement** was a source of new land for farming. Since the Middle Ages, the **open field system** of farming had been prevalent in most of Europe. Under this system, each village or manor had some large fields, known as the **commons,** that were divided into small strips for cultivation by the peasantry. In 1700, most farmland in Europe and at least half in Britain were in these common open field strips. In addition, these open common areas were available for grazing animals, gathering firewood, and foraging.

Samuelson's Self-delivery Reaping-machine.

The development of reapers powered by animals such as horses or oxen relieved people of one of the most difficult tasks in agriculture.

Credit: Getty Images

The open field system ended with the enclosure movement of the late-18th century. In Britain, Parliament passed the **Enclosure Acts** to hasten the process, allowing wealthy landholders to purchase the common areas, consolidate them into single farms, and enclose those farms with fences. Before long, much of the agriculture in Great Britain took place on commercial farms. By 1850, nearly all British agricultural lands had been enclosed.

With enclosure, large-scale farmers could now plow and plant huge parcels of previously uncultivated land. On the other hand, enclosure brought ruin for small-scale farmers and peasants, many of whose families had lived in the same village for centuries and who depended on the commons for survival. Though the results were horrendous for these small farm families, the new system did increase food sources. In addition, it provided an inexpensive pool of labor for the coming Industrial Revolution.

Transportation

To transport their increasing supply of food, Britain and other parts of Western Europe were improving their internal transportation systems. Nations built new roads and widened existing ones, creating turnpike networks suitable for wheeled transportation. They strengthened bridges, linked canals and waterways, and gradually lifted road tolls—a remnant of feudal times. Eventually, European nations established railroad networks. All of these developments made it easier and less expensive to transport food to urban areas. Food transportation also was facilitated by the widespread adoption of a sterile canning process developed by French chef Nicolas Appert (1749–1841) at the request of Napoleon Bonaparte, who desired to improve the food supply for his field troops.

Improvements in Health

Along with the Agricultural Revolution, Europe's growing population was better-nourished and healthier, for two additional reasons:

- advancements in medical science, including new understanding of disease transmission and the development of inoculation

- developments in engineering, resulting in cleaner water, safer food, better sewage disposal, and improved hygiene

The Danger of Infectious Diseases

Recurrent episodes of infectious disease had caused major rises in Europe's death rates. For some diseases, such as tuberculosis, the bacteria that caused them could be found all over Europe. Other diseases, such as malaria, were confined to certain regions or climates. The worst diseases were **epidemic** in nature, sweeping through the continent in periodic waves and then mysteriously subsiding, only to reappear later. Some epidemics, such as typhus and typhoid fever, spread as a result of unsanitary conditions and primarily affected the poor.

The epidemic of the **bubonic plague**, or Black Death, wiped out a third of the European population in the 14th century and then reappeared at approximately 20-year intervals until the early-18th century. In 1665, plague reduced the population of London by 16 percent, and in the years between 1710 and 1720, it killed half the city of Danzig, almost half of Prague, Copenhagen, and Stockholm, and a third of Marseilles. Historians do not know why the plague ended. Theories include immunity through repeated exposure, decline in the rats that carried the disease, isolation of infected individuals or areas, improved sanitation, and genetic mutations in the bacteria responsible for the disease.

The most devastating epidemic disease was **smallpox**, affecting all levels of society and changing the course of history, as it killed off members of royal families. In the late-17th and 18th centuries, smallpox epidemics were a leading cause of death in Europe and Britain, eliminating as much as 13 percent of the population each generation. Those who survived the disease were left disfigured and often blind.

The Anti-Epidemic Campaign

In the 17th century, the Scientific Revolution inspired many physicians to apply new techniques to investigating and treating infectious diseases. By looking at not only the patient, but also the patient's environment, scientists discovered that unsanitary conditions, particularly in crowded urban areas, were connected to epidemics, and vocal public health campaigns arose.

Near the end of the 19th century, smallpox was still killing as much as 10 to 20 percent of Europe's population. To combat it, *variolation*—an inoculation procedure of infecting someone with live smallpox virus taken from a blister of someone with a mild form of the disease—was introduced in Britain by **Lady Mary Wortley Montagu** (1689–1762), who had learned about it when she lived in Turkey. However, Edward Jenner (1749–1823) developed a safer alternative—the world's first vaccine—in 1796. Jenner had noticed that milkmaids who had cowpox, a similar but less virulent disease, did not get smallpox. He determined that giving people cowpox protected them from smallpox. With his new vaccine, Edward Jenner became known as the "father of immunology." Thanks to his treatment, smallpox soon declined across Europe and has since been eradicated worldwide.

Other Health Practices

Additional practices against disease became important during this period, including quarantining and improved personal hygiene. Rising standards of living and the increased food supply led to improved overall health, which meant stronger resistance to disease. The availability of silk and cotton cloth meant more sanitary bedding and clothing. A growing preference for tea and coffee meant that people often boiled water before drinking it. On the other hand, increased urbanization facilitated the spread of disease, as the growth of cities brought new public health and sanitation concerns.

Advancing a Market Economy

The population explosion in the late-18th century occurred because of improvements in the food supply and reductions in infectious disease. Occasional famines still occurred, but for the most part, there was sufficient food to sustain the population by the mid-18th century.

The Agricultural Revolution also was important in advancing the market economy. Farmers could sell their surplus first in regional markets, eventually nationally, and later internationally, thanks to improvements in transportation. By the mid-19th century, most food grown in Western Europe was produced to be sold rather than for consumption by the farmer. Agriculture was thus changing from a means of subsistence to a competitive business. This was a key part of the shift toward **capitalism,** an economic system in which individuals and businesses make decisions based on the pressures of the market, rather than on tradition or because of government orders.

At the same time, the advancements of the Agricultural Revolution meant that fewer people were needed to produce food, leading to an enormous disruption in the labor force, as peasants had to migrate to urban areas in search of work.

The Consumer Revolution

Unsurprisingly, the demographic changes brought great social change. Lower mortality and better nutrition meant Europeans, particularly in Western Europe, were healthier than ever. In addition, education levels were rising, and culture was becoming more accessible to a greater number of people.

By the end of the 18th century, a high proportion of Europeans experienced unprecedented levels of relative material prosperity. For centuries, life for most Europeans had been dominated by scarcity. Now a **Consumer Revolution,** propelled by the disposable income of the growing middle class, swept across Europe, bringing both a powerful desire for consumer goods and an unfamiliar ability to afford at least some of them, particularly among city-dwellers.

Increase in Commercial Production In preindustrial Europe, the household had traditionally been the site of production for most people. Now, however, a population of merchants, financiers, and wage earners—anyone no longer dependent on the land for livelihood—shared a common bond. They embraced consumption to satisfy *desire* rather than *necessity*, and the wealthy saw luxury items and fashion as a way to display their economic status. This attitude was emulated by the masses but with cheaper fashions and edibles, ensuring that the consumer revolution carried through to all levels of society.

Household goods and products began to shift from being mostly homemade to mostly commercially produced. Consumerism, in turn, brought jobs and stimulated commerce, creating even more wealth. The new consumer economy eventually became a permanent feature of capitalist economies worldwide.

Consumer Goods for the Home A number of factors resulted in an increased supply and variety of consumer goods, among them increased trade, both within Europe and with Asia and the American continents. Those who could not afford imported luxury goods made up a market for lower-cost domestic imitation items, allowing them to emulate the upper classes. Asian-imported ceramics, particularly Chinese **porcelain**, were so popular that imports could not keep up with demand, sparking a domestic ceramic industry. Entrepreneur Josiah Wedgwood (1730–1795) developed less expensive imitation ceramics that became very popular. Wedgwood's success was built not only on quality but also on his understanding of the new consumer market.

OCEAN TRADE BY EUROPEANS IN THE 19TH CENTURY

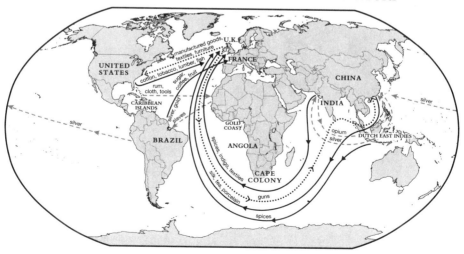

He realized that items used by the upper class would become desired by the middle class. When Queen Charlotte, wife of George III, purchased some of his ceramics, he convinced her to let him use her name in advertising.

In addition to porcelain dishes, other household consumer items in great demand included mirrors, cotton and linen goods, silks, decorative prints, and jewelry. These took on increasing importance as status symbols for the owner. Consumers desired these items for their usefulness but even more for their ability to confer social status. Demand for such consumer items inspired domestic glass making as well as silk and cloth manufacturing.

Food and Drink Some of the most popular commodities of the 17th and 18th centuries were consumables. Europeans were able to obtain coffee, hot chocolate, tea, and liqueurs. Sugar, once an exotic luxury item, became widely available and inexpensive as a result of slavery in the New World, and the consumption of sugar skyrocketed among all social classes.

New Leisure Venues Soon, **coffeehouses** and other public spaces sprang up, allowing the shared social consumption of these new beverages. Located mostly in urban areas, these venues served as a meeting place for all classes of male society, encouraging a healthy exchange of ideas. Women sometimes were proprietors or servers at coffeehouses, but otherwise, they were unwelcome. The coffeehouse began to decline in popularity during the 1800s as homes grew increasingly comfortable and privacy became more desirable; some coffeehouses later evolved into private men's clubs. As an alternative to coffeehouses, **lending libraries** opened, making books and other print materials available to those who could not afford to buy them.

In villages and more rural areas, **taverns** and alehouses were places to socialize, converse, dine, and drink alcohol. Taverns that offered sleeping accommodations to travelers were called *inns.* In fact, until the end of the 18th

"HA, HA! YOU MUST LEARN TO LOVE ME."
Vide " The Bottle Imp."

This British cartoon suggests, based on the expressions on the faces of the family, that not everyone was pleased with the food they were importing.

Credit: Getty Images

century, when the first restaurants began to appear in France, inns and taverns were the only places to dine outside of the home. They were popular meeting places to conduct business affairs and hold meetings, so they were sometimes referred to as "public houses" or "pubs."

As Europe grew increasingly urban, there was a dramatic increase in the number of **theaters** and **opera houses**, designed to cater to a new and broader audience—the growing middle class.

Changing Attitudes and Identities The growing desire for consumer goods changed not only spending behavior, but also society's attitude toward labor; as individuals—particularly women—needed money to purchase the new goods they desired. Work outside the home—wage-earning labor—was necessary to maintain the household and purchase the consumer items.

Spurred by demographic growth in the 18th century, the Consumer Revolution resulted in a new type of social identity. Once people had the opportunity to choose from a variety of consumer goods, those goods became more than just functional items. The goods began to represent one's individuality and social position. The family unit, in general, had shifted from a unit of production to one of consumption. Consumer goods became increasingly important in the home, the locus of domestic life.

Family and Private Life

During the 18th and early-19th centuries, the reduction in child mortality and increase in life expectancy formed the demographic foundation for new attitudes toward marriage, children, and families. The growing money economy was creating a new middle class with education and financial means, and its impact on marriage and family institutions was enormous. The Enlightenment had brought a rethinking of old attitudes toward childhood and education. During this period, many long-held social patterns were rethought, though others remained in place.

Concern for Privacy

A new concept of the home reflected the shifting attitudes of consumers. Formerly, a typical home might consist of a few rooms that served multiple functions. With the advent of the Consumer Revolution, homes began to be designed with specific rooms for specific functions, each decorated appropriately. Privacy became a central focus, leading to developments such as the **boudoir**. Originally intended as a quiet space for prayer, by the second half of the 18th century, the boudoir became a private retreat set aside specifically for the wife—a place for her to dress, read, relax, and entertain, "free" from her husband and from the traditional role assigned to her. The evolution of the boudoir reflects the emerging concept of **domesticity,** the idea of the home as a private sphere distinct from the encroachments of the public world. It served as a refuge from outside influences.

This new concept of domestic space was reflected in the sentimental novel, a popular-18th century literary genre that celebrated feeling as opposed to reason. It sought an emotional response from readers. The main characters were often females, and virtue was a main theme. The women were either virtuous or their virtue was imperiled or lost. (For more on these authors and others of their time, review Chapter 11.)

- The novels of **Samuel Richardson** (1689–1761), such as *Pamela* and *Clarissa,* emphasized the vital role private domestic spaces served in the lives of his female characters.

- **Jonathan Swift** (1667–1745), in the poem "The Lady's Dressing Room," used a fragrant boudoir as a metaphor for the female body.

- Later examples include the works of **Jane Austen** (1775–1817), **Charlotte Brontë** (1816–1855), and **George Eliot** (1819–1880). Their heroines followed the social rules of the time, but their observations and private emotions were refreshingly acute and independent.

Jane Austen wrote books for a popular audience. Her books and movies based on them remain so popular that she was portrayed on British currency.

Credit: Getty Images

Marriage and Birth Patterns

The **European marriage pattern** tended to limit population growth, at least for non-nobility. Its main features were late marriage age, small age difference between husband and wife, and the establishment of a nuclear household after marriage that is separated from both spouses' parents. People could not marry until they had enough resources to start their own independent households. Those unable to acquire such resources might never marry at all.

Consequently, the European marriage pattern represented an important check on population growth rates. However, this situation began to change following the Vital Revolution. The changes were experienced differently depending on social position. More and rural peasants were forced to migrate to urban areas looking for work. This also released them from some of the social constraints imposed by families and village traditions. At the same time, the growing middle class was less troubled by financial considerations, making it possible for men and women to marry for status, companionship, or even love.

Children of Unwed Parents By the second half of the 18th century, the rate of babies born to parents not married to each other (sometimes called illegitimate births) began to show a rapid and dramatic increase. In Britain, France, and Germany, statistics suggest that fewer than 1 percent of babies were born out of wedlock in 1600; by 1800, this had increased to around 3 to 6 percent; by 1850, it was 20 percent or even higher. These figures indicate increased sexual activity between unmarried people, particularly those in urban areas who were removed from the control of family and community authorities. Despite the surge in births outside of marriage, unwed mothers still suffered brutal social stigma that could leave them with no recourse but prostitution.

Foundling Hospitals Despite opposition from both the Catholic Church and the Church of England, some couples practiced birth control to avoid pregnancy. However, unwanted pregnancies continued to occur. No public financial support was available for unwed mothers. Killing an infant was a capital crime for which a number of women were hanged in the 18th century. The first foundling hospital —an institution that cared for unwanted children—was established in 1739 in Britain. Parliament announced that the hospital would accept all abandoned children it received, but that policy was quickly overturned when almost 15,000 arrived within the first year. Conditions at the hospital were harsh, with only about a quarter of children surviving to adulthood.

Birth and Infancy Childbirth, which almost always took place in the home, was dangerous, with high maternal and fetal mortality rates. However, more and better food and less infectious disease meant that once born, more children survived infancy. By the end of the 18th century, the traditional family pattern of many births and many infant deaths was shifting toward a pattern of fewer births and fewer infant deaths.

There was considerable variation in infant care both among different social classes and in different countries. Particularly in France, but also in Scandinavia, many women chose not to breastfeed, believing it to be unpleasant and bad for the mother's health. Instead, they hired other women to breastfeed their infants, called *wet-nurses*. Wealthy women hired wet-nurses to live in their homes, while working women who could not maintain a live-in wet-nurse might send their babies off to live with hired wet-nurses, often for years.

Wet-nursing was popular even though it greatly increased the risk of infant mortality. Some women preferred it, some women had no alternative, and in any case, it was standard practice. In his influential novel *Emile*, Enlightenment philosopher **Jean-Jacques Rousseau** (1712–1778) urged mothers to breastfeed their own infants, as one important step in a comprehensive plan for nurturing and educating children.

Changing Views of Childhood Before the 18th century, the concept of childhood as a developmental stage did not really exist. Children were regarded as small adults. In the upper classes, children were strictly disciplined, while in the lower classes children were expected to work, just as adults did.

The Enlightenment elevated childhood and coincided with the rise of a middle class possessing more resources to devote to children. **John Locke** discussed the development of children in his concept of *tabula rasa,* or blank slate, which included the belief that behavior and personality were learned.

In *Emile,* Rousseau similarly argued that children were born innocent and childhood should be a privileged period before the hardships of adulthood. Young children should focus on play, exercise, fresh air, and freedom. Boys should then learn a craft to nurture hand-eye coordination. Formal education should be delayed until they reached their teens. Education for girls should focus on the skills they would need to be wives and mothers.

Artistic representations of children from this period reflected this Enlightenment attitude toward children. The painting *The Age of Innocence,* by Sir Joshua Reynolds (1723–1792), which shows a barefoot young girl sitting outside, absorbed by the natural beauty, was deeply admired by the public.

Education Before the Enlightenment, education had been mostly a privilege of the upper class, and university education focused on certain professions, such as law or medicine. The Scientific Revolution led to increased interest in education. As print materials became widely available during the Enlightenment, the demand for literacy rose. The 17th-century Czech educator John Amos Comenius (1592–1670) developed the first comprehensive system of universal education, and his ideas were extremely influential on Enlightenment thinkers.

In the late-18th century, Prussia became the first nation to implement compulsory universal education. The Prussian education system provided free compulsory public education for boys and girls ages 6 to 13; it also required teacher training, a universal curriculum, and mandatory kindergarten. The Prussian system was widely seen as effective and efficient and became a model for many other nations. The curriculum, which included folk tales and national history, all taught in a common language, encouraged the development of a shared national identity.

France's educational system dated to the Roman Empire, but it served a small part of the populace and remained under church control. As early as the 17th century, convent schools operated by orders of nuns such as the Ursulines educated girls from the lower class as well as from the aristocracy.

During the French Revolution, rebels seized church properties, including schools. Enlightenment intellectual and politician **Nicolas de Condorcet** (1743–1794) developed a plan for a universal state educational system. The revolutionary government did establish new public schools for young men. However, it could afford to maintain them only briefly. Not until 1802 did Napoleon lay the foundation for a modern school system in France. His goal was to produce loyal, unquestioning citizens. He left many elementary schools in the control of the church but established state-supported secondary schools that used a common curriculum taught in French. A system of universal secular elementary education was not fully in place in France until the 1880s.

Austrian **Empress Maria Theresa** (1740–1780) mandated in 1775 that all children ages 6 to 12 must attend school. Schools shared a unified curriculum and required teachers to complete training. The system was two-track, permitting only upper-class boys to continue on to secondary school.

Life in Cities

The Agricultural Revolution meant fewer workers were needed to produce food and many people could no longer make a living farming. Cities offered economic opportunities, and people seeking work flocked to them.

As cities grew, they opened museums for art, history, and science to display objects that had been held by wealthy landowners or religious institutions. They started publicly funded orchestras, which quickly took the place of ones sponsored by nobles.

Urban Growth Patterns

In 1500, only a very few European cities, mostly in the Mediterranean area, had populations of more than 100,000. For the next 150 years, growth of towns and cities was slow but steady. Between 1650 and 1750, however, a few major cities began to expand rapidly, notably Paris, Amsterdam, and most spectacularly, London. Large urban areas became concentrated in the north of the continent. Certain features of 18th-century city life confronted everyone.

- Cities were overcrowded and congested. There was not enough housing. Streets were too narrow for all the carts, carriages, and pedestrians.

- Cities were dirty. Human and animal waste was poured out of windows. Horse manure filled the streets. Sanitation was poor. Sewage systems, if they existed, were rudimentary. Water was impure and air was polluted from coal and wood that heated and lit homes and shops.

- Cities were noisy. Streets swarmed with noisy horse-drawn carriages, vendors, and even livestock.

Though city dwellers had higher incomes and more dependable food supplies than rural dwellers, their mortality rates were higher. This resulted from infectious disease, which spread rapidly in crowded and unsanitary areas.

Nonetheless, urban populations continued to grow with the steady arrival of new migrants. And city life did improve over time, as cities made efforts to provide drainage, light outdoor areas at night, and clean public streets regularly. Cities also undertook large-scale public works projects to build new sewage systems, roads and avenues. These works required higher taxes.

The Wealthy and the Poor

In the 19th century, city life also held many attractions. There was the allure of cultural and social activities. The flourishing market economy meant shops and vendors with captivating new fashions, foods, and consumer goods. The urban wealthy could enjoy a luxurious lifestyle.

Such pleasures were not available to the urban poor, however. They lived in crowded, unheated, filthy slums. Their constantly growing population meant a chronic labor glut; competition for work pushed wages down. Poverty was widespread and dire. The close conditions of urban living made it obvious that wealth and opportunity were not equally available to all. Unsurprisingly, there was great discontent among the urban lower classes. Many urban areas experienced **riots** in response to events that increased the misery of the poor, such as an increase in the price of bread, the main item in their diet.

As cities continued to grow, so did the problems of the urban poor. Crime was rampant. Prostitution was prevalent, as was begging. Many poor city dwellers turned to drinking gin, relatively inexpensive and readily available, to assuage their suffering.

Public Response to Poverty Since the early 1600s, England had a system in place to administer assistance to the poor through local church parishes. By the 1800s, however, the tremendous increase in the number of poor and their concentration in urban areas strained this system to the breaking point. In response, Parliament passed the **Poor Law Amendment Act** in 1834. Under the new law, neither money nor services of any kind would be given to the needy unless they agreed to enter the *workhouse system*. Workhouses would provide subsistence shelter and food and in return, residents had to move into the workhouse and provide unpaid labor. This was meant to reduce the cost to the public of providing for the poor. Conditions in the workhouse were intentionally unpleasant, to further reduce costs and provide an incentive for people to find some way to support themselves.

Novelist **Charles Dickens** (1812–1870) vividly described the harsh conditions inside workhouses, most notably in *Oliver Twist*. Public inquiries eventually led to a loosening of rules in some areas but the workhouse system itself stayed in existence through the 19th century.

The Fight Against Sexually Transmitted Diseases Parliament also passed the **Contagious Disease Acts** (CD Acts) in 1864, after an investigation into the prevalence of sexually transmitted diseases in the British armed forces.

Under the new law, plainclothes police officers watched for and arrested women they suspected of prostitution. Those who could not prove their innocence (guilt was assumed) would then be subjected to regular compulsory physical inspections every two weeks to determine whether they were infected with venereal disease. Anyone found to be carrying disease would be placed in "lock hospitals" for three months.

The CD Acts did little to prevent spread of venereal disease, because the people who visited prostitutes were not subject to examination. However, the acts did galvanize women of different classes, who widely viewed the forced examinations as degrading and unfair. Led by the feminist and suffragist **Josephine Butler** (1828–1906), they united in an organized campaign to repeal the Acts and finally achieved success after 16 years.

While working with women targeted by the CD Acts, Butler discovered a flourishing sex slave trade in young British girls being sold on the European continent. She organized a second campaign, resulting in the passage of laws to raise the age of consent for legal sexual activity and help prevent girls from being forced into prostitution.

Evaluating Urbanization

Historians evaluating urbanization of the early industrial period have engaged in a **standard of living debate**. Economic historians focus on the steady overall rise in living standards and greater life expectancy. Social historians look instead at the destruction of centuries-old village traditions and the misery of the urban poor. Both agree that mass migration created a potential large-scale inexpensive urban workforce that would be crucial to support the Industrial Revolution (see Chapter 13).

HISTORICAL PERSPECTIVES: WHY DID PEASANTS MOVE TO CITIES?

In 1909, Max Weber, Georg Simmel, and Ferdinand Tönnies were among the founders of the German Sociological Association. Their leadership in this field was based on their publications about the *social impact* of urbanization, more so than about the process by which cities formed. The phenomenon of rapid urbanization resulting from industrialization came to be generally accepted by sociologists and historians. The commonly held narrative explained that enclosures reduced opportunity for peasants in the countryside, while factories drew peasants to urban areas with opportunities as unskilled laborers using new machinery. In 1899, statistician Adna F. Weber argued that though migration was not new, and that mortality rates prevented exponential growth of cities, the economic organization—in this case capitalism leading to new production and transportation technology—largely was responsible for the pace of urbanization.

Greater Ease of Moving By the 1970s, historians and social scientists developed models of economic and demographic transition, but cultural geographer Wilbur Zelinsky wanted to look beyond those models and their use of fertility statistics to understand the motives behind the demographic transition.

Zelinsky considered all types of migration, including to the Americas and other colonies. In all cases he came to the same conclusion, which he defined as "mobility transition." His hypothesis posited that prior to modernization, most people remained in stable self-sufficient communities that limited movement, and that movement was for the elites or the result of disaster. Modernization and industrialization provided opportunities for average people to move, by minimizing their local commitments and providing distant opportunities. As a result, great numbers of people moved.

Impact of the Industrial Revolution By the 21st century, scholars living in an unprecedented era of globalization noticed that people were on the move long before modernization. Scholars such as Jan Lucassen and Steven Hochstadt became part of what economic historian Jan de Vries called, "revolt of the early modernists" who found that mobility was the norm. It was not constrained, as Zelinsky argued. Hochstadt's study of German migration between 1820 and 1989 revealed that German cities were large prior to industrialization and population actually fell after World War I. This directly challenged Zelinsky's correlation between the liberating elements of modernization and urbanization. From the perspective of historians living in a global age, the cause for growth in the 19th century was that as international markets grew, rural industrialization no longer remained competitive and larger urban areas developed.

KEY TERMS BY THEME

Geography
Little Ice Age

Social Structures
demographic patterns
subsistence diet
epidemic
bubonic plague
smallpox
Lady Mary Wortley Montagu
coffeehouse
lending library
tavern
theater
opera house
boudoir
domesticity

Samuel Richardson
Jonathan Swift
Jane Austen
Charlotte Brontë
George Eliot
European marriage pattern

Technology
Agricultural Revolution
crop rotation

Movement
Columbian Exchange

Economics
enclosure movement
open field system
commons
Enclosure Acts

capitalism
Consumer Revolution
porcelain
Charles Dickens
standard of living debate

Governance
Jean-Jacques Rousseau
John Locke
Nicolas de Condorcet
Empress Maria Theresa
riots
Poor Law Amendment Act (1834)
Contagious Diseases Acts (1864)
Josephine Butler

Questions 1–3 refer to the following passage.

"I am going to tell you a thing that I am sure will make you wish your self here. The Small Pox so fatal and so general amongst us is here entirely harmless by the invention of engrafting (which is the term they give it). There is a set of old Women who make it their business to perform the Operation... with a large needle (which gives you no more pain than a common scratch) and puts into the vein as much venom as can lye upon the head of her needle, and after binds up the little wound with a hollow bit of shell... Every year thousands undergo this Operation, and the French Ambassador says pleasantly that they take the Small Pox here by way of diversion as they take the Waters in other Countries...

[You] may believe I am very well satisfied of the safety of the Experiment since I intend to try it on my dear little Son . . . . I am Patriot enough to take pains to bring this useful invention into fashion in England, and I should not fail to write to some of our Doctors... about it if I knew any one of 'em that I thought had Virtue enough to destroy such a considerable branch of their Revenue for the good of Mankind. . . .Perhaps if I live to return I may, however, have courage to war with 'em."

Lady Mary Wortley Montagu, Letter to Sarah Chiswell,
writing from Turkey, April 1, 1717

1. Which attempted cure for smallpox does Montagu describe?

   a) A procedure similar to Jenner's cow pox inoculations

   b) A plan to bring the less-deadly Turkish small pox to England

   c) A series of check-ups with doctors

   d) A treatment of wounds using shells

2. The writer viewed the practice described as which of the following?

   a) Barbarous and frightening

   b) Effective and worth emulating

   c) Interesting and amusing

   d) Effective only in Turkey

3. How does the experience of Lady Montagu in Turkey fit in with larger trends in European history?

   a) The ideas of Jean-Jacques Rousseau

   b) The enclosure movement

   c) Anti-epidemic campaigns

   d) The Colombian Exchange

Questions 4 and 5 refer to the following passage.

"Happily for him, a love of the theatre is so general, an itch for acting so strong among young people, that he could hardly out-talk the interest of his hearers. From the first casting of the parts to the epilogue, it was all bewitching, and there were few who did not wish to have been a party concerned, or would have hesitated to try their skill . . . .

[The] inclination to act was awakened, and in no one more strongly than in him who was now master of the house; and who having so much leisure to make almost any novelty a certain good, had likewise such a degree of lively talents and comic taste as were exactly adapted to the novelty of acting. The thought returned. "Oh for the Ecclesford theatre and scenery to try something with"...Henry Crawford, to whom, in all the riot of his gratifications it was yet an untasted pleasure. Was quite alive at the idea..."Let us be doing something. Be it only half a play, an act, a scene; what should prevent us? Not these countenances, I am sure," looking towards the Miss Betrams; "and for a theatre, what signifies a theatre? We shall only be amusing ourselves. Any room in this house might suffice." . . . .

[N]othing in the world could be easier than to find a piece which would please them all. [Edmund] was determined to prevent it, if possible, though his mother, who equally heard the conversation which passed at table, did not evince the least disapprobation."

Jane Austen, *Mansfield Park,* 1814

4. The entertainment discussed in the passage came about most directly because of which of the following?

   a) The end of the bubonic plague

   b) The Commercial Revolution

   c) The French Revolution

   d) Changes in marriage patterns

5. What does involvement in theatrical performances indicate about the middle class in the 19th century?

   a) They were focused on managing wealth.

   b) They were generally poorly educated.

   c) They had increasing leisure time.

   d) They were politically rebellious.

Questions 6–8 refer to the following passage.

"New schools are being opened, and inspectors have been appointed to see that the instruction does not degenerate into vain and sterile examinations. The *lycees* and the secondary schools are filling with youth eager for instruction. The polytechnic school is peopling our arsenals, ports, and factories with useful citizens. Prizes have been established in various branches of science, letters, and arts, and in the period of ten years fixed by his Majesty for the award of these prizes there can be no doubt that French genius will produce works of distinction."

Napoleon's statement to the Legislative Body,
December 31, 1804

6. What can be inferred from the passage about one of Napoleon's central motivations for overhauling the French educational system?

   a) He wanted more citizens who could run the operations of the empire.

   b) He wanted more candidates from the class of nobles.

   c) He wanted exams to focus more on literature and philosophy.

   d) He wanted women to have equal access to education.

7. What emerging relationship between church and state is reflected in the passage?

   a) Religious values were an essential part of the educational system.

   b) The church and the state were equal partners in the educational system.

   c) The state assumed primary responsibility for education.

   d) Religious education was forbidden.

8. Napoleonic educational reforms most clearly tried to establish

   a) universal childhood education

   b) higher education for the laboring class

   c) a system of schools for secondary and higher education

   d) greater diversity in higher education

SHORT-ANSWER QUESTIONS

1. Use the passage below to answer all parts of the question that follows.

"Consumer demand grew, even in the face of contrary real wage trends, and the productive achievements of industry and agriculture in the century before the Industrial Revolution could occur because of reallocations of the productive resources of households. In England, but in fact through much of Northwestern Europe and Colonial America, a broad range of households made decisions that increased both the supply of marketed commodities and labor and the demand for goods offered in the marketplace."

De Vries, Jan. "The Industrial Revolution and the Industrious Revolution." *The Journal of Economic History*, 1994.

a) Describe ONE way the changes described above benefitted rural workers in 18th-century Europe.

b) Describe ONE way the changes described above harmed rural workers in 18th-century Europe.

c) Explain how the changes described above facilitated the development of the Industrial Revolution in 18th-century Europe.

2. Answer all parts of the question that follows.

a) Explain ONE cause of the decrease in child mortality in Europe during the 18th century.

b) Explain ONE effect on family structures of the decrease in child mortality in Europe during the 18th century.

c) Explain ONE effect on demographic patterns of the decrease in child mortality in Europe during the 18th century.

LONG ESSAY QUESTIONS

1. Evaluate the extent to which the Agricultural Revolution of the 18th century contributed to demographic shifts in European society.

2. Evaluate the extent to which European family life changed during the 18th century.

REFLECT ON THE CHAPTER ESSENTIAL QUESTION

1. In one to three paragraphs, explain what factors shaped the experiences of everyday life in the 18th century.

An AP essay should present opposing viewpoints—and information to refute them. *Refute* means to argue against something and explain why it is not a correct or complete point of view.

If you've ever prepped effectively for a debate or a mock trial, this is exactly the skill you employed. Historical essay writing is no different. Being able to acknowledge viewpoints that do not support your thesis shows your ability to handle complexity. Writing a short paragraph near the end of your essay about opposing viewpoints allows you to return effectively to your thesis in the conclusion and provide it with new insights.

Identify the words or phrases in each passage that show a different viewpoint is being acknowledged.

1. Admittedly, the movement of many people to cities resulted in greater awareness of poverty and crime, but cities continued to offer economic opportunities that rural living couldn't provide.

2. Many people assume that the concentration of poor people in cities was an unrelieved urban problem; however, new laws and institutions attempted to create a healthier and safer environment.

3. Some fault the growth of cities for eroding traditional community values. What they fail to consider is that at the same time, child and infant mortality were dropping, leading to greater emphasis on the nuclear family.

4. While there is evidence that the consumer revolution did not result in a better standard of living for all, there also is evidence that major segments of society benefitted from improved products available for the home and new venues for leisure activities.

Place the topic sentences below in the best order to organize an essay that acknowledges opposing viewpoints, based on the following thesis statement.

5. Thesis statement: The experiences of everyday life were shaped by demographic, environmental, medical, and technological changes.

   a. Better weather conditions, the availability of more farmland, and improved transportation helped stabilize the balance between population and food supply.

   b. Prior to the 18th century, populations were regularly decimated by waves of plague and starvation, but that largely ended by 1730 as a result of several factors.

   c. Despite the manufacture of goods being skewed toward the aristocracy, resulting in problems of supply and demand, overall the quality of living improved for most people due to a wider range of consumer goods and technologies.

PERIOD 2: Review

DOCUMENT-BASED QUESTION 1

Directions: Question 1 is based on the accompanying documents. The documents have been edited for the purpose of this exercise. You are advised to spend 15 minutes planning and 45 minutes writing your answer.

In your response you should do the following:

- **Thesis:** Make a defensible claim that establishes a line of reasoning and consists of one or more sentences found in one place.
- **Contextualization:** Relate the argument to a broader historical context.
- **Document Evidence:** Use content from at least six documents.
- **Outside Evidence:** Use one piece of evidence not in the documents.
- **Document Sourcing:** Explain how or why the point of view, purpose, situation, or intended audience is relevant for at least three documents.
- **Analysis:** Show the relationships among pieces of historical evidence and use them to support, qualify, or modify an argument.

1. Analyze the causes and effects of humans' views of themselves and the world around them during the Scientific Revolution (1550s to 1700s).

Document 1

Source: Claudius Ptolemy (100 C.E.–168 C.E.), astronomer in Alexandria, Egypt. This diagram shows Ptolemy's view of the universe, with the sun and planets orbiting the earth.

Credit: Getty Images

Document 2

Source: Nicolaus Copernicus, Dedication of *On the Revolutions of the Heavenly Bodies* to Pope Paul III, (1543)

I can easily conceive, most Holy Father, that as soon as some people learn that in this book which I have written concerning the revolutions of the heavenly bodies, I ascribe certain motions to the Earth, they will cry out at once that I and my theory should be rejected. For I am not so much in love with my conclusions as not to weigh what others will think about them, and although I know that the meditations of a philosopher are far removed from the judgment of the laity, because his endeavor is to seek out the truth in all things, so far as this is permitted by God to the human reason, I still believe that one must avoid theories altogether foreign to orthodoxy.

Accordingly, when I considered in my own mind how absurd a performance it must seem to those who know that the judgment of many centuries has approved the view that the Earth remains fixed as center in the midst of the heavens, if I should, on the contrary, assert that the Earth moves; I was for a long time at a loss to know whether I should publish the commentaries which I have written in proof of its motion, or whether it were not better to follow the example of the Pythagoreans and of some others, who were accustomed to transmit the secrets of Philosophy not in writing but orally, and only to their relatives and friends. . . .

Therefore, when I considered this carefully, the contempt which I had to fear because of the novelty and apparent absurdity of my view, nearly induced me to abandon utterly the work I had begun.

Document 3

Source: Tycho Brahe, a model of the universe, 1596. The earth is at the center. The sun and moon revolve around it, and the planets revolve around the sun.

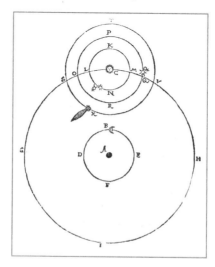

Document 4

Source: Johannes Kepler, *A New Astronomy,* 1609.

Gravity is a mutual corporeal disposition among kindred bodies to unite or join together; thus the earth attracts a stone much more than the stone seeks the earth. . . .

For it follows that if the earth's power of attraction will be much more likely to extend to the moon and far beyond, and accordingly, that nothing that consists to any extent whatever of terrestrial material, carried up on high, ever escapes the grasp of this mighty power of attraction.

The sphere of the attractive virtue which is in the moon extends as far as the earth, and entices up the waters; but as the moon flies rapidly across the zenith, and the waters cannot follow so quickly, a flow of the ocean is occasioned in the torrid zone towards the westward. If the attractive virtue of the moon extends as far as the earth, it follows with greater reason that the attractive virtue of the earth extends as far as the moon and much farther; and, in short, nothing which consists of earthly substance anyhow constituted although thrown up to any height, can ever escape the powerful operation of this attractive virtue.

Document 5

Source: Galileo Galilei, *The Starry Messenger,* 1610, Venice

ASTRONOMICAL MESSAGE: Which contains and explains recent observations made with the aid of a new spyglass concerning the surface of the moon, the Milky Way, nebulous stars, and innumerable fixed stars, as well as four planets never before seen, and now named THE MEDICEAN STARS. . .

It is a very beautiful thing, and most gratifying to the sight, to behold the body of the moon, distant from us almost sixty earthly radii, as if it were no farther away than two such measures—so that its diameter appears almost thirty times larger, its surface nearly nine hundred times, and its volume twenty-seven thousand times as large as when viewed with the naked eye. In this way one may learn with all the certainty of sense evidence that the moon is not robed in a smooth and polished surface but is in fact rough and uneven, covered everywhere, just like the earth's surface, with huge prominences, deep valleys, and chasms. Again, it seems to me a matter of no small importance to have ended the dispute about the Milky Way by making its nature manifest to the very senses as well as to the intellect. Similarly it will be a pleasant and elegant thing to demonstrate that the nature of those stars which astronomers have previously called "nebulous" is far different from what has been believed hitherto. But what surpasses all wonders by far, and what particularly moves us to seek the attention of all astronomers and philosophers, is the discovery of four wandering stars not known or observed by any man before us. Like Venus and Mercury, which have their own periods about the sun, these have theirs about a certain star that is conspicuous among those already known, which they sometimes precede and sometimes follow, without ever departing from it beyond certain limits.

Document 6

Source: Francis Bacon, Dedication to King James I, *The Great Instauration,* 1620

To our most serene and mighty prince and the lord, James I, by the grace of God, king of Great Britain, France, and Ireland, Defender of the Faith, etc., most serene and mighty king:

    This regeneration and instauration [renewal] of the sciences is with justice due to the age of a Prince surpassing all others in wisdom and learning. There remains for me to but to make one request, worthy of your majesty, and very especially relating to my subject, namely, that, resembling Solomon as you do in most respects, in the gravity of your decisions, the peacefulness of your reign, the expansion of your heart, and, lastly, in the noble variety of books you have composed, you would further imitate the same monarch in procuring the compilation and completion of a Natural and Experimental History, that shall be genuine and rigorous...

    In short, as I will in its proper place describe: that, at length, after so many ages, philosophy and the sciences may no longer be unsettled and speculative, but fixed on the solid foundation of a varied and well considered experience. I for my part have supplied the instrument, the matter to be worked upon must be sought from things themselves.

Document 7

Source: John Locke, *Essay Concerning Human Understanding,* 1689.

Let us then suppose the mind to be, as we say, white paper, void of all characters, without any ideas: —How comes it to be furnished? Whence comes it by that vast store which the busy and boundless fancy of man has painted on it with an almost endless variety? Whence has it all the materials of reason and knowledge? To this I answer, in one word, from EXPERIENCE. In that all our knowledge is founded, and from that it ultimately derives itself. Our observation employed either, about external sensible objects, or about the internal operations of our minds perceived and reflected on by ourselves, is that which supplies our understandings with all the materials of thinking. These two are the fountains of knowledge, from whence all the ideas we have, do spring. . . .

    Sense and intuition reach but a very little way. The greatest part of our knowledge depends upon deductions and intermediate ideas: . . . The faculty which finds out the means, and rightly applies them, to discover certainty in the one, and probability in the other, is that which we call reason. For as reason perceive the necessary and indubitable connexion of all the ideas or proof one to another, in each step of any demonstration that produces knowledge; so it likewise perceives the probable connexion of all the ideas or proofs one to another, in every step of a discourse, to which it will think assent due. This is the lowest degree of that which can truly be called reason.

Directions: Question 2 is based on the accompanying documents. The documents have been edited for the purpose of this exercise. You are advised to spend 15 minutes planning and 45 minutes writing your answer.

In your response you should do the following:

- **Thesis:** Make a defensible claim that establishes a line of reasoning and consists of one or more sentences found in one place.
- **Contextualization:** Relate the argument to a broader historical context.
- **Document Evidence:** Use content from at least six documents.
- **Outside Evidence:** Use one piece of evidence not in the documents.
- **Document Sourcing:** Explain how or why the point of view, purpose, situation, or intended audience is relevant for at least three documents.
- **Analysis:** Show the relationships among pieces of historical evidence and use them to support, qualify, or modify an argument.

2. Analyze the continuities and changes in the attitudes toward leadership and political ambition demonstrated in France from 1789 to 1795.

Document 1

Source: Camille Desmoulins, Speech at the Bastille, July 14, 1789

There is one difference between a monarchy and a republic, which alone should suffice to make people reject with horror all monarchical rule and prefer a republic regardless of the cost of its establishment. In a democracy, tho the people may be deceived, yet they at least love virtue. It is merit which they believe they put in power as substitutes for the rascals who are the very essence of monarchies. The vices, concealments, and crimes which are the diseases of republics are the very health and existence of monarchies. Cardinal Richelieu avowed openly in his political principles, that "kings should always avoid using the talents of thoroughly honest men." Long before him Sallust said: "Kings can not get along without rascals; on the contrary, they should fear to trust the honest and upright." It is, therefore, only under a democracy that the good citizen can reasonably hope to see a cessation of the triumphs of intrigue and crime; and to this end the people need only to be enlightened....There is yet this difference between a monarchy and a republic: the reigns of Tiberius, Claudius, Nero, Caligula and Domitian all had happy beginnings. In fact, all reigns make a joyous entry, but this is only a delusion.

Document 2

Source: Declaration of Rights of Man and Citizen, August 26, 1789

Therefore the National Assembly recognizes and proclaims, in the presence and under the auspices of the Supreme Being, the following rights of man and of the citizen:

Men are born and remain free and equal in rights. Social distinctions may be founded only upon the General Good.

The aim of all political association is the preservation of the natural and imprescriptible rights of man. These rights are liberty, property, security, and resistance to oppression.

Liberty consists in the freedom to do everything which injures no one else; hence the exercise of the natural rights of each man has no limits except those which assure to the other members of the society the enjoyment of the same rights….

Law is the expression of the General Will. Every citizen has a right to participate personally, or through his representative, in its foundation. It must be the same for all, whether it protects or punishes. All citizens, being equal in the eyes of the law, are equally eligible to all dignities and to all public positions and occupations, according to their abilities, and without distinction except that of their virtues and talents."

Document 3

Source: The Women's March on Versailles, October 5, 1789

Credit: This image is in the public domain in the United States. en.wikipedia.org. Bibliothèque nationale de France

Document 4

Source: Henri Grégoire, a Jacobin member of the New National Convention, 1791

Not one of us would ever propose to retain in France the fatal race of kings. We all know but too well that dynasties have never been anything else than rapacious tribes, who live on nothing but human flesh. It is completely necessary to reassure the friends of liberty. We must destroy this talisman whose magic power is still sufficient to stupefy many men. I move accordingly that you sanction, by a solemn law, the abolition of royalty.

Document 5

Source: George Jacques Danton, 1792

At such a moment this National Assembly becomes a veritable committee of war. We ask that you concur with us in directing this sublime movement of the people, by naming commissioners who will second us in these great measures. We ask that any one refusing to give personal service or to furnish arms shall be punished with death. We ask that a set of instructions be drawn up for the citizens to direct their movements. We ask that couriers be sent to all the departments to notify them of the decrees that you proclaim here. The tocsin we are about to ring is not an alarm signal; it sounds the charge on the enemies of our country. To conquer them we must dare, dare again, always dare, and France is saved!

Document 6

Source: Maximilien Robespierre addressed the National Convention, May 7, 1794

Now, in these circumstances, the first maxim of our politics ought to be to lead the people by means of reason and the enemies of the people by terror… The basis of popular government in time of revolution is both virtue and terror. Terror without virtue is murderous, virtue without terror is powerless. Terror is nothing else than swift, severe, indomitable justice – it flows, then, from virtue.

Document 7

Source: This painting shows Napoleon visiting with the orphans of soldiers who received special recognition for their service to France.

NAPOLEON VISITING THE ORPHANS OF THE LEGION OF HONOR.

Credit: Getty Images

PERIOD 3: c. 1815 to c. 1914

Period Overview

Between 1815 and 1914, Europe was relatively peaceful compared to the war-filled 16th, 17th, and 18th centuries. This was also a period of tremendous economic growth and changes in family structure.

Industrial Revolution By the mid-18th century, the developments in agriculture and science in previous centuries had created the foundation for some of the most dramatic changes in European history. These began in Great Britain. By replacing human and animal power with new machines that used the power of moving water of streams and of steam created by burning coal, humans could produce far more goods at far lower costs than ever before.

These changes in technology and economics rippled through everyday life. Whereas most people before had lived on farms and worked in agriculture, people flocked to cities to take new jobs in factories and offices. Instead of everyone working at home, adults, mostly men but some women as well, left the house to work in these new jobs. The women who remained at home became the center of family life. Further, machine-made clothes, tools, and housewares became so plentiful that people could easily purchase them rather than make their own by hand.

Expanded Government Industrialization led to growth in government, both to promote trade and to solve problems. In the midst of the great material wealth produced by industries, people still suffered. Workers led short, hard lives. Radicals such as Karl Marx argued that the solution was that the workers who created the wealth should own the means to produce it as well. Others argued for reforms to improve the lives of workers by opening schools, building sewers, and allowing workers to form unions.

States and Cultures In politics, boundaries in Europe were redrawn. In 1815, Europe included a mix of large, multi-ethnic empires and tiny states, all formed with little regard to culture. By 1914, many of the tiny states had consolidated to form the modern states of Germany and Italy. The large empires still existed, but were under attack from people who wanted independence.

Overseas Expansion In the early 19th century, Europeans expanded their influence into Asia and Africa, desiring the resources for use in industry and markets where they could sell their goods. Africans and Asians had mixed responses. Some welcomed European technology and ideas, but many fought back against political and economic control.

Industrialization also influenced philosophy and the arts. Some artists looked back to the medieval times before industrialization revolutionized life. Others wanted to portray the new world as realistically as possible—crowded, dirty cities. Artists who were part of the Romantic movement became skeptical of the power of reason to explain everything—they looked to the subconscious, to emotions.

Key Concepts

3.1 The Industrial Revolution spread from Great Britain to the continent, where the state played a greater role in promoting industry.

   I. Great Britain established its industrial dominance through the mechanization of textile production, iron and steel production, and new transportation systems in conjunction with uniquely favorable political and social climates.

   II. Following the British example, industrialization took root in continental Europe, sometimes with state sponsorship.

   III. During the second industrial revolution (c. 1870–1914), more areas of Europe experienced industrial activity, and industrial processes increased in scale and complexity.

3.2 The experiences of everyday life were shaped by industrialization, depending on the level of industrial development in a particular location.

   I. Industrialization promoted the development of new classes in the industrial regions of Europe.

   II. Europe experienced rapid population growth and urbanization, leading to social dislocations.

   III. Over time, the Industrial Revolution altered the family structure and relations for bourgeois and working-class families.

   IV. A heightened consumerism developed as a result of the second industrial revolution.

   V. Because of the continued existence of more primitive agricultural practices and land-owning patterns, some areas of Europe lagged in industrialization while facing famine, debt, and land shortages.

3.3 Political revolutions and the complications resulting from industrialization triggered a range of ideological, governmental, and collective responses.

   I. Ideologies developed and took root throughout society as a response to industrial and political revolutions.

   II. Governments, at times based on the pressure of political or social organizations, responded to problems created or exacerbated by industrialization.

   III. Political movements and social organizations responded to problems of industrialization.

3.4 European states struggled to maintain international stability in an age of nationalism and revolutions.

    I. The Concert of Europe (or Congress System) sought to maintain the status quo through collective action and adherence to conservatism.

    II. The breakdown of the Concert of Europe opened the door for movements of national unification in Italy and Germany as well as liberal reforms elsewhere.

    III. The unification of Italy and Germany transformed the European balance of power and led to efforts to construct a new diplomatic order.

3.5 A variety of motives and methods led to the intensification of European global control and increased tensions among the Great Powers.

    I. European nations were driven by economic, political, and cultural motivations in their new imperial ventures in Asia and Africa.

    II. Industrial and technological developments (i.e., the second industrial revolution) facilitated European control of global empires.

    III. Imperial endeavors significantly affected society, diplomacy, and culture in Europe and created resistance to foreign control abroad.

3.6 European ideas and culture expressed a tension between objectivity and scientific realism on one hand, and subjectivity and individual expression on the other.

    I. Romanticism broke with Neoclassical forms of artistic representation and with rationalism, placing more emphasis on intuition and emotion.

    II. Following the revolutions of 1848, Europe turned toward a realist and materialist worldview.

    III. In the later 19th century, a new relativism in values and the loss of confidence in the objectivity of knowledge led to modernism in intellectual and cultural life.

The Industrial Revolution changed how manufacturing companies employed people. Instead of hiring people who could make textiles or other goods in their own homes, companies hired them to work in enormous factories. This drawing shows dozens of workers in a jewelry factory in Paris.

Credit: Getty Images

13

The Industrial Revolution

*"The opening of a foreign trade, by making them acquainted with new
objects . . . sometimes works a sort of Industrial Revolution in a
country . . . inducing those who were satisfied with scanty comforts
and little work, to work harder for the gratification of their new tastes,
and even to save, and accumulate capital."*

—John Stuart Mill (1806–1873)

Essential Question: Why did the Industrial Revolution begin in Great Britain
and then spread to the continent?

British philosopher John Stuart Mill lived through one of the greatest
revolutions in European history. During his lifetime new technological
developments in manufacturing, transportation, and communications played a
powerful role in transforming Europe's economy from one largely dependent
upon agriculture to one that revolved around the production of goods, or
industry. Known as the **Industrial Revolution**, the era proceeded in two stages.

The initial Industrial Revolution began in the textile industry in Britain
in the mid-18th century and later spread to the European continent. Britain's
natural resources, including coal and iron, combined with its social, economic,
and political structure, made it ideal for industrial development. By the 1850s,
Britain had achieved industrial dominance in Europe and the world. Between
1850 and 1870, France and Prussia were becoming more industrialized as
well. Yet industrialization proceeded more slowly in those two countries, so
governments took a more prominent role in supporting change.

From about 1870 to 1914, a **second industrial revolution** occurred. Often
called the Age of Steel, it featured more complex technologies, such as the
internal combustion engine. It extended the reach of industrialization through
Russia and Eastern Europe. Up to that time, Russia's reliance on serfdom had
delayed industrialization in Eastern Europe, as tsars such as Catherine II and
Alexander I did not support industrialization. Eastern European countries also
lacked the raw materials such as coal, which limited their ability to industrialize.

By 1914, industrialization had spread throughout Europe and was
increasing in other parts of the world. In particular, the United States and Japan
were heavily industrialized.

Great Britain's Industrial Dominance

Great Britain established the lead in the Industrial Revolution through the mechanization of textile production, the development of steam power, increased coal mining, and the production of **wrought iron** (the molded form of iron used for building iron objects) and steel. The development of railroads in Britain sped the transportation of raw materials to factories and of finished goods to consumers. Another key to Britain's industrialization was that no location was more than a few miles from a canal, a river, or the coast. In addition, Britain's Parliamentary democracy enabled manufacturers and **industrialists** to influence government policies through their representatives, or members of Parliament. Britain had a growing middle class and the British social climate favored inventors, businessmen, and **entrepreneurs**—those who could create wealth rather than inherit it.

The Textile Industry

In 1764, English inventor James Hargreaves developed the spinning jenny, which dramatically increased the production of cloth thread. Before the spinning jenny, women spun thread mostly at home, using a spinning wheel with a single spindle, or spool. Production was slow and the demand for thread by textile weavers was often greater than the supply. Hargreaves's jenny, however, had eight spindles and thus allowed a single worker to produce eight times as much thread. Eventually, machines similar to spinning jennies were attached to waterwheels, and waterpower was used to spin thread. In 1785, Edmund Cartwright invented a water-powered loom to weave cloth.

Capitalism and the Rise of the Factory With the use of water-powered spinning wheels and looms, textiles could be produced in large quantities, or **mass produced.** Textile workers no longer worked at home or in small workshops. Instead, they labored together in textile mills in groups as large as three or four hundred. Opening a textile mill required **capital**, or money and other resources set aside for building a business. Often, new owners borrowed money from banks in the form of loans they would have to repay from the profits of the mill. Private individuals also invested in new companies or contributed money in exchange for a share of future profits. These individuals would receive a portion, or share, of the mill's profit at the end of the year. The mill owners generated profits by selling finished goods.

In Britain, private individuals, not the king or the state, owned the mills. This system of private ownership of industry became known as **capitalism**. The textile manufacturing industry created a new class of well-to-do factory owners. Unlike aristocrats, their wealth came from business, not inherited land. Eventually, textile mills became known as manufactories, or simply **factories** because they manufactured goods.

Cotton Becomes King Britain had an abundant supply of wool from sheep. However, **consumers**, people who purchase goods or services, increasingly favored cotton cloth. Compared to wool, cotton was lighter, cooler, and easier to dye bright colors and patterns. Cotton was grown in Britain's colonies in India and the American South. Raw, fluffy cotton bolls contained seeds and had to be cleaned, or combed, slowly by hand before they could be spun into thread. In 1794, American inventor Eli Whitney unveiled a machine called the cotton gin that removed seeds from cotton bolls, revolutionizing the production of cotton cloth. Large quantities of combed cotton could now be imported from America or India and woven in Britain. By the end of the 18th century, Britain was exporting finished cotton cloth to its American colonies and to the other countries of Europe.

Steam Power Changes Manufacturing In 1769, James Watt of Scotland patented the **steam engine**, a revolutionary technology that used steam from water heated by a coal fire to power numerous devices. The pressure from built-up steam moved a system of small plungers, or pistons, attached to gears and shafts to generate energy to operate machines. By 1800, steam power had begun to replace waterpower in textile factories. Factories no longer had to be located near a stream or river. Instead they could be anywhere, as long there was a steady supply of coal to keep the steam engines moving. By 1835, there were more than 1,000 steam-powered looms in Britain.

Coal was transported to factories over land by carts or via water. In the early 19th century, the British Parliament sponsored the construction of canals expressly for the transport of coal. Steamboats carrying cargo traveled the nearly 2,000 miles of canals that had been dug by 1815.

Railroads

Steam power soon had another important use. In 1816, George Stephenson invented a **locomotive** powered by steam that ran along iron rails. The railway industry had become a major component of the Industrial Revolution. By 1830, 51 miles of rails had been laid in Britain. Rail transport soon eclipsed canals. By 1850, British railways encompassed more than 6,000 miles, uniting all regions of the country. Trains carried raw materials to factories and goods from factories to consumers in cities, or to ports for export abroad.

George Stephenson's locomotive, constructed in 1829, was a breakthrough in land transportation. Like steam ships, it used the expansive power of steam to produce rotary motion.

Credit: Getty Images

OLD MODES OF LOCOMOTION.—STEPHENSON'S LOCOMOTIVE "THE ROCKET," 1829.

People, as well as goods, traveled by rail. Improved transportation helped create a sense of common culture and national identity. Greater mobility led to increased trade and migration, which increased links between regions. In addition, the growth of mass production and mass consumption reduced differences in regional dialects, dress, and other customs. Before the Industrial Revolution, all goods from cloth to soap to dishes to nails were produced by hand, so they were expensive. Manufacturing reduced the prices for many goods, so they became available to many people for the first time and **consumerism**—promoting the buying of goods and services—became part of the economic fabric. Local variations of goods decreased, and people recognized that they had much in common with one another. While economic class differences remained strong, cultural differences declined. People increasingly identified with their country rather than with city or region.

Coal

Beginning in the 19th century, coal became the major source of energy in Britain. Coal stoves rather than wood-burning fireplaces heated homes and buildings. More important, railroads and factories needed coal for fuel. Britain had abundant coal reserves, especially in the regions of northeast and central England, southeast Scotland, and Wales. However, coal mining was a difficult and dangerous job. Workers often died in cave-ins, floods, or from inhaling the poisonous gases that accumulated underground. The demand for coal, however, drew millions of men and women to the mines. In 1750, Britain produced about 3 million tons of coal. By 1816, production reached 16 million tons. Then it approximately doubled every 20 years for the following century.

Iron and Steel

During the Industrial Revolution, demand for iron soared. Railroads needed iron to build tracks and locomotives. Steam engines and furnaces and all kinds of tools were made of iron. The military needed iron for weapons, including cannons and cannon balls. Bridges were made of wrought iron, while buildings had iron staircases, railings, and other fixtures.

Coke Smelting Coal played an important role in the production of iron. **Coke,** a solid form of coal bricks, provided the steady burning fuel needed to smelt, or extract, iron ore from rocks and melt it into bars, called pig iron. These bars could then be bent, rolled, and molded into wrought iron to use in building machines and in construction. Since people often found iron deposits near coal seams, the iron industry became closely tied to coal-producing regions.

The Growth of the Iron Industry Smelting and molding iron could be a time-consuming process. In 1783, Henry Cort, a former British naval officer, improved the production of wrought iron with the invention of his puddling furnace and roller mechanism that could shape iron while it was still soft and malleable. Cort became known as the father of Britain's iron industry. Between 1780 and 1790, Britain produced about 70,000 tons of iron. Between 1855 and 1859, it produced 3.5 million tons. By the early 20th century, Britain was the greatest iron-producing nation in the world, smelting more than 8.7 million tons between 1900 and 1904.

Steel In 1856, English inventor **Henry Bessemer** patented the **Bessemer process**, a method for mass-producing steel, a combination of iron and carbon that is more durable and more resistant to rust than pure iron. Bessemer relied on huge furnaces and hot air pumps that removed impurities from pig iron via a chemical process called oxidation. Bessemer's invention revolutionized the production of steel, and Britain became a leader in steel production. A combination of glass and iron struts could also produce entire structures, including the **Crystal Palace** of the **Great Exhibition of 1851**, and London's Paddington Station, completed in 1854.

The Great Exhibition of 1851 In 1851, Britain celebrated its economic progress by staging the Great Exhibition of the Works of Industry of All Nations. The centerpiece of the exhibit was the magnificent Crystal Palace, a multistory glass and steel structure the length of three city blocks.

As host country of the Great Exhibition, Britain mounted the largest exhibits. Among the inventions displayed were a steam-powered hammer, a hydraulic press, early bicycles that were known as velocipedes, rubber-tubed hearing aids, a high-speed printing press, and a massive railway locomotive. More than 6 million people attended the Exhibition. The Palace and its exhibits were intended to impress the world with Britain's industrial strength.

Political Power and Social Class

As John Stuart Mill suggested in the quotation that opened this chapter, the Industrial Revolution caused people to work and save money for the future. Previously, people had little to save for. Most goods were so expensive that they were out of reach for most people. However, industrialization made goods affordable, so people had a reason to work hard and save money. Mill believed this was a great benefit to society.

Not everyone agreed with Mill's positive view of industrialization. Some people, known as Luddites, were so angry at how mechanization had replaced human labor that they destroyed machinery.

More generally, the Industrial Revolution also created enormous social class differences. Gaps between the richest and poorest members of society meant that many people could not enjoy the benefits of prosperity. For many thousands of people, the Industrial Revolution led to a life of tedious work with long hours and little reward. However, others found new opportunities for upward social mobility and education. And while life was especially harsh for the first generation or two that lived in cities, by the end of the 19th century, poorer city dwellers did see an improvement in their standard of living.

The Growth of the Middle Class The Industrial Revolution encouraged the growth in Britain of a **middle class**, people who were neither peasants, nobles, nor clergy. They were merchants, clerks, factory managers, and others. They were, in general, wealthier and better educated than peasants but without the traditional status and power of nobles and clergy. Compared to the working class, the middle class of the late 19th century led lives that seemed luxurious, living in comfortable houses often with servants waiting on them.

As middle-class people accumulated more wealth, they could pursue higher education. Literacy increased and with it the desire for books, newspapers, and magazines. People became more aware of events beyond their immediate geographical region. Improved transportation and communications helped create a greater sense of common culture and national identity. Differences in regional dialects, dress, and other customs continued to decline with the growth of **mass production** and **mass consumption**.

The Repeal of the Corn Laws Reforms enacted by Parliament in 1832 gave more power to the House of Commons. This chamber represented merchants and manufacturers more than did the aristocratic House of Lords By the 1840s, Britain's middle class was powerful enough to challenge the **Corn Laws**, which placed a high tariff on imported grains. These laws kept the price of wheat, also known as corn, high. High wheat prices benefited aristocratic landowners, but made bread expensive for everyone. In 1846, the Anti-Corn League, a reform movement led by Sir Robert Peel and members of the middle class, pressured Parliament to repeal the Corn Laws. Removing the tariffs meant that the price of wheat would be based primarily on supply and demand. (For more on the Corn Laws, see Chapter 15.)

Increasing Trade After the repeal of the Corn Laws, Britain began to import increasing quantities of grain from the United States and European nations. British farmers could not compete with the cheap imported grain, and many of them began to leave the countryside for factories, accelerating the dominance of manufacturing over agriculture in the British economy.

The Anti-Corn League also supported the larger issue of **free trade**, a policy of few restrictions or taxes on trade. The merchant class did not want Parliament to limit their right to import and export goods. The repeal of the Corn Laws led to the relaxing of trade laws in general and further increased the importance of industry. The change symbolized a major shift in power in British politics, from the land-based aristocrats to the merchants. Throughout the 19th century, British **tariffs**, or taxes on imported goods, decreased. By 1900, Britain led Europe in both manufacturing and trade.

Patents and Rewards for Inventors

The British government recognized the importance of inventors to the economy through its support of **patents**, licenses issued by the government that allow inventors to control and sell the rights to their inventions for a period of time. Patents enabled inventors to profit from their work, thus encouraging inventors to be creative. While the British patent system dated back to the Middle Ages, in 1852, new laws enabled inventors to obtain patents more rapidly, giving inventors greater motivation to develop new devices and mechanisms.

Britain also supported inventors through the use of incentives, or financial rewards, given for new inventions or improvements to old ones.

In 1754, William Shipley, a drawing teacher, established the Society for the Encouragement of Arts, Manufactures and Commerce. The Society issued a challenge asking people to solve particular problems in fields such as manufacturing, chemistry, agricultural production, or engineering, and offered cash prizes to people whose solutions succeeded best. Innovators developed better machinery for textile production and for lumber milling. The Society started as a private organization and acquired government sponsorship through a royal charter in 1847.

Industrialization on the Continent

Industrialization took place more slowly on the European continent, in part because the British government protected its industries by closely guarding its inventions from foreign discovery and made it illegal for anyone to take blueprints for power looms, engines, and other devices outside the country. During the late 18th and early 19th century, continental Europe was also beset by revolutions, wars, and border disputes that made it difficult for governments to focus on economic development. Many nations also suffered from a lack of natural resources, especially coal and iron. Extreme focus on the aristocratic market left many of the middle and lower classes without growth and further slowed industrialization.

Continental European governments were more autocratic than democratic. When the continent did industrialize, military leaders and aristocrats often took the lead in initiating economic and financial programs.

Industrialization in France

Industrialization in France took place mostly after 1815. Unlike Great Britain, France did not have large reserves of coal and iron. Most of the coal and iron fields were concentrated in the north, close to the Belgian border. France had experienced limited growth in manufacturing during the mid-18th century, especially around the region of Lyon. Luxury goods such as silk, woven tapestries, porcelain, and carved furniture formed the basis of France's modest industrial expansion. Wealthy aristocrats purchased most of these goods.

The French Revolution of 1789 and the violence that followed disrupted the country's economic development, and manufacturing declined. Though the revolution had promised democracy, the government proved too unstable to fulfill its aims. In 1799, the French general Napoleon Bonaparte seized power, turning the country into a military dictatorship.

Napoleon's Reforms Napoleon laid the groundwork for France's industrial growth. His army needed weapons and uniforms, so iron and cloth production increased to meet the demands of the military. In addition, Napoleon supported many innovations that helped modernize France, especially in education and transportation. His administration established schools that taught engineering, science, architecture, and mathematics. He initiated the construction of new roads, bridges, and canals that helped unify the nation.

Among his major achievements was the completion in 1810 of the Saint Quentin Canal, a waterway joining a network of rivers and other waterways connecting the coal and iron fields of northern France to the capital city of Paris. Additional canals connected to ports and allowed barges to transport grain and other goods across the country.

Napoleon also established the **Bank of France**, the country's national bank and main financial institution. The Bank helped fund government infrastructure projects, including the expansion of the railroad. As in Britain, government support helped industry develop.

British Technology Helps France After the French deposed Napoleon in 1815, the country entered a period of renewed industrial growth. Many French aristocrats who had escaped to England during the French Revolution began to return, bringing English technology with them. During the 1830s, France finally acquired access to British weaving technology and started to use looms with multiple spindles, reviving the French silk industry. The cities of Lille and Rouen in northern France became centers for cotton manufacturing. The Alsace region of northeast France proved rich in deposits of coal and iron and began to attract manufacturers.

The introduction of the steam engine increased the demand for coal. Industrialist François de Wendel began to use steam engines to mine coal. He also introduced the British method of smelting iron, and his family became one of the major manufacturers of heavy machinery during the 19th century.

French Railroads The French began to build railroads shortly after the British introduced them in 1816. By 1827, France had constructed the first railway line on the continent. It ran about 11 miles (18 km), carrying coal and iron from mines to a nearby river. In 1832, it expanded and added passenger cars. Demand for iron increased as France's railroads grew. In 1838, French ironworkers completed the first locomotive made entirely in France.

Railroad lines expanded throughout France during the second half of the 19th century. The government, rather than private investors, sponsored most of the expansion. In 1879, the government launched the **Freycinet Plan**, a program that called for making railroads accessible to nearly every town and village in France.

Trade Agreements and Tariffs The French government tried to protect its industries from competition by controlling the importation of goods. To do so, the government levied high tariffs on imports. Sometimes it banned the importation of certain goods altogether. This changed in 1860, when a British member of Parliament, Richard Cobden, convinced the French government that free trade would improve their labor market. France and Britain signed a treaty easing trade between the two nations and reducing French tariffs on British goods. The era of French-British free trade lasted until France returned to its earlier protectionist policies and imposed tariffs once more in 1892.

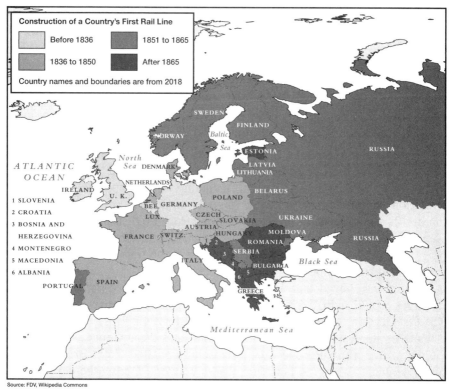

Source: FDV, Wikipedia Commons

Industrialization in Prussia

Before the age of Napoleon, the name "Germany" referred to a region in north central Europe that consisted of more than 300 separate kingdoms, free cities, and other states. Many were part of the Holy Roman Empire, but they maintained their separate identities. From 1815 to 1867, many of these states consolidated and became loosely united in the **German Confederation**. However, they did not form a single country.

In the 18th century, Prussia focused on building a strong military to protect itself from Europe's two most powerful armies, those of France and Russia. It emerged as one of the dominant German states.

Then, as the Industrial Revolution spread through Europe, Prussia became even stronger. Its large deposits of coal and iron helped it become the first German state to industrialize. Prussian textile mills, using British techniques, began operating in 1786. By 1837, Prussia had more than 1,000 mills. In 1794, the first coke-smelting furnace started operating in Silesia, a region in what is now southwestern Poland. A few years later, the Ruhr Valley, an area straddling the Rhine River in Western Germany, became a center of iron production. The introduction of the steam engine in the 1830s spurred the demand for iron and coal. By 1850, Prussia was producing around 529,000 tons of iron and mining

6 million tons of coal per year to support its railroads and manufacturing industries. Prussia had become a leader in industrialization.

The Zollverein Agreement *by mid-1800s* Political divisions reduced trade and slowed the economic growth of German states in the early 19th century. In 1834, guided by an ambitious Prussian monarchy, several German states signed the Zollverein Agreement. The goal of this arrangement was eliminating the customs, or taxes, paid on goods imported from one German state to another and promoting German unity. In 1871, Prussia finally united the German states (except Austria) into the German Empire.

List's National System In a set of ideas known as the **National System**, German economist **Friedrich List** (1789–1846) argued for government involvement in economic growth, including tariffs and investments in education and infrastructure. List, a supporter of German unification, believed that tariffs would protect German industries from English imports. But once Germany was on an equal footing with England, List believed, free trade could be gradually reintroduced. List's ideas provided the framework for later free trade agreements among European nations.

List also believed that an extensive network of government-controlled rail lines would help German unification and increase government power. The first German railroad line opened in 1835. In 1842, Prussia's government established the Railroad Fund to finance rail lines throughout German lands. Germany, like all of Europe except densely populated Great Britain, relied on government support to build its railway network. During the next decade most major German cities became connected by rail, with Berlin emerging as a railway hub and leading urban center. By the time Germany unified in 1871, it had more than 11,000 miles of railway.

Slower Growth in Southern Europe

As Britain, France, and Prussia industrialized, southern Europe remained largely agrarian with few factories and railroads. Portugal, Spain, southern Italy, and Greece lacked significant deposits of coal and iron. In addition, their economies featured large landowners who used peasants or serfs to work the land. Landowners had little interest in industrial development that might lure people to work in factories. Because the landed elites controlled the governments, no states sponsored initiatives to construct railroads.

Life in southern Europe remained as it had been for hundreds of years. Many used little cash and banks had little role in the economy. Throughout the 19th century, Britain, France, and Germany grew wealthier and stronger faster than did southern Europe. This pattern would continue into the 20th and 21st centuries.

However, Russia, began to industrialize. It built railroads to connect major commercial centers. The Trans-Siberian Railroad transported goods and materials between Moscow and the Pacific Ocean, a distance of over 5,700 miles. It enabled Russia to trade more easily with East Asian countries.

Russia's coal, iron, and steel industries developed along with its railways, mostly in the 1890s. Russia became the world's fourth largest steel-producing nation by 1900. Still, Russia's economy remained largely agricultural until the Communists took power in 1917.

To accumulate the money needed to invest in railroads and factories, Russia increased its grain exports. It did so even in years when it had too little to feed its own people. One government minister noted that the peasants might starve but the country would export.

The Second Industrial Revolution, 1870–1914

From around 1870 to 1914, Europe underwent a dramatic expansion of manufacturing, transportation, and trade that became known as the second industrial revolution. New innovations in manufacturing increased the mass production of goods. Steel became a major industry. Electricity revolutionized urban centers and provided a new source of power for manufacturing. Chemical engineering introduced new materials including galvanized rubber and plastics. The invention of the **internal combustion engine** ushered in an age of vehicles powered by gasoline, diesel oil, and other liquid fossil fuels.

Mechanization and the Factory System

The expansion of factories increased the demand for the machines that created products. These machines needed to be standardized in size, shape, and function so that if one part broke down it could easily be replaced. The second industrial revolution saw a rise in the manufacture of machine tools, those used to shape metal and build other machines.

Manchester, England During the second industrial revolution, Manchester, England, became one of the world's most industrialized cities and a center for the manufacture of machines used in the production of textiles and other consumer goods. The construction of deep canals in the 1880s and 1890s brought cargo ships directly into Manchester to be loaded for export.

In 1898, Manchester created the world's first **industrial park**—an area designated expressly for manufacturing. In 1902, the British branch of the U.S.-based Westinghouse Electric Company opened a factory in the park. In 1911, the Ford Automobile Company opened its first British factory there. Manchester's role in industry gave rise to the term **Manchester capitalism**, the idea that free trade could raise the living standard of all workers.

The Krupps The **Krupp family** of Essen, Germany, began manufacturing steel in 1810, specializing in weapons. The government subsidized much of the Krupp business. In the 1840s, the Krupps invented a new method for making steel. In 1847, they produced the first steel cannon. Other countries began to purchase Krupp weapons. Soon, Krupp was one of the world's wealthiest manufacturers. In 1862, Krupp built the first Bessemer process furnace on continental Europe. They added their own improvements to the process to develop purer steel. In the 1890s, Krupp developed steel combined with nickel, thin enough for the construction of ships. These steel-sided vessels became models for ocean liners and cargo carriers. Krupp also grew to become one of the world's largest railroad suppliers.

In 1872, Alfred Krupp, the company's president and owner, presented the *General Directive*, one of the first systematic plans for the management of a large modern company. It described the specific duties and responsibilities of all employees, established a formal hierarchy, and outlined employee benefits and regulations for working conditions.

Die Hüttenwerke von Krupp in Essen. (Nach Originalzeichnung.)

While the steel industry took off first in Great Britain, other countries quickly followed. In Germany, the steel works owned by the Krupp family became enormous in the country's economic development and the rise of its military power in the 19th and 20th centuries.

Credit: Getty Images

Electricity

The second industrial revolution was also an electric revolution. For most of history, electricity, such as lightning strikes or sparks of static electricity, were sources of curiosity or danger. The first practical use for electricity was in communications. In the 1840s, the American inventor Samuel Morse introduced the **telegraph**, a method of sending messages along an electric wire using a series of taps that made long or short sounds, which he termed "dashes" and "dots." For the first time, humans could transmit complicated information faster than a human or an animal could travel. It allowed almost instantaneous communication across hundreds or thousands of miles. In the 1870s, the laying of the first successful trans-Atlantic telegraph wire connected Britain with the United States.

Electrical Generators Transform Urban Life The development of electric generators in the 1880s led to the establishment of the **electric grid**, a system of supplying cities and towns with electric power for lighting, streetcars, and trolleys. With the use of electric light, offices, schools, libraries, restaurants, and factories could remain open at night. City life entered a 24-hour cycle of work and play.

Electricity Speaks Scottish American inventor Alexander Graham Bell patented the first **telephone** in 1876. Telephones did not become widely available, however, until the early 20th century. Telephone communications relied on a central "switchboard," or exchange where workers connected wires manually. As telephone lines spread, thousands of young women acquired jobs as telephone operators, making the telephone part of a new movement toward jobs and economic independence for women in the United States and Europe.

Wireless communication, or **radio**, first evolved in the 1890s. In 1894, Italian physicist and inventor Guglielmo Marconi invented a device he called the "wireless" telegraph. He received a British patent for his invention in 1896 and relocated to England. Marconi's wireless only transmitted signals, not human voices.

The first wireless voice transmission was accomplished by the Brazilian inventor Landell de Moura in 1900, and on December 25, 1906, Americans working for the Westinghouse Corporation broadcast the first radio program from a station on the coast of Massachusetts. Marconi capitalized on these new developments by opening the world's first radio factory in 1912. The new forms of communications enabled people to transmit ideas, inventions, and news rapidly across the globe, and the world became more interconnected.

Chemical Engineering

The second industrial revolution brought new uses for chemicals. Vulcanization, the process of hardening rubber by treating it with sulfur, made rubber far more valuable. It could be used to make many materials waterproof, including a coating for electrical wires.

In 1907, a chemist in New York, Leo Baekeland, developed a mixture of the chemicals phenol and formaldehyde to produce a hard, smooth material he named Bakelite. This material was the world's first plastic. Bakelite proved to be practical material for many modern devices including radios, telephones, phonographs, and cameras.

Chemical engineering also improved the textile industry. In 1894, Frederick Cross of England and his colleagues invented a fiber from wood pulp they called viscose. A little more than a decade later, the English textile manufacturing company Courtaulds opened the first factory devoted exclusively to the production of chemical, or synthetic, cloth.

Important Inventions, 1876 to 1907		
Year	Inventor	Invention
1876	Alexander Graham Bell	Patented the first telephone
1894	Guglielmo Marconi	Invented the wireless telegraph, a precursor to the radio
1894	Frederick Cross	Engineered viscose, an early synthetic cloth
1906	Landell de Moura	Sent the first wireless voice transmission
1907	Leo Baekeland	Created Bakelite, the world's first plastic

Governments and Corporations Try to Manage Markets

During the second industrial revolution, many countries experienced economic instability that led to a downward spiral or depression. Between 1873 and 1879, both Western Europe and the United States struggled with an economic crisis.

The Long Depression Several factors caused the economic crisis historians now call the Long Depression. Wars between Germany and France had destabilized both countries. Germany demanded monetary reparations from the defeated French, which the French had difficulty paying. Yet in a growing economy, people increasingly relied on money to buy and sell goods. However, the supply of money, which was based on the amount of gold each country held, did not increase fast enough. Money remained in short supply. Like anything in short supply, it became more valuable, and people had a hard time borrowing to expand or even operate a farm or business. Investment dried up for the railway building booms in Germany and the United States. Investors went into a panic over existing investments, and many workers faced unemployment. From 1873 to 1896, the rate of growth in production declined, unemployment rose, and prices in general fell. It was the world's most severe global economic crisis since the start of industrialization.

Responses to the Depression Nations tried to stabilize their economies through **protectionism**, with high tariffs to protect their own industries. Tariffs had been a successful strategy for economic growth for countries as they began to industrialize. However, the lack of trade caused manufacturers and merchants to go out of business, leading to even more widespread unemployment and social unrest.

In need of cash, people sought to withdraw their money from banks causing a "run" on the banks. Because banks had money out on loan before the crisis, they could not return all deposits and would sometimes go out of business. Although most nations had recovered somewhat by 1879, similar crises occurred periodically throughout the 1880s and 1890s. In response to these upheavals, both businesses and governments tried to develop strategies to survive economic uncertainty.

Trusts and Monopolies Throughout the Industrial Revolution, manufacturers had always tried to balance supply with demand. A surplus of goods would lead to a drop in price that would cut into profits, while a shortage might raise the price beyond what consumers were willing to pay. Sometimes corporations would try to set prices by joining together in **cartels** or **trusts.** Rather than competing on the open market these groups of companies would privately agree to set their prices at a certain level. Such price setting became illegal in many nations, and governments would punish companies that engaged in it.

A **monopoly** exists when one company buys up all its competitors. As a company grew, one way it might try to control the market was through a monopoly. That company would then control the entire market for the product and could set whatever price it wished. Consumers could not purchase from any other company, because all the competition had been eliminated. Again, governments tried to control monopolies by passing laws against them.

Not all monopolies were outlawed, however. The government might decide that in a certain industry one single company could provide better service than many companies, particularly when the cost of starting a business was very high. For example, electric companies and phone companies needed to build vast and costly networks of wires to carry electricity or phone calls, so once a company built such a network rarely could another company challenge its control of a market. Since those companies lacked competition, governments often regulated them.

Tariffs and Other Government Policies Traditionally, governments tried to protect their native industries by placing tariffs on foreign imports. High tariffs, however, could lead to trade wars, with each country raising tariffs to punish the other. **Free trade agreements** between individual states could allow for the mutual exchange of goods with few or no tariffs. This meant a trading partner had a **most favored nation** status. Free trade agreements could also be used to support political and military alliances. While freer trade created more competition for producers, it often reduced prices for consumers.

The Influence of Banks The influence of banks grew as the economies of industrialized nations became more complex and sophisticated. Large banks acquired considerable political and social influence. They could decide which companies and individuals were most worthy of loans and which would be denied credit.

Banks could also make loans to governments for infrastructure projects and other state-sponsored programs. In addition, banks helped international trade through currency conversion. Different nations used different monetary systems. If an American company sold goods to Britain, those goods would be purchased with British pounds. A bank would then covert the pounds into American dollars for the company to use.

For most of human history, people did not expect progress. Technology and ideas changed so little from one generation to the next that parents assumed their children would lead lives similar to theirs. This expectation changed in the Enlightenment.

Trust in Reason The Marquis de Condorcet was a prominent Enlightenment writer and philosopher (see Chapter 10). Condorcet popularized the idea that humankind had the ability to constantly improve. He expressed this view in his book *Sketch for a Historical Picture of the Progress of the Human Mind* (1795). He thought that the human mind had already evolved through nine stages. He predicted it would eventually reach a tenth stage of peaceful equilibrium around the world. While Condorcet acknowledged that there were limits to the population and amount of cooperation a civilization could support, he asserted that, by the time humankind reached that stage, science would have kept pace and would resolve such issues.

World War I Challenges Progress On the verge of another traumatic event, as World War I began, activist lawyer Victor S. Yarros pointed out how widespread, yet recent, the idea of progress was. Yarros explained that it was unheard of in the ancient world, but popularized by Enlightenment thinkers such as Condorcet. From those thinkers stemmed the belief that progress was constant, steady, and certain—that the world would always get better. However, in 1913, scholars began to question that notion. Yarros referred to the work of French scholar, M. Faguet. In response to the idea of progress, Faguet wrote, "I think it is absurd by its very definition to know whether anyone is advancing toward a goal." Faguet argued that mere movement is not progress, and the theory that humanity constantly and consistently improves is "sheer delusion, a prejudice, not only useless, but dangerous."

But not all early 20th-century scholars were so critical of the idea of progress. American philosopher, educator, and social critic John Dewey presented a more measured analysis of progress. Although Dewey began his career viewing the world in the same terms as Condorcet, his views became more complex. He believed that progress could continue, but that people had to plan and work for it.

Dangers of Progress By the 21st century, some thinkers argued that the population might be about to outstrip the ability of the earth to support it. One such scholar is Ronald Wright. In *A Short History of Progress* (2004), he made the point that the belief in human progress is not predetermined, nor, necessarily positive. Instead, Wright described "progress traps" into which both large and small civilizations fell because their populations outstripped the ability of their environment to sustain them. Rather than believing, as Condorcet did, that humans become smarter over generations and develop the ability to think their way out of their environmental problems, Wright declared that some fall prey to the same traps time and again, such as by producing technology that destroys the very environment that nurtures progress. No civilization has ever ultimately dodged these traps and survived, although the Egyptians and Chinese made the longest run at about 3,000 years.

Optimism However, Steven Pinker resurrected the argument for progress in his 2018 book, *Enlightenment Now*. Pinkerton challenged the "progress traps" of Wright and suggested instead that humans have reached the point predicted by Condorcet. He believed that scientific, analytical thinking had improved life for most people, reduced the number of nuclear weapons in the world, and given people the capacity to resolve the challenges of global climate change.

KEY TERMS BY THEME

Technology
Industrial Revolution
second industrial revolution
wrought iron
mass produced
steam engine
locomotive
coke
Henry Bessemer
Bessemer process
Crystal Palace
Great Exhibition of 1851
internal combustion engine
industrial park
telegraph
electric grid
telephone
radio

Economics
industrialists
entrepreneurs
capital
capitalism
factories
consumers
consumerism
middle class
mass production
mass consumption
Corn Laws
free trade
tariffs
patents
National System
Friedrich List
Manchester capitalism
Krupp family
protectionism
cartels
trusts
monopoly
free trade agreements
most favored nation

Questions 1 and 2 refer to the passage below.

"[T]here was a host of other background causes, some as fortuitous [fortunate] as the immense resources of coal and iron ore [on] which the British sat; others as purposeful as the development of a national patent system which deliberately sought to stimulate and protect the act of invention itself. In many ways, England was 'ready' for an Industrial Revolution. But perhaps what finally translated the potentiality into actuality was the emergence of a group of new men who seized upon the latent opportunities of history as a vehicle for their own rise to fame and fortune....

These were all men interested in expansion, in growth, in investment for investment's sake. All of them were identified with technological progress, and none of them disdained the productive process....They brought with them a new energy, as restless as it proved to be inexhaustible. In an economic, if not a political, sense, they deserve the epithet 'revolutionaries,' for the change they ushered in was nothing short of total, sweeping, and irreversible."

> Robert L. Heilbroner, American economic historian,
> *The Making of Economic Society,* 1980

1. A historian agreeing with Heilbroner's central argument about the causes of British industrialization would likely emphasize which of the following?

    a) James Watt's improvement on earlier models of the steam engine as a critical breakthrough

    b) The importance of the enclosure movement in creating a surplus of food and labor

    c) The British government's ban on Indian textiles to protect domestic industries from competition

    d) The role of the Napoleonic Wars in disrupting economic development in continental Europe

2. A historian arguing *against* the revolutionary nature of industrialization would likely cite which of the following as evidence?

    a) The private-public partnerships that helped expand the rail system

    b) The pace of population growth and urbanization that accompanied industrial change

    c) Violent riots by unemployed handloom weavers who sought to destroy new textile machinery

    d) The continued existence of cottage industry alongside factory production for much of the 19th century

Questions 3–5 refer to the chart below.

Output of Coal in European Countries, 1820–1900					
Year	United Kingdom	France	Germany	Belgium	Russia
1820	18	1	1	Not available	Not available
1840	34	3	4	4	Not available
1860	81	8	17	10	Less than 1
1880	149	19	59	17	3
1900	229	33	150	23	16

Data in millions of metric tons.

Source: B. R. Mitchell, *European Historical Statistics 1750–1970*

3. Which of the following factors best accounts for the increase in coal output in France and Germany during the 19th century?
   a) The collectivization of agriculture and creation of government-owned mines
   b) The removal of tariffs to allow capital and labor to move freely between countries
   c) British investment in coal-mining technology in continental Europe
   d) State sponsorship of national industries and railroad construction

4. The lag in Eastern European coal production was most likely a result of which of the following?
   a) The dominance of the traditional landed aristocracy
   b) The development of alternate sources of energy for mining
   c) British use of patents to restrict the spread of steam engine technology
   d) Inadequate population growth to sustain an industrial workforce

5. The pace of German industrialization between 1880 and 1900 contributed most directly to which of the following?
   a) The formation of a British-German alliance against France
   b) A new wave of imperial expansion and competition for colonies
   c) Germany's displacement of Britain as the leading maritime power
   d) The overthrow of the German monarchy by revolutionaries

Questions 6–8 refer to the passage below.

"The civilization, political education and power of nations depend chiefly on their economical condition and reciprocally; the more advanced their economy, the more civilized and powerful will be the nation, the more rapidly will its civilization and power increase, and the more will its economical culture be developed....

The system of import duties is consequently not, as has been said, an invention of speculative minds; it is a natural consequence of the tendency of nations to seek for guarantees of their existence and prosperity, and to establish and increase their weight in the scale of national influence."

Friedrich List, German economist, *National System of Political Economy*, 1841

6. The economic ideas expressed in this passage are best understood in the context of which of the following?
   a) Emperor Wilhelm II's desire to establish German colonies in Africa and Asia
   b) Conservative opposition among Germans to the upheavals of 1848
   c) Liberal efforts to help German industries compete with British manufacturing
   d) Romantic writers' appeal to a common German language and cultural identity

7. Based on the ideas in this passage and the context in which it was created, the author would have most likely supported which of the following?
   a) The establishment of social welfare programs for elderly and unemployed Germans
   b) The banning of German socialist parties
   c) The initiation of wars by Bismarck to unify Germany
   d) The formation of the Zollverein, a German customs union

8. The ideas in this passage most directly challenge the principles of
   a) laissez-faire
   b) capitalism
   c) Social Darwinism
   d) industrialization
   e) mercantilism

SHORT-ANSWER QUESTIONS

1. Use the passage below to answer all parts of the question that follows.

"Industrial Revolution implies industrialization—that is, both the absolute growth of industry, and its expansion relative to the other sectors of the economy, those being agriculture and service. . . . Many of the changes which characterized industrialization in Britain were not new, but they were unprecedented in scale. Nowhere else, at least in Europe, had ever seen the volume of industry... by 1850. Nowhere else had ever seen the concentration of machines which by then existed in the factories."

Charles More, *Understanding the Industrial Revolution*, 2000

a) Describe ONE piece of evidence that *supports* More's argument regarding the effects of the Industrial Revolution in England.

b) Describe ONE piece of evidence that *undermines* More's argument regarding the effects of the Industrial Revolution in England.

c) Explain ONE example of how the second industrial revolution (1870–1914) provoked an argument similar to those described by More.

2. Answer all parts of the question that follows.

a) Describe ONE reason for the delay in industrialization in France from 1780–1850.

b) Describe ONE reason for the delay in industrialization in Eastern Europe from 1780–1850.

c) Describe ONE reason for the expansion of industrialization in Prussia or Germany in the mid-19th century.

LONG ESSAY QUESTIONS

1. Evaluate the most significant factors that made Great Britain a leader in the Industrial Revolution.

2. Evaluate the most significant effects of the growth of the middle class during the Industrial Revolution.

REFLECT ON THE CHAPTER ESSENTIAL QUESTION

1. In one to three paragraphs, explain why the Industrial Revolution began in Great Britain and spread to the continent.

WRITE AS A HISTORIAN: MAKE CONNECTIONS

A key skill needed when writing as a historian is the ability to make connections: between events, time periods, themes, and even contextual backgrounds. To make a persuasive argument requires not only supporting it with evidence but also showing how it is related to other parts of history:

- make connections across different time periods (for instance, showing a link between the Industrial Revolution in the 18th century and the idea of imperialism in the 19th century)
- make connections across different geographical regions (for instance, showing how the Industrial Revolution in Europe benefited from slavery in the Americas)
- make connections between similar events or issues (for instance, showing how the Industrial Revolution in Great Britain influenced industrial development in France)

Another way to extend an argument is to make connections between various contexts. For instance, if the prompt asks for social factors regarding a specific event or issue, you could also introduce the economic or political contexts that support the social factors. For example, a prompt might ask about the influence of the Industrial Revolution on the role of women in society. You could extend this by adding context that explains how changes in the method of producing goods influences social change.

For the prompt below, describe whether each statement is connected to it by the context of time periods, geographical regions, similar events, or related themes.

Prompt: Explain how Britain's supplies of coal and iron ore promoted industrial growth.

1. As Britain moved to large-scale mechanization, the standard of living improved consistently for the general populations of industrialized nations worldwide for perhaps the first time in history.

2. Britain's Industrial Revolution was influential as far away as the United States, where people sought the methods to create their own textiles. Americans "borrowed" ideas for building textile mills from the British, but Eli Whitney's cotton gin made the raw materials plentiful and cheaper for the British.

3. Innovation extended to other fields, such as agriculture. Farming used less labor thanks to seed drills, ploughs, and threshers.

4. By the 19th century, coal became a cheap and efficient fuel source for producing iron using hot blast furnaces. This availability of iron, in turn, led to the development of machine tools and engine technology. The pace of innovation became exponential.

14

Industrialization and Everyday Life

"Rattle me out of bed early, set me going, give me as short a time as you like to bolt my meals in, and keep me at it. Keep me always at it, and I'll keep you always at it, you keep somebody else always at it. There you are with the Whole Duty of Man in a commercial country."

—Charles Dickens, *Little Dorrit*, 1857

Essential Question: How did industrialization shape everyday life?

Industrialization reshaped nearly every aspect of daily life, first in Northern and Western Europe and eventually throughout the world. Social classes became more distinct, and people in each class developed their own outlook based on their economic role. As workers moved from farms to factories, they had to learn to follow strict schedules, working a set number of hours at a repetitive task often in unsafe conditions and for very low pay. Factory work also separated workers from their homes and families, since the home was no longer the focus of working life.

Those who remained on farms were forced to change how they worked as well. Many became tenant farmers, growing crops for others on commercial farms. Improvements in transportation, including railroads, steamships, and better roads and harbors, prompted these commercial farms to produce for distant markets rather than for their own consumption.

Meanwhile, a new middle class gained power and influence, creating a demand for consumer goods that further spurred industrialization. Urban areas became centers of education and culture that reflected middle-class interests and values. For this new middle class, a comfortable home served as a shelter from the larger society—a place where women and children could find shelter from the so-called masculine world of work.

Most important, social classes were linked with each other through the processes of production and consumption of goods. Charles Dickens believed that many in the lower class produced far more than their low wages enabled them to consume. Dickens, the author of the quotation that begins this chapter and the most famous English novelist of the mid-19th century, had been poor as a child. He sympathized with the plight of those with little money. Many of his novels depict characters from the lower class who, against all odds, rise to the ranks of the middle class—something that rarely actually happened. In real life, **social mobility**, or moving from a poorer and less influential class to a wealthier and more prestigious one, was extremely difficult.

However, industrialization did generate some improvements for all social classes. Mass production and improvements in transportation made obtaining material goods easier than ever. Progress in medicine and public health increased the average life span in industrialized areas. Education and literacy increased, first for the middle class and later for the working class.

Industrialization also resulted in more leisure time for many families. Parents and children could visit public spaces and institutions such as parks, libraries, and museums. For many families, these replaced the at-home activities common in agrarian communities.

Rise of New Social Classes

Industrialization created new types of work. People filling these new jobs did not fit into the feudal classes, such as peasants and nobles.

The Working Class The members of the **working class,** or **proletariat,** worked largely in manufacturing, mining, and related industries, such as railroads and steamship travel. Many working-class people lived in homes they rented from their employers or in a new type of housing that first appeared during industrialization— multifamily dwellings called **tenements,** in which several families would crowd into buildings, often forced to share kitchen and toilet facilities. Few working-class families owned real estate. Working-class women and children often had to work to help support the family.

In England, as industrialization grew, the number of industrial workers skyrocketed during the 19th century. In 1750, about 60 percent of all males worked in farming, but by 1900 that had declined to about 12 percent, even though agricultural production doubled during that period. By 1900, nearly 80 percent of the population in industrialized countries worked on commercial farms, in factories, or as domestic servants.

The Middle Class Members of the **middle class,** or the **bourgeoisie,** in contrast, worked in professional occupations such as business management, law, medicine, banking, government civil service, and higher education. Many middle-class families owned their own homes, and communities of single-family dwellings, or **suburbs,** on the edges of cities expanded to accommodate the growing middle class during the late 19th and early 20th centuries. Few middle-class women worked outside the home. Children attended school or were tutored at home. A small number of middle-class families accumulated enormous wealth through the ownership of factories, mines, railroads, and steamship lines. Toward the end of the 19th century, these families began to form a new upper-class "aristocracy," purchasing large country estates and building mansions that rivaled those of the traditional aristocrats.

Class-Consciousness Among Workers

The term **class-consciousness** means that members of a social class were aware of which class they belonged to and consciously identified with that class and its interests. They spoke of themselves as members of a class and saw their lives through the lens of class distinctions.

This class-consciousness was especially true of the proletariat. Working-class people often left their homes to seek work in factories and mines. In doing so, they also distanced themselves from their **extended families**. Without their family network nearby, they had to rely on one another for help and support. Young people in factories found that their closest relationships were those with whom they worked. On their rare days off, workers would spend their much valued leisure time together. New activities to relax became popular:

- performances at **vaudeville** theaters, where audiences could see a variety of musicians, dancers, magicians, and actors in a single show
- sports, such as boxing matches, horse races, and team games such as rugby and football (known in the United States as soccer)
- excursions, on bicycles or on foot, into the countryside or to a beach
- picnics and other leisure activities in new urban parks

Spending both work and leisure time together created solidarity among people who did physical labor in factories and mines. They began to see themselves as a distinct social class, and they wanted political representation.

On August 16, 1819, about 70,000 people gathered in St. Peter's Fields in Manchester, England, to demand reforms in Parliament, such as expanding the right to vote. Efforts to break-up the gathering resulted in 15 deaths. This event, known as the **Peterloo Massacre,** demonstrated to many working people that they needed to unite to defend their interests. They became more willing to join **labor unions,** organizations of workers that could negotiate with employers to improve wages and working conditions. Many workers also formed **mutual-aid societies**, groups that helped members in times of need.

Class-Consciousness in the Middle Class

Members of the new middle class tried to distinguish themselves from the working class by adopting the styles and **social mores**, or customs, of the aristocratic classes as they became seen as the "new bourgeoisie." Middle-class families invested deeply in their homes. Luxury items such as works of art, china dishes, fine wooden furniture, woven rugs, and window drapes enhanced bourgeois homes as conspicuous consumption—the public display of luxury goods purchased— became part of the culture. Middle-class families often entertained at home and employed servants to cook and clean for them.

As did working-class families, middle-class families mainly socialized with one another. When they traveled, members of the bourgeoisie chose resorts and hotels where they could socialize with other middle-class families. In England, the city of Bath with its hot springs was a traditional vacation spot for the bourgeoisie. In Germany, the town of Baden-Baden served a similar function. Social life was also a way to establish business connections, which would further solidify middle-class wealth. Many middle-class families attempted to act like the aristocracy by attending theater, ballet, the symphony, and horse races.

Many middle-class men joined private clubs whose members shared investment opportunities and business advice with one another. Some joined **fraternal organizations,** also known as brotherhoods, organizations of people with common interests and ambitions. Once a man joined such an organization, he could depend on his "brothers" for a loan or a job reference. Many of these organizations, such as the Freemasons, started out as professional guilds for skilled workmen. As the guilds themselves declined and disappeared, the organizations continued to flourish as a means of mutual support. In this way, they helped strengthen the bonds among the middle class.

The intertwined triangle and circle, with an "all-seeing eye" in the center, was one of the many symbols used by the Freemasons. This building is in Venice. It was completed in 1790. Credit: Getty Images

Middle-Class Philanthropy

As members of the middle class began to accumulate wealth, they had new opportunities to take on roles formerly carried out only by the elite. For example, middle-class people formed **philanthropic,** or charitable, organizations. Some of these organizations endowed museums, symphonies, schools, operas, and other cultural institutions.

Others focused on charity. Many middle-class women provided aid at orphanages and helped the poor and working class by distributing food and clothing and training children for domestic service or factory jobs. While these charities did not lift people out of poverty, they did provide basic care at a time when there were few government programs in industrialized nations that addressed the needs of the poor.

Several charitable groups were religion based. One of the best known was the Salvation Army, founded in London in 1865 to provide shelter to the homeless and unemployed. As part of the Social Gospel movement, it also encouraged the people it served to become Christians or to deepen their Christian faith.

Population Growth and Urbanization

Industrialization brought rapid population growth to Europe, particularly in cities, and urbanization changed the face of Western Europe. Rural populations dwindled as cities grew.

These shifts led to changes in politics and economics. Political power became concentrated in cities. Governments began to invest in such projects as sewage systems to improve urban life. Rural areas, meanwhile, grew weaker and their people had less say in government policies. People saw cities as centers of opportunity and wealth. Even those with few resources were eager to make the transition from country to city in search of jobs and, ultimately, a better life.

The Growth of Western Europe's Urban Population, 1750–1900					
Year	Population Living in Urban Areas	Population Living in Rural Areas	London	Paris	Berlin
1800	20%	80%	1,200,000	580,000	172,500
1850	35%	65%	2,650,000	1,050,000	419,000
1900	55%	45%	6,500,000	3,500,000	1,500,000

Effects of Overcrowding

As cities grew, urban problems increased. Most city residents were poor and working class. Five or more people might live in a single tenement "flat," or apartment, of one or two rooms. Some rooms did not have windows, fresh air was scarce, and stairways lacked lighting. Residents had to share bath facilities. Mice, rats, and other vermin proliferated. Contagious diseases such as tuberculosis, cholera, and typhus spread rapidly in such overcrowded conditions.

Lack of Housing Some people could not afford any housing at all and they lived on the margins of society as beggars. Some eked out a living as peddlers, sleeping on the streets. Such dire poverty forced many men into a life of crime, and women often turned to prostitution for survival. Orphanages, **workhouses** (see Chapter 22), and debtors' prisons served as last resorts for those who had nowhere else to go.

Poor Public Infrastructure During the first half of the 19th century, cities did not have the **infrastructure**—the basic physical structures needed for a process—to provide clean water. Tenements lacked toilets and running water. People depended on public pumps and wells for drinking water. Raw sewage was often disposed of as it had been in the Middle Ages, dumped on the street. It then found its way into these water sources. Even if it was carried away from homes, it was often dumped in or near the rivers that provided the water people drank.

In the mid-19th century, the Thames, the main river flowing through London, was so polluted with industrial and human wastes that it was viewed as carrying death. The city had grown rapidly and did not have the public infrastructure to handle discharge from factories and sewage.

Credit: Getty Images

THE " SILENT HIGHWAY"-MAN.
"YOUR MONEY OR YOUR LIFE!"

Other Health Issues Cold and damp housing fostered respiratory problems. Lack of access to sunlight was particularly hard on children. Sunlight produces the vitamin D needed for strong bones. With so little of it, children developed crippling bone diseases such as rickets. Cholera, tuberculosis, and typhoid fever sometimes reached epidemic levels of infection. Industrial accidents also took many lives.

For most urban dwellers, life was dangerous and difficult. Yet during the last half of the 19th century, trends in agriculture and health care enabled the population to grow. Despite the hardships, the standard of living began to improve by the end of the century, even for the working class.

Reasons for Population Growth

Despite the terrible living conditions in the growing cities, one important reason that population grew was increased progress in agricultural productivity through better agricultural practices:

- Crop rotation increased harvests of grains and vegetables.

- The cast-iron plow (1803) allowed farmers to sow crops in deeper furrows, preventing seeds from being blown away.

- The mechanized reaper, developed by Cyrus McCormick (1837), enabled farmers to harvest crops faster and with less labor. In fact, McCormick had demonstrated years earlier that one worker using an early version of his reaper could do the work of 12 men with scythes.

- The steel plow (1837) made farming even more efficient.

The Beginning of Public Health In the 19th century, scientists were just beginning to understand infections and how diseases spread. Progress in medicine and health remained slow, but a few breakthroughs did help establish better living conditions, even among the poor. The introduction of the **smallpox vaccine** in 1796 by Dr. Edward Jenner of England slowed the progress of one of history's most deadly diseases.

In 1854, Dr. John Snow of London made a map showing where cholera victims lived and where public pumps were located. Dr. Snow's map showed the locations of the 578 deaths during a September 1854 cholera outbreak. He quickly realized that cholera was being spread by contaminated water from public pumps. People slowly realized that higher taxes to pay for public sanitation would improve health. In 1869, the city of London began to build a sewage system that would dispose of waste and provide clean drinking water. Other European cities eventually followed suit, building networks of water mains that helped prevent cholera and other waterborne diseases.

Pasteur and the Germ Theory One of the biggest medical breakthroughs of the 19th century came when **Louis Pasteur** of France developed his **germ theory** of disease. Born in 1822, Pasteur studied chemistry in Paris. In 1849, he used a microscope to identify tiny organisms he called "germs" that he believed were responsible for the putrefaction, or rotting, of food and liquids.

At first, the medical establishment ridiculed Pasteur. Few doctors believed that nearly invisible organisms could spread disease. It took several years for Pasteur's ideas to take hold. However, by the 1870s, most physicians accepted Pasteur's research. Pasteur developed two vaccines, one for rabies and another for anthrax. In addition, he gave his name to **pasteurization,** a process used to kill bacteria in milk by heating it to a high temperature. Understanding microorganisms such as bacteria and viruses transformed medicine and paved the way to the discovery of new treatments and drugs in the 20th century.

The Antiseptic Method and Bacteriology Additional 19th-century medical advances also helped slow the spread of disease. The **antiseptic method,** the practice of never allowing germs to enter a medical operating procedure, was pioneered by British physician Joseph Lister (1827–1912). The field of **bacteriology,** the study of bacteria, was founded by German physician Robert Koch (1843–1910) and others. He identified specific bacteria that caused tuberculosis and cholera.

Increase in Life Span Prior to the Industrial Revolution, the average life span in Britain was about 40 years. During the early 19th century, infant mortality was very high. About one out of three children died in infancy. The

Louis Pasteur and Joseph Lister were recognized around the world for their contributions to human health. Each was honored with a stamp by an African government.

Credit: Getty Images

average life span of an industrial worker had actually decreased to about 30 years of age. Improvements in nutrition and medicine increased the average life span in Western Europe during the second half of the 19th century. By 1900, it had risen to 47 for men and 50 for women.

Not all social classes shared equally in the benefits of progress. Middle-class people had access to better food and sanitation and worked on jobs that were less physically demanding than people in the working class. As a result, middle-class people lived longer.

Family Structure and Relationships

Over time, the Industrial Revolution altered the family structure and personal relationships for both bourgeois and working-class families. Overall, family units became smaller, and multigenerational households became less common. The norm became the **nuclear family,** which consisted mainly of two generations—parents and their children living in a single home.

In addition, in an industrialized society, family and work occupied **separate spheres,** or areas of life. Instead of everyone working at home and integrating work with family life, the adults increasingly worked outside the home. As a result, the home took on less of an economic function and more of a comforting and nurturing one. This separate-sphere arrangement was particularly true for men in middle-class families.

Changes for the Working Class

In a rural farming society, people had always depended on the family to work the land. Children learned skills from the adults. Craft workers, such as blacksmiths and furniture makers, often worked from home. Men could not marry until they either inherited land or could support a family with a skill; women had to have a dowry to enter a marriage.

However, once people started working in factories, they were often separated from their families. Family members no longer worked together. Each employed individual brought his or her wages home. Workers' wages were low and a family usually needed many workers just to pay for necessities like food, clothing, and shelter. Even apprentices left their rural families to live and work with masters in large cities.

Working-Class Childhood Children in factories labored at a single task all day long and rarely had the chance to learn new skills. Some working-class families relied entirely on the labor of their children. Many factory owners preferred child workers because they worked for less than one-half the wages paid to men. In some industries, the owners preferred children because smaller hands could perform the fine work needed in manufacturing textiles. Many young boys worked at the very dangerous job of bobbin boy, delivering empty bobbins to women spinning thread and removing bobbins when they were full. Some bobbin boys worked 14 hours a day, six days a week.

Once these children grew too old for their jobs, they might find themselves unemployed and unwanted. In urban areas, unemployed children were often expected to fend for themselves, by begging, scavenging for scrap material to sell, or even stealing to survive. Conditions for working children contributed to the growth of reform movements.

Working-Class Women and Marriage Working-class women, too, were often expected to work for wages as well as cook, clean, and care for any young children in the home. When a mother worked outside the home, small infants were often left in the care of a neighbor rather than with a grandparent or relative. By the late 19th century, the most common jobs for working-class women were as domestic servants. Working-class men worked long hours, and many had little time for family life. As labor unions sought reforms in the late 19th century, many called for a shorter workday not just to give workers a break from physical labor but also to help them find time for family life.

Middle-Class Families Become the Social Ideal

Beginning in the late 19th century, working-class people looked to the middle class as an example of the ideal family life. Like middle-class people, they strove to make their homes the center of their lives and to provide their children with greater education and the opportunity for social mobility.

As the 19th century progressed, the middle-class family developed clearly defined gender roles in what became known as **the cult of domesticity.** A husband and father who worked outside the home supported the family. Women did not join the workforce. Rather, they stayed home and cooked, cleaned, and cared for the children. Within these gender roles, the main goal of the wife and mother was to make the home a shelter for her husband and children as well as for herself. Home life revolved around the emotional relationships between family members. Middle-class people believed a home should provide a warm and caring atmosphere for the family.

Children in middle-class homes often remained dependent upon their parents until their late teens or early twenties. Sons did not enter the workforce until they had graduated from secondary school or college. Daughters usually remained at home until they married.

Middle-Class Marriage and Family Life With the rise of the middle class during the 19th century, the "ideal" family was one whose members were bound to one another primarily by love and affection. Although many families never succeeded in reaching such an ideal state, the image of the warm and loving family proved a powerful image in 19th- and early 20th-century culture. Novelists such as Jane Austen and Charlotte Brontë (see Chapters 11 and 12) presented characters who married for love, not money. Young people, who grew up reading these novels, believed that they should have the right to marry whomever they chose, rather than let their parents arrange a marriage for them.

Once people married, they tended to have large families. Childbearing and child-rearing were the main roles for women, and motherhood was considered a woman's highest achievement.

For most of the 19th century, birth control was limited and highly controversial. However, the introduction of some basic methods of birth control at the turn of the 20th century made it possible for some couples to limit the size of their families. Birth control was mainly available to middle-class women. With fewer children, parents could invest more time and money in each child. Education became increasingly important and smaller families ensured greater social mobility for the middle class.

Class Distinctions Remained Based on Economics Economic prosperity remained important to the middle class. Most people married within their own social class because the classes rarely mixed with one another. Marriages between middle-class and working-class people were relatively rare and frowned upon by most middle-class families. Even within the middle class, wealthier families tended to marry into one another. The daughter of a small shopkeeper, for instance, was not likely to wed the son of a man who owned a steamship line or railroad. Yet within these restrictions, men and women aimed for a **companionate marriage**—one in which both spouses regarded one another as friends and companions striving toward the same goals in life.

Social Reform and Family Life

People responded to the problems that came with industrialization by demanding that the government impose reforms. The first reforms protected women and children, who were seen as the most vulnerable members of society. Reformers sought to limit the types of jobs women and children could perform and the number of hours they could work. During the first half of the 19th century, Britain's Parliament passed three acts regulating industrial work: the **Factory Act of 1833,** the **Mines Act of 1842,** and the **Ten Hours Act of 1847.**

The Factory Act of 1833 The Factory Act of 1833 was the first attempt to protect working children. The act declared that no child under the age of 9 could be employed in a factory or mine. Children between the ages of 9 and 13 could work up to nine hours a day. Children between 14 and 18 could work up to twelve hours a day. No child could work between 8:30 at night and 5:30 in the morning. In practice, these restrictions made little difference because lighting in factories was very limited before the widespread use of electricity. Further, children were supposed to receive at least two hours of schooling each day. They had to provide a certificate stating that they had the equivalent of that schooling the prior week.

The weaknesses of the act rapidly became apparent. Many families lied about the age of their children in order to obtain work certificates, and employers made little effort to verify the true ages of those they employed. Even a child as young as 4 or 5 could get a piece of paper giving a false age of 9 or 10. Children and teens old enough to work rarely had time for school, and schools for working children did little to prepare them for better jobs. Certificates for education were readily granted. When government factory inspectors found manufacturers violating the law, they had little power to punish them. Many owners employing underage children received only small fines or no punishment at all.

Nevertheless, the act did have some influence. It made people aware of the need to protect children from some of the worst aspects of industrialization. Further, it introduced the idea that the welfare of children was the government's responsibility.

The Mines Act of 1842 Like the Factory Act, the Mines Act of 1842 represented another attempt to regulate the treatment of women and children in industry. Under this act, no boy under the age of 10 could be employed in coal mines in Britain. In addition, women and girls were banned from working in mines entirely. Legislators felt that mine work was too difficult and even degrading for females. Rather than improving conditions for all workers, they simply chose to ban women. Although the ban was meant to protect them, many working-class women felt threatened by the new law. While work in mines was grueling and exceedingly dangerous, women in mining districts had few other job options. If they could not work in the mines, their families would suffer.

As with the Factory Act, many workers and employers disregarded the rules. Small boys continued to work in the mines. Women sometimes dressed as men or came to the mines as "substitutes" when their husbands and sons were sick or injured. Only when the miners' unions secured higher wages for men in the early 20th century did it become economically possible for women and children to leave the mines entirely.

The Ten Hours Act of 1847 At the beginning of the Industrial Revolution, workers did not have any set hours. They worked as long as the employer needed them, often from dawn to dusk. Work shifts of twelve to fifteen hours were common. During the 19th century, a campaign for the ten-hour day became a major theme for labor unions and reformers. In 1847, after several failed attempts, reform-minded members of Parliament finally passed a bill limiting the number of hours women and children between 13 and 18 could work to ten hours a day on weekdays and eight hours a day on weekends. Children under the age of 13 were banned from working entirely. As with previous laws, the Ten Hours Act proved hard to enforce. Economic need forced many women to accept longer hours, and children under the age of 13 continued to work as long as their families needed the income.

Rise of Consumerism

During the last half of the 19th century, the industrialized nations of Europe experienced a dramatic increase in the number of consumer goods available on the market. Ready-made clothing, processed foods, books, furniture, and even toys spurred the rise of **consumerism,** a lifestyle that revolved around the purchase of consumer goods. In urban areas, **department stores,** sometimes called emporiums, catered to middle-class shoppers by providing a wide array of goods within a single establishment. Shopping became a leisure activity for many middle-class women, and successful department stores catered to their tastes. Some stores even added restaurants, beauty salons, and theaters to their premises to make shopping an all-day experience for their customers.

Marketing and Advertising

As consumer culture grew in the second half of the 19th century, merchants developed new ways of reaching customers. Women, because they did most of the family shopping, became the prime movers of consumer culture. Advertisements in magazines and newspapers were often aimed toward women and used illustrations to promote products. These advertisements played upon the role the woman was expected to fulfill in the family, reminding her that a good wife and mother might want to purchase "only the best" soap, fabric, or canned foods for her loved ones.

Shopping by Mail

Railroads and steamships transported goods across countries and continents, and catalogs enabled merchants to reach consumers. Welshman Sir Pryce Pryce-Jones created the first known **mail-order catalog** around 1861. He established a company called the Royal Welsh Warehouse in the city of Newtown. From there he shipped clothing to customers as far away as Russia and Australia. Even Florence Nightingale and Queen Victoria became customers of his.

Other business owners followed the example of Pryce-Jones. In the United States, with vast rural areas, catalog sales to customers on farms and in small towns were very profitable. The Sears, Roebuck and Company and the Montgomery Ward Company became retail giants. Through catalogs they sold everything from canned fruits to boots to pianos. The mail-order business enabled families in remote areas to purchase the goods that signified an urban middle-class lifestyle.

Consumerism and the Home

The increase in consumer goods redefined home life, especially for the middle class. The invention of the first **refrigerated railroad cars** by William Davis of the United States in 1868 enabled fresh foods to be shipped from country to city. Once purchased, those foods could be stored in zinc-lined iceboxes designed to keep provisions cold even during the hottest days. The spread of electricity transformed the kitchen. Cleaner, more efficient electric stoves replaced coal stoves. Women began to cook with time-saving canned foods and prepared mixes. Rubber and the plastic material known as linoleum were used to construct easy-to-clean counters and floors. In the early 20th century, electric refrigerators and freezers allowed people to keep food fresh for long periods of time. Other aspects of home life were also transformed:

- The gramophone, an early record player invented by Thomas Edison in 1877, changed how people interacted with friends. For the first time, people could hear recorded music, and "gramophone parties" became a popular form of entertainment toward the end of the 19th century.

- In the early 20th century, the introduction of mass-produced incandescent light bulbs and electrification further revolutionized home life. With artificial light, people could socialize at night as easily as they could during the day.

- The development of the radiator to distribute steam heat also made homes warmer in the winter. With light and heat, the middle-class family could enjoy evenings together.

By the early 20th century, the middle-class home had come to symbolize both **progress** and comfort. For many people, these consumer goods were indeed proof that the Industrial Revolution had created a better way of life.

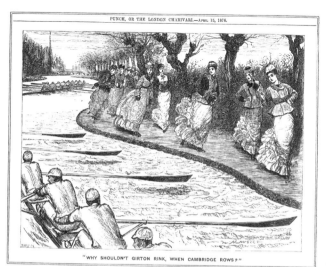

PUNCH, OR THE LONDON CHARIVARI—April 15, 1876.

"WHY SHOULDN'T GIRTON RINK, WHEN CAMBRIDGE ROWS?"

The middle class had more leisure time than the working class and performed less physical work than did agricultural workers. As a result, with the growth of the middle class came a growth in new forms of entertainment, such as rowing and skating.

Credit: Getty Images

Nonindustrialized Europe and the Hungry '40s

Compared to the industrialized areas of Northern and Western Europe, Southern and Eastern Europe remained more dependent on agriculture. Though serfdom had ended in the Habsburg Empire in 1848 and in Russia in 1861, most people remained poor and landless. They usually rented land from or were employed by landlord, receiving "pay" in the form of food and shelter. The landowners formed an elite that continued to dominate politics and society. As the 19th century progressed, peasants suffered from **famine**, an extreme and widespread shortage of food, when crops failed because the region's economy offered few alternatives to agriculture.

Societies dependent upon agriculture provided little financial cushion for most people when crops failed. In the mid-19th century, poor agricultural practices, combined with absentee landlords and a growing population, created conditions leading to famines.

Urban areas in Southern and Eastern Europe were smaller and more isolated than those of Western and Northern Europe. Manufactured goods were imported and available only to the wealthy elite. In many regions, relationships between peasants and aristocrats there had changed little since the Middle Ages. The harsh economic conditions found in Southern and Eastern Europe, often combined with religious or political persecution, forced the poor and oppressed to migrate to places such as the United States and Latin America.

The Irish Potato Famine

Made a part of the United Kingdom in 1801 and governed as a colony, Ireland was located in Western Europe but was economically more similar to the nonindustrialized countries of Southern and Eastern Europe. With few sources of coal, the Irish relied on a substance called peat, a dense, dirt-like layer of partially decomposed plant matter dug out of the ground. Since the plant matter had not fully decomposed, it could be burned for fuel and heat. Although Ireland had a small linen industry based on the cultivation of the fibrous plant flax, there was little attempt at full-scale industrialization.

The British regarded Ireland as a source of produce for their own workers. Irish farms and estates cultivated grain, potatoes, and dairy products, most of which were exported to England by English landlords. The Irish people for the most part remained poor. During the **Potato Famine** of the 1840s and 1850s, thousands of Irish men and women migrated to the United States and Canada.

Causes of the Famine Potatoes originated in the Americas. They first arrived in Europe in the 1600s. Nutritious and easy to cultivate in Ireland's poor soil, they rapidly replaced other foods as a staple among the Irish poor farmers. By the 1840s, most rural Irish relied almost entirely upon potatoes for nourishment. Around 1846, a disease known as blight began to destroy the crops. Parliament, committed to laissez-faire, did little to aid the Irish. Food shortages drove up prices (see Chapter 13).

Most Irish land belonged to English aristocrats who spent little time in

Ireland. They thought little about the suffering of their tenants, whom they viewed as an inferior people. Religion caused a further separation. Most English landowners were Protestants while nearly all Irish tenants were Catholics. For centuries, anti-Catholic laws had prohibited most Irish from owning land or voting. Some of these restrictions had been removed in the 19th century, but the legacy of religious discrimination persisted.

When the blight struck, landlords had little sympathy for the Irish. They continued to demand rent even after the crops failed. They evicted peasants who could not pay. Starving, homeless people wandered the Irish countryside.

One form of aid was the workhouse, built to house homeless people and provide them work. The British government built 163 workhouses in Ireland, but with little industry in Ireland, there was nothing for people to do to earn a living. Some were hired to build stone fences, known as famine walls. The fences were not really needed, but the British were reluctant to provide food to people unless they worked. Most of the workhouses were overcrowded, leading to unsanitary conditions and the spread of disease. Death rates in Ireland soared.

The Effect of the Famine on Population The Irish potato famine lasted approximately four years, from 1845 to 1849. Between 1841 and 1851, Ireland's population decreased 20 percent. In the mid-1800s, nearly 1 million people died of starvation and disease. Nearly 2 million more people **emigrated** to the United States, Britain, Canada, or Australia. Many never reached their destination. Vessels carrying Irish immigrants were called "coffin ships" because so many passengers, weakened by hunger and sickness, died en route. Economically, the country remained poor for many decades, with most people dependent on subsistence farming and fishing for a livelihood.

From Famine to Independence The famine aggravated political tensions between Ireland and Britain. When starving Irish farmers rioted to protest the lack of British aid, the government sent armed troops to suppress them.

Irish anger at British treatment continued to simmer. In the later 19th century, many Irish joined a vigorous campaign demanding **Home Rule**, a policy allowing Irish self-government within the United Kingdom. A group called **Irish Unionists,** primarily Protestants who saw Home Rule as a threat to their power, opposed this movement. Finally, in 1914, after decades of Irish pressure, Parliament passed a Home Rule bill.

However, when World War I broke out, Parliament delayed the bill's enactment. A small group of Irish rebels, tired of waiting peacefully for Home Rule, hoped to spur a national uprising to demand independence while Englad was focused on the war against Germany. The rebels seized the main post office in Dublin, an event known as the **Easter Rising of 1916**. But no revolution followed. The rebels were quickly defeated and 15 were executed. Irish anger at the executions, though, caused the country to explode in outrage. Years of fighting followed. In 1922, a peace agreement created the **Irish Free State**, which included most of Ireland, where Catholics dominated. However, in the northern six counties, known as Ulster, most people were Protestants. This region remained part of the United Kingdom.

Slow Change in Russia

Even after the abolition of serfdom in Eastern Europe and Russia, the peasants remained extremely poor. In Russia, the tsar ruled as an absolute monarch and traditional roles in society changed very slowly.

Tsar Alexander II recognized that serfdom undercut Russia's power. It reduced the incentive for people to work hard, try new farming techniques, and take initiative. It produced men who made poor soldiers, and it created little wealth to fund a strong military. So, despite the opposition of many nobles, he issued the **Emancipation Edict of 1861** that started a slow process of gradually abolishing serfdom. It technically allowed ordinary people to own land and participate in local government. Most peasants, however, lacked money to buy land. They had little education. Many chose to remain on the estates where they were born and continued to work for the landowners by renting small plots of land. Overall their lives changed little after emancipation.

HISTORICAL PERSPECTIVES: DID INDUSTRIALIZATION RAISE THE STATUS OF WOMEN?

The Industrial Revolution caused upheavals throughout society. Historians have disagreed on whether these changes resulted in a higher or lower status for women.

Status in the Pre-Industrial Economy In the early 20th century, women in Europe were fighting for the right to vote. In this context, with concern about the rights of women, economic historian Alice Clark investigated the respect for women's economic contributions to the pre-industrial economy. She found that, beginning in 17th-century England, the economic contribution of women in the pre-industrial economy raised their status. Clark noted that women contributed greatly to family production and survival. The domestic labor provided by women to make cloth, produce products, and raise crops avoided the need to purchase these items. These contributions enabled the view of rural residents that they were self-sufficient.

This domestic industry soon evolved into family industry, in which some family members might work for wages, but the family as the unit of production remained largely intact. Clark argued that women's status changed with the rise of capitalism in the 18th and 19th centuries. The family was no longer seen as an economic unit. Rather, men who worked outside the home were the primary source of wealth for the family. As such, men had a larger role in the public sphere, both economically and politically. Therefore, men demanded protections in the public sphere. In contrast, women focused on the domestic sphere and had little influence in the public sphere. Based on this loss of status, Bridget Hill, a historian writing in the late 20th century, concluded that the pre-industrial world had been a "golden age" for women.

New Ways to Define Status Successes by feminists in the 1970s and 1980s provided the setting in which some historians noticed gains made by women in the Industrial Revolution. While women might have been isolated, they also took on new responsibilities and status. According to historians Eleanor S. Riemer and John C. Fout, women tended to the spiritual and moral needs of their families. These responsibilities paved the way for entry into the public sphere as many middle-class women looked to use these skills beyond the home and apply them to society at large. Middle-class women worked to assist struggling working-class women and established the temperance movement, for example. In this way, social engagement led to pressure for a political voice, and with that, the status of women did increase.

The Broader Role of Women Katrina Honeyman, a British economic historian writing in the late 20th and early 21st century, focused on the actual role of women and children in the success of the Industrial Revolution. Unlike Clark, who considered declining economic contribution as a sign of declining status, Honeyman explained that employers who paid women less could use the extra money to further invest in technology and increase overall productivity. Honeyman argued that reduced wages combined with the marginalization of women was a defensive strategy used by men to maintain their own status. As a result, reforms improved economic opportunities only for male breadwinners, reduced job opportunities for women in the public sphere, and cut back on the opportunities for women to attend universities.

KEY TERMS BY THEME

Economics
tenements
workhouse
infrastructure
consumerism
department stores
mail-order catalog
famine
Potato Famine

Social Structures
social mobility
working class
proletariat
middle class
bourgeoisie
class-consciousness
extended families

Peterloo Massacre
labor unions
mutual-aid societies
fraternal organization
philanthropic
nuclear family
separate spheres
cult of domesticity
companionate marriage

Geography
suburbs

Continuity and Change
vaudeville
social mores

Technology
smallpox vaccine

Louis Pasteur
germ theory
pasteurization
antiseptic method
bacteriology
refrigerated railroad cars

Governance
Factory Act of 1833
Mines Act of 1842
Ten Hours Act of 1847
emigrate
Home Rule
Irish Unionists
Easter Rising of 1916
Irish Free State
Emancipation Edict of 1861

Questions 1 and 2 refer to the passage below.

"Gentlemen who supported the present measure . . . professed their object to be the welfare of the labouring community . . . held that the common sense of the working classes was capable of enabling them to take care of themselves; if it were not, let them be educated and better taught. . . . On every side he heard of their claims for universal suffrage; . . . yet these very men, who were the loudest in demanding the suffrage, which would enable them to take a part in deciding on the affairs of the nation, would appear, by this Bill, to say they were incapable of directing their own affairs; and, therefore, they desired the interference of legislation... which should restrain the operations of the working classes, by laying down laws and regulations which were to prevent them from carrying on their labour as seemed to them best? . . .

The Bill of the hon. [Honorable] Member seemed to require that as to the working classes there should be one measure for everybody. . . . If England alone had to supply the whole world with manufactures, he should not fear any consequences. . . . If the competition so created [in America] and going on were to continue, he apprehended that those who were asking for the limitation of labour to eight or ten hours, would find eight or ten hours to be much to their inconvenience. . . . It was well known that after defraying the expenses of individual labour and interest on capital, owners of mills . . . had therefore to calculate, besides having the competition of the Continent and of America . . . whether they could . . . obtain a proper and fair amount of profit."

> House of Commons debate over the Factories Bill
> (Ten Hours Act), February 10, 1847

1. What is the main argument in the passage against limiting the number of hours a factory laborer could work?

    a) It takes away the control workers have over their own choices.

    b) It creates a hierarchy of workers.

    c) It forces mill owners to pay unnecessary overtime wages.

    d) It prevents workers from earning a living wage.

2. The goal of the bill described in the source was most similar in the type of reform it advocated to which other bill?

    a) The Irish Home Rule Bill

    b) The Corn Laws

    c) The Emancipation Edict

    d) The Mines Act of 1842

Questions 3– 5 refer to the passage below.

"Equally important has been the influence of the Railway—now the principal means of communication in all civilized countries. This invention has started into full life within our own time. The locomotive engine had for some years been employed in the haulage of coals; but it was not until the opening of the Liverpool and Manchester Railway in 1830, that the importance of the invention came to be acknowledged. The locomotive railway has since been everywhere adopted throughout Europe. In America, Canada, and the Colonies, it has opened up the boundless resources of the soil, bringing the country nearer to the towns, and the towns to the country. It has enhanced the celerity [speed] of time, and imparted a new series of conditions to every rank of life."

Samuel Smiles, *Men of Invention and Industry*, 1884

3. Which general economic change in society was most directly encouraged by the development described in the passage?

   a) The need for horses and canals increased.

   b) The degree of social mobility increased.

   c) The size of labor unions increased.

   d) The ties between rural and urban areas increased.

4. Which development was helped most by railroads?

   a) It facilitated the movement of people from crowded cities to rural areas in order to meet agrarian labor needs.

   b) It was a means of overcoming the effects of the Corn Laws in Ireland.

   c) It allowed for the cheaper and more efficient transportation of raw materials and manufactured goods.

   d) It created economic competition between England and France to produce less expensive locomotives to sell in European markets.

5. Which best explains the context for the change described in the passage?

   a) New forms of entertainment emerged that appealed to factory workers.

   b) New technology was improving the lives of middle-class families.

   c) New efforts by the government began to improve public health.

   d) New laws regulated industrial work.

Questions 6–8 refer to the following passage.

"The work of undermining the population is going on stealthily, but steadily. Each succeeding day witnesses its devastations—more . . . deadly than the plague. We do not say that there exists a conspiracy to uproot the 'mere Irish;' but we do aver [charge], that the fearful system of wholesale ejectment [removing people from their land], . . . which we daily behold, is a mockery of the eternal laws of God—a flagrant outrage on the principles of nature. Whole districts are cleared. Not a roof-tree is to be seen where the happy cottage of the labourer or the snug homestead of the farmer at no distant day cheered the landscape. . . .

Those who laboured to bring those tracts to the condition in which they are—capable of raising produce of any description—are hunted like wolves, or they perish without a murmur. The tongue refuses to utter their most deplorable—their unheard of—sufferings. The agonies endured by the 'mere Irish' in this day of their unparalleled affliction are far more poignant than the imagination could conceive, or the pencil of a Rembrandt picture."

> *Tipperary Vindicator* [Irish newspaper], quoted in *The Illustrated London News*, December 16, 1848

6. According to the writer of the passage, how did the British government react to the Irish Potato Famine?

   a) English landlords suspended payments owed by the Irish tenant farmers.

   b) The British government sent supplies of free wheat to help the Irish.

   c) The British government did little to alleviate the effects of the famine.

   d) Queen Victoria made an official visit to Ireland to lend emotional support.

7. Which historical development most directly created the conditions for the crisis discussed in the passage?

   a) The Industrial Revolution aided British exploitation of Ireland.

   b) The French Revolution created British fear of Irish republicanism.

   c) The Romantic movement led the British to focus on nature's beauty.

   d) The Napoleonic wars made the British less concerned about large-scale suffering.

8. Which was a consequence of the Irish famine?

   a) Potatoes became the primary crop in Ireland.

   b) The Catholic religion lost its influence in Ireland.

   c) English control was accepted by the Irish.

   d) It increased political tensions and Irish nationalism.

SHORT-ANSWER QUESTIONS

1. Use the passage below to answer all parts of the question that follows.

"In sum, the sexual division of labour at home, which was already distinctly gendered in the seventeenth century, appears to have been further accentuated over the course of our period [eighteenth and nineteenth centuries] as a result of economic and ideological changes which undermined men's participation in domestic life, and . . . removed work opportunities for some wives."

R. Shoemaker, *Gender in English Society 1650–1850*, 2014

a) Explain ONE specific reason for the development of "separate spheres" that took place during the 19th century.

b) Describe ONE specific example of the changing role of men in the workplace in the second half of the 19th century.

c) Describe ONE specific example of the changing role of women in the workplace in the second half of the 19th century.

2. Answer all parts of the question that follows.

a) Describe ONE significant change in conditions for the working classes from 1800–1850.

b) Describe ONE significant continuity in conditions for the working classes from 1800–1850.

c) Explain ONE significant cause for the change or continuity identified in part a or part b.

LONG ESSAY QUESTIONS

1. Evaluate the extent to which the Industrial Revolution altered workers' positions within the family and society.

2. Evaluate the most significant difference in family life between countries that experienced industrialization and countries that remained agrarian.

REFLECT ON THE CHAPTER ESSENTIAL QUESTION

1. In one to three paragraphs, explain how industrialization shaped everyday life.

One effective way to extend an argument in a historical essay is to connect it to another discipline such as economics, geography, or the arts. You might also connect course themes, such as Individual and Society (IS) with Poverty and Prosperity (PP), or you could show the interrelationships among social and cultural history for a concept such as Social Darwinism.

When making a connection to another discipline, use a transition word, such as *similarly, likewise,* or *also.* As you write, remember to explain your ideas thoroughly to establish clear connections between your thoughts.

Another way to make connections among different disciplines or fields of inquiry is by referencing the DBQ documents. You may encounter a political cartoon or a paragraph from a scientific treatise or an excerpt from a law. Explaining the context and importance of such diverse sources allows you to extend your answer and show mastery of more than just straightforward historical dates and events.

In the statements below, identify any transition words that signal a connection to another discipline or field and identify the area of connection being made.

1. Europe experienced rapid urbanization during the Industrial Revolution as people moved to cities to take factory jobs. Technological advances transformed society in other ways as well. Self-conscious economic classes (such as the bourgeoisie and the proletariat) arose and led to social divisions between the working and middle classes.

2. Economic changes resulted in distinctive class-based cultures of dress, speech, values, and customs. Because middle-class women, in particular, embraced new socially conscious values, legislation changed in response. For the first time, society provided for universal schooling and protections for women and children laborers in mines and factories.

3. Family life evolved. Couples began to use birth control and had fewer children but were able to care for them better. Companionate marriages became common even among the working classes. As a result of these shifts, cities and philanthropists responded by creating family spaces: parks, beaches, sporting venues, libraries, theaters, and museums.

4. Industrialization and mass marketing increased both supply and demand for many consumer goods, including clothing, processed foods, and labor-saving devices. At the same time, new and efficient methods of transportation, such as steamships, railroads, and refrigerated railroad cars, all made it possible to distribute these goods, leading to improved quality of life for both sellers and consumers.

15

Political Responses to Industrialization

Workers of the world unite; you have nothing to lose but your chains.

—Karl Marx *Manifesto of the Communist Party* (1848)

Essential Question: What responses did the problems of industrialization provoke in how people thought and governments acted?

The word **politics** refers to all activities relating to government, including the rivalries among those who vie for power. Greek philosopher Aristotle (384 B.C.E.–322 B.C.E.) declared, "Man is a political animal." Aristotle recognized that a stable, functioning government needed the work of many citizens.

In Europe's rapidly growing industrialized societies, few people could avoid the influence of political movements. These movements played an enormous role in public life among all classes during the Industrial Revolution. To paraphrase Aristotle, man *and woman* truly proved to be political animals.

The Emergence of New Ideologies

In response to the turmoil of the Industrial Revolution and the French Revolution, Europeans explored many political theories and ideas of government. Some supported absolute monarchies while others promoted constitutional monarchies or republics. As the working class grew, people explored varieties of socialism and communism. A few people argued that the lack of any centralized government was the best system of all. In general, though, average citizens began taking on larger roles in public life than before.

Liberalism and the Rights of the Individual

One very influential new theory was **liberalism,** the political philosophy that emphasizes the rights of the individual and the idea that the government should have a limited role in the everyday lives of citizens. According to classical liberal theory, anything not expressly forbidden by law is allowed. Liberalism was introduced in England in the 17th century by the philosopher **John Locke**, who advocated the idea of the social contract, the theory that governments rule only with the consent of the governed (see Chapter 10).

Popular Sovereignty Locke's work inspired a movement toward **popular sovereignty**, a doctrine that the people, rather than just the monarch or nobles, should hold the greatest, or sovereign, power in society. This idea conflicted with reality in 19th-century Britain. At that time, most people could not participate in government. The British Parliament consisted of two houses. The House of Lords was a group of aristocratic men who inherited their positions. The House of Commons consisted of commoners, those who had no aristocratic titles or estates. Members of their districts elected representatives to the House of Commons. However, before 1832 only men over the age of 21 who owned land worth a certain amount of money could vote. These qualifications described less than 20 percent of the adult male population.

Reform Acts and Voting Rights As the middle class grew in the 19th century, members of it began to agitate for greater enfranchisement. They argued, demonstrated, and sometimes rioted. In 1832, Parliament responded by passing the **Great Reform Act of 1832**. This bill extended the vote to some middle-class men who did not own property—those who paid at least 10 pounds (10£) a year in rent. As a result, about 20 percent of Britain's adult male citizens could vote. The act favored rural regions, as Conservatives feared giving cities too much power. Over the following century, additional reform bills would expand voting rights to adults, including women (see Chapter 16).

THE ELECTION.
THE POLLING.

This engraving by William Hogarth provides a lively look at the way elections took place in the 18th century. To vote, a person had to announce in public how they were voting. The right-hand side of the image shows a campaigner attempting to bribe a voter.

Credit: Getty Images

Victory over the Corn Laws As voting rights spread, the middle class began to exercise its power by pressuring Parliament to enact laws favorable to middle-class interests. In 1839, Richard Cobden, a textile merchant and writer, organized the **Anti-Corn Law League**, opposing high taxes on imported wheat and the laws that regulated the wheat trade. (Recall that wheat also was known as "corn" then.) The wheat taxes favored the British aristocrats who rented their land to wheat farmers but raised the cost of wheat and wheat products for urban dwellers. When crops in England failed, the cost of imported wheat remained high, leading to scarcity and food riots.

Petitions were one of the main public-opinion tactics used by the Anti-Corn Law League to influence Parliament. A **petition** was a formal document signed by citizens requesting lawmakers to take action on a certain issue. Petitioning the government was an old and popular tradition in Britain dating back to the 17th century. In 1843, the House of Commons received approximately 34,000 petitions, most of which concerned the Corn Laws. In 1846, the League convinced British Prime Minster Peel to support the repeal of the Corn Laws, representing a major victory for the middle class and helping increase the power of the House of Commons, which represented the middle class.

Personal and Social Good Liberals argued that repeal of the Corn Laws was an example of **enlightened self-interest**, the idea that a person can see how acting for the good of society also benefits himself or herself. The middle class pushed for the repeal, but it also helped the poor and working classes by making food less expensive. The success fostered a coalition between middle-class politicians and the working class.

Whig Party Most liberal politicians belonged to Britain's Whig Party. Founded around 1688, the Whig Party promoted limited government. The Whigs controlled Parliament when it passed the Great Reform Act of 1832 and when it repealed the Corn Laws in 1846. In 1859, the Whigs joined other groups to create Britain's Liberal Party. Liberals believed in free trade, voting rights, and social reforms—all of which they hoped would promote greater stability and economic prosperity for all classes.

Jeremy Bentham and Utilitarianism One British philosopher who contributed to the ideas later associated with liberalism and the Liberal Party was **Jeremy Bentham**. Born in London in 1748, he studied law at Britain's prestigious Oxford University. After receiving his degree, he abandoned his legal career to travel, write, and promote social reform. His writing focused on philosophy, politics, and economics.

In 1789, he published his first book, *An Introduction to the Principals of Morals and Legislation,* outlining his "theory of utility." The goal of all laws, he declared, "must be the greatest happiness of the greatest number [of people.]" Bentham thought that the government should enact legislation that promoted and protected the well-being of most of the population. The value of every law, he believed, could be measured by how much good it accomplished.

Bentham's idea became known as **utilitarianism**. According to utilitarianism, any action is "right" that promotes happiness or well-being for all those affected. Utilitarianism thus contradicted Christian teachings and other ideas about ethics which held certain acts as inherently or always wrong.

Acting upon his utilitarianism, Bentham supported many causes. Among these were prison reform, education for women, religious freedom, and the humane treatment of animals. His ideas attracted many followers. Utilitarianism gave birth to the concept of the "greater good," which shaped many 19th-century social reform movements.

John Stuart Mill and Liberalism Among those influenced by Bentham's works was the politician and writer **John Stuart Mill**. His father believed he could make Mill a genius through early, intense instruction. By the age of 8 he could read and write in both Greek and Latin. By 12 he was adept in algebra, geometry, natural history, physics, economics, and astronomy. In his teens Mill was reading works on utilitarianism and law.

However, by the age of 20 Mill's studious upbringing had left him severely depressed. He wanted to devote himself to social reform. For a year, he desperately tried to understand how he could be happy in a world with so much injustice. Reading the poetry of William Wordsworth, a writer inspired by the beauty of nature, helped revive Mill's spirits. He came to believe that everyone was entitled to seek happiness as long as he or she did no harm to others, in a condition he termed **social liberty**.

Mill joined the Liberal Party and was elected a Member of Parliament in the House of Commons in 1865, becoming one of Britain's most influential Liberal leaders. He worked to expand voting rights and to expose corrupt government practices. In addition, he supported free speech, equal rights for women, and the abolition of slavery. His book, *The Subjection of Women,* published in 1861, was the first work in the English language to assert that women should have the same rights as men to vote, hold property, and pursue professional careers. His other works include *Principals of Political Economy, On Liberty,* and *Considerations on Representative Government.*

Mill often called himself a utilitarian who considered the greatest good for the greatest number. However, he also believed that governments should protect individual liberties, even from a democratic majority.

Chartism and the Working Class

Working-class people also were heavily involved in political movements. In Britain, a working-class movement known as **Chartism** campaigned for voting rights for all men regardless of wealth or property. The movement got its name from a document called the **People's Charter** written by William Lovett in 1839.

Lovett, a self-educated cabinetmaker, had become involved in radical politics in London. His charter called for **universal suffrage**, by which he meant allowing all men to vote regardless of wealth. It also called for redrawing voting districts, which gave extra representation to rural areas and reduced representation from urban areas. Lovett and his followers sought to reform the poor laws and labor laws that they felt oppressed working people. The Chartists organized mass meetings that drew thousands of men and women.

In 1842, the Chartists presented Parliament with a petition of between 2 million and 3 million signatures calling for political reforms. Parliament ignored the petition. Around the same time, Chartists also engaged in violent clashes with police, and many Chartist leaders were imprisoned. The movement declined after 1850, but its influence continued in subsequent ideological movements such as socialism and Marxism. Many reforms advocated by the Chartists were eventually enacted in the last half of the 19th century.

Flora Tristan One of the people inspired by the Chartists was **Flora Tristan**. The child of an aristocratic Peruvian father and a French mother, Tristan was a vocal advocate for the rights of workers in general. She was one of the early leaders in Europe in the fight to win the right of women to vote.

Conservatism and the Status Quo

In the 19th century, **conservatism** was a movement of people who believed that governments were most stable when based on traditional sources of power such as the monarchy, the church, and the army. They were suspicious of mass movements and feared giving too much power to common people. Conservatives worried that people with little education and little property to protect might disrupt the economy and create social chaos. As a result, conservatives believed that authority was best concentrated in the hands of the upper classes. Change should happen slowly. It should not be pushed by government.

One of the most fundamental differences between liberals and conservatives concerned human nature. Conservatives focused on the imperfections of humanity. In contrast, liberals were more optimistic that humans could improve themselves and the world.

Leaders of Conservatism

Many conservatives developed their ideology in response to the French Revolution (1789–1799). They watched in horror as a revolution that started as an attempt to reform a corrupt monarchy disintegrated into violence and civil war. They saw the dictatorial rule of Napoleon as the only way to restore order. Events in France, conservatives insisted, demonstrated that mass movements could not produce progress. Distrust of such movements was one of the beliefs developed by a series of 19th century conservative thinkers.

Burke of Great Britain Born in Ireland in 1730, **Edmund Burke** is considered the father of modern British conservatism. In some ways, Burke was a progressive. Like John Locke, he subscribed to the idea of a social contract between rulers and the ruled. He believed that even the king should obey the laws, a concept known as **limited monarchy**. He was sympathetic to the American colonies and believed that Britain could have avoided the American Revolution if the king had been more lenient and willing to listen to the colonists' complaints. Burke stopped short of advocating true democracy, however. He did not believe most people were capable of governing themselves.

In his book *Reflections of the Revolution in France* (1790), Burke argued that traditional authority was part of a **natural order** that enabled humans to flourish. Human society needed the structure imposed by a strong but responsible government. Without such authority, people would inevitably become selfish and violent. Freedom for the masses would lead only to civil strife. In Burke's view, respect for tradition and authority was the safeguard against chaos. Burke's vision of a well-regulated society under the leadership of a small group of elite rulers was shared by other European politicians.

Maistre of France Born in southeastern France in 1753, **Joseph de Maistre** attended Catholic schools and became a French politician and lawyer. Initially, he supported the French Revolution. However, he quickly became alarmed by the violence and the anti-clerical sentiments of the revolutionaries, who believed the Catholic Church was too powerful. Maistre believed that all political authority should be based on religious and moral teachings. After the Revolution, he supported a return to monarchy and declared that only a strong Christian leader could maintain social order in France.

Metternich of Austria One of the most powerful diplomats of the 19th century, **Klemens von Metternich** descended from an aristocratic family. He served as Austria's minister of foreign affairs for four decades beginning in 1809. Metternich was alarmed by both the French Revolution and Napoleon's rise to power. He opposed democracy because he believed that it would weaken Europe and lead to costly revolutions and wars. Only a strong, centralized government, he argued, could result in prosperity and peace. Such a government could be effectively controlled only by a monarch.

Conservatives Reestablished Control

Though conservative in his political philosophy, Metternich had more progressive ideas about international cooperation to promote peace. To build international coalitions, he organized congresses, or formal meetings, at which European powers could discuss issues and settle their differences.

The most important of these meeetings was the **Congress of Vienna** in 1815, after the defeat of Napoleon. European leaders gathered under Metternich's leadership to try to end the centuries of war that had ravaged the continent. Metternich's plan was known as the **Concert of Europe,** a movement by leaders to restore "legitimacy" and a "balance of power" to the continent based on the principles of 19th-century conservatism:

- the right of monarchies to rule

- the rights of landed aristocracies

- the need for an organized religion

- the danger of liberal nationalist movements

Congress of Vienna Preserves Conservatism A key element of promoting stability was to create a balance of power among the rival states of Europe, with no state strong enough to dominate all others. This required dividing territory in a way that each state felt secure. The territorial provisions of the Congress of Vienna included the following:

- Russia acquired most of Poland as well as Finland.

- Prussia acquired parts of many German states.

- Austria acquired parts of some German states and northern Italy.

- Great Britain's control of colonies in Africa and Asia was confirmed.

- A new German Federation (37 states) replaced the Holy Roman Empire.

- The Dutch Republic and the Austrian Netherlands (today's Belgium) were combined to form the Kingdom of Netherlands.

- The Kingdom of Sardinia was restored and given land in northern Italy.

- The Kingdom of Sicily acquired Naples.

EUROPE AFTER THE CONGRESS OF VIENNA, 1815

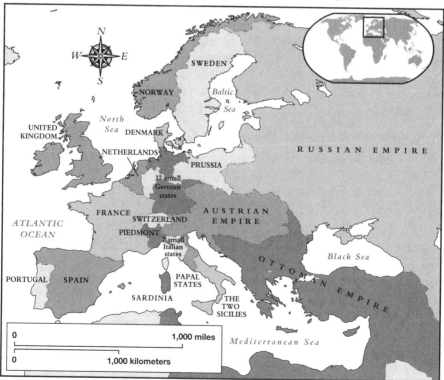

While the Congress of Vienna reestablished conservative control in Europe generally, it did not resolve all differences. Leaders tried to combat liberalism and nationalism in their own state.

Austria Preserves Conservatism In 1819, just a few years after the conclusion of the Congress of Vienna, a radical student organization murdered a German dramatist. In response, Austria's government issued the Carlsbad Decrees, which were designed to suppress liberal and nationalist tendencies within the German states. They banned nationalist organizations, expanded press censorship, fired liberal university professors, and disbanded radical student organizations. Despite the repressive decrees, German nationalism grew stronger. The decrees were enforced until 1848.

Russia Maintains an Autocratic State In the early 19th century, Russia remained one of the most conservative empires in Europe. Its rulers, called tsars, continued to claim they ruled by divine right. The country had a rural, agricultural economy. The tsars enforced strict censorship, suppressed demands for constitutional reform, and defended serfdom. They relied on the secret police to imprison or deport anyone suspected of dissent. With a singular focus on preserving their authority, the tsars suppressed any change, creating a stagnant empire.

France Attempts to Restore the Monarchy At the end of the Napoleonic Wars, Europeans recognized the Bourbon Dynasty as the rightful rulers of France. For several years, the restored monarchy was limited by a constitution. However, in 1824, Charles X inherited the throne and ruled as an absolute monarch. Charles X strengthened his power by compensating nobles who had lost land in the French Revolution as well as enforcing the death penalty for those who stole from the Catholic Church. In addition, he dissolved the legislature and enforced strict censorship, angering liberals within France.

Revolutionaries Battle the Status Quo

While monarchs wanted a return to conservative ideals, liberals and nationalists in various nations sought to implement reforms in the early 19th century. Many of these movements had little success at first in their efforts to alter political systems and borders.

Greek Independence Movement From 1821 to 1832, the **Ottoman Empire** experienced a continuous rebellion by Greek citizens who desired independence. The Ottoman Empire, a conservative monarchy, had ruled Greece since the 15th century. While the Ottomans ruled with a measure of religious toleration, they required the Greeks to serve in the military and pay additional taxes. Starting in the 1700s, more conservative Ottoman rulers, or sultans, began ordering the destruction of ancient Greek temples and relics.

In 1821, a Greek nationalist group established a small military force. While initially defeated, the Greek cause later attracted the naval support of Great Britain, France, and Russia. Each of these states was eager to weaken the Ottomans for their reasons. Russia, as always, wanted access to a warm-water port, while France and Great Britain were determined to thwart Russian ambitions and acquire land for themselves. After a series of battles, the coalition defeated the Ottoman Empire, which then recognized Greece as an independent state in 1832. The victory by the Greeks was the first of many nationalist secession movements that would disrupt the balance of power in Eastern Europe later in the century.

Decembrists Revolt in Russia Near the end of 1825, Tsar Nicholas I inherited the Russian throne. A secret society of Russian officers who had served in the Napoleonic Wars and had been influenced by liberal ideals saw the transition in rulers as a chance to establish a representative government. Known as the Decembrists, they and a few thousand soldiers attempted to overthrow the new tsar. They were crushed in less than a month. In response, the tsar intensified the Russian police state, further suppressing dissenters.

July Revolt in France In 1830, the French citizens became frustrated by the autocratic policies of King Charles X. That summer, demonstrations began in the streets of Paris, and violence erupted. More than 500 citizens and soldiers were killed in three days. In response to the revolts and facing a hostile Chamber of Deputies, Charles abdicated and fled to England.

A distant cousin of Charles, Louis-Philippe, assumed the throne. Seeing what had happened to his relative, he assumed the title of Louis-Philippe, the "Citizen King." Louis-Philippe reigned as a constitutional monarch and extended civil liberties. Most importantly, he doubled the number of French men with access to voting rights to 170,000, which still represented only 5 percent of the population. While the July Revolution did not create a republic, it did move France from autocratic rule to a constitutional monarchy.

Nationalist Movement in Italy In the 1830s, the Italian peninsula was divided politically among several kingdoms and city-states. While some of these were independent, others were controlled by France or Austria. In general, they were monarchies or other forms of autocratic states. Culturally, the peninsula was also divided, with people speaking various regional languages that could be traced back to Latin, but which were as different as French and Spanish. Nationalist leaders such as **Giuseppe Mazzini** envisioned a region free from foreign influence, united as a single state with a republican form of government. However, Mazzini's efforts to start revolutions and to unify the region in the 1830s were unsuccessful.

Alternatives to Capitalism

Socialism is a political and economic system under which the **means of production**—the ways people gather raw materials and manufacture goods—are owned or controlled by society and used for the public good. Socialism does not outlaw all private property, but it does promote regulations governing the acquisition and distribution of property. Unlike capitalism, in a socialist state, the economy is not governed primarily by the principle of supply and demand. The government is closely involved in the production and distribution of wealth. It might also promote social welfare and pass laws regarding health care, education, housing, and employment.

Utopian Socialism

Modern socialism originated during the early 19th century when social reformers tried to address the inequalities between workers and factory owners. Some of these reformers sought to create an ideal, or utopian society.

The Ideals of Saint-Simon French writer and philosopher **Henri Saint-Simon** first introduced the idea of **utopian socialism** in the early 19th century. Saint-Simon was fascinated by science and engineering. He believed that scientists and engineers, working together with businessmen, could transform society for the better. Factories would become clean, efficient, beautiful places to work, and all manufacturing would be devoted to creating things useful to society. Saint-Simon was deeply religious and believed that his new society would be based on the Christian ideals of brotherhood and charity.

Though Saint-Simon never had the opportunity to put his ideas into practice, his writing attracted a large following and became a major influence on socialism and social reform throughout Europe.

Intentional Communities Among Saint-Simon's most active followers were **Charles Fourier** of France and **Robert Owen** of Britain. Both advocated the establishment of **intentional communities**—small societies governed by the principles of utopian socialism. In these societies, all property would be owned communally, and every aspect of life, including work, education, and leisure time, would be governed by the rules of the community.

Owen established a prototype for a utopian community in New Lanark, England, around 1800. He instituted eight-hour days in the community's textile mills, founded free public schools and day care for children, and opened a store that sold goods to workers at minimal cost. Though New Lanark attracted a great deal of interest, few people in Europe formed similar communities.

The United States, where land was cheaper, was more receptive to Owen's ideas. Among the American communities founded on utopian socialism were New Harmony, Indiana; Brook Farm, Massachusetts; and Oneida, New York.

The Scientific Socialism of Karl Marx

German-born historian and economist Karl Marx shared some of the goals of the utopian socialists. However, he criticized them for failing to understand how capitalism worked in practice. He wanted to develop a model of socialism that reflected the same systematic approach that scientists used. Marx became one of the first close observers and critics of European capitalism. He and one of his supporters, Friedrich Engels, summarized their ideas in *Communist Manifesto*. Published in 1848, it was a short book written for a broad audience. Marx's more detailed analysis of the modern economy, *Capital,* formed the basis of the body of thought known as **Marxism**.

Marx's View of History Marx based his predictions for a revolution on his study of the past. Most historians of his time focused on politics or religion. Unlike them, Marx emphasized the importance of technology. He thought technology shaped economics, which then shaped politics and other aspects of culture. That is, he thought a society based on handmade goods and horsepower would generate one type of political system. A society based on large factories and steam engines would produce another.

Marx also saw history as an unending story of class struggle. He defined a class by its relationship to how goods and services were produced. For example, some classes, such as slaves and peasants, performed physical labor. Others, such as merchants and lawyers, did mental labor.

Since technology was constantly evolving, economics and politics were always changing to catch up. This gap created contradictions in every social system. Resolving them could be violent, but would always lead to a new system. This change was inevitable. How it happened would be affected by individual leaders and temporary conditions, but the underlying forces were unstoppable. Their belief that history followed laws, just as physics or chemistry did, became known as **historical determinism**.

Marx's View of His Era Marx was struck by the sharp contradiction between the impressive abundance capitalism produced and the dreadful misery many workers lived in. While he often supported reforms advocated by middle-class leaders, he saw them as weak efforts that failed to address the roots of inequality. He thought that the working class, which he labeled the **proletariat,** would gain **class-consciousness**, an awareness of their place in the socioeconomic structure and a recognition that they all shared a similar plight. The proletariat would then overthrow the middle-class industrialists who profited from their labor, which he labeled the **bourgeoisie**.

The proletarian revolution would replace most privately owned factories, banks, and businesses with ones owned collectively. This socialism would be a step toward **communism,** in which all property used to produce goods would be owned collectively, and all classes would disappear.

Since Marx believed that revolutions would be led by the proletariat, they would happen only in wealthy, industrialized countries, such as those in Western Europe. However, the development of labor unions and social reforms reduced the interest in revolution. The first major communist revolutions occurred in two relatively poor countries, Russia and China, in the 20th century.

The Evolution of Nationalism

Nationalism as it emerged in the early 1800s was a strong, emotional attachment to one's ethnic or cultural group. In its emphasis on emotion, it was a challenge to the focus on reason associated with the Enlightenment. It began as a cultural movement, focusing on art, literature, and music. For example, the **Brothers Grimm** collected folktales from German and other cultures to bring out the richness and beauty of those traditional cultures.

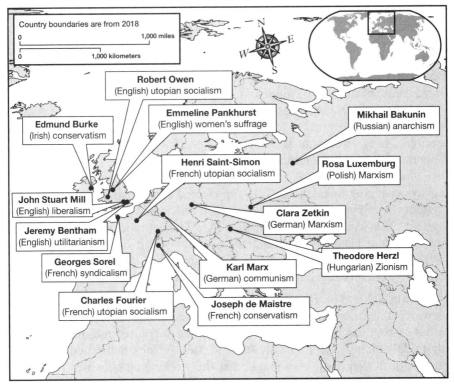

Ideas of cultural pride quickly took on political meanings as well. These were expressed in many ways:

- By emphasizing the culture of common people, it became associated with democracy. This was a threat to the ruling monarchs of Europe.

- The focus on one's own cultural group led each group to demand its own state. This made it a threat to break apart the multi-ethnic empires based in Austria, Russia, and Turkey.

- The interest in culture also meant that people who shared a culture but not a state wanted to unite under one state. Germans and Italians were the largest examples of people living divided among multiple states.

- The importance of cultural unity gave leaders a way to instill a sense of nationalism in people who lived in their state but did not share their culture. For example, when the Hungarians won independence from the Austrians, they tried to make everyone in the new country—most of whom were not ethnically Hungarians—learn the Hungarian language.

In the 20th century, another type of more extreme form of nationalism emerged. It contributed to the rise of dictatorial systems such as fascism in Italy, Germany, and other countries (see Chapter 21).

The success of nationalism is evident in a modern map of Europe. Most states in Europe are organized as nation-states in which one culture is dominant. For example, most people in Poland identify as culturally Polish. Further, most people who are culturally Polish live in Poland. A few countries are not nation-states. For example, Belgium is divided between French-speaking Walloons and Dutch-speaking Flemish.

Ideological Responses to Industrialization			
Movement	Beliefs	Important Individuals	Examples of Significance and/or Impact
Liberalism	• Popular sovereignty • Individual rights • Social reform • Enlightened self-interest	• John Locke • Richard Cobden • Jeremy Bentham • John Stuart Mill • Edwin Chadwick • Josephine Butler	• Increased voting rights, Anti-Corn laws, rise of Whig and Liberal Parties • Rise of utilitarianism
Chartism	• Universal male suffrage	• William Lovett	• Many Chartist reforms enacted in last half of 19th century
Conservatism	• Importance of tradition • Trust in traditional political and religious authorities • Fear of the chaos of mass movements	• Edmund Burke • Joseph de Maistre • Klemens von Metternich	• Rise of the dictator Napoleon to restore order in post-Revolutionary France • International congresses, which helped Europe stay mostly at peace from 1815 to 1914
Utopian Socialism	• Redistribution of wealth	• Henri Saint-Simon • Charles Fourier • Robert Owen	• "Intentional communities" in France, Britain, and United States
Marxist Socialism	• Social control of the means of production	• Karl Marx • Friedrich Engels • Clara Zetkin • Rosa Luxemburg	• Communist revolution in Russia, 1917
Anarchism	• Abolition of government • Creation of a society of voluntary cooperation from all members	• Mikhail Bakunin • Georges Sorel	• Violent underground revolutionary actions
Nationalism	• Loyalty to one's nation • Making state and cultural boundaries match	• Grimm Brothers • Giuseppe Mazzini • Mayor Karl Leuger	• Developments ranging from liberal reforms to racial and anti-Semitic oppression

The Growth of Government

Industrialization and the rise of new social classes required new forms of government. People in both the middle and working classes sought to influence government through public opinion and mass political parties. Generally, conservative parties favored authoritarian governments, while more liberal parties favored increased suffrage and popularly elected governments. Labor unions became politically active as workers joined socialist parties or formed their own labor parties.

Urbanization and industrialization created complex social issues, requiring governments to expand their powers and increase the size of their bureaucracies. In addition, the rise of nationalism made governments aware of the need to secure their borders and maintain their laws, all leading to a stronger government presence in the lives of ordinary people. In Britain, liberals led social reform; while in continental countries such as France, socialists played a greater role in pushing governments to institute new policies and reforms.

As governments grew, the rights of women and minorities became social issues. Women began to demand the right to vote. Jews, the largest religious minority in Europe, acquired new rights but also faced growing hostility and intolerance from nationalist movements.

Liberalism and Reform in Britain

In Britain, the government promoted several liberal reforms that helped average citizens and increased their sense of national loyalty. Faced with the threat of worker revolts and increasing unrest, the British Parliament became increasingly involved in the day-to-day lives of its citizens. Further, by increasing voting rights, the government gave a wider range of citizens the sense that they had a voice in social policies.

Improving the Public Sector Several reforms addressed infrastructure, housing, public health and education. Reforms were especially crucial in overcrowded and unsanitary urban areas. **Edwin Chadwick**, a follower of utilitarian Jeremy Bentham, led many efforts to reform the Poor Laws. These laws jailed people simply for being unemployed. He also helped establish public health standards. In particular, his report titled "Sanitary Conditions of the Labouring Population of Great Britain," published in 1842, was influential. It was a landmark in the development of public support for the idea that the government in an industrial society should protect the health of its citizens.

Between 1848 and 1913, Parliament enacted a series of reforms that improved life for the working class. Reforms helped increase loyalty to the government and decrease the possibility of armed class struggle. Between 1880 and 1896, real wages (wages adjusted to inflation, or the relative amount of goods and services they could purchase) rose approximately 45 percent. Reforms also gave the British Liberal Party a boost over the rival Conservative Party. In 1906, the Liberal Party won a majority of seats in Parliament, mostly as a result of support from working class voters.

Actions in Response to Industrialization	
Movement	**Examples of Significance and/or Impact**
1833	Abolition of slavery in the British Empire
1848	Public Health Act passe in response to cholera epidemic, paving the way for clean water and sewage control
1850	Public Libraries Act establishes free public libraries
1855	Work begins on London's infrastructure for a subway
1863	World's first underground rail line opens in London
1870	Education Act establishes free elementary schools for all children
1889	Employment of children under 10 is outlawed
1890–1892	Slums cleared for new housing in cities and towns
1908	National old age pensions introduced
1913	Sickness, maternity, and unemployment compensation benefits introduced

Philanthropy and Social Reform In addition to government initiatives. private **philanthropies**, or charities, also addressed poverty and inequality. Many reformers were inspired by their religious faith. For example, some Christians joined the social gospel movement. Rather than focusing directly on individual salvation, they focused on improving social conditions. They believed that feeding the hungry, improving housing for the poor, and organizing labor unions would enable people to become devout Christians.

Often, educated middle-class women spearheaded these efforts. In 1869 **Josephine Butler** began her work on behalf of women and girls who had been forced into prostitution. Butler established industrial schools to give females vocational skills and campaigned against human trafficking through which women and girls were sold into sexual slavery.

Women also helped lead the **temperance movement**, an organized attempt to ban the sale and consumption of alcoholic beverages. Though the movement never achieved its aims, it did succeed in placing taxes on the sale of liquor.

Other social reforms supported by women included the **Sunday School Movement**, founded in 1795, which provided basic education for working class children. By 1850 more than 2 million children were enrolled in weekly Sunday School classes, most of which were taught by women.

Women's Suffrage in Britain As women became more involved in reform, they began to question their own status. In 1850, a group of British women led by **Barbara Smith Bodichon** began to meet to discuss women's rights. Eventually known as "the Ladies of Langdon Place," they called for women's suffrage and also for married women to have the right to control their own property. In 1856, Bodichon gathered 26,000 signatures on a petition for women's property rights. A year later, in 1857, Parliament passed the Married

Women's Property Act, which enabled married women to control their own property. In 1869, Bodichon helped Emily Davis found Girton College, Cambridge, the first institution to offer higher education to women in Britain.

In the early 20th century, a strong women's suffrage emerged in Britain, picking up on the ideas of Flora Tristan. In 1903, **Emmeline Pankhurst** and her daughters Christabel, Adela, and Sybil formed the **Women's Social and Political Union** (WSPU) to promote women's suffrage. The Pankhursts went far beyond writing petitions. They organized huge rallies. In June 1908, nearly 500,000 women assembled in London's Hyde Park to demand the vote.

The Hyde Park demonstrators were physically attacked, harassed by police, and even arrested. In prison, the suffragists went on hunger strikes to protest their treatment. The wardens then fed them by force, a violent and degrading process intended to punish the women for their disobedience rather than nourish them. Emmeline Pankhurst herself was arrested at least eight times during her campaign for the vote.

While her militancy alienated some allies, Pankhurst forced the Liberal Party to take women's suffrage seriously and include it in their party platform. In 1918, Parliament passed an act allowing all men over the age of 21 and all women over the age of 30 to vote. In 1928, the act was amended to allow every citizen over 21 to vote, making voting a universal right for all adults in Britain.

Suffrage supporters in Great Britain drew attention to their cause by getting arrested.

Credit: Getty Images

While elements of capitalism existed long before Adam Smith, he is often viewed as the first thinker to argue for capitalism as a system of organizing the entire economy. Like the *philosophes* of his time, Smith's goal was to protect the public good. With this goal, he criticized governments for regulating trade too strictly. However, he also feared that an economy with no effective government would harm the public. So, he did not oppose all government intervention in the economy. As capitalism developed, government often played an important economic role. Historians have disagreed on the relationship between government and economic growth.

The Need for Bureaucracy By the early 20th century, governments in Europe and the United States were beginning to regulate businesses more closely and to provide more assistance to the poor, elderly, and unemployed. In *Economy and Society* (1922), sociologist Max Weber argued that as modern capitalism became more complex, society relied on an efficient and professional bureaucracy to make rational choices. Whether the growth of a bureaucracy was something Smith would have supported or not, Weber argued that it was what actually happened.

Why Capitalism Developed Slowly For most of the late 20th century, the main rival to capitalism was communism. By the end of the century, almost all communist countries had abandoned that ideology and adopted some form of capitalism. The success of capitalism raised the question of why the system took so long to emerge. In *Capitalism through the Ages: A Grand Tour* (2011), historians Larry Neal and Jeffrey J. Williamson

invited historians to share their answers. To Neal, the answer involved the time necessary to coordinate respect for private property rights, establish enforceable contracts, maintain markets responsive to prices, and have a supportive government. These were all activities that Smith supported, but they took many decades or centuries to develop.

Neal and Williamson claimed that prior to the 17th century, societies might put some of these elements into place, but corrupt or inept governments made investment too risky to be worthwhile. Only after the 17th century did government intervention support economic growth. For example, both Alexander Hamilton's investment in infrastructure in the United States and Prussia's investment in universal primary education represented such intervention. To explain why not every nation became capitalist and why not all who tried succeeded, Neal and Williamson looked beyond the West. They claimed that the early capitalist societies relied on the resources and markets of the not-yet industrialized nations. As a result, they corrupted those governments and exploited their resources, making it impossible for those economies to develop.

KEY TERMS BY THEME

Civic Ideals
politics
liberalism
John Locke
popular sovereignty
petition
People's Charter
universal suffrage
enlightened self-interest
Jeremy Bentham
utilitarianism
John Stuart Mill
social liberty
conservatism
Edmund Burke
limited monarchy
natural order
Joseph de Maistre
temperance movement
Barbara Smith Bodichon
Emmeline Pankhurst
Women's Social and
   Political Union

Economics
socialism
means of production
Henri Saint-Simon
utopian socialism
Charles Fourier
Robert Owen
intentional communities
historical determinism
proletariat
class-consciousness
bourgeoisie
communism
Clara Zetkin
Marxism
Rosa Luxemburg
anarchism
Mikhail Bakunin
Georges Sorel
syndicalism

Governance
Great Reform Act of
   1832

Anti-Corn Law League
Chartism
Klemens von Metternich
Congress of Vienna
Concert of Europe
Ottoman Empire
Flora Tristan

Identity
nationalism
Brothers Grimm
Giuseppe Mazzini
Edwin Chadwick
philanthropies
Josephine Butler
Sunday School
   Movement
Zionism
Theodore Herzl

This statue of Jacob and Wilhelm Grimm was erected 1896 in the city of Hanau to honor two of the people who promoted German cultural nationalism.

Credit: Getty Images

Questions 1–3 refer to the passage below.

"The Governments, having lost their balance, are frightened, intimidated, and thrown into confusion by the cries of the intermediary class of society, which, placed between the Kings and their subjects, breaks the scepter of the monarch, and usurps the cry of the people—the class so often disowned by the people, and nevertheless too much listened to, caressed and feared by those who could with one word reduce it again to nothingness.

We see this intermediary class abandon itself with a blind fury and animosity... to all the means which seem proper to assuage its thirst for power, applying itself to the task of persuading Kings that their rights are confined to sitting upon a throne, while those of the people are to govern, and to attack all that centuries have bequeathed as holy and worthy of man's respect—denying, in fact, the value of the past, and declaring themselves the masters of the future... [This class] takes possession of the press, and employs it to promote impiety, disobedience to the laws of religion and the State, and goes so far as to preach murder as a duty for those who desire what is good."

Klemens von Metternich, Letter to Tsar Alexander I of
Russia, 1820

1. The political conditions described by Metternich were largely the result of which of the following developments?

    a) The abolition of serfdom in Russia

    b) The dissolution of the Austrian Empire

    c) The French and Industrial Revolutions

    d) The spread of Marxism among the Russian working class

2. Based on the context in which the passage was written, which group did Metternich believe posed the largest threat to the political order in 1820?

    a) Liberals

    b) Peasants

    c) Factory workers

    d) Anarchists

3. Which statement best describes how the views of most 19th-century leaders differed from those of Metternich?

    a) They became less responsive to public opinion.

    b) They were more inclined to use violence against political opponents.

    c) They had fewer concerns about domestic unrest.

    d) They were more likely to agree to political reforms.

Questions 4–6 refer to the passages below.

"In other nations humanity comes after nationality. Among the Slavs nationality comes after humanity. Scattered Slavs, let us be a unified whole, and no longer mere fragments. Let us be all or nothing. Who are you, a Russian? And you, a Serb? And you, a Czech? And you, a Pole? My children, seek unity! Say: I am a Slav!"

Ján Kollár, Slovak poet and early advocate of
Pan-Slavism, 1829

"The danger that Austria has to face is the diversity of language and race in the empire. Our Slavic nationalities are likely at a moment of dangerous crisis to develop pro-Russian tendencies."

Count Friedrich Ferdinand von Beust, Austrian foreign
minister and imperial chancellor, 1887

4. The ideas expressed by Kollár most clearly show the influence of which of the following?

   a) Romantic nationalism

   b) Marxist socialism

   c) Social Darwinism

   d) Anti-Semitism

5. The danger facing Austria described by von Beust was part of a larger trend that also was a danger for which state?

   a) Great Britain

   b) Turkey

   c) Germany

   d) Italy

6. The unification of several groups of Slavs into the single state of Yugoslavia would have been supported by

   a) both Kollár and von Beust

   b) neither Kollár nor von Beust

   c) only Kollár

   d) only von Beust

Questions 7–8 refer to the following passage.

- "The purpose of establishing censorship is to give useful, or at least harmless, for the good of the Fatherland, works of literature, sciences and arts, when publishing them through book printing, engraving and lithography.

- From this it follows that all books, essays, words, geographic and topographical maps, drawings, plans, paintings, portraits and musical notes published inside the State are subject to the Censorship.

- The duty of the Censorship in reviewing all these works is to protect the Shrine, the Throne, the authorities, the laws of the Fatherland, the customs and honor of the people . . . from everyone, not only malicious and criminal, but also unintentional assassination...

- The Chief Directorate of the Censorship is entrusted to the Minister of National Enlightenment.

- To help him in resolving the most important Censorship cases, and the top management of the Censors, the Supreme Censorship Committee is established."

Russian Tsar Nicholas I, Charter of Censorship, 1826

7. The Charter of Censorship represents which important aspect of post-Napoleonic Europe?

   a) Nationalism

   b) Conservatism

   c) Romanticism

   d) Revolution

8. Which leader or thinker would most likely have agreed with the ideas expressed by Nicholas I?

   a) John Stuart Mill

   b) Prince Klemens von Metternich

   c) Karl Marx

   d) Emmeline Pankhurst

SHORT-ANSWER QUESTIONS

1. Use the passage below to answer all parts of the question that follows.

> The foundations of modern socialist thought were laid during the first half of the 19th century in the writing of a number of thinkers, chiefly French, British, and German, who attempted in their various ways to show how a radical improvement in the condition of the working classes could be brought about. . . .
> It became a common practice, at this time, to mock the efforts of these early pioneers and dismiss them as expressions of a naïve utopianism. . . .
> The designation of 'utopian' has since entered into the conventional vocabulary of the history ideas, and is now used without question.
>
> Keith Taylor, *The Political Ideas of*
> *the Utopian Socialists,* 1982

a) Explain ONE 19th-century liberal perspective that supports Taylor's argument regarding the naïveté of Utopian Socialists.

b) Explain ONE 19th-century Marxist perspective that supports Taylor's argument regarding the naïveté of Utopian Socialists.

c) Explain ONE 19th-century conservative perspective that supports Taylor's argument regarding the naïveté of Utopian Socialists.

2. Answer all parts of the question that follows.

a) Describe ONE political event or policy in the 19th century that was a response to a problem of industrialization.

b) Describe ONE event or policy used by women in the 19th century to respond to a problem of industrialization.

c) Describe ONE event or policy used by nongovernmental reformers in the 19th century in response to a problem of industrialization.

LONG ESSAY QUESTIONS

1. Evaluate the extent to which the Industrial Revolution impacted the political systems of Britain and France.

2. Evaluate the extent to which political thought and ideologies prior to 1815 were different from political thought and ideologies during the period from 1815 to 1914.

REFLECT ON THE CHAPTER ESSENTIAL QUESTION

In one to three paragraphs, explain how the problems of industrialization provoked ideological, governmental, and collective responses.

One of the most basic, and most controversial, skills of a historian is the ability to identify causation, which includes recognizing both causes and effects. Historians clarify causation in many ways:

- distinguishing between the most important, or primary, causes and effects, and less important, or secondary ones
- distinguishing between short-term and long-term causes and effects
- evaluating the relative historical importance of causes and effects
- using words such as *because, consequently, therefore,* and *which*

For instance, one primary cause of the Industrial Revolution in Great Britain was that the region had natural resources such as coal mines, iron fields, good natural harbors for shipping, rivers to use as canals for transportation, and safety from invasion due to its being an island nation. A secondary cause was that these natural resources encouraged the rise of steam-powered factories.

A short-term effect of the Industrial Revolution was the migration of people off the farms in search of jobs. A long-term effect was the creation of a new social class structure composed of a small wealthy class, a growing middle class, and a large poor and laboring class.

In each pair of sentences, select the one that best expresses historical causation.

1. **a.** The Industrial Revolution was characterized by factories that used steam power and were able to mass-produce goods.

   b. The Industrial Revolution resulted in numerous social transformations.

2. **a.** A desire to transform society inspired suffrage movements.

   b. The women's suffrage movement believed that the fate of women was tied to the fate of the working class.

3. **a.** Though it was difficult to enforce, the Education Act made school attendance mandatory for children up to age 10.

   b. Images and stories of children working in mines and factories aroused people's sympathies and led to the passage of protective legislation.

4. **a.** Rebelling against the social restrictions of the Cult of Domesticity, women lobbied for suffrage.

   b. Emmeline Pankhurst, one of the more radical suffragettes, founded the Women's Social and Political Union.

5. **a.** Miserable conditions in factories led to the creation of unions and protests for better wages, working hours, and safety conditions.

   b. Union membership rose from around 100,000 in the 1850s to about a million people by the 1870s.

16

Nationalism, Revolutions, and International Stability

"Union between the monarchs is the basis of the policy which must now be followed to save society from total ruin."

—Klemens von Metternich, *Political Faith*, 1820

Essential Question: How did European states struggle to maintain international stability in an age of nationalism and revolution?

The **balance of power** among countries in Europe had weakened in the 1700s, resulting in devastating wars. Following the defeat of Napoleon in 1815, the diplomatic gathering known as the **Congress of Vienna** attempted to restore that balance. In the Congress, the leaders of Austria, Great Britain, Prussia, and Russia met under the leadership of Austria's **Klemens von Metternich** and formed an alliance. The assembled leaders supported conservative ideals of monarchy rather than constitutional monarchy, hierarchy rather than equality, and tradition rather than reform.

Revolutions, War, and Reform

Nonetheless, throughout the 1800s, revolutionary movements, nationalistic leaders, and socialist demands challenged conservatism and the balance of power. By the late 1800s, nationalism and antagonistic alliances heightened international tensions in Europe directly before World War I.

Revolutions of 1848

While the beginning of the 19th century saw isolated regional resistance movements against conservative governments, 1848 featured an outbreak of revolutions across the continent. These revolutions were spurred by economic hardship and political discontent and caused a breakdown in the Concert of Europe established by Metternich at the Congress of Vienna.

Revolution Strikes France First When Louis-Philippe became king of France in 1830, he promised to rule as a constitutional monarch. Yet, as king, he blocked many attempts at expanding voting rights. In response, opposition

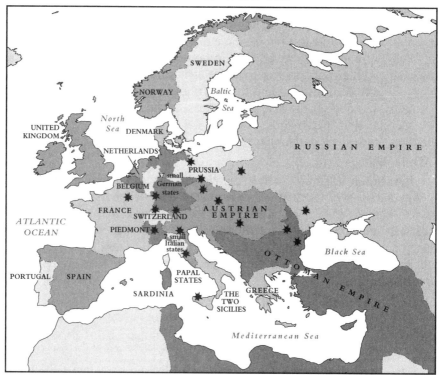

leaders organized and began demanding a more liberal government. At the same time, Paris experienced a bread shortage. Initially, workers, students, and the unemployed rallied together, built barricades, and protested the conservative king. After the military opened fire and killed 50 citizens, Parisians took to the streets, building more than 1,500 barricades. Louis-Philippe abdicated the throne, and the provisional government declared a republic in France. The French Republic quickly passed laws creating a property tax, ending the death penalty, and allowing for freedom of the press.

While French citizens were excited to create a new government, the revolution failed because of class division. The working class became concerned the middle class was ignoring their demands for **national workshops** across the country, which provided work for the unemployed. In the summer elections, mostly middle-class professionals were elected to the National Assembly, and these men closed the national workshops. About 10,000 workers took to the streets and rioted.

While the Army and National Guard defeated the workers, the National Assembly voted Louis-Napoleon, the nephew of Napoleon, president of France—a vote favoring order rather than liberty. In 1852, Louis-Napoleon declared himself Emperor **Napoleon III** and reestablished an authoritarian government in France.

Revolution in the German States Inspired in part by the 1848 uprising in France, demonstrators in Prussia and the German states began calling for civil liberties and constitutional reforms. The demonstrations spread to Berlin, where Frederick William IV used force to respond. By the middle of March, hundreds were dead. However, the king promised to create a constitutional monarchy. At the Frankfurt Assembly, delegates from each German state were sent to create a constitution and to unify the German states. The process in Frankfurt was slow, as the delegates discussed what groups to include in this new German state. Meanwhile, in Berlin, the monarchy regained control, and the king crushed the remaining protesters, refusing to accept the Frankfurt Constitution.

Revolution in Conservative Austria Austria also experienced rebellion in the summer of 1848. Austria's government struggled to maintain control of its multi-ethnic empire, as nationalities such as Hungarians, Poles, Czechs, and Serbs sought self-rule. In addition, students in Vienna demanded a more liberal government and began rioting in the streets. As a result, Metternich, the architect of the Congress of Vienna, resigned from office. His resignation led to further revolts:

- In Hungary, the dominant ethnic group, known as the Magyars, demanded autonomy under the leadership of Louis Kossuth.

- In Prague, Czechs also demanded self-rule.

- Italians fought to be part of the Italian Confederation in Northern Italy.

Austria's Habsburg monarchy, with Russian help, subdued the Magyar revolt, put down the Czech demands, and installed a conservative monarchy under Francis Joseph (reigned 1848–1916).

Credit: Getty Images

The revolutions of 1848 drove Metternich from office after almost 40 years as one of Europe's most influential diplomats. His opposition to liberalism and nationalism first brought him success but then under cut his power.

Short-Term Results In the mid-19th century, the results of uprisings of 1848 and 1849 looked like a failure. The movements scattered throughout Europe did not share a clear ideology. They were not coordinated with each other. They did not have strong military backing. They were divided by ethnicity. The rebels never kept power for long.

In addition, most governments reacted by becoming more conservative. For example, in Russia, Tsar Nicholas I expanded the use of secret police. He hoped to uncover and crush any further attempts at rebellions before they started. In France, the government banned the writing of novelists, anarchists, and others considered dangerous.

In response to the harsher government policies, many people who were sympathetic to the uprisings emigrated. Some went to Great Britain, which was generally more tolerant of dissenters than most of Europe. Many moved to the United States. In the United States, German immigrants would later become important supporters of the Union in the American Civil War.

To some, the failures of 1848 provided more evidence that republicanism would not take hold in Europe. The English had tried a republican government in the 1640s under Oliver Cromwell, and it had ended in a terrible civil war. The French had also tried republicanism in the late 18th century, and again it had resulted in extensive bloodshed.

Long-Term Results The long-term impact of 1848 and 1849 is harder to determine. The reforms advocated in 1848 included such changes as greater voting rights, more freedom for the press, and more self-rule for ethnic groups within empires. Eventually, advocates for these goals would be successful.

The Crimean War

While the revolutions of 1848 were mostly unsuccessful in creating political change across Europe, the uprisings did challenge the status quo and cause Europeans to question political systems and the balance of power in Europe.

Causes of the Crimean War In 1853, the nations of France, Russia, Great Britain, and the Ottoman Empire met on the Crimean Peninsula to fight the bloodiest European war between the end of the Napoleonic conflicts in 1815 and the start of World War I in 1914. The war erupted for two main reasons:

- Religion: The Muslim sultan of the Ottoman Empire had granted extra privileges in Jerusalem to French Roman Catholics. Leaders of the Russian Orthodox Church wanted the same privileges but were denied.

- Politics: Emperor Napoleon III of France and Tsar Nicholas I of Russia wanted to prove their military strength, and the weakening Ottoman Empire provided a way to do so. Great Britain did not support the expansion of Russian power and sought to maintain a balance of power in Europe.

In October 1853, the sultan of the Ottoman Empire refused to cede territory to the Russian Empire and declared war. In response, the French and British came to the aid of the Ottoman Empire, hoping to intimidate Russia into backing down. Great Britain also opposed the increased territory Russia would gain if it were victorious, which would affect the balance of power. However, Russia continued to demand land from the Ottoman Empire. In response, the Ottomans formally started the **Crimean War.**

Mass Politics and Warfare Over the next 18 months, the Crimean War resulted in more than a million casualties. Critics attacked it as a useless war fought by incompetent generals. Compared to previous European wars, the conflict in Crimea was followed closely and quickly by civilians on the home front through newspapers. While the *London Times* provided the most detailed coverage, other papers also benefited from changes that brought in readers:

- Greater freedom of the press allowed journalists to write more freely.

- Increased literacy meant that more people could read news of the war.

- The telegraph allowed journalists to get news to the home front rapidly.

- The camera allowed people to see photos of battle scenes.

As civilians knew more, governments had to be more sensitive to public perception and opinion.

Effects of the War The publicity given the Crimean War exposed the weakness of the Ottoman Empire, the growing importance of mass politics, and the increased importance of military technology. The war also demonstrated the struggle of European states to maintain stability in an age of nationalism.

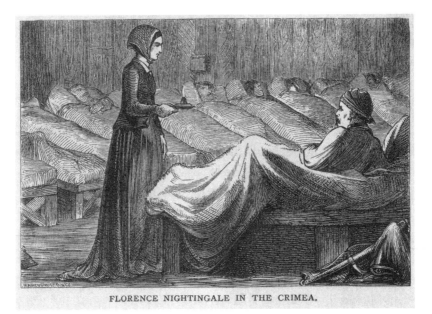

FLORENCE NIGHTINGALE IN THE CRIMEA.

The medical care provided for wounded soldiers in the Crimean War by Florence Nightingale and others reflected the greater opportunities for women and the increasing use of scientific knowledge.

Credit: Getty Images

Popular Nationalism Strengthens the State

A new generation of conservative leaders in France, Italy, and Prussia recognized the power of nationalism and used it to strengthen the state. These "neo-conservatives" used the cultural nationalism aroused by the Napoleonic conquest of Europe and transformed it into a political movement designed to create unified states. Napoleon III of France manipulated nationalism to ensure a unified nation, and other leaders like **Otto von Bismarck** in Prussia and Cavour in Italy used nationalism to unify the state.

Napoleon III in France Following the French Revolution of 1848, the French attempted to establish another republic with a strong executive branch. In the elections of 1848, Louis-Napoleon, the nephew of Napoleon, campaigned to "defend religion, property and the family, the eternal bases of all social order."

A dark-horse candidate, Louis-Napoleon won almost 75 percent of the vote. As president, he possessed the power to declare war, make laws, and sign treaties. However, the law barred him from running for a second term. So, in 1852 he used a direct vote, as his uncle had done, to approve his decision to crown himself Emperor Napoleon III of France. With his new title, he ruled as an autocrat even as he granted the importance of nationalism and mass politics.

Creating Modern Paris Under Emperor Napoleon III, civil servant **Georges-Eugène Haussmann** oversaw massive changes in Paris to adapt the city to the industrial age. Haussmann oversaw projects to widen boulevards, construct larger stores, and build a central train depot.

One of the emperor's purposes in the redesign was to clear spaces by tearing down the closely built buildings that made the streets of Paris narrow and hard to navigate. For many years, protesters had constructed barricades to block French troops and police on the narrow streets. The wide boulevards now made it easier to move government forces and to keep protesters from building effective barricades.

Napoleon III undertook other projects that he believed would modernize France and promote prosperity:

- building railroads, ports, and canals to stimulate trade

- increasing international trade by opening French markets

- supporting the creation of new banks

- encouraging ship building

- backing the construction of the Suez Canal in Egypt

The emperor's public projects won him support. They created jobs that stimulated the economy. Further, since bread prices were low, people who worked could afford to eat. His political reforms also made him popular. They looked impressive even if they did not result in true political liberty.

Reform in Eastern Europe

For multi-ethnic empires in Eastern Europe such as Austria and Russia, nationalism increased tensions. Ethnic groups that dominated a particular region advocated for self-determination. In addition, conservative leaders in those states feared liberal and socialist reforms. Nevertheless, the revolutions of 1848 and the Crimean War caused these nations to recognize the need for a change in their political, economic, or social system in order to compete with Western Europe.

Austria-Hungary's Dual Monarchy Following the revolutions of 1848, the Austrian monarchy attempted to suppress Hungarian culture, but with little success. The Ausgleich Compromise of 1867 established the **dual monarchy of Austria-Hungary** under Francis Joseph. This dual monarchy recognized the political power of the Hungarians, the largest ethnic minority in the empire.

Austro-Hungary shared the same ministers for foreign policy, finance, and defense. However, the dual monarchy provided autonomy for Hungary by creating two capitals and two official languages. The status of Hungary was made more complex by the diversity in that region. Most people in Hungary identified as non-Hungarian ethnic groups, such as Ruthenians or Slovaks and did not speak the Hungarian language.

Comparing Austria and Hungary		
Trait	**Austria**	**Hungary**
Largest Ethnic Group	Germans were the majority of the population	Magyars (Hungarians) were the largest group, but not a majority
Capital	Vienna, also the main capital of the empire	Budapest, though divided into separate cities of Buda and Pest until 1873
Religion	Mostly Roman Catholic	Mixture of Catholics and Protestants

While the dual monarchy recognized the Hungarians, both the Hungarians and Austrians continued to neglect the other minority groups. For example, while Hungarians voted and served in the Parliament, Croatians and Romanians lacked representation. In addition, Hungarian became an approved language in schools, but languages such as Czech and Polish were not permitted.

By establishing the dual monarchy, the empire had hoped to stabilize itself by reconfiguring national unity and recognizing Hungarians as an official minority group. While the empire lasted into the 20th century, the dual monarchy would collapse as a result of World War I, as other ethnic groups within the Austro-Hungarian Empire sought self-determination.

Russian Reforms Under Alexander II Russia's failures in the Crimean War caused the country's leaders to reflect on how weak their country had become. While Russia possessed a large empire and army, the sheer size of its army no longer made it powerful. Russia lacked industrialization and innovation and so it was becoming weak.

Russia's Tsar **Alexander II** (r. 1855–1881) recognized these problems. He supported efforts to reform Russia's social system, infrastructure, and legal code in order to maintain its role on the international stage. However, aristocrats stubbornly resisted calls to end serfdom. In 1861, Alexander, as Russia's absolute ruler, took action. He issued the Emancipation Manifesto, abolishing serfdom in Russia. The process for peasants actually obtaining land, however, was very complicated, with peasants having to remain on the land until payment schedules could be established. Most had to make "redemption payments" to the government over a lengthy period of time to actually receive the land.

More Local and National Reforms To increase autonomy at the local level, Alexander II created the Zemstvo, elected councils meant to address local issues. Unfortunately, the Zemstvo did not create social equality because the local nobility manipulated the system to maintain their power.

At the national level, Alexander II implemented independent courts and demanded equality before the law. In order to modernize, he encouraged and financed the construction of the railroad industry. By 1916, the Trans-Siberian Railroad stretched from Russia's western border in Europe to its eastern borders in Asia. Alexander also set out to modernize the Russian military, introducing conscription, or a draft, for the first time in the Russian army.

Despite Alexander's power, reforms moved slowly. Many peasants were frustrated, and many working-class people felt that Russia needed more radical change. In 1881, a terrorist faction of radicals assassinated the tsar.

Russia Attempts Reform Again Following the assassination of Alexander II, his son, Alexander III (r. 1881–1894), assumed the throne. While the new tsar rejected liberal political reforms, he did support industrialization. Under his finance minister, **Sergei Witte,** Russia modernized its economy:

- It passed a protective tariff to assist Russian industry.

- It placed Russia on the gold standard.

- It sped up construction of the Trans-Siberian Railroad.

- It improved education related to commerce and technology.

Witte's economic reforms brought changes, but most Russians continued to live in poverty under an oppressive government. In 1905, Russia lost a war against Japan, and the defeat ignited the **Revolution of 1905.** Many Russians wanted a more liberal government, in part to compete in the modern age. Tsar Nicholas II (r. 1894–1917) appointed Witte to frame liberal reforms; Witte crafted the October Manifesto, which gave Russians the right to citizenship, freedom of speech, and universal suffrage for men. Russia created a representative body, the Duma, in which leaders could express their grievances. Nevertheless, the tsar maintained his power with the right to veto any law, and within a short time suffrage was restricted.

In the Duma, **Peter Stolypin,** a conservative monarchist, passed agrarian reform to help the peasants. He wanted to end the open-field system (see

Chapter 4) and replace it with a system of small landowners, thus creating a higher standard of living for peasants. Stolypin believed that a prosperous peasant class would stabilize Russia and prevent revolution.

Suffrage Expansion in Great Britain

The 1832 Reform Bill expanded the rights of men to vote slightly. In 1867, Parliament passed the Second Great Reform Act, extending voting rights to men in urban areas who did not own property. This gave industrial workers more political influence. A subsequent act in 1884 removed almost all restrictions on voting, enabling about 60 percent of all men over the age of 21 to cast ballots in local and parliamentary elections.

National Unification Movements

While nationalist movements broke up the Austro-Hungarian and Ottoman Empires, they brought unification elsewhere. Nationalistic movements among Italians and among Germans led to the creation of the modern countries of Italy and Germany in the 1860s and the 1870s. As unified states, Germany and Italy emerged as important powers, both in Europe and on the world stage.

Mazzini, Cavour, and Garibaldi Unify Italy

The process of Italian unification succeeded in the second half of the 19th century because a handful of leaders overcame foreign opposition and traditional regional loyalties. For example, **Giuseppe Mazzini** was an ardent nationalist who envisioned all of the Italian peninsula united into one state. He faced two major obstacles to uniting the region:

- Austria and France controlled several Italian states, and they opposed losing their influence.

- Conservative leaders, particularly Russia's tsar and Prussia's king, feared the creation of any powerful, liberal, republican state.

- The people of the peninsula were divided by culture. Less than 5 percent spoke what is today considered Italian. Most spoke a regional language, German, or French as their primary language.

Mazzini led several small uprisings, but had little success. His importance was his inspirarion to later nationalists.

Cavour's Diplomatic Strategy Camillo Benso, known as **Count Cavour,** was from Piedmont, a region in what is now northwestern Italy. He grew up under French rule and speaking French. His goal was to expand Piedmont's control over northern Italy under a constitutional monarchy. He had little interest in ruling southern Italy and was skeptical of republicanism. Cavour rose to the position of prime minister under the Piedmont monarch, **Victor Emmanuel II**. Among his successes were that he improved banking practices, reduced the power of the Catholic Church, and increased access to education.

RIGHT LEG IN THE BOOT AT LAST.

Garibaldi. "IF IT WON'T GO ON, SIRE, TRY A LITTLE MORE POWDER."

Garibaldi was one of the most influential nationalists in the 19th century. Besides his leading role in uniting Italy, he fought for the independence of Brazil and Uruguay and was considered as a possible general for the Union in the American Civil War.

Credit: Getty Images

Cavour advanced the interests of Piedmont through skilled, if often dishonest, diplomacy. He carefully played Europe's most powerful states, particularly France and Austria, against each other. His style was known as **realpolitik,** the practice of acting for political power rather than for a religious, moral, or ideological goal. Through a series of wars, alliances, and betrayals, Cavour's Piedmont won control over most of northern Italy.

The Heroic Garibaldi The third great Italian leader was a charismatic military figure, **Giuseppe Garibaldi.** He was known throughout the Atlantic world because of his exploits on behalf of various South American independence movements. Later in his life, during the American Civil War, the Union considered offering him a position as a general. He declined because the Union refused to make the war explicitly about abolishing slavery.

In Italy, his success came in the southern states. His rebel army, known as the Red Shirts, combined with his appeals to popular nationalism, unified the region. He considered attacking Rome, where French armies protected the pope. Instead, he chose to hand over Naples and all the lands in southern Italy to King Victor Emmanuel II, whom Cavour had made ruler of most of northern Italy. As a result, one monarch controlled almost the entire peninsula.

Italian Unification Completed In 1861, Victor Emmanuel II declared himself king of Italy. The new country began to form a constitutional monarchy with parliament. Rome was added when Napoleon III withdrew French forces to fight in the Franco-Prussian War. In 1871, Rome became the capital of the newly unified Italy, finalizing the unification process.

Bismarck's Realpolitik Unites Germany

Otto von Bismarck of Prussia was somewhat similar to Cavour. Both were masters of realpolitik who used war and deceit to unify states under the leadership of his own region. However, compared to Cavour, Bismarck was far more conservative. He believed in authoritarian rule under a strong monarch. By relying on diplomacy, industrialization, and political manipulation, Bismarck created a German powerhouse that threatened the balance of power in Europe. Bismarck's goal was to create a united Germany without Austria being a part of it. This was known as "kleindeutsch" (lesser Germany) versus "grossdeutsch" (greater Germany). He was not eager to include Austria for several reasons:

- Bismarck was a devout Protestant, and Austria was mostly Roman Catholic.

- Austria was poorer than many of the northern German states.

- Bismarck believed an independent Austria could be a diplomatic ally for his German state.

Bismarck's Successful Foreign Policy While the revolutions of 1848 had failed to create a united Germany, nationalism continued to grow in the German states. The Prussian monarchy led the movement. Bismarck emerged as the conservative politician to negotiate unification, relying on industrialized warfare to bring other German states together under Prussian leadership. These wars included the three in the table below.

Prussian Wars Leading to Unification	
War	**Features**
War with Denmark, 1864	• Bismarck provoked and won a short war with Denmark. • Prussia and its allies won control of three provinces. • Popular support for Bismarck's coalition increased.
Seven Weeks War, 1866	• Bismarck provoked and won a short war with Austria. • Prussia unified northern and central German states. • A lenient peace treaty encouraged Austria's neutrality in future military engagements.
Franco-Prussian War, 1870	• Bismarck provoked and won a short but deadly war with France. • Prussia unified northern and southern German states. • France had to pay a heavy indemnity and lost the provinces of Alsace-Lorraine on the German-French border.

Bismarck's Domestic Policy While Bismarck employed a successful foreign policy, he also needed to maintain internal unity. From 1871 to 1890, Bismarck served as the chancellor of Germany. To create a modern industrial state, he instituted a new legal code and a national constitution. In the new constitution, the king of Prussia became the emperor of the entire empire.

Bismarck actively promoted economic innovation and growth. German inventors created the internal combustion engine and the electric train. Berlin installed a telephone network. Coal and iron production as well as the size of the railroad network increased sharply. In 1879, Bismarck concluded that high-tariff countries were more prosperous than low-tariff countries. So, he passed the "iron and rye" tariff, which partially protected German manufacturers and farmers from foreign competition. Under Bismarck, cities also flourished, and the economy competed with other industrial European powers.

While Bismarck tried to create a conservative, centralized state, he met opposition from Catholics and socialists in Germany. First, Bismarck feared the power of the Catholics in the southern states, who represented 40 percent of the population. He sought to diminish the power of Catholicism by creating a program called *Kulturkampf* (culture struggle), passing laws that expelled the Jesuits, ended Catholic education, and introduced civil marriage.

However, Bismarck soon backed off the conflict with Catholics. He was increasingly concerned about socialist demands from the working class in response to industrialization. To reduce the spread of socialism, he passed laws that banned socialist newspapers and abolished trade unions. At the same time, he tried to undercut the appeal of socialists by implementing innovative programs such as nationalized health care and old-age insurance. These programs provided a model that other industrialized countries followed. Nevertheless, the socialist movement continued to gain support.

Bismarck's Dismissal Earlier in his career, Bismarck had successfully used three wars to unify Germans under Prussian leadership. After unification, Bismarck's major goal in both domestic and foreign policy had been to consolidate and strengthen the power of Germany. Domestically, at times, he had sided with liberals and at other times with conservatives.

In foreign policy, Bismarck viewed France as Germany's most significant rival. He thought France might want revenge after its defeat in the Franco-Prussian War. To prevent this, Bismarck created a web of alliances with other states in an effort to isolate France. For example, he negotiated agreements with Russia and Austria. He supported their influence in eastern Europe. In return, he hoped they would not support a French war against Germany.

However, he was ultimately unable to overcome the political and religious divisions within the country. Further, he opposed later wars as destabilizing. In 1890, Kaiser Wilhelm II (also known as emperor and as William) dismissed Bismarck and adopted a more aggressive foreign policy stance. The Kaiser was determined that Germany would achieve the status he believed it deserved. In contrast, Bismarck promoted a restrained foreign policy designed to prevent conflict that could weaken Germany.

Conflict and Reform in France

Like Germany and Britain, France had politically active working-class and middle-class movements. In the early 19th century, Napoleon had sought to create national unity in France by instituting public education, building infrastructure, and enacting a body of laws known as the Napoleonic Code (see Chapter 8). After Napoleon's exile in 1815, a series of monarchs and emperors ruled France. Reforms introduced in 1830 limited the power of the throne and created a constitutional monarchy. Laws expanded voting rights, allowing more men to vote for representatives to the nation's General Assembly. Overall, conservative parties in France favored the monarchy and tried to limit citizen participation in government, while socialist and liberal parties supported workers' rights and popular sovereignty.

The Revolution of 1848 In 1848, a series of liberal uprisings spread throughout Europe. Their causes varied, but all involved mass protests against established governments. In France, when the government attempted to limit political gatherings by working-class and middle-class political groups, people responded with riots. The government collapsed. Replacing it was one known as the Second Republic. The leader of the new government was **Napoleon III,** nephew of the first Napoleon.

Knowing he had wide support, Napoleon III extended voting rights to all adult men. He also pledged financial relief to help unemployed workers. However, he was not committed to liberal government. Playing on middle-class fears of working-class movements, he declared himself emperor in 1852. His government became increasingly authoritarian. As workers felt more alienated from the government, the radical socialist and anarchist parties grew stronger.

In 1860, losing popularity, Napoleon III again shifted his policies, hoping to regain support and increase French nationalism. He gave the General Assembly greater power, relaxed restrictions on civil liberties, and opened France to free trade and better relations with Britain.

The Revolution of 1870 In 1870, Napoleon III believed war with Prussia would rally the country behind him and that France would be victorious. However, the war led to his downfall. Joining the battle himself, Napoleon III was taken prisoner and then overthrown in a bloodless revolution in Paris.

In 1871, elections supported a republican monarchy that called itself the Third Republic. However, a combined group of socialist and anarchist workers, fearing that the new government would be more monarchist than republican, barricaded streets in Paris in an attempt to create their own separate society, which they called the **Paris Commune**. They demanded reforms in education, welfare, and rights for women. After bloody clashes with the police, the Commune was defeated. But the determination of the Commune cannot be underestimated; up to 10,000 insurrectionists gave their lives when the government troops crushed it.

Few of the reforms the Paris Commune called for were enacted, but it did serve as an inspiration for later worker revolts in Russia. Many of the Commune's leaders remained in French politics and were elected to the National Assembly where they represented socialist parties.

Women's Rights in France French women had been active in politics since at least the French Revolution. For most French feminists, the campaign for women's rights was part of the larger struggle for workers' rights. One of first women to call for female suffrage in France after Olympe de Gouges was **Flora Tristan**, a writer of mixed Peruvian and French heritage. As a young woman, she was drawn toward Saint-Simon's ideas of utopian socialism. Tristan believed that the political emancipation of women was essential for true social revolution. In 1843 she published an essay, "The Workers' Union," in which she called for a national union of all working-class men and women.

Tristan died in 1844, but her writings helped the French labor movement grow. In 1848, nearly 8,000 workers commemorated her death by marching to her grave. As they marched, they sang a song she had published in "The Workers' Union." Despite the efforts of women like Tristan, women's suffrage was slow to come in France. French women did not have full rights to vote until the end of World War II in 1945.

The Transformation of Paris In the 1850s, France had enjoyed a period of relative peace and stability. Emperor Napoleon III decided to celebrate his reign by completely renovating the city of Paris, France's largest city and national capital. Paris was an old city, plagued by slums, narrow streets, poor water systems, and crumbling bridges. The Emperor wanted to see the city become a more modern metropolis and hired Georges Haussmann to oversee the project.

In the largest urban renewal project up to that time, Haussmann, a civil servant, completely redesigned the Parisian infrastructure, creating wide boulevards, public parks and plazas, a system for gas lighting, and new water mains to bring fresh water to the city. The new water supply and drainage improved sanitary conditions for the working class and eliminated the city's foul odor. The wider boulevards allowed people and goods to move through the city more easily. The boulevards also had a military purpose, replacing many narrow streets where anti-government rebels might build barricades and allowing police and troops to move rapidly to any part of the city.

The main part of the construction work took nearly 20 years, and some parts were not completed until the 1920s. The huge financial costs made Haussmann very unpopular with some legislators, but most historians agree that his work was a success. Haussmann was an urban visionary who turned Paris into one of the most attractive cities in Europe and made it a model for urban planners throughout the world. Haussmann went on to redesign Vienna and other cities as well.

Jews and Anti-Semitism in Europe

Throughout most of European history, Jews were subject to **anti-Semitism**, or discrimination and persecution based on their religion, often forbidden from owning property or practicing certain professions. Some municipalities, such as the city of Venice, required Jews to live in specified areas and forced them to obey a curfew at night. The Enlightenment, with its emphasis on individual liberties and rights, brought wide-scale changes to Europe's Jewish population. During the French Revolution, the Revolutionary government issued an edict granting Jews full citizenship. After Napoleon took over the French government, he extended emancipation to Jews in all the countries he conquered. By the mid-19th century, Jews in most Western European countries enjoyed equal rights and were fully integrated into the economy.

The Dreyfus Affair Integration and emancipation did not mean that anti-Semitism had disappeared, though. Even if Jews did not face legal discrimination, they still faced suspicion and hostility from the majority who often regarded them as "outsiders." In 1894, **Alfred Dreyfus**, a Jewish captain in the French Army, was accused of passing sensitive military information to Germany. He was tried and convicted of treason, although the government had little evidence against him. However, because he was Jewish, he made a convenient scapegoat. Some people found blaming him easy because he belonged to minority group.

For more than ten years the Dreyfus Affair split French society. Some people defended Dreyfus and condemned anti-Semitism. Others blamed Jews for social problems and claimed that Dreyfus showed that Jews could not be trusted. Advocates for religious liberty prevailed, and Dreyfus was pardoned in 1906. By that time, the issued raised by the Dreyfus Affair had spread beyond France to other regions of Europe. Jews throughout Western Europe, even in countries that seemed to accept religious diversity, found their loyalty questioned. Vienna's mayor openly appealed to anti-Semites and introduced laws restricting Jewish immigration from Russia and Eastern Europe.

While some French magazines portrayed Dreyfus as a traitor, most French later looked back on the treatment of Dreyfus as a disgraceful example of anti-Semitism.

Credit: Getty Images

Pogroms Pan-Slavism, the idea that Eastern and east-central Europe should belong to people of Slavic origin, forced many Jews from their homes. In Russia, pogroms, or violent attacks against Jews, destroyed lives, businesses, and property, causing thousands of Jews to immigrate to America.

Zionism Other Jews determined that they should have a homeland of their own, a concept known as Zionism. The most important early leader of Zionism was Theodore Herzl. Born in Hungary in 1860, he grew up in an assimilated German-Jewish family—one deeply absorbed into German society. He admired German culture and believed that Jews should become part of the larger European society. The Dreyfus Affair, however, opened his eyes to the persistence of anti-Semitism in Europe. Herzl later claimed that his reaction to the Dreyfus Affair inspired his interest in Zionism. Some historians dispute this claim, stating that Herzl had explored the idea of a Jewish state even before the arrest of Dreyfus.

Herzl's book, *Der Judenstat (The Jewish State),* published in 1895, was one of the first documents to declare that Jews should have a nation-state of their own. Herzl felt that without their own state, Jews would remain at the mercy of others. He wanted a place where Jews would be guaranteed the right to practice their own religion and form their own government. At first, Herzl did not stipulate where the Jewish state should be, even speculating that it might be established in South America or Africa.

In the early 1900s, though, Herzl and his followers came to believe that the region known as Palestine was the most likely place for a Jewish state. Most Jews regarded the land around the city of Jerusalem as the traditional Jewish homeland. Jews had lived there for centuries and many traveled there to see the ancient city. The British, who controlled Palestine, supported the creation of a "national home" for Jews there. The Zionist movement continued, even after Herzl's death in 1904, and Jewish immigration to Palestine grew throughout the 1920s and 1930s. In 1948, the Jewish state of Israel was established. Israelis considered Herzl one of their nation's founders and celebrate his birthday as a national holiday.

Revolutionary Options

The ideas of Karl Marx spread throughout Europe in the late 19th century. While they challenged some of the basic ideas of capitalism, the theory of anarchism challenged the idea of government itself.

Women as Socialist Leaders

Clara Zetkin Marx and Engels believed that women and men should be equal. This idea attracted a number of women who supported both gender equality and labor reform. In Germany, **Clara Zetkin** became a leading advocate of Marxism, the political term for Marx's ideas. Born into a middle-class family, she was impatient with the limited roles for women in bourgeois society and felt more drawn toward the labor movement and workers' rights.

In 1878, she joined Germany's Socialist Workers' Party. A dedicated feminist, she supported women's suffrage and edited a socialist newspaper for women. She later joined Germany's Communist Party. Zetkin was a strong advocate of international workers' movements, and she believed that all workers had the same interests regardless of where they lived. She opposed nationalism, and her resistance to the rise of Germany's fascist Nazi party in the 1930s made her a hero to many Europeans after World War II.

One of the most famous women in the socialist movement, **Rosa Luxemburg** was born in Poland and became involved in socialist workers' movements in her teens. Her political activity attracted the attention of the authorities. To escape arrest, she fled to Switzerland, and later to Germany, where she became a citizen at the age of 28 and joined Germany's communist party. Luxemburg was a dramatic speaker who believed that workers had the right to take up arms against a government that oppressed them. In 1914, she helped organize the radical socialist group, the Spartacus League. The League opposed Germany's participation in World War II and was part of the failed German Revolution of 1918–1919. Luxemburg was then executed in a wave of anti-communist violence that swept through Germany.

Revolutions Against the Tsar

Russia began to industrialize only in the last decades of the 19th century. In Russia, industrialization favored the aristocratic classes who still owned most of the land. Unlike Western Europe, Russia lacked a strong middle class to stabilize society. In 1905, the loss to Japan in the Russo-Japanese War demonstrated how far behind Russia remained in their efforts to industrialize. A peaceful march by demonstrators in St. Petersburg was met with gunfire by the tsar's troops. More than 1,000 people were killed or wounded, in what many consider the first phase of the **Russian Revolution**. In 1917, suffering the disastrous effects of World War I, Russia underwent a more violent revolution that replaced the Tsar with a Communist government. Within a few years, Russia became the Soviet Union, also known as the USSR.

Socialism arose as a response to capitalism. Early utopian socialists believed that cooperation was superior to competition. Many believed that the government should intentionally distribute goods among social classes and that communities should have control over the businesses that generate wealth. Marxist-socialists believed the existing order must be overthrown and replaced by a system of pure communism (where all property would be owned collectively and goods distributed according to need). Although communism promised greater equality and freedom to the working classes in Russia, the new government was actually a dictatorship and most people remained powerless. The Soviet Union officially dissolved in 1991. Since that date Russia has continued to struggle with issues of democracy versus dictatorship.

Anarchism and Syndicalism

Anarchism is the theory that all forms of government should be abolished. Anarchists believe that society should be based on the voluntary cooperation of all members. The word *anarchy* comes from ancient Greek and means "without a chief or ruler." The modern philosophy of anarchism evolved in the 19th century in response to industrialization. Like utopian socialists, anarchists believed that people could live without national governments or states to oversee them. However, unlike utopians, anarchists did not advocate withdrawal from society. Many thought that capitalism could be overthrown only by force and became swept up in violent underground movements.

Mikhail Bakunin Born into a noble family in Russia, **Mikhail Bakunin** was drawn to socialism and communism through his study of philosophy. As a young man he traveled to France where he met many socialist leaders including Marx. Bakunin supported the violent overthrow of established governments and the destruction of property owned by capitalists. His political activities landed him in prison many times. In 1849, Swiss authorities arrested him and sent him to Russia where was imprisoned and later exiled to Siberia. He was allowed to leave Siberia in 1861 and moved to Italy. While there, he developed what he called his "anarchist creed."

Bakunin had become disillusioned with socialism and communism. He believed that once capitalist governments were overthrown, socialist leaders would simply take over the power of government for themselves. A socialist government, he declared, was no better than any other form of government. Bakunin wanted to see all forms of government and centralized authority abolished. He wanted all property controlled by groups of workers who ran their own communities. This idea became known as **collective anarchism**.

Bakunin also believed that revolution could be accomplished not by mass movements but by small, tightly knit groups that operated secretly or "underground." Bakunin's ideas were mostly rejected by the larger socialist movement, but his concept of anarchism did remain influential in Spain and Italy, where anarchist groups flourished in the 1930s.

Georges Sorel and Syndicalism Born in France in 1847, **Georges Sorel** developed ideas that influenced anarchism as well as other social revolutionary movements. He believed that once capitalism was overthrown, all property should be transferred to labor unions. The unions would then organize workers into small, self-supporting groups. This idea became known as **syndicalism**.

Sorel originally had trained as an engineer but abandoned his profession to study philosophy and economics. His studies led him to the topic of myths and their role in society. Sorel came to believe that all movements needed to create their own myths in order to inspire their followers. He likened these myths to religion and believed that the working class needed a mythology of its own that would encourage violent revolution. Violence, Sorel wrote, could be a creative as well as a destructive force. He believed that violent revolution could erase the old forms and create space for new societies to grow.

Sorel died in 1922. Though he had supported Alfred Dreyfus and rejected anti-Semitism, anti-Semitic and other racist and fascist movements later adapted some of his ideas about myths. Sorel also was highly critical of other socialists, whom he believed exploited the Dreyfus trial for their own ends.

A New Diplomatic Order

The balance of power in Europe shifted under the force of nationalism. Germany and Italy emerged as new powers, as Austria, Russia, and Turkey tried to crush nationalist uprisings. Bismarck had served as the initial architect of a complex system of alliances that attempted to maintain the status quo. Over time, conflicts in the Balkans and antagonistic alliances increased tensions in Europe, paving the way for the massive conflict now known as World War I.

Alliances Increase Tension

The European powers desired to maintain the balance of power in Europe. As nationalism and unification challenged the status quo, governments began making alliances to demonstrate their military might and assure their protection.

Bismarck's Alliance System To ensure the success of a unified Germany, Bismarck had engineered a series of alliances that created a new diplomatic order in Europe. He also wanted to isolate Germany's longtime rival France so that Germany would not get pulled into a multinational war. To accomplish these goals, Bismarck negotiated the following treaties.

European Treaties Creating Alliances		
Alliances	**Date**	**Purpose**
Three Emperors' League • Germany • Austria-Hungary • Russia	1873–1887	Spheres of influence for Austria-Hungary and Russia were determined to avoid conflict in the Balkans. Also preempted an alliance of Austria-Hungary, Russia, and France, which could threaten Germany.
Reinsurance Treaty • Germany • Russia	1887	Secret treaty after the collapse of the above promising that Germany and Russia would remain neutral if the other got into a war with another major party. Exceptions were if Germany attacked France or Russia attacked Austria.
Dual Alliance • Germany • Austria-Hungary	1879–1918	Germany and Austria-Hungary promised to support each other if attacked by Russia.
Triple Alliance • Germany • Austria-Hungary • Italy	1882–1915	Allies promised mutual support if attacked. Italy would remain neutral in a war between Germany and Austria-Hungary.

1878 Congress of Berlin Bismarck organized the major powers of Europe in the **Congress of Berlin of 1878** to solve the growing tensions in the Balkan states resulting from the Russo-Turkish War. Bismarck wanted to stabilize the Balkans in order to appease Great Britain, Austria-Hungary, and the Ottoman Empire, while trying to diminish Russian gains.

As a result of the 1878 Congress, Romania, Serbia, and Montenegro gained independence, and Austria-Hungary took over Bosnia and Herzegovina. Russia believed the Congress failed to sufficiently help the Slavic people, causing tension between Austria-Hungary and Russia. Bismarck desired to create stability and maintain the balance of power, but the Congress created more antagonism in the region.

Alliances Create Antagonism Following Bismarck's 1890 dismissal to attain the kaiser's goal of a more aggressive military policy, Germany allowed its Reinsurance Treaty with Russia to lapse. Meanwhile, Austria-Hungary and Germany drew closer. Russia soon signed a defensive alliance with France (1894). Great Britain and France signed a series of agreements known as the Entente Cordiale, and in 1907 Britain and Russia signed an Anglo-Russian Convention, ending their rivalry in Central Asia. The system of alliances became an increasing source of tension, as Europe divided into two main factions—the **Triple Alliance** and the **Triple Entente.** Bismarck had created the alliance system to maintain the status quo and peace. However, by the early 20th century, the alliances created antagonism across Europe.

Individually, states could justify making these alliances. Germany feared a British naval blockade in the event of a war, while the British and French feared a growing German military. Together, the results of the alliances increased the danger for all of Europe.

Nationalist Conflicts in the Balkans

Bismarck recognized the growing instability in the Balkans and hoped to create stability through an international conference. Unfortunately, at the turn of the 20th century, tensions in the Balkans escalated as the Great Powers supported regional groups, and nationalism threatened the stability of the Balkans.

Ethnic Tensions The **Balkans,** in southeastern Europe, had always been a multi-ethnic region. For centuries, the Ottoman Empire and Austria-Hungary had consolidated the territories in the region. As nationalism sparked unification movements in Europe, it also ignited independence movements in the Balkans. For example, the Slavic people throughout the region were unified under the policy of **Pan-Slavism,** a belief that all Slavic people should be free and united. Russia supported Pan-Slavism, motivated in part by a desire to gain warm-water ports in the eastern Mediterranean.

Annexation of Bosnia-Herzegovina Austria-Hungary feared the growing power of nationalistic movements in the region. In 1908, Austria-Hungary annexed **Bosnia-Herzegovina.** Reluctantly, both Serbia and Russia recognized the acquisition, as they both lacked the military strength to win a war. This event empowered Austria-Hungary to take an aggressive stance in the Balkans. Serbia recognized its own weakness on the international stage, leading to the rise of radical nationalist groups. Organizations such as the terrorist group Black Hand called for war against Austria-Hungary in order to win Serbian independence.

The Balkan Wars In 1912 and 1913, the **Balkan Wars** erupted twice, as the Ottoman Empire crumbled. Independent states such as Serbia, Greece, and Bulgaria fought alongside Russia to ensure independence for Ottoman territories in Europe. A month after the end of the First Balkan War, the Second Balkan War began among the former allies because of tensions over the borders created by the peace settlement. Bulgaria was defeated by an alliance of Balkan states, thus losing territory and leading to escalating nationalist tensions in the region.

HISTORICAL PERSPECTIVES: WHAT CAUSED NATIONALISM?

For most of human history, people felt their primary loyalty was to the local city or small region where they lived, or to a particular monarch who ruled over them. In the past two centuries, this changed. People began to identify more with their nation, all the people who shared their basic culture. The nation was larger than a city or region and more general than just one leader. Historians have disagreed on why this change occurred.

The Importance of Culture As liberalism and democracy spread in Europe during the 19th century, French writer Jules Michelet began to write history that focused more on common people than on great leaders. He saw the rise of nationalism as an expression of the demands of masses of people who shared elements of a culture, such as language, religion, ethnicity, and traditions that had existed far back into history. In his view, common people pushed their leaders to either break up or unite states so that cultural and political boundaries matched.

The Importance of Forgetting Another French scholar of the 19th century, Ernest Renan, saw nationalism quite differently. To him, it depended not only on shared history, but also on forgetting events that had divided people. For example, before the French Revolution, the kingdom was a coalition of various regions and languages. Only after the event did people identify with the French people as a whole and begin to speak the same language. To achieve this, they had to leave behind the religious and regional conflicts that had long divided them.

The Importance of Elites In the 1960s, historians began to focus more on how common people lived and what they felt. They found that the common people— the poor and poorly educated—were not the first advocates of nationalism. Rather, the wealthy and well-educated elites were. They developed an idea of cultural unity and then worked to get others to accept it. Political scientist and historian Benedict Anderson, in *Imagined Communities* (1983), argued that nations were not natural but created. As they were, they took the place of religion in unifying people. He explained that "the symbolism and fervor of religion was replaced with the nation, and people were willing to make the ultimate sacrifice for their nation." These nation-states had become the key organizing principle of global politics and so ingrained in the understanding of the world that it became nearly impossible to imagine a world without them.

KEY TERMS AND NAMES

Identity
national workshops
Balkans
Pan-Slavism
anti-Semitism
Alfred Dreyfus
Triple Alliance
Triple Entente
Bosnia-Herzegovina
Balkan Wars
Governance
balance of power
Congress of Vienna
Klemens von Metternich

realpolitik
Napoleon III
Paris Commune
Flora Tristan
Crimean War
Otto von Bismarck
Georges-Eugène Haussmann
dual monarchy of Austria-Hungary
anarchism
Mikhail Bakunin
collective anarchism
Georges Sorel

syndicalism
Alexander II
Sergei Witte
Revolution of 1905
Peter Stolypin
Giuseppe Mazzini
Count Cavour
Giuseppe Garibaldi
Victor Emmanuel II
Congress of Berlin of 1878
Clara Zetkin
Rosa Luxemburg

Questions 1–3 refer to the following passage.

"It is impossible to determine a concrete, universal, and obligatory norm for the internal development and political organization of every nation. The life of each nation is subordinated to a plethora [large number] of different historical, geographical, and economic conditions, making it impossible to establish a model of organization equally valid for all.

Any such attempt would be absolutely impractical. It would smother the richness and spontaneity of life which flourishes only in infinite diversity and, what is more, contradict the most fundamental principles of freedom. However, without certain absolutely essential conditions the practical realization of freedom will be forever impossible. These conditions are . . .

- Abolition of classes, ranks, and privileges; absolute equality of political rights for all men and women; universal suffrage.

- Abolition, dissolution, and moral, political, and economic dismantling of the all-pervasive, regimented, centralized State, the alter ego of the Church, and as such, the permanent cause of the impoverishment, brutalization, and enslavement of the multitude."

Mikhail Bakunin, "Political Organization," State and Anarchy,
1873

1. Which of the following set of ideas had the most influence on Bakunin?
   a) Conservatism
   b) Communism
   c) Nationalism
   d) Romanticism

2. Which of the following ideas would have been influenced by Bakunin's ideas of collective anarchism seen in the above excerpt?
   a) Syndicalism
   b) Capitalism
   c) Communism
   d) Socialism

3. Which individual would have agreed most with the ideas in this passage?
   a) Georges Sorel
   b) Peter Stolypin
   c) Clara Zetkin
   d) Flora Tristan

Questions 4 and 5 refer to the following political cartoon.

The figure in the toboggan represents Russian Tsar Nicholas I, who reigned from 1825 to 1855.

Credit: John Leech, "Montagne Russe A Very Dangerous Game," wood engraving, *Punch* 27 (1854): 127

4. What is the broader context of the "dangerous game" that the cartoonist thought the Russian tsar was playing in 1854?

   a) The tsar was among Europe's Christian leaders who were under attack from other Christians over theological issues.

   b) The tsar was one of several Europe's imperialist leaders who were involved in wars in overseas colonies.

   c) The tsar was allied with other conservative rulers in Europe who were opposed to liberal political reforms.

   d) The tsar was part of a group of European reformers who were risking rebellions because they wanted to change government very quickly.

5. Why would a political cartoon like this one have been more effective in Britain during the mid-19th century than in earlier times?

   a) British nationalism was in decline in the 19th century.

   b) Britain had begun compulsory public education in the 19th century.

   c) The British public was more aware of world events because of the use of the telegraph and battle scene photography.

   d) The British public strongly supported the government's diplomatic and military efforts in the Middle East.

Questions 6–8 refer to the following passage.

"Italy's misfortunes are of long standing... But it is certainly true that they must be attributed primarily to the political influence exercised among us for centuries by foreigners. The principal obstacles to our freeing ourselves from this distressing influence are the internal divisions, the rivalries, even hostility among the members of the great Italian family. Next comes the distrust between the national princes and the most energetic segment of the population. This segment has a desire for progress, which is often too great, a lively national spirit, and a strong patriotism—all of which makes it, if not the principal instrument, the indispensable auxiliary of all efforts for emancipation...

All history proves that no people can attain a high degree of intelligence and morality unless its spirit of nationalism is strongly developed...

The intellectual life of the masses moves within a highly restricted circle of ideas. Of those which they can acquire, the most noble and elevating other than religious ones are the concepts of patriotism and nationality. If the political circumstances of a country prevent these concepts from being manifest or give them false direction, the masses are plunged into a state of deplorable inferiority. But that is not all; if a people cannot be proud of a nationality a feeling of personal dignity exists only incidentally among a few privileged individuals. The majority, occupying the humblest social positions, need a feeling of national greatness to acquire a consciousness of their own dignity."

Count Camillo di Cavour, "On Railroads in Italy," 1846

6. The movement Cavour was most supporting in this passage was
   a) conservatism
   b) autocracy
   c) liberalism
   d) nationalism

7. Who probably disagreed most with the views expressed in the passage?
   a) Garibaldi
   b) Bismarck
   c) Metternich
   d) Mazzini

8. Which of the following states had the most influence in the Italian regions that Cavour wanted to unite?
   a) Russia
   b) Austria
   c) Prussia
   d) Ottoman Empire

1. Use the passage below to answer all parts of the question that follows.

"The Germans of the Age of Nationalism had no liberal statesman, . . . not even a Cavour. . . . to direct their national energies into democratic channels. Instead, they had Bismarck. What the revolution of 1848 failed to do, his revolution of 1866 accomplished. It laid the foundations of a unified German nation-state. . . . Solitary voices crying in the wilderness of national self-satisfaction warned Bismarck's admirers in vain against overestimating power and underestimating liberty. For 1866 failed even more disastrously than 1848 in securing liberty and infusing nationalism with the spirit of democracy.

Hans Kohn, The Mind of Germany, 1960

a) Explain ONE piece of evidence that supports Kohn's view of the relationship between events in 1848 and 1866 in Germany.

b) Explain ANOTHER piece of evidence that supports Kohn's view of the relationship between events in 1848 and 1866 in Germany.

c) Explain ONE piece of evidence that opposes Kohn's view of the relationship between events in 1848 and 1866 in Germany.

2. Answer all parts of the question that follows.

a) Describe ONE cause of the Crimean War.

b) Explain ONE short-term effect of the Crimean War on the Russian Empire.

c) Explain ONE long-term effect of the Crimean War on the balance of power in Europe.

LONG ESSAY QUESTIONS

1. Evaluate two of the following leaders' approaches toward nationalism in the 19th century: Metternich, Bismarck, Napoleon III, Cavour, Mazzini, Francis Joseph, Garibaldi.

2. Evaluate the extent to which nationalism undermined the balance of power in Europe during the 19th century.

1. In one to three paragraphs, explain how European states struggled to maintain international stability in an age of nationalism and revolution.

WRITE AS A HISTORIAN: EVALUATE RELATIVE SIGNIFICANCE

A first step in writing a history essay—or writing in general—is deciding what is important enough to include. Not all information is equally important. For instance, which had greater relative significance: Napoleon's decision to invade Spain or his decision to invade Russia? In part, the answer depends on context. A historian writing about Spain and a historian writing about Russia might make different decisions. A historian writing a biography might decide the invasion of Russia was more important because it destroyed much of Napoleon's army.

Three criteria you can use to evaluate relative historical significance are to understand:

- how crucial the issue was when it occurred

- how lasting its consequences were

- how representative the issue was in symbolizing larger trends

Consider also whether the issue or event had global, national, or local significance.

When you are writing, issues of lasting global significance often form the main ideas, or topic sentences of paragraphs. The supporting details will be the less significant national and local events that led up to the history-changing moments.

Rank each of the following events using the following scale of significance:

- *1: little global impact; mostly local significance*

- *2: mostly national significance*

- *3: large international or global significance*

1. Napoleon III advocated French nationalism.

2. The king of Sardinia led a revolution in Sicily in 1848.

3. Revolutionaries fomented events such as the War of Greek Independence.

4. The revolutions of 1848 led to the breakdown of the Concert of Europe.

5. The decline of the Ottoman Empire prompted the Crimean War.

6. Russia undertook internal reforms to achieve modern industrialization.

7. Tsar Alexander II ordered the emancipation of Russian serfs.

8. German Kaiser Wilhelm II dismissed Chancellor Bismarck.

9. The Great Powers militarized and formed complex alliances.

10. An assassin murdered Archduke Franz Ferdinand in Sarajevo.

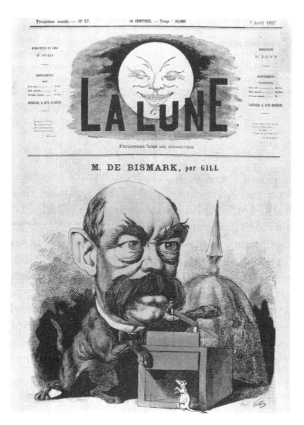

Otto von Bismarck was a favorite of cartoonists. His bushy eyebrows, large mustache, and spiked helmet (shown on the side) made him very recognizable. Here, a French artist portrayed him as a cat, a commentary on Bismarck's ability to plan carefully before leaping into action.

Credit: Getty Images

Global Control and European Tensions

"Gentlemen, we must speak more loudly and more honestly! We must say openly that indeed the higher races have a right over the lower races . . . I repeat, that the superior races have a right because they have a duty. They have the duty to civilize the inferior races..."

—French Premier Jules Ferry, "On French Colonial Expansion," Speech to French Chamber of Deputies, 1884

Essential Question: What caused the intensification of European efforts at global control and the resulting tensions among the Great Powers?

At the beginning of the **Age of Imperialism**, the expansion by European powers into Asia and Africa increased global tensions. During the **Berlin Conference of 1884–1885**, the European powers established guidelines for the "carving up" of Africa for colonization. Germany's Otto von Bismarck had called the conference to maintain peace and stability among the European powers. Bismarck's role as a broker for stability eventually led to his dismissal in 1890 by Kaiser Wilhelm II. The Kaiser sought a more aggressive foreign policy than Bismarck desired.

In Asia, European nations and businesses also sought access to raw materials and new markets. By the turn of the 20th century, colonial exploitation, global markets, and resistance movements created increased tensions throughout the world, as European countries established new colonial empires.

Motives of Imperialism in Africa and Asia

The Industrial Revolution had a dramatic impact on Europe's economy. Industrialized powers desired access to raw materials such as oil, diamonds, rubber, and manganese to fuel their factories. They also desired new markets in which to sell their mass-produced goods. In the 19th century, imperialist European states competed with each other to control Africa and Asia in order to obtain raw materials and sell finished products. Europeans justified the subjugation of people around the world by portraying them as racially and culturally inferior.

Search for Raw Materials and Markets

As European colonies in North America and South America sought and acquired their independence, European governments and capitalists focused on new markets in Asia and Africa, both of which provided Europeans with access to needed natural resources, markets to sell their manufactured goods, and sources for new investment such as railroads.

Trade with China Since the 18th century, European powers had been trading in Asia. In China, European nations hoped to create a favorable balance of trade with the Chinese —a total value of exports greater than the value of imports—in order to gain fair prices on Chinese goods such as tea, silk, and porcelain. Tea accounted for 60 percent of England's trade with China. However, the British produced no goods that the Chinese wanted to buy, making it difficult to achieve a favorable balance of trade. But then the British began smuggling the addictive drug opium into China in the early 1800s. Chinese leaders protested, but the British defended their actions on the principle of free trade. When a Chinese official destroyed a large quantity of opium seized from British traders, the British started the Opium War against the Chinese. The British won the war, and the Chinese were forced to accept the following terms in the Treaty of Nanking in August of 1842:

- British took control of Hong Kong until 1997.

- China opened five ports of trade to the British.

- China compensated Britain $21 million in silver.

From this point on, China gradually became more and more accessible to European powers. While China became a vital market to Europeans, many Chinese never forgave their government for failing to protect them from the opium trade. China's humiliating defeat in the Opium War would contribute to a rebellion against European imperialism in the late 1890s and to the overthrow of the Qing Dynasty in 1911.

England in India Following the Seven Years' War, the British East India Company acquired sole rights to trade in India. In 1857, Indians rebelled unsuccessfully against British dominance in the **Sepoy Rebellion.** (This event, also known as The Indian Rebellion of 1857, the Sepoy Mutiny, The Indian Uprising, and The First War of Indian Independence, is discused later in this chapter). Britain's Queen Victoria then took direct control of India in order to protect this vital territory, allowing Britain to profit greatly from the export of India's tea, indigo, coffee, and cotton. Moreover, with more than 300 million Indian subjects, the British were able to sell manufactured goods to the Indian people, creating additional profit for factories in Great Britain. While Britain exploited India's natural resources and subjects, it also invested in railroad construction and increased access to education for the people of India.

Looking to Africa For centuries, Europeans had considered Africa south of the Sahara as the "dark continent," because they lacked accurate maps and knowledge of the interior. The British and Dutch began to explore Africa in the 19th century. By 1914, Europeans controlled all of Africa except Liberia and Ethiopia. They used Africans as poorly paid miners or farm workers. In central Africa, King Leopold II of Belgium used the Congolese as slave labor.

National Rivalry

Rivalries between European nations fostered imperial competition, as the great powers of Europe fought for strategic locations that offered **human capital** (workers), geographical advantages, and natural resources. In particular, Great Britain, the leader of the Industrial Revolution, competed with France and Germany (after Kaiser Wilhelm II dismissed his Chancellor Bismarck and began his aggressive foreign policy) for territory in Asia and Africa.

The Berlin Conference In 1884–1885, **Otto von Bismarck** of Germany hosted the Berlin Conference to ensure the peaceful expansion of European powers into Africa. As industrialized European nations sought the natural resources available in Africa, tensions mounted among European nations such as Belgium, Great Britain, and France as each nation wanted valuable land in Africa, in a process that became known as the "Scramble for Africa."

Bismarck, considered an "honest broker" with little interest in African territory for Germany, negotiated a peaceful and orderly conference to divide up the African continent. Bismarck sought stability in order to consolidate German strength and keep France from forming threatening alliances.

During a series of meetings in Berlin, the leaders of the European powers peaceably agreed to colonial boundaries and trade arrangements in Africa. In addition, the powers agreed to the free movement of goods on Africa's major rivers such as the Niger River and the Congo River.

| Current Names of Countries Formerly Colonized ||
Imperial Power	Countries Today
Great Britain	• Egypt • Sudan • Nigeria • Zimbabwe • South Africa
France	• Algeria • Morocco • Niger • Mali
Germany	• Namibia • Tanzania
Portugal	• Angola • Mozambique
Belgium	• Congo
Italy	• Somalia

Nationalistic Motives With more than 11 million square miles of territory, Great Britain possessed the largest empire in the world by the beginning of the 20th century. Great Britain had acquired valuable territory in strategic locations such as India, Egypt, and South Africa. Despite its power, Great Britain faced competition from the French and Germans for overseas power:

- During the Scramble for Africa, France had solidified its claims on most of West Africa. In addition, it acquired large parts of North Africa, which contained vital natural resources such as iron ore and petroleum.

- At the Berlin Conference, Bismarck negotiated for territory in central Africa, where Germany exploited the mining industry. In addition, this central African territory blocked Great Britain's hopes of creating a railroad from Cairo, Egypt to Cape Town, South Africa.

As each European power became stronger, tension over the control of colonies increased. In particular, Germany began to threaten Great Britain's dominance. Germany was rapidly building its industrial base. This made it more dependent on international trade and a stronger potential military foe. In addition, after Wilhelm II dismissed Bismarck in 1890, Germany adopted a more aggressive foreign policy.

Myths of Cultural and Racial Superiority

As the European powers expanded into Africa and Asia, imperialists justified this expansion and subjugation by claiming cultural and racial superiority. Europeans believed they were civilizing the world by spreading their Western ideals to "less developed" peoples. Europeans assumed that other civilizations were less civilized.

The White Man's Burden In the late 19th century, Herbert Spencer, a British sociologist and anthropologist, began applying, however incorrectly, Darwin's principles of evolution to social groups. Spencer used Darwin's idea of "survival of the fittest" in comparing cultures. Spencer stressed that different ethnicities and classes had progressed to be more advanced and sophisticated than others. This idea, called **Social Darwinism,** provided European nations with the rationale that they were actually *helping* less developed Asian and African peoples by colonizing them.

Rudyard Kipling, a British subject living in India, exemplified this attitude in his poem **"The White Man's Burden"** in 1899. Kipling described the native people as "Half-devil and half-child," insisting that European powers must "Send forth the best ye breed" to end famine, laziness, and disease in less developed parts of the world.

Mission Civilisatrice Imperialists stressed that the colonization of Africa and Asia was a "civilizing mission," as Europeans spread the ideals of Western civilization across the world. The French term *Mission Civilisatrice,* meaning

"The Civilizing Mission," was not a new concept. It had been employed in the Age of Exploration and supported during the Enlightenment. Europeans stressed the importance of indoctrinating indigenous peoples around the world to accept Western ideals of religion and government.

For example, the French, under the leadership of Jules Ferry, wanted to "civilize" France's West African colonies by teaching Christianity, requiring people to speak French, and encouraging the adoption of French fashion. The French colonial administration hoped that if people adopted French culture, they would also share French values about equality and liberty.

While initially occupied with West Africa, the French government also saw an opportunity to colonize Southeast Asia. This region, heavily influenced by Indian and Chinese culture, was known as Indochina. Today, it includes the countries of Vietnam, Laos, and Cambodia.

The creator of this drawing suggested that over time, Darwinism would make people taller, smarter, and more attractive.

Credit: Getty Images

Industrial and Technological Developments

As the second half of the 19th century progressed, the industrial and technological developments in Europe aided the expansion of global empires. In particular, during the **Second Industrial Revolution** (see Chapter 13), Europeans acquired the technological tools and scientific means to more effectively establish empires in Asia and Africa.

Development of Military and Medical Technologies

While European powers possessed smaller armies than the native people, Europeans were able to conquer large amounts of land because of developments in weaponry and medicine.

    Advances in Weaponry Military technology gave Europeans the ability to conquer larger but less well-armed people who used primitive weaponry. Their technology allowed European nations to use less manpower and fewer economic resources in the process of building global empires. Two important phases of the revolution in weaponry were:

- The muzzle-loading musket was upgraded to a rifled barrel—a spiraled barrel, spinning the bullet and thus creating greater accuracy—and oblong, or **Minié bullets**, also improving accuracy.

- Two new weapons—the **breechloader Maxim gun** (easier to load than the musket and able to fire eleven bullets per second) and the **machine gun**—both increased firing speed and accuracy and reduced the need for larger military forces.

The development of weapons such as the Maxim gun made war more deadly than previously. The British used it widely in the colonial conflicts.

Credit: Getty Images

Advances in Microbiology In the 19th century, medical science expanded rapidly as scientists employed the scientific methods and research to make improvements in disease prevention and reduce the mortality rate. Research by Louis Pasteur and Joseph Lister was ground breaking. (To review these improvements in medical treatments, see Chapter 14.) Advances in medical care had an important impact on military power. They allowed European militaries to vaccinate troops and provide a healthy surgical environment for injured soldiers. Microbiology thus decreased battlefield mortality rates, which made the military more effective and efficient.

Preventing Malaria In Africa, the disease **malaria** had prevented Europeans from exploring the interior of the continent. While dysentery and yellow fever also contributed to European morality, malaria was the primary disease that killed Europeans. With limited immunity, Europeans could conduct trade only on the coasts of Africa. In the 19th century, French scientists discovered a treatment for malaria by extracting **quinine** from the bark of a tree found in South America. With the mass production of the treatment, Europeans were able to enter the African interior without fear of contracting malaria. Medical science had provided European explorers and capitalists with the biological tools to exploit the African interior.

Improvements in Communication and Transportation

As European colonial empires expanded across Asia and Africa, Europeans developed innovations in communication and transportation, allowing them greater access to colonial territories. Technologies such as the **telegraph** (see Chapter 13) brought faster communication, while steamships allowed Europeans to move people and goods with greater speed.

Advances in Transportation Technology To improve access to colonial possessions, European powers increased their speed and navigation with the railroad and steamship. The steamship gave European soldiers, explorers, and capitalists the ability to travel up and down rivers without relying on wind or currents. Macgregor Laird, a British explorer and proponent of steam power, noted, "By his [James Watt's] invention every river is laid open to us, time and distance are shortened." Over time European powers armed the steam-powered boats, turning them into **gunboats**.

Once European powers acquired colonial possessions, they invested time and money into building **infrastructure**—in particular, railroads. Railroads allowed Europeans to create rapid transportation networks within colonial territories in order to move raw materials and resources to ports more quickly. In India, the British Empire built 22,000 miles of railroad. In Africa, the railroad allowed Europeans to connect rivers and lakes with a clear transportation route. By 1907, the industrial powers had built 168,000 miles of railroad tracks beyond Europe and the United States.

Opening the Suez Canal Europeans had begun using canals to connect waterways in the early 19th century. In 1869, the **Suez Canal** opened, connecting the Mediterranean Sea with the Red Sea and Indian Ocean. European ships no longer needed to travel around Africa to gain access to Asian ports. Instead, a three-day trip on the Suez Canal shortened the voyage to India by more than 5,000 miles, allowing easier movement of goods and troops. In 1887, electric lighting was added to the canal allowing for safer and faster travel.

Advances in Communication Technology The telegraph and undersea cable transformed European communications with their colonial empires. In the early 19th century, people used the system of "dashes" and "dots" known as Morse Code (see Chapter 13) to transmit messages by telegraph over long distances. While the telegraph was initially used only across land, European and American capitalists and inventors developed undersea cables to communicate across bodies of water such as the Atlantic Ocean. By the 1860s, people on the European continent could communicate relatively rapidly with their counterparts in North America, and by 1890, Great Britain could communicate with all of its Asian and African colonies. A sender could relay a message from India to England in only five hours. European powers thus had "instant" communication with their colonies.

Imperial Tensions and Debate

Imperial conquest affected European society and diplomacy by increasing domestic and international tensions. While diplomacy initially allowed for the "peaceful carving up" of Africa, over time, imperialism strained European alliances. In Europe, critics began to debate the ethics and economic value of imperialism, while artists and writers used their skills to intensify the debate.

Diplomatic Tensions Increase

Bismarck had successfully held the Berlin Conference and utilized alliances to maintain the balance of power and ensure peace in Europe at the beginning of the Age of Imperialism; but by the turn of the 20th century, diplomatic tensions among Great Britain, France, and Germany had become strained, resulting in conflicts in Sudan and Morocco. (To review the increasingly aggressive foreign policy of Germany's Kaiser Wilhelm II, see Chapter 16.)

Fashoda Crisis In 1898, British-French tensions escalated in Africa over railroads. France wanted rail lines to unify an African empire from the Niger River in West Africa to the Nile River in East Africa. Britain wanted to create a railroad network from Cairo, Egypt, to Cape Town, South Africa.

The two great powers came into conflict in Fashoda, Sudan, in what became known as the **Fashoda Crisis**. There, British and French colonial authorities disputed the ownership of the territory, and both nations sent military forces into the region. Within a few days, France withdrew its military and conceded the territory to Britain, recognizing the strength of Great Britain's military as well as the need for a strong European ally in future wars, given the increasing competition from Germany. In 1904, France and Britain agreed to the **Entente Cordiale** (see Chapter 16), recognizing French and British colonial territories and formally acknowledging British-French friendship.

Moroccan Crises Tension between Germany and France escalated over a territorial dispute in **Morocco**. Since the 19th century, France had wanted to control North African territories, as evidenced by their acquisitions at the 1884 Berlin Conference. As part of the 1904 Entente Cordiale, Britain recognized France's sphere of influence in Morocco, and France recognized Great Britain's sphere of influence in Egypt. A sphere of influence is an area of control over a foreign territory, often for commercial purposes.

Germany disliked the British-French agreement and in 1905 and 1911 supported Moroccan rebellions against French rule. The crisis ended with Morocco becoming a *protectorate*—a country that is controlled and protected by a more powerful country—of France. The dispute over Morocco did not bring war, since Germany did not have the support of its allies, while France had backing from Britain. However, tensions between Germany and France intensified as a result of the conflict, further strengthening the alliance between France and Britain.

Debates over Colonial Acquisition

While many Europeans supported imperialism, disagreements about it affected European society and culture, as writers and artists debated the necessity and ethics of colonial empires. Writers **Joseph Conrad** and **E. D. Morel** documented the mistreatment of Africans and questioned the morality of imperialism. **John A. Hobson** and **Vladimir Lenin** wrote about and debated the economic viability of imperialism. European visual artists, influenced by non-Western cultures, created stylist changes that also brought to light the colonization and treatment of non-Western cultures.

Conrad and Morel While European capitalists and governments benefited from the new markets and abundance of raw materials, others debated the ethics of imperialism. In the 1890s, novelist Joseph Conrad visited the Belgian Congo and witnessed the harsh realities of imperialism. In 1899, he published the story ***Heart of Darkness*** depicting the immoral treatment of the Congolese by King Leopold II of Belgium. Conrad described how European colonizers abused and starved the native peoples of Africa.

At the same time, E. D. Morel, a shipping clerk in England, recognized the unethical trading practices in the Congo. The Berlin Conference had set the rules for the Congo as a "free trade" region; yet, the Belgians were shipping in large amounts of illegal military supplies. After further investigation, Morel noted that Belgian capitalists were stripping the Congolese of their economic autonomy by restricting free trade and abolishing fair wages. In 1902, Morel made his first public speech on the mistreatment of the Congolese. While Conrad and Morel would not effect change in their lifetimes, their desire to educate the public on the implications of imperialism would impact future generations.

Hobson While figures such as Conrad and Morel objected to imperialism from an ethical standpoint, some economists criticized imperialism because they believed it was not a profitable or sound economic policy. In 1902, British economist John A. Hobson published *Imperialism: A Study,* arguing that imperialism "jeopardized the entire wealth of the nation" and insisting that imperialism made the European economy dependent on unstable markets. Moreover, Hobson believed that imperialism required European nations to invest in foreign infrastructure as well as spending larger amounts on the military. Hobson thus believed that imperialism was not beneficial in the long run for European powers.

Lenin While Hobson outlined detrimental economic effects of imperialism on capitalist nations, Vladimir Lenin stressed philosophical reasons against imperialism. Lenin declared that imperialism was "the monopoly stage of capitalism." As a prominent Communist Party leader in Russia in the early 20th century, Lenin wanted to expose the exploitation of colonized people. In his essay "Imperialism, the Highest Stage of Capitalism," Lenin insisted that European nations plundered the world for their own self-interest and that imperialism would inspire a global revolution against capitalism.

Gauguin and Picasso As well as influencing writers of the time, encounters with non-Western cultures also influenced the styles and subject matter of visual artists, further stoking debates over colonialism. From 1880 to 1905, Post-impressionist artists like **Paul Gauguin** and **Pablo Picasso** gained inspiration from and used non-European subjects in their art, expressing their visions through the striking use of color and light. **Primitivism** thus emerged as an artistic style, as artists sought to illustrate the unblemished "perfection" of native peoples living in a more "natural" state than Europeans. Gauguin used his art to illustrate the beauty of what he called the "savage instinct," untainted by Western civilization. In the 1890s, Gauguin traveled through the Pacific and spent time in Tahiti, where he was inspired to portray the native women in works such as "Sacred Spring, Sweet Dreams" and "Seed of the Areoi."

Shortly before Gauguin died, Pablo Picasso became exposed to his works, and the beauty of their simplified forms. Exposure to Gauguin's primitivism caused Picasso to reconsider form and beauty beyond the social and artistic conventions of his era. Disillusioned with his own society, Picasso became inspired by primitivism and studied non-European art forms such as African masks. While Picasso never left Europe, non-European art and subjects inspired him to paint forms in a new manner as seen in "Les Demoiselles d'Avignon" in 1907. Picasso both manipulated the form of the subject and altered the subject itself, which would lead to the early 20th century artistic movement known as Cubism, featuring abstract images based on geometric forms.

Colonial Challenges to Imperialism

While imperialism had both positive and negative effects on the colonizing European nations, they were not the only regions affected by change. Asian and African nations may have benefitted to some extent from modernized societies and economies, but not without dramatic problems. Nationalist movements in colonized regions challenged European imperialism and sought self-determination with varying degrees of success.

Resistance in Africa

Some African nations and localized groups resisted European imperialism. In the case of the **Zulus**, their attempts to rebel against the British eventually failed while the **Ethiopians** successfully defeated Italian troops.

Zulu Resistance In 1843, the British occupied Natal and Zululand in Southern Africa. Zulu miners there worked in Britain's profitable diamond mines. In 1872, the leader of the Zulu people decided to resist British rule and organized 40,000 men into a disciplined army. The British demanded the Zulus disarm, but by 1879, when the Zulus continued to maintain a defensive posture, the British sent in military personnel to suppress the Zulus. Initially, the British suffered defeats by the native forces, but after six months the British defeated the Zulu and forced them to surrender. By the end of the century, Great Britain formally annexed Natal and Zululand, and Zulu resistance to British imperialism ended.

Ethiopia Resists Successfully Ethiopia represents one of the most successful attempts to resist European imperialism in Africa. The emperor of Ethiopia recognized that European nations, especially Italy, wanted to control East Africa. To ensure that Ethiopia could defend itself, the emperor purchased modern weapons such as rifles from France and Russia, who profited from the sale of these weapons. However, Italy claimed Ethiopia as a protectorate and Italian troops began to occupy parts of the region. Ethiopia declared war on Italy. At the Battle of Adwa (1896), Ethiopian forces defeated the Italian troops, leading to Italy's eventual withdrawal. Ethiopia successfully defeated the Italians and maintained their independence into the 20th century.

Resistance in Asia

Similarly to Africa, Asian nations experienced some limited success when challenging European imperialism, particularly in India and China. Japan represented one of the few successful movements that prevented European occupation through imitation of Western modernization.

Sepoy Rebellion Since the 1600s, the British East India Company had operated profitable trading ports in India. The Industrial Revolution made India especially important to the British economy, because India provided raw materials such as cotton for British factories. India also provided markets for British manufactured goods. India was the "Jewel in the British Crown."

Over time, the British gained powerful influence over Indian politics. By 1857, the British East India Company staffed a private army with British officers and **sepoy**, or Indian soldiers, who were mostly Hindus or Muslims. British officers had little contact with the sepoy.

The sepoy were discontented with the growing presence of Christian missionaries and felt that Great Britain was attempting to undermine their Hindu and Islamic faiths. Yet the discontent went well beyond the sepoy. Much of Indian society resented British rule, the rapid pace of Westernization, and the degrading of their own rulers and traditions.

In 1857, the sepoy mutinied after hearing unconfirmed rumors that the British were coating cartridges in beef or pork fat, which violated the sacred tenets of both Hindus and Muslims. The mutiny began in March 1857 with a single attack. It spread across Delhi, Agra, Kanpur, and Lucknow. Initially, the British military had only 23,000 troops, which limited their ability to suppress the mutiny. Over time they were successful. The British defeated the sepoy and officially declared peace in July of 1858.

However, reprisals may have continued for as long as a decade. Historians do not agree on the number of deaths during the rebellion, but some estimate that 100,000 Indians may have been killed during reprisals.

While the mutiny was unsuccessful, it caused the British to increase their political and military presence in India. The British government, instead of allowing the British East India Company to rule India, made India an official colony. British rule over India would last until 1947.

Boxer Rebellion By the late 19th century, European powers and Japan were "carving up" China, each seeking a sphere of influence. While the Qing Empress still ruled, she felt threatened by these foreign assaults on her country.

In 1898, she gave some support to attacks on foreigners in port cities. Carrying out these attacks were members of the Society of Righteous and Harmonious Fists. Since this group was also known as the Boxers, their actions became known as the **Boxer Rebellion**. They recruited economically depressed peasants angered by growing foreign power in their country. Many were particularly offended by Christian missionaries, whom they felt disrespected their traditions.

Eight countries or colonies sent forces into China to put down the Boxer Rebellion: Japan, the United States, Great Britain, India, France, Germany, Austria, and Italy.

Credit: Wikimedia Commons

France awarded medals to soldiers who helped
defeat the Boxer Rebellion in China.

Credit: Getty Images

In 1900, the Boxers attacked the capital city of Peking, today known as Beijing, targeting signs of European culture, such as Christian churches. In response, an international force of about 19,000 soldiers, made up mostly of Japanese and Russians put down the rebellion by late 1901. The uprising had significant results:

- Deaths in the rebellion may have totaled 100,000 people.

- The involvement of Japan marked a turning point in Japanese imperialism in the core of China. This imperialism would continue until World War II ended in 1945.

- Europeans forced the Chinese government to pay more than $330 million in reparations, a tremendous sum. It was the equivalent of about a year's income for China's central government.

Japan Modernizes Japan's involvement in China was part of its rapid development into a world power. Starting in the 17th century, Japan had mostly isolated itself from trade with Western powers. Then, in 1853, heavily armed American ships, led by Commodore Matthew Perry, sailed into Edo, now called Tokyo. They threatened Japan that they would return and attack the country if it did not allow more foreign trade. Unprepared for battle, the Japanese submitted. They opened two ports for trade with European and American merchants.

Within Japan, the concession to foreigners set off a furious debate. How could Japan protect iteself from industrialized powers while keeping its own culture? The debate led to the overthrow of the government, an event known as the **Meiji Restoration**. A new emperor was seated in 1868. Under him, Japan sent officials to Europe and America to learn how to grow strong enough to protect itself. The government built schools, factories, railroads, a navy modeled on Great Britain's, and an army modeled on Germany's. Japan's military power enabled it, between 1894 and 1905, to defeat China and Russia in wars, as well as to help crush the Boxers.

Japan also learned from Europeans that powerful countries should possess colonies. It formally seized Korea in 1905. This was the first step in creating an East Asian empire—a move that would contribute to the start of World War II.

In the politically and economically competitive environment of the 19th century, modernity seemed to demand the building of empires. The underlying assumption among European powers was that empire promoted economic growth and projected political strength.

Problems with Imperialism By the early 20th century, as the struggles of the workers and the burden of imperialist wars began to take its toll, anti-imperialism gained support. The most popular of those British writers, J.A. Hobson argued in his book *Imperialism: A Study* (1904) that the capitalist system might have been flawed but was not beyond reform. One flaw was imperialist competition for new resources and markets. The accumulation of capital in the hands of a few capitalists who sought greater profit put pressure on government to take over underdeveloped nations and to protect access to them. Hobson then explained how this was justified, based on the needs of a growing population or hopes for quick profits, but that those supporting this greed for territorial acquisition did not consider the associated political and economic costs.

Throughout his prolific career Hobson explained how capitalists demanded protection and support from their government. He further explained that this occurred at a time of great nationalist competition, which meant that protection brought militarism, international tension and war, as demonstrated initially in the Boer War and to a greater extent in the First World War. To Hobson, the colonies that the imperialists demanded did not benefit their nation economically, as the costs of maintaining the empire were too great and the inequalities emerging at home and abroad reflected further flaws.

Hobson believed that the system could be improved through greater global cooperation and planning. In contrast, Vladimir Lenin explained that the imperialist conflicts would cause capitalist nations to destroy each other and usher in the era of communism in his book *Imperialism, The Highest Stage of Capital Development* (1917).

Benefits to Some In the late 20th century, historians revisited the roots of the world economy and the emerging global system. Although French historian Fernand Braudel popularized the idea of a world economy, it was Immanuel Wallerstein, an American social scientist, who popularized the world-systems theory. This theory builds on the work of Hobson and Marxists, such as Lenin, who noted the system's inequality. However, Wallerstein described a much more dynamic system, made up of two main regions:

- The core included highly-developed nations that accumulated capital and demanded resources and markets from undeveloped or lesser-developed regions
- The periphery consisted of regions that provided resources and markets as well as labor needed by the core

Wallerstein traced the roots of this world-system to the mid-16th century. Colonialism became the means by which peripheral states became incorporated into the world economy. However, Wallerstein noted that politics and culture vary within the world economy, so nations could be semi-peripheral at some point and possibly move to core—or the other way around, with Spain as a key example. Although this world-system caused inequalities, its dynamic nature maintained its durability.

KEY TERMS BY THEME

Economics
Age of Imperialism
human capital
John A. Hobson
Vladimir Lenin

Governance
Sepoy Rebellion
Berlin Conference of
   1884–1885
Otto von Bismarck
Fashoda Crisis
Morocco
Boxer Rebellion
Meiji Restoration

Global Exchange
imperialist

Identity
Social Darwinism
The White Man's Burden
Mission Civilisatrice
Joseph Conrad
E. D. Morel
Heart of Darkness
Paul Gauguin
Pablo Picasso
Primitivism
Zulus
Ethiopians
sepoy

Technology
Second Industrial
   Revolution
Minié bullets
breechloader Maxim
   gun
machine gun
malaria
quinine
telegraph
gunboats
infrastructure

Geography
Suez Canal

Questions 1 and 2 refer to the image below.

Georges Dascher, "The French Colonies," the front page of a French school notebook, c. 1900

1. Which of the following most directly led to the spread of ideas such as those expressed in the image?

   a) The desire to disseminate the ideals of the French Revolution

   b) Competition for consumer markets during the second industrial revolution

   c) The cultural influence of Romantic writers and artists

   d) Efforts by Jesuit missionaries to revive Catholicism

2. The colonial relationship depicted in this image was most directly undermined by which of the following?

   a) Ethiopia's defeat of Italy

   b) Britain's defeat of the Zulus

   c) Britain's defeat of the Sepoy Rebellion

   d) The defeat of the Boxer Rebellion by international forces

Questions 3–5 refer to the passage below.

- "Laying of a [telegraph] cable from Kiachow [China] to Port Arthur `[Manchuria], with connection with the Russian-Siberian cable

- German coaling and cable stations in the Red Sea, the West Indies, and near Singapore

- Complete possession of Samoa

- More subsidized German steamship lines to Kiaochow and Korea

- Understanding with France, Spain, Portugal, and the Netherlands about the laying of an independent cable from West Africa through the Congo to German East Africa, Madagascar, Batavia, and Tongkin to Kiaochow

- Development of harbor of Swakopmund and railroads to Windhoek [in German Southwest Africa]"

The Program of the Pan-German League, a German
nationalist organization, 1898

3. The Program of the Pan-German League is best understood within the context of which of the following developments?

   a) The formation of the European Steel and Coal Community

   b) Bismarck's enactment of anti-socialist laws

   c) Germany's shift toward a more antagonistic foreign policy under Wilhelm II

   d) The use of *laissez-faire* policies to stimulate economic growth

4. The policies described in the passage best exemplify which of the following aspects of imperialism?

   a) The frequency of military confrontations between the Great Powers

   b) The technological infrastructure that facilitated imperial expansion

   c) The use of scientific theories as a rationale for colonial domination

   d) The creation of a complex system of alliances to maintain a balance of power

5. In addition to the factors described in the passage, which of the following had the greatest impact on European imperial expansion in the late 19th century?

   a) Improvements in air travel

   b) The development of synthetic fertilizers

   c) The invention of dynamite and other explosives

   d) Advances in medicine to combat disease

Questions 6–8 refer to the passage below.

"Seeing that the Imperialism of the last three decades is clearly condemned as a business policy, in that at enormous expense it has procured a small, bad, unsafe increase of markets, and has jeopardised the entire wealth of the nation in rousing the strong resentment of other nations, we may ask, 'How is the British nation induced to embark upon such unsound business?' The only possible answer is that the business interests of the nation as a whole are subordinated to those of certain sectional interests that usurp control of the national resources and use them for their private gain. This is no strange or monstrous charge to bring; it is the commonest disease of all forms of government. The famous words of Sir Thomas More are as true now as when he wrote them: 'Everywhere do I perceive a certain conspiracy of rich men seeking their own advantage under the name and pretext of the commonwealth.'

Although the new Imperialism has been bad business for the nation, it has been good business for certain classes and certain trades within the nation. The vast expenditure on armaments, the costly wars, the grave risks and embarrassments of foreign policy, the stoppage of political and social reforms within Great Britain, though fraught with great injury to the nation, have served well the present business interests of certain industries and professions."

John A. Hobson, British economist, *Imperialism: A Study*, 1902

6. Hobson's critique of imperialism is best understood in context of which of the following?

    a) Growing public support for decolonization in Africa and Asia

    b) Rising imperialist tensions in the years leading up to the First World War

    c) The increased popularity of fascist parties during the Great Depression

    d) Modern philosophical movements that emphasized human irrationality

7. Which claim about the colonial system did Hobson challenge most directly?

    a) That believers in Social Darwinism were correct

    b) That imperialists were civilizing colonial subjects

    c) That governments benefited from ruling larger territories

    d) That British prosperity relied on natural resources from colonies

8. Hobson's view of imperialism most likely would have been shared by which of the following groups in the early 20th century?

a) Socialists

b) Christian missionaries

c) Industrialists

d) Right-wing nationalists

SHORT-ANSWER QUESTIONS

1. Use the passage below to answer all parts of the question that follows.

"New Imperialism has long been the object of controversy among historians because of its extraordinary speed and scope; by account, the land area of the world controlled by Europeans increased from 35 percent in 1800 to 84.4 percent in 1914…In their fascination with the motivations of the imperialists, most historians took for granted that the European powers and the United States had the technical…means to turn their ambition into reality…Technology is now widely recognized as a necessary, if not sufficient, explanation for the New Imperialism in Africa and Asia."

Daniel Headrick, *Tools of Empire*, 1981

a) Explain how ONE piece of evidence supports Headrick's argument regarding the reason for New Imperialism from 1870-1914.

b) Explain how ONE piece of evidence undermines Headrick's argument regarding the reason for New Imperialism from 1870-1914.

c) Explain ONE example from the Age of Exploration in the 15th or 16th century that provoked a similar argument described by Headrick.

2. Answer all parts of the question that follows.

a) Describe ONE example of how imperial encounters with non-European peoples influenced the styles and/or subject matter of artists from 1870-1914.

b) Describe ONE example of how imperial encounters with non-European peoples influenced the styles and/or subject matter of writers from 1870-1914.

c) Explain ONE example from the Age of Exploration (1500-1700) on how encounters with non-European peoples influenced European culture or society.

LONG ESSAY QUESTIONS

1. Evaluate the major reason for a change in European attitudes toward imperialism after 1870.

2. Evaluate ONE important change between European expansion during the European Age of Exploration (16th-18th centuries) and the New Imperialism of the 19th century.

REFLECT ON THE CHAPTER ESSENTIAL QUESTION

1. In one to three paragraphs, explain what caused the intensification of European efforts at global control and the resulting tensions among the Great Powers.

WRITE AS A HISTORIAN: IDENTIFY CONTINUITY AND CHANGE

Historians often write about continuity and change over time—what remains constant and what evolves. One historian might view European imperialism as evidence of continuity in history: people have been fighting and exploiting others as far back in history as we have evidence for. Another historian might view imperialism in the context of change: the weapons and tactics of 19th century Europeans differed greatly even from those of 17th century Europeans. Some have argued violence of all sorts, including imperialism and war, has been slowly decreasing in human society. Writing clearly and powerfully about continuity and change over time is a required skill on the AP exam.

To think and write like a historian, practice understanding historical events in terms of continuity and change over time. Look for ways that people or societies stay the same. Look for the turning-point events that signal important shifts. Then consider how these two forces of continuity and change interacted. International trade was an example of continuity during the period of imperialism. However, the development of steam-powered ships and locomotives brought change as these technologies revolutionized trade.

Also examine "ripple effects"—the series of changes that spread out from a main effect. How often have merchants, armies, or missionaries moved into a region and affected its history in ways both large and small? Such details often set into motion the big patterns that keep repeating, such as the rise of empires, forced migrations, the spread of diseases, and exchanges of ideas and cultures.

Which three of the statements below best illustrate continuity?

1. The search for raw materials and markets for manufactured goods fostered imperialist expansion in Asia and Africa, much as it had earlier in the Americas.

2. This latest wave of imperialist expansion was once again fueled by economic rivalries among European powers.

3. Revolutionary advancements in weaponry combined with the development of capitalism combined to ensure European domination over less-developed regions.

4. Even as European former colonies in Central and South America gained independence, new colonial uprisings sprang up, such as the creation of India's Congress Party and the Boxer Rebellion in China.

5. Thanks to better medical techniques such as quinine for malaria and use of antiseptics, Europeans were more successful at adapting to life overseas.

Which of the following topic sentences best addresses the reasoning skill of continuity and change over time?

6. a. The "new imperialism" of the late 19th and early 20th centuries was promoted in European nations by interest groups that included politicians, military officials and soldiers, missionaries, explorers, journalists, and intellectuals.

   b. Millions of Europeans carried their culture abroad to the Americas and elsewhere through emigration and helped create a variety of mixed cultures around the world.

   c. The European imperial outreach of the 19th century was in some ways a continuation of three centuries of colonization, but it also resulted from the economic pressures and necessities of a maturing industrial capitalist economy.

18

Tension between Objectivity and Subjectivity

"I cannot send you my explanation of the word 'Romantic,' because it would be 125 sheets long."

—Friedrich Schlegel, in a letter to his brother Wilhelm, 1793

Essential Question: Explain the tension between ideas of objectivity and scientific realism and the ideas of subjectivity and individual expression.

The 150-year period from the late 18th century through the early 20th century featured an ideological struggle between two worldviews. **Objectivity** emphasized facts with little interpretation. **Subjectivity** encouraged emotions with more interpretation. Each part of the period was a direct response to, and a reaction against, the period immediately before it. In art, literature, and science, when objective, universal ways of thinking became the norm, the pendulum would soon swing back toward subjective, skeptical questioning.

Throughout this period, artists became social activists. Scientists made discoveries that would forever change humans' relationship with the world around them. Musicians created masterpieces that transcended notes on a page. Philosophers developed social and economic theories that continue to be tested and questioned. The tension between objectivity and subjectivity only served to propel great art and thinking forward.

Romanticism in Art, Music, and Writing

The Enlightenment emphasized the principles of logic, reason, and rationalism. It was followed by the **Romantic period**, which lasted from the late-18th to mid-19th century. Romanticism was a backlash against the Enlightenment's rationalism and materialism, foreshadowed by Rousseau's interest in introspection and feelings. (See Chapters 10, 11, and 12.) Romanticism chose subjective emotion and creativity over objective logic and reason.

Romanticism was also a rejection of the **Neoclassical** style—a popular movement during the Enlightenment that employed Classical themes and linear design. Romanticism rejected Neoclassicism's standards of order and balance, replacing them with greater appreciation of imagination and emotion.

Looking Inward Romantics of the 19th century tended to avoid fields of politics and science, instead expressing themselves through art, music, and literature. They also were historians, but they documented the world around them in more creative and expressive ways. Romantics encouraged **introspection**, or a deep focus on the self and one's emotions. They examined human personality and moods, and they were fascinated by the personalities of exceptional figures such as mythic heroes. The great figures of the Romantic period focused on the purity of nature as a way to abandon what they considered to be the corruption of their modern society.

Individual Expression By the end of the Romantic era, a new view of the artist had emerged. Artists of all kinds—from painters and sculptors to composers and authors—now were seen as supremely individual creators. Their work was not dictated by the church or a state and was limited only by their own imaginations. Creative spirits were valued over a strict adherence to formal rules and traditional procedures. There was now a new emphasis on imagination as a gateway to a higher spiritual truth.

Romanticism in Art

Artists of the Enlightenment attempted to depict reason and order. Their compositions were filled with traditional mythological figures and symbolism that praised logic and reason. Romantic artists broke from such conventions to emphasize less tangible subjects such as emotion, nature, and individuality.

Landscapes British artists such as J. M. W. Turner (1775–1851) and John Constable (1776–1837) used effects of light, atmosphere, and color to awe at the grandeur of the natural world. Their landscapes reflected one aspect of nationalism: pride in the beauty of one's homeland.

The German painter most famous for his landscapes was Caspar David Friedrich (1774–1840). He preferred to show vast, mysterious landscapes and seascapes. For example, *The Wanderer Above the Sea of Fog* (1818), portrays a solitary individual looking outward over a turbulent sea. Friedrich shows the individual from behind. As a result, the viewer cannot see the individual's face to know whether he is feeling awe, fear, domination, or some other emotion.

Politics While many Romantics were more fascinated by nature than by human events, others focused on individual heroism, battle scenes, and dramatic conflict. Some expressed strong nationalism in their works:

- **Francisco Goya** (1746–1828), a Spanish painter, portrayed dramatic, sometimes violent scenes of historical conflict. Among his best known works was *The Third of May* (1808). It shows Spanish rebels being executed by a French firing squad during the Napoleonic wars.

- **Eugène Delacroix** (1798–1863), of France, often painted contemporary scenes in vibrant colors. His work, *Liberty Leading the People* (1830) reflected the zealous committment to equality and liberty of the revolutionaries in France in 1830.

Romanticism in Music

Just as Romantic artists strove to free themselves from the confines of the preceding Enlightenment period, so did Romantic composers and musicians. They prized originality and individuality in their compositions. They worked to be less formulaic, and they freely experimented with various styles that could showcase personal emotional expression.

- Ludwig van Beethoven (1770–1827) was trained in the Classical style. However, his increasing use of dramatic changes in pitch and volume and innovative harmonies marked him as one of the first composers in the Romantic style. His nine symphonies and many sonatas remain widely preformed today.

- Frédéric Chopin (1810–1849) wrote primarily for piano. He took advantage of improvements in the piano design that allowed a greater range of volume and tone quality.

- Building on the work of early Romantics, Russian composer Pyotr Ilyich Tchaikovsky (1840–1893) wrote impressive symphonies and other works, including a ballet, *The Nutcracker.* Like many Romantics, he was influenced by national pride. His best-known work might be *The 1812 Overture,* a tribute to Russian bravery in stopping the invasion by Napoleon.

Historical Influences and Wagner Beethoven, Chopin, Tchaikovsky, and other Romantic composers often included folk melodies in their works. Using these tunes was one more expression of nationalism in the 19th century.

Few composers drew upon traditional culture as much as **Richard Wagner** (1813–1883) did. Wagner combined Germanic and Nordic mythology, expressive music, and the cult of the hero to create that represented German nationalism. Because of this, long after his death, he became a favorite among extreme German nationalists, including many Nazis.

Though Wagner drew upon the past for content, the form of his music was innovative. Compared to previous composers, he used far larger orchestras and choruses, wrote much longer pieces, and used innovative harmonies. Listener found his works awe-inspiring, even if they found them exhausting and, at times, filled with clashing sounds they were not used to hearing. His most famous work was the *The Ring of the Nibelung,* a set of four operas. A performance of the full Ring cycle takes about 15 hours spread over four days.

Romanticism in Literature

Much of the inspiration for literature during the Romantic period came from premodern times. Writers looked back to a world before industrialization and the emphasis on reason reshaped how people related to each other and to the natural world. Writers such as **Sir Walter Scott** were attracted to the medieval romance and folklorists such as the Grimm brothers resurrected traditional tales. Others, including **William Blake, William Wordsworth, Percy Bysshe**

Shelley, and John Keats, emphasized their emotional reactions to beauty, nature, or the spiritual world. Mary Shelley wrote *Frankenstein,* a work that explored emotional and supernatural realms, representing another move away from the Enlightenment's reason and science. (See Chapter 15.)

Many Romantic writers took inspiration from the growth of cultural nationalism. Throughout their work, they encouraged the development:

In 2012, the United States issued a stamp of Boris Karloff's famous portrayal of the monster created by Dr. Frankenstein in a 1931 movie.

Credit: Getty Images

- **Johann Wolfgang von Goethe** (1749–1832) was one of the most influential German writers in history. People considered his works, such as his play, **Faust,** as expressions of an essential and distinctive spirit of the German people.

- **Lord Byron** (1788–1824), an English poet and satirist, admired both nationalism and classical Greek culture. He beliefs inspired him to fight on behalf of the Greeks in their war for independence from the Ottoman Turks. He died in the conflict in 1824, at the age of 36.

- **Victor Hugo** of France (1802–1885) was a prolific writer whose novel *Les Misérables* provided a sympathetic account of the lives of the poor and outcast people of France.

Materialism in Philosophy, Science, and Economics

Romantic and liberal ideas inspired anti-monarchical revolutions across Europe in 1848. The failure of the uprisings to replace royal authority is reflected in the name for the period from 1837 to 1901. They are known as the **Victorian Era,** after Queen Victoria of England, whose reign spanned these years.

Materialism is the philosophy that all matter—including the human mind and its consciousness—are the result of physical processes of nature and the human body. Materialism is closely related to **physicalism**, because of the latter's belief that the awareness of the human mind is the by-product of physical processes, such as the biochemistry of the human brain.

Philosophy of Positivism

Positivism is the philosophy that science alone provides knowledge. It emphasizes the rational and scientific analysis of nature and human affairs. It is based on two principles:

- Knowledge is based on sensory experience, not on intuition.

- Knowledge reflects data that can be observed, not on faith.

While hints of positivism can be seen in ancient philosophy and in some works of medieval European thought, the roots of positivism lie most clearly in the Enlightenment and its clear focus on reason.

Science of Charles Darwin

During the Enlightenment, scientists viewed the world as stable and orderly. For example, Isaac Newton and others proposed unchanging laws to explain how planets moved. Biologists categorized species. However, the ideas of Charles Darwin's undermined this view. His emphasis on gradual but nonstop change in animals caused scientists in all fields to rethink their focus on stability.

Charles Darwin (1809–1882) was an English naturalist who formulated a bold theory after returning from a voyage around the world in 1837. More than two decades later, he published *On the Origin of Species* (1859), a book that stated that species change—evolve—by a process of **natural selection**. Members of a species that have traits that help them survive in a particular environment will have more offspring than members without that trait. Eventually, all members of the species will be born with that trait. Darwin's work became the foundation of modern evolutionary studies.

Darwin's work initially shocked Victorian society by suggesting that animals and humans shared common ancestry. Many Christians thought his ideas about changes in species and shared ancestry went against the teachings of the Bible. However, his focus on evidence rather than religious tradition appealed to the rising class of professional scientists. By the time of his death in 1882, the theory of evolution had spread through all of science, literature, and politics.

The Economics of Karl Marx

The ideas of Karl Marx about history reflected the intellectual currents of his period. Marx was a materialist because he focused on physical processes such as how people produced goods. In contrast, other historians focused on abstract ideas, such as those who saw history as the story of freedom. Marx's ideas were positivist because he attempted to ground them in the facts of history. Finally, like Darwin, Marx tried to find laws underlying change.

Realist Art and Literature

While Hugo's *Les Misérables* expressed the drama typical of Romantic literature, it also pointed toward a new development. Writers and painters were examining the struggles of common people in their own country. They created **Realist** art and literature, the accurate, detailed, depiction of nature and contemporary life. Realism rejected imaginative fantasies in favor of strict observation. Painters and writers of this style depicted the lives of ordinary people. Creating a clear depiction of the world around them meant that Realists also drew attention to the social problems of their time.

Realist Art

Artists in the Romantic period prized emotion over subject matter, but the pendulum swung back during the Realist period. Artists of the 19th century strove to depict life as accurately as possible. Some used their work to make political statements about the living conditions of those around them, especially the working poor.

France was the center of European Realism, especially through the work of Gustave Courbet. In works such as *Burial in Ornans*, he emphasized the material nature of life. This was in contrast to the long tradition of European painting that at least showed the influence of the spiritual world. Courbet was strongly opposed to any idealization in his art, and he urged other artists to make the commonplace and contemporary their focus as well. From France, the movement spread to other parts of Europe, especially Russia and Germany. It then crossed the Atlantic to the United States.

Realist Painters and Print Artists		
Individual	**Works**	**Legacy**
Gustave Courbet 1819–1877 France	• *The Artist's Studio* • *The Stone Breakers*	Incorporated political views into his art
Jean-François Millet 1814–1875 France	• *The Gleaners*	Portrayed the dignity of French peasants
Ilya Repin 1844–1930 Russia	• *Barge Haulers on the Volga*	Connected Russian art to the European mainstream for the first time
Adolph von Menzel 1815–1905 Germany	• *History of Frederick the Great* • *Iron Rolling Mill*	Developed illustration as an important art form
Honoré Daumier 1808–1879 France	• *The Laundress* • *Gargantua*	Created satirical caricatures, paintings, sculptures, and lithographs

The Gleaners (1857) by French painter Jean-François Millet is among the most famous Realist paintings. It portrayed the hard labor by women working in the fields.

Credit: Getty Images

Realist Literature

Just as Realist painters wanted to show the world the actual conditions of those on the bottom of the social order, so too did novelists. Honoré de Balzac, for example, attempted to create an almost encyclopedic portrait of the whole range of his French society. As such, his series *La Comédie humaine*, or *The Human Comedy*, pioneered the Realist movement in literature.

Realism entered the mainstream of European literature during the 1860s and 1870s. Authors emphasized strict objectivity, avoiding implausible, exotic elements. They detached themselves from their subject matter, unlike the deeply connected Romantic authors who preceded them. Realism writing had a very clear, very emotionally restrained criticism of the social environment and values of the time.

One significant result of literary Realism was **Naturalism**, a late 19th- and early 20th-century movement that aimed at an even more accurate representation of reality. Naturalistic authors emphasized **scientific determinism**, or the belief that all natural events and social changes are determined exclusively by the events that preceded them. The French novelist Émile Zola was the leading author of the Naturalist movement.

Realist Writers		
Individual	**Works**	**Legacy**
Honoré de Balzac 1799–1850 France	• *The Human Comedy* • *The Unknown Masterpiece*	Helped establish the traditional form of the novel
Gustave Flaubert 1821–1880 France	• *Madame Bovary* • *Sentimental Education*	Marked the shift in French literature from Romanticism to Realism
Charles Dickens 1812–1870 England	• *Tale of Two Cities* • *A Christmas Carol* • *David Copperfield*	Portrayed the lives of the poor, sometimes based on his own childhood
George Eliot (Mary Ann Evans) 1819–1880 England	• *Middlemarch* • *Silas Marner*	Described the emptiness of middle-class domestic life and marriage
Leo Tolstoy 1828–1910 Russia	• *War and Peace* • *Anna Karenina*	Delved deeply into the psychology of his characters
Émile Zola 1840–1902 France	• *Les Rougon-Macquart* • *J'accuse*	Depicted social injustice and promoted political liberalization in France
Thomas Hardy 1840–1928 England	• *Tess of the d'Urbervilles* • *Jude the Obscure* • *Wessex Tales*	Wrote about his native Wessex and the working class with sympathy

Modernism in Intellectual and Cultural Life

Realism was most influential during the Victorian Era, a period of strict morals and social conventions. In reaction to these limits, the **Modernism** movement embraced industrialization, social change, and scientific advancement. The Modernists pioneered new ideas in psychology and political theory. Their goal was to move beyond the Realists' strict interpretations of the world around them to find less literal modes of expression.

Irrationalism

The philosophy of **Irrationalism** moved beyond rational interpretations of humans and their surroundings to focus instead on their impulses. Irrationalists believed that conflict and struggle led to progress and suggested that life did not need to be explained only by rational methods of science, but also by the spirit. Irrationalism explored humans' biological roots through evolution.

- **Friedrich Nietzsche** (1844–1900) was a German who questioned the fundamental, cultural values of Western philosophy and morality. He influenced a wide range of artists and politicians with his examination of how individuals can lead meaningful lives.

- **Georges Sorel** (1847–1922) was a French philosopher who argued that social change required revolutionary action. His ideas were later used by dictators to support totalitarian action.

- **Henri Bergson** (1859–1941) was a French philosopher who emphasized change and evolution. He inspired a group of thinkers known as process metaphysicians.

Natural Sciences

Developments in the natural sciences such as quantum mechanics and Einstein's theory of relativity undermined the physics of Isaac Newton as an objective way to describe nature. Modernist scientists placed human thought and presence at the center of their practices.

Sigmund Freud Austrian neurologist **Sigmund Freud** was the founder of **psychoanalysis**, a therapeutic technique related to the study of the unconscious mind. Freud's work helped create psychology as an independent discipline, separate from either philosophy or neurology. Psychoanalysis led to investigations of human behavior that gradually revealed the need for more subtle methods of analysis. Freud also delved into the human psyche and wrote about the power of irrational motivations and humans' ongoing struggle between the conscious and unconscious parts of their minds.

Albert Einstein While Isaac Newton regarded scientists as observers, Albert Einstein believed scientists must be central to their own scientific realities. His theories were less objective than strict Newtonian mechanics. Einstein's theory of relativity, for example, his life's greatest work, relies on the relationship between humans and their environment, time, and space. Einstein is generally considered the most influential physicist of the 20th century.

Natural Scientists		
Individual	**Works**	**Legacy**
Max Planck 1858–1947 Germany	Developed **quantum theory**, which revolutionized the understanding of atomic and subatomic processes	Changed how people understood space and time and contributed to the study of thermodynamics
Marie Curie 1867–1934 Poland and France	Developed a way to isolate pure radium as well as the element polonium	Became the first woman to win a Nobel Prize and developed the theory of radioactivity

Modern Art

Realist artists sought to depict their subjects accurately. However, in a world with photography, painters felt less need to portray the world exactly as it appeared In contrast. This shift led to **Modern art**, a style that was more subjective, abstract, and expressive than most European art throughout history. It included several movements:

- **Impressionism** emphasized light and color as the true subjects of their work. It reflected the influence of African and Japanese traditions.

- **Post-Impressionism** focused more on order than on light and color.

- **Expressionism** focused on portraying the internal feelings of the artists rather than showing a subject accurately. The content often looked somewhat realistic, but modified in order to focus on a mood.

- **Fauvism** emphasized vibrant rather than realistic colors.

- **Cubism** abandoned the need for subject matter altogether in an attempt to depict three-dimensional subjects on a two-dimensional plane.

The rapid evolution of art made the late 19th and early 20th centuries a time of experiment and controversy. Traditional content, such as portraits of aristocrats and landscapes, gave way to depictions of the activities of common people. Then artists began to downplay the importance of content altogether, emphasizing light or color or emotion. Art became nonrepresentational. The shifts in style and content excited some museum goers and angered others.

Van Gogh's series of paintings of sunflowers, like those of many modern artists, focused more on the process of creativity than on the subject matter.

Credit: Wikimedia Commons.

Modern Artists			
Individual and Country	**Style**	**Works**	**Legacy**
Claude Monet (1840–1926) France	Impressionism	• *Impression, Sunrise* • *Water Lilies (series)* • *Haystacks (series)*	Focused on the use of light and color by painting the same scene at different times of day
Edgar Degas (1834–1917) France	Impressionism	• *Woman with Chrysanthemums* • *The Dance Class*	Depicted everyday life in Paris
Henri Matisse (1869–1954) France	Fauvism	• *Woman with a Hat* • *La Danse*	Used brilliant colors to evoke strong reactions among viewers
Paul Cézanne (1839–1906) France	Post-Impressionism	• *The Bathers* • *The Card Players*	Took a step toward representational art with paintings the emphasized the painting itself rather than the subject matter
Vincent Van Gogh (1853–1890) Netherlands and France	Post-Impressionism	• *The Starry Night* • *Sunflowers*	Used forceful brushwork to express emotion more than subject matter
Pablo Picasso (1881–1973) Spain and France	Cubism and others	• *Les Demoiselles d'Avignon* • *Guernica* • *Untitled sculpture in Chicago*	Represented multiple perspectives in one painting

HISTORICAL PERSPECTIVES: WHAT DID FRANKENSTEIN REPRESENT?

Mary Shelley's Gothic thriller, *A Modern Prometheus,* is better known as the story of Dr. Frankenstein and the creature he brought to life. Literary critics and historians have debated the tale's meaning since it was written.

Dangers of Modernity In 1818, few could believe an 18-year-old woman could create such a complex story that artfully intertwined the work of the leading scholars. Instead they saw Mary Shelley as a passive vessel describing the world of her feminist mother, Mary Wollstonecraft, her radical father, John Godwin, and Romantic poet husband, Percy Bysshe Shelley. Despite growing up in this modern/liberal environment, early interpretations of Mary Shelley's Victor Frankenstein and his Monster described the story as a conservative or at least moderate cautionary tale, warning against the excesses of the French Revolution and even the abolition of slavery.

Over time, the cautionary tale against modernity grew stronger, especially with James Whale's iconic 1931 film *Frankenstein*. Whale not only changed the interpretation, but the genre from Gothic to the first work of science fiction. As such, Whale showed a story that warned against the uncontrollable danger of a selfish drive for scientific accomplishment. However, almost 100 years later, Elizabeth Young, an expert in literature and gender relations, found evidence to show the persistence of a "black Frankenstein" metaphor first used by anti-abolitionists, seen throughout political cartoons of the late 19th century, and captured in the final scene of Whale's movie, when the Monster was lynched.

A Victim Deserving Empathy In the 1970s, as historians tried to understand the history of the masses, it seemed fitting that George Levine edited *The Endurance of 'Frankenstein': Essays on Mary Shelley's Novel*, in which scholars explored who Mary Shelley was and how her life shaped the lives of her characters. In one such essay, Lee Sterrenburg, a professor of English, "got into the mind" of Mary Shelley, as was his specialty. This analysis revealed that Mary Shelley did not just observe but broke with Enlightenment rationalism and saw with her own Romantic mind. She opened the door to subjective understandings of the world and empathy for the Monster.

A Tale of Feminism In this same series of essays, Ellen Moers used Muriel Spark's 1951 biography of Mary Shelley to provide a feminist interpretation. Through this biographical feminist lens, Moers noted parallels between Mary Shelley's life and that of Frankenstein and his Monster. Moers paid attention to Mary Shelley's formative experiences as a motherless child and a mother of stillborn children. Moers suggested that it was a combination of these uniquely female life experiences and constant reading of the intellectuals of her time that shaped the story of the unnamed monster. Suggesting that maybe the early metaphors were accurate to the extent that the struggle between Victor Frankenstein and his Monster were those same personal struggles faced by Mary and the liberal ideas swirling around her (but not to the degree that she was fully anti-revolution or anti-abolition). Again the notion that circumstances made the Monster do horrible things, instead of the Monster being inherently evil, surfaces.

By the novel's 200th anniversary, all of these interpretations of Mary Shelley's Monster prove that whatever her Monster meant to her, it continues to have meaning. Whether it is to explore liberal-conservative tension, the power of science, the impact of traumatic experiences, or as has been noted most recently, to remind people that even those who may look like Monsters are people, too.

KEY TERMS BY THEME

Identity

objectivity

subjectivity

Continuity and Change

Romantic period

Neoclassical

introspection

Victorian Era

materialism

physicalism

positivism

natural selection

naturalism

scientific determinism

modernism

irrationalism

psychoanalysis

quantum theory

Modern art

Impressionism

Post-Impressionism

Expressionism

Fauvism

Cubism

nonrepresentational art

Picasso startled viewers with his innovative portrayal of people. This one, *Three Musicians,* was completed in 1921.

Credit: Wikimedia Commons.

Questions 1–3 refer to the painting below.

'The Lord on high is mightier than the noise of many waters, yea, than the mighty waves of the sea.'

Wood engraving from a painting by J. M. W. Turner, *The Shipwreck* (1805). Tate Gallery, London.

Credit: Getty Images

1. The painting by Turner above, as well as works by artists such as Goya and Delacroix, are examples of the artistic movement known as

   a) Neoclassicism

   b) Impressionism

   c) Romanticism

   d) Mannerism

2. As demonstrated in the painting, how was this artistic movement in opposition to certain principles of the Enlightenment?

   a) It provided exact and detailed images.

   b) It emphasized the natural over the human-made.

   c) It suppressed emotional responses.

   d) It celebrated the rule of reason.

3. Which of the following authors is considered a literary exponent of this same movement?

a) Percy Bysshe Shelley

b) Charles Dickens

c) William Thackeray

d) Honoré de Balzac

Questions 4 and 5 refer to the following passage.

"In demanding from a citizen contributions for the mitigation of distress . . . the state is . . . reversing its function, and diminishing that liberty to exercise the faculties which it was instituted to maintain. Pervading all nature we may see at work a stern discipline, which is a little cruel that it may be very kind. That state of universal warfare maintained throughout the lower creation, to the great perplexity of many worthy people, is at bottom the most merciful provision that the circumstances admit of. The poverty of the incapable, the distresses that come upon the imprudent, the starvation of the idle, and those shoulderings aside of the weak by the strong, which leave so many "in shallows and in miseries," are the decrees of a large, farseeing benevolence. It seems hard that an unskillfulness, which with all its efforts he cannot overcome, should entail hunger upon the artisan. It seems hard that a laborer incapacitated by sickness from competing with his stronger fellows, should have to bear the resulting privations. It seems hard that widows and orphans should be left to struggle for life or death. Nevertheless, when regarded not separately, but in connection with the interests of universal humanity, these harsh fatalities are seen to be full of the highest beneficence—the same beneficence which brings to early graves the children of diseased parents, and singles out the low-spirited, the intemperate, and the debilitated as the victims of an epidemic."

Herbert Spencer, *Social Statics*, 1851

4. This passage can best be tied to what scientific theory espoused about this same period of time?

a) theory of natural selection

b) the germ theory

c) Marxist socialism

d) theory of relativity

5. What system found support in the author's Social Darwinism?

a) Progressivism

b) Imperialism

c) Reformism

d) Scientism

Questions 6–8 refer to the following passage.

"To examine the effects of violence it is necessary to start from its long-term consequences and not from its immediate results. . . .

We have the right to conclude from this that [union-related] violence, perpetrated in the course of strikes by proletarians who desire the overthrow of the State, must not be confused with the acts of savagery. . . .

The immense successes obtained by industrial civilization ha[ve] created the belief that, in the near future, happiness will be produced automatically for everybody. . . .

The optimist in politics is an inconstant and even dangerous man, because he takes no account of the great difficulties presented by his projects; . . . He frequently thinks that small reforms of the political system and, above all, of government personnel will be sufficient to direct the movement of society in such a way as to mitigate those evils of the modern world which seem so hideous to sensitive souls. . . . Yet men who are participating in great social movements always picture their coming action in the form of images of battle in which their cause is certain to triumph."

Georges Sorel, *Reflections on Violence*, 1908

6. What do people such as Sorel and other anti-capitalists advocate in order to achieve societal transformation?

   a) measured political reforms

   b) acts of savagery

   c) proletariat strikes

   d) automatic changes

7. Which school of philosophy is best represented by this passage?

   a) Irrationalism

   b) Realism

   c) Romanticism

   d) Expressionism

8. Which thinkers would most likely agree with the ideas expressed in this passage?

   a) Planck and Curie

   b) Delacroix and Turner

   c) Nietzsche and Bergson

   d) Wagner and Chopin

SHORT-ANSWER QUESTIONS

1. Use the passage below to answer all parts of the question that follows.

"Classicism assumes the existence of a perfect order, hidden but discoverable beneath the chaos of human experience. But the assumption is not often justified by the world around us, and certainly was not justified by the succession of events in France for several decades after 1789—the tumult of the Revolution, the hysteria of the Terror, the bloody grandeur of Napoleon's triumphs, the shattering disillusion after his fall, and all the subsequent corruption and dissension. Yet classical artists continued to put a premium on balance, precision, and rule in a world that was lopsided, confused, and unpredictable. The romantics would have none of their outworn formulas."

J. Canaday, *Mainstreams of Modern Art*,1959

a) Describe the main idea expressed in the passage by Canady.

b) Explain ONE piece of evidence supporting the main argument.

c) Explain ONE piece of evidence contradicting the main argument.

2. Answer all parts of the question that follows.

a) Describe ONE continuity between the themes of Realist artists and writers and those of earlier European artists and writers of the 18th and 19th centuries.

b) Describe ONE change between the themes of Realist artists and writers and those of earlier European artists and writers of the 18th and 19th centuries.

c) Explain ONE important reason for the continuity or change outlined in part a or b.

LONG ESSAY QUESTIONS

1. Evaluate the extent to which scientific advancements influenced artistic expression and the search for truth during the 19th century.

2. Evaluate the extent to which Modernism differed from Romanticism.

REFLECT ON THE CHAPTER ESSENTIAL QUESTION

1. In one to three paragraphs, explain the tension between the ideas of objectivity and scientific realism and the ideas of subjectivity and individual expression.

Some historical events have far more impact than others. These turning points mark the end of one period and the beginning of another. The choice of turning points reflects what a historian considers important. An art historian might focus on shifts in content or style in painting. A historian focused on economics might select changes in how people produced goods. AP® European history is divided into four periods:

- Circa 1450 to 1648 (invention of the printing press to the Peace of Westphalia)

- Circa 1648 to 1815 (formation of nation-states to the defeat of Napoleon)

- Circa 1815 to 1914 (Congress of Vienna to the start of World War I)

- Circa 1914 to 2001 (World War I to the 9/11 attacks)

To write using specific evidence, refer to historical periods and movements that occur within them. Knowing why they exist and how they were named gives you a clue about their significance. Delving further into specific art and music of the time can help enrich your word choice and descriptions.

For each statement, identify the movement's name and its time frame. Then, in your own words, explain in one sentence how it reflected other changes.

1. Romanticism emerged in late 18th-century Europe. This movement placed an emphasis on individual heroism, glorification of nature, and the importance of emotion. It was a response to the classicism and scientific rationalism of the Enlightenment, as well as to industrialism, which was causing population growth and urban problems. *The Third of May* by painter Francisco Goya and "Liebesträum No. 3" by composer Franz Liszt are two artistic expressions of the Romantic era.

2. The artistic movement known as Realism began after the revolutions of 1848. It was a rejection of Romanticism, drama, and emotionalism. Instead, it focused on real-life, sometimes ugly, portrayals that reflected social, economic, and political realities. It relied on direct observation of an increasingly modern world. *The Third Class Carriage* by Honoré Daumier and "Un Bel Di Vedremo" from *Madame Butterfly* by composer Giacomo Puccini both depicted Realism in life.

3. Modernism was a philosophical as well as artistic movement that arose in reaction to huge transformations in Western society. Influencing factors included industrialization, urbanization, and the horrors of World War I. Modernism rejected religion and the certainty of Enlightenment ideals. It focused on defying conventions. *Les Demoiselles d'Avignon* by artist Pablo Picasso and *Pierrot Lunaire* Op. 21 by composer Arnold Schoenberg clearly illustrated the fragmentations of the modern world.

PERIOD 3: Review

DOCUMENT-BASED QUESTION 1

Directions: Question 1 is based on the accompanying documents. The documents have been edited for the purpose of this exercise. You are advised to spend 15 minutes planning and 45 minutes writing your answer.

In your response you should do the following:

- **Thesis:** Make a defensible claim that establishes a line of reasoning and consists of one or more sentences found in one place.
- **Contextualization:** Relate the argument to a broader historical context.
- **Document Evidence:** Use content from at least six documents.
- **Outside Evidence:** Use one piece of evidence not in the documents.
- **Document Sourcing:** Explain how or why the point of view, purpose, situation, or intended audience is relevant for at least three documents.
- **Analysis:** Show the relationships among pieces of historical evidence and use them to support, qualify, or modify an argument.

1. Evaluate the significant factors that led to the development of industrial competition in Europe between 1800 and 1890.

Document 1

Source: Napoleon Bonaparte, The Berlin Decree, November 21, 1806.

That this monstrous abuse of the right of blockade has no other aim than to prevent communication among the nations and to raise the commerce and the industry of England upon the ruins of that of the continent. That, since this is the obvious aim of England, whoever deals on the continent in English goods, thereby favors and renders himself an accomplice of her designs. That this policy of England, worthy of the earliest stages of barbarism, has profited that power to the detriment of every other nation.

We have consequently decreed and do decree that which follows: All commerce and all correspondence with the British Isles are forbidden. Consequently letters or packages directed to England or to an Englishman or written in the English language shall not pass through the mails and shall be seized.

Every individual who is an English subject, of whatever state or condition he may be, who shall be discovered in any country occupied by our troops or by those of our allies, shall be made a prisoner of war.

Trade in English goods is prohibited, and all goods belonging to England or coming from her factories or her colonies are declared lawful prize....Half of the product resulting from the confiscation of the goods and possessions declared a lawful prize by the preceding articles shall be applied to indemnify the merchants for the losses they have experienced by the capture of merchant vessel.

Document 2

Source: Debate in Parliament on the British Corn Laws, 1814

The Petition characterized the Report of the committee as a proposition which had for its object the raising the import price of corn, and compromising the commercial interests of the country for the temporary interests of the landlords; and as "an unhallowed attempt to bring ruin and devastation on the country, to annihilate the manufactures, and force our artizans to emigrate to countries where the means of subsistence were more easily obtained." The greatest caution and deliberation in legislating upon this important subject. It was but last year that it was asked, could any person expect to live to see corn so low as 10s. 6d. a bushel. Gentlemen had only to look to the present price, and the change that took place would sufficiently prove the necessity of proceeding with all possible care.

Document 3

Source: The Peterloo Massacre, 1819. On August 16, 1819, about 70,000 people gathered in St. Peter's Fields in Manchester, England, to demand reforms in Parliament. When officials tried to arrest the speakers, officers attacked the crowd, killing 15 people and injuring hundreds more.

Credit: Getty Images

Document 4

Source: Resolutions of the Select committee of the House of Commons on Artisans and Machinery, 21 May 1824, Hansard's *Parliamentary Debates,* New Series, XI, 813-814.

European Economic Growth, 1830 –1890			
Country	1830	1860	1890
Great Britain	$375	$500	$800
Germany	$225	$325	$500
France	$225	$325	$500
Italy	$225	$250	$250
Russia	$200	$200	$200

Amounts are estimates of GDP per capita in 1960 U.S. dollars.

Source: Adapted from Paul Bairoch, "Europe's Gross National Product: 1800–1975," Journal of European Economic History, 5 (2), 286.

Document 5

Source: Friedrich List, German economist, "The National System of Political Economy," 1841

I saw clearly that free competition between two nations which are highly civilised can only be mutually beneficial in case both of them are in a nearly equal position of industrial development, and that any nation which owing to misfortunes is behind others in industry, commerce, and navigation, while she nevertheless possesses the mental and material means for developing those acquisitions, must first of all strengthen her own individual powers, in order to fit herself to enter into free competition with more advanced nations. In a word, I perceived the distinction between cosmopolitical and political economy. I felt that Germany must abolish her internal tariffs, and by the adoption of a common uniform commercial policy towards foreigners, strive to attain to the same degree of commercial and industrial development to which other nations have attained by means of their commercial policy.

Document 6

Source: Prince Albert, describing the Great Exhibition, 1851

Man is approaching a more complete fulfillment of that great and sacred mission which he has to perform in this world... to conquer nature to his use... In promoting [the progress of the human race], we are accomplishing the will of the great and blessed God.

Document 7

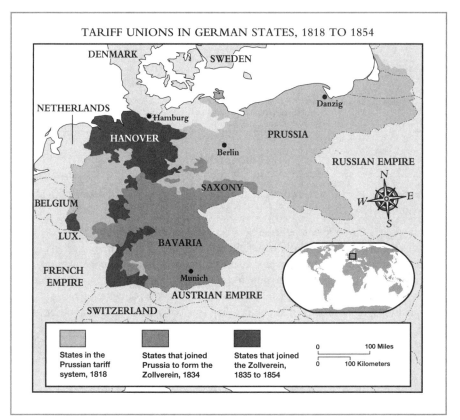

TARIFF UNIONS IN GERMAN STATES, 1818 TO 1854

DOCUMENT-BASED QUESTION 2

Directions: Question 2 is based on the accompanying documents. The documents have been edited for the purpose of this exercise. You are advised to spend 15 minutes planning and 45 minutes writing your answer.

In your response you should do the following:

- **Thesis:** Make a defensible claim that establishes a line of reasoning and consists of one or more sentences found in one place.
- **Contextualization:** Relate the argument to a broader historical context.
- **Document Evidence:** Use content from at least six documents.
- **Outside Evidence:** Use one piece of evidence not in the documents.
- **Document Sourcing:** Explain how or why the point of view, purpose, situation, or intended audience is relevant for at least three documents.
- **Analysis:** Show the relationships among pieces of historical evidence and use them to support, qualify, or modify an argument.

2. Evaluate the extent to which revolutionary movements in Europe from 1823 to 1832 were successful.

Document 1

Source: Pietro Mauromichali, Greek rebel leader, 1821

Reduced to a condition so pitiable, deprived of every right, we have, with unanimous voice, resolved to take up arms, and struggle against the tyrants. . . . In one word, we are unanimously resolved on Liberty or Death. Thus determined, we earnestly invite the united aid of all civilized nations to promote the attainment of our holy and legitimate purpose, the recovery of our rights, and the revival of our unhappy nation. With every right does Hellas, our mother, whence ye also, O Nations, have become enlightened, anxiously request your friendly assistance with money, arms, and counsel, and we entertain the highest hope that our appeal will be listened to; promising to show ourselves deserving of your interest, and at the proper time to prove our gratitude by deeds.

Document 2

Source: Pavel Pestel, Russian leader, 1823

The desirability of granting freedom to the serfs was considered from the very beginning; for that purpose a majority of the nobility was to be invited in order to petition the Emperor about it. This was later thought of on many occasions, but we soon came to realize that the nobility could not be persuaded. And as time went on we became even more convinced, when the Ukrainian nobility absolutely rejected a similar project of their military governor.

Document 3

Source: In the French Revolution of July 1830, King Charles X (left) was replaced with Louis Phillipe (right).

Credit: (Left) Robert Lefèvre - originally uploaded on de.wikipedia. (Right) Getty Images.

Document 4

Source: Giuseppe Mazzini's "Instructions to the Members of Young Italy," 1831

Young Italy is a brotherhood of Italians who believe in a law of Progress and Duty, and are convinced that Italy is destined to become one nation—convinced also that she possesses sufficient strength within herself to become one, and that the ill-success of her former efforts is to be attributed not to the weakness, but to the misdirection of the revolutionary elements within her—that the secret of force lies in constancy and unity of effort. They join this association in the firm intent of consecrating both thought and action to the great aim of re-constituting Italy as one independent sovereign nation of free men and equals.

Document 5

Source: Thomas Campbell, "The Pleasure of Hope," a poem on the Polish uprising against Russia, 1831

Peal'd her loud drum, and twang'd her trumpet horn;
Tumultuous horror brooded o'er her van,
Presaging wrath to Poland — and to man!
Warsaw's last champion from her height survey'd
Wide o'er the fields, a waste of ruin laid,—
Oh! Heav'n! he cried, my bleeding country save!—
Is there no hand on high to shield the brave?—
Yet, though destruction sweep these lovely plains,
Rise, fellow men! our country yet remains!
By that dread name we wave the sword on high,
And swear for her to live! — with her to die!"

Document 6

Source: The English Electoral System, 1831

Credit: George Cruikshank, "The System Works So Well, " 1831. The British Museum.

The House of Commons is shown as a water mill. The waterwheel bears the names of rotten boroughs. Underneath lies the corpses of the poor, and from the mill pours a stream of benefits of being MPs, which they stuff in their pockets, while praising the system and opposing reform.

Document 7

Source: Princess Dorothea Lieven, the wife of the Russian ambassador, on the Passing of the 1832 Reform Bill

I was absolutely stupefied when I learnt the extent of the Reform Bill. The most absolutely secrecy has been maintained on the subject until the last moment. It is said that the House of Commons was quite taken by surprise; the Whigs are astonished, the Radicals delighted, the Tories indignant. This was the first impression of Lord John Russell's speech, who was entrusted with explaining the Government Bill. I have had neither the time nor the courage to read it. Its leading features have scared me completely: 168 members are unseated, sixty boroughs disfranchised, eight more members allotted to London and proportionately to the large towns and counties, the total number of members reduced by sixty or more.

PERIOD 4: c.1914 to the Present

Period Overview

Since 1914, the world has changed more than in any comparable time period in human history. Two enormous wars, rapid population growth, and amazing technological changes have made the period one of constant change.

Wars and Global Efforts for Peace The devastation of World War I (1914 to 1918) led to economic and political problems that prepared the way for totalitarian governments, racism, more violence, and a terrible economic collapse in the 1930s. These problems led to far worse destruction and suffering in World War II (1939 to 1945).

Following World War II, much of the world divided into rival camps. The United States and Western Europe were liberal and democratic. The Soviet Union and Eastern Europe were communist. Adding to the constant tension between the two sides were efforts of colonies in Southeast Asia, India, and most of Africa to assert their independence. The European colonial powers eventually agreed to independence, but sometimes only after a bitter war.

After World War II, Great Britain, Germany, Sweden, and many other Western and Southern European countries increased government-funded benefits such as health care and unemployment assistance. By increasing both benefits and taxes to pay for them, they continued expanding the role of government in everyday life. In Eastern Europe, countries remained dominated by the Soviet Union until about 1989, just as the Soviet system was beginning to collapse.

War and Beliefs In 1914, most Europeans found a balance among their beliefs in progress, reason, and religion. While these beliefs had begun to be challenged by intellectuals, it was only during and after World War I that such challenges became widespread. The seemingly senseless slaughter of soldiers during the war, made worse by improved military technology such as machine guns and airplanes made people question the value of their past beliefs. As wars and atrocities continued in the 20th century, people wondered what, if anything, was true. Neither science nor religion seemed to have answers. Art became increasingly experimental, more concerned with self-expression than in representing reality.

Despite these problems, advances in public health and medicine resulted in rapid population growth. Improvements in production and inventions such as the car and the computer made the economy more efficient and people more prosperous than ever before in world history. Women fought for equality, winning the right to vote and greater opportunities for careers. After World War II, European states began to break down national barriers, increasing trade and political cooperation. The result was the most peaceful, and prosperous, half century in many centuries.

Key Concepts

4.1 Total war and political instability in the first half of the 20th century gave way to a polarized state order during the Cold War and eventually to efforts at transnational union.

    I. World War I, caused by a complex interaction of long- and short-term factors, resulted in immense losses and disruptions for both victors and vanquished.

    II. The conflicting goals of the peace negotiators in Paris pitted diplomatic idealism against the desire to punish Germany, producing a settlement that satisfied few.

    III. In the interwar period, fascism, extreme nationalism, racist ideologies, and the failure of appeasement resulted in the catastrophe of World War II, presenting a grave challenge to European civilization.

    IV. As World War II ended, a Cold War between the liberal democratic West and the communist East began, lasting nearly half a century.

    V. Nationalist and separatist movements, along with ethnic conflict and ethnic cleansing, periodically disrupted the post–World War II peace.

    VI. The process of decolonization occurred over the course of the century with varying degrees of cooperation, interference, or resistance from European imperialist states.

4.2 The stresses of economic collapse and total war engendered internal conflicts within European states and created conflicting conceptions of the relationship between the individual and the state, as demonstrated in the ideological battle between and among democracy, communism, and fascism.

    I. The Russian Revolution created a regime based on Marxist–Leninist theory.

    II. The ideology of fascism, with roots in the pre–World War I era, gained popularity in an environment of postwar bitterness, the rise of communism, uncertain transitions to democracy, and economic instability.

III. The Great Depression, caused by weaknesses in international trade and monetary theories and practices, undermined Western European democracies and fomented radical political responses throughout Europe.

IV. Postwar economic growth supported an increase in welfare benefits; however, subsequent economic stagnation led to criticism and limitation of the welfare state.

V. Eastern European nations were bound by their relationships with the Soviet Union, which oscillated between repression and limited reform, until the collapse of communist governments in Eastern Europe and the fall of the Soviet Union.

4.3 During the 20th century, diverse intellectual and cultural movements questioned the existence of objective knowledge, the ability of reason to arrive at truth, and the role of religion in determining moral standards.

I. The widely held belief in progress characteristic of much of 19th-century thought began to break down before World War I; the experience of war intensified a sense of anxiety that permeated many facets of thought and culture, giving way by the century's end to a plurality of intellectual frameworks.

II. Science and technology yielded impressive material benefits but also caused immense destruction and posed challenges to objective knowledge.

III. Organized religion continued to play a role in European social and cultural life despite the challenges of military and ideological conflict, modern secularism, and rapid social changes.

IV. During the 20th century, the arts were defined by experimentation, self-expression, subjectivity, and the increasing influence of the United States in both elite and popular culture.

4.4 Demographic changes, economic growth, total war, disruptions of traditional social patterns, and competing definitions of freedom and justice altered the experiences of everyday life.

I. The 20th century was characterized by large-scale suffering brought on by warfare and genocide, but also by tremendous improvements in the standard of living.

II. The lives of women were defined by family and work responsibilities, economic changes, and feminism.

III. New voices gained prominence in political, intellectual, and social discourse.

IV. European states began to set aside nationalist rivalries in favor of economic and political integration, forming a series of transnational unions that grew in size and scope over the second half of the 20th century.

19

Two World Wars

"I have nothing to offer but blood, toil, tears, and sweat. We have before us an ordeal of the most grievous kind. We have before us many, many long months of struggle and of suffering. You ask, what is our aim? I can answer in one word: Victory."

—Winston Churchill, speech to the British people, May 13, 1940

Essential Question: How did war in the first half of the 20th century give way to the Cold War?

During the first half of the 20th century, Europe engaged in two massive wars. Both involved a number of nations and spread across more than one continent. Because of their size and scope, these wars became known as **World Wars**. In World War I fighting lasted from 1914 to 1918. In World War II war was declared in 1939 and ended in 1945. Winston Churchill, the author of the quote above, lived through both wars, as a British battalion commander in World War I and later as prime minister of Britain during World War II. During the World War II, his speeches helped inspire Britons to withstand the German assault upon their country.

At the end of World War II in 1945, the balance of global power had permanently shifted from Western Europe to the United States and the Soviet Union. Western Europe would no longer dominate world politics and economic development. The United States would emerge as the leader of the democratic or "free" West, while the USSR (United Soviet Socialist Republics) would control the communist or Eastern Bloc. Aided by the United States, Western Europe would rebuild and become a more stable and unified region.

World War I as a European Conflict

A number of factors converged to cause World War I. Although Europe had been more peaceful in the 19th century than it had been for many centuries, France was eager regain the provinces of Alsace and Lorraine near the French-German border. The provinces had changed hands as a result of France's humiliating defeat in the Franco-German War in 1871. Germany's desire to expand its territory and influence had alarmed Britain and Russia for years as well. A series of agreements among France, Russia, and Britain became, in effect, an **alliance** to counter growing German power. (See Chapter 16 for more on alliances.) Germany and Austria-Hungary had been allied to one another for many years. Smaller nations in Europe felt pressured to take sides. **Militarism,** the arming of European countries, grew as every nation began to accumulate arms for both offensive and defensive purposes. From 1890-1910 defense expenditures had more than doubled among major European powers. Nationalism had dramatically increased, especially since the unification of Italy and Germany in the second half of the 19th century. In addition, movements such as pan-Slavism had caused unrest, especially within the Balkan region of the Habsburg Empire. Citizens wanted a strong government that would protect and promote their interests.

The War in Europe

The road to World War I began with the assassination of Austrian Archduke Franz Ferdinand by a Serbian nationalist in Sarajevo on June 28, 1914. A month later, Austria declared war on Serbia. In response, Serbia's ally Russia mobilized its forces, thereby heightening tensions around Europe. Germany, hoping to gain a quick victory over unprepared adversaries, declared war on Russia and France on August 1. Germany's subsequent invasion of neutral Belgium brought Great Britain into the war on France and Russia's side.

PUNCH, OR THE LONDON CHARIVARI.—March 27, 1918.

A WALK-OVER?

The Kaiser. "THIS IS THE DOORMAT OF OUR NEW PREMISES."
Emperor Karl. "ARE YOU QUITE SURE IT'S DEAD?"

Emperor Karl of Austria (left) was more fearful of arousing Russia (represented by the bear) than was Kaiser Wilhelm II of Germany (right). The assassination of Austrian Archduke Ferdinand set off a chain of events that resulted in World War I.

Credit: Getty Images

Ultimately 32 states fought in the war. The two sides were known as the Central Powers and the Allies. The Central Powers consisted of Germany, Austria-Hungary, and the Ottoman Empire, soon joined by Bulgaria. France, Britain, and Russia led the Allies; Italy, although a member of the Triple Alliance, joined the allies in 1915, as did the United States in 1917. The war was fought on two fronts. The Western Front stretched for 400 miles from Belgium through France. The Eastern Front extended for 1,000 miles along Russia's border from the Baltic to the Black Sea.

[margin handwritten: I was promised land, didn't get any]

The Western Front

[handwritten: quickly defeat F then bring all troops towards R → plan]

Germany invaded Belgium in August 1914 and swiftly overwhelmed the small country. By the end of the month German forces had invaded France, but the offensive bogged down, and the Western Front turned into **trench warfare.** *[handwritten: new technique]* Each side dug protective trenches into the earth from which they could emerge to attack the other. The space between the trenches was called **no man's land.** Trenches could stretch for miles. Soldiers might live in the trenches for months at a time. They endured cold, wet, and unsanitary conditions. Contagious diseases spread easily. Many men suffered from trench foot, a crippling foot condition caused by the damp and cold.

Between 1914 and 1916 the German army confronted British and French forces in a series of battles in central France. Major engagements included the Marne, Verdun, Ypres, and the Somme. Both sides suffered staggering numbers of soldiers killed and wounded. Soldiers dug in on each side, and the war seemed to reach a **stalemate**. In 1917, the United States entered the war, tilting the advantage toward the Allies. *[handwritten: → last hope of winning]*

[margin handwritten: high # of deaths, almost no land gained]

The Germans launched one last offensive at the Second Battle of the Marne on the outskirts of Paris in July 1918. They hoped to force Britain and France to negotiate peace before large numbers of American soldiers arrived. But the German army was too exhausted to succeed. On November 11, 1918, Germany signed an **armistice** treaty with the Allies, bringing World War I to an end.

The Eastern Front

[handwritten: mobilized troops faster than G thought they could]

The war on the Eastern Front began on August 17, 1914, when Russia invaded Germany. Austria-Hungary rapidly joined on the side of the Germans and invaded Poland (part of the Russian Empire at the time). Although the Russians repelled the Austrian advance, Germany increased its forces on the Eastern Front.

By 1915, Germany and Austria-Hungary had seized all or most of the Russian territories of Poland, Latvia, and Lithuania. The offensive stalled, however, as the Germans fell short of supplies and the Russians were able to establish a nearly 800-mile defensive line stretching southeast from the Baltic Sea to the border with Romania.

In mid-1916, the Russian army rallied and regained much of its lost territory, but victory was costly. About 1 million Russian soldiers died, were wounded or taken prisoner, or deserted. As the hardships of war mounted, Russian soldiers began to mutiny. The political turmoil that followed led to the Russian Revolution and Russia's withdrawal from the war in 1917.

World War I Timeline	
Date	**Event**
1914–1915	
July 28, 1914	Archduke Franz Ferdinand assassinated.
August 4, 1914	Germany invades Belgium.
September–October 1914	Battles of the Marne and Ypres begin.
November 1914	War expands to Turkey.
May 7, 1915	German submarines sink *Lusitania*.
1916–1917	
Februry 1916	Battle of Verdun begins.
July 1916	Battle of the Somme begins.
March 15, 1917	Tsar Nicholas of Russia abdicates.
April 6, 1917	United States enters war against Germany.
December 1917	Russia withdraws from the war.
1918–1919	
November 11, 1918	Germany signs armistice agreement.
January 1919	Paris Peace Conference.
June 28, 1919	World War I officially ends.

New Technologies in Weapons

New technologies contributed to the mass casualties seen in World War I. Machine guns killed and maimed thousands of soldiers. Poison gas blinded and suffocated its victims. Gas masks became part of every soldier's equipment. Barbed wire protected trenches. Attacking soldiers slowed by or entangled in the spiky wire were easy targets for enemy machine gunners. Armored tanks could cross open terrain, crushing anyone and anything in their path.

Armies deployed airplanes in combat for the first time. Pilots engaged in one-on-one combat with machine guns mounted in the cockpit. By the end of the war, both sides used planes to drop small bombs on enemy targets, the first form of aerial bombardment. At sea, German submarines sank enemy warships and merchant vessels. The Germans expertly developed their submarine, or U-boat, program, deploying more than 100 of the vessels, during the course of the war.

Protest and Insurrection

Stalemate on the battlefront demoralized the troops. On both sides soldiers began to feel abandoned by their respective leaders. Some men **mutinied** and openly refused to fight. Others began to sabotage equipment or desert their posts. One of the largest mutinies took place among French soldiers during the Second Battle of Aisne in 1917. Soldiers in 136 regiments refused to man the front lines. Thousands deserted. Around 40,000 men participated in various acts of mutiny. General Henri Petain finally brought the rebellion to a halt. Twenty-six men were executed. The rest returned to their posts.

The cost of the war sparked unrest at home, too. In Russia and Ireland revolutions began to remake European society and politics.

Easter Rebellion in Ireland For decades the Irish had sought to free their island from British rule. Despite their differences with Britain, though, thousands of Irish soldiers enlisted to fight with the British in World War I. Heavy losses in the trenches increased resentment at home. Many Irish believed that the British had no intention of honoring the Irish Home Rule Bill that had been passed by the British parliament but "temporarily" suspended with the outbreak of WWI. On April 23, Easter Sunday, 1916, a rebellion broke out in Dublin, Ireland's capital. A week of street fighting between Irish rebels and British troops ended with the uprising crushed. Around 1,350 people had been killed or wounded. The British executed 15 rebel leaders. In 1922, a treaty divided Ireland into the Irish Free State and British Northern Ireland. Conflict would continue to plague Ireland for most of the 20th century.

Russian Revolution Russia's war with Germany left the country drained and impoverished. Workers went on strike. Riots broke out. After going to the Eastern Front to personally command the war effort, Tsar Nicholas II returned home. Unable to establish order, Tsar Nicholas II abdicated his throne in March 1917, and a provisional government took over. However, the new government's weak leadership and insistence on continuing the war effort made it vulnerable. In October the Bolshevik party seized power. Vladimir Lenin, a communist leader, controlled the new government.

In December 1917, Russia and Germany negotiated an armistice, a cessation of fighting, and the March 1918 Treaty of Brest-Litovsk officially marked the end of Russia's war. Lenin had agreed to the terms of the treaty in return for Germany's help in returning him to Russia from exile in Switzerland. In 1922, Russia became the Soviet Union, the world's largest communist country. Relations between the Soviet Union and Germany remained tense. The two countries would confront one another again in World War II.

World War I as a Global Conflict

The war in Europe quickly spread to the Middle East, North Africa, and Asia. Japan declared war on Germany and seized Germany's colony in China. Arabs began to revolt against the Ottoman Empire in the Arabian Peninsula. By the end of 1914, World War I was truly a global conflict.

Armenian Genocide In 1915, the Ottoman government began a systematic program to seize Armenian land and deport Armenians from Turkey. The Armenians were a Christian minority who lived mainly in northeastern Turkey. Turkey's Muslim rulers feared that the Armenians were potential traitors who would betray the empire if they had a chance to win autonomy.

Ottoman authorities encouraged ethnic Turks to rise up against their Armenian neighbors. Many Armenians were murdered outright, while others died of hunger, thirst, and disease on the forced march from their homes to camps in the deserts of Syria and Iraq. Between 1915 and 1916, an estimated 1 million or more Armenians died. Many Armenians and their supporters have described the actions of the Turks as **genocide**, an attempt at complete extermination of all people in an ethnic or religious group. The Turkish government has denied the charge of genocide.

Arab revolt against the Turks Although both Arabs and Turks were Muslim, the Arabs regarded the Turks as oppressors. As the Ottoman Empire weakened, Arab tribes in the Arabian Peninsula organized attacks on Ottoman posts. The British supported the Arabs and supplied them with weapons and advisors led by the famous Lawrence of Arabia, Colonel T.E. Lawrence. Emir Faisal of Arabia drove the Ottomans from the cities of Mecca and Medina. In Syria and Lebanon, Arab nationalists overthrew Ottoman rulers.

After the war, however, Britain betrayed earlier promises to support Arab nationalism, and the Arabs failed to establish independent states.

Japanese Aggression in the Pacific Japan declared war on Germany in 1914. Japanese troops seized many of Germany's island territories in the South Pacific as well as territory on mainland China. In 1916, Russia helped Japan extend its reach into Manchuria. Japan attended the Peace Conference in Paris but did not gain any territory. Anti-Japanese sentiment forced the Japanese out of China. These frustrations of Japan's territorial ambitions fueled its desire for an empire. In 1933, Japan returned to Manchuria, beginning its imperialist collision course with the United States and World War II in the Pacific.

The Balance of Power Shifts

After World War I, the balance of power shifted. The United States emerged as a world leader. The Austro-Hungarian Empire disbanded and split into several smaller states. Under the **mandate** system, authorized by the peace treaty, victor nations took control over Middle Eastern territories once ruled by the Ottoman Empire. They also acquired Germany's colonies in Africa and the Pacific.

France and Britain controlled the regions of Palestine and Syria. Britain, France, Belgium, and Australia governed Germany's former possessions in Africa. The dissolution of the Ottoman Empire led to the creation of the modern state of Turkey, under the leadership of Kamal Ataturk, in 1923. Turkey became an independent state. Although sympathetic to the Allies, it did not participate in World War II.

The Peace Settlement

The peace conference convened in Paris on January 4, 1919. The United States, Great Britain, France, and Italy led the negotiations. These countries, known as the "big four," wanted to establish long-term peace in Europe and beyond. At the forefront of this movement was U.S. President Woodrow Wilson. In early 1918, Wilson had introduced his "Fourteen Points," an idealistic vision for postwar peace and security in Europe and beyond. In many ways, the points delivered what Wilson called "peace without victory"—a resolution to the war in which humiliation, resentment, and a desire for revenge could be avoided.

However, the stunning ravages of the war put the leaders of Britain (David Lloyd-George) and France (George Clemenceau) in a much less charitable frame of mind. They insisted Germany accept guilt for starting the war and pay heavy **reparations** to the victorious nations. They hoped to cripple Germany's ability to wage war in Europe ever again.

The Terms of the Treaty

already impacted by the war & its effects

The Treaty of Versailles required Germany to give up 10 percent of its land and all of its foreign colonies. The nation was forced to disarm. The Germans had to officially accept responsibility for the war and pay a total amounting to $37 billion U.S. dollars to the victorious nations. Germans resented these terms. Economic difficulties made it almost impossible for them to meet their payments. The democratic Weimer Republic, established after the war, could not, at first, rebuild the economy or stabilize German society. Extreme nationalist groups readily exploited the unrest, and Germany began to move toward fascism.

The League of Nations → weak, no US (Senate refused), w/o US =

Created as part of the Treaty of Versailles, the League of Nations was intended as a forum where nations could try to resolve their differences. Its charter, or covenant, was based in part on Wilson's Fourteen Points. Wilson believed an international organization supported by a majority of nations could prevent future wars. One of the League's main goals was international **disarmament**, for without weapons, nations could not fight wars. Both the treaty and the covenant went into effect on January 10, 1920.

The first meeting of the League's General Assembly took place in Geneva, Switzerland, on November 15. The League never lived up to its high ideals. The Assembly was plagued by suspicion. No nation trusted the others enough to give up its arms. Wilson, who had refused to take any Senate leaders to Paris with him, could not now convince the Senate to ratify the Versailles Treaty. Without U.S. support the League remained weak. Germany and the Soviet Union were also nonparticipants. Though the League continued to exist legally, it had little influence. The League of Nations officially disbanded in 1946 when it was replaced by the United Nations.

New States Emerge in Europe

The collapse of the Austro-Hungarian Empire after World War I led to the formation of several new states. Austria, Hungary, Poland, Czechoslovakia, and Yugoslavia all emerged from parts of the former empire. Though most of these states wanted to be democratic, political unrest and economic crises created instability and left them vulnerable to authoritarian movements.

- **Poland** Poland became an independent republic in 1918. In 1926, Josef Pilsudski overthrew the government and became dictator. Many Poles welcomed his rule, believing he could enforce order and unity.

- **Czechoslovakia** Czechoslovakia was formed by the unification of the Czech Republic and Slovakia. Of all the new nations formed after World War I it was, by far, the most democratic and prosperous.

- **Hungary** Hungary split from Austria in 1918. In 1920, the victorious nations of World War I forced Hungary to surrender most of its territory. The country became increasingly **totalitarian**—a centralized government led by a dictator, allowing no opposition.

- **Yugoslavia** In the Balkan region, the Serbs, Croats, and Slovenes emerged under the control of the ruling Serbian dynasty. Dissatisfaction and struggle among the ethnic groups led to the declaration of a royal dictatorship in 1929 and the renaming of the country: Yugoslavia.

Extremism Spreads Throughout Europe

During the 1920s and 1930s, **fascism**, an extreme form of nationalism, spread throughout Europe. In many nations, fascism was simply one political ideology among many, but in Italy first and then Germany, fascist movements took control of the government completely. Benito Mussolini and his fascist gang, known as the *Blackshirts*, gained control of the Italian government through legal means.

Adolf Hitler, leader of the National Socialist German Workers Party (Nazi Party), became chancellor of Germany in 1933. Despite its "socialist" name, the Nazis were militant fascists. Hitler was a rabid racist and **anti-Semite**, one who promotes discrimination of Jews, who stoked ethnic prejudice and religious bigotry to divide Germans. He told Germans they had been victimized by the Treaty of Versailles and had no obligation to honor its terms. With the inherent weakness of the Weimar constitution, he was also able to gain control of the government.

Mussolini welcomed Hitler as an ally. In spring 1939, Germany and Italy declared the Pact of Steel, cementing their mutual political and military support. Two years later Japan joined the alliance, and the three nations—Germany, Italy, and Japan—became known as the Axis powers. The rise of fascism placed the free nations of Europe and the rest of the world in grave danger.

Appeasement and Expansion

The war-weary French and the British feared another costly war with Germany. Neither country wanted to sacrifice a new generation of soldiers to combat. As a result, both countries followed a policy of **appeasement** toward Hitler. They granted him what he wished in return for peace. The United States, too, had little interest in confronting the German dictator. Americans wanted to focus on their own problems. The economic depression of the 1930s left the country struggling with high unemployment. Isolationist policies restricted immigration and encouraged people to turn away from Europe and its conflicts. In addition, deep distrust and political differences between the Soviet Union and the capitalist nations made it difficult for them to present a united front against the fascist states. Germany, Italy, and Japan took advantage of the fear, isolationism, and discord to begin expanding their military power and annexing new territory.

Remilitarization of the Rhineland The Treaty of Versailles forbid Germany from arming the Rhineland, a German region bordering France and Belgium. In March 1936, Hitler sent troops to the region. He wanted to test whether Britain and France were committed to enforcing the treaty. When neither nation challenged him, he accelerated his drive toward rearmament and focused his plans for expansion into Austria and Eastern Europe.

Italian Invasion of Ethiopia Italy had maintained colonies in East Africa since the late 19th century. In October 1935, Italy invaded the independent state of Ethiopia. The Italian conquest of Ethiopia threatened the British, who controlled the Suez Canal in Egypt. Although the League of Nations condemned Italy's actions, member nations enacted only token economic sanctions against Italy.

Annexation of Austria On March 12, 1938, Germany annexed Austria. Nazis had influenced Austrian politics for several years, and Nazi propaganda had generated strong support for Germany in Austria. Many Austrians welcomed the Germans. In a plebiscite, or **referendum**, conducted in October,

[handwritten margin note: basically let it do whatever he wanted. Horrors of WWI. People still remembered]

a near total majority of Austrians declared themselves in favor of unification with Germany, a questionable vote that merely reinforced an established fact.

Munich Agreement In an effort to avoid conflict, Great Britain and France agreed to let Germany annex the border regions of Czechoslovakia known as Sudetenland. Germany claimed that these areas had been settled by ethnic Germans and did not actually belong to Czechoslovakia. In return, Germany promised to maintain peace in Europe and leave the rest of Czechoslovakia alone. Britain, France, Italy, and Germany all signed the Munich Agreement on September 30, 1938. Less than a year later in March 1939, Germany openly violated the Munich Agreement by seizing the Czechoslovakian states of Moravia and Bohemia. Though alarmed, Britain and France still did not challenge Hitler.

Fearing it would be the next target of German aggression, Poland turned to France and Britain for protection. Both nations pledged to defend Poland's borders if it was attacked by Germany.

[handwritten margin note: Surprised other nations]

Nazi–Soviet Non-Aggression Pact The Soviet Union was not ready to engage in another major war with Germany. On August 23, 1939, the two nations signed a non-pact, promising that they would not attack one another for ten years. They also agreed that they would divide Poland between them. This pact essentially gave Germany the freedom to invade Poland a week later without fear of any opposition from the Soviet Union. In return, Germany allowed the Soviet Union to take control of the eastern part of Poland and did not protest the Soviet invasion of Finland or the Soviet annexation of the Baltic states and Romania. The pact dissolved with the German invasion of the Soviet Union in 1941.

World War II

World War II took place in two major regions of the globe, or **theaters of war**—the Theater of Europe and the Theater of the Pacific. The war pitted the Axis powers against the Allies. The Axis powers consisted mainly of Germany, Italy, and Japan. All had fascist governments dedicated to military conquest. Adolf Hitler of Germany, Benito Mussolini of Italy, and General Hideki Tojo of Japan led the Axis nations. The major nations of the Allies were Great Britain, the United States, and the Soviet Union. The British Commonwealth nations of Canada, Australia, and New Zealand also fought with the Allies. Winston Churchill of Britain, Franklin D. Roosevelt of the United States, and Josef Stalin of the Soviet Union led the Allies. Britain and the United States were both democracies, while the Soviet Union was a Communist dictatorship. The three nations decided to put their political differences aside, however, to combat a common enemy.

World War II Begins

In 1937 Japan invaded and conquered a large part of eastern China, instigating the initial phase of the war in the Pacific. The Japanese then began to expand their empire across the region, seizing Guam and Wake Island. In Europe, Germany prepared to seize Poland. Germany relied on a strategy called **blitzkrieg**, or lightning war. Blitzkrieg used a combination of tanks, troops, and air power to overwhelm the opposition's defenses as rapidly as possible. Once the Germans broke through enemy lines, they used maximum force to intimidate the civilian population and crush the opposing army. German officers became experts in blitzkrieg tactics. Between 1939 and 1941, Germany conquered Poland, Yugoslavia, Greece, and most of Western Europe including France, Belgium, Norway, Denmark, and the Netherlands.

Polish Campaign of 1939 World War II began in Europe with the German invasion of Poland on September 1, 1939. In the face of such blatant Nazi aggression, Britain and France could no longer avoid war. Honoring their commitment to Poland, they declared war on Germany two days later on September 3. They could do little to help Poland, though. On September 27, Poland surrendered. The Soviet Union invaded Poland from the east, quickly occupying that half of the country.

France Surrenders After quickly gaining control of the "Low Countries" (Belgium, Netherlands, and Luxembourg), Germany invaded France in May 1940. France surrendered to Germany on June 24, 1940. Marshall Pétain signed the armistice on behalf of France. In return for his cooperation, Hitler gave him official control of southern France, which became known as Vichy France, named for the town that was home to Pétain's collaborationist government. Germany controlled northern France, including the city of Paris. In theory, Vichy was a free state. In reality, it was a **puppet state** of the Nazis. Pétain simply enacted Nazi laws. After France's surrender to Germany, General Charles de Gaulle began to organize a French army in exile. In France, a strong resistance movement worked to undermine German rule and helped the Allies by providing intelligence on German movements.

Operation Barbarossa On June 22, 1941, Germany launched Operation Barbarossa, a three-pronged invasion of the Soviet Union. Hitler had never intended to honor his non-aggression pact with Stalin. He needed Russia's natural resources, especially iron, coal, and oil, to support his army. He also saw the Soviet Union as a threat to his control of Eastern Europe. More than 3 million soldiers attacked the Soviet Union. The Eastern Front stretched nearly 1,500 miles from the Baltic Sea in the north to the Black Sea in the south.

Germany anticipated an easy victory. The Soviets, however, rallied after a series of initial losses and put up surprising resistance, forcing the Germans to endure a Russian winter. Soviet forces repelled a German attack on Moscow in the winter of 1941. Germany continued to occupy parts of the Soviet Union until 1944, but they were never able to subdue the country completely.

The Holocaust

Anti-Semitism had a long history in Europe before 1800. In the 19th and 20th centuries, the debate became more intense. The legacy of the Enlightenment supported tolerance, so some people opposed discrimination against Jews. However, as societies focused more on the concept of race, people debated whether some people were racially superior to others. For Hitler and the Nazis, anti-Semitism was a core part of their belief that Germans were "Aryans," northern European who formed a superior race. They viewed Jews as inferior, and they blamed Jews for Germany's economic problems after World War I. Nazis referred to **"Jewish Question,"** the issue of how to end Jewish influence in Germany.

Nuremberg Laws Beginning in 1935 Hitler's government enacted a series of laws that denied German Jews their citizenship and civil rights. Known as the **Nuremberg Laws**, these acts forbade marriages between Jews and non-Jews. Jews could no longer employ non-Jews or work in certain businesses. Jewish doctors could not treat non-Jewish patients. Eventually the laws were extended to mean that Jews could not attend public schools or universities or mingle in public places with non-Jews. Jews had to carry identity cards at all times. Later, the Nazi government required all Jews in Germany and German-occupied territories to wear a yellow star on their clothes.

Kristallnacht On the night of November 9–10, 1938, the Nazi government unleashed a wave of **pogroms**, or organized assaults on Jews. In Germany, Austria, Poland, and Czechoslovakia, mobs attacked Jewish homes, businesses, and synagogues. They smashed windows, looted goods and burned buildings. Called Kristallnacht, or the Night of Broken Glass, these attacks left many Jewish communities in ruins. At least 91 individuals died, and around 30,000 Jewish men were rounded up and deported to concentration camps. An estimated 7,500 Jewish-owned businesses were destroyed, and at least 270 synagogues were burned. By the end of 1939, more than 100,000 Jews had fled Germany and Austria.

Foreign Responses to Persecution Anti-Semitism was so accepted in Europe and the United States that other government did little to stop the Nazis. However, Jews resisted when they could, and some non-Jews tried to help them escape to other countries. Some countries, including the United States, accepted only a small number of refugees. Most Jews who did leave went to nearby countries that were later overrun by the Nazis. By October 1941, Jewish emigration was officially forbidden.

Wannsee Conference and the Final Solution On January 20, 1942, Nazi officials met in Wannsee, a neighborhood near Berlin, to plan the "final solution" to the Jewish Question. They decided to murder all Jews. Their plan was an example of genocide.

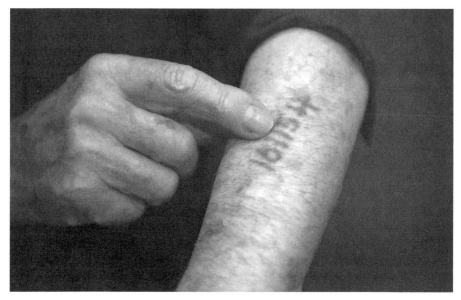

The Nazis tattooed an identification number on each person sent to a concentration camp.

Credit: Getty Images

Labor Camps and Death Camps During World War II, the Nazis operated about 40,000 camps. Most were prisons and slave labor sites where people were worked until they died. Camp inmates died of starvation, cold, sickness, beatings, and gunshot wounds. In several camps Nazi doctors performed cruel experiments designed to see how people reacted to brutally cold temperatures, drowning, diseases, and other deadly conditions.

A few of the sites were **concentration camps,** camps designed for the purpose of killing human beings. In the largest of these camps, Auschwitz, Nazis murdered more than 1 million Jews.

Persecution and Resistance Many Jews were killed in gas chambers in the concentration camps. Others died in mass executions, especially in the Soviet Union and Eastern Europe. On September 29–30, 1941, Nazi forces shot 33,771 Jews and buried them in a mass grave at Babi Yar, outside the city of Kiev in Ukraine. In several cities Jews were forced into overcrowded areas called **ghettos**. Walled off from the larger city, they were denied food, water, and basic sanitation services.

In Warsaw, Poland, approximately 400,000 people were packed into an area of 1.3 square miles. At least 83,000 died of starvation and disease. Thousands of others were deported to death camps. In April 1943, several hundred resistors staged a revolt, attacking German soldiers with homemade grenades and weapons smuggled in from the outside. The uprising took the Germans by surprise, temporarily driving them away. The revolt lasted four weeks. In the end, the Germans captured and killed almost all of the rebels. A small number were able to escape and find shelter outside the ghetto. When the Soviet forces liberated Warsaw from Nazi control in 1945, approximately 11,500 Jews in the entire city had survived out of an original population of around 350,000. While the uprising had failed, it served as an inspiration to Holocaust survivors throughout Europe and is still commemorated in Israel today.

Before Hitler's rise to power, approximately 9 million Jews lived in Europe. Between 1933 and the end of the war in 1945, an estimated 6 million, or two thirds, would die. Jews referred to this slaughter as the *Shoah,* a Hebrew word meaning destruction. In the 1950s historians translated this as the **Holocaust,** a word derived from Greek meaning sacrifice or burnt offering.

In addition to murdering Jews, Nazis murder about 5 million other people. They singled out groups they viewed as inferior for death. Among these were Slavs (including Poles and Soviet prisoners of war), Roma (formerly known as Gypsies), gay men, lesbians, and people with mental and physical disabilities. The Nazis also massacred socialists, communists, and others politically opposed to them.

The Allied Victory

The United States entered World War II with the Japanese bombing of Pearl Harbor, Hawaii, on December 7, 1941. Immediately after the attack, the United States declared war on Japan; Germany and Italy declared war on the United States, which then responded in kind.

Although Germany had a highly trained army, the Allies enjoyed significant advantages. The Unites States was rich in natural resources, especially oil. The United States had a large population that could be mobilized for war and manufacturing industries that could produce weapons and other war materials.

Britain Holds Out Under the leadership of Winston Churchill, the British had proven that they had the will to resist Germany. They had withstood severe aerial bombardment during the Battle of Britain from July to November 1940. The battle took place almost entirely in the air, and Britain's Royal Air Force had demonstrated that it had the skill and determination to protect the British Isles from German invasion.

Russian Endurance Russians also resisted the German onslaught. In December 1941, Soviet forces drove Germans from Moscow. During the Siege of Leningrad, which lasted from September 1941 to January 1944, Soviet civilians and military endured brutal conditions rather than surrender to the Nazis. The most significant battle took place at Stalingrad. The Germans launched a massive attack in the summer of 1942 in an effort to seize the Volga River and the oil fields of the Caucasus. By the spring of 1943 the Germans had lost the entire 6th Army (over 750,000 casualties) and the Soviet Union held Stalingrad. From that point the Germans were on the defensive on the Eastern Front.

The War in North Africa Hitler regarded the conquest of North Africa as key to the control of the shipping lanes of the Mediterranean and the Suez Canal. He wanted access to the oil fields of the Middle East in order to fuel German tanks and planes, and he wanted to deny that oil to the British. After a four-year battle for North Africa, the Allies won control of the region in 1943.

The War in Italy After the conquest of North Africa, the Allies turned to Italy. If they could seize the airfields in Rome, they could launch bombing raids on Berlin from there instead of London. The shorter distance would conserve fuel and lives. British and American troops invaded the island of Sicily in July 1943, a few months before Mussolini was overthrown. After a year of hard fighting, the Allies controlled Rome.

World War II Timeline	
Date	**Event**
1933	
January 1933	Hitler appointed chancellor of Germany.
1938–1941	
November 1938	Germany and Italy sign the Rome-Berlin Axis.
March 1938	Germany annexes Austria.
September 1938	Munich agreement signed.
September 1939	Germany invades Poland; World War II begins.
May-June 1940	Germany invades and defeats France.
September 1940	Germany, Italy, and Japan sign the Tripartite Pact.
December 1941	United States enters the war.
June 1941	Germany invades Soviet Union.
1944–1945	
June 1944	Allies land in France.
January 1945	Soviets begin liberation of Eastern Europe.
February 1945	Allied leaders hold the Yalta Conference.
May 7, 1945	Germany surrenders.
August 6 and 9, 1945	United States drops atomic bombs on Japan.
September 22, 1945	Japan surrenders; World War II ends.

The War in Western Europe On June 6, 1944, Allied troops, led by U.S. General Dwight D. Eisenhower and British General Bernard Montgomery, landed on Normandy Beach on the coast of France. Known as **D-Day**, the invasion was the first step in the Allied effort to liberate Western Europe from Nazi control and ultimately defeat Germany. Approximately 175,000 Allied troops faced 850,000 German soldiers. The two sides fought for over a month. Air support tipped the battle in the Allies' favor. Allied bombing raids pushed the Germans back.

On July 25, the Allies broke through German lines. Within a month, Allied forces had liberated most of France, Belgium, and the Netherlands. In December the German army attempted to stop the Allied advance at the Battle of the Bulge in Belgium. Although the Allies suffered high casualties, the German assault failed. The Allies continued their advance on Berlin from the west.

Meanwhile, Soviet forces drove the Germans out of Eastern Europe. They marched toward Berlin from the east. Facing certain defeat, Hitler and several of his high-ranking officers committed suicide. On May 7, 1945 the German army surrendered to Allied forces. The war in Europe was over.

The Yalta Conference On February 4, 1945, Roosevelt, Stalin, and Churchill met at Yalta in the state of Crimea in order to discuss the defeat of Germany and the Allied occupation of Germany. They agreed on the following:

- France should take part in the administration of Germany after the war

- Germany as a whole, and Berlin in particular, would be divided into four occupation zones administered by Great Britain, the Soviet Union, the United States, and France

- Eastern European countries liberated from Germany would be allowed to hold free elections

Stalin also agreed that the Soviet Union would join the Allies in the war in the Pacific against Japan.

All parties agreed that Germany would be required to pay reparations, but the reparations would not be excessive, and the civilian population would be allowed to rebuild their country as long as they accepted the terms of the Allied victory.

However, the Soviets did not fully honor the promise of free elections in Eastern Europe. Stalin wanted pro-Soviet governments in that region to serve as a buffer between the Soviet Union and Germany. Even before the end of the war, it became clear to Roosevelt and Churchill that Eastern Europe would become part of the communist **bloc** of nations. Nevertheless, the Yalta Conference did foster peaceful cooperation among the Allies in Western Europe and helped set the terms for the German surrender.

The End of the Pacific War In July 1945, the Allied Powers met at Potsdam, Germany, to discuss outlining Japan's terms of surrender. The Allies and some Japanese leaders recognized that Japan was almost defeated. In August, the United States dropped atomic bombs on Hiroshima and Nagasaki. Japan formally surrendered on September 2.

Estimated Casualties in World War I and World War II		
Category	World War I	World War II
Military Deaths	10 million	23 million
Military Injuries	22 million	25 million
Civilian Deaths	9 million	49 million

Source: www.nationalww2museum.org/students-teachers/student-resources/research-starters/research-starters-worldwide-deaths-world-war

By telling the story of the past, history helps people define what is important to them. Efforts to remember the Holocaust have shaped not only how people recall the Nazi period in German history, but also horrific events in general.

The First Memories In the first two decades after World War II, the Holocaust did not receive as much attention as it later would. One reason for the lack of attention was the Cold War. For example, in East Germany, sites such as Buchenwald served as memorials to the triumph of the German Communist Party over the fascists. This view highlighted the Marxists rather than the Jews killed by the Nazis. In the United States, according to historian Peter Novick, people focused more on a new enemy, the Soviet Union, and a new ally, West Germany, rather than on the atrocities committed in the war.

Memories began to change in the 1960s. People inside and outside of Germany wanted to preserve the stories of survivors and victims. The publication of *The Diary of Anne Frank* in 1962 provided the world with an individual story that people could identify with. It was a personal tale of courage and suffering that was easier to grasp than the overwhelming facts of the entire Holocaust.

New Attitudes Among Germans By 1992, the 50th anniversary of the Wannsee Conference, Germany had committed itself to confronting its past. The country's president reminded all Germans at the opening of the Holocaust Museum that they had a special commitment to ethnic toleration. This commitment became evident by the willingness of many Germans to take in refugees from Syria and elsewhere in the 2010s.

Changes in Commemoration Scholar Jay Winter studied how the memorials people created after World War II compared to those created after World War I. Those built after the first war seemed to draw upon medieval Christian themes and metaphors often associated with the end of the world, known as the Apocalypse. They often promoted democratic values. For example, many tributes included an alphabetical listing of names of those who died, without including the social or even military rank.

The reaction to the horrors of the Holocaust caused people to rethink the long history and structure of commemoration. The victims were Jews, not Christians. Further, they were innocent civilians, not soldiers going off to fight for their country or some other purpose. Winter wrote, "Sites of memory are places where people affirm their faith that history has meaning. What kind of site is appropriate where the majority of people see no meaning at all in the events being marked in time and space?" In 2017, Winter explained how memorial spaces became "flattened-out spaces for mourning and contemplation of the horror of war." World War II memorials in Europe today represent Europe's respect for human rights and peace, and the greatest atrocities have their own memorials.

KEY TERMS BY THEME

Identity
anti-Semite

Geography
no man's land

Governance
alliance
armistice
bloc
appeasement

concentration camp
disarmament
totalitarian
fascism
ghetto
Holocaust
mandate
militarism
pogrom

puppet state
referendum
reparations
stalemate
theater of war
trench warfare
World War

Technology
blitzkrieg

This Soviet memorial to victory of World War II is in Volgograd. The city, then known as Stalingrad, was the site of the one of the turning points of the war. In a five-month battle, the Soviets suffered approximately as many casualties as the United States suffered the entire war. The Soviet victory permanently weakened the German military.

Credit: Getty Images

Questions 1–3 refer to the passage below.

"The cannon fodder loaded onto trains in August and September is moldering in the killing fields of Belgium... Across the ocean stretch thousands of greedy hands to snatch it up. Business thrives in the ruins. Cities become piles of ruins; villages become cemeteries; countries, deserts; populations are beggared; churches, horse stalls. International law, treaties and alliances, the most sacred words and the highest authority have been torn in shreds. Every sovereign 'by the grace of God' is called a rogue and lying scoundrel by his cousin on the other side. Every diplomat is a cunning rascal to his colleagues in the other party. Every government sees every other as dooming its own people and worthy only of universal contempt. There are food riots in Venice, in Lisbon, Moscow, Singapore. There is plague in Russia, and misery and despair everywhere. Violated, dishonored, wading in blood, dripping filth— there stands bourgeois society... Today's world war is entirely a competitive struggle amongst fully mature capitalisms for world domination, for the exploitation of the remaining zones of the world not yet capitalistic."

Rosa Luxemburg, *The Junius Pamphlet: The Crisis in German Social-Democracy*, 1915

1. The conditions described in this passage were most directly a result of which development?

   a) The strains of a military stalemate and total war

   b) The economic crisis generated by the Great Depression

   c) The use of blitzkrieg warfare

   d) Government efforts to incite revolution in enemy nations

2. Luxemburg's attitude toward the war implies that she was most influenced by which ideology?

   a) Liberalism

   b) Marxism

   c) Romanticism

   d) Nationalism

3. Sentiments similar to those expressed in this passage led most directly to which result?

   a) The acceptance by Germany of war guilt in the Versailles Treaty

   b) The desire of women to take jobs in war industries

   c) The entry of the United States into World War I

   d) The outbreak of a revolution that overthrew the Russian tsar

THE BALKANS, 1913

4. Comparing this map with one of the same region a century earlier would highlight the importance of

   a) conservativism in reaction against the Englightenment

   b) nationalism in reaction against multiethnic empires

   c) socialism in reaction against capitalism

   d) anarchism in reaction against the growth of government

5. How would a map of this region look different a decade later?

   a) Serbia, Montenegro, and parts of Austria-Hungary would combine to form a new state.

   b) Serbia, Bulgaria, and part of Greece would be part of the Ottoman Empire.

   c) Serbia and Montenegro would be part of Austria-Hungary.

   a) Serbia, Albania, and Romania would each be divided into smaller states.

Questions 6–8 refer to the cartoon below.

"Why should we take a stand about someone pushing someone else when it's all so far away. . ."

David Low, "Increasing Pressure," *Evening Standard,* a British newspaper, February 18, 1938
Credit: https://archive.cartoons.ac.uk/record.aspx?src=CalmView.Catalog&id=DL1304

6. The British policy depicted in the cartoon had which of the following effects on European politics in the period before World War II?

   a) It helped European economies recover from the Great Depression.

   b) It reaffirmed the peace settlement made by the Treaty of Versailles.

   c) It allowed fascist states to rearm and expand their territory.

   d) It encouraged loyalty from subjects of the British Empire.

7. Which of the following was the most significant factor in contributing to the British attitude in the cartoon?

   a) The losses and devastation caused by World War I

   b) Confidence in the diplomatic influence of the League of Nations

   c) The establishment of a British alliance with the Soviet Union

   d) The presence of a significant German population in Britain

8. Which of the following best describes the purpose of the cartoon?

   a) To mock the weakness of other European countries

   b) To encourage British isolationism

   c) To criticize the British policy of appeasement

   d) To glorify German military strength

1. Use the passages below to answer all parts of the question that follows.

Passage 1

It is my purpose, as one who lived and acted in these days, to show how easily the tragedy of the Second World War could have been prevented…We shall see how the counsels of prudence and restraint may become the prime agents of mortal danger; how the middle course adopted from desires for safety and a quiet life may be found to lead direct to the bull's-eye disaster… It is the fact that whereas "appeasement" in all forms only encouraged their aggression and gave the Dictators more power with their people.

Winston Churchill, *The Gathering Storm,* 1948

Passage 2

In analyzing appeasement, it is necessary to examine the role of the British prime minister, Neville Chamberlain, who was not as foolish as some have imagined…The Western democracies have been denounced for their failure to go to war against Germany before 1939. Such accusations fail to take into account the public mood and the lack of military preparedness on the part of France or Great Britain. It is important to realize that the Western leaders who had to make the decision for war or peace had grave doubts about the capabilities of their armed forces.

Keith Eubanks, *The Origins of World War II,* 1969

a) Describe ONE major difference between Churchill's and Eubank's interpretations of the origins of World War II.

b) Describe ONE historical event or development from 1930 to 1939 that could be used to support Churchill's interpretation.

c) Describe ONE historical event or development from 1930 to 1939 that could be used to support Eubank's interpretation.

2. Answer all parts of the question that follows.

a) Describe ONE similarity in the causes of World War I and World War II.

b) Describe ONE difference in the causes of World War I and World War II.

c) Explain why results of World War I and World War II differed.

LONG ESSAY QUESTIONS

1. Evaluate the extent to which developments in the Balkans were the most significant factor leading to World War I.

2. Evaluate the extent to which the Germans and French viewed the Versailles Treaty differently.

REFLECT ON THE CHAPTER ESSENTIAL QUESTION

1. In one to three paragraphs, explain how war and instability in the first half of the 20th century gave way to the Cold War.

WRITE AS A HISTORIAN: EVALUATE TURNING POINTS

The move from one period into another is based on some significant event or change. Some events appear inevitable. For instance, World War II might seem to be destined to occur because of the Treaty of Versailles and the weakness of the League of Nations. However, no events in history were truly inevitable. People always made choice. This is the idea of *contingency*, that history happened as it did because multiple factors came together.

You can highlight the role of contingency by asking what might have happened if someone had made a different decision. If the assassin of Franz Ferdinand had decided not to carry out the act, would World War I still have happened? Historians cannot answer "what if" questions with confidence, but trying to answer them shows how important a decision can be.

Develop "what if" questions for the statements below to suggest how these turning-point events might have had different results than they actually did.

1. World War I destroyed Europe's balance of power, and the Treaty of Versailles created instability in which extremist ideologies emerged. The breakdown of that settlement led to World War II.

2. Newly established postwar democracies in central and Eastern Europe were too weak to provide stability, leading to failed states.

3. The Nazi government in Germany undertook the annihilation of Jews from the whole continent (the Holocaust), as well as the murder of other targeted groups of Europeans.

4. The uneasy alliance between Soviet Russia and the West during World War II gave way after 1945 to a Cold War between the democratic capitalist states of Western Europe allied with the United States and the communist bloc of Eastern Europe dominated by the Soviet Union.

20

Nationalism and Transnationalism

"From Stettin in the Baltic to Trieste in the Adriatic, an iron curtain has descended across the continent. Behind that line lie all the capitals of the ancient states of central and eastern Europe. . . . all these famous cities and the populations around them lie in the Soviet sphere . . . ."
—Winston Churchill, speech in Fulton, Missouri, March 5, 1946

Essential Question: How did Europe become both more polarized and more open to transnational efforts after World War II?

After the destruction and devastation of World War II, Europe became polarized between states aligned with the United States and liberal democracy and those aligned with and dominated by the communist **Soviet Union**, also known as the **Union of Soviet Socialist Republics (USSR)**. (See Chapter 21 for information on the formation of the Soviet Union.) This polarization lead to efforts that were **transnational**, ones that linked participants across country boundaries, especially in the areas of trade and military defense. After the collapse of the Soviet Union in 1991, some transnational efforts were able to bridge the gap between the former enemies.

The Cold War in Europe and the World   *common enemy*

During World War II, Western democracies in Europe and the United States allied with the communist Soviet Union in an effort to defeat Nazism. Political differences between liberal democracy and communism were put aside in order to focus on the Allies' main goal. As the defeat of Germany became certain in 1945, Allied leaders began to talk about the peace process and these differences once again became prominent. The United States and the Soviet Union emerged from the war as the two political and military superpowers, and they had very different visions for the postwar world. Neither side was willing to engage in another massive battle on the ground. Instead, tensions led to a **Cold War** in which conflicts played out in propaganda campaigns, secret operations, limited military conflicts, and an arms race. The Cold War lasted for about 50 years. (See Chapter 21 for more information on the ideological differences among democracy, communism, and fascism.)

The Division of Europe

better than
LON

American President **Franklin Roosevelt** and British Prime Minister **Winston Churchill** had made the establishment of the **United Nations (UN)** a priority during World War II. They hoped this new international organization would be more effective than the League of Nations had been in mediating disputes among nations. **Joseph Stalin** of the Soviet Union negotiated with the other Allied leaders on certain aspects of the UN's makeup. In the end, concessions were made and the basis for the UN Charter was laid. Divisions between West and East were soon reflected, however, in the workings of the UN, as the United States and the Soviet Union each had veto powers in the Security Council and would not approve decisions that conflicted with their interests. Several specific issues soon led to the division of Europe.

Eastern Europe For the United States and Great Britain, the principle of **self-determination** was paramount, and they advocated for free elections in the countries of Eastern Europe that had been liberated from the Nazis by the Soviet Union. Stalin was adamant that the nations of Eastern Europe remain under Soviet influence. He recognized that free elections would result

purpose: protect

in governments that were less than friendly to the Soviets. He also believed that Soviet security depended on buffer states in Eastern Europe to protect it from Western aggression. Therefore, pro-Soviet governments were put in place in Poland, Romania, Bulgaria, and Hungary.

to stop the spread of communism

After Soviet-influenced countries in Eastern Europe supported communists in a civil war in Greece, in 1947 the United States proclaimed the **Truman Doctrine**, which offered financial aid to any country that was threatened by communist takeover. These events led to a decisive division of Europe into West and East. Following Winston Churchill's speech (quoted at the start of the chapter), the West referred to the countries under Soviet domination as the **Iron Curtain** countries.

invisible line drawn through Europe

This monument in Hungary recalls the period when Eastern Europe was under Soviet power and separated off from the rest of Europe.

Credit: Getty Images

Germany The question of what to do with Germany was also a source of conflict among the Allies. All agreed that the country and the city of Berlin would be partitioned among France, Great Britain, the United States, and the Soviet Union. The three Western Allies wanted to combine their three zones into one state under democratic principles. In Berlin, the three Western zones would become a free city that was located within the Soviet zone of Germany.

The Soviets wanted to stop these Western plans and gain control of all of Berlin. To this end, they set up a blockade of the Western zones in Berlin to prevent the West from moving supplies into the area by land. The Western Allies did not want to risk a military confrontation with the Soviets and ultimately began the Berlin Airlift. Through this operation, supplies were flown into the Western zones every day between February 1948 and May 1949, when the Soviets finally lifted the blockade. After that time, two states were created in Germany, the West German Federal Republic and the German Democratic Republic, generally referred to as East Germany. The division of Europe into East and West was complete.

The Cold War on a Global Stage

In 1949 the Cold War moved to a global stage. In that year, communists gained control of the government of China and increased the West's concerns about the spread of communism. The United States and the Soviet Union never fought direct military battles against one another. Instead the war involved four major types of conflict.

Propaganda Campaigns Because the Cold War was a war between different ideologies, an important part of the "fight" was the effort to persuade people around the world of the superiority of each side's ideas and values. For the West, those values were focused on democracy, political freedom, and the benefits of a capitalist economy. The Soviets promoted the values of a communist system, such as the end of class differences and the benefits of a planned, collective economy. Both sides used a variety of means to promote their messages.

The United States used mass media to promote the benefits of a Western lifestyle to people in Eastern Europe and the Soviet Union. The Voice of America and Radio Free Europe were two government-sponsored programs that broadcast Western news and culture throughout the Soviet bloc. These programs provided an alternative to the messages that were put out by state-sponsored media in communist countries. The Soviets made every effort to jam these radio signals but were largely unsuccessful.

Soviet messages focused on the corruption and greed of Western countries, portraying them as economic imperialists. They also pointed to problems of class and race in the United States. Stalin saw efforts by the United States to supply aid to European countries to rebuild after World War II as efforts to make those countries dependent on the United States. Soviet propaganda posters often evoked images of Lenin and other early communist leaders to encourage citizens in the East to make sacrifices for communist ideals. The

Soviets also emphasized their strengths in developing weapons and space technology. (See Chapter 22 for a comparison between life in Western and Eastern Europe during the Cold War era.)

Covert Actions The nature of the Cold War led to **covert actions**—hidden or shadowy operations that were not openly carried out by the governments of the nations involved. Much of this activity was in the form of espionage, or spying. The main intelligence agencies involved in spying were the Soviet KGB, the American Central Intelligence Agency (CIA), and the British Secret Intelligence Service (SIS), usually referred to as MI6. All of these agencies grew out of organizations that had been active during World War II.

Each agency recruited people to infiltrate its counterpart in other countries in order to gain secret information, such as plans for weapons development or Cold War strategies. For example, before World War II, the Soviets recruited four college students from Cambridge University in England who supported the communists in the fight against fascism. During the Cold War, these young men gained influential positions within the British government but were actively working for and supplying information to the KGB.

The CIA was also involved in covert actions to influence governments to be more favorable to the United States. For example, it intervened in Italian elections in 1947–1948 to prevent communists from taking control of the Italian government. In a similar way it sought to weaken the Communist Party in France. In addition to gathering foreign intelligence, the KGB spied on and terrorized its citizens who might be opposed to the Soviet regime.

Limited "Hot Wars" The ideological Cold War was accompanied by actual "hot wars" in Asia, Africa, Latin America, and the Caribbean. These military conflicts resulted in the deaths of many millions of people. They were sometimes referred to as proxy wars because the armies of other countries were proxies, or stand-ins, for the two superpowers. Most focused on spreading or stopping the spread of communism. For example, in the 1970s, the United States supported anti-communist forces in a civil war in Angola in southwest Africa, while the Soviet Union and Cuba supported the communist forces.

Two of the biggest confrontations were the **Korean War** and **Vietnam War** in Asia. In both instances, the countries were split into a north with a communist government and a south with a pro-U.S. government. When North Korea invaded South Korea in 1950, the United States, with the support of the United Nations, sent troops to counter the move. North Korea received support from the Soviet Union and later China. The opposing sides fought to a stalemate. An armistice in 1953 left the Korean peninsula divided.

The division in Vietnam occurred in 1954 after the Vietnamese succeeded in defeating the French, who had controlled the country for almost a century. The United States supported the weak and corrupt government of South Vietnam and in the 1960s began to send increasing numbers of military advisors and troops to fight communist guerrillas, the Viet Cong, as well as troops sent from North Vietnam. Both the Soviet Union and China supported the Vietnamese communists. The United States was unsuccessful in defeating the communist

THE GLOBAL COLD WAR

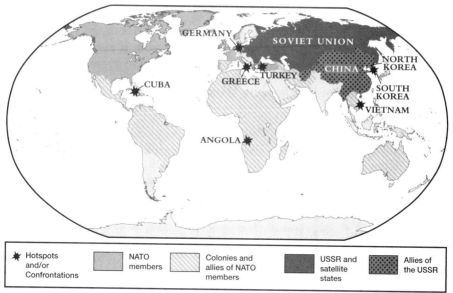

Hotspots and/or Confrontations · **NATO members** · **Colonies and allies of NATO members** · **USSR and satellite states** · **Allies of the USSR**

forces. It withdrew from the country in 1973; North Vietnam soon gained control, uniting the country under a communist government in 1975.

Arms Race When the Soviets exploded their first atomic bomb in 1949 in response to the atomic bombs developed by the United States, a **nuclear arms race** became a key component of the Cold War. Both sides were intent on developing increasing numbers of ever more powerful weapons. The nations knew that if they launched a nuclear attack, the other side would be able to retaliate and destroy them. Therefore, neither side wanted to risk an unwinnable nuclear war that would destroy much of the world.

The threat of nuclear war reached its peak during the Cuban Missile Crisis. The Soviets had supported the communist government of Fidel Castro on the island of Cuba since 1959, and the United States had been unsuccessful in its efforts to overthrow that government. In 1962, the Soviets decided to place nuclear missiles in Cuba—only 90 miles off the coast of Florida. When a U-2 spy plane photographed Soviet missiles in Cuba, President John F. Kennedy ordered a blockade of the island and demanded the removal of the missiles already there. Ultimately, the Soviet leader Nikita Khrushchev agreed to recall the ships carrying the missiles if Kennedy agreed not to invade Cuba.

After this scare, the two countries established a telephone hotline to allow rapid communication. In 1963, they also agreed to ban the testing of nuclear weapons in the atmosphere. However, the arms race continued for most of period until the collapse of the Soviet Union in 1991.

Non-Aligned Movement Some countries, such as India, Indonesia, and Yugoslavia, wanted to avoid taking sides in the U.S.-Soviet conflict. Known as the Non-Aligned Movement, they stayed out of military alliances with either superpower and tried to benefit from good relationships with both.

(handwritten margin note, left: who, CFA)

(handwritten margin note, right: also agreed to take US missiles out of Turkey)

Economic and Political Integration

The Cold War split Europe into East and West. Countries on both sides were closely linked to one of the two superpowers. In both Western and Eastern Europe, countries also realized the benefits of being part of an integrated group.

The United States Influences Western Europe

The United States had a vested interest in supporting the countries of Western Europe that had democratic governments. For this reason, it announced the closely linked policies of the Truman Doctrine and the **Marshall Plan** to provide economic support to help European countries rebuild and become economically stable to prevent them from falling under communist influence. (See next page for information on the Soviets' economic plan.) The military, political, and economic influence of the United States in Europe led to the creation of world monetary and trade systems and a geopolitical military alliance. (See Chapter 20 for information on the Truman Doctrine and Chapter 22 for information on the Marshall Plan.)

NATO During the Cold War, European nations could not act independently in the area of foreign policy because they were so closely tied to the superpowers. No one country in Western Europe could stand up to aggression from the Soviet Union. In 1949, 10 nations of Western Europe signed a treaty with the United States and Canada to form the **North Atlantic Treaty Organization (NATO)**. The member countries pledged to support one another if any of them were attacked.

Early Monetary and Trade Systems A conference to plan for the economy after the end of World War II was held at Bretton Woods, New Hampshire, in July 1944. The United States and Great Britain led the conference, and representatives of 43 countries, including the Soviet Union, attended. The purpose of the conference was to avoid the economic problems that developed after World War I that led to the rise of fascism and the Great Depression. (See Chapter 21 for information on these economic issues.) Out of the conference came the **International Monetary Fund** to help facilitate currency exchange and trade and the **World Bank** to provide loans for trade and rebuilding. In 1948, 23 countries signed the **General Agreement on Tariffs and Trade (GATT)** to reduce barriers to world trade.

The Common Market The Marshall Plan encouraged the countries of Western Europe to cooperate with one another in order to maximize the benefits of U.S. aid and boost post-war recovery. Early cooperative efforts expanded over time. In 1951, France, West Germany, the Netherlands, Belgium, Luxembourg, and Italy created an organization, the European Coal and Steel Community (ECSC), to eliminate trade barriers on steel and coal. In 1957, the same six countries signed a treaty that created the **European Economic Community (EEC)**, often known as the **Common Market**, which promoted free trade within the EEC. By the 1960s, the Common Market was a trading force that was close in size to the United States.

The European Union The Common Market integrated more European economies in the 1970s and 1980s with the addition of Great Britain, Ireland, Denmark, Spain, Portugal, and Greece. The organization was then called the **European Community** and was the world's largest trading bloc. Europeans then sought to create a political union as well as wan economic one, with an executive body and a Parliament. The **Maastricht Treaty** of 1991 founded the **European Union**, which was ratified by all members in 1994. In 1999, 11 member countries agreed to accept the **euro** as a common currency.

The Soviet Union Dominates Eastern Europe

The Soviet Union dominated the European countries east of the Iron Curtain militarily, politically, and economically. The Soviets responded to the efforts of the United States in Western Europe by establishing their own organizations to integrate the countries of the Soviet bloc.

Council for Mutual Economic Assistance (COMECON) The Soviets refused to participate in the Marshall Plan, and in 1949, they created COMECON to strengthen economic ties among the countries in the Soviet bloc. Later, other countries in Eastern Europe and other communist countries, including Cuba and Vietnam, became part of COMECON. After Stalin's death in 1953, the Soviets used COMECON to promote industrial specialization among member countries as part of the planned economy. The purpose was to minimize duplication of production and competition in manufacturing among member nations.

Warsaw Pact In 1955, the Soviets signed a treaty known as the **Warsaw Pact** with Albania, Bulgaria, Czechoslovakia, East Germany, Hungary, Poland, and Romania to create a military alliance with its satellite countries. Through it, the Soviet Union increased its dominance over satellite countries. The pact forced all member nations to supply a certain number of troops each year and gave control of those forces to the Soviet Union. In 1956, when Poland and Hungary began to reject Soviet policies, the Soviets reacted with force. The Soviets also cited the Warsaw Pact when it used troops to crush an uprising in Czechoslovakia in 1968. (See Chapter 22 for more information on these uprisings.)

The Integration of Eastern and Western Europe

The rejection of communist rule in many of the Eastern bloc countries began in 1989 after Soviet leader Mikhail Gorbachev introduced the policies of *glasnost,* or "openness," and *perestroika,* or "restructuring." A variety of political and economic factors, including the costs of the Cold War arms race, led to the final collapse of the USSR in 1991. (See Chapter 22 for more on the causes of the collapse of communism.) With the collapse of communism, the Cold War ended and the Warsaw Pact dissolved. All the members in the pact at that time, except Russia, later joined NATO.

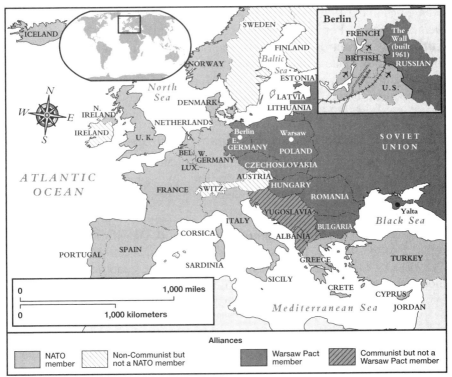

After the collapse, countries in Eastern Europe rejected the planned economies of Soviet times and began to establish capitalist economies. The transition to market economies was difficult. As consumers, citizens grappled with higher prices as state subsidies ended. As workers, citizens faced unemployment as state planning ended. However, the expansion of economic freedom allowed for more innovation and opportunities for people to make decisions about their own careers.

As former Eastern bloc countries moved toward greater political and economic freedom, many applied to join the European Union. Between 2004 and 2007, 10 former Eastern bloc countries became members.

In the realm of politics, the end of Soviet dominance in Eastern Europe led to both greater integration and new divisions. East and West Germany were reunited even before the official collapse in 1991, beginning with free elections held in March 1990. The countries merged their economies in July and their governments in October of that year.

In Czechoslovakia, ethnic differences led to the separation of the country into two states, the Czech Republic and Slovakia, in 1993. The separation was peaceful. (See Chapter 22 for more information on the collapse of the Soviet Union and its aftermath in Europe.)

Nationalist and Separatist Movements

Beginning in the 1990s, Europe experienced a resurgence of nationalism even as the integration of Western and Eastern Europe proceeded. For example, the violent dissolution of Yugoslavia in the 1990s was fueled by ethnic conflict and nationalist and separatist movements. The dissolution began with declarations of independence from both Slovenia and Croatia in June 1991. **Serbian** nationalists under the leadership of Slobodan Milošević fought to maintain and expand Serb areas of Croatia and **Bosnia-Herzegovina**, which declared its independence in March 1992.

In their efforts to drive **Bosnian Muslims** from the territory, the Serbian army killed 250,000 and forcibly removed another two million people from their homes. This effort to create an ethnically homogeneous territory through violence is called **ethnic cleansing**. In a similar effort in the late 1990s, Milošević's forces drove hundreds of thousands of **ethnic Albanians** from the province of **Kosovo**. (See Chapter 22 for more information on the conflict in Yugoslavia.)

Chechnya The breakup of the Soviet Union in 1991 led to independence for many former Soviet republics, including Ukraine, Lithuania, and Azerbaijan. The small, petroleum-rich, and mostly Muslim republic of **Chechnya** in the southwestern part of Russia also declared its independence in November 1991. Leaders advocated for Chechen nationalism and opposed Russia. Russian troops invaded Chechnya in 1994 to forcibly bring the republic back into the Russian Federation, formed after the dissolution of the Soviet Union. By 1997, when a peace treaty was signed, about 100,000 Chechens had been killed and 400,000 had become homeless.

Soviet troops returned in 1999, when Russian president **Vladimir Putin** accused Chechens of bombings that killed Russian civilians. Though Chechen involvement was not proved, Russia maintained control over the republic. In 2003, the new Chechen constitution reaffirmed the republic's membership in the Russian Federation; the presidents of the republic have been appointed by Russia since that time.

Basques The ethnic **Basque** people of northern Spain and part of southwestern France also have sought a separate national identity dating back to the period before World War II. The Basques, who have a language and culture distinct from the rest of Spain, had historically enjoyed a certain level of autonomy. However, the Spanish dictator **Francisco Franco**, who came to power in the 1930s and ruled until 1975, took this away. (See Chapter 21 for more information on Franco.) Some of the autonomy was returned by later Spanish governments.

The group **ETA**, whose name stands for Basque Homeland and Liberty, formed in the 1960s to resist Franco and fight for an independent Basque state. During and after the Cold War, ETA engaged in attacks that resulted in the deaths of more than 800 people. Support for ETA decreased in the 21st century. In May 2018, the group announced its intention to formally disband.

Currrent Separatist Movements in Europe		
Country	**Region**	**Location of Region**
Denmark	Faroe Islands	Islands in the north Atlantic Ocean
United Kingdom	Scotland	Northern part of the island of Britain
Belgium	Flanders	Northern region, near the Netherlands
Germany	Bavaria	Southern Germany, near Austria
Italy	South Tyrol	Northern Italy, in the Alps
Italy	Veneto	Northeastern Italy, near the Adriatic Sea
France	Corsica	Island in the Mediterranean Sea
Spain	Catalonia	Northeastern Spain, near France
Spain	Basque Country	North central Spain, in the Pyrenees

Source: Rick Noack, "Europe Has Plenty of Secessionist Movements Like Catalonia." *Washington Post*, October 11, 2017. washingtonpost.com

Decolonization Replaces European Empires

European colonial empires, amassed in Asia and Africa during the 18th and 19th centuries, finally came apart in the 20th century. Decolonization took decades in many cases, as European imperialist states had varying reactions to the process—ranging from cooperation to resistance and interference. The two world wars played a major role in the move to end European control over their empires.

Principle of National Self-determination

Nationalist forces were among the causes of World War I. At the end of the war, four major empires were dismantled: the German, Austro-Hungarian, Ottoman, and Russian. In Europe, some former territories within these empires became independent states. (See Chapter 21 for more information on the consequences of the breakup of these empires.)

    National Self-determination During the peace process, President **Woodrow Wilson** of the United States advocated the principle of national self-determination. He believed that the people of a given territory should be able to decide their own form of government without interference from outside states. Though he was not successful in getting this principle included in the charter of the League of Nations, Wilson's ideas struck a chord with many nationalists around the world. These nationalists believed that they would benefit from new policies and freedoms. People in French and British colonies were disappointed when it soon became clear that reality did not match the promises of self-determination.

    British India The **Indian National Congress** was the main group in India advocating for national independence. After World War I, many argued that India's wartime service to the empire strengthened its case for independence.

Almost 1.5 million Indians had volunteered to provide fighting troops and support services for the British, mostly in Africa and the Middle East. Britain promised a gradual increase in self-governance but always insisted that India remain part of the empire. The Indian nationalists refused to accept what they saw as insufficient concessions.

French African Colonies In a similar way, France used hundreds of thousands of colonial subjects from West and North Africa to fight on the Western Front during World War I. Many Africans also worked in French factories as battle losses created a shortage of French workers. The French often drafted Africans into its armed forces. French reforms after World War I did little to encourage nationalists in its African colonies.

The Mandate System

The League of Nations did try to establish some international control over colonies after World War I. The **mandate system** was set up so that League-supervised European powers would take administrative responsibility for former colonies of the German and Ottoman empires. The Middle East was a key region where the mandate system took effect.

Middle East Mandates During World War I, the Allies had promised independence to many Arab territories in the Middle East in exchange for their support in fighting the Ottoman Empire. Yet when the empire was dismantled during the peace process, Great Britain and France were awarded control of these former Turkish territories as mandates. As a result of the mandate system, Turkey's power in the Middle East was severely limited, while that of France and Great Britain grew.

The British mandates in the Middle East were **Iraq** and **Palestine**, which included present-day Jordan and Israel. The French mandates in the region were **Syria** and **Lebanon**. These mandates were all considered to be close to independence, yet the British and the French remained actively involved in the region until after World War II.

Mandates and Oil One major reason for the ongoing presence of these European powers was the recognition of the strategic importance of the Middle East and its oil. As World War I progressed, oil became increasingly important to fuel ships, trucks, tanks, and planes. Countries also realized oil would be important after the war as a fuel and a lubricant for the civilian economy.

Before the war, German and British oil companies had invested in the Turkish Petroleum Company (TPC), which was exploring for oil in the region that became Iraq. During the peace negotiations, Germany lost all rights to this company. The victors in the war—Great Britain, France, and the United States negotiated with each other for control of the oil. In 1928, private oil companies in the three countries agreed that they would work together to develop the oil fields in the Middle East region that had formerly been controlled by the Ottoman Empire.

Nationalist Movements and Delayed Independence

Indigenous nationalist movements in many Asian and African colonies began before World War I and grew stronger immediately after it. These movements were generally repressed until after World War II. In 1945, the principle of national self-determination became part of the UN Charter. In addition, most European states were so weakened by World War II that they could no longer maintain control over their colonies. For example, after resisting the move for decades, Great Britain granted independence to India in 1947. But for a variety of reasons, independence for many colonies was delayed for decades.

Indochina The French had been reluctant to relinquish control of their colonies in Indochina, or Southeast Asia. In Vietnam, the **Viet Minh**, strong nationalist guerillas under the leadership of **Ho Chi Minh**, defeated the French in 1954 at the battle of Dien Bien Phu. The French then granted independence to Laos and Cambodia. They divided Vietnam into two countries until elections could be held in 1956. However, Vietnam then became the site of a long proxy war between the United States and the Soviet Union. Vietnam finally became independent under a communist government in 1975.

North Africa Though France granted independence to Morocco and Tunisia in 1956, it was reluctant to do the same for **Algeria**, in large part because two million French citizens had settled there. In Algeria as in Vietnam, nationalist guerillas fought the French in a long war that deeply divided citizens in France. France finally agreed to Algeria's independence in 1962.

Southern Africa In southern Africa, several countries gained independence peacefully. By 1960, the French, British, and Belgians had given up direct control of most of their colonies. However, Portugal fought longer to keep control of its African colonies, including **Angola**. After 14 years of fighting, Angola declared its independence in 1975 when a coup disrupted the Portuguese government. However, Angola lacked stability. Three different groups had been fighting for independence, with groups being supported by the Soviet Union and Cuba, the United States, China, and Zaire (now the Democratic Republic of the Congo). Much of this international interest resulted from the Cold War and the spread of communism. After independence, Angola endured a long civil war that ended in the mid-1990s.

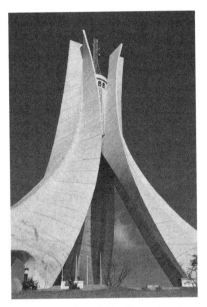

The Martyrs' Memorial in Algiers, Algeria, was opened in 1982 to pay respect to all the Algerians who died in the fight for independence from France.

Credit: Getty Images

Effects of Decolonization Even after decolonization, European influence remained strong in many former colonies. As these countries dealt with poverty and factional disputes, they remained dependent on the West and Japan for technology and financial aid. In addition, many former colonial subjects migrated to Europe seeking economic opportunities. Migration due to decolonization especially affected Great Britain, France, and the Netherlands.

In the first decades after World War II, Europe needed migrant labor to help it rebuild. About 10 million people migrated to Western Europe between 1950 and 1973. However, when economic times grew tighter in the 1970s, many European countries found that workers they considered temporary residents wanted to become permanent citizens. Ethnic and racial tensions between immigrants and native populations grew over time as Europe found its ideas about its identity changing.

HISTORICAL PERSPECTIVES: WHAT CAUSED THE COLD WAR?

The causes of the five-decade struggle between the United States and the Soviet Union after World War II are many. Historians continue to weigh them.

The Soviet Union In the 1940s and 1950s, the orthodox, or mainstream, historians of the Cold War argued that Stalin and his uncompromising totalitarian ways caused the conflict. Arthur Schlesinger Jr. expressed this view in numerous works throughout the 1960s, including the article "Origins of the Cold War" (1967). He saw capitalism and communism as incompatible ideologies. Schlesinger pointed to Lenin's view that all capitalist societies were destined to follow the road to communism and the Stalin's creation of a totalitarian state as the key factors in causing the Cold War. Schlesinger did recognize changes in the Soviet Union after Stalin's death. The process of "de-Stalinization," he thought, might lead to the Soviets' willingness to compromise, which would reduce tensions.

The United States By the 1960s, the Cold War spread to the Third World, most notably Vietnam. As a result historians became more critical of the American role in the cause and course of the Cold War. These revisionist historians focused on the U.S. pursuit of a capitalist agenda that made diplomatic decisions based on economic needs and a desire to dominate the global economy.

Among the most controversial revisionists were Gabriel and Joyce Kolko. They argued that the demands of a growing capitalist economy depended on an expansionist American foreign policy. Further, economic pressures demanded resistance to leftist movements everywhere because they threatened this system. The Kolkos used the role of the United States in Eastern Europe in the aftermath of World War II of evidence of this behavior. Some revisionists argued that if the United States had recognized the Soviet need for security, Stalin would have been more willing to compromise.

Refocusing on the Soviets In the later years of the Cold War, the most famous of Cold War historians, John Lewis Gaddis, shared the post-revisionist view that misunderstandings on both sides escalated the Cold War. However, once the wall came down and access to the Soviet archives became available, Gaddis revisited his views in 1998 and again in 2005 stating that it was in fact Russia's fault. In his 2005 book, *The Cold War,* Gaddis finds much evidence in telegrams to justify American policy decisions. Based on his research in the Soviet archives, Gaddis placed blame for the Cold War squarely on the internal workings of the Soviet system: "Soviet leaders had to treat the outside world as hostile because otherwise they could not excuse the dictatorship without which they did not know how to rule."

KEY TERMS BY THEME

Governance

Soviet Union

Union of Soviet Socialist Republics (USSR)

Cold War

Franklin Roosevelt

United Nations (UN)

Winston Churchill

Joseph Stalin

national self-determination

Truman Doctrine

Iron Curtain

covert actions

"hot wars"

Korean War

Vietnam War

nuclear arms race

Marshall Plan

North Atlantic Treaty Organization (NATO)

Warsaw Pact

Mikhail Gorbachev

glasnost

perestroika

Vladimir Putin

Iraq

Palestine

Syria

Lebanon

Viet Minh

Ho Chi Minh

Algeria

Angola

Economics

International Monetary Fund

World Bank

General Agreement on Tariffs and Trade (GATT)

euro

Council for Mutual Economic Assistance (COMECON)

Continuity and Change

European Economic Community (EEC)

Common Market

European Community

Maastricht Treaty

European Union

Identity

transnational

Serbian

Bosnia-Herzegovina

Bosnian Muslims

ethnic cleansing

ethnic Albanians

Kosovo

Chechnya

Basque

Woodrow Wilson

Indian National Congress

mandate system

Francisco Franco

ETA

Questions 1–3 refer to the passage below.

The statements contained in the North Atlantic treaty [that created NATO] that it is designated for defense and that it recognizes the principles of the United Nations organization serve aims which have nothing in common, either with the tasks of self-defense of the parties to the treaty or with real recognition of the aims and principles of the United Nations organization.

Of the great powers, only the Soviet Union is excluded from among the parties to this treaty, which can be explained only by the fact that this treaty is directed against the Soviet Union. .

The North Atlantic pact is designed to daunt the states which do not agree to obey the dictate of the Anglo-American grouping of powers that lay claim to world domination, though the untenability of such claims was once again affirmed by the second World War which ended in the debacle of Fascist Germany, which also had laid claim to world domination.

Soviet Monitor, April 1949

1. Which of the following influenced the formation of NATO?

   a) the World Bank

   b) Marshall Plan

   c) COMECON

   d) Warsaw Pact

2. The develop of which organization or agreement reflected the point of view expressed in the passage?

   a) the European Economic Community

   b) the Council for Mutual Economic Assistance

   c) the Warsaw Pact

   d) the Maastricht Treaty

3. The writer's point of view in the passage most clearly reflected concerns shaped by which development?

   a) the spread of nationalism

   b) the trend of decolonization

   c) the outbreak of war in Korea and Vietnam

   d) the nuclear arms race

Questions 4–6 refer to the passage below.

"While [U.S. secretary of state] Kissinger was trying to sort out the cease-fire, he met with his State Department senior staff to give them his assessment of the situation since the war broke out. This gave him a chance to vent some steam about issues that troubled him, such as the question of his advice on preemption and the attitude of West European allies who, he argued, were behaving like 'jackals' because they 'did everything to egg on the Arabs.'

Kissinger reviewed the immediate prewar intelligence estimating on the Arab-Israeli conflict ('no possibility of an attack'), the 'new elements' in Arab strategy, overall U.S. strategy, interpretations of Soviet conduct, the decision for a major U.S. airlift, U.S. early efforts toward a cease-fire, and Resolution 338. On the basic U.S.-Israeli relationship during the war, Kissinger explained his balancing act: 'we could not tolerate an Israeli defeat' but, at the same time, 'we could not make our policy hostage to the Israelis.' Thus, 'we went to extreme lengths to stay in close touch with all the key Arab participants.' The progress of the war, so far had been a 'major success' in part because it validated the importance of détente: 'without the close relationship with the Soviet Union, this thing could have easily escalated.'

Washington, however, not Moscow, was in the catbird seat; the Israelis had won, Soviet clients had lost, and a peace settlement depended on Washington. The United States was in a 'position where if we behave wisely and with discipline, we are really in a central position.'"

Henry Kissinger, Staff Meetings Transcript, October 23, 1973

4. According to the passage above, prewar intelligence indicated that
   a) a Syrian attack on Israel would happen very soon
   b) European nations were encouraging the Arabs to attack Israel
   c) an Israeli attack on Egypt was likely
   d) an Arab attack on Israel was unlikely

5. As expressed above, the relationship between which two countries was considered most important in limiting the Israeli-Arab conflict?
   a) the USSR and the United States
   b) Great Britain and Egypt
   c) France and Syria
   d) the United States and Israel

6. Which term best describes the conflict discussed above?
   a) cold war
   b) guerilla war
   c) proxy war
   d) ethnic war

Questions 7–8 refer to the passage below

"For the past three years Algeria has been the theatre of an atrocious war. Blood flows profusely, increasing both mourning and hatred... Before anything else, you must know the truth that they are trying to hide from you.

[T]he demands of a people to its own national life is natural and legitimate... The Algerians will not stop fighting until they are free...Despite the presence of 500,000 French soldiers, despite the horrible repression... 'pacification' has failed...

The Algerians aren't making war on the French people or the Europeans of Algeria, but on FRENCH COLONIALISTS. Besides, isn't it true that many European Algerians participate in this struggle alongside their Moslem brothers? They are Communists, liberals, Christians.

No! The Algerians don't want to throw you into the sea!...

Contrary to what colonialist propaganda wants you to believe, the future Algerian Republic will not be theocratic. The different Algerian national organizations have expressed this: it will be democratic and social...

Who is responsible?...

It is the colonialists, the big bosses, the big landowners... and financiers.

Yesterday they served Hitler and Vichy in the name of French Sovereignty. Today, fearing defeat, they are preparing their fall-back position, exporting their capital, buying land in France and South America...

This horrible face of colonial war explains the fact that exasperated patriots answer by the bomb and the grenade. And how can we forget that there were several tens of victims of these attacks, while colonialist barbarism has already caused SEVERAL HUNDRED THOUSAND DEAD, among the Algerians?"

Letter to the Europeans of Algeria, Algerian Communist Party, 1957

7. What was a main objective of the Algerian nationalists?

a) Establishment of a Muslim state

b) Expulsion of French citizens

c) Elimination of colonial rule

d) Collectivization of large estates

8. How did the Algerian communists defend the violent tactics used by the nationalists?

a) It was a powerful means of demonstrating Algerian resolve.

b) It was a rational effort to get the Nazis out of Algeria.

c) It was an essential method for introducing collective land ownership.

d) It was a justified response to French brutality.

SHORT-ANSWER QUESTIONS

1. Use the excerpt below to answer all parts of the question that follows.

"Similarly, resistance to the United States and the Soviet Union did not grow exclusively out of anti-American and anti-Soviet sources. Quite the contrary, many of the most effective critics of the superpowers emerged from Cold War institutions, especially political parties and universities. Postcolonial personalities certainly had their roots in local traditions and experiences, but they also drew on rhetoric, ideas, and resources from dominant international institutions. Decolonization was, at least in part, a product of the Cold War."

> J. Suri, "The Cold War, Decolonization, and Global Social Awakenings: Historical Intersections." *Cold War History*, 2006.

a) Describe ONE way in which the Cold War contributed to decolonization.

b) Describe ONE cause other than the Cold War that contributed to decolonization.

c) Explain ONE result of decolonization in a specific African or Asian location.

2. Answer all parts of the question that follows.

a) Describe ONE aspect of decolonization in Asia and Africa during the period 1914–1925.

b) Describe ONE aspect of decolonization in Asia and Africa during the period 1945–1955.

c) Describe ONE aspect of decolonization in Asia and Africa during the period 1960–1980.

LONG ESSAY QUESTIONS

1. Evaluate the various ways that nationalism caused instability within Europe from 1914 to 2014.

2. Evaluate the different goals of nationalist movements prior to and after 1945.

REFLECT ON THE CHAPTER ESSENTIAL QUESTION

1. In one to three paragraphs, explain how Europe became both more polarized and more open to transnational efforts after World War II.

Demonstrating that you understand the basis for continuity and change is essential when writing an AP essay. There are a variety of ways to track and mark continuity and change.

- By a concept, such as the Cold War
- By historical events, such as World War II
- By years, such as the 20th century or the 1950s
- By influential individuals, such as the Stalin era
- By developments in historical evolution, such as capitalism or communism
- By geographically specific events, such as Francisco Franco's fascist regime in Spain
- By comparative label, such as the more industrialized countries

Marking the start of a significant change is an attempt to make sense of historical time periods, to determine an era's beginning and end points, its characteristics, its causes and effects. Periods may reflect major trends in technology, science, religion, the arts, or popular culture. Or periods may be concrete, such as the beginning and end of a specific war or political reign. Sometimes, a single individual is so powerful that an era is based entirely on that person's influence.

Choices about identifying the bases for change in history can actually shape the way we think about it. These choices might give higher value to one group, one narrative, or one geographic region over another. Thinking critically about how subjective the basis for identifying change is can enrich the content of your essay.

In the statements below, which words indicate various models of marking time periods?

1. Military and worker insurrections in Russia set the stage for Lenin's Bolshevik Revolution and the establishment of a communist state.

2. Under Stalin, the Soviet Union engaged in rapid economic modernization, as demonstrated by Collectivization and the Five-Year Plan.

3. Fascism gained hold in the environment of bitterness and economic instability of the post-World War I era.

4. The Great Depression undermined Western European democracies and fomented radical political responses throughout Europe.

5. During the Marshall Plan years, the U.S.-financed extensive reconstruction of Western and Central Europe.

6. The expansion of cradle-to-grave social welfare programs in the post-World War II era was funded by high taxes, which became a contentious political issue in Europe.

7. Following a long period of economic stagnation, Mikhail Gorbachev's internal reforms of *perestroika* and *glasnost* attempted to prevent the collapse of the Soviet Union.

8. The rise of new nationalisms in the late 20th century resulted in war and genocide in the Balkans and instability in some former Soviet republics.

The Berlin Airlift Memorial honors the effort by the United States and Western European countries to break a blockade imposed by the Soviet Union on West Berlin in 1948 and 1949.

Credit: Getty Images

Ideological Clashes in the Interwar Years

"Fascism is the complete opposite of Marxian socialism . . . . Fascism combats the whole complex system of democratic ideology, and repudiates it, whether in its theoretical premises or in its practical application."

— Benito Mussolini, 1932

Essential Question: What factors and events caused ideological battles among democratic, communist, and fascist states?

The power of central governments increased throughout Europe during World War I. By the end of the war, the Russian, German, Austro-Hungarian, and Ottoman empires had collapsed. The new democratic governments that followed tended to be weak because there was no history of democratic institutions in these countries. These political changes led to internal conflicts in many European states, exacerbated by severe economic problems and ethnic tensions. Different ideas soon emerged about the relationship between the individual and the state.

Responses to Industrialization

Among these ideas, **communism** advocated ownership of the means of production by the **proletariat** or working class with the ultimate goal of a classless society. As these ideals became reality, communists believed, individuals would be freed from oppressive labor to develop their full human potential, and the state would eventually cease to exist. Communism is an extreme form of **left-wing** ideology. **Fascism** espoused a strong central government with dictatorial control over the economy and the lives of individuals. Fascism is an extreme form of **right-wing** ideology. These ideologies conflicted with **liberal democracy**, which characterized the governments of several western European states. In liberal democracies, individuals were free to elect government leaders and develop their individual self-interests through a capitalist economy. These ideological conflicts led to World War II and continued throughout the 20th century.

Three Approaches to Modern Industrial Society			
Policy Area	Communism	Capitalism	Fascism
Economics	Believed businesses should be owned or managed by the government	Believed businesses should be owned privately and compete with each other	Believed businesses should be owned privately and that government should restrict competition
Internationalism and Nationalism	Supported internationalism by opposing colonialism and calling for global worker solidarity	Supported a mixture of nationalism and internationalism	Supported nationalism strongly by urging each nation to pursue its unique interests
War and Peace	Believed that international peace would follow the defeat of capitalism	Expressed mixed attitudes toward war and peace	Opposed peace on the belief that it weakened society
Equality	Supported both political and economic equality	Supported political equality but not economic equality	Opposed both political and economic equality
Religion	Rejected religion and advocated atheism	Allowed individual religious liberty	Viewed religion as a way to promote national unity

The Russian Revolution and Lenin

In Russian, both reformers and revolutionaries were influenced by the German intellectual **Karl Marx**. Among these was a lawyer, **V. I. Lenin** (1870–1924). Even before he studied Marx closely, Lenin was a revolutionary, committed to overthrowing the tsarist government. While he adopted most of Marx's ideas, he modified them in important ways. For example, Marx thought that a socialist revolution could happen only in a wealthy, highly industrialized country. Lenin disagreed. He believed that even Russia, a poor, peasant-dominated country, could become socialist. Further, Lenin thought that a successful revolution would always depend on a small group of dedicated revolutionaries who could lead the masses. His modifications of Marx's ideas became known as **Marxist-Leninist ideology**. (See Chapters 15 and 18 for more on Marx and Marxism.)

Lenin led the **Bolshevik** faction of the Russian Social Democratic Party. While some socialists believed in gradual, peaceful change, the Bolsheviks called for immediate, violent change. They became the basis for the modern **Communist Party**, which controlled Russian throughout the 20th century.

War Supports Revolutionary Change

The **Russian Social Democratic Party** led a revolution against the rule of **Tsar Nicholas II** in 1905; however, little real change occurred as a result. Although the tsar agreed to create a **Duma**, or elected legislature, that group never gained the power to create a true constitutional monarchy. Russian society remained hierarchical with extremes of social inequality. The industrialization that began in the 1890s created many social problems with people living and working in poor conditions in the crowded cities of Moscow and St. Petersburg. Peasants were largely excluded from land ownership, and food shortages were common. The demands of World War I made these long-standing problems worse and brought Russia to the brink of collapse. Because of this weakened condition, a revolutionary minority, the Bolsheviks, was able to gain control of the country.

The March Revolution Russian industries were unprepared for wartime production. With so many men in the military, women held many factory jobs. After working long hours, these women then had to stand in long lines to buy meager amounts of food. On March 8, 1917, about 10,000 women demonstrated under the banner "Peace and Bread" on the streets of the capital city of Petrograd (formerly, and again today, known as St. Petersburg). A general strike shut down the city's factories on March 10. When the tsar ordered troops to disperse the crowds, many of the troops joined the demonstrators instead.

After the Duma met on March 12, the tsar agreed to abdicate on March 15. The moderates in the Duma then established the **Provisional Government**, which represented the middle-class and liberal aristocrats rather than workers and peasants. The government wanted to continue the war as a matter of national honor. However, the lower classes wanted the war to end immediately.

At the same time, the Provisional Government faced competition from the **soviets**, councils that represented workers, peasants, and soldiers. The first soviet formed in Petrograd in March. Others quickly formed within the army and then other areas. These soviets, composed mainly of radical socialists, represented the interests of the lower classes.

Lenin Returns to Russia Lenin had been involved in anti-government activity since 1887 and active in Marxist organizations since 1893. In 1897, the government had punished him by sending him for a number of years to **Siberia**, a remote region with extreme climate in the eastern part of Russia. After 1900, he lived mostly in exile in Switzerland. Lenin saw the formation of the Provisional Government as an opportunity for the Bolsheviks to seize power. He returned to Russia in April 1917 and laid out his plans for revolution.

Lenin believed that the Bolsheviks could use the soviets to overthrow the Provisional Government. He had the Bolsheviks gain control of the largest soviets in Petrograd and Moscow. At the same time, the Bolsheviks began to use propaganda to gain the support of the people. **Propaganda** uses emotional language, distortion of facts, or scare tactics to persuade others to support a particular point of view. Bolshevik propaganda revolved around three slogans:

- Peace, Land, Bread

- Worker Control of Production

- All Power to the Soviets

Lenin had a reputation as a powerful speaker.

Credit: Getty Images

The Bolshevik Revolution

The Petrograd soviet promoted insurrection in the military by directing soldiers to obey only orders that came from newly elected committees of soldiers rather than from the officers who had been in charge. This action created chaos in the army. The Provisional Government was unable to undertake a new military offensive in July as many peasant soldiers deserted and returned to their homes. Although an attempt by soldiers and workers to overthrow the government failed at that time, conditions revealed how weak the government was.

By late October 1917, the Bolshevik party's membership had grown substantially, and the Bolsheviks had gained slim majorities in the Petrograd and Moscow soviets. Lenin believed that the time was right for the Bolsheviks to seize control. He overcame resistance in his party with the help of **Leon Trotsky** (1877–1940). Trotsky had once been a member of the more moderate Menshevik faction of the Social Democratic Party but had become an ardent supporter of revolution. On November 6–7, the Bolsheviks easily took control of the Winter Palace in Petrograd where the Provisional Government had its headquarters.

Lenin soon established the Council of People's Commissars, which held true power in the country. He quickly enacted laws to give peasants control of land and workers control of factories in order to keep the masses of people supporting the Bolsheviks, who soon became known as **Communists**. Lenin then disbanded the Constituent Assembly, which had been elected under the Provisional Government and in which the Bolsheviks had a minority of seats.

On March 3, 1918, Bolshevik-led Russia agreed to give the Baltic territories and some other lands that were part of the Russian empire to Germany in the Treaty of Brest-Litovsk, which ended its involvement in World War I. Shortly after this treaty was signed, Lenin moved the Russian capital to Moscow because it was farther from Germany. In July 1918, Tsar Nicholas II and his family were executed. In about one year, Russia had moved from an autocratic government led by the tsar to a new form of authoritarian rule under the Communists.

[handwritten margin note: ended involvement due to chaos (Russian Rev.)]

Civil War

Although lower-class Russians wanted peace, the treaty that ended their country's involvement in World War I did not bring it to them. Instead the country was plunged into a long civil war because numerous forces opposed the Bolsheviks, who were called the **Reds**. Red was the color of the Communist flag. Opponents, called the **Whites**, included not only members of the bourgeoisie and aristocracy who opposed communism but also other socialist factions that opposed Lenin, including the Mensheviks and the Social Revolutionaries. Troops from the Allies fighting in World War I also became involved. Their initial goal was to bring Russia back into the war against Germany, although they remained in the country after World War I ended in November 1918.

For a time, the Whites seemed close to success. By 1921, however, the Communists had regained control of the country. There were several reasons why the Communists were ultimately successful.

- The Red Army was more disciplined and effective under the leadership of Leon Trotsky and had better field positions.

- The Whites could not agree on a united political strategy. Some wanted the return of the tsarist government; others wanted a more democratic form of government.

- The Communists were unified around the goal of creating a new order in Russian society.

- The Communists modified their principles during the war in order to win and maintain their power. For example, they took steps such as nationalizing banks and industries, forcibly taking grain from peasants, and creating a centralized government bureaucracy controlled by the Bolsheviks. They used a secret police force to eliminate all opposition to the party. These and similar economic and political policies that characterized the economy and society during the civil war together became known as **war communism**.

- The Communists appealed to Russians' patriotism to fight against Allied troops that were portrayed as foreign invaders.

Lenin's New Economic Policy

In 1921, Lenin saw that Russia was on the brink of economic collapse after years of war and strict government control of the economy. Peasants and workers threatened to revolt against the policies that had been put in place during the civil war. For example, peasants began holding back food from the government. A two-year drought that began in 1920 resulted in widespread famine that killed millions of people.

To address these conditions, Lenin introduced his **New Economic Policy (NEP)** in March 1921. The NEP was basically a modified form of a free-market or small-scale capitalist economy. Peasants were allowed to sell their produce on the open market. Private ownership of retail shops and other small businesses was permitted. The state retained control of larger industries, banks, and mines. By 1922 the economy and harvests had improved, and the country was more stable.

The Soviet Union under Stalin

During Lenin's NEP era, Russia joined with three other territories to form the **Union of Soviet Socialist Republics (USSR)** or **Soviet Union** in 1922. In that same year, Lenin suffered a series of strokes, and he died in 1924. Before his first stroke, Lenin appointed **Joseph Stalin** (1879–1953) as general secretary of the Communist Party. Before his death, Lenin expressed doubts about Stalin, but Lenin's declining health prevented him from removing Stalin from his position.

Lenin's death set off a power struggle within the **Politburo**, a group of seven men that controlled the Communist Party. One group, led by Leon Trotsky, wanted an end to the NEP and favored the rapid industrialization of the Soviet Union and "international revolution"—the expansion of communism around the world. Other members of the Politburo, including Stalin, wanted to focus on developing "socialism at home"—creating a strong communist state in the Soviet Union and supported the continuation of the NEP. Stalin and Trotsky were fierce political rivals.

As general secretary, Stalin made thousands of political appointments at the local and regional level. These appointees became Stalin's strong supporters because they depended on him for their jobs. Eventually Stalin declared his decision to focus on creating a strong communist state in the Soviet Union and forced all his rivals out of the party. By 1929, Stalin had complete control of the party and established a dictatorship of unprecedented power over the country that lasted until his death.

Rapid Economic Modernization

Although Stalin disagreed with Trotsky on the idea of a worldwide communist revolution, he did favor a program to push for the Soviet Union's rapid modernization. Stalin's first five-year plan, launched in 1928, was designed to transform the Soviet Union from a mainly agricultural country to an industrial powerhouse. A second plan followed in 1933. Under these plans, the government took control of industry and emphasized production of chemicals, heavy equipment, and weapons rather than consumer goods such as clothing. The steel and oil industries were particularly important. New cities for these industries quickly grew in areas with large iron ore and coal deposits. The rate of economic growth was 14–20 percent per year. The Soviet Union also built the largest electric power plant in Europe during this period. This rapid growth and change had severe repercussions for the Soviet people.

Consequences of Economic Modernization

Such rapid industrial growth caused millions of new workers to join the labor force and move into industrial cities. Millions of people lived in terrible conditions because the government spent too little on housing for workers during this period. In addition, workers' wages fell by 43 percent between 1928 and 1940. The government also passed laws that limited workers' ability to move freely about the country. The government used propaganda to encourage workers to sacrifice for the good of the socialist state they were creating.

The government also reorganized agricultural production to finance industry and feed the huge numbers of urban workers. These changes led to suffering for millions in the countryside. In his repressive actions, Stalin made it clear he would stop at nothing to achieve his goals.

Liquidation of the Kulaks Under the NEP, a new class of wealthy landowning peasants known as **kulaks** had emerged. About two million kulaks employed other peasants to farm on their land for wages. Communists saw the kulaks as capitalists who did not belong in their society. Stalin's response was the **collectivization** of agriculture, eliminating private farm ownership and forcing people onto large **collective farms** controlled by the state.

Propaganda stressed the importance of communal values. The text of this 1933 poster from Uzbek, Tashkent, is "Strengthen working discipline in collective farms."

Credit: Wikimedia Commons

The peasants strongly resisted the move to collective farms. They hid or destroyed their crops and even killed their livestock rather than turn them over to state control. Stalin responded by expanding the process of collectivization to include all private farms, not just the wealthiest kulaks. By 1934, virtually all of the Soviet Union's 26 million peasant households had been moved to 250,000 collective farms. Most of the crops grown on these farms were sold to the state at low prices. Peasants were allowed to have very small private plots to grow food for themselves. The peasants' actions and the state's response had devastating consequences.

Famine in the Ukraine The destruction of crops and livestock led to famines that were created by human action rather than by weather or crop failures. These famines in 1932 and 1933 were especially devastating in the Ukraine, one of the Soviet Union's most fertile farming regions. An estimated 7–10 million peasants died as a result of these famines. The government took much of the crops that were grown to feed industrial workers or use for industry. Although peasants starved, industry grew.

Purges of Political Rivals Stalin was determined to eliminate anyone who stood in the way of his policies and goals. He especially focused on his political rivals, termed *Old Bolsheviks,* who had supported Lenin and might oppose Stalin's decisions. During the period of terror known as the **Great Purge** of 1936–1938, many of these Old Bolsheviks were put on trial and condemned to die. Other perceived enemies of the state were also purged at this time, including members of the Communist Party, five "Marshals" of the army (the highest-ranking members), and labor unions along with diplomats, intellectuals, and even ordinary citizens. As many as eight million people may have been arrested; millions were sent to Siberia where they died in forced labor camps.

Repression Under Stalin Stalin's actions resulted in an oppressive political system. He strengthened the Communist Party organization, and anyone who tried to stand in his way could be exiled to Siberia. In a climate of fear, people were encouraged to spy on one another, and the secret police arrested millions of people. Stalin's government also ended the liberal social policies instituted after the 1917 revolution. It outlawed abortion, made divorce more difficult, and treated homosexuality as a crime.

Women in Stalin's Russia Stalin encouraged families to have more children in order to increase the Soviet population. However, at the same time, the government encouraged Soviet women to take jobs outside their homes. The Russian newspaper *Pravda* took pride, in 1929, of how the Russian woman "stands in the most advanced ranks of our working collective . . . [i]n the factory workshop and at the controls of the state ships, in the cooperatives and at the shooting range, in the nursery school and at the thundering machinery, everywhere the tractors of our increasingly strong state farms and collective farms go . . . in none of these places have the working women of the Soviet Union been forced into last place."

Women in Higher Education in the 1930s				
Type of Institution	Soviet Union	Germany	England	Italy
All higher education	38%	14%	26%	14%
Industrial institutes	2%	4%	2%	1%
Agricultural institutes	32%	2%	13%	1%

Source: Adapted from "Women in the Soviet Union and Capitalist Countries," *Zhenshchina v USSR* (Moscow, 1936).

Fascism and Authoritarian Rule

The roots of fascism could be seen in the heightened nationalism and increasing militarism in Europe in the pre–World War I era. During that same era, the rise in socialism and the increase in violent labor strikes alarmed conservative leaders. Though they appreciated how capitalism created great wealth, they worried that it created great instabililty and bitter social conflict.

After the war, there was bitterness over the Treaty of Versailles, especially in Italy and Germany. (See Chapter 20 for more on the Treaty of Versailles.) The revolution in Russia sparked fears that communism was a threat to other countries. Political uncertainty appeared as countries tried to transition to democracy in the context of economic instability. These conditions led to an increase in popularity for the ideology and promises of fascism.

Dictatorships and Propaganda

As communist leaders had done in Russia, fascist dictators also used propaganda to attract followers from those who were disillusioned about conditions in their countries. These dictators of the 1920s also used modern technology such as radio and movies to spread their propaganda quickly to wide audiences. In their messages they rejected democratic institutions, promoted charismatic leaders, and glorified war and nationalism. They presented fascism as the system that would bring order and glory to their countries.

Charismatic Leaders Both **Benito Mussolini** (1883–1945) in Italy and **Adolf Hitler** (1889–1945) in Germany were charismatic leaders who created a **cult of personality** around themselves. Mussolini called himself *Il Duce,* a leader with the strength of iron whose decisions were always correct. Hitler was the *Führer,* a visionary leader who demanded unconditional loyalty from his followers, including a willingness to die for him.

Both men wore military uniforms, had special symbols, and surrounded themselves with elite squads of soldiers and police—known as the **Blackshirts** in Italy and the **Brownshirts** in Germany—who terrorized the population. At mass rallies, their speeches whipped crowds into frenzies. The Italian and German states became identified with their supreme leaders who put themselves above the country's democratic institutions.

Use of New Technology Hitler was more successful than Mussolini at using the new technologies of radio and film to spread his propaganda, although both men used newsreels to convey stories that showed them in a most positive light. Hitler soon learned that the sound of his voice over the radio was sufficient to create the feelings of fervent enthusiasm that he achieved among crowds present at mass rallies, allowing millions of people to feel they were present at the rallies.

Hitler's minister of propaganda, **Joseph Goebbels** (1897–1945), used film as an important tool in his work. For example, *The Triumph of the Will* was an important documentary about the 1934 Nazi rally at Nuremberg. The director **Leni Riefenstahl** used thirty-two different cameras to capture images of Hitler flying into the city for the rally, driving through the streets cheered by adoring crowds, and addressing crowds of soldiers and civilians. Such images reinforced Hitler's claims about the widespread support for his ideas.

Italy and Germany were on different sides during World War I, but similar conditions in both countries after the war allowed fascist dictators to come to power. Both Mussolini and Hitler exploited postwar bitterness and economic instability, used terror to control the population, and manipulated the new democracies in their countries, which were generally unpopular.

Mussolini in Italy

The results of World War I made Italians bitter. The war had been costly for Italy, both financially and in human lives. Yet, though Italy was on the winning side, the Treaty of Versailles did not give Italians all the land they desired. Then, post-war economic problems caused severe inflation and unemployment.

Rise of the Blackshirts In 1919, Mussolini, a former socialist, formed a political group, the *Fasci di Combattimento ("League of Combat")*, whose name later gave rise to the term *fascism.* Mussolini soon saw that if he switched from left-wing to right-wing positions, he could take advantage of the fear caused by instability in the country. The new parliament was unable to govern successfully, and strikes by industrial and agricultural workers created a climate of violence and class warfare. Mussolini gained the support of middle-class business owners and large landowners by opposing communism and strikes and appealing to Italian national pride. The Blackshirts, squads of armed supporters, violently attacked labor organizations and workers. The government supported the Blackshirts as a way to oppose communism.

The Promise of Order The Fascists portrayed themselves as the party that would bring order to the country, and they soon gained power. In 1922, the king named Mussolini prime minister after the Fascists had marched on Rome and threatened to take it by force. The Fascists won 65 percent of the vote in a national election in 1923 and gained a majority in parliament. Although the Fascists had manipulated the election, the large victory seemed to indicate the growing popularity of Fascism. By the end of 1926, Mussolini established a complete dictatorship as the free press and other political parties were eliminated. Although the army, the monarchy, and the Catholic Church retained some independence from the Fascist state, Mussolini ruled Italy as a totalitarian dictator until his death at the end of World War II.

was not a total totalitarian dictator tho

HItler in Germany

The defeat of the German empire in World War I led to the creation of the democratic **Weimar Republic**. The Republic lacked strong leadership and was unable to control such institutions as the army, judiciary, and government bureaucracy. Wealthy aristocrats and business owners still wanted an imperial government. Germans were bitter about the burden of paying war reparations demanded in the Treaty of Versailles. In addition, severe inflation in the early 1920s caused many people to lose their life savings. Members of the middle-class were increasingly attracted to right-wing parties, especially when the worldwide economic crisis of the 1930s, the **Great Depression**, created severe economic hardship. (The Great Depression is explained later in this chapter.)

Hitler's Emergence Amidst the postwar political and economic weakness of Germany, extremism became the path for Adolf Hitler and his supporters to rise to power. As an unsuccessful young artist living in Vienna from 1908 to 1913, Hitler came in contact with such men as Karl Lueger, mayor of Vienna, who influenced his ideas about German nationalism, anti-Semitism, and leadership of a mass movement through emotional manipulation.

After serving in World War I, Hitler entered politics in Munich. He gained control of a small right-wing party and in 1921 changed its name to the **National Socialist German Workers' Party** or **Nazi Party**. In November 1923, Hitler and the Nazis staged an armed uprising, the **Beer Hall Putsch**, in Munich, hoping to cause the collapse of the Weimar Republic. The uprising was unsuccessful, and Hitler was arrested, charged with treason, and sentenced to five years in prison.

Finding Supporters While in prison, Hitler concluded that the way to overthrow the Republic was to manipulate its democratic institutions. During his imprisonment he wrote *Mein Kampf (My Struggle)*, in which he laid out his anti-Semitic ideas and his plans for expanding German territory.

Hitler also showed an understanding of how to organize mass movements through propaganda. After serving one year in prison, Hitler quickly reestablished himself as the unquestioned leader of the Nazi Party. He first focused on establishing the party organization throughout the country and increasing its membership. By 1929, Hitler realized that the Nazis' greatest success would come from appealing to the middle-class in small towns and rural areas rather than workers in large cities.

As Germany began to experience severe economic problems and unemployment in the early 1930s, extremist parties such as the Nazis and communists won support. The **Reichstag,** or German parliament, was no longer able to govern effectively. Increasingly, right-wing elites in business, the aristocracy, the military, and the bureaucracy saw Hitler as the leader who could restore order and prestige to Germany through a totalitarian government. These elites persuaded President Hindenburg to appoint Hitler as chancellor in January 1933.

Taking Power Once in power, Hitler quickly created the governmental framework for Nazi control over Germany. A key supporter, Hermann Göring, took control of the police. He replaced non-Nazis with members of Hitler's Storm Troops, making Nazi terror part of the government. Hitler persuaded the president to give the government emergency powers after a fire in the Reichstag building in February. Under these powers, citizens lost their rights.

Then, after elections in March 1933, Hitler pushed the Reichstag to pass a law suspending the constitution for four years so he could address Germany's problems. The parliament thus gave Hitler the powers of a dictator under the appearance of democracy. The Nazis held totalitarian control under Hitler's rule until his death at the end of World War II in 1945.

Franco and the Spanish Civil War

After World War I, the Spanish parliamentary monarchy was weak. For example, a military dictator controlled the country between 1923 and 1930. The beginning of the Great Depression then caused severe economic problems that led to the government's collapse. The king lost support and left the country.

In his place, a new Spanish Republic was formed. The government was extremely unstable as parties on the left and right fought for control. In 1936, the **Popular Front**, a coalition of left-wing groups, took control. The army refused to accept the authority of the Popular Front. Under the leadership of **General Francisco Franco** (1892–1975), it led a violent revolt against the government. The bloody **Spanish Civil War** resulted.

In a number of ways, the Spanish Civil War was a testing ground for World War II. It was a clash between Fascists and the Popular Front's left-wing republicans, workers' groups, and Communists. This anticipated the clash in World War II between an alliance of Fascists and an alliance of Western democracies and Communists. Though it was a war between opposing factions within Spain, other countries became involved, as they would in the European-wide war:

- Franco received weapons, money, and troops from right-wing, fascist governments in Italy and Germany.

- The Popular Front received some support from the Soviet Union, and 40,000 volunteers from Western democracies fought for it. However, the governments of Western democracies did not intervene in the war.

The Spanish Civil War provided both sides the opportunity to test new weapons and tactics they would use in World War II.

Over time, Franco's forces prevailed over the Popular Front and the war came to an end in March 1939. Franco then instituted a totalitarian government in Spain that lasted until the mid-1970s. Although Spain's government was not fascist, Franco exhibited the characteristics of a fascist dictator, and Spain largely supported the fascist governments in Italy and Germany.

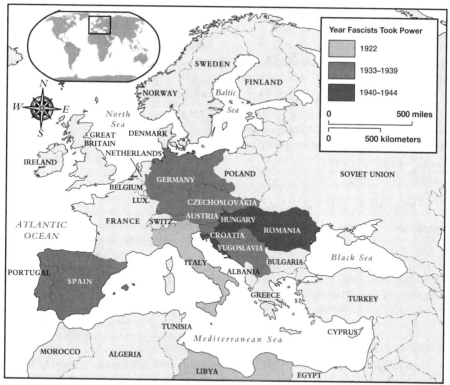

SPREAD OF FASCISM IN EUROPE, 1922–1944

Authoritarian Dictatorships

World War I created a number of new states in central and eastern Europe, including Austria, Czechoslovakia, Poland, and Yugoslavia. These new states established parliamentary democracies; several existing countries, including Bulgaria, Greece, Hungary, and Romania, also established more democratic forms of government in the early 1920s. However, most of these new democracies soon gave way to authoritarian dictatorships.

In general, these states had little tradition of democracy and weak middle-classes. Many of these countries were largely rural, and large landowners were not in favor of peasants' rights or the redistribution of land. Ethnic differences were also a source of conflict in many states. Many people, especially the landowners and the churches, saw authoritarian governments as a way to maintain the old social order. For example, the kings of Bulgaria and Yugoslavia established authoritarian governments in the 1920s.

The fascist governments in Italy and Germany provided attractive models for other states. For example, a strong fascist movement grew up in Romania. The king responded by establishing authoritarian rule. A military dictatorship then took control of the country with the outbreak of World War II. Czechoslovakia was the only state in the region that remained democratic. It had a stronger democratic tradition, middle-class, and industrial economy.

The Great Depression

The Great Depression was a major factor in undermining Western European democracies. The Depression began in the United States in 1929 and quickly spread to Europe. One reason for the rapid spread was that most countries determined the value of their currency based on its worth in a fixed amount of gold, a monetary practice known as the *gold standard*. There was no flexibility to let the value of a currency and its exchange rate with other currencies change as economic conditions changed. Weaknesses in international trade also contributed to the Depression. As citizens faced rising unemployment and hunger, radical political responses to the crisis spread throughout Europe.

Worldwide Economic Weaknesses

There were many causes of weak economies throughout the world after World War I. Tied to the gold standard, the currencies of countries had **depreciated**, or declined in value, after the war. European countries had spent billions of dollars waging the war, leading to massive debt and the need to borrow for rebuilding. Countries on the losing side, especially Germany, were burdened by the requirement to pay huge reparations to the victors, especially France and Britain. European economies had barely recovered from the war by 1922. Then other problems weakened the economies further.

Overproduction Countries had geared up agriculture and manufacturing production to meet the requirements of total war. When demand fell after the war, overproduction led to declining prices. Farmers and businesses had to cut back production to adjust to this situation. Many had gone into debt to increase production during the war and now did not have the revenue to pay off that debt.

Tariffs and Trade By the mid-1920s, many European countries began to impose tariffs on imports to protect their domestic agricultural and manufacturing sectors, interfering with the free flow of goods and hindering trade. These nationalistic tariff policies led to higher prices for imported goods or closed markets to some foreign goods completely. In addition, countries in Europe that had their factories and infrastructure damaged during the war lost out on trade to the United States. For example, British coal, steel, and textile industries all declined after the war and high unemployment resulted.

Speculation In the United States, stock prices rose faster than other prices during the 1920s; investors began to put more money into the stock market in the hopes of reaping huge returns. Prices rose rapidly, and more and more people were tempted to invest in the market, often buying on margin, meaning that they were borrowing a large portion of the money needed to buy stocks. Such investors believed that they could pay back their borrowing from the profits they made. Stock prices rose beyond the value of the companies' worth, revealing the underlying weakness in the economy.

Financial Collapse

The Dawes Plan of 1924 had reduced German war reparations and provided a $200 million loan for German recovery. The plan had also encouraged United States investment in Europe. American bank loans to Germany created prosperity in 1924–1929. In 1928, investors began diverting capital from Europe to invest in the U.S. stock market. When stock prices started to decline, investors lost confidence and pulled their money quickly out of the market. This selling off of stocks caused the 1929 stock market crash in October.

As a result of the crash, capital stopped flowing from the United States to Europe. This loss of capital in turn led to the collapse of major banks in Germany and other parts of central Europe. Without American funds, trade and industry declined and unemployment increased. Individual countries' economies were affected by the problems of international banks.

Attempts to Overcome the Great Depression

Western democracies tried a variety of economic and political strategies to overcome the Great Depression. However, their results fell short. Extremist movements weakened democracy throughout the continent.

Rethinking Economic Theories and Policies The traditional government response to a typical economic depression was a policy of balanced budgets, which required lowering wages and raising protective tariffs, in order to let the depression run its course. During the Great Depression, however, this approach tended to make the situation worse. Britain changed one policy by going off the gold standard in 1931; this change began the nation's recovery.

The British economist **John Maynard Keynes** (1883–1946) proposed a new and different economic approach. Instead of balanced budgets and tariffs, he advocated increased government spending to increase consumer demand, even if this spending resulted in budget deficits. For example, he stated that government spending on infrastructure projects could help create jobs, giving consumers more money to spend and thus provide a reason for other businesses to hire workers to produce more products. Such a program required greater government involvement in the economy, and British politicians did not have the will to do that in the 1930s.

Forging Political Alliances Several European governments found it necessary to forge political alliances among parties that usually competed rather than cooperated. For example, in Britain a **National Government** was formed in 1931 that was a coalition of all three parties—Conservative, Liberal, and Labour. This coalition government was successful in cutting unemployment from about 3 million in 1932 to about 1.6 million in 1936, using traditional economic policies.

France felt the effects of the Depression later than other countries did because its economy had more balance between agriculture and industry.

However, fascist groups in France became stronger as the Depression worsened. The French **Popular Front** government formed in 1936 was a response to the rise of fascism. This coalition government included Communists, Socialists, and Radicals, all left-wing groups. The Popular Front was unable to effectively solve France's economic problems, however. By 1939, France and Britain were the only major European countries with democratic governments.

German Extremism Germany suffered more from the Great Depression than any other European nation. By the end of 1930, almost 4.5 million people were unemployed; the number had increased to 6 million two years later. The Weimar Republic's inability to deal with this level of economic suffering and the fear that followed in its wake opened the door for Hitler's Nazi Party to come to power. The Nazis held out the hope of restoring Germany to order and prosperity.

HISTORICAL PERSPECTIVES: WHAT WAS THE APPEAL OF FASCISM?

When Italian fascism first emerged in the early 20th century, Mussolini focused on regaining the lost glory of the Roman Empire from two millennia earlier. Similarly, other fascist-style leaders often looked to the past for inspiration. However, historians have argued that the appeal of fascism was more than just returning to a time in the past.

Fascism's Connections to Traditions In his book *The Fascist Revolution* (1999), George L. Mosse argued that fascism did not win support by looking at the distant, pre-modern past. Nor did it offer a revolutionary new ideology. Rather, it combined elements of 19th- and 20th-century ideologies, including Romanticism, liberalism, socialism, Darwinism, and modern technology. Because it picked up ideas that were already spreading, it attracted followers quickly. It promised a better future and created an illusion of political participation. Mosse noted that fascism had not originally included racism, nor was racism essential to it.

Fascism's Appeal to Modernists Roger Griffin, in *The Nature of Fascism* (1999) and in *Fascism: The Sense of a Beginning under Mussolini and Hitler* (2010), focused on how fascism appealed to fear. In the aftermath of World War I, people were anxious that the modern world was becoming decadent. To Griffin, early 20th century Europeans were desperate for a better world, rejecting the failing one. In this environment, the modernist styles of Mussolini and Hitler and their calls for social revitalization proved attractive. Fascism offered strength and confidence to people who felt little of either.

Fascism at the Right Place and Time Robert O. Paxton wrote *The Anatomy of Fascism* (2004) as a culmination of a lifetime of study of European history. While Mosse and Griffin emphasized cultural concerns, Paxton looked more closely at the influence of changes in political, social, and economic structures.

Paxton noted first that although political participation was on the rise, most people still lacked a voice. Fascists criticized this failure of democracy and welcomed the voiceless to their mass politics. Paxton was careful to point out that the fascist movement was possible only because existing political alternatives to capitalism—communist or socialist—failed to provide people with real hope. Existing policies were also unable to solve the economic and social crises of the time.

However, even this cluster of circumstances was not enough for fascism to arise, according to Paxton, since Mussolini and Hitler were around for a number of years before people found their messages attractive. It was only when they combined their message with the nationalism resulting from frustrations after World War I that the fascists gained traction, while existing political elites continued to struggle.

KEY TERMS BY THEME

Economics
communism

proletariat

Karl Marx

V. I. Lenin

Marxist-Leninist
 ideology

New Economic Policy
 (NEP)

kulaks

collectivization

collective farm

Great Depression

depreciate

John Maynard Keynes

Governance
left-wing

fascism

right-wing

liberal democracy

Bolshevik

Russian Social
 Democratic Party

Communist Party

Russian Revolution

Tsar Nicholas II

Duma

Provisional Government

soviet

Siberia

propaganda

Leon Trotsky

Communists

Reds

Whites

war communism

Union of Soviet Socialist
 Republics (USSR)

Soviet Union

Joseph Stalin

Politburo

Great Purge

Benito Mussolini

Adolf Hitler

cult of personality

Joseph Goebbels

Leni Riefenstahl

Fasci di Combattimento

Blackshirts

Brownshirts

Weimar Republic

National Socialist
 German Workers'
 Party

Nazi Party

Beer Hall Putsch

Mein Kampf

Reichstag

Popular Front (Spain)

General Francisco
 Franco

Spanish Civil War

National Government
 (Britain)

Popular Front (France)

Questions 1 and 2 refer to the passage below.

"The situation in the army has not changed and may be described as a complete lack of confidence in the officers and the higher commanding personnel. The belief is growing among the soldiers that they cannot be punished for what they do . . . . To this must be added a general weariness, an irritability, and a desire for peace at any price. . . . The press of the political parties is no longer influencing the soldier masses. Again and again one hears the orders of the Provisional Government severely criticized. The committee of the 95th Regiment . . . declared Kerensky a traitor . . . .

An intensive agitation is being conducted in favor of an immediate cessation of military operations on all fronts. Whenever a whole regiment or battalion refuses to carry out a military order, the fact is immediately made known to other parts of the army through special agitators."

Russian Army Intelligence Report, October 1917

1. The conditions referred to in the passage led most immediately to

   a) the abdication of Tsar Nicholas II

   b) the creation of a liberal republic in Russia

   c) the Bolshevik takeover of the government

   d) Stalin's purges of political and military rivals

2. The report best supports which of the following conclusions?

   a) The backing for revolutionary change was largest in Russia's major cities.

   b) The Provisional Government's commitment to the war effort undermined its legitimacy.

   c) Widespread domestic discontent led to the collapse of the Soviet Union.

   d) The Bolsheviks' victory in the Russian Civil War resulted from the military weaknesses of their opponents.

Questions 3–5 refer to the poster below, created by the Soviet government in 1932.

This poster describes how collectivization should be accomplished at the end of the five-year plan.

Credit: Getty Images

3. The poster best reflects which of the following goals of the Soviet government during the 1930s?

   a) To encourage migration from the countryside to the cities

   b) To increase agricultural efficiency by establishing centralized state-run farms

   c) To prioritize agricultural development over heavy industry

   d) To win the support of peasants by redistributing aristocratic land to rural families

4. The developments reflected in the poster can best be seen as a continuation of which of the following?

   a) Lenin's mixture of socialism with free-market principles

   b) Alexander II's emancipation of the serfs

   c) The expansion of the social welfare state

   d) Increasing state authority over the economy during World War I

5. The policy represented in the poster had which of the following effects in the Soviet Union?

a) It ended the era of centralized economic planning.

b) It increased the political influence of the kulaks.

c) It expanded the use of state repression.

d) It eliminated famine in the countryside.

Questions 6–8 refer to the passage below.

"A new way of approaching the study of the Holocaust is implicit in much of the unparalleled, widespread public discussion about various aspects of the Holocaust that has been taking place for the last two years. The old paradigm consists of abstract, faceless structures and institutions . . . and allegedly irresistible external forces (totalitarian terror, the exigencies of war, social psychological pressure). This paradigm effaces [eliminates] the human actors and their capacity to judge what they were doing and make moral choices. . . . This is being challenged by a view that recognizes the Holocaust was brought about by human beings who had beliefs about what they were doing, beliefs which they developed within a highly specific historical context, and who made many choices about how to act. . . . The heretofore [previously] dominant question of 'What compelled them to act against their will?' is being replaced by the question of 'Why did these people choose to act in the ways that they did?' "

Daniel Jonah Goldhagen, American historian, "The Paradigm
Challenged," questia.com,1998

6. Which event or trend in the 1990s might help explain the change that Goldhagen described among scholars studying the Holocaust?

a) The efforts to reduce barriers separating European countries caused historians to focus less on divisive issues of the past.

b) The reunification of Germany caused historians to focus more on pre-20th century German history than on recent history.

c) The break-up of Yugoslavia caused historians to focus more on the decisions that led to ethnic violence.

d) The end of the Cold War caused historians to focus more on differences between Germans and Russians.

7. Goldhagen's emphasis in his study of the Holocaust is most similar to which of the following ideas?

a) Romanticism, because it also highlighted individual action

b) Darwinism, because it also studied slow change over a long time

c) Communism, because it also demonstrated the importance of class

d) Liberal democracy, because it also grew out of the Enlightenment

8. Which set of actions from German history is most directly comparable to the ones studied by Goldhagen?

a) The choices made by individual Germans in the Thirty Years' War

b) The response of German intellectuals to Napoleon

c) The leadership of Bismarck in unifying Germany

d) The decisions by the German government in World War I

SHORT-ANSWER QUESTIONS

1. Use the passage below to answer all parts of the question that follows.

Totalitarian movements use and abuse democratic freedoms in order to abolish them. This is not just devilish cleverness on the part of the leaders or childish stupidity on the part of the masses . . . . Through these republics, totalitarian leaders motivated the indifferent masses . . . . Above the state and behind the facades of ostensible power, in a maze of multiplied offices, underlying all shifts of authority and in a chaos of inefficiency, lies the power nucleus of the country, the superefficient and super-competent services of the secret police. The emphasis on the police as the sole organ of power, and the corresponding neglect of the seemingly greater power arsenal of the army, which is characteristic of all totalitarian regimes, can still be partially explained by the totalitarian aspiration to world rule and its conscious abolition of the distinction between a foreign country and a home country, between foreign and domestic affairs . . . .

Hannah Arendt, "Origins of Totalitarianism," 1951

a) Explain how ONE piece of evidence supports Arendt's argument regarding the rise of totalitarianism from 1917–1939.

b) Explain how ONE piece of evidence <u>undermines</u> Arendt's argument regarding the rise of totalitarianism from 1917–1939.

c) Explain ONE difference between rulers in the Age of Absolutism (1600–1789) and totalitarian leaders as described in Arendt's argument.

2. Answer all parts of the question that follows.

a) Describe ONE significant change in the role of the state in the economic or political development of the Russian Empire/Soviet Union from 1914–1939.

b) Describe ONE significant continuity in the role of the state in economic or political development of the Russian Empire/Soviet Union from 1914–1939.

c) Explain how ONE economic or political development affected the Soviet Union's involvement in World War II.

LONG ESSAY QUESTIONS

1. Evaluate the extent to which Lenin fostered change in Russian society and economics.

2. Evaluate the extent to which economic factors led to the rise of totalitarian regimes in Germany and Italy.

REFLECT ON THE CHAPTER ESSENTIAL QUESTION

1. In one to three paragraphs, explain what factors and events caused the ideological battles between and among democracy, communism, and fascism.

WRITE AS A HISTORIAN: MAKE AN ARGUMENT

The ability to support a defensible claim is the heart of writing a historical essay. You start by carefully examining a question (the prompt) and then formulating an argument (your thesis statement). The thesis doesn't simply rephrase the prompt; it answers the question by offering a complex interpretation based on your historical knowledge. This is called *argumentation*, which along with the ability to analyze historical evidence, is one of the two major practices assessed in the writing portion of the AP exam.

You prove your thesis with multiple pieces of specific historical evidence, using proper nouns (people, places, events, geographical locations) and years/time periods. The evidence is organized into paragraphs consisting of topic sentences (main points) and at least three relevant supporting ideas each, with all paragraphs tying back to the thesis.

When creating an effective argument, you need to analyze your evidence—not simply list it. You can apply the 4 C's reasoning skills you've learned—contextualization, comparison, causation, and continuity/change over time—to explain evidence, determine its relative significance, and organize it chronologically. You can also evaluate the reliability of documents.

In defending a claim, a good writer also acknowledges opposing ideas and viewpoints—usually toward the end of the essay–and then effectively argues against them. Finally, the conclusion of the essay can provide a new viewpoint that extends the thesis, possibly taking a look ahead at what came next in history as a result of the events in the essay.

Whether you are writing the long-essay question (LEQ), a short answer, or a document-based question (DBQ), your first goal is to articulate a defensible claim. Your second is to make an argument for it.

For each prompt below, identify which statement summarizes the argument that most directly addresses the prompt.

1. Analyze how post-World War I conditions contributed to the rise of fascist ideologies.

   a. Fascism gained popularity because charismatic leaders exploited the post-war bitterness many felt because of how they suffered during the fighting and from the peace settlement.

   b. Post-World War I conditions contributed greatly to the rise of fascist ideologies because leaders used propaganda and terror tactics to sway their own people.

2. Explain the role the Great Depression played in European politics in the 1930s.

   a. The Great Depression was caused by weaknesses in international trade and monetary theories and practices.

   b. The economic upheavals of the Great Depression undermined Western European democracies and fomented radical political responses.

22

Western Prosperity and Eastern Communism

"Our policy is not directed against any country or doctrine but against hunger, poverty, desperation, and chaos."

—George C. Marshall, June 1947

Essential Question: How did economic growth and political conflict influence Europe in the second half of the 20th century?

World War II had seen the temporary alliance of Western democracies with the Soviet Union in order to defeat fascism. After the war, however, the ideological conflict between democracy and communism hardened into the Cold War between the United States and the Soviet Union. This conflict was also reflected in the different types of economies that developed in Western and Eastern Europe. These differing economic systems continued to reflect conflicting conceptions of the relationship between the individual and the state.

Economic Growth and the Welfare State

Even in the democracies of Western Europe, governments became more involved in managing economic decisions during World War I, the Great Depression, and World War II. This practice continued after World War II as governments actively managed their economies and used the benefits of post-war growth to provide increased social welfare benefits to their citizens. The growth of the welfare state revealed a new relationship between individuals and the state, one in which the state assumed some responsibility for basic needs of individuals. Economic hard times later in the 20th century led to some criticism and limitation of the welfare state.

Marshall Plan Stimulates Growth

The **Marshall Plan** was proposed in 1947 as a way to help Europe rebuild its infrastructure and industry from the devastation of World War II. The American Secretary of State, George C. Marshall, and others believed that restoring economic stability in Europe would prevent communism from becoming stronger in Europe and keep European countries from falling under the influence of the Soviet Union. The plan offered $13 billion for economic recovery programs. The Soviet Union and other states of Eastern Europe under its influence, often called **satellites**, refused to participate in the Marshall Plan.

Western Europe Recovers For the countries of Western Europe, funds from the United States under the Marshall Plan provided a strong stimulus for rapid economic recovery and growth. The funds were used for the purchase of new equipment and raw materials for construction projects and the revival of industry. By 1950, European industry was producing 30 percent more than it had before World War II. The steel industry's output was 70 percent higher than before the war. This economic growth continued through the 1960s, aided, in part, by the nations' economic cooperation in the Common Market.

The post-war economic recovery in Germany has often been referred to as an "economic miracle." West Germany was smaller than pre-war Germany, yet by 1955 its gross national product (GNP), or total economic output, was higher than pre-war GNP. Unemployment was low, and wages doubled between 1950 and 1965. In Italy, the economy recovered in a similar fashion. Italian growth in producing automobiles, electrical appliances, and office machinery was an example of the increasing importance of consumer goods to the new economy.

Rise of Consumerism As Europe's economy grew stronger, **consumerism**, the theory that individuals should buy more goods in order to expand the economy, grew in importance both economically and culturally. Being able to buy more became a key sign of upward mobility. The middle-class grew as large numbers of people took jobs as supervisors, administrators, and technicians, creating a larger market for consumer goods. At the same time, wages for all workers increased so that working-class families were able to acquire some of the trappings of a middle-class lifestyle, such as televisions and home appliances. Buying on installment by making monthly payments for purchases allowed more people to buy these expensive goods. Increase in automobile ownership was the main indicator of the growth of consumerism. Between 1948 and 1960, the number of automobiles in Europe grew from 5 million to 45 million.

GDP Per Capita, 1960 and 2017		
Country	1960	2017
Denmark	21,076	61,582
Italy	10,868	34,878
United Kingdom	13,827	42,514
Portugal	4,506	23,117
Spain	7,360	32,406
Countries now using the Euro	10,809	40,089
World	3,697	10,634

Data given in constant 2010 U.S. dollars.

Source: Adapted from the World Bank at data.worldbank.org

Expansion of Social Welfare Programs

European economic growth gave governments funds to help provide welfare benefits for their citizens. Although these programs were politically popular when times were good, changing economic conditions led to contentious political debates about social welfare in the late-20th century.

Creation of the Welfare State Even before the Marshall Plan was introduced, Britain's newly elected Labour Party government began implementing a **welfare state** that provided a wide range of social benefits to all citizens. In 1946, laws were passed to provide benefits for subsidized health care, unemployment insurance, and old age pensions. Even conservative governments expanded the welfare system in the 1950s and early 1960s with a program to build affordable housing.

The British system became the model for other European states. In addition to the benefits first introduced in Britain, European states in Western Europe provided benefits for children in the form of direct payments to families for each child. They also sought to increase educational and employment opportunities by creating more universities and providing free or low-cost tuition.

These social programs required high taxes and high government expenditures, which grew over time. Average spending on social services grew from about 17 percent of gross national product in 1967 to close to 50 percent by the 1980s. Most people accepted the high taxes because they liked the benefits that the programs provided. The welfare state not only increased the role of the government in people's lives but also showed that the state wanted to promote better lives for its citizens.

Challenges to the Welfare State Decades of economic growth in Europe came to an end with recessions in 1973–1974 and 1979–1983. With reconstruction after the war complete, jobs in the building trades declined. As countries around the world experienced difficult economic times, demand for European goods declined, which also led to job losses. During such challenging times, European governments began to face difficult choices about continuing the high level of spending on social welfare programs. For example, in 1982, West Germany's coalition government split apart over the question of reducing such spending.

When **Margaret Thatcher** became prime minister of Britain in 1979, she vowed that she would cut taxes and limit social welfare programs. She did not do away with basic health and welfare benefits but did make cuts in government spending in order to curb inflation. These spending cuts were seen as harmful in the northern industrial parts of the country, where unemployment increased as the government began to end its substantial subsidies to businesses. In her second term, she battled the National Union of Mineworkers over the closing of 20 coal mines that the government said were unproductive. The strike lasted for a year, but in the end the miners returned to work with no concessions being made. Probably Thatcher's main legacy was the privatization of many industries, often with mixed results.

The Soviet Bloc

Although Western European governments were actively involved in managing their economies and even had national control over some industries, their economies also maintained many aspects of free-market capitalism. The situation was quite different in the **Soviet bloc**, nations of Eastern Europe that were closely bound to the Soviet Union, which exerted tremendous control over all aspects of life in the region. Albania and Yugoslavia were the only countries of Eastern Europe that had communist governments but were somewhat independent of the Soviet Union. At times Soviet control was very repressive. At other times, it included limited economic and social reforms.

Centrally Planned Economies

Soviet bloc countries all featured **planned economies** in which a central committee of the Communist Party in Moscow determined what was produced, how much was produced, and where it was produced and sold. Joseph Stalin's five-year plans of the 1930s were prime examples of planned economies in the Soviet Union. After World War II, Stalin returned to these policies in order to rebuild industry in the Soviet Union. Once again, the state's plans focused on the growth of heavy industry at the expense of working and living conditions for ordinary people. These plans put little emphasis on consumer goods. Prices were kept low, but food, medicine, and consumer goods were often in short supply. Shoes and clothing were often of poor quality.

Credit: Getty Images

One of the most common symbols used in the Soviet Union was the hammer, representing industry, and the sickle, representing agriculture. Together, factory workers and farmers were to build a strong, prosperous country.

Credit: Getty Images

Planned Economies in the Stalinist Era Communist leaders in the Soviet bloc countries of Central and Eastern Europe followed Stalin's model in their own countries with similar five-year plans focused on heavy industry and collectivized agriculture. The Soviet Union itself mandated certain features of the economies in Soviet bloc countries. The Council of Mutual Economic Assistance, COMECON (1941–1949), was set up first to combat the Marshall Plan and then to assure that the economies of the Soviet Bloc benefited the Soviet Union. For example, after the war, the Soviets confiscated factories, railroad stock, and livestock in countries such as East Germany, Romania, Poland, Bulgaria, and Hungary and shipped them to the Soviet Union. In addition, each country was directed to focus on certain industries. One five-year plan in Czechoslovakia, for example, focused on machine building, chemicals, and metallurgy. The Soviet Union also mandated trade terms with the satellite nations that forced the satellites to increase their trade with the Soviet Union on terms that benefited the Soviets more than the satellites.

[handwritten margin note: for SU's benefit only]

Social Welfare Programs As part of these planned economies, the state provided extensive social welfare programs, such as affordable housing and health care. However, the quality of these social services was often poor and the quantity insufficient. Affordable housing consisted of huge apartment buildings that were generally poorly constructed and extremely crowded; often more than one family shared a small apartment. However, people who had experienced conditions before and during World War II still saw these conditions as an improvement. In the early years after the Russian Revolution, the Soviets improved life expectancy, but the health care system deteriorated over time as governments failed to continue to make improvements to an aging system.

The Soviets greatly improved education with special emphasis on science and technology. Students attended free public schools that included Communist indoctrination along with their studies. Students were educated to fill the jobs needed in the state-run industries. Generally only children of elite members of the Communist Party had access to a university education.

Weaknesses of Planned Economies The Soviet's centrally planned economy achieved some rapid industrial growth, but at great cost. Disruptions in agriculture resulted in massive famines that killed millions in Ukraine and central Asia. The government restricted the freedoms of individual citizens, giving priority to what it decided was the good of the state. For example, people often had a limited choice about where they could live or work. The system was slow to respond to changes in technology and in demand for goods, so it became less and less efficient. By World War II, the Soviet economy was beginning to stagnate.

Suppression of Dissent The Communists suppressed dissent by anyone who disagreed with their ideas and policies. The Communist Party soon became the only political party allowed in Soviet bloc countries. Yet only a small percentage of the population belonged to the party. All forms of intellectual expression in art, literature, and science had to conform to the state's political goals. The Communists threatened to close any private organizations, such as soccer or chess clubs, that they feared could be used to organize political opposition to them. This level of suppression of dissent was reinforced by state terror. Stalin made the recruitment of secret police a priority in planning Communist takeovers of the governments of Eastern Europe.

Limits on Travel The governments of the Soviet bloc also severely limited freedom of travel and emigration. A prime example of this policy is the construction of the **Berlin Wall** in 1961. As people in East Germany began to experience the reality of the Soviet planned economy, many of them wanted to emigrate to the West. Moving from East Berlin to West Berlin provided the easiest access to West Germany and the rest of Western Europe. An estimated 2.5 million people fled East Germany through Berlin between 1949 and 1961, many of them skilled workers and professionals.

The East German leaders realized that the loss of these individuals would threaten their economy, so they built a barrier to prevent freedom of movement. The original wall, built in August 1961, was later strengthened into a 15-foot high concrete barrier topped with barbed wire, monitored by armed guards, and supplemented by electrified fences. The wall eventually stretched 28 miles across the city of Berlin and 75 miles around West Berlin to create a barrier between the city and the Soviet state of East Germany in which it was located. Between 1961 and 1989, only about 5,000 people successfully fled East Berlin by crossing the wall.

Changes under Khrushchev

Stalin's death in 1953 led to a struggle for leadership of the Communist Party in the Soviet Union. By 1956, **Nikita Khrushchev** emerged as the supreme leader. However, Khrushchev ruled in a very different way from Stalin.

De-Stalinization Policies Khrushchev gave a speech at a closed session of the 20th Party Congress in 1956 in which he denounced many of Stalin's most abusive practices, such as purges of his political enemies and his oppressive leadership style. He then embarked on a series of new policies referred to as **de-Stalinization**. Under these policies, Khrushchev eased some political restrictions:

- allowing greater freedom of expression by artists and writers

- allowing people to read what they wanted

- decreasing the power of the secret police

- releasing some political prisoners

In addition, Khrushchev also revised some economic policies to make the system more flexible and more rewarding to average Soviets:

- shortening the work week to about 40 hours

- giving workers more freedom to move from place to place

- allowing certain people to change jobs

- putting more resources into producing consumer goods in order to improve people's standard of living

- allowing more local decision-making about agriculture

- embarking on a plan to grow corn and increase farming in the region east of the Ural Mountains

However, these economic policies failed to meet their goals, and the Soviet Union's growth rate slowed dramatically between 1953 and 1964.

Revolts in Eastern Europe As part of his de-Stalinization policies, Khrushchev agreed that the Soviet government in Moscow would give more autonomy to the communist governments in Eastern Europe. In addition, he eased travel and trade restrictions in Eastern Europe. However, the slowing-down of the Soviet economy and people's growing frustrations over restrictions of their individual rights led to a series of revolts in Eastern Europe.

Revolts in Eastern Europe, 1956–1968			
Country	**Leader**	**Causes**	**Result**
Poland, 1956	Wladyslaw Gomulka	• Workers staged protests. • Poland rejected the Soviet choice for prime minister.	• Gomulka supported the Soviet Union. • Poland remained in the Warsaw Pact.
Hungary, 1956	Imre Nagy	• Hungary wanted to be a non-Communist, independent, and neutral country with free elections.	• Soviet troops invaded Hungary. • Soviets executed Nagy and installed Janos Kader as leader.
Czechoslovakia, 1967–1968	Alexander Dubcek	• Writers protested against censorship. • The government eased censorship during the **Prague Spring**. • Czechs wanted to leave the Soviet bloc.	• The Soviets sent Warsaw Pact troops to put down the revolt. • The Soviets announced they would intervene to defend communism.

The Collapse of Communism

The Soviet Union remained one of the world's two superpowers throughout the 1970s and early 1980s. Under the leadership of **Leonid Brezhnev** (1906–1982), the head of the Communist Party after Khrushchev's forced retirement in 1964, the Soviet Union retained **hegemonic**, or unified and dominant, economic and political control over the countries of Eastern Europe in the Soviet bloc. Brezhnev favored the status quo rather than experimentation or reform. He advocated the Soviet Union's right to use military force to hold off threats to socialism in socialist countries. Intervention in Czechoslovakia in 1968 shows this policy in action.

In the 1970s, tensions with the United States eased under the policy of **détente**. The Soviets and the Americans felt roughly equal in their nuclear weapons programs. They and 33 other nations signed the Helsinki Accords in 1975 in which participating nations agreed to respect one another's sovereign equality and refrain from using force, among other nonbinding agreements. As Brezhnev felt that Russia's diplomatic relationships with the United States had become more relaxed, he allowed more access to Western popular culture. There was still little tolerance for dissent. Communism seemed strong, and its rapid collapse in the late 1980s was surprising to many. Economic problems were a major reason for this collapse.

The End of Soviet Control

Brezhnev continued to emphasize heavy industries in the Soviet economy. The Soviets surpassed the United States in producing cement, coal, iron, and steel, but overall the economy slowed down. Weaknesses in the nature of planned economies, including the huge bureaucracy needed to manage the economy, led to inefficient use of resources and a lack of productivity. Also, Soviet workers were guaranteed jobs, so they had no incentive to work hard or innovate. Similar problems led to declines in agricultural productivity, which were worsened when severe weather led to bad harvests in the mid-1970s. The Soviet Union was forced to import grain from the United States in order to feed its people.

After this long period of economic stagnation, by 1980 the Soviet Union was in serious trouble. Economic decline combined with a decline in overall health, including increases in the rates of infant mortality and alcoholism, led to a sense within the nation that the communist system was starting to fail. A few reformers within the Communist Party wanted to address these problems in a direct way after Brezhnev's death in 1982. When older reformers soon died, the younger **Mikhail Gorbachev** (b. 1931), who had grown up under the rule of Khruschev, became the leader of the Communist Party in the Soviet Union in 1985.

Gorbachev's Reforms Although the Soviet Union continued to be strong in technology related to space exploration and weapons, it fell behind the United States in the development of computers and remained far behind in the production of consumer goods. The Soviet people were aware that their standard of living had gotten worse. In 1986, Gorbachev spoke about the need for changes in Soviet society. His program of reforms was built around the idea of **perestroika**, or economic restructuring. He wanted to introduce elements of a free-market economy to the Soviet Union, including some private property. It was difficult to implement his ideas as some people wanted rapid and widespread change, and others wanted to introduce change more slowly. Trying to implement change halfway was not successful, however.

Gorbachev realized he could not change the economy without changing Soviet society. He then introduced the idea of **glasnost**, or openness. He encouraged members of the Communist Party and ordinary people to discuss openly what was working and what wasn't working in the Soviet system. State news media and artists presented information about problems and protests.

Glasnost also led to changes in the political system. Dissidents were freed from prison. Elections became competitive for the first time as two candidates were able to run instead of only one. In addition, political parties other than the Communist Party became legal. The Soviet state was no longer identified with the Communist Party, and Gorbachev established the new position of president of the Soviet Union. This position became more powerful than that of general secretary of the Communist Party. Gorbachev became the first president in March 1990.

The Soviet Union's Collapse Gorbachev's reforms had been designed to make the Soviet system more flexible. However, these reforms had unexpected effects that weakened the Soviet Union and ultimately led to its collapse. For example, the Soviet Union was made up of 15 different republics, which included 92 nationalities and 112 languages recognized by the state. When the Communist Party was strongly in control, ethnic tensions were kept in check. Under glasnost, ethnic groups began protesting examples of discrimination, and violence often erupted. Many of these ethnic republics also began to develop feelings of nationalism and desired independence from Soviet control. These feelings were especially strong in Azerbaijan and Georgia between the Black and Caspian seas; Estonia, Latvia, and Lithuania on the Baltic Sea in the northwest; landlocked Moldavia; and Uzbekistan in the southeast. Lithuania declared its independence in March 1990.

Gorbachev tried to find a balance between conservative and liberal forces in Soviet society. He created the new office of president (which actually had more power than the general secretary of the Communist Party), and **Boris Yeltsin** was elected as the first president in June 1991. In August, conservative forces attempted a coup by arresting Gorbachev. However, Yeltsin and thousands of others resisted, and the coup was unsuccessful. Nonetheless, the republics' push for independence accelerated. In December, Ukraine, Russia, and Belarus declared that the Soviet Union no longer existed.

Satellites Break Free Perestroika and glasnost had consequences within the Soviet bloc as well as within the Soviet Union itself. In 1989, Gorbachev stated that the Soviet Union would no longer intervene with its military to support communist governments in Soviet bloc countries as it had done earlier in Hungary and Czechoslovakia. With the collapse of the Soviet Union, there was an end to its ability to maintain hegemonic control over the satellite countries of Eastern and Central Europe.

As change happened in the Soviet Union in the late 1980s, it also happened throughout the Soviet bloc. In Poland, for example, severe economic problems in the early 1980s led to the rise of **Solidarity**, a labor movement led by Lech Walesa (b. 1943) that represented almost one-third of the Polish population. This movement had the support of the Catholic clergy and Pope John Paul II, a Pole who became the first non-Italian pope in hundreds of years when he was elected in 1978. In 1981, the communist government arrested Walesa and established military rule. However, economic problems continued to grow, and workers demonstrated in large numbers in 1988. At that point the government had to agree to free elections, which had not been held in Eastern Europe since 1948. In 1990, Solidarity formed a new coalition government with Lech Walesa as president.

The division between East and West in Germany, symbolized and enforced by the Berlin Wall, was one of the most visible examples of Soviet control in Eastern Europe. East Germany's extremely repressive communist government, which made use of a feared secret police force, had ruled since 1971. In 1988, severe economic problems and the repressive government motivated huge numbers of people to leave East Germany. Demonstrations and the flight of refugees from the country continued to grow throughout 1989. The communist

In 2008, Czechs posted replicas of posters and graffiti first made in the 1968 protest against the Russian invasion of their country. "Hanba" means "shame."

Credit: Getty Images

COUNTRIES FORMED FROM THE SOVIET UNION

government could no longer function—even with a show of support from Gorbachev in a visit to East Berlin in October 1989— and gave in to this popular pressure. On November 9, 1989, the border to the West was opened, and the Berlin Wall began to fall. The Christian Democrats won the free elections held in March 1990 and favored rapid unification with West Germany. By October 1990, the reunification of Germany was complete.

New Nationalisms Rise in Central and Eastern Europe

Although there was a strong feeling of excitement throughout Central and Eastern Europe after the revolutions of 1989 and the collapse of the Soviet Union in 1991, change did not come easily. New nationalisms led to the formation of new countries and governments that often had to deal with ethnic tensions. In addition, the transition to free-market economies brought difficult changes as people tried to adjust to a new way of life. Outcomes varied from country to country.

Peaceful Revolutions Most of the revolutions in the Soviet satellites in 1989 were peaceful. For example, even under communist rulers, Hungary had gradually instituted economic reforms since its attempt to break with the Soviet Union in 1956. The country was still affected by the economic problems common to Eastern Europe in the 1980s, and opposition to the communist government grew. When elections were held in March 1990, a coalition government was formed and committed to a democratic government and free-market economy.

Czechoslovakia's government had been less reform-minded than Hungary's, and opponents had little success in challenging the Communists until 1988–1989. At that time, demonstrations of up to 500,000 people showed that the government had little support. The dissident playwright Vaclav Havel was appointed president in December 1989 and became a strong advocate for democracy. Czechoslovakia was able to peacefully resolve ethnic differences between Czechs and Slovaks. In 1993, two new countries were formed: the Czech Republic and Slovakia.

War in the Balkans The death of Marshall Tito eventually resulted in the collapse of the country of **Yugoslavia**, which had been created during the peace process after World War I. (See Chapter 19 for more information on the creation of Yugoslavia.) Tito had ruled Yugoslavia with an iron fist since taking power after WWII, keeping the many ethnic and national groups at bay. Although a communist country, Yugoslavia under Tito had always followed a policy of nonalignment, refusing to follow Soviet doctrine. After his death, separatist groups on the Balkan Peninsula wanted to establish the independent republics of Slovenia, Croatia, **Bosnia-Herzegovina**, and Macedonia. The extreme Serbian nationalist and communist leader Slobadan Milošević opposed them in the name of protecting Serb minorities within those republics.

Under Milošević's leadership, the Serbian army attacked Croatia and Bosnia-Herzegovina, brutally taking control of large tracts of territory and carrying out genocide, or **ethnic cleansing**, against **Bosnian Muslims** who were massacred by Bosnian Serb forces. The war finally ended with a peace agreement in 1995 that resulted in new boundaries being drawn.

COUNTRIES FORMED FROM YUGOSLAVIA

Another war broke out in the Balkans in 1998 with a fight over the independent status of **Kosovo**, a province in the southern part of Serbia. Brutal clashes occurred between Milošević's Serbian forces and **ethnic Albanians** who formed the majority of Kosovo's population. The Serbs carried out ethnic cleansing against the ethnic Albanians. The United Nations made Kosovo a protectorate in 1999; Kosovo declared its independence from Serbia in 2008.

Political Instability When the Soviet Union ceased to exist in 1991, 11 of the 15 republics became part of a loose confederation called the Commonwealth of Independent States (CIS). Estonia, Latvia, Lithuania, and Georgia refused to become part of the CIS. The ethnic issues and nationalist sentiments that had led to calls for independence under glasnost continued to cause political instability in some of the former Soviet republics. For example, ethnic tensions led to armed clashes within Georgia and between Georgia and Russia over regions that wanted independence from Georgia.

The largest of the former Soviet republics, Russia, also faced political instability and ethnic conflicts after the dissolution of the Soviet Union. President Boris Yeltsin faced challenges in making the transition to a free-market economy. When the government no longer controlled prices, severe inflation occurred, and the standard of living declined. Oligarchs, a small group of wealthy Russians (many of whom were former Communist Party officials), gained control of many of the nation's businesses.

In addition, many Communist Party members had become members of Russian parliament and, along with nationalists, they often opposed Yeltsin's policies even when the majority of the people favored them. Demonstrations and clashes with groups who opposed Yeltsin were frequent throughout his presidency in the 1990s. Yeltsin's use of force against rebels in **Chechnya**, which wanted independence from Russia, also contributed to political instability within Russia.

HISTORICAL PERSPECTIVES: WHY DID THE COLD WAR END?

The rapid end of the Cold War surprised many analysts in Europe and the United States. They had not realized how internally weak the Soviet Union was. Historians have tried to identify the underlying reasons for this weakness and why the reaction was to accept radical change without violence.

Pressure from Citizens American historian Robert J. McMahon, who specialized in the study of foreign policy, noted that President Ronald Reagan faced foreign criticism for his policies. In 1980, 2.5 million West Germans signed the "Krefeld Appeal" in which they stated, "Atomic death threatens us all—no atomic weapons in Europe." Throughout the early 1980s Europeans demonstrated against American nuclear proliferation.

David Cortright, an American historian and political scientist, noted the role of domestic politics. In 1993, he published *Peace Works: The Citizen's Role in*

Ending the Cold War. He argued that a variety of citizen groups, from scientific to religious, successfully put pressure on U.S. President Ronald Reagan to end nuclear proliferation and the Cold War. For example, in 1983, the Catholic bishops of the United States stated that Reagan's nuclear policy was immoral, That same year, ABC aired a show entitled "The Day After," demonstrating the impact of a nuclear attack in Kansas—100 million American casualties. According to Cortright, "the combination of domestic and foreign opposition forced the Reagan administration to pursue a more peaceful relationship with the Soviet Union that did not involve fear of nuclear attack."

Credit to Reagan Unlike McMahon and Cortright, American historian John Lewis Gaddis gave Reagan more credit for his willingness to question the need for the Cold War. Most politicians and diplomats at the time accepted a bipolar world as status quo. However, Reagan asked if the Cold War was necessary and what it might take to end it. While others criticized Reagan's role in prolonging the Cold War by accelerating nuclear spending, Gaddis described Reagan as a nuclear abolitionist who, in order to abolish nuclear weapons, needed a Soviet leader willing to negotiate. When Gorbachev showed willingness, Reagan responded.

Gorbachev Lost the Cold War Vladislav M. Zubok, an expert on Soviet leadership, argued that Leonid Brezhnev failed to improve the lives of Soviets enough to make communism appealing in the Eastern Bloc. This meant that Eastern Europeans saw the Soviets as dominating rather than protecting them. Brezhnev's failure illustrated the weaknesses of the Soviet system. Gorbachev hoped to stabilize the Soviet system without the use of force by opening the USSR and its satellites ideologically and diplomatically to the West. However, when Gorbachev agreed to reduce the nuclear tension with the United States, he gave up his only leverage to unite the communist world. Zubok argued that this failure meant Gorbachev ended the Cold War by losing it.

KEY TERMS BY THEME

Governance

Marshall Plan

satellite

Margaret Thatcher

Soviet bloc

Berlin Wall

Nikita Khrushchev

de-Stalinization

Leonid Brezhnev

hegemonic

détente

Mikhail Gorbachev

glasnost

Boris Yeltsin

Solidarity

Czech Republic

Yugoslavia

Bosnia-Herzegovina

Bosnian Muslims

Kosovo

Chechnya

Identity

ethnic cleansing

ethnic Albanians

Economics

consumerism

welfare state

planned economy

perestroika

Questions 1–3 refer to the passage below.

"The world situation is very serious . . . . In considering the requirements for the rehabilitation of Europe the physical loss of life, the visible destruction of cities, factories, mines and railroads was correctly estimated, but . . . this visible destruction was probably less serious than the dislocation of the entire fabric of European economy . . . . [T]he rehabilitation of the economic organization of Europe quite evidently will require a much longer time and greater effort than had been foreseen. . .

The truth of the matter is that Europe's requirements for the next three or four years of foreign food and other essential products—principally from America—are so much greater than her present ability to pay that she must have substantial additional help, or face economic, social and political deterioration of a very grave character. . . .

It is logical that the United States should do whatever it is able to do to assist in the return of normal economic health in the world, without which there can be no political stability and no assured peace . . . . Any assistance that this Government may render in the future should provide a cure rather than a mere palliative."

George C. Marshall, speech at Harvard University, 1947

1. The excerpt above reflects a policy that was responsible for

   a) expanding U.S. influence in South America

   b) financing of an extensive program of reconstruction in Europe

   c) overthrowing communist governments in Eastern Europe

   d) creating a new economic system

2. Which best describes the context in which Marshall gave this speech?

   a) The development of atomic weapons had caused so much fear among Europeans that countries were unwilling to work together.

   b) The Berlin Blockade had stopped the movement of essential goods throughout Europe.

   c) World War II had devastated the economies of much of Europe.

   d) A drought in 1946 had resulted in the spread of starvation in Europe.

3. Which European country viewed the policies described in the speech above as a threat to its economic and political status?

   a) Germany

   b) France

   c) Great Britain

   d) The Soviet Union

Questions 4–5 refer to the photograph below.

The graveyard at Srebrenica includes more than 6,000 Bosnian Muslims who were massacred in July 1995.

Credit: Getty Images

4. Which challenge in maintaining a government does the photo above reflect?

   a) The danger of famine from inefficient use of agricultural resources

   b) The violence that could occur in multi-ethnic regions

   c) The risks faced by countries that did not align with the Soviet Union

   d) The consequences of emphasizing rapid industrial development

5. Which best describes the context that contributed to the events reflected in the photo above?

   a) The power vacuum left by the death of Josip Broz (Tito)

   b) The Soviet attempt to increase its influence in the Balkans

   c) The Greek fear of a Muslim takeover

   d) The Czechoslovakian withdrawal from communist control

Questions 6–8 refer to the passage below.

"The Director of Central Intelligence [Allen Dulles] . . . said that the Soviet repression in Hungary had been ruthless and brutal to the last degree [adding] . . . the Soviet admission that they had now 200,000 troops deployed in Hungary . . . .

Mr. Dulles . . . describe[d] the European reaction to what the Soviets had done in Hungary, concluding that these Soviet actions had reduced Soviet prestige in Western Europe to its lowest point in many years. He ended with the prediction that the rebellion in Hungary would be extinguished in a matter of days, if not of hours. Nevertheless, the Soviets would be faced with a problem in Hungary for many, many years to come. In turn, the situation presents the United States with the problem of what more we can do . . . .

The President also cited [Soviet] Premier Bulganin's message to him received this morning, in which Bulganin stated in effect that what was going on in Hungary was none of the business of the United States . . . .

Mr. Dulles replied that not very much in the way of unfavorable reaction had occurred in Asia . . . . [F.B.I. Secretary J. Edgar Hoover stated that] if the British and French had not at this particular time decided to move into Suez, things would not have happened as they did in Hungary. If the British and French had stayed out of Egypt and the Soviets had nevertheless moved against Hungary, they would have been ruined in the eyes of world public opinion. Secretary Hoover doubted if they would under the circumstances have dared to move against Hungary."

> Memorandum of Discussion at the 303rd Meeting of the
> National Security Council, Washington, November 8, 1956

6. The events in Hungary referred to in this source were caused most immediately by which of the following?

   a) A U.S. confrontation with the Soviet Union over Cuba

   b) Outbreak of war between Egypt and Israel

   c) The ascension to power of Imre Nagy who wanted to end Soviet domination

   d) Western European challenges to Soviet control of East Berlin

7. The actions by the Hungarians that the Soviets were responding to were encouraged by

   a) the French response to an Algerian revolt

   b) the discussion of a French-British alliance

   c) the U.S. response to a Polish uprising

   d) the speech by Khrushchev denouncing Stalinism

8. The Soviet actions in Hungary as described in this excerpt were most like the actions of countries following which concept?

a) nationalism

b) imperialism

c) self-determination

d) decolonization

SHORT-ANSWER QUESTIONS

1. Use the following excerpt to answer all parts of the question that follows.

"The Hungarian Revolution of 1956 is one of the great historical events of the twentieth century. It was an unplanned, leaderless, spontaneous explosion brought on by a confluence of fateful errors. In late October and early November of 1956 the world's attention was riveted on the uprising in Budapest and the revolution which quickly enveloped the whole country; even more so when it was all brutally crushed by the Soviet Union in what seemed like just a few days."

J. P. Matthews, *Explosion* (2007)

a) Describe ONE other event from Eastern Europe that was similar to the actions of Hungary or the Soviet Union described in the passage.

b) Describe ONE event from outside Eastern Europe that was similar to the actions of Hungary or the Soviet Union described in the passage.

c) Explain ONE reaction from the Soviet Union or a Warsaw Pact member that had a result different from the one described.

2. Answer all parts of the question that follows.

a) Briefly describe ONE continuity in Communist Party control of the Soviet Union from 1956 to 1991.

b) Briefly describe ONE change in Communist Party control of the Soviet Union from 1956 to 1991.

c) Explain ONE reason for the change identified in part b.

LONG ESSAY QUESTIONS

1. To what extent were the political experience between Eastern and Western Europe similar between 1945 and 1992?

2. Evaluate the extent of changes that occurred in Eastern Europe after 1992.

1. In one to three paragraphs, explain how economic growth and political conflict influenced Europe in the second half of the 20th century.

WRITE AS A HISTORIAN: ORGANIZE AN ESSAY

When writing an essay answering a historical question, analyze the sources and use your knowledge of their context to explain big ideas and create defensible arguments. Organize your thoughts so they are clear to the reader.

The following questions are based on this prompt: Analyze how the Cold War both maintained continuity and fostered change in the relationship between Europe and the rest of the world.

1. Which statement is the better thesis statement?

a. During the Cold War struggle between the United States and the USSR. European countries used their wealth to continue exerting their power in international affairs even as they developed new ways to work together through international institutions.

b. Although some historians see the Cold War as an ideological fight only between the two superpowers, it also sustained established patterns in European traditions of dealing with other countries.

2. Select the *three* ideas that could best be the basis of topic sentences.

a. An examination of new Cold War alliances and how they compared to alliances and military build-ups leading to both world wars

b. An explanation of how the Cold War divided Europe into opposing factions, noting how economic differences shaped foreign policies

c. A survey of America's political climate during the Cold War, including the McCarthy hearings and spy scandals

d. An analysis of how European countries continued to have close relationships with lands they had once colonized

e. A review of the events leading up to the construction of the Berlin Wall and to its destruction.

3. Which reasoning skill does this prompt focus on?

4. If you were to explain how World War I, the rise of communism, and World War II laid the groundwork for the Cold War, which reasoning skills would you be using?

23

Knowledge, Truth, and Moral Standards

"A world that can be explained even with bad reasons is a familiar world. But, on the other hand, in a universe suddenly divested of illusions and lights, man [every human] feels an alien, a stranger."

—Albert Camus, *The Myth of Sisyphus*, 1955

Essential Question: Why did some people in the 20th century question the objectivity of knowledge, the value of reason, and the role of religion?

The history of European thought and culture in the 20th century reveals a change from the optimism and belief in progress that characterized much of the 19th century. Science and reason had made great strides in solving human problems since the Age of Enlightenment. A variety of intellectual and cultural movements throughout the 20th century, however, began to question whether objective knowledge about the world was possible, and these ushered in the Age of Anxiety. Many saw the limits of reason in reaching the truth, especially about human experiences. In addition, organized religion's role in determining standards of morality was called into question.

Challenges to the Belief in Progress

Even before World War I, some philosophers, writers, and artists began to question Europeans' widely held belief in progress. These cultural leaders explored the weaknesses in European life and saw that some kind of disaster was approaching, and this view created a sense of anxiety among cultural leaders. After two world wars, the sense of anxiety spread to more people. By the end of the 20th century, more intellectual frameworks for understanding the world had emerged.

General Confidence in Science and Technology

At the outbreak of World War I, most Europeans were still confident that science and technology could solve problems and answer questions that affected people's lives. This confidence was based on personal experience of an improved standard of living, which included better schools and urban environments, as well as new inventions such as electric lights and automobiles. Although new scientific and psychological theories created some uncertainty, confidence persisted because the new ideas at first touched only a relatively small group of intellectuals.

New Theories about Physics Throughout the 19th century, most scientists saw their work as the application of existing scientific laws to solve problems in a mechanical universe. The laws were based on Isaac Newton's conception of the universe. Matter, space, and time were thought to be objective realities independent of the scientists studying them. The atom, which was perceived as hard and solid, was considered the smallest unit of matter. (See Chapter 1 for more information on Isaac Newton.)

Around the turn of the 20th century, however, scientists began to question whether atoms were the basic building blocks of matter when they discovered **subatomic particles** such as protons and electrons. These discoveries created uncertainty about the Newtonian view of the universe.

In 1905, **Albert Einstein** pushed these ideas even further when he published a paper that included his **theory of relativity**. Einstein's theory claimed that space and time were not independent of human observers and were linked together in what he called the *space-time continuum.* Einstein also posited that matter was not something solid but was a different form of energy. Although Einstein's ideas were not generally accepted until the 1920s, they led to exploration into the energy contained in the atom, opening the door to the atomic age later in the century. After World War I, the challenges continued to expand, as scientists gained increased knowledge about the atom and the potential energy that it contained.

Recognizing Uncertainty Earlier scientists and ordinary people believed that with enough knowledge, accurate predictions could be made about the way the world worked. In 1927, however, **Werner Heisenberg** (1901–1976), a German physicist, questioned this belief. He argued that scientists could not accurately predict the path of an electron's movement because the act of observing that movement with light affected the electron's path. His conclusion was known as the **uncertainty principle**.

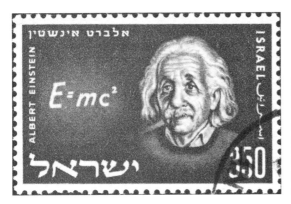

Albert Einstein, with his unruly hair and bushy mustache, became one of the best-known faces in the world in the 20th century. His simple formula summarizing the relationship among energy, mass, and the speed of light became famous, though hard for many people to fully understand.

Credit: Getty Images

By the mid-1970s, so-called *new physics* provided alternative frameworks for understanding the physical sciences that acknowledged chaos and uncertainty in the behavior of particles.

Psychology The physical world was not the only realm in which new ideas began to create a sense of uncertainty and anxiety. In 1900, **Sigmund Freud**, a physician from Vienna, published new ideas about the human mind in *The Interpretation of Dreams.* In this work, Freud presented the theory that human behavior was not always motivated by reason but was often driven by unconscious forces, including past experiences or inner urges of which people are generally unaware. According to Freud, the *ego*, the center of human reason, and the *superego,* the higher realm of conscience and social norms, struggled to control the unconscious forces of the *id.*

Freud thought that much of this struggle revolved around the repression of sexual urges, stemming from experiences in childhood. Through hypnosis and analysis of dreams, Freud began the practice of **psychoanalysis**, in which therapists help patients become aware of the contents of their unconscious and resolve psychological conflicts. These ideas about the irrational foundation of much human behavior undermined the optimistic belief that human reason would lead to unending progress in society. As with physics, however, these ideas had a limited impact before World War I.

Challenges to Reason from New Philosophies

After two world wars and worldwide economic depression, people's confidence in science and reason was profoundly shaken. These catastrophic events revealed beyond doubt that science could lead to destruction as well as progress, and human beings could act in irrational and cruel ways. In the period after World War II, these feelings of despair were expressed in new philosophical ideas that challenged the optimistic ideas of rational science.

Existentialism The underlying premise of **existentialism** is that God is no longer present in the world. The German philosopher **Friedrich Nietzsche** (1844–1900) had already expressed this premise when he proclaimed in the late 19th century the death of God and along with it the values and purpose of life associated with God. According to his *nihilist* viewpoint, life had no purpose or meaning. Without God's presence and universal moral standards, humans could rely only on themselves. Two French philosophers were the main spokespeople for existentialism.

Jean-Paul Sartre (1905–1980) said that human beings first existed and then created who they were through their actions. Existentialism emphasized that individuals should take responsibility for their lives. People must decide on their own values and then act accordingly. How people interacted with one another was central to the ethics of existentialism. Sartre himself fought in the Resistance against the Nazis in Paris; it is no surprise that he felt that "never were we freer than under the German occupation." What he meant was that he found meaning through struggle and purpose in his own actions.

Albert Camus (1913–1960) described humans who felt alienated from their world and who saw life as absurd and meaningless. Yet he believed they could make a choice to create meaning in their lives. Both of these philosophers stressed the need for individuals to become authentic human beings in an age that had become depersonalized.

Postmodernism In the 1950s, intellectuals began using the term **postmodernism** to mean the general reaction to the ideas of the modern period, which lasted from the Scientific Revolution of the 16th century through the middle of the 20th century. In addition to its use in philosophy, postmodernism referred to movements of the late 20th century in architecture, art, and literature. (See later pages in this chapter for more on 20th century art.)

In philosophy, postmodernism was a reaction to the certainty about the world expressed in the ideas of the Enlightenment. Postmodernism was skeptical about humans' ability to know anything for certain about the world apart from the individual's perception of it. Therefore, it questioned the existence of objective truth and the ability of reason to discern it. In general, postmodernists claimed that language, scientific theories, and historical analysis do not represent universal principles or objective truths but constructions by particular minds in a particular time and place. In addition, they saw that the application of science and technology did not always make society better. Postmodernists saw that logic and reason had used these tools for terrible purposes, especially in the atrocities of World War II.

Evolving Attitudes Toward Reason		
Philosophy	**Years**	**Ideas**
Enlightenment	c. 1685–1815	• Application of reason and the scientific method to political, social, economic, and religious institutions • A rational questioning of prevailing institutions and patterns of thought • A general belief that human progress was possible
Modernism	c. 1900–1970	• Doubt that reason was sufficient to explain people and nature • A belief that people need to take responsibility for their lives • A sense of despair and anxiety about a depersonalized world
Postmodernism	c. 1970–present	• Questioning of objective truth and the role of reason in determining it • A belief that ideas once thought objective were instead the creation of humans in a social and political context • A belief that science and reason were not inherently a force for good

Postmodernism's belief that all truth was relative to the observer of an action or event was a direct echo of Einstein's and Heisenberg's ideas about the observing scientists' effect on physical phenomena that they studied.

The Benefits and Costs of Science and Technology

Science and technology made life better for many people. Inventions such as home appliances made life easier. Improvements in transportation included the railroad, the automobile, and the airplane. From the assembly line to computers, people used technology to make workplaces more efficient. All of these technological advances had both benefits and costs. Especially in the areas of medical advances and military technology, many people questioned whether the costs outweighed the benefits.

Medicine became increasingly scientific in the 20th century. New medical theories and technologies improved the quality of life for many and increased life expectancy. For example, the development of *antibiotics*, medications that fight bacteria, allowed for the successful treatment of many types of infection. Continued development of *chemotherapy* drugs improved cancer treatment and increased survival rates. Knowledge about the *genes* that make up an individual's hereditary traits led to social experiments in population control and new diagnostic tests and treatments that could be tailored to individual patients.

These advances, however, raised a variety of questions, and people did not always agree on how to address them. These questions, and responses to them, ranged across religious, political, and philosophical perspectives.

Social Questions

As life expectancy increased, the percentage of the population that was elderly also increased. The aging population, along with new but expensive drugs and technologies, increased the cost of health care. Because most European nations had established some sort of national health system, health care costs were a high cost for government. For example, in Germany by the early 21st century, health care accounted for more than 10 percent of the country's gross domestic product, and 77 percent of that was financed through the government. National health systems were designed to provide care to everyone. Europeans debated how to finance advanced technologies and treatments and allocate them fairly.

A related social issue was unequal medical care within the European Union. Each country set its own health care policies. For example, in countries such as Greece, Spain, and Portugal that faced government cutbacks during the economic crisis that began in 2009, life expectancy decreased, and doctors sought better opportunities in other countries. For these reasons, patients often traveled throughout Europe seeking better care than they could find in their home countries.

Moral Questions

Changes in philosophy and technology raised questions about truth and morality. If all knowledge was relative to the observer, could any moral standard apply to all people in all circumstances? If all actions had unpredictable results, could any statement about cause and effect be considered true? The lack of agreement on morality and truth sometimes ignited fierce controversies over new technologies that enabled people to intervene in the basic processes of life.

Birth Control By the 1990s, contraceptive pills were the most common method used by Europeans to prevent pregnancy. Often, pills were provided for free or at low cost by government health programs.

Abortions In the 1960s and 1970s, many countries in Europe reduced restrictions on abortions. In most countries, women could obtain abortions, but the conditions varied widely. Strongest opposition to abortion came from the Roman Catholic Church on moral grounds.

Eugenics In the early 20th century, some people began to advocate for policies, known as **eugenics**, which they argued would improve the genetic quality of the human race. For example, they supported forced sterilization for people with disabilities. The Nazis adopted this policy as part of their plan for "racial hygiene" to promote the Aryan "master race." Because of the association of eugenics with the Nazis, it was widely rejected.

Fertility Treatments Medical efforts to help couples conceive children began in the 19th century. In England in 1978, the first child was born through in vitro fertilization. In this process, an egg is fertilized outside a woman's body and then placed inside her uterus to develop. While some people thought the process was unethical, others welcomed the possibility of helping couples have children.

Genetic Research European researchers were leaders in genetic research to explore how changes in a person's genes might be used to cure certain diseases such as cystic fibrosis and leukemia. This research generated debate about the possibility of dangerous side effects of using genes. Some feared it would lead to human cloning, or the production of human embryos that are genetically identical to a parent.

Stem Cell Research Other aspects of genetic research, such as stem cell research, have been debated as well. *Stem cells* are general cells that can divide and change into specialized cells such as blood cells or skin cells. Some scientists saw in stem cells the potential to treat many diseases, while other people objected to the use in research of human embryos that were discarded during the process of fertility treatments.

Military Technologies

As in other fields, science and technology changed the nature of warfare in the 20th century. European countries strove to develop weapons and surveillance technologies that would give them an advantage over their rivals. However, these new technologies resulted in devastation and dangers for not only the continent of Europe but also for the world.

Industrialized Warfare Modern military technologies made World War I different from all previous wars. Factories of each combatant nation produced sophisticated weapons such as machine guns and ammunition in mass quantities. Railroads transported these war materials and troops rapidly. As the war dragged on, new deadly technologies were developed, including poison gas, tanks, and the first use of military aircraft. These technologies were developed further during World War II, when aircraft supplemented railroads for transporting supplies and troops, and aerial bombardment devastated cities throughout Europe and Asia.

Development of Nuclear Weapons Development of the atomic bomb took military technology to a new level. As scientists learned more about the secrets of the atom, they were developing the knowledge necessary for the production of nuclear weapons and power. Once they understood how to split the atom into its component parts, they learned to release the energy that resulted in a variety of ways. Atomic weapons, first used by the United States against Japan in World War II, had a destructive potential far beyond other types of weapons. (See Chapter 19 for more information on atomic weapons in World War II.)

Electricity from Nuclear Power Although the first use of nuclear energy was destructive, its use to provide power generation had great potential to meet a growing demand for electricity. Nuclear power plants were first developed in Europe in the late 1950s. In 2015, about 27 percent of electricity in the European Union came from nuclear power. However, nuclear power comes with risks, including the release of radioactive material from waste disposal and accidents at nuclear power plants. The 1986 disaster at the Chernobyl nuclear power plant in Ukraine released more radioactivity into the atmosphere than the bombs at Hiroshima and Nagasaki. Contamination of soil and water had long-lasting effects on people and livestock.

A memorial to the victims of Chernobyl, in Korostren, Ukraine

Credit: Getty Images

Genocide The extermination of millions of people, including six million Jews, in the Holocaust in the Nazi death camps showed the ultimate industrialization of death and the use of military technology to commit genocide. German technical experts set up the camps like efficient factories that destroyed rather than created, as people were moved to them and through them in a brutal and impersonal way. Railroads, deadly gas chambers, and huge crematoria all played a role in this carnage.

Nuclear Weapons Concerns The devastation of Hiroshima and Nagasaki showed the destructive power of nuclear weapons technology. The Soviet Union developed its first atomic bomb in 1949. Soon the United States and the Soviet Union became involved in a nuclear arms race as each sought to move ahead of its rival in the growth of its nuclear arsenal.

The arms race became even more deadly with the development of a new category of weapons. In the bombs used at Hiroshima and Nagasaki, the energy came from nuclear fission, the splitting of atomic nuclei. In the new bombs, the energy came from fusion, the combining of atomic nuclei. These new bombs were known as hydrogen or thermonuclear weapons. In November 1952, the United States detonated the first hydrogen bomb. In August 1953, the Soviets responded with a successful test of their hydrogen bomb.

The two superpowers recognized the tremendous danger posed by a nuclear war. They came to believe that the best way to prevent a war was to protect the ability of a country to retaliate. They reasoned that a country would not use nuclear weapons first if it understood that its opponent could launch a nuclear attack in response. The desire to prevent war led to several arms control agreements. The first major one came in 1963. The Soviet Union and the United States agreed to ban atmospheric testing of nuclear weapons.

During the Cold War, **nuclear proliferation**, the spread of nuclear weapons, became a growing concern. In 1968, the United States, the Soviet Union, France, the United Kingdom, and China signed the **Nuclear Nonproliferation Treaty** to try to limit the spread of nuclear weapons to other countries. The treaty did not limit peaceful uses of nuclear technology. Despite this treaty, several countries later acquired nuclear weapons. Among these were India, Pakistan, and North Korea. The threat of nuclear war remained.

Modern Challenges to Religion

As European society modernized in the 19th century, the role of organized religion in people's lives declined. As more people moved into urban environments, they became detached from the village churches that had been central to their lives. In addition, many European rulers in the late 19th century sought to curb the power of the churches.

Europe continued to become more secular as science and reason grew in importance. Some biblical scholars used new scientific and historical information to challenge the literal truth of the Bible. While some churches looked for ways to incorporate new ideas, others sought to maintain traditional beliefs. In the 20th century, as new ideas in science and philosophy questioned the belief in a rational, orderly universe, religious renewal provided an alternative viewpoint.

Christian Responses to Totalitarianism

Totalitarian governments in Central and Eastern Europe sought to replace Christianity with the ideologies of fascism and communism. These governments found different ways of dealing with the churches, and the churches responded in a variety of ways.

Fascism and the Church When Mussolini came to power in Italy in 1926, he established a totalitarian government. However, he found that he needed to work with existing institutions, including the Catholic Church. In 1929, the fascist state recognized the independence of Vatican City and declared the Catholic Church as the only official religion in Italy. The Catholic Church also received grants of money. In exchange, the pope recognized Mussolini's government and encouraged Italians to support it.

Germany As Hitler rose to power, some protestant German clergy spoke out against him. **Dietrich Bonhoeffer** and **Martin Niemöller** first objected to the state's interference in matters of religious organization. Then they began to take strong stands against the state's anti-Christian and anti-Semitic views as well. Both were sent to concentration camps for their opposition. Bonhoeffer was executed, and Niemöller only narrowly escaped execution.

The Soviet Union Communism was an atheistic ideology that oppposed all religion. (Marx is often quoted as writing, "Religion is the opiate of the people.") Lenin and Stalin systematically attacked the **Russian Orthodox Church**, the largest in the Soviet Union, closing churches and sending clergy to labor camps or killing them. However, during World War II, Stalin reopened thousands of churches to appeal to people's patriotism in the fight against the Nazis. Khrushchev renewed attacks on the church and thousands of churches were closed. After the collapse of the Soviet Union, Russians were again able to worship. The Russian Orthodox Church thrived despite the decades of opposition to it by the Communist government.

Poland During Stalin's era, the Roman Catholic Church in Poland was persecuted just as the Russian Orthodox Church had been. After 1956, however, Poland's Communist government and the Catholic Church reached a compromise. The government agreed to allow the Church to conduct its religious mission as long as it stayed out of politics. Although the Church was still strongly anti-Communist, it accepted these terms.

When dissidents began to speak up against the Communist government in the 1970s, the church was in a difficult position. However, more clergy began to sympathize with dissidents and workers. In 1978, a Polish cardinal became **Pope John Paul II**. The following year, the pope made an eight-day visit to Poland and drew huge enthusiastic crowds. The pope was a strong supporter of social justice and peace, and the Catholic Church in Poland became a strong supporter of the **Solidarity** movement that emerged in 1980. The support of the Catholic Church was an important factor in Solidarity's ultimate success and the downfall of the communist government in 1989. (See Chapter 22 for more information on Solidarity.)

Reform in the Catholic Church

The meeting of the **Second Vatican Council**, the first such meeting of the Roman Catholic Church since 1870, was the major instrument of Catholic reform in the 20th century. **Pope John XXIII** (1881–1963) called the council, which began in 1962 and was continued under **Pope Paul VI** until 1965. One of the main goals of the council was to make the church more responsive to concerns of the modern world.

To that end, the council redefined some of the church's doctrine and practices. For example, the church allowed the celebration of the mass in vernacular languages rather than in Latin and encouraged greater participation by lay people in the liturgy and in the church. The church also emphasized the Bible as the foundation of its teachings and encouraged Catholics to read the Bible rather than relying on clergy to interpret it for them. In addition, bishops were given a more active role in advising the pope.

The council also began to redefine the church's relations with other religious communities. Many non-Catholic observers attended the council. The pope affirmed the close relationship between Christianity and Judaism and condemned anti-Semitism. Catholics were allowed to attend services and pray with other Christian denominations and were encouraged to be friendly with non-Christian faith communities. In 1965, the Roman Catholic and Eastern Orthodox churches, divided since the 11th century, issued a proclamation expressing a desire for some reconciliation between them.

Immigration and Religion

A variety of factors affected Europe's religious makeup in the 20th century, which had traditionally been characterized as Judeo-Christian. The Holocaust and repression in the Soviet Union led to the death or emigration of millions of Jewish citizens from Europe during and after World War II. At the same time many Jews left, decolonization after World War II brought many people from the former colonies into Europe seeking better economic opportunities. For example, immigrants came to the United Kingdom from India, Pakistan, and the Caribbean and to France from North Africa. In the 1950s and 1960s, many European nations encouraged immigrants to come to Europe as guest workers to meet a severe labor shortage. Many of these newcomers practiced Hinduism, Buddhism, and Islam. (See Chapter 20 for more information on decolonization and Chapter 24 for more information on guest workers.)

Starting in the early 1970s, economic conditions caused governments to discourage immigration. Yet from the 1980s onward, economic, political, and ecological conditions in many parts of Asia, Africa, and the Middle East led to an increase in immigrants and refugees coming to Europe.

THE MUSLIM POPULATION OF EUROPE, C. 2017

1 SLOVENIA
2 CROATIA
3 BOSNIA AND HERZEGOVINA (51%)
4 MONTENEGRO
5 KOSOVO (96%)
6 MACEDONIA
7 ALBANIA (57%)

Muslims as a Percentage of the Population

Less than 5 percent
5 percent to 10 percent
10 percent to 40 percent
Over 40 percent

0   500 miles
0   500 kilometers

Source: World Factbook

Growth of the Muslim Population The minority religion that grew the most with increased immigration to Europe was the Muslim population. Muslims were around 1 percent of the population of many European countries in 1970, although France's Muslim population was 3.9 percent of the total. In 2016, the overall Muslim population of Europe was about 5 percent, with France having the highest proportion at 8.8 percent. Germany and the United Kingdom each had slightly more than 6 percent.

Debates about Religion In spite of increased immigration, Europe remained predominantly Christian, with about 75 percent of the population identified as Christians in 2010. However, nearly 20 percent identified as "unaffiliated," marking a growth in Europe's secularism.

Europe's secularism created a strong separation between church and state. The rapid growth of Islam as a larger minority religion caused debate and conflict about the role of religion in social and political life. For example, many countries debated whether Muslim girls should be allowed to wear headscarves in schools. One study in 1997 showed that a large majority of Europeans agreed that immigrants who wished to be fully accepted into society needed to give up any part of their religion or culture that conflicted with European laws. In politics, some countries allowed immigrants to vote and run for local office, while others have made it increasingly difficult for them to become naturalized citizens.

Experimentation and Subjectivity in the Arts

Trends in 20th-century art followed the patterns seen in science, psychology, and philosophy, questioning objective knowledge and rational truth. Emphasis on the individual's perspective led to a growth of subjectivity and self-expression. As science challenged beliefs about the universe, artists in all fields experimented with new forms and subjects. After 1945, the United States replaced Europe as the dominant influence in both elite and popular culture.

New Movements in the Arts

The visual arts, architecture, and music showed many similarities as they evolved throughout the 20th century. In all three fields, artists radically shifted **aesthetics**—principles governing the nature of beauty—by introducing new ideas of what was beautiful. Following the lead of psychologists such as Freud, artists explored subconscious and subjective states in a variety of media. Many artists also satirized Western society and its values in their work.

Visual Arts A major theme in new movements in the visual arts was an independence from Realism and a break with the past. One influential style, Cubism, began in 1907 and became very influential. **Cubism** is a style of art in which a subject is taken apart and reassembled to show many different perspectives, often through the use of geometric shapes. Pablo Picasso became the most famous Cubist artist.

The eggs sitting on top of the Dali Theatre and Museum, located in the northeast corner of Spain, reflect Dali's playful view of the world.

Credit: Getty Images

Futurism, an Italian art movement between 1909 and 1916, glorified the machine age. Representing different perspectives as the Cubists did, Futurist painters used multiple images and splashes of vibrant color to capture the frenzy of modern life. Although Futurism lasted only a short time, it had a strong influence on the movements that followed.

Dadaism—whose name origin is uncertain—began in Switzerland in 1916 as a form of protest against the perceived purposelessness of life in the midst of World War I; it became strongest in Germany. This art movement created a type of anti-art by satirizing traditional aesthetics. For example, French artist Marcel Duchamp used the image of the famous Mona Lisa by Italian Renaissance artist Leonardo da Vinci and drew a mustache on her. Like Cubism and Futurism, Dadaism incorporated overlapping images, including photomontages, in an experimental way.

In Paris in 1924, Dadaism gave rise to **Surrealism**, which also protested against older forms of art and Realism. Rather than focusing on the external world, Surrealism, influenced by the psychological theories of Sigmund Freud, focused on the emotions and the unconscious mind by portraying objects as they might appear in dreams and fantasies with unusual shapes and relationships. The most-well known Surrealist painter was **Salvador Dali** (1904–1989) from Spain.

Like Surrealism, **Abstract Expressionism** explored the emotions and the unconscious but with even less of a connection to Realism. This movement began before World War I. One of its founders was the Russian artist Vasily Kandinsky (1866–1944). It became the dominant art movement after World War II. By then New York City had replaced Paris as the capital of the Western art world, reflecting the growing influence of the United States on elite culture. The American painter Jackson Pollock (1912–1956), a leading Abstract Expressionist, was best known for his paintings consisting of drips of color that created explosive patterns. Although some artists embraced postmodernism and a return to Realism in painting, Abstract Expressionism remained strong throughout the century, with European artists such as Anselm Kiefer (b. 1945) showing that American artists were not as dominant in the 1980s as they had been earlier.

After World War II, the United States and Britain led the way in the **Pop Art** movement. Pop artists sought a break from both traditional and contemporary art and turned to the world of popular culture—movies, TV, and advertising, for example—for inspiration. Iconic works from the pop art movement include American Andy Warhol's series of painting of Campbell's Soup cans.

Architecture Change in architecture in the first half of the 20th century was largely driven by the slogan "form follows function," which expressed the idea that design flowed from a building's purpose. Efficiency and lack of extraneous ornamentation were the hallmarks of this architecture. For example, the **Bauhaus** school founded in 1919 in Berlin by Walter Gropius sought to integrate fine arts and crafts into sleek designs. Many of Gropius's buildings looked like boxes made of stainless steel and glass.

The Bauhaus building in Dessau, Germany, was closed by the Nazis when they came to power, and it was damaged by bombings during World War II. However, the building was restored and designated a landmark because of the influence Bauhaus architects had on modern design.

Credit: Getty Images

In the 1960s, postmodernism became an important influence in architecture, as many architects and designers rebelled against what they saw as the sterile and boring qualities of many modern buildings. Architects referred back to historical styles and incorporated ornamentation in the outside of buildings, sometimes in a playful or satirical way. The American architect Robert Venturi was an early thinker and designer of this style. Postmodernism spread from America to Europe and the rest of the world. The Spaniard Santiago Calatrava was one of many influential European architects who embraced postmodernism.

Music On the eve of World War I, **Igor Stravinsky** (1882–1971) shocked the musical world with his composition *The Rite of Spring*. Stravinsky's music incorporated primitive rhythms and dissonant sounds that challenged the traditional aesthetics of Western musical forms used for centuries. Stravinsky's work also reflected an interest in the irrational that characterized other art forms of the period. He had a great influence on composers throughout the century.

In the period between the wars, **Arnold Schoenberg** (1874–1951) from Vienna took experimentation even further when he began to write *atonal* music, which was built on twelve notes and was not written in a particular key. His work was similar to the emergence of abstract painting. Schoenberg's work had little acceptance until after World War II, when it influenced the development of *serialism,* a form of composition that emphasized the intellectual and mathematical aspects of music rather than emotion and intuition.

Richard Strauss (1864–1949) was a German composer and conductor whom some regarded as backward-looking for his use of traditional tonalities, in contrast to Schoenberg. However, he extended the boundaries of traditional harmonies and pioneered orchestration techniques that had a great influence on other composers, especially those of film scores. Strauss's composition *Also Sprach Zarathustra,* inspired by a philosophical novel of Nietzsche, was famously used as the opening to the film *2001: A Space Odyssey.*

Writers Challenge Conventions

Writers also challenged the conventions of their art form throughout the 20th century. Franz Kafka (1883–1924), a German-speaking Jew who was born in Prague, challenged convention by combining lucid prose with fantastical elements. The beginning of his novella *The Metamorphosis* demonstrates this combination: "When Gregor Samsa woke up one morning from unsettling dreams, he found himself changed in his bed into a monstrous vermin." Many other writers questioned traditional Western values, especially in the face of wars and new ideas about the human mind and human behavior. In their work, they often chose to address controversial social and political issues.

Response to War After serving in the German army during World War I, **Erich Maria Remarque** (1898–1970) wrote his famous novel *All Quiet on the Western Front*, an emotionally accurate and critical portrayal of the experiences of German soldiers in the war. After moving to Switzerland in 1930, Remarque wrote a number of other works critical of unquestioning patriotism and the horrors of war. His works were burned by the Nazis, and he moved to the United States in 1939.

Stream of Consciousness Another literary trend that emerged in the 1920s came from an interest in exploring the unconscious, as Surrealism had done in the visual arts. Writers used a technique known as **stream of consciousness**, which presented a character's inner thoughts as they occurred in the form of an unspoken monologue. Readers often had to piece together the meaning that the author conveyed in this way.

For example, the Irish writer **James Joyce** (1882–1941) used this technique to explore the minds of ordinary people in Dublin in the course of a single day in his novel *Ulysses*. The British author **Virginia Woolf** (1882–1942) used her own version of this technique in novels such as *Mrs. Dalloway* to reveal the world in which her characters lived. In her work, Woolf also challenged traditional roles for women, who were generally expected to be wives and mothers rather than artists.

Theater Jean-Paul Sartre was a literary writer and playwright as well as a philosopher. His play *No Exit*, written in 1944, was a dramatic expression of his existentialist ideas, which he had articulated in the same year in his nonfiction *Being and Nothingness*. In *No Exit,* three characters are confined in a hotel room representing hell. They are forced to face themselves through the perceptions of the others, creating an environment of eternal pain.

After World War II, the disillusionment with life in Europe was strongly expressed in literature in the **Theater of the Absurd**, which Sartre's work inspired. The Irish playwright **Samuel Beckett** (1906–1990) challenged the conventions of theater in works such as *Waiting for Godot,* in which nothing seemed to happen as two characters waited for the mysterious Godot to appear. It was clear to the audience that the action was not intended to portray reality. Beckett and other playwrights even questioned whether language was capable of communicating with accuracy about the real world.

American Cultural Influences

After World War II, the United States emerged as one of two world superpowers—a leader economically, militarily, and politically. It also became an increasingly strong influence on European culture. In elite culture, American influence was particularly strong in the visual arts and architecture. Technology and popular culture from the United States generated both enthusiasm and criticism.

Movies Film was a primary medium for bringing American popular culture to Europe. Charlie Chaplin's *Modern Times*, for example, a slapstick comedy from 1936 that skewered industrialization and provided escapism during the Great Depression, earned more money in other countries, especially Great Britain, than in the United States. By the 1960s, the European market accounted for 40 percent of the income for Hollywood filmmakers. At the same time, many European filmmakers made movies that were popular in art houses and independent cinemas in both Europe and the United States. Directors in Sweden, Italy, and France made movies that were more experimental than those that came out of Hollywood.

Television This new technology became widely available in the United States after the war and spread to Europe and other parts of the world in the 1960s. Along with private automobiles and home ownership, television became the hallmark of a middle-class American lifestyle. As the technology spread, American broadcasters sold their programming to European countries at very low prices. For example, the British Broadcasting Corporation (BBC) could buy American programs for a small fraction of what it cost to produce their own programs. Most European governments had state-controlled television and eventually established quota systems to limit the amount of American programming, which continued to be very popular. However, commercial television began to grow in Western Europe in the 1980s.

Popular Music While European composers such as Stravinsky and Schoenberg led the revolution in classical music in the 20th century, several innovations in popular music came from America and were based on African-American music. These styles included blues, jazz, rock and roll, and rap. For example, rock and roll began in the United States in the 1950s built on the rhythm and blues music of black performers, including Little Richard and Chuck Berry, and adapted by white performers such as Elvis Presley. In the

1960s, rock and roll became a worldwide phenomenon as American music inspired British groups, including the Beatles, who became wildly popular in the United States and elsewhere. This reciprocal influence also occurred in the 1970s when the punk movement that started in New York spread to Britain and back to the United States.

New Technologies In the 1960s, Marshall McLuhan, an important media critic, wrote about the potential of new communication technologies such as satellites and personal electronics to transform the way people around the world consumed and exchanged culture. For example, DVDs made films from the United States and Europe available in people's homes, not just their movie theaters. Satellites allowed viewers to watch sporting events such as the Olympics as they happened. American broadcasters supported by corporate advertising revenue mostly financed such television events and revealed another way that the United States continued to influence popular culture.

HISTORICAL PERSPECTIVES: WHAT CAUSED SECULARIZATION?

The role of religion in European culture changed significantly between the 16th century and the 21st century. In the 16th century, wars between Catholics and Protestants resulted in the deaths of millions, and everyday life centered on religious practices. By the 21st century, only a few European religious leaders had significant political power, and most Europeans did not attend religious services regularly. Life had become more secular.

Science and the State One explanation for secularization was suggested by the 19th-century French intellectual Auguste Comte. He was heavily influenced by the ideas of the Enlightenment. Comte believed that science and reason had replaced religion in shaping how Europeans thought. Further, he argued that the state increasingly took on the traditional social roles of religion. For example, the state regulated individual behavior and promoted social unity. Comte predicted that other societies that adopted Europe's Enlightenment values would inevitably become more secular as well.

Continued Strength of Faith In the late 20th century, American sociologists began to challenge Comte's prediction. Starting around 1980, observers noted that the role of religion in politics was increasing. In this context, some sociologists questioned the idea that secularization, at least as described by Comte, was inevitable. In the United States, a country founded at the height of the Enlightenment and with a strong tradition of scientific research, support for religion remained widespread. Rodney Stark, an American sociologist especially interested in Catholicism, found that in the 1980s American church membership had never been higher. To Stark, this indicated that religion could remain strong in a modern country.

And the United States was not alone. Even though many values of the Enlightenment, such as a reliance on reason, had spread throughout the world, religion remained a powerful force in South America, Africa, and India. Even in countries such as China and Russia that were officially atheist for several decades, interest in religion surged in the 1990s.

Religion in the 21st Century The ongoing power of religion around the world caused scholars to relook at the data. José Casanova, a professor of sociology and theology at Georgetown University in Washington, DC, in a 2006 article titled "Rethinking Secularization," suggested that Europe might be exceptional in the way it became more secular. Even as religious institutions, such as churches, lost influence, people continued to have strong personal beliefs. In an age of globalization, people were more exposed to religions from around the world rather than just the one their parents followed. Enlightenment values of religious liberty and individual choice might go together with continued importance of religion.

KEY TERMS BY THEME

Technology

subatomic particles

Albert Einstein

theory of relativity

Werner Heisenberg

uncertainty principle

birth control

eugenics

nuclear proliferation

Nuclear Nonproliferation Treaty

Identity

Sigmund Freud

psychoanalysis

existentialism

Friedrich Nietzsche

Jean-Paul Sartre

Albert Camus

postmodernism

aesthetics

Cubism

Futurism

Dadaism

Surrealism

Salvador Dali

Abstract Expressionism

Pop Art

Bauhaus

Igor Stravinsky

Arnold Schoenberg

Richard Strauss

Erich Maria Remarque

stream of consciousness

James Joyce

Virginia Woolf

Theater of the Absurd

Samuel Beckett

Governance

Dietrich Bonhoeffer

Martin Niemöller

Russian Orthodox Church

Pope John Paul II

Solidarity

Second Vatican Council

Pope John XXIII

Pope Paul VI

Questions 1–3 refer to the passage below.

"We modern civilizations have learned to recognize that we are mortal like the others. We had heard tell of whole worlds vanished, of empires foundered with all their men and all their engines, sunk to the inexplorable depths of the centuries with their gods and laws, their academies and their pure and applied sciences, their grammars, dictionaries, classics, romantics, symbolists, their critics and the critics of their critics. We knew that all the apparent earth is made of ashes, and that ashes have a meaning. We perceived, through the misty bulk of history, the phantoms of huge vessels once laden with riches and learning. We could not count them. But these wrecks, after all, were no concern of ours.

[The ancient civilizations] Edam, Nineveh, Babylon were vague and splendid names; the total ruin of these worlds, for us, meant as little as did their existence. But France, England, Russia, these names, too, are splendid. And now we see that the abyss of history is deep enough to bury all the world. We feel that a civilization is fragile as a life. The circumstances which will send the works of Keats and the works of Baudelaire [two modern poets] to join those of Menander [an ancient Greek poet whose works were lost until the 19th century] are not at all inconceivable; they are found in the daily papers."

Paul Valéry, French writer, On European
Civilization, 1919

1. This passage is best understood within the context of which event?

   a) The collapse of the French Republic after the Nazi invasion

   b) Economic misery generated by the Great Depression

   c) Anxiety about the possibility of nuclear war

   d) The trauma and destruction of the First World War

2. The sentiment expressed in this passage contributed most directly to

   a) Leninism

   b) Relativism

   c) Existentialism

   d) Futurism

3. Valéry's reference to ancient civilizations best reflects which of the following developments in 20th-century European culture?

   a) Declining confidence in the progress of Western civilization

   b) A renewed interest in classical arts and philosophy

   c) The use of history to promote extreme nationalism

   d) Growing concerns about the influence of American consumerism

Questions 4–5 refer to the image below.

Poster for International Day Against Nuclear Tests.
Credit: Getty Images

4. This image is best understood within the context of which political trend?

   a) Declining state spending on infrastructure and civilian defense

   b) Rising Cold War tensions and the acceleration of the arms race

   c) Growing faith in democratic governments and parties

   d) Increasing debates over the role of religion in public life

5. This image is best understood within the context of which intellectual trend?

   a) Increasing doubts about the power of science to solve the problems faced by humans

   b) Growing disillusionment among the "lost generation" of artists and writers

   c) Rising interest in psychoanalysis as taught by Freud

   d) Declining influence of American popular culture in Europe

Questions 6–8 refer to the passage below.

"All of France's children, whatever their history, whatever their origin, whatever their beliefs, are the daughters and sons of the republic . . . .

It cannot be tolerated that under the cover of religious freedom, the laws and principles of the republic are challenged. Secularism is one of the great achievements of the republic. It is a crucial element of social peace and of national cohesion. We cannot allow it to be weakened. We have to work to consolidate it . . . .

In all conscience, it is my view that the wearing of clothes or of symbols which conspicuously demonstrate religious affiliations must be banned in state schools."

French President Jacques Chirac, Speech, December 17, 2003

6. The debate expressed in the passage most directly resulted from which of the following?

a) Increased immigration to France from its former colonies

b) The revival of Catholicism after the Second Vatican Council

c) The commemoration of the 200-year anniversary of the French Revolution

d) Gains in women's and minorities' participation in higher education

7. Chirac's speech reflects which of the following developments of this period?

a) Tensions between national sovereignty and membership in the European Union

b) Concerns about how to define European identity in a multicultural society

c) Attempts to reconcile religious and scientific explanations for natural phenomena

d) Pressure on the French state to acknowledge the injustices of colonialism

8. Sentiments similar to those expressed in this passage contributed most directly to which of the following?

a) The creation of large-scale guest worker programs

b) A French vote to exit the European Union

c) The rise of extreme nationalist political parties

d) The eradication of organized religion

1. Use the passage below to answer all parts of the question that follows.

"Contemporary scholars often describe modernism, understood as a cosmopolitan movement in literature and the arts reflecting the crisis of representation, as having arisen in Europe in the middle of the nineteenth century and developing up to, and even after, the Second World War . . . .The crisis of representation evident in modernism has its roots in other crises: of faith, of reason, of liberalism, of empire."

Pericles Lewis, *The Cambridge Companion to European Modernism*, 2011

a) Describe ONE example in the arts that supports Lewis's argument regarding new movements in European art during the 20th century.

b) Describe ONE example in literature that supports Lewis's argument regarding new movements in European art during the 20th century.

c) Describe ONE example in science that supports Lewis's argument regarding new movements in European art during the 20th century.

2. Answer all parts of the question that follows.

a) Identify ONE way in which the Christian churches challenged modern secularism in the second half of the 20th century.

b) Explain ONE similarity between the role of organized religion in Eastern Europe and in Western Europe from 1950 to 1991.

c) Explain ONE difference between the role of organized religion in Eastern Europe and in Western Europe from 1950 to 1991.

LONG ESSAY QUESTIONS

1. Evaluate the extent to which scientific research promoted new views among Europeans in the years from 1914 to 1945.

2. To what extent did new technologies change the lives of Europeans in the years from 1914 to 2005?

REFLECT ON THE CHAPTER ESSENTIAL QUESTION

1. In one to three paragraphs, explain why people questioned the objectivity of knowledge, the value of reason, and the role of religion in the 20th century.

The following activities will help you review ways you can evaluate evidence and allow for opposing viewpoints.

For the following statements, choose the two best pieces of evidence. If a piece of evidence seems biased or inaccurate or does not support the statement, do not choose it for this exercise.

1. The major trend of 20th-century European thought and culture moved from an optimistic view that modern science and technology could solve the problems of humankind to the formation of eclectic and sometimes skeptical movements that doubted the possibility of objective knowledge and of progress.

   a. a sample from the writings of existentialist author Jean-Paul Sartre

   b. examples of post-modernist architecture and urban planning concepts

   c. a Cubist painting by Pablo Picasso

   d. the outcomes of the Second Vatican Council

   e. photographs and writings about anti-nuclear war demonstrations

2. By the mid-20th century, dramatic new medical technologies prolonged life but created new social, moral, and economic problems.

   a. writings of the 21st-century anti-vaccine movement

   b. a description of the role eugenics played in Nazi Germany

   c. a table of abortion statistics from 1980 to 2000

   d. examples of changing the genes of animals

   e. an explanation of the benefits of fertility treatments

For the following statements, which evidence could best be used to demonstrate an opposing viewpoint?

3. It was a mistake to develop nuclear weapons.

   a. an examination of wars since 1945

   b. statistics on deaths at Hiroshima and Nagasaki

4. Military technologies made genocide more possible.

   a. photographs of the Nazi death camps

   b. a comparison of the Holocaust and examples of ethnic cleansing in Europe since 1945

24

Freedom, Justice, and Everyday Life

"I do not know with what weapons World War III will be fought, but World War IV will be fought with sticks and stones."

—attributed to Albert Einstein, c. 1947

Essential Question: What changes altered experiences of everyday life?

The 20th century brought significant change to the European continent. Two total wars and migration affected populations. Globalization and consumerism affected people's everyday lives. For the first time, more people lived in cities than in the rural countryside. Economic growth increased the number of women in the workforce and changed how Europeans spent their free time. Many of the cultural changes that began during the two world wars continued in the second half of the century. More women received formal education and took jobs outside their homes, and new political parties and initiatives took shape.

Human Suffering and Human Progress

The first half of the 20th century was filled with human suffering, economic devastation, and a continent left in ruins. In part because of how overwhelming those years were, the second half of the century brought incredible improvements in the standard of living.

World War I

The men who survived World War I—or the Great War or the War to End All Wars, as it was called in the 1920s and 1930s—returned to a Europe of economic, social, and cultural uncertainty.

World War I was a **total war**—one in which nations dedicate all their resources to winning and target not only enemy combatants but also the entirety of the enemy country. World War I is often considered the first total war, and it had consequences that the working class in Europe had never seen. States were forced to direct resources—financial, material, and human—into war-related industries. The working class, therefore, began working jobs in heavy industry. Women's work also changed. Women left textile and commercial food processing jobs for employment in metalworking and munitions factories. Female workers were also becoming highly skilled in positions traditionally held by men.

This surge of women in the workplace was short-lived, however. When men returned from the war, they reclaimed the jobs taken by women. For example, in 1917, women made up more than 40 percent of France's industrial workforce. However, by 1926, that percentage had dropped to just under 29. Nonetheless, the experience of women during the war had opened the door to women in the workforce.

As work became more concentrated in large factories in big cities, so did the working-class population. A great divide soon opened between those workers and the governments sponsoring the war effort. Worker frustration grew as food supplies and official rations dropped and the number of working hours grew. Increasing numbers of soldiers returning home wounded—or not returning at all—only added to discontent with governments. One result of this widespread frustration was a wave of strikes and revolutions in various parts of Europe. Strikes usually began over wages and food rations and then quickly became politicized as workers demanded an end to the war.

Councils In the midst of these strikes and revolutions, workers in some countries established **councils** (called *soviets* in Russia), or democratic forms of worker representation. At the end of a great rally, workers would elect delegates to represent their interests to employers and the state. The councils from different factories in a city would convene and constitute the city council. Usually workers elected well-respected local leaders, shop stewards, or other union representatives to the councils.

Lost Generation The young adults of Europe and America during World War I became known as the **Lost Generation**. They were "lost" because many of them were cynical or disillusioned with the world after the war and were either unwilling or unable to establish a settled life. The values this generation inherited from its parents were no longer relevant in the postwar world. The new society they were suddenly a part of seemed hopelessly materialistic and without a moral compass.

The term "Lost Generation" was coined by American writer Gertrude Stein and made popular by American writer Ernest Hemingway in his novel *The Sun Also Rises*, which captures this postwar disillusionment. The Lost Generation also refers to Stein, Hemingway, and other American writers who came of age during World War I, settled in Europe after the war, and established themselves as writers in the 1920s.

Great Depression At first the European economy after World War I was very fragile. It was built on a delicate combination of international loans (largely from the United States), payments of reparations, and relatively weak foreign trade. After the Dawes Plan was established to help Germany pay reparations to the Allies, European economies began to improve. Then, on October 29, 1929, the New York Stock Exchange crashed. The result was an economic collapse now known as the **Great Depression**. By 1932, the economies of Europe were performing at levels that were half those of 1929. Jobs became scarce as the economy contracted. Without work, many families fell into abject poverty.

Unemployment in Europe During the Great Depression					
Country	Austria	France	Germany	Poland	United Kingdom
1929	225,000	9,000	2,484,000	177,000	1,204,000
1930	239,000	14,000	3,041,000	289,000	1,694,000
1931	304,000	72,000	4,744,000	373,000	2,666,000
1932	417,000	347,000	6,034,000	360,000	2,660,000
1933	456,000	356,000	5,599,000	280,000	2,821,000

Source: Lionel Robbins, *The Great Depression* (New York: Macmillan, 1936), 213.

World War II

Daily life was especially challenging for the German people after World War I. Germany was already in debt during the war, so the **Treaty of Versailles** that ended World War I left them in economic ruins. The treaty not only humiliated Germans by forcing them to accept full responsibility for the conflict, but it also forced them to pay many billions of dollars in **reparations**, money paid to make amends for a wrong. To pay the staggering reparations and support German workers who went on strike after France and Belgium took over the industrial Ruhr region, the **Weimar Republic**—the German government in place between the two world wars—inflated the value of German currency to the point that it became worthless. Even wheelbarrows of cash were not enough to buy daily food.

From the ashes of World War I, the Great Depression, and the ineffective Weimar Republic, Germany was receptive to the message of a leader such as Adolf Hitler and his Nazi Party. These factors ultimately led to

Under the Weimar Republic, German currency declined so much in value that burning it was cheaper than purchasing firewood or coal.

Credit: Library of Congress

the second historically large war of the 20th century and even more human suffering, especially for the Jewish population. The Holocaust ultimately resulted in the mass murder of 90 percent of Jewish Poles and two-thirds of the Jewish population of Europe. (For more on discrimination against Jews under the Nazis and the Holocaust, see Chapter 19.)

Ethnic Migrations

For most of the 19th century and first part of the 20th century, Europeans had been emigrating to lands around the world. People, mostly from rural areas, were fleeing poverty. They saw opportunities for themselves and their children in countries such as the United States, Argentina, Brazil, South Africa and Australia.

During the second half of the 20th century, migration patterns reversed. As Europe emerged from the chaos and destruction of World War II, it became a prosperous region. Migrants from around the globe, many from former colonies, streamed into Europe. By the end of the century, Europeans found themselves living in multiethnic and multireligious communities.

Diversity created tensions in many European countries in the last half of the 20th century and the early 21st century. Some native-born citizens complained that immigrants did not assimilate as immigrants of the past had attempted to do. On the other hand, some immmigrants felt discriminated against because of their religion, ethnicity, or traditions. For example, France had a long debate on whether it should be legal for women to cover their face in public. For some Muslim women, this was an issue of religious liberty and cultural practice. For some French, covering one's face represented a security threat.

Postwar Populations The Jewish population suffered more dramatically than any other during World War II. But war took a toll on the general population as well, especially in Germany and Russia. Germany suffered heavy losses during the war, both in lives and industrial power. Nearly 9 percent of the population was killed, or as many as 7.5 million people. The country's cities were severely damaged by Allied forces' bombings at the end of the war, and agricultural production was only 35 percent of what it was before the war. The population of Russia was devastated by World War II. More than 15 percent of the population—or roughly 16.8 million people—died during the war. China suffered more than 20 million casualties.

Class Hierarchies During the postwar era, there was much less of a division between people living in the city and those living in the country. Rural areas and occupations still existed, of course, but the lines between cities and villages blurred after 1945 as people's lives became more similar. The lines between classes therefore also changed after the war. Europe saw a tremendous rise in the impact of its middle class. Managers and experts replaced property owners and title holders in positions of authority. Western Europeans suddenly had upward mobility, or the ability to move from one class to another by means of one's own abilities and aspirations.

Consumer Culture

The rise of Europe's middle class and its involvement in an increasingly global economy exposed people to new goods, ideas, and practices. After World War II, mass-production technologies that were perfected in munitions factories were turned to producing consumable products at rates never before seen. A new consumer culture was emerging. In it, domestic comforts such as electricity, indoor plumbing, plastics, and synthetic fibers made life easier.

Many historians attribute the rise in a consumer-driven Europe to a desire to emulate American-style consumerism. The postwar years saw unprecedented prosperity both in the United States and Europe. That, coupled with ongoing and rapid industrialization, only fueled the European consumer boom. The era has been called the Age of the Automobile because of the widespread availability of commodities and the new liberated, mobile style of life.

Communication and Transportation

Two world wars had devastated Europe and demanded full attention on survival. During the second half of the 20th century, however, Europeans' focus was no longer on survival on the home front or victory at war. Rather, people focused on the ease of domestic life and the technology that could achieve it.

Radios and Television Technology in the home became a great social equalizer. No longer did people need to visit the theater or cinema for entertainment, which only the better off could afford. Instead, mass production of radios and televisions brought entertainment directly to living rooms, regardless of social class or standing. Millions of people from all walks of life could enjoy the same entertainment experience simultaneously. Tastes converged across classes and cultures, from the most remote rural areas to the busiest city centers. The 1954 World Cup, for example, was broadcast throughout Europe by the newly created Eurovision network. The wide audience for that game demonstrated not only the proliferation of the television in the lives of all Europeans, but also the common way people chose to spend their new abundance of leisure time.

Telephones and Computers Other technological innovations also swept through Europe after the wars. The telephone made it easier for individuals to communicate and for businesses to be productive. Later, the cell phone made such communication even easier and widespread. Few innovations were as influential as the computer. Early computers existed as early as the 1940s, but they were large, cumbersome, and slow. From the late 1950s to the mid-1970s, the computer grew from a purely scientific instrument to an integral part of enterprises. Computers made for home use became widespread in the 1980s.

The computer's related technology, the Internet, emerged in the United States in the 1970s, but it was not available to the general population until the 1990s. As unifying as radio and television may have been, the Internet is an unparalleled equalizer. In most countries, many people have access to a wide range of information and can connect with most other people at any time. By the beginning of the 21st century, approximately 360 million people were estimated to have access to the Internet. As pervasive as the Internet's influence was at the time, that was still only 6 percent of the world's total population.

Transportation As advances in communication connected people remotely, transportation advances connected them physically. Throughout Europe at the beginning of the 20th century, populations clustered around railroad destinations. With automobile ownership, populations became even more mobile. Infrastructure that once built airplanes to bomb enemies instead built airplanes to transport leisure travelers across countries and over oceans. The world was becoming smaller, and social movements were beginning to take shape.

The Influence of Feminism

During the early 20th century, daily life in Europe was focused on survival. Many women left their traditional roles as mothers and caretakers to work in munitions factories and other male-dominated fields. As Europeans moved beyond the conflicts and settled into the second half of the century, women began to have opportunities and choices as never before. Feminist movements emerged throughout Europe as women's advocates fought for their causes.

Roles of Women

Women on both sides of the conflict during World War II joined the armed services in large numbers. Hundreds of thousands of women served in auxiliary—or support—positions such as nurses, ambulance drivers, and office workers. They also played significant roles in resistance movements, which often took them into enemy territory. Women in Yugoslavia even fought alongside men on the front lines. In Russia, almost 800,000 women served in the armed forces, some as pilots and snipers. In Britain, more than 640,000 women served in the armed forces during World War II. At first, only single women, aged 20 to 30, were called to serve, but by mid-1943, almost 90 percent of single women and 80 percent of married women were working in factories or directly with the armed forces.

War also brought an increased demand for labor on the home front. Women made up much of the shortfall. The British workforce grew by half a million between 1939 and 1943, and women—many of whom had previously been unemployed—contributed 80 percent of that. This surge of women into the workforce happened during World War I as well, but women left the workforce as soon as men returned from war. After World War II, however, the change was more lasting. Unemployment in Britain was wiped out. In the Soviet Union, where women were already widely employed before World War II, more than half the labor force was female by 1942.

Childcare Facilities Before the two world wars, there was little or no need for anyone outside the home to take care of children. Wealthy families hired live-in help. But as women increasingly left the home to go to work, the need for childcare outside of homes grew. State-led expansion of Early Childhood Care and Education (ECCE) services first emerged in the Russian Federation in the early 20th century to encourage women to participate equally in work and public life. In both Russia and Western Europe, such programs also served to provide an education at as young an age as possible. These programs eventually led to preschool programs and modern-day kindergarten.

Efforts of Feminists

World War I brought about women's **suffrage**, or the right to vote, through much of Europe. The recognition of the vital contribution women made to the war effort led to the widespread belief that women should be granted the right to vote. The battle was harder fought in some countries than others. France didn't allow women to vote until 1944, Italy in 1946, Belgium in 1948, and Greece in 1952. In neutral Switzerland, women didn't gain the right to vote until 1971.

But beyond voting rights, women's status at home and in the workplace was little changed in the early 20th century. Society after World War I was male-dominated. Women were still largely discriminated against in the labor market, especially married women. If paid employment was available, it was only in "women's jobs," such as nursing, teaching, and secretarial work. In education, too, women continued to struggle. While more women began to study at universities between 1900 and 1940, the percentage was still small. In Spain and Greece, for example, only about 7 percent of university students were female.

Second-Wave Feminism The first wave of feminism in the 19th and early 20th centuries focused mostly on public issues, such as women's suffrage and legal rights. Building on these achievements, **second-wave feminism**, or the women's movement, addressed more personal issues, including family, sexuality, and professional ambition. It was largely a response to the postwar ideal of the domesticated housewife and the inherent limitations that ideal placed upon women. Second-wave feminism peaked in the 1960s and 1970s, after it had successfully expanded choices for women both inside their homes and in the workplace.

Simone de Beauvoir French writer, philosopher, and feminist Simone de Beauvoir is best known for her 1949 book *Le Deuxième Sexe*, or *The Second Sex*. In it, she writes about the need to abolish what she called the myth of the "eternal feminine." To her, this myth was the traditional view of women that limited their opportunities for intellectual development and for work opportunities. She also wrote about the need for women to be politically active, to engage in debate and advocate for equality. De Beauvoir advanced the concept that all individuals—regardless of gender—should be afforded the same opportunities. Her works became a staple of feminist literature.

Women throughout Europe protested against inequality in the workplace. The German words on this sign say "Equal pay for equal work for men and women."

Credit: Getty Images

Population Growth

In 1913—before World War I—almost 500 million people lived in Europe. By 1950—after World War II—this figure reached almost 600 million. However, the growth varied by country. The countries that suffered the highest loses in war, such as Poland and Germany, grew more slowly. The Soviet population, for example, was 26 million smaller in 1946 than it had been in 1941.

Changes in the birth rate had mixed impact on the size of the population. The absence of men during war, combined with the death of so many men in battle, reduced birth rates during both major wars. Then, following each war, couples that had put off having children during war began to have children again. Many countries had a **baby boom**—a sharp increase in the birth rate. To some extent, this made up for the decline in birth rate during the wars.

The short-term effects of the war occured within a longer term decline in birth rates. The spread of birth control and education about family planning reduced the size of families. To counter this trend, some states provided families with financial incentives to have more children. The Soviets began making such payments as early as 1936.

The significant cause of population growth was a steep decline in death rates. In 1910, life expectancy at birth in Western Europe was around 55 years. Forty years later, people were more commonly living to be 65 or older. The fall in the mortality rate was largely the result of the greater emphasis on public hygiene and advances in medicine. Better treatment of sewage, improvements in housing, and campaigns to improve health and nutrition for pregnant women all contributed. So did improvements in drugs and health care. In particular, growing knowledge about **neonatalism**, or the care of infants, helped more children survive the dangerous months following birth.

Options for Women

Many states throughout Europe created job opportunities for women. Initially, these jobs were in fields traditionally dominated by females. For example, right after World War II, Britain's newly created National Health Service first employed women as nurses, midwives, and clerical staff. Opportunities soon emerged throughout Britain in fields such as banking, textiles, and light industries such as electronics. The overall proportion of women in the British workforce increased from 46 percent in 1955 to 51 percent in 1965. Still, jobs were typically segregated by gender, with work categorized as "women's work" typically paying less money than other jobs. Many women also still faced the "marriage bar," which prevented married women from entering the workforce.

By the 1960s, attitudes toward women—both in employment and in general—started to shift noticeably. Employers began to allow married women to work for wages, at least part-time. Countries passed laws making it illegal to fire a woman if she became pregnant. Divorce laws became more lenient throughout Europe, and women's studies programs emerged at colleges and universities. Record numbers of women ran for—and started winning— political office. Wome were becoming more integrated into the workforce, a trend that continued into the 21st century.

The Pill In the 1950s, family planning advocate Margaret Sanger raised $150,000 to fund research for a **birth control pill**, a pill that a women could be taken to prevent pregancy. In 1960, the pill, as it became known, was approved for use in the United States. It was soon available throughout much of Europe. The pill provided women with much greater control over their own fertility and helped families plan when to have children. However, it was controversial. The Roman Catholic Church and some other religious groups opposed the use of the pill.

Scientific Fertilization Alternate methods of fertilization gave women a different type of freedom. The process of **in vitro fertilization (IVF)** fertilizes the egg outside the woman's body and then implants the embryos. Women who wish to have children on their own are able to do so without a male partner, needing only a male donor. Couples who are unable to conceive children naturally also have IVF as an option.

Women in Politics

Thanks in large part to suffrage movements and second-wave feminism, women in the latter half of the 20th century began to obtain political power. Throughout Europe, women attained political positions previously held only by men.

Margaret Thatcher of Great Britain Margaret Thatcher was the leader of the Conservative Party and became the country's first female prime minister in 1979. Her stated goal was to break with what she considered to be the failed practices of the Labour Party. The term **Thatcherism** became synonymous with her economic policies, including cuts in public spending and tax cuts for high-income earners. The term is still used to describe such policies.

Another of Thatcher's goals was to make Britain more competitive in the global marketplace by reducing the number of trade unions and privatizing parts of the economy that were under government control. Her attempts to privatize such institutions as the National Health Service were not popular, though she was still elected to a third term. She ultimately resigned in 1990 amid conflicts within her own party over European integration.

Mary Robinson of Ireland Mary Robinson became the first female president of Ireland in 1990. As president, Robinson worked to convey to the rest of the world a more modern image of Ireland, and she did so by taking on a more prominent role than had past presidents. Robinson was strongly committed to human rights. She was the first head of state to visit Somalia after its civil war in 1992. Two years later, she was the first to visit Rwanda after a period of genocide.

Shortly before Robinson's term as president expired, she took up the post of United Nations High Commissioner for Human Rights (UNHCHR). In that role, she made human rights at both the national and regional levels priorities of her office.

Édith Cresson of France Édith Cresson was the first female premier of France, serving from May 1991 to April 1992. Cresson worked to improve France's industrial competitiveness and to reduce social inequities. She was replaced after just one year, however, because of rising unemployment and declining support for her Socialist Party.

In 1995, Cresson was appointed to serve as European Commissioner for Science, Research, and Education. She and the entire European Commission resigned in 1999 because of alleged fraud and corruption.

New Voices in Society

As feminism found its foothold in the world that emerged after the two world wars, so did many other political, intellectual, and social movements. As individuals became more empowered, new voices found a place in European society.

Environmentalism and Green Parties

By the 1960s, the rapid industrialization of the previous century had created significant environmental problems. Environmentalists argued that Europe was bound for ecological disaster if it failed to adopt practices that were more sustainable. They challenged the traditional economic and political establishment to adopt policies that were sensitive to the environment.

This movement included not only environmental conservation but also broader issues of lifestyle. The oil crisis of 1973, for example, in which a ban on oil trade drove down fuel supplies and drove up prices, helped spark the European environmental movement.

To try to gain a voice in political policy, environmentalists formed Green Parties—political parties whose main focus is on the environment or ecology-oriented ideals. Such parties began to form in the 1970s. An umbrella organization known as the **European Greens** was founded in Brussels, Belgium, in January 1984.

The first and most successful Green Party was **die Grünen**, founded in West Germany primarily by Herbert Gruhl and Petra Kelly in 1979. The party was formed by a collective of roughly 250 separate environmental groups. Its primary goal was to rally public support around the issues of nuclear energy and pollution. By the end of the 1980s, almost every country in Western and Northern Europe had its own version of the Green Party.

Other Political and Social Movements

Several other movements rose alongside the feminists and Greens after World War II. Though the groups all had different aims, each was fighting for some sort of social change. Most of the movements saw some degree of success, though some brought about more change than others.

Youth Revolts of 1968 A generation that had experienced neither economic depression nor total war came of age in the 1960s. It was also the first generation to grow up under the threat of nuclear destruction. The combination of forces created tensions between older and younger people around the world known as the generation gap.

As a movement, young people criticized existing institutions and beliefs while also calling for greater political and personal freedoms. Students felt that leadership—either of their governments or educational institutions—was more interested in global security than in providing opportunity. In this period, for the first time, echoes from the United States had an important effect on student action in Europe.

Several events led to massive student unrest in 1968. The year opened with young people in Czechoslovakia protesting against Communist Party rule. Their action there inspired movements in Rome and Paris. In France, the May student revolts against consumerism, capitalism, and traditional values sparked labor strikes as well, with 11 million workers walking off their jobs. Other student outbreaks soon followed, from London to Yugoslavia. The student movements produced few immediate concrete gains, but they raised awareness of persistent class divisions that seemed to prevent real democracy from taking hold in Europe. The students' efforts also highlighted gender divisions that would spark the women's movement.

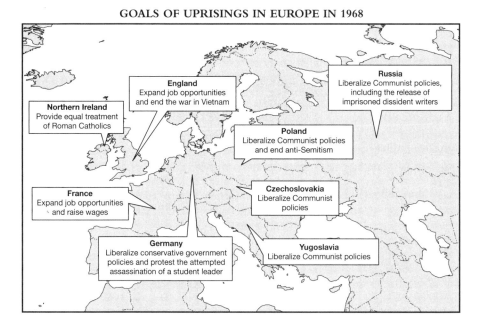

Gay and Lesbian Movements Organized movements for gay, lesbian, bisexual, and transgender (LGBT) people may have started after other movements in Europe, but individuals in this group had a long history of struggle. Discrimination was widespread and legal. Aversion therapy—or the practice of attempting to rid an individual of homosexual tendencies—was practiced in most Western countries from the 1950s to the 1960s, often using painful electric shock therapy.

In France, the beginning of the gay liberation movement is commonly identified as May 1, 1971. A small group of protestors interrupted France's popular May Day celebrations. A decade later, in 1981, there were mass demonstrations against laws that supported discrimination against LGBT people. Since 1995, gays and lesbians have obtained full legal rights throughout Europe, although social rights have not been achieved everywhere.

Immigrants as Targets

Because of the economic growth of the 1950s and 1960s, many "guest workers" from southern Europe, Asia, and Africa immigrated to Western and Central Europe. After the economic downturn of the 1970s, these workers and their families often became targets of anti-immigrant agitation and extreme nationalist political parties. In France, for example, the right-wing National Rally political party supports French nationalism and controls on immigration, and it has been accused of encouraging **xenophobia**, or an intense fear or dislike of people from other countries, and anti-Semitism. The Freedom Party of Austria, founded in 1956, also argued for stricter controls on immigration and has warned against the "over-foreignization" of Austrian society.

European Integration

After decades of global conflict, several factors contributed to European countries' desire for greater cooperation. For the French in particular, such cooperation was a means to keep an eye on Germany, a country that occupied it twice in the 20th century. There was also a growing sense that economic rationalization and cooperation were needed to end wasteful competition and ease tensions between nations. Concerns about the Soviet Union further encouraged unity.

Steps to a Unified Europe

After World War II, Europeans took explicit steps toward reducing nationalism. The measures European leaders put into place were designed to promote both economic and political integration. Leaders hoped that integration would lead people to see peace as in their self-interest.

Further, these meassures tried to change how people thought about themselves. The goal was to establish a shared European identity. Just as the development of nationalism in the 19th century had overcome regional divides, internationalism might overcome national divides.

To aid in Europe's postwar economic recovery, the United States provided $13 billion, or roughly $140 billion in modern-day currency. As part of the **Marshall Plan**, the United States stipulated that European nations must spend the money cooperatively. The first step in European unification, the **Organization for European Economic Cooperation (OEEC)**, was established to administer Marshall Plan funds.

Member states France, West Germany, Italy, Belgium, Luxembourg, and the Netherlands continued to work together toward postwar economic recovery. The European Coal and Steel Community (ECSC) was established in 1951. It combined and administered Europe's vital steel and coal resources and also established an assembly—later named the **European Parliament**—as well as a court. It also collected tax income. The main architect of the ECSC was Robert Schuman of France, who hoped that it would make war between France and Germany "not merely unthinkable, but materially impossible."

In 1957, the original member nations of the ECSC signed the Treaty of Rome, which established the **European Economic Community (EEC)**, more commonly referred to as the **Common Market**. Britain, Ireland, and Denmark later joined the EEC in 1973. They lifted almost all trade restrictions among the member states. In 1986, the Single European Act allowed citizens to move freely among the member nations.

The Maastricht Treaty of 1991 led to the establishment of a common currency, the **Euro**, though the actual paper currency and coins didn't go into circulation until 2002. The treaty also allowed European nations to cooperate in areas such as security and environmental affairs, and it also resulted in a name change from EEC to the **European Union (EU)**.

Modern Europe

Membership in the EU became a perpetual balancing act. People in each country had to weigh the benefits against the costs.

EU membership provided countries with many advantages. For example, tax-free trade allowed businesses to sell their products more easily in a wider market. Free movement for citizens across borders made travel for work and tourism easy. Sharing a common currency made every financial transaction simpler. Greater political cooperation made addressing cross-border problems, such as pollution, more effective. These advantages help explain why Europe under the EU had its most peaceful and prosperous period in many centuries.

However, many countries disliked some of the restrictions on their autonomy. For example, no member could use the death penalty. Wealthier countries sometimes resented helping support poorer ones. Economic integration brought greater stability and prosperity overall, but it also meant that an economic problem in one country could have greater impact on other countries. Further, some countries feared the loss of their own distinct culture. They wanted to protect their language and their traditions from becoming just part of a general European one.

Another difficulty EU member nations faced was determining if, when, and how to leave. In 2016, British citizens voted to exit the EU. This move became known as **Brexit**. Negotiations between Britain and the rest of Europe over separation proved very complicated.

The vote on whether to remain in the European Union was hotly contested in the United Kingdom. Some viewed the EU as a continuation of Churchill's policies of working closely with European allies. Others supported leaving because they thought membership infringed on the country's independence.

Credit: Getty Images

Credit: Getty Images

Modern nation-states began to emerge with Great Britain and France in the 18th century. In the following two centuries, nation-states spread throughout Europe and other parts of the world. By World War II, nationalism reached a new level of intensity in the governments of Italy, Germany, and Japan. However, following the war, nationalism seemed to decline. Scholars who study nation-states disagreed on how long nation-states were likely to last.

The Impact of Globalization Between the end of World War II and the 1980s, Europeans broke down national barriers to make trade and movement easier. In this context, in 1989, British historian Eric Hobsbawm predicted that nation-states would decline around the world. He argued that nation-states developed along with capitalism and played an important role in globalization. They provided the order and organization necessary for states to participate in the global economy. However, Hobsbawm believed that the world was embarking on a new era of globalization marked by the free flow of goods and capital. In this new era, the time for nation-states was passing.

Hobsbawm's theory gained support in the 1990s. For example, French diplomat Jean-Marie Guéhenno based his book, *The End of the Nation-State,* on the rising power of supranational organizations such as the European Union and United Nations. However, it was not until the explosion of the Internet that Hobsbawm's point about the diminishing power of the nation-state in a borderless world was clearly demonstrated.

The Continued Need for Nation-States In the 1990s and the first decade of the 21st century, nationalism reasserted its power in Europe. In conflicts in the Balkans and in reactions against globalization, Europeans demonstrated their desire for nation-states. In 2011, Hedva Ben-Israel, a historian of European nationalism, argued that Hobsbawm and Guéhenno were wrong. She believed that nation-states will remain. Ben-Israel pointed out that the nation-state emerged as a response to the decline of feudalism. It united people under the government of their choosing, promising equal citizenship. The community that developed around that government forged its own cultural identity, one with a language and history that is preserved and shared through an organized educational system. Nationalism and the accompanying nation-states are not another 19th-century ideology that defined modern societies, nor merely a cultural identity, but rather a form of political organization that continues to evolve. Ben-Israel noted that no matter how interconnected the world might become, one global government seems impossible. In light of this, success in a competitive, globalized world requires the stability that only a nation-state can provide.

Political economist Dani Rodrik shared this view, stating that it may be popular to argue for the end of the nation-state, but nation-states are "the best placed entity to regulate and legitimize markets." Without such regulation, Rodrik warned about the challenges of globalization and misplaced patriotism used to address them.

The Return of the City-State The Brexit vote in 2016 seemed to support the argument that people would resist globalization and wanted more local control. Jamie Bartlett, a British social media analyst, argued that nation-states might indeed decline, but not as Hobsbawm predicted. Bartlett did not believe that greater global cooperation would bring about the end of nation-states. Rather, he suggested that nation-states were a relic of the 19th century, and they would prove too inefficient to operate in a fast-paced global world. He explained that nation-states could not control information, crime, businesses, borders, or even money supplies, but he also argued that international organizations could not control these either. Instead, Bartlett explored the possibility of the reemergence of city-states. He looked back to the success of Venice and the Hanseatic League centuries earlier. As the world continued to distribute and decentralize, the future "looks far brighter for the modern, connected, agile city."

KEY TERMS BY THEME

Governance

total war

councils

Treaty of Versailles

Weimar Republic

Thatcherism

European Greens

die Grünen

xenophobia

Marshall Plan

European Parliament

European Union (EU)

Brexit

Identity

Lost Generation

suffrage

second-wave feminism

baby boom

neonatalism

birth control pill

in vitro fertilization (IVF)

Economics

Great Depression

reparations

Organization for European Economic Cooperation (OEEC)

European Economic Community (EEC)

Common Market

Euro

MULTIPLE-CHOICE QUESTIONS

Questions 1–3 refer to the passage below.

"The restrictions that education and custom impose on [a] woman limit her grasp of the universe . . . . The girl today can certainly go out alone, stroll in the Tuileries; but I have already said how hostile the street is: eyes everywhere, hands waiting: if she wanders absentmindedly . . . an unpleasant incident can quickly occur; she must inspire respect by the way she dresses and behaves: this concern rivets her to the ground and [to] self. 'Her wings are clipped.' At eighteen, T. E. Lawrence went on a grand tour through France by bicycle; a young girl would never be permitted to take on such an adventure . . . . Yet such experiences have an inestimable impact: this is how an individual in the headiness of freedom and discovery learns to look at the entire world as his fief . . . .[The girl] . . . never stands up in front of it, unique and sovereign. . . .

Women's actions have never been more than symbolic agitation; they have won only what men have been willing to concede to them; they have taken nothing; they have received. . . . [T]hey lack the concrete means to organize themselves into a unit that could posit itself in opposition. . . . [U]nlike the proletariat, they have no solidarity of labor or interests; they even lack their own space . . . . They live dispersed among men, tied by homes, work, economic interests, and social conditions to certain men—fathers or husbands—more closely than to other women."

Simone de Beauvoir, *The Second Sex,* 1949

1. De Beauvoir described women as the "second sex" because

a) they were created after men according to the Bible

b) they have been defined in relation to men

c) they have accomplished much less than men

d) they lack the ambition to be as prominent as men

2. The above passage is a reflection of an understanding that

a) women's roles were formed by association with other women

b) women's encounters in the world were fostering new creativity

c) women's societal roles still faced inequality

d) women's relationships provided an opportunity for significant change

3. Which most shifted the perspective on women's roles in society?

a) Women's economic production during World War II

b) Increased resistance to women's suffrage

c) The postwar baby boom

d) The increase in women's life expectancy

Questions 4–5 refer to the timeline below.

Oral Contraceptives in Great Britain	
Date	**Development**
1960	First large-scale trials of oral contraceptive pills were conducted.
1961	Pills were approved for use but were available only to married women. They were high-dosage pills that contained seven times the level of hormones as pills today.
1974	Clinics could prescribe pills for single women.
2011	Approximately 70 percent of adult women had used oral contraceptive pills at some point in their lives.

4. What trend in society might be partially explained by the developments described in the chart?
   a) A decrease in the birth rate
   b) A decrease in the age of marriage
   c) An increase in the divorce rate
   d) An increase in the marriage rate

5. The developments described in the chart were part of which larger historical development after 1945?
   a) A decrease in the number of women who worked outside the home
   b) A decrease in the role of government research and regulation in everyday life
   c) An increase in conflicts between men and women over the role of women in society
   d) An increase in the importance of science and technology in everyday life

Questions 6–8 refer to the two passages below.

"The movement of coal and steel between member countries will immediately be freed from all customs duty . . . . Conditions will gradually be created which will spontaneously provide for the more rational distribution of production at the highest level of productivity."

Robert Schuman, Schuman Declaration, May 9, 1950

"British citizens are able to travel, study, work, retire, get fairer legal redress and obtain free medical help anywhere in Europe, without restrictions. We work together better to stop international gangs bringing drugs, terrorism and illegal immigrants into our country. It provides a network of trade, aid and cooperation that covers most of the world, giving us greater influence, stability and prosperity."

British Foreign Secretary Jack Straw, message to House of
Commons, June 16, 2004

6. The organization discussed in the first passage was formed because of a desire to

   a) prevent France and Germany from going to war

   b) stop the trading of goods such as drugs across the European continent

   c) offer a viable alternative to the United Nations

   d) provide a means to address the post-World War II rise of the Soviet Union

7. One difference between the organizations discussed in these two passages is that the one described by Straw

   a) focused on forming a military force that fought in areas such as Bosnia

   b) reached out to Eastern European countries, including the Czech Republic

   c) required that the United Kingdom end its use of its own currency

   d) included the United States and Canada as members

8. A historian could use these two passages to support which argument about Europe between 1945 and 2004?

   a) Nations were breaking apart because of ethnic tensions.

   a) Europeans were identifying more strongly with their nation.

   b) Local governments were taking over functions that national governments had performed before World War II.

   c) Nation-states were becoming less important and international organizations were becoming more important.

SHORT-ANSWER QUESTIONS

1. Use the passage to answer all parts of the question that follows.

"After World War II the German economy lay in shambles. The war, along with Hitler's scorched-earth policy, had destroyed 20 percent of all housing. Food production per capita in 1947 was only 51 percent of its level in 1938, and the official food ration set by the occupying powers varied between 1,040 and 1,550 calories per day. Industrial output in 1947 was only one-third its 1938 level. Moreover, a large percentage of Germany's working-age men were dead. . . .[O]bservers thought that West Germany would have to be the biggest client of the U.S. welfare state; yet, twenty years later its economy was envied by most of the world. And less than ten years after the war people already were talking about the German economic miracle."

> David R. Henderson, "German Economic 'Miracle,'"
> *The Concise Encyclopedia of Economics*

a) Explain ONE piece of evidence that supports Henderson's argument regarding the German economic miracle following World War II.

b) Explain ONE piece of evidence that supports why a similar transformation did not occur in at least one other part of Europe following World War II.

c) Provide ONE argument to explain the difference between your responses in parts a and b.

2. Use the passage to answer all parts of the question that follows.

"Around 1950, participation in higher education worldwide was still very low for both sexes but, still, enrollment rates for men were more than double those for women. From the 1960s onwards, participation in tertiary [post-secondary] education rapidly expanded. Initially, this expansion disproportionately involved men, leading to a widening of the gender gap in higher education. However, from the 1970s onwards, the gap began to shrink."

> Jan Van Bavel, "The Mid-Twentieth Century Baby Boom
> and the Changing Educational Gradient in Belgian Cohort
> Fertility," *Demographic Research,* March 2014

a) Describe ONE cause for low female participation in post-secondary education in Europe prior to 1950.

b) Describe ONE cause for the increase in female participation in post-secondary education in Europe after 1950.

c) Explain ONE political, social, or economic factor that contributed to the cause you identified in part b.

LONG-ESSAY QUESTIONS

1. Evaluate the impact of modern feminist movements on the daily life of women post-1945.

2. Evaluate the extent to which European political and economic integration created a more unified Europe.

REFLECT ON THE CHAPTER ESSENTIAL QUESTION

1. In one to three paragraphs, explain the changes that altered experiences of everyday life.

WRITE AS A HISTORIAN: WRITE AN ESSAY

This chapter summarizes the skills that are useful for writing essays for the AP® exam. More generally, they are helpful in thinking and communicating clearly about history.

Time Periods

Period 1: c. 1450 to c. 1648

Period 2: c. 1648 to c. 1815

Period 3: c. 1815 to c. 1914

Period 4: c. 1914 to the Present

Practices

Practice 1: Analyze historical evidence, including primary and secondary sources

Practice 2: Argument development

Reasoning Skills

Skill 1: Contextualization

Skill 2: Comparison

Skill 3: Causation

Skill 4: Continuity and Change over Time

Themes

Interaction of Europe and the World (INT)

Poverty and Prosperity (PP)

Objective Knowledge and Subjective Visions (OS)

States and Other Institutions of Power (SP)

Individual and Society (IS)

National and European Identity (NI)

Free Responses and Essays

Part I has **three short-answer questions** – two on required topics (1600-2001) and one for which you choose between two topics (1450-1815 or 1815-present). All three questions ask you to describe or explain examples of historical evidence. Forty minutes total, worth 20 percent of the exam.

- Question 1 asks you to analyze secondary sources (respond to a historian's argument).

- Question 2 assesses the skill of either causation or continuity and change over time. You will probably be asked to respond to a stimuli, either a primary source or a visual.

- Question 3 assesses whichever skill was not used for Question 2. You will be asked to respond to general propositions about European history.

Part II has **one document-based question** (topics from 1600-2001). Sixty minutes (includes a 15-minute reading period), worth 25 percent of the exam.

- You must incorporate all or most of the seven documents into your answer.

- You need to explain authorship and significance of the documents (view, purpose, point of view, audience, and context).

Part II has **one long-essay question**. You get to choose from three options, all of which feature the same theme and reasoning skill (period choices are 1450–1648, 1648–1914, and 1815–present). The questions focus on large-scale topics from the course. Forty minutes, worth 15 percent of the exam.

Which of the following strategies might be most useful in reviewing European history? Choose all that apply.

1. Take timed practice exams to pace yourself on the writing portions.

2. Create study note cards with brief outlines for a essays on core topics.

3. Read history essays, and evaluate whether they are well-written and persuasive.

4. Review the special features of your textbook to be sure you know specific historical events, their time frames, and important vocabulary.

5. Look at sample documents from DBQs across different periods. Practice interpreting the documents in them.

PERIOD 4: Review

DOCUMENT-BASED QUESTION 1

Directions: Question 1 is based on the accompanying documents. The documents have been edited for the purpose of this exercise. You are advised to spend 15 minutes planning and 45 minutes writing your answer.

In your response you should do the following:

- **Thesis:** Make a defensible claim that establishes a line of reasoning and consists of one or more sentences found in one place.
- **Contextualization:** Relate the argument to a broader historical context.
- **Document Evidence:** Use content from at least six documents.
- **Outside Evidence:** Use one piece of evidence not in the documents.
- **Document Sourcing:** Explain how or why the point of view, purpose, situation, or intended audience is relevant for at least three documents.
- **Analysis:** Show the relationships among pieces of historical evidence and use them to support, qualify, or modify an argument.

1. Explain the ideas associated with the interwar years and the various consequences of these ideas.

Document 1

Source: Rudolph Nadolny, speech accepting the Nobel Prize in physics on behalf of Albert Einstein, December 10, 1922

Since Professor Einstein is prevented by his journey to the Far East from receiving the high honors of the Nobel Prize himself, I have the task and the honor of receiving his prize from the hands of the King. . . .

But I may be able to draw a parallel between what concerns us tonight and what is subject to my competence—not that in politics relativity is at least as valid as in space—but that the Nobel Foundation, by encouraging and rewarding the pursuit of the highest goals of humanity, the cultural community of nations, is also an international political organ, and that Alfred Nobel, by placing the scientific achievement at such a high level he raised his pedestal above the peoples, and at the same time made his country the refuge of his ideas, to unite the peoples in cultural competition, to perform diplomatic service in the best sense, combining the highest service of the Fatherland with the noblest service of humanity. . . . The Nobel Prize winner Einstein is not only a scholar and researcher, but also an enthusiastic priest of reconciliation.

Document 2

Source: Adolf Hitler, *Mein Kampf,* 1925

The fact that intelligent sections of the community regard the German collapse primarily as an economic catastrophe, and consequently think that a cure for it may be found in an economic solution, seems to me to be the reason why hitherto no improvement has been brought about.

No improvement can be brought about until it be understood that economics play only a second or third role, while the main part is played by political, moral and racial factors. Only when this is understood will it be possible to understand the causes of the present evil and consequently to find the ways and means of remedying them. . . .

The most facile [simplistic], and therefore the most generally accepted, way of accounting for the present misfortune is to say that it is the result of a lost war, and that this is the real cause of the present misfortune. . . . The apostles of world conciliation habitually asserted . . . the resurgence of the German people—once "militarism" had been crushed. Did not these self-same circles sing the praises of the Entente and did they not also lay the whole blame for the sanguinary [bloody] struggle on the shoulders of Germany? Without this explanation, would they have been able to put forward the theory that a military defeat would have no political consequences for the German people? . . . Is not that so, you miserable, lying rascals? That kind of impudence which is typical of the Jews was necessary in order to proclaim the defeat of the army as the cause of the German collapse.

Document 3

Source: Albert Camus, *The Stranger*, 1942

Nothing, nothing had the least importance and I knew quite well why. [The priest], too, knew why. From the dark horizon of my future a sort of slow, persistent breeze had been blowing toward me, all my life long, from the years that were to come. And on its way that breeze had leveled out all the ideas that people tried to foist on me in the equally unreal years I then was living through. What difference could they make to me, the deaths of others, or a mother's love, or his [the priest's] God; or the way a man decides to live, the fate he thinks he chooses, since one and the same fate was bound to "choose" not only me but thousands of millions of privileged people who, like him, called themselves my brothers. Surely, surely he must see that? Every man alive was privileged; there was only one class of men, the privileged class. All alike would be condemned to die one day; his turn, too, would come like the others'. And what difference could it make if, after being charged with murder, he were executed because he didn't weep at his mother's funeral, since it all came to the same thing in the end?

Document 4

Source: Benito Mussolini, *My Autobiography*, 1928

My labor had not been easy nor light. . . . When, in parliament, I delivered my first speech of November 16, 1922, after the Fascist revolution, I concluded by invoking the assistance of God in my difficult task. Well, this sentence of mine seemed to be out of place! In the Italian parliament . . . the name of God had been banned for a long time. Not even the Popular party—the so-called Catholic party—had ever thought of speaking of God.

In Italy, a political man did not even turn his thoughts to the Divinity. And, even if he had ever thought of doing so, political opportunism and cowardice would have deterred him, particularly in a legislative assembly. It remained for me to make this bold innovation! And in an intense period of revolution! What is the truth? It is that a faith openly professed is a sign of strength. I have seen the religious spirit bloom again; churches once more are crowded, the ministers of God are themselves invested with new respect. Fascism . . . is doing its duty.

Document 5

Source: Sigmund Freud, *Civilization and Its Discontents,* 1930

It is impossible to escape the impression that people commonly use false standards of measurement—that they seek power, success and wealth for themselves and admire them in others, and that they underestimate what is of true value in life. And yet, in making any general judgment of this sort, we are in danger of forgetting how variegated the human world and its mental life are. There are a few men from whom their contemporaries do not withhold admiration, although their greatness rests on attributes and achievements which are completely foreign to the aims and ideals of the multitude. One might easily be inclined to suppose that it is after all only a minority which appreciates these great men, while the large majority cares nothing for them. But things are probably not as simple as that, thanks to the discrepancies between people's thoughts and their actions, and to the diversity of their wishful impulses. . . .

This brings us to the more general problem of preservation. . . . The subject has hardly been studied as yet; but it is so attractive and important that we may be allowed to turn our attention to…a destruction of the memory-trace—that is, its annihilation—that everything is somehow preserved and that in suitable circumstances . . . it can once more be brought to light. Let us try to grasp what this assumption involves by taking an analogy from another field. We will choose as an example the history of the Eternal City. Historians tell us that the oldest Rome was the *Roma Quadrata,* a fenced settlement on the Palatine. . . . Of the buildings which once occupied this ancient area he will find nothing, or only scanty remains, for they exist no longer. The best information about Rome in the republican era would only enable him at the most to point out the sites where the temples and public buildings of that period stood. Their place is now taken by ruins, but not by ruins of themselves but of later restorations made after fires or destruction.

Document 6

Source: Gino Severini, *The Accordion Player*, 1919

Document 7

Source: W. H. Auden, "Dance of Death," 1933

It's farewell to the drawing room's civilised cry
The professor's sensible where-to and why
The frock-coated diplomat's social aplomb
Now matters are settled with gas and bomb.

  The works for two pianos, the brilliant stories
  Of reasonable giants and remarkable fairies
  The pictures, the ointments, the frangible wares
  And the branches of olive are stored upstairs.
  For the Devil has broken parole and arisen
  He has dynamited his way out of prison
  Out of the well where his Papa throws
  The rebel range, the outcast rose. . . .

The fishes are silent deep in the sea:
The skies are lit up like a Christmas tree
The star in the west shoots its warning cry
"Mankind is alive but mankind must die."

So good-bye to the house with its wallpaper red,
Good-bye to the sheets on the warm double bed
Good-bye to the beautiful birds on the wall,
It's good-bye, dear heart, good-bye to you all.

Directions: Question 1 is based on the accompanying documents. The documents have been edited for the purpose of this exercise. You are advised to spend 15 minutes planning and 45 minutes writing your answer.

In your response you should do the following:

- **Thesis:** Make a defensible claim that establishes a line of reasoning and consists of one or more sentences found in one place.
- **Contextualization:** Relate the argument to a broader historical context.
- **Document Evidence:** Use content from at least six documents.
- **Outside Evidence:** Use one piece of evidence not in the documents.
- **Document Sourcing:** Explain how or why the point of view, purpose, situation, or intended audience is relevant for at least three documents.
- **Analysis:** Show the relationships among pieces of historical evidence and use them to support, qualify, or modify an argument.

2. Evaluate the extent to which Cold War politics affected international affairs during the period 1949–1989.

Document 1

Source: Fidel Castro, speech to a group of farmers and farmworkers, February 24, 1959

Let us not speak about promises but about realities. The peasants had always lived under terror, they did not have faith because they had been deceived, they did not have hope. . . . While the enemy [the troops supporting Batista] took away everything, stole everything, and did not pay for what they took, in spite of the many millions they had, the Rebel Army did the opposite. Nothing stopped Batista's Army from stealing personal belongings from the peasants, which were sold later. When they did not find anything to take, they just burned the houses. How little they thought about the efforts that had been needed to build them! How easily they burned houses! How easily they murdered people! The conduct of the Rebel Army gained little by little the peasants' confidence, their love, and gave them faith in the final victory. We never took anything from the peasants without paying for it, we never invaded their houses. The Rebel Army never took anything that had not been spontaneously offered. Never a rebel soldier humiliated a peasant.

Document 2

Source: Winston Churchill, speech, Fulton, Missouri, March 5, 1946

A shadow has fallen upon the scenes so lately lighted by the Allied victory. Nobody knows what Soviet Russia and its Communist international organization intends to do in the immediate future, or what are its limits, if any, to their expansive and proselytizing tendencies. I have a strong admiration and regard for the valiant Russian people and for my wartime comrade, Marshal Stalin. . . . It is my duty, however . . . for me to state the facts as I see them to you. . . . From Stettin in the Baltic to Trieste in the Adriatic, an iron curtain has descended across the continent. Behind that line lie all the capitals of the ancient states of Central and Eastern Europe, Warsaw, Berlin, Prague, Vienna, Budapest, Belgrade, Bucharest and Sofia, all these famous cities and the population around them lie in what I must call the Soviet sphere, and all are subject in one form or another, not only to Soviet influence but to a very high degree . . . of control from Moscow. . . . If the Western democracies stand together in strict adherence to the principles of the United Nations Charter . . . no one is likely to molest them. If however they become divided or falter in their duty . . . then indeed catastrophe may overwhelm us all.

Document 3

Source: Lord Ismay, Secretary General of NATO, Rome, October 18, 1952

[Unity] binds the 14 nations of the Atlantic Alliance together. I stress the word unity because that is what matters more than anything else: that is the real answer to the threat of aggression, that is what potential enemies fear more than anything else; that is what they want to destroy more than anything else. We must be on guard against the sometimes persuasive whispers and insinuations of propagandists who seek to magnify our differences and try to drive a wedge in our unity. Nations cannot afford to stand alone to be picked off one by one. We have the eloquent evidence of countries that formerly were free, independent, and important members of the Western European community, who now have fallen under the domination and imperialistic exploitation of the Soviet. Clearly we must arm up to the limit in order to be as strong as possible as rapidly as possible, but not at the expense of national bankruptcy. We cannot afford, through excessive haste to avert the hot war, to lose the cold one. Our alliance, it cannot be too often repeated, is purely defensive. Not a ship, not a plane, not a gun will ever be used except in self-defense. And no one knows better than the Soviet General Staff that the forces we plan are of a magnitude which can never be put to offensive or aggressive purposes.

Document 4

Nuclear Weapons Stockpiles, 1945 to 2015		
Year	United States	Soviet Union
1945	6	0
1955	3,057	200
1965	31,982	6,129
1975	27,826	19,055
1985	24,237	39,197
1995	12,144	27,000
2005	10,295	17,000
2015	7,100	7,700

Source: Hans M. Kristensen and Robert S. Norris, "Global Nuclear Stockpiles, 1945–2006," *Bulletin of the Atomic Scientists,* July 1, 2006; data for 2015 from Arms Control Association, armscontrol.org.

Document 5

Source: Belgrade Declaration, the first conference of the Non-Aligned Movement, 1961

Imperialism is weakening. Colonial empires and other forms of foreign oppression of peoples in Asia, Africa and Latin America are gradually disappearing from the stage of history. Great successes have been achieved in the struggle of many peoples for national independence and equality. . . . The governments of countries participating in the Conference resolutely reject the view that war, including the "cold war," is inevitable as this view reflects a sense both of helplessness and hopelessness and is contrary to the progress of the world. They affirm their unwavering faith that the international community is able to organize its life without resorting to means which actually belong to a past epoch of human history.

Document 6

Source: A West German soldier is standing in front of the Berlin Wall, with an armed East German soldier sitting on top of the wall

Credit: Library of Congress

Document 7

Source: *Izvestia,* the newspaper for expressing views of the Soviet government, March 13, 1947

On March 12, President Truman addressed a message to the U.S. Congress asking for 400 million dollars to be assigned for urgent aid to Greece and Turkey, and for authority to send to those countries American civil and military personnel, and to provide for the training by Americans by specially picked Greek and Turkish personnel. . . .

Commenting on Truman's message to Congress, the *New York Times* proclaims the advent of "the age of American responsibility." Yet what is this responsibility but a smokescreen for expansion? The cry of saving Greece and Turkey from the expansion of the so-called "totalitarian states" is not new. Hitler used to refer to the Bolsheviks when he wanted to open the road for his own conquests. Now they want to take Greece and Turkey under their control, they raise a din about "totalitarian states." This seems all the more attractive since, in elbowing in itself, the U.S.A. is pushing non-totalitarian Britain out of yet another country or two.

AP® European History
Practice Exam

Section 1

Directions: Each of the questions or incomplete statements below is followed by four suggested answers or completions. Select the one that is best in each case.

Questions 1–4 refer to the passage below.

"I think that in discussions of physical problems we ought to begin not from the authority of scriptural passages but from sense experiences and necessary demonstrations; for the holy Bible and the phenomena of nature proceed alike from the divine Word the former as the dictate of the Holy Ghost and the latter as the observant executrix [a female who carries out orders of another] of God's commands. . . .

From this I do not mean to infer that we need not have an extraordinary esteem for the passages of holy Scripture. On the contrary, having arrived at any certainties in physics, we ought to utilize these as the most appropriate aids in the true exposition of the Bible and in the investigation of those meanings which are necessarily contained therein, for these must be concordant [in agreement] with demonstrated truths. I should judge that the authority of the Bible was designed to persuade men of those articles and propositions which, surpassing all human reasoning could not be made credible by science, or by any other means than through the very mouth of the Holy Spirit. . . .

But I do not feel obliged to believe that the same God who has endowed us with senses, reason and intellect has intended us to forego their use and by some other means to give us knowledge which we can attain by them. He would not require us to deny sense and reason in physical matters which are set before our eyes and minds by direct experience or necessary demonstrations."

Galileo Galilei, letter to the Grand Duchess of
Tuscany, 1615

1. This passage most clearly demonstrates the influence of which development in how people thought about the world?
   (A) The interest in original translations of the Bible by Christian humanists
   (B) The promotion of reasoning and experimentation by thinkers during the Scientific Revolution
   (C) The reliance on classical Greek and Roman sources by Renaissance scholars
   (D) The emphasis on the authority of scripture by Protestant reformers

2. This passage best demonstrates which of the following about scientific thinkers in the 17th century?
   (A) They continued to hold religious worldviews as they pursued scientific inquiry.
   (B) They received substantial support from kings and emperors.
   (C) They developed mathematical models to prove scientific ideas.
   (D) They rejected the role of divine forces in the creation of humans and the universe.

3. Ideas such as the ones conveyed in this passage contributed most directly to which of the following developments?
   (A) The Romantic emphasis on intuition and emotion
   (B) The Social Darwinist belief in the natural superiority of Western civilization
   (C) The Positivist application of science to solve social problems
   (D) The Enlightenment philosophies of skepticism and deism

4. Which event is most useful in providing the context for describing the the risks that Galileo was taking by writing this letter?
   (A) The rise to power of Louis XIV, the Sun King, who became the king of France in 1643
   (B) The development of the idea of mercantilism, particularly in England and France, in the 16th century
   (C) The conflict that drove the Thirty Years' War in central Europe between 1618 and 1648
   (D) The influence of the Ottoman Empire in southeastern Europe in the 17th century

Questions 5–8 refer to the chart below.

Copies of Books Printed in Europe		
Period	**Total Number**	**Number per person in Western Europe**
1301–1400	3 million	less than 0.1
1401–1500	5 million	less than 0.1
1501–1600	210 million	0.2
1601–1700	540 million	0.5
1701–1800	990 million	0.8

Source: Adapted from www.OurWorldInData.org/data/media-communications/books. Data from Eltjo Buringh and Jan Luiten van Zanden, "Charting the 'Rise of the West,'" *Journal of Economic History,* 2009

5. Which trend in Europe provides the most important part of the context for the trend shown on the table?

   (A) The increased use of Latin as the primary written language for scholars

   (B) The spread of humanist ideas into northern Europe

   (C) The rising power of the Holy Roman emperor

   (D) The expansion of educational opportunities for women

6. A historian might use the data in the table to support the claim that the number of printed books was

   (A) one sign of the development of centralized nation-states after the Peace of Westphalia

   (B) a major cause in the expansion by European states of their overseas colonial empires

   (C) a significant factor in the spread of the ideas of Martin Luther and John Calvin

   (D) a direct result of the spread of industrialization from Great Britain to other parts of Europe

7. The information in the table describes a change that contributed most directly to which development?

(A) The expansion of capitalist investment through joint-stock companies

(B) The establishment of republican governments based upon written constitutions

(C) The passage of new laws relaxing state censorship and protecting freedom of the press

(D) The publication of scientific writings that challenged classical learning

8. Which claim is best supported by the change in the number of books per person printed in Western Europe between 1300 and 1600?

(A) The total population was declining, so the demand for books was decreasing.

(B) The rise of absolute monarchs to power in several states caused publishers to reduce the production of books.

(C) Rapid economic changes increased the demand for workers who were able to read books.

(D) More people were becoming able to read, which had an effect on the demand for books.

"The chief cause that I fell out with the pope was this: the pope boasted that he was the head of the Church, and condemned all that would not be under his power and authority; for he said, although Christ be the head of the Church, yet, notwithstanding, there must be a corporal head of the Church upon earth. With this I could have been content, had he but taught the gospel pure and clear, and not introduced human inventions and lies in its stead. Further, he took upon him power, rule, and authority over the Christian Church, and over the Holy Scriptures, the Word of God; no man must presume to expound the Scriptures, but only he, and according to his ridiculous conceits; so that he made himself lord over the Church, proclaiming her at the same time a powerful mother, and empress over the Scriptures, to which we must yield and be obedient; this was not to be endured. They who, against God's Word, boast of the Church's authority, are mere idiots. . . .

We, through God's grace, are not heretics, but schismatics, causing, indeed, separation and division, wherein we are not to blame, but our adversaries, who gave occasion thereto, because they remain not by God's Word alone, which we have, hear, and follow."

Martin Luther, *Against Catholicism*, 1535

9. Which statement best describes the political and economic context in which Luther wrote this passage?

(A) German rulers were angry about the power of the pope.

(B) Nation-states were emerging throughout Europe.

(C) The conditions of peasants was improving because serfdom was being abolished.

(D) The economy was changing because the Industrial Revolution was beginning.

10. Which of the following would Luther most likely oppose?

(A) The employment of priests by the church

(B) The reading of the Bible during worship services

(C) The election of a new Holy Roman emperor

(D) The granting of indulgences for money

11. Which individual would most likely share the point of view about the Bible expressed by Luther in this passage?

(A) Erasmus

(B) Johann Tetzel

(C) Charles V

(D) Philip II of Spain

"Others again have propounded other reasons why there are more superstitious women found than men. And the first is, that they are more credulous; and since the chief aim of the devil is to corrupt faith, therefore he rather attacks them…The second reason is, that women are naturally more impressionable, and more ready to receive the influence of a disembodied spirit; and that when they use this quality well they are very good, but when they use it ill they are very evil. The third reason is that they have slippery tongues, and are unable to conceal from the fellow-women those things which by evil arts they know, and since they are weak, they find an easy and secret manner of vindicating themselves by witchcraft…All wickedness is but little to the wickedness of a woman. And to this may be added that, as they are very impressionable, they act accordingly…

And it should be noted that there was a defect in the formation of the first woman, since she was formed from a bent rib, that is a rib of the breast, which is bent as it were in a contrary direction to a man. And since through this defect she is an imperfect animal, she always deceives."

Heinrich Kramer, *Malleus Maleficarum*, 1487

12. Which statement most accurately describes the context in which Kramer articulated his views on women?

    (A) The economic upheaval taking place that threatened many people

    (B) The public humiliation of women by religious leaders as a way to increase their own status

    (C) Communities' punishment of women as part of ceremonies to honor saints

    (D) The persecution of women because they opposed blood sports

13. Which of the following developments contributed to increasing numbers of women accused of being witches?

    (A) *La Querelle des Femmes* raised questions about roles for women.

    (B) Women had been seen as responsible for abolishing Carnival.

    (C) Women were viewed as intellectually equal to men.

    (D) Religious leaders needed a reason to close nunneries.

14. Which statement best explains the context for the passage?

    (A) Women were demonstrating resistance to the Reformation.

    (B) Fear of witchcraft was strongest in Italy, where Latin was the dominant language.

    (C) Social upheaval was leading to the suppression of certain groups.

    (D) Technology was changing the role of women in agriculture.

Questions 15–17 refer to the following passage.

"The King's Army marched on the right hand of the Battle, and the Dukes on the left, and advanced in Battle array against our Enemy; who began to play dispitfully with his ordnance upon us which we cared not much for, but advanced forward with our ordinance likewise playing before us. They seeing us marching towards them, they advanced likewise towards us, and came so close to one to an other that joining battalions together, wee came to push of pike and disputed the business so long, till it pleased God, that wee routed them, and gave us the victory, by putting the Enemy to a retreat with the Kings own Army, but the Duke's Army was viley beaten back, and began to make a shameful flight, so that wee were forced to send our horse men after these that were beaten, and to relieve the Duke's men with our foote, which doing, we putt all the Enemy at last to flight, and followed the execution very hotly till it was dark night, and till wee could not see to pursue them any further, for which victory immortal thanks be given to God."

Major Forbes, a Scottish mercenary fighting for the
King of Sweden, 1631

15. The actions described by Major Forbes can be used as evidence for which of the following?

    (A) A resumption of religious warfare after the Peace of Westphalia

    (B) A military revolution that led to new forms of warfare

    (C) A return to traditional forms of fighting battles against knights in armor

    (D) The adoption of one single form of Christianity in Western Europe

16. What aspect of European warfare does the excerpt most directly illustrate?

    (A) Louis XIV's alliances with the clergy and middle class

    (B) The Habsburgs' attacks on powerful nobles

    (C) Gustavus Adolphus's military ranking and flexible formations

    (D) Louis XIII's greater fortifications and firepower

17. Which of the following was a long-term result of conflict discussed in the passage?

    (A) The forces of the Holy Roman Empire were defeated.

    (B) Sweden lost significant territory.

    (C) Troop movements had limited effect on civilian populations.

    (D) The Catholic League became a powerful force in France.

Questions 18–21 refer to the following passage.

"Women, wake up; the tocsin [alarm] of reason is being heard throughout the whole universe; discover your rights. The powerful empire of nature is no longer surrounded by prejudice, fanaticism, superstition, and lies.The flame of truth has dispersed all the clouds of folly and usurpation. Enslaved man has multiplied his strength and needs recourse to yours to break his chains. Having become free, he has become unjust to his companion. Oh, women, women! When will you cease to be blind? What advantage have you received from the Revolution? . . . . [u]nite yourselves beneath the standards of philosophy; deploy all the energy of your character, and you will soon see these haughty men, not groveling at your feet as servile adorers, but proud to share with you the treasures of the Supreme Being. Regardless of what barriers confront you, it is in your power to free yourselves; you have only to want to."

Olympe de Gouges, *Declaration of the Rights of Woman and Female Citizen*, 1791

18. Which statement about the Declaration of the Rights of Man is most useful in explaining the context in which de Gouges was writing?

    (A) It had declared strong support for the rights of all women.

    (B) It had proposed rights just for women of the nobility.

    (C) It had encouraged wives to support their husbands.

    (D) It had not extended equal rights to women.

19. In this excerpt, de Gouges was addressing which group?

    (A) All women of France

    (B) Women of the French peasantry

    (C) Women of the French bourgeoisie

    (D) Women of the French royal court

20. Which would be an ideal result, according to de Gouges?

    (A) Women controlling government, while men controlled the home

    (B) Women controlling the home, while men controlled government

    (C) Women and men sharing control of government and society

    (D) Women being in full control of government and society

21. Which individual held views most similar to those in this excerpt?

    (A) James I of England

    (B) Mary Wollstonecraft of Great Britain

    (C) Louis XIV of France

    (D) Marie Antoinette of France

Questions 22–25 refer to the map below.

THE EXPANSION OF THE AUSTRIAN HABSBURG EMPIRE, 1525–1805

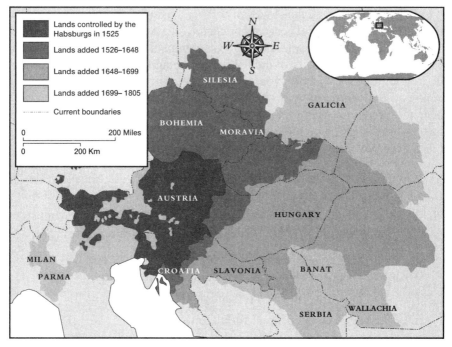

22. Which was the most important part of the context of events in Europe that contributed to the shift in Habsburg lands shown on this map?

(A) The growth of Russia power in the 17th and 18th centuries

(B) The impact of the Peace of Westphalia starting in the middle of the 17th century

(C) The decline in the power of the Swedes starting in the early 18th century

(D) The partitions of Poland in the late 18th century

23. Which event or trend within the Habsburg empire contributed to the shift shown on this map?

(A) The religious reforms by Emperor Joseph II in the late 18th century

(B) The Habsburg's successful defense of Vienna in the late 17th century

(C) The desire of the Habsburgs for peaceful relations with the tsars who controlled Russia in the 18th and 19th centuries

(D) The Habsburg monarchy's failure to implement absolutist government in the 18th century

24. The map provides the best evidence for which aspects of warfare and diplomacy in the 18th century?

(A) The organization of professional state-controlled militaries became the decisive factor in warfare.

(B) After 1648, balance of power played an important role in structuring diplomatic and military objectives.

(C) Expansion and diplomacy was still shaped by dynastic interests, in which ruling families sought to maintain and extend their influence.

(D) The growth of a commercial economy gave Western European states greater military resources than Central and Eastern European powers.

25. The change in the Austrian Habsburg Empire shown on this map was most like the change in which other state in the same time period?

(A) Great Britain

(B) Germany

(C) Italy

(D) Russia

Questions 26–28 refer to the following passage.

"A little before noon on the 16th August, the first body of reformers began to arrive on the scene.... in the town of Manchester. These persons bore two banners, surmounted with caps of liberty, and bearing the inscriptions, 'no corn laws', 'annual parliaments', 'universal suffrage', 'vote by ballot.' . . . The congregated multitude now amounted to a number roundly computed at 80,000. . . . The cavalry dashed into the crowd. . . . The people began running in all directions; and from this moment the yeomanry lost all command of temper; numbers were trampled under the feet of men and horses; many, both men and women were cut down by sabers; several, and a peace officer and a female in the number, slain on the spot. The whole number of persons injured amounted to between three and four hundred."

The Peterloo Massacre, *The Annual Register*, 1819

26. Followers of which ideology would have been most in support of the actions taken against the reformers?

(A) Conservatism

(B) Liberalism

(C) Romanticism

(D) Democracy

27. Why was Manchester an appropriate location for the gathering described in the above passage?

(A) The city was a port for mass emigration.

(B) The city had seen an influx of workers to its factories.

(C) The city was a center of the Agricultural Revolution.

(D) The city had a radical newspaper that fomented protest.

28. One long-term result of the event described in the passage was which of the following?

(A) A break-up of the trade union movement

(B) An increase in chronic unemployment

(C) The suppression of the free press

(D) The expansion of the right to vote

"I have attempted…to resume in the briefest possible manner the main features of the Italian war effort on sea, on land, in the air and in the field of economics and finance. There remains the home front proper, which is mainly concerned with the feelings and reactions of the population as a whole. I have in previous [dispatches] given in some detail accounts of the development of public opinion in this country. In the early part of the year the Abyssinian adventure was by no means generally popular throughout Italy – in many quarters, indeed, it was the reverse. The position is changed today. After one month of war in East Africa, the whole of the Italian people stand, as I have said, solidly behind their leader, and the general feeling is one of single and fervent loyalty to Italy. Some few admit that she is technically wrong; the great majority are hardly in their consciences aware even of the technical breach. The intervention of the League, which is, of course, in Italian eyes, the intervention of Great Britain, has indeed had the most remarkable effect. The Abyssinian adventure is now widely popular, and the threat of sanctions has unified the Italian people to a degree which has astonished many observers."

Eric Drummond, British ambassador to Rome,
memo, November 1935

29. How accurately did the statement above reflect British ideas about intervention in the war in Ethiopia?

(A) Accurately, because the British strongly supported the League of Nations' opposition to the Italian invasion of Ethiopia

(B) Accurately, because the British actually controlled the policies of the League of Nations

(C) Not accurately, because the British and French hoped to gain Italian support against Hitler

(D) Not accurately, because the British were prepared to invade Italy as a response to Italian aggression

30. How did the Italian invasion of Ethiopia reflect developments in European politics at that time?

(A) The rise of fascism was characterized by increasing territorial takeovers.

(B) The rise of fascism was characterized by non-European expansionism.

(C) The opposition to fascism was strengthening the League of Nations.

(D) The opposition to fascism was spreading, except in Spain.

Questions 31–34 refer to the image below.

Front page of *Votes For Women*, a British newspaper published by the Women's Political and Social Union, June 1913. Below each figure is a list of the states in the United States and the countries in which women had the right to vote.

31. This image could best be used to illustrate which of the following trends in the early 20th century?

(A) The growth of a cult of domesticity

(B) The rise of marketing and mass consumerism

(C) The shift from laissez-faire to interventionist government policy

(D) The importance of mass politics and media

32. Based on the imagery and intended audience, what was the most likely purpose for the newspaper?

(A) To encourage women to be patient with the political process

(B) To convince men that suffrage would make women better caretakers

(C) To portray women's suffrage as an inevitable outcome of social progress

(D) To appeal to working-class women to join the feminist movement

33. Which of the following helps explains the trend shown in this newspaper page?

(A) Women's participation in World War I won support for the suffrage movement.

(B) The growth of the welfare state after World War II reflected a growing sense that all people should participate in society.

(C) One result of industrialization was a rapid expansion in the roles open to women in society.

(D) Government in Europe and elsewhere wanted to secure women's loyalty during the Cold War.

34. Which movement occurred at the same time as the one portrayed?

(A) The spread of the welfare state through Europe

(B) The spread of colonial independence

(C) An increase in the number of disarmament treaties

(D) An increase in the power of empires in Central and Eastern Europe

Questions 35–37 refer to the image below.

Credit: George
Elgar Hicks,
*The Sinews of
Old England*
(1857). commons.
wikimedia.org.

35. Which development provides the best context for the scene depicted?

(A) The development of tenements in large industrial cities

(B) The building of manorial estates

(C) The decline of the middle-class family model

(D) The rise of the nuclear family model

36. In the context of the mid-1800s, which may best explain why the artist placed the figures at the threshold of the cottage?

(A) It represented the meeting of rural and urban life.

(B) It showed that higher living standards were emerging.

(C) It showed the growing equality of men and women.

(D) It marked the boundary between the spheres of women and men.

37. What development in the 19th century portrayed life very differently from its portrayal in the painting?

(A) Romanticism

(B) Realism

(C) Nationalism

(D) Liberalism

Questions 38–39 refer to the map below.

ITALIAN STATES PRIOR TO 1871 UNIFICATION

38. The changes that occured by the end of 1871 for the states shown on the map most clearly demonstrate which idea?

(A) The appeal of socialism

(B) The importance of Romanticism

(C) The spread of nationalism

(D) The influence of industrialization

39. The states shown on the map went through a process in the 1860s and 1870s that was similar to what was occuring at that time in

(A) Spain

(B) Germany

(C) Austria-Hungary

(D) Russia

"IRISHMEN AND IRISHWOMEN: In the name of God and of the dead generations from which she receives her old tradition of nationhood, Ireland, through us, summons her children to her flag and strikes for her freedom. . . . Having resolutely waited for the right moment to reveal itself, she now seizes that moment, and supported by her exiled children in America and by gallant allies in Europe, but relying in the first on her own strength, she strikes in full confidence of victory. We declare the right of the people of Ireland to the ownership of Ireland and to the unfettered control of Irish destinies, to be sovereign and indefeasible. The long usurpation of that right by a foreign people and government has not extinguished the right, nor can it ever be extinguished except by the destruction of the Irish people.... Standing on that fundamental right and again asserting it in arms in the face of the world, we hereby proclaim the Irish Republic as a Sovereign Independent State."

Proclamation of an Irish Republic, Easter 1916

40. According to the above passage and your knowledge, why were the Irish prepared to take armed revolutionary action?

(A) European allies had secretly provided them with military training.

(B) The British had failed to implement the Irish Home Rule bill.

(C) The German military had encouraged them to rebel.

(D) The Irish had extensive experience in local constabulary actions.

41. What was a primary factor that led the Irish revolutionaries to believe, as they declared in the above passage, that it was the "right moment" for insurrection?

(A) They had the support of the American nation.

(B) They had sufficient numbers of revolutionaries.

(C) England's resources were involved in the war on the continent.

(D) Heavy losses in the trenches created resentment and reprisal.

42. Which of the following accurately reflects the Irish attitudes toward the rebellion against British rule?

(A) Most Irish supported the union between their country and Great Britain.

(B) Catholics were more likely than Protestants to support rebellion.

(C) Nearly everyone in Ireland wanted independence, even if they opposed rebellion.

(D) People became less supportive of rebellion after several rebel leaders wer executed.

Questions 43–45 refer to the table below.

Unemployment Rate in Britain and Germany, 1920–1940		
Year	Britain	Germany
1920	2.0%	3.8%
1930	11.2%	15.3%
1932	15.6%	30.1%
1934	11.9%	14.9%
1936	9.4%	8.3%
1938	9.3%	2.1%
1940	3.3%	not available

Source: https://www.encyclopedia.com/education/news-and-education-magazines/global-impact-1929-1939

43. Which contributed most to the change in German unemployment between 1930 and 1932?

(A) An increase in state spending on social welfare programs

(B) The dependence on American loans and investment to settle reparations after World War I

(C) The introduction of laborsaving machinery

(D) An increase in labor strikes and factory shutdowns

44. Which caused the change in the German economy shown on the chart between 1932 and 1938?

(A) The emigration of large numbers of Germans to the United States

(B) The expansion of Germany's colonial markets

(C) The Nazis' rearmament and remilitarization program

(D) The establishment of the European Coal and Steel Community

45. Which of the following accurately reflects the relationship between British and German unemployment in the years shown in the table?

(A) British unemployment was caused by factors different from those causing unemployment in Germany.

(B) British unemployment was not as bad as unemployment in Germany, but it was slower to recover.

(C) Unemployment rose faster and recovered faster in Britain than it did in Germany.

(D) The Great Depression had as large an effect on Britain and Germany as it had on the United States.

Questions 46–48 refer to the passage below.

"Every Englishman knows that they are a mere handful in this country and it is the business of every one of them to befool you in believing that you are weak and they are strong. This is politics. We have been deceived by such policy so long. What the new party wants you to do is to realize the fact that your future rests entirely in your own hands. . . .

This is boycott and this is what is meant when we say, boycott is a political weapon. We shall not give them assistance to collect revenue and keep peace. We shall not assist them in fighting beyond the frontiers or outside India with Indian blood and money. We shall not assist them in carrying on the administration of justice. We shall have our own courts, and when time comes we shall not pay taxes. Can you do that by your united efforts? If you can, you are free from tomorrow."

Indian nationalist Bal Gangadhar Tilak, speech to the
Indian National Congress, 1907

46. The passage best illustrates which of the following trends in the early 20th century?

(A) Colonial subjects' use of mass media to influence European public opinion

(B) The growing financial burdens of maintaining a colonial empire

(C) Resistance of indigenous nationalist movements to imperialism

(D) The conscription of colonial troops in the world wars

47. Organizations similar to the Indian National Congress were most influenced by

(A) Western educational and political values

(B) Fascist ideologies

(C) the methods of European anarchists

(D) the writings of Karl Marx

48. The activities described in the passage shared a goal with which of the following changes in the 20th century?

(A) The willingness of European governments to extend democratic rights to their colonial subjects

(B) The economic impact of the Great Depression and the world wars

(C) The proliferation of new ideas through the Internet

(D) The formation of the European Union

Questions 49–51 refer to the image below.

Credit: Replica of the painting by Pablo Picasso, *Guernica,* 1937. Guernica was heavily bombed by Franco's forces in the Spanish Civil War.

49. The image exemplifies which of the following trends in 20th-century art?

(A) Increasing experimentation and subjective interpretations of reality

(B) A return to classical methods of painting and composition

(C) The creation of visual works that portray life in striking realism

(D) Using images from popular culture to satirize Western consumerism

50. Based on the imagery and context, Picasso was most likely influenced by which of the following ideas?

(A) The revival of religious sentiment after World War I

(B) Freudian theories emphasizing the irrationality of human behavior

(C) Growing concerns about the possibility of nuclear war

(D) Soviet critiques of Western imperialism and capitalism

51. Based on the painting *Guernica,* Picasso is most similar to which intellectual tradition?

(A) He was similar to Jacques-Louis David, Wolfgang Mozart, and others in the Neoclassical tradition in their ideas about proportion and harmony.

(B) He was similar to Francisco Goya, Victor Hugo, and others in the Romantic tradition in their ideas about the relationship between art and politics.

(C) He was similar to William Blake and Mary Shelley, and others in the Romantic tradition in their ideas about the supernatural.

(D) Picasso was similar to Jean-François Millet, Gustave Flaubert, and others in the Realist tradition in their ideas about everyday life.

Questions 52–53 refer to the map below.

WORLD WAR II IN EUROPE, JANUARY 1942

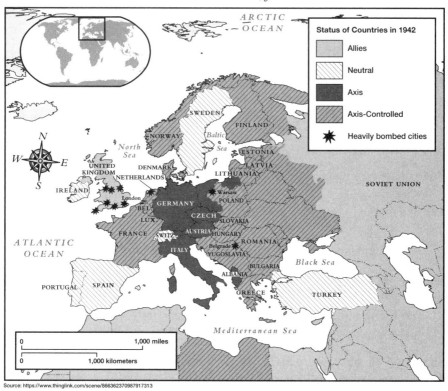

Source: https://www.thinglink.com/scene/866362370987917313

52. Which of the following contributed most to the pattern of Axis conquest shown on the map?

(A) The support for Nazism within the countries Germany conquered

(B) Germany's use of armies that were far larger than those of any other European country

(C) The greater industrial capacity of the Axis countries compared to most countries on the European continent

(D) The British policy of neutrality up to 1942

53. Which of the following contributed most to a reversal of the patterns shown on the map?

(A) The creation of the Marshall Plan

(B) The League of Nations

(C) The military mobilization of the Soviet Union

(D) The use of nuclear weapons

Questions 54–55 refer to the passage below.

"The Berlin Wall has collapsed. This entire era in the history of the Socialist system is over. . . .

But the main thing is the GDR [German Democratic Republic, or East Germany], the Berlin Wall. For it has to do not only with 'socialism' but with the shift in the world balance of forces. This is the end of Yalta . . . of the Stalinist legacy and the 'defeat of Hitlerite Germany.'

That is what Gorbachev has done. And he has indeed turned out to be a great leader. He has sensed the pace of history and helped history to find a natural channel.

A meeting with [U.S. president] Bush is approaching. Will we witness a historic conversation? There are two main ideas in the instructions [I was given] to prepare materials: the role of two superpowers in leading the world to a civilized state and the balance of interests. But Bush might disregard our arguments."

Anatoly Chernyaev, diary, November 10, 1989

54. Based on the writer's reference to other leaders, which of these would he most likely support?

(A) Glasnost

(B) Warsaw Pact

(C) Five-year plans

(D) Collectivization

55. Based on events of 1989 to 1992, the predictions made by this writer turned out to be

(A) quite accurate for the Soviet Union and Eastern Europe

(B) mostly accurate for the United States and China

(C) mostly inaccurate for Russia and China

(D) quite inaccurate for the countries of Eastern Europe

Section I

Directions: Use the passage below to answer all parts of the question that follows.

"The Germans accepted [Nazism] as a last act of desperation. A nation which appreciated its own excellent qualities and high abilities thought its existence menaced by chaos. It could not understand the reasons for this plight and refused to acquiesce. Millions of Germans from all classes and occupations felt the crisis to be so acute that the Nazis were quickly transformed from a small group of crackpots into a mass party led by a messiah determined upon action to restore the vigor and rightful glory of the German people. The ingredients of [Nazism] were derived in sufficient strength from the German past to be acceptable as German."

> Eugene N. Anderson, "Freedom and Authoritarianism
> in German History" in *The Struggle for Democracy
> in Germany,*, 1949

1. a) Explain how ONE piece of evidence supports Anderson's argument regarding the causes of the success of the Nazis in Germany.

b) Explain how ONE piece of evidence undermines Anderson's argument regarding the causes of the success of the Nazis in Germany.

c) Explain ONE example of a development in another European country that resulted in a development similar to those described by Anderson.

Use the passage below to answer all parts of the question that follows.

"Our blood is too hot; we prefer to wear armor which is too heavy for our slender body; but we should use it nonetheless. The eyes of Germany are fixed not upon Prussia's liberalism but upon her armed might. Bavaria, Wurttemberg, and Baden [three German states] may indulge in liberal experiments; therefore no one will assign to them Prussia's role. Prussia must harbor and maintain her strength for the favorable moment—a moment which has already, on one occasion, slipped by; Prussia's boundaries, as drawn by the Vienna treaties, are not suitable for a healthy state life. The great questions of the day will not be decided by speeches or by majority decisions—that was the mistake of 1848 and 1849—but by blood and iron!"

> Otto von Bismarck, speech to the Prussian House of
> Representatives, 1862

2. a) Describe ONE significant change in German history represented by the ideas stated by Bismarck.

b) Describe ONE significant continuity in German history represented by the ideas stated by Bismarck.

c) Explain ONE significant effect of the changes in German history that resulted from the ideas stated by Bismarck.

Choose EITHER Question 3 OR Question 4.

3. a) Describe ONE significant cause of the rise of commerical capitalism starting in the 1600s.

b) Describe ONE significant effect of the rise of commercial capitalism starting in the 1600s.

c) Explain how the expansion of global trade influenced the early development of capitalism.

4. a) Describe ONE significant cause of the growth of imperialism starting in the 1800s.

b) Describe ONE significant effect of the growth of imperialism starting in the 1800s.

c) Explain how the growth of imperialism influenced international relations starting in the 1800s.

Section II

PART A: DOCUMENT-BASED QUESTION

Directions: Question 1 is based on the accompanying documents. The documents have been edited for the purpose of this exercise. In your response you should do the following:

- Respond to the prompt with a historically defensible thesis or claim that establishes a line of reasoning.
- Describe a broader historical context relevant to the prompt.
- Support an argument in response to the prompt using at least six documents.
- Use at least one additional piece of specific historical evidence (beyond that found in the documents) relevant to an argument about the prompt.
- For at least three documents, explain how or why the document's point of view, purpose, historical situation, and/or audience is relevant to an argument.
- Use evidence to corroborate, qualify, or modify an argument that addresses the prompt.

Source: AP® European History Examination, 2018

1. Evaluate the extent to which Enlightenment ideas supported the development of liberal ideas in European society from the late 17th century to the late 18th century.

Document 1

> **Source:** John Locke, *An Essay Concerning Human Understanding*, 1689
>
> Since it is the understanding that sets man above all other animals and enables him to use and dominate them, it is certainly worth our while to enquire into it. The understanding is like the eye in this respect: it makes us see and perceive all other things but doesn't look in on itself. To stand back from it and treat it as an object of study requires skill and hard work. Still, whatever difficulties there may be in doing this, whatever it is that keeps us so much in the dark to ourselves, it will be worthwhile to let as much light as possible in upon our minds, and to learn as much as we can about our own understandings. As well as being enjoyable, this will help us to think well about other topics.

Document 2

Source: Baron de Montesquieu, *The Spirit of Laws*, 1748

There is no word that has admitted of more various significations, and has made more different impressions on human minds, than that of Liberty. Some have taken it for a facility of deposing a person on whom they had conferred a tyrannical authority; others for the power of choosing a person whom they are obliged to obey; others for the right of bearing arms, and of being thereby enabled to use violence, others in fine for the privilege of being governed by a native of their own country or by their own laws. . . .

There is ultimately a formula: a large state must be an autocracy, a medium sized states must be ruled as a kingdom and a small state can be ruled as a Republic....There is also an ultimate formula that the English have achieved after their Glorious Revolution: an ultimate balance of power between the Monarch as an Executive power, the Parliament as the Legislative and the Judicial Branch.

Document 3

Source: Voltaire, *Candide*, 1759

"Do you believe," said Candide, "that men have always massacred each other as they do to-day, that they have always been liars, cheats, traitors, ingrates, brigands, idiots, thieves, scoundrels, gluttons, drunkards, misers, envious, ambitious, bloody-minded, calumniators, debauchees, fanatics, hypocrites, and fools?"

"Do you believe," said Martin, "that hawks have always eaten pigeons when they have found them?"

"Yes, without doubt," said Candide.

"Well, then," said Martin, "if hawks have always had the same character why should you imagine that men may have changed theirs?"

Document 4

Source: Jean-Jacques Rousseau, *Emile, or On Education*, 1762

Hold childhood in reverence, and do not be in any hurry to judge it for good or ill. . . .

You are afraid to see him spending his early years doing nothing. What! Is it nothing to be happy, nothing to run and jump all day? He will never be so busy again all his life long. . . . What would you think of a man who refused to sleep lest he should waste part of his life? You would say, "He is mad; he is not enjoying his life, he is robbing himself of part of it; to avoid sleep he is hastening his death." Remember . . . that childhood is the sleep of reason. . . .

Although memory and reason are wholly different faculties, the one does not really develop apart from the other. Before the age of reason the child receives images, not ideas; and there is this difference between them: images are merely the pictures of external objects, while ideas are notions about those objects determined by their relations.

Document 5

Source: Adam Smith, *The Wealth of Nations*, 1776

The greatest improvements in the productive powers of labor, and most of the skill, dexterity, and judgment with which it is directed or applied, seem to be results of the division of labor.
It will be easier to understand how the division of labor affects society in general if we first look at how it operates in some particular manufactures. . . .

In the large manufactures that are destined to meet the needs of the great body of the people, every branch of the work employs so many workmen that they can't be collected into a single workshop; so that we can't see more at one time than those employed in one branch. In such manufactures the work may be divided into many more parts than in the smaller ones, but the division is much less obvious and has accordingly been much less noticed.

Document 6

Source: Immanuel Kant, "What is Enlightenment," 1784

Enlightenment is man's leaving his self-caused immaturity. Immaturity is the incapacity to use one's intelligence without the guidance of another. Such immaturity is self-caused if it is not caused by lack of intelligence, but by lack of determination and courage to use one's intelligence without being guided by another. Sapere Aude [which is Latin for "dare to know"]! Have the courage to use your own intelligence! [This] is therefore the motto of the enlightenment.

Document 7

Source: Statue of David Hume in front of a church in Edinburgh, Scotland.

Credit: Getty Images

PART B: LONG ESSAY QUESTIONS

Directions: Answer Question 2 OR Question 3 OR Question 4.

In your response you should do the following.

- Respond to the prompt with a historically defensible thesis or claim that establishes a line of reasoning.

- Describe a broader historical context relevant to the prompt.

- Support an argument in response to the prompt using specific and relevant examples of evidence.

- Use historical reasoning (e.g., comparison, causation, continuity or change over time) to frame or structure an argument that addresses the prompt.

- Use evidence to corroborate, qualify, or modify an argument that addresses the prompt.

Source: AP® European History Examination, 2018

Question 2. Evaluate the extent to which the idea of the divine right of monarchs differed from the idea of the social contract.

Question 3. Evaluate the extent to which the organization of empires in mid-19th century Europe differed from the organization of nation-states in mid-19th century Europe.

Question 4. Evaluate the extent to which the ideology of facism differed from the ideology of communism.

Index

Antagonism, 367
Antibiotics, 517
Anti-Corn Law League, 286, 327
Anti-epidemic campaign, 253–254
Anti-Semitism, 361–363, 434
Antiseptic method, 309
Antoinette, Marie, 159
Antwerp, 59
Apocalypse, 444
Appeasement, 434–435
Arab revolt, against Turks, 433
Architecture, 10–13, 525
Arendt, Hannah, 491
Argumentation, 492
Aristocracy, 80, 135–138, 157, 197, 304
Aristotle, 12, 15
Arkwright, Richard, 197
Armenian genocide, 432
Armistice, 428
Arms race, 455
Arouet, François-Marie (Voltaire), 210
Art
    Baroque movement, 233–234
    Baroque style, evolution away from, 234–235
    experimentation and subjectivity in, 524–529
    neoclassicism, 235–236
    Romanticism in, 399
Artisans, 76, 91
Asia, 386–388. *See also* East Asia; Southeast Asia; specific countries
    Resistance in, 386–388
Astrolabe, 53
Astrology, 19
Astronomy, new ideas in, 15–16
Atheism, 229, 230
Atlantic Ocean, 59, 183, 186
Atlantic Ports, 59
Atlantic trading system, 61
Attitudes, 257
Auden, W. H., 561
Augustan Age, 235
Austen, Jane, 236, 258, 266, 312
Austria
    annexation of, 436–437
    revolution in, 350
Austria-Germany, 330

Austria-Hungary, 354
Authoritarian dictatorships, 483
Authoritarian rule, 479, 483
    authoritarian dictatorships, 483
    fascist dictatorships and propaganda, 479–480
    Franco and Spanish Civil War, 482
    Mussolini and Hitler, rise of, 480–482
Aztec(s), 56, 61
Aztec Empire, 56

B

Baby boom, 541
Bach, Johann Sebastian, 234
Bacon, Sir Francis, 17, 18, 208, 273
Bacteriology, 309
Baekeland, Leo, 293
Bainton, Roland H., 48
Bakewell, Robert, 251
Bakunin, Mikhail, 336, 365
Balance of power, 111, 134, 348, 433
Balkan(s), 505
    Congress of Berlin of 1878, 367
    nationalist conflicts in, 367–368
    war in, 368, 505
Bank of Amsterdam, 74
Bank of England, 198
Banks, influence of, 295
Baroque
    art, 14–15, 233, 248
    music, 234
Baroque Art (Carl and Charles), 247
Baroque movement, 233–234
Basque, 457
Bastille Day, 161, 162
Battle of Adwa, 386
Battle of Britain, 441
Battle of the Bulge, 442
Battle of Vienna, 146
Bauhaus, 523
Bayle, Pierre, 229
Beccaria, Cesare, 212, 214
Beckett, Samuel, 526
Beer Hall Putsch, 479
Behrendt, Stephen D., 69
Being and Nothingness (Sartre), 527

Department(s), 163
Department stores, 314
Depreciate, 482
Der Judenstaat (Herzl), 363
Descartes, René, 18
Desmoulins, Camille, 274
De-Stalinization, 497
Détente, 499
Deterrence theory, 212
Devasating disease, 77
Dewey, John, 296
d'Holbach, Baron, 229
Di Cavour, Count Camillo, 372
Dialogues Concerning Natural Religion
    (Hume), 229
Bartolomeu Dias, 54
Dickens, Charles, 262, 406
Diderot, Denis, 211, 214, 229
Die Grünen, 544
Diet of Augsburg, 108
Diet of Worms, 30
Diplomacy, 106–108
    Britain and France, colonial rivalry,
        148
    end of Ottoman expansion, 146
    French, 111
    Prussian and Habsburg rulers,
        145–146
    Spain, 112
    Sweden, 111
    wars of Louis XIV, 147
Diplomatic order
    Balkans, nationalist conflicts in,
        367–368
    tension, alliances increase, 366–367
Diplomatic tensions, 383–384
Directory, 167
Disarmament, 432
Discourse on the Origin of Inequality
    (Rousseau), 224
The Discourses (Machiavelli), 8
Disease. *See* Infectious disease
Divergence, 149
Dividends, 74
Dividing the World, 54
Divine right, 134
Doctrine, Truman, 450, 454

Domestic policy, 358–359
Domesticity, 257
Dowry, 92
Doyle, William, 179
Dreyfus Affair, 362
Dreyfus, Alfred, 362, 365
Dual monarchy of Austria-Hungary, 354
Dubois, François, 130
Duchamp, Marcel, 525
Duma, 470
Dupin, Amantine Lucile Aurore, 239
Dutch, 40–41, 191
Dutch East India Company, 62, 74, 144,
    191
Dutch "Golden Age," 234
Dutch oligarchy, 144
Dutch Republic, 144
Dutch resistance, in Spanish
    Netherlands, 115
Dutch Revolt, 115
Dutch War, 147
Dutch War for Independence, 115
Dutch West India Company, 62

E

Early Childhood Care and Education
    (ECCE) services, 542
Early modern period, 90
East India Company, 191
East Indies, rivalries in, 190–191
Easter Rising of 1916, 317
Eastern communism
    Central and Eastern Europe, new
        nationalisms rise in, 504–506
    Marshall Plan, 494–495
    social welfare programs, expansion
        of, 496
    Soviet bloc, 497–500
    Soviet control, end of, 501–504
Eastern Europe, 452. *See also specific
    countries*
    new nationalisms rise in, 504–506
    reform in, 354–356
    revolts in, 500
    serfdom in, 80
    troubles in, 40

G

Galen, 16, 17

Galilei, Galileo, 16, 23, 272

Garibaldi, Giuseppe, 357

The Gathering Storm (Churchill), 449

Gauguin, Paul, 385

Gay and lesbian movements, 547

Gender, 76, 92–93

Gender in English Society 1650–1850 (Shoemaker), 323

General Agreement on Tariffs and Trade (GATT), 454

"General Directive" (Krupp), 292

General will, 212

Geneva, 32, 83

Genoa, 74

Genocide, 432, 439, 520

Gentry, 75, 109

Geocentric universe, 15

Geometric perspective, 10

Géricault, Théodore, 398

Germ theory, 309

German
  extremism, 486
  revolution in, 350

German Territories, 108

German Workers' Party, 436

Germany
  Bismarck's realpolitik unites, 357–359
  Cold War, 453
  totalitarianism, 521

Ghetto, 437

Girl with a Pearl Earring (Vermeer), 235

Girondins, 164

Glasnost, 455, 500

Global control
  colonial acquisition, debates, 384–385
  communication and transportation, 382–383
  diplomatic tensions increase, 383–384
  imperialism. *See* Imperialism
  military and medical technologies, 381–382

Global exchanges
  African slave trade, 61
  Atlantic states, competition from, 62–63
  Columbian Exchange, 59–61
  Economic power, shifts in, 58–59
  european powers, rivalries among, 64

Glorious Revolution, 197, 217
  England, 143–144

Goebbels, Joseph, 478

Gold Coast, 53

Gold standard, 484

Golden Age, 82, 234

Goldhagen, Daniel Jonah, 490

Gorbachev, Mikhail, 455, 499

Gould, J. D., 88

Government policies, 295

Goya, Francisco, 399

Gramophone, 315

Grand Embassy, 136

Great Britain. *See* Britain

Great Depression, 481, 482, 535–536
  attempts to overcome, 485–486
  financial collapse, 485
  worldwide economic weaknesses, 484

Great Exhibition of 1851, 285

Great Fear, 161

The Great Instauration (Bacon), 273

Great Northern War, 136

Great Plague, 77

Great Purge, 476

Great Reform Act of 1832, 326, 327

Greek and Roman Political Institutions, 7

Greek Independence Movement, 332

Green Parties, 546

Grégoire, Henri, 276

Grimm Brothers, 239, 342

Grimm's Fairy Tales (Wilhelm), 239

Gross, Leo, 116

Grotius, Hugo, 110

Guerrilla war, 172

Guerrilla warfare, 168

Guilds, 76, 193

Gunboats, 382

K

Kafka, Franz, 527
Kandinsky, Wassily, 525
Keats, John, 238, 239, 401, 402
Kennedy, John F., 455
Kepler, Johannes, 16, 272
Keynes, John Maynard, 483
Khrushchev, Nikita, 497–498
King Charles I, 114
King Ferdinand and Queen Isabella, 55
King Henry IV, 107
King James I, 67
Kissinger, Henry, 466
The Kitchen Maid (Vermeer), 234
Kleindeutsch, 358
Koch, Robert, 309
Kohn, Hans, 373
Kollár, Ján, 344
Korean War, 452
Kosovo, 457, 504
Koyama, Mark, 243
Kristallnacht, 439
Kristensen, Hans M., 564
Krupp, Alfred, 292
Krupp family of Essen, 291
Krupps, 291–292
Kulaks, 475
Kulturkampf, 359

L

La Comédie humaine, 405
Labor camps, 440
Labor unions, 305
Laissez-faire, 219
Lake Poets, 239
Land conversions, 196
Land use, 250
Landlord, 76
Large city-states, 7
Las Casas, Bartolomé de, 56, 68, 126
Las Meninas (Velásquez), 234
The Last Supper (da Vinci), 11
Late Baroque, 235
Lawrence, Colonel T. E., 433
Le Chapelier Law, 193
League of Nations, 434, 460, 461

Lebanon, 459
Left-wing ideology, 469
Lending libraries, 215, 256
Lenin, Vladimir, 384, 385, 389, 470–472
Letters on the English (Voltaire), 229
Letters to Atticus (Cicero), 5
Leuger, Mayor Karl, 362
Levée en masse, 165
Leviathan (Hobbes), 209
Levine, George, 410
Lewis, Pericles, 534
Liberal democracy, 469
Liberal government, 83
Liberal Party, 328
Liberalism, 328, 337, 350, 368
    and reform in Britain, 338–340
    and rights of the individual, 325–328
Lieven, Dorothea, 424
Life span, 309–310
Lima, 57
Limited monarchy, 329
Limited-liability corporation, 199
Liquidation, of kulaks, 477
Lisbon, 59
List, Friedrich, 290, 300, 419
Lister, Joseph, 309, 310, 382
Literature, romanticism in, 401–402
Little Ice Age, 77, 94, 249
Little, Richard, 528
Locke, John, 209–210, 214, 231, 260,
    273, 325
Locomotive, 283
Logan, George M., 85
London, 74, 75, 81
Long depression, 294
Long Parliament, 113
Lord Byron, 401, 402
Lord Ismay, 563
Lorenzo the Magnificent, 11
Lost Generation, 535
Louis XIII, 114
Louis XIV, 111, 122, 138–139, 147
Louis XVI, 158, 232
L'Ouverture, Toussaint, 167–169
Low, David, 448
Lucassen, Jan, 264
Luther, Martin, 28–31, 37, 115, 128
Luxemburg, Rosa, 336, 364, 446

N

Nadolny, Rudolf, 558
Napoleon Bonaparte, 167, 267, 277,
    287–290, 417
    curtailment of rights under, 170–171
    domestic reforms under, 169–170
    end of era, 173
Napoleon III, 330, 349, 353, 360
Napoleonic Code, 169, 178
Napoleonic Wars, 171
National Assembly, 160, 166
National Convention, 164, 166
National Convention (Robespierre), 276
National Government, 483
National Health Service, 544
National markets, 195
National rivalry, 378–379
National Security Council, 510
National self-determination,
    450,460–461
National Socialist German Workers'
    Party, 479
National System, 290
National System of Political Economy
    (List), 300
*The National System of Political
    Economy* (List), 419
National unification movements
    Bismarck's Realpolitik unites
        Germany, 357–359
    France, conflict and reform in,
        359–361
    Mazzini, Cavour, and Garibaldi
        unify Italy, 356–357
National workshops, 349
Nationalism, 231, 241–242, 335–337,
    353, 368, 429, 550–551
    Cold War, Europe and world,
        451–455
    decolonization. *See* Decolonization
    Eastern and Western Europe,
        integration of, 457–458
    in German States, 172
    nationalist and separatist
        movements, 459–460
    Soviet Union, 457
    United States, 456–457

Nationalist movement, 333, 459–460,
    462–463
NATO. *See* North Atlantic Treaty
    Organization (NATO)
Natural law, 18, 110, 208, 209
Natural order, 330
Natural philosopher, 15
Natural religion, 228–230
Natural rights, 210
Natural science, 17, 407–408
Natural selection, 401
Naturalism, 10, 405
The Nature of Fascism (Griffin), 486
Navigating the Age of Exploration
    (Widmer), 70
Navigation, 52
Navigation Acts, 187
Nazi Party, 479
Nazis, 444
Nazi–Soviet Non-Aggression Pact, 437
Neal, Larry, 341
Nederman, Cary J., 242
Neoclassical art, 248
Neoclassical style, 397
Neoclassicism, 235–236
Neonatalism, 542
NEP. *See* New Economic Policy (NEP)
Nepotism, 30
Netherlands, 62, 63, 115
New Amsterdam, 62
The New Cambridge Modern History
    (Elton), 43
New crops, 251
New cultural institutions, 261
New Economic Policy (NEP), 474
New France, 63
New leisure venues, 256
New monarchies, 106
New Spain, 56
New warfare, 111–112
New World, 56
New York, 62
Newton, Isaac, 16, 18, 207, 514
Nicholas I, Tsar, 333, 345, 351, 370, 371
Nicholas II, Tsar, 432, 470
Niemöller, Martin, 519
Nietzsche, Friedrich, 407, 513
Nine Years' War, 147

W

Wagner, Richard, 400
Waiting for Godot (Beckett), 528
Wallerstein, Immanuel, 389–390
Wannsee Conference, 439
War communism, 473
War of 1792, 163
War of the Spanish Succession, 147
War of the Three Henrys, 39–40
Wars. *See also specific wars*
    in Balkan, 505
    and beliefs, 425–426
    Dutch War, 147
    Eighty Years' War, 144
    English Civil War, 38, 112–114
    European Wars, 145–148
    French and Indian War, 148
    and global efforts for peace, 425
    guerrilla war, 172
    hot wars, 454
    Korean War, 454
    Napoleonic Wars, 171
    Second Hundred Years' War, 148
    Spanish Civil War, 482
Warsaw Pact, 455
Water frame, 197
Water meadows, 196
Watt, James, 283
Watteau, Jean-Antoine, 235
Wealth of Nations (Smith), 84
Weaponry, 381
Weber, Adna F., 263
Weber, Max, 83, 263
Weimar Republic, 479, 536
Welfare state, 494
Wesley, John, 230
West Indies, 56
Western Allies, 453
Western Europe, 65
    economic and political integration, 456–458
    troubles in, 40–41
    war in, 442–443
Western prosperity
    Central and Eastern Europe, new nationalisms rise in, 504–506

Marshall Plan, 494–495
social welfare programs, expansion of, 496
Soviet bloc, 497–500
Soviet control, end of, 501–504
Westphalia, 116–117
Wet-nursing, 260
The Whig Interpretation (Butterfield), 242
Whig Party, 327
The White Man's Burden, 379
Whites, 473
Whitney, Eli, 197, 283
Widmer, Ted, 70
Wilhelm II, Kaiser, 359, 429
William III, 143
William IV, Frederick, 350
William of Orange, 143
Williams, Andrea, 201
Williams, Jeffery J., 341
Wilson, Woodrow, 433, 447, 458
Winter, Jay, 444
Wireless communication, 293
Witchcraft, 97–98
Witte, Sergei, 355
Wollstonecraft, Mary, 213, 214
Woman Question, 93
Women
    on Age of Reason, 213–214
    capitalism, 363–364
    feminism, 541–542, 544
    in French Revolution, 165–166
    intellect and education, 93–94
    prominence of, 98
    rights, in France, 360–361
    suffrage, 339
    working-class, 311
Women's March on Versailles, 162, 275
Women's Social and Political Union (WSPU), 340
Woolf, Virginia, 525
Wordsworth, William, 239, 246, 402
Workers' wages, 193
Workhouse system, 262
Workhouses, 307